BLACKSTONE'S

CHILD LAW INDEX

CASE PRECEDENTS 1900-1997

BLACKSTONE'S

CHILD LAW INDEX

CASE PRECEDENTS 1900-1997

Dr Maxwell Barrett

BLACKSTONE PRESS LIMITED

First published in Great Britain 1998 by Blackstone Press Limited,
Aldine Place, London W12 8AA. Telephone: 0181-740 2277

ISBN: 1 85431 853 5

British Library Cataloguing in Publication Data
A CIP catalogue record for this book is available from the British Library

Typeset by Style Photosetting Limited, Mayfield, East Sussex
Printed by Bell and Bain Limited, Glasgow

CONTENTS

INTRODUCTION

> 'The decisions . . . of courts are held in the highest regard, and are not only preserved as authentic records in the treasuries of the several courts, but are handed out to public view in the numerous volumes of *reports* which furnish the lawyer's library.'[1]

So wrote Blackstone in 1765. Since then those 'numerous volumes of reports' to which he makes reference have multiplied in number to a level that is surely beyond anything he ever imagined. And it is not just that the total number of reports being published has increased in the past two and a half centuries. Mirroring the present tendency among lawyers towards ever greater specialisation into ever more specific fields of legal expertise has been a growing tendency among publishers in recent years to bring out law reports that concentrate on particular subject areas.

All of this has placed lawyers in something of a predicament. Even if it were economically feasible to subscribe to each of the many series of law reports and legal periodicals that have been or become available during this century alone (and even the most generously funded library would surely baulk at such an enormous expense) the amount of overlap in coverage between the different sources could well mean that those cases to which particular lawyers need access are already handsomely covered in the publications to which they or their chambers or firm presently subscribe and that outside reference is so occasional it could be met by a reasonably priced publication which would not only index the reports to which those lawyers or their chambers or firms now subscribe but contain additional comprehensive references to alternative reports and journals that feature relevant case-law and to which occasional recourse might be necessary.

Economic feasibility aside, there is the matter of convenience. However well prepared they are on entering court every barrister and many solicitors have on occasion found themselves on their feet addressing or pressing a perhaps unanticipated argument which they wished they could support by reference to a convincing precedent. That precedent may well exist somewhere among the many sources of case-law now available. Indeed oftentimes a barrister or solicitor may have a very good notion of when a relevant case was decided or with what subject-matter the relevant case was concerned but simply cannot remember its name. Standing before the court, away from law reports and legal periodicals practitioners would at such times undoubtedly find a one-stop, single-volume index relevant to the subject area being litigated, detailing the location and content of many thousands of cases and drawn from a very wide array of sources to be of real usefulness.

Of course such an index would also be of enormous benefit back in the office. It would in a single self-contained book provide lawyers with a cost-effective, hassle-free, easy-to-use means of accessing in their particular subject area many thousands of cases in many thousands of law report and law journal volumes and so open up a whole new world of precedents for them to call in aid when seeking to buttress whatever case they are called upon to make. And with lawyers working ever longer hours, many of them at home, such a reference work that gave immediate access to thousands of cases would be of considerable help there too.

[1] Blackstone, *Commentaries on the Laws of England* (Dawsons of Pall Mall, 1966), Volume I, p.71.

Such a reference work now exists. The publication of the first eight volumes of *Blackstone's Index of Case Precedents*, each volume being an entirely self-contained index to cases in one of eight subject areas means that there is now a reasonably priced, convenient and readily usable one-stop reference source for legal practitioners, academic lawyers and legal students who are seeking to locate a specific twentieth century precedent or trying to discover whether there is a relevant and helpful precedent in a particular area of the law.

Embracing Child Law, Criminal Law, Evidence, Family Law, Marriage Breakdown, Road Traffic Law, Sentencing, and Tort these first eight volumes of *Blackstone's Index* contain over 120,000 references to more than 40,000 cases decided by the English and Welsh courts (and by the Privy Council) throughout the twentieth century. Within the various volumes cases are listed alphabetically as well as by subject. The court which decided each case is also identified. In addition case-entries are followed by brief one or two sentence 'pointers' which seek to indicate in a little greater detail the content of the many decisions that have been indexed. These pointers do not, it should be noted, attempt to summarise the *ratio decidendi* of each case or indeed to encapsulate the entire array of issues that have been considered in a case. They are intended merely to provide a modicum of assistance to the reader in deciding whether it is worth moving on from having unearthed a case in *Blackstone's Index* to actually reading it in its entirety in a case report.

The *Blackstone's Index* is uniquely comprehensive in indexing not only law reports but legal journals and periodicals as well. Cases have been extracted from the *All England Law Reports, Cox's Criminal Cases, the Criminal Appeal Reports, Criminal Appeal Reports (Sentencing), Criminal Law Review (Case and Comment), Family Court Reporter, Family Law Reports, Justice of the Peace Reports, Law Journal, Law Journal County Court Reporter, Law Journal Newspaper County Court Appeals, Law Journal Newspaper County Court Reports, Law Journal Reports, Law Reports (Appeal Cases, Chancery Division, Family Division, King's/Queen's Bench Division, Probate, Divorce* and *Admiralty Division*), *Law Times Reports, New Law Journal, New Law Journal Reports, Road Traffic Reports, Solicitors Journal, Times Law Reports* (old and new series), *Weekly Notes, Weekly Reporter* and *Weekly Law Reports.*

In short *Blackstone's Index of Case Precedents* represents a uniquely powerful low-cost reference tool through which the legal wisdom of the twentieth century is made readily available to lawyers heading into the twenty-first. In addition to publishing each volume of the work as a separate self-contained and easy-to-use book all eight volumes have been published on CD-ROM.

HOW TO USE BLACKSTONE'S CHILD LAW INDEX

This volume contains references to those Child Law cases decided by the English and Welsh courts (and the Privy Council) during the twentieth century which have been reported in the wide array of reports and periodicals that form the basis of *Blackstone's Index of Case Precedents*.

Like each other volume of a *Blackstone's Index* this volume is a self-contained reference source. In other words users of *Blackstone's Child Law Index* will not be referred to any other volume in their quest for a particular Child Law case.

On the whole *Blackstone's Child Law Index* embraces those areas of law that would feature in a typical Child Law syllabus at university. As with all volumes of the Index cases principally or entirely concerned with points of practice have not been included.

Blackstone's Child Law Index is divided into two Parts. In Part I cases are grouped into subject categories. In Part II cases are listed alphabetically. Readers looking for cases by topic are recommended to consult Part I. Readers with a rough (or indeed exact) idea of a case name and who wish merely to discover where a specific case is located ought to consult Part II.

Each case is succeeded by a brief 'pointer'. The 'pointer' gives a better idea of what exactly each case is concerned with. It cannot be overemphasised that the 'pointer' does not represent an attempt to summarise the entirety of a case nor does it seek to give a one or two line *ratio decidendi* for each case. It is meant merely to provide a flavour of what has been decided in each case and to thereby enable the reader to make a somewhat more informed choice as to whether it is worth consulting a comprehensive account of the case in the relevant source or sources to which the reader is referred

The Subject Index Cases in the subject index are grouped into generic categories such as ADOPTION, FOSTERING, WARD. Cases are then listed under a variety of highly specific sub-headings. This has the double advantage that readers can either look up all the cases in a loosely defined area of interest or alternatively can very quickly zone in on the few cases decided in a much more tightly defined area of interest.

Either way the subject index is perfectly easy to use. It is preceded by two Tables of Contents. The first (entitled 'Generic Headings') lists the broad categories into which cases have been divided (ADOPTION, FOSTERING, WARD). The second (entitled 'Generic Headings with Sub-Headings') lists the much more specific headings under which cases are listed within each generic category ('ADOPTION (ward)', 'FOSTERING (publicity)', 'WARD (medical treatment)'). The reader can turn to the 'Generic Headings with Sub-Headings' page, see in what generic category the case or type of case being looked for is most likely to be found and turn to the appropriate part of the subject index. Alternatively the reader can move on to (if the reader has not in fact gone straight to) the 'Generic Headings with Sub-Headings' page, find out the sub-headings under which cases are listed, decide which sub-heading most closely matches the reader's subject of inquiry and turn to the page indicated. As with any dictionary or index a degree of creative thinking may very occasionally be required of the reader in judging which category or sub-heading best matches the case or genre of case the reader is seeking to locate.

HOW TO USE BLACKSTONE'S CHILD LAW INDEX

The Alphabetical Index The alphabetical index generally follows the traditional format adopted in the contents of case reports. Hence case names are on the whole listed both in forward and in reverse order so. Thus *C* v *C (No 2)* appears as *C* v *C (No 2)* and *C (No 2), C* v. However cases involving absolutely identically named parties (such as *Francis* v *Francis*) are listed only in forward order.

Users should note that while every reasonable care has been taken to ensure that the case names and citations in the text of this work are accurate and that the text of the work is correct insofar as it indicates what was decided in each case mentioned the author accepts no responsibility for loss occasioned to any person acting or refraining from acting as a result of material contained in this publication.

ABBREVIATIONS USED

The following abbreviations are used in the text:

AC	*Law Reports (Appeal Cases)*
All ER	*All England Reports*
CA	Court of Appeal
CCA	Court of Criminal Appeal
CCR	Crown Cases Reserved
CC Rep	*Law Journal County Court Reports*
Ch	*Law Reports (Chancery Division)*
Cox CC	*Cox's Criminal Cases*
Cr App R	*Criminal Appeal Reports*
Cr App R (S)	*Criminal Appeal Reports (Sentencing)*
CrCt	Crown Court
Crim LR	*Criminal Law Review*
CyCt	County Court
FamD	*Law Reports (Family Division)*
FCR	*Family Court Reporter*
FLR	*Family Law Reports*
HC ChD	High Court (Chancery Division)
HC FamD	High Court (Family Division)
HC KBD	High Court (King's Bench Division)
HC PDAD	High Court (Probate, Divorce and Admiralty Division)
HC QBD	High Court (Queen's Bench Division)
HL	House of Lords
JP	*Justice of the Peace Reports*
KB	*Law Reports (King's Bench Division)*
LJ	*Law Journal/Law Journal Reports*
LJNCCR	*Law Journal Newspaper County Court Reports*
LJNCCA	*Law Journal Newspaper County Court Appeals*
LTR	*Law Times Reports*
Mag	Magistrates' Court
NLJ	*New Law Journal/New Law Journal Reports*
PC	Privy Council
Police Ct	Police Court
PDAD	*Law Reports (Probate, Divorce and Admiralty Division)*
QB	*Law Reports (Queen's Bench Division)*
RTR	*Road Traffic Reports*
SJ	*Solicitors Journal*
TrTb	Transport Tribunal
TLR	*Times Law Reports*
WN	*Weekly Notes*
WR	*Weekly Reporter*
WLR	*Weekly Law Reports*

In addition the following letters are sometimes indicated alongside:

1. dt, g, i, t

These letters when they appear immediately after a page number indicate that the source to which the reader is being referred contains an additional reference to a British newspaper report of the case concerned.

dt = *Daily Telegraph*
g = *The Guardian*
i = *The Independent*
t = *The Times*

2. ccr

Not all County Court cases noted by the *Law Journal* were published separately from the main body of the *Journal*. Those notes of County Court reports contained within the *Journal* itself are indicated in the text of this *Index* by prefacing the page number from the relevant volume of the *Law Journal* with the abbreviation 'ccr' to show that the case is contained in the County Court Reporter section of the *Journal*.

3. LB

These letters may appear before the page number in a reference to the *Solicitors Journal* and indicate that the reference is to a page number in the *Lawyer's Brief* section of the relevant *Solicitors Journal*.

5. wr

These letters may appear before the page number in a reference to the *Solicitors Journal* and indicate that the reference is to a page number in the *Weekly Reports* section of the *Solicitors Journal*.

ACKNOWLEDGMENTS

Writing the first eight volumes of *Blackstone's Index of Case Precedents* has been a challenging task rendered all the easier by the consistent kindness of family and friends and the very real generosity of many other people who have freely given their advice and assistance throughout the period in which the volumes were prepared.

My parents, Michael and Della Barrett, yet again provided me with that unqualified encouragement and support which they have afforded me in the past. My two brothers, Conor and Dr Gavin Barrett were similarly helpful.

In addition to my parents and brothers I was privileged throughout the period of writing the various volumes of the Index to have a close coterie of generous people around me who were eager to provide me with whatever assistance I needed. My very good friend Jennifer Powell proved herself to be a remarkable bastion of support to whom I owe a particular debt of gratitude. I am also deeply grateful to Sue Bate, the Law Librarian at Manchester University whose unfailing and undeserved kindness towards me has immeasurably facilitated and speeded the completion of this work. Professor Frank B. Wright, my onetime doctoral and later post-doctoral research supervisor at the European Occupational Health and Safety Legal Research Centre willingly provided useful and much-appreciated advice whenever it was solicited. My old friend Dr Jonathan Rush, not only undertook the onerous technical task of formatting the Index for publication both in book and CD-form but was a constant bedrock of support in many other ways. Bryan and Josie Hallows provided me with a warm and welcome retreat in the Cheshire countryside and so much more besides. So far as places to retreat to with my work were concerned I was in fact rather spoiled for choice with — regrettably as yet unavailed of — offers coming in from Duncan Lennox in San Francisco and from Anna Retoula, Christos Retoulas and Constantina Scholidi in Greece. Others among this 'support team' of friends included Fr Des Doyle, Fr Ian Kelly, Fr John McMahon, Stephano Pistillo and Martin Wai-Chung Leung. I must also acknowledge the very great assistance given to me by the library staff at Cambridge University, Manchester University, Salford University and Trinity College Dublin.

Last but far from least I would like to record my special thanks to Agapi Kapeloni, who when I began this work was my girlfriend, who somewhere along the way found herself changed in status to that of honorary research assistant and whose latest and most agreeable change in status was to become my wife.

Finally, I have taken reasonable care to ensure that the case names and citations in the text of this work are accurate and that the text of the work is correct insofar as it indicates what was decided in each case mentioned. However, I accept no responsibility for loss occasioned to any person acting or refraining from acting as a result of material contained in this publication.

The Index of Case Precedents embraces cases from the turn of the twentieth century through to the early Autumn of 1997.

Dr Maxwell Barrett,
Dublin,
Feast of the Immaculate Conception, 1997.

GENERIC HEADINGS

GENERIC HEADINGS WITH SUB-HEADINGS

ADOPTION (non-patrial)
ADOPTION ('parent')
ADOPTION (parentage)
ADOPTION (progress reports)
ADOPTION (prohibited degrees)
ADOPTION (property)
ADOPTION (provisional)
ADOPTION (publicity)
ADOPTION (religion)
ADOPTION (residence)
ADOPTION (revocation)
ADOPTION (step-parent)
ADOPTION (succession)
ADOPTION (surrogacy)
ADOPTION (taking child outside jurisdiction)
ADOPTION (ward)
ADOPTION (welfare)
AFFILIATION (corroboration)
AFFILIATION (general)
AFFILIATION (legitimacy)
AFFILIATION (maintenance)
APPRENTICE (general)
APPROVED SCHOOL ORDER (general)
BAIL (general)
BIRTH (concealment)
BIRTH CERTIFICATE (general)
BIRTH CERTIFICATE (transsexual)
BLOOD TEST (general)
BLOOD TEST (guardian)
BLOOD TEST (legitimacy)
BLOOD TEST (parental responsibility order)
BLOOD TEST (paternity)
CARE/CUSTODY (abduction)
CARE/CUSTODY (access/contact)
CARE/CUSTODY (adoption)
CARE/CUSTODY (adulterer)
CARE/CUSTODY (child sex abuse)
CARE/CUSTODY (child-minder)
CARE/CUSTODY (confidentiality)
CARE/CUSTODY (consent)
CARE/CUSTODY (contempt)
CARE/CUSTODY (contribution)
CARE/CUSTODY (cruelty)
CARE/CUSTODY (discharge)
CARE/CUSTODY (disclosure)
CARE/CUSTODY (discovery)
CARE/CUSTODY (divorce)
CARE/CUSTODY (education)
CARE/CUSTODY (emergency protection order)
CARE/CUSTODY (estoppel)
CARE/CUSTODY (ethnicity)
CARE/CUSTODY (evidence)
CARE/CUSTODY (expert evidence)
CARE/CUSTODY (foetus)
CARE/CUSTODY (foreign decree)
CARE/CUSTODY (fostering)
CARE/CUSTODY (general)
CARE/CUSTODY (grandparent)
CARE/CUSTODY (guardian)
CARE/CUSTODY (habitual residence)
CARE/CUSTODY (harbouring)
CARE/CUSTODY (hearsay)
CARE/CUSTODY ('household')
CARE/CUSTODY (homosexual)
CARE/CUSTODY (HIV-testing)
CARE/CUSTODY (ill-treatment)
CARE/CUSTODY (injunction)
CARE/CUSTODY (interim)
CARE/CUSTODY (interview)
CARE/CUSTODY (joint)
CARE/CUSTODY (legitimacy)
CARE/CUSTODY (maintenance)
CARE/CUSTODY (mental health)
CARE/CUSTODY (mother)
CARE/CUSTODY (neglect)
CARE/CUSTODY (non-parent)
CARE/CUSTODY (Official Solicitor)
CARE/CUSTODY (parental responsibility)
CARE/CUSTODY (place of safety order)
CARE/CUSTODY (privilege)
CARE/CUSTODY (provisional)
CARE/CUSTODY (publicity)
CARE/CUSTODY (religion)
CARE/CUSTODY (residence)
CARE/CUSTODY (residential assessment)
CARE/CUSTODY (secure accommodation)
CARE/CUSTODY (split)
CARE/CUSTODY (step-parent)
CARE/CUSTODY (supervision order)
CARE/CUSTODY (surname)
CARE/CUSTODY (surrogacy)
CARE/CUSTODY (temporary)
CARE/CUSTODY (transsexual)
CARE/CUSTODY (ward)
CARE/CUSTODY (welfare)
CARE/CUSTODY (wishes of child)
CARE/CUSTODY (withdrawal of application)
CARE/CUSTODY (witness)
CARE/INTERIM (general)
CAUTION (general)
CHILD (publicity)
CHILD ABUSE REGISTER (general)
CHILD OF THE FAMILY (foetus)
CHILD OF THE FAMILY (general)
CHILD SEX ABUSE (adoption)
CHILD SEX ABUSE (case conference)
CHILD SEX ABUSE (general)

WARD (interview)
WARD (legitimacy)
WARD (maintenance)
WARD (medical expert)
WARD (medical treatment)
WARD (Official Solicitor)
WARD (place of safety order)
WARD (publicity)
WARD (religion)
WARD (secure accommodation)
WARD (social worker)
WARD (soldier)
WARD (sterilisation)
WARD (supervision)
WARD (surety)
WARD (surrogacy)
WARD (witness)
WELFARE REPORT (general)
WILFUL NEGLECT (general)

SUBJECT INDEX

Re H and others [1997] 2 All ER 225; [1997] 2 WLR 563; [1997] 2 FCR 257; [1997] 1 FLR 872 HL On what constitutes acquiescence to removal/retention of child for purposes of Child Abduction Convention (as implemented).

Re K [1995] 3 FCR 473; [1995] 1 FLR 977 HC FamD Six-month delay in seeking return not acquiescence to taking of child; return ordered despite child's objections; application to hear oral evidence refused.

Re K [1997] 2 FLR 212 HC FamD On proving consent to removal of child (here from US to UK).

Re M [1996] 1 FLR 315 HC FamD Non-return of child settled in England whose removal from Greece (to which father acquiesced) not wrongful under Greek law/whose return entailed risk of physical or psychological harm.

Re O [1997] 1 FLR 924 HC FamD Father found to have consented to/acquiesced in removal of 'abducted' child: no order for return made.

Re R [1993] 2 FCR 461; [1994] 1 FLR 190 HC FamD Maintaining contact with children not acquiescence to their retention: return of abducted/wrongfully retained children ordered.

Re R [1995] 2 FCR 609; [1995] 1 FLR 716 CA No clear/definite expression of acquiescence so no acquiescence found; return of children ordered despite their stated wish to remain in England with mother (abductress).

Re S [1994] 2 FCR 945; [1994] 1 FLR 819; [1994] TLR 80 CA On determining whether there has been acquiescence.

Re S [1994] 1 FLR 82; (1993) 137 SJ LB 188; [1993] TLR 406 HC FamD Where one/other parent agreed to children remaining in jurisdiction for certain time/sought to keep them there for all time there was no acquiescence to their retention even inside period agreed to.

Re T [1992] 2 FCR 92 HC FamD Where Child Abduction proceedings started, stopped, re-started/principally used to secure return of mother not child there was acquiescence to non-return of child.

Re T (C) [1992] 2 FCR 92 HC FamD Where Child Abduction proceedings started, stopped, re-started/principally used to secure return of mother not child there was acquiescence to non-return of child.

Re Z (A) [1993] 1 FLR 682 CA Acquiescence to 'abduction' established so no order for return.

W v W [1992] 2 FCR 502 HC FamD Was acquiescence to non-return of children where father (unaware of Child Abduction Convention) agreed to mother keeping children.

ABDUCTION (care/custody)

Jenkins v Jenkins (1980) 1 FLR 148 CA Return of child to parent granted custody to be ordered where other parent 'snatches' child.

Re B (1983) 4 FLR 472; (1982) 132 NLJ 1172 CA Interim care and control of children to mother pending resolution of wardship/'kidnapping' proceedings appropriate.

Re L (1983) 4 FLR 368 CA Interim care and control order made in favour of mother who 'kidnapped' own child from United States and had him made ward of court.

Re T [1968] 3 All ER 411; [1968] Ch 704; (1968) 112 SJ 639; [1968] 3 WLR 430 CA Generally court will not countenance wardship/custody actions on foot of kidnapping by parent.

ABDUCTION (consent)

Re B [1995] 2 FCR 505; [1994] 2 FLR 249; (1994) 138 SJ LB 109; [1994] TLR 267 CA Consent to taking of child invalid as obtained by fraud; on meaning of 'rights of custody' in Child Abduction Convention, art 1(b).

Re C [1996] 3 FCR 222 HC FamD Father who stood by during considerable and lengthy preparations made by mother to remove children from US to UK held to have consented to removal.

Re K [1995] 3 FCR 697; [1995] 2 FLR 211 CA Father's consent to removal meant could not claim wrongful restraint.

Re W [1995] 1 FLR 878 HC FamD On evidential basis required to establish 'consent' defence contained in Hague Child Abduction Convention, art 13(a).

ABDUCTION (contact)

Re B (No 1) [1994] 1 FCR 389 HC FamD On relationship between contact/residence orders jurisdiction of court and Child Abduction Convention jurisdiction.

Re T and others [1993] 3 All ER 127; [1993] 2 FLR 617; [1993] 1 WLR 1461 HC FamD Procedure for contact order concerning child abducted by parent from abroad.

ABDUCTION (contempt)

Adami v Adami (1929) 73 SJ 557 HC PDAD Contemnor-husband who had removed child to France released on condition that would not leave country without leave of court, would surrender passport/permit, would not himself, or through another, interfere with child.

Re B [1994] 2 FCR 1142; [1994] 2 FLR 479 CA Improper that Algerian father (abductor) who was not in contempt when attended court be committed to prison until children brought to British Embassy in Algiers.

Re G (1967) 111 SJ 702 HC ChD Contemnor to be released from prison once 'kidnapped' daughter returned to jurisdiction (child to be placed with foster mother pending wardship hearings.

ABDUCTION (delay)

Re G [1996] 1 FCR 173; [1995] 2 FLR 410 HC FamD Non-return of children where was inordinate delay in seeking return (children two and a half years in jurisdiction).

Re K [1995] 3 FCR 473; [1995] 1 FLR 977 HC FamD Six-month delay in seeking return not acquiescence to taking of child; return ordered despite child's objections; application to hear oral evidence refused.

W v W [1993] 2 FCR 644; [1993] 2 FLR 211 HC FamD Return of child to country of habitual residence not ordered; ten-month delay in non-abducting parent seeking return of child was acquiescence to wrongful retention.

ABDUCTION (disclosure)

Re B [1995] 2 FCR 601; [1995] 1 FLR 774 CA On duty of solicitor (to whom client-abductor has confided his location and that of abducted children) to whom court makes order to disclose all documents pertaining to abductor's location.

ABDUCTION (foreign custody order)

Re K [1990] FCR 524; [1990] 1 FLR 387 HC FamD Recognition/registration/enforcement of Belgian custody order allowed.

Re L [1992] 2 FCR 821; [1992] 2 FLR 178 HC FamD Pre-Child Abduction Convention foreign custody order recognised/registered/enforced in England.

ABDUCTION (general)

A v A [1995] 1 FLR 341 HC FamD Court could make order in respect of abducted child who was expected but had not yet arrived in jurisdiction.

B v K [1993] 1 FCR 382 HC FamD Expressed desire of older children not to return respected by court: return of younger brother consequently not ordered.

C v C [1989] 2 All ER 465; [1989] 1 WLR 654 CA Parent's right to stop child's removal from Australia a right of custody for purpose of Convention on Child Abduction; Convention does not preclude child's return to country because exposed to grave personal risk where arises from mother's refusal to return.

C v S [1990] 2 All ER 449; [1990] 2 FLR 442 (also HL); [1990] TLR 414 CA No wrongful abduction where father has no rights in respect of child when child taken; no wrongful retention where child not habitually resident in jurisdiction from whence taken.

D v D [1994] 1 FCR 654; [1994] 1 FLR 137 CA On applying principles of Child Abduction Convention to case where inapplicable.

Evans v Evans [1989] FCR 153 CA On bringing applications under Child Abduction Convention: return of child ordered.

M v M (1983) 4 FLR 603 CA Children 'kidnapped' by mother returned to Italian father as their long-term interests demanded it (mother a hard-drinking liar).

N v N [1995] 1 FCR 595; [1995] 1 FLR 107 HC FamD Return ordered in case where psychological risk to children in return/non-return considerable.

R v Berry (Thomas Clive) [1996] 2 Cr App R 226; [1996] Crim LR 574 CA On application of defence that are child's natural father in context of child abduction case where man was taking child in honest but mistaken belief that was own child.

R v Colville-Hyde [1956] Crim LR 117 Assizes On necessary elements of offence of abduction.

R v Duguid (1907-09) XXI Cox CC 200; (1906) 70 JP 294; (1906) 41 LJ 335; [1906] 75 LJKB 470; (1906) XCIV LTR 887; (1905-06) 50 SJ 465; (1905-06) XXII TLR 506; (1906) WN (I) 100 CCR Was criminal conspiracy on part of person agreeing with mother to remove her child from lawful custody.

R v Griffin [1993] Crim LR 515 CA On respective roles of judge/jury in child abduction case; was possible to find attempted abduction where had arranged boat trip and went to school to request control of children in local authority care.

R v Leather (John Holdsworth) (1994) 98 Cr App R 179; [1993] Crim LR 516; [1994] 1 FCR 877; [1993] 2 FLR 770; (1993) 137 SJ LB 54; [1993] TLR 18 CA On what it means to remove child from lawful 'control' (Child Abduction Act 1984, s 2(1)).

R v Mousir [1987] Crim LR 561 CA On what is meant by removing child from 'lawful control' for purposes of Child Abduction Act 1984.

R v Powell (1914-15) XXIV Cox CC 229; (1915) 79 JP 272 CCC Need not intend to forever deprive parent of child to be convicted of child abduction.

R v Tegerdine [1983] Crim LR 163 CA Putative father was guilty of abduction of child albeit that did so from concern for child.

Re A (1981) 131 NLJ 1212 CA Return of children to Italian father in Rome ordered of English mother who had taken the children to England.

Re A [1988] 1 FLR 365 CA Return of child to foreign jurisdiction ordered where was not grave risk that same would expose child to psychological harm.

Re A-K [1997] 2 FCR 563; [1997] TLR 123 CA Valid order for supervised contact with children at Royal Courts of Justice plus requirement that father surrender his passport to his solicitors where was danger father might otherwise abduct children.

Re B [1992] TLR 520 HC FamD Mother could seek return of children to Germany (from whence taken by father) even though took part in post-abduction family law action in England (place to whence children taken).

Re B [1992] 2 FLR 1 CA Exceptionally can make ex parte interim residence order in respect of abductee and non-abducted children on application by non-abducting parent.

Re B [1993] 2 FCR 607 CA Discharge of committal/care/return orders in respect of child whose return to jurisdiction was sought.

Re B [1994] 2 FCR 404 HC FamD On determining which court has jurisdiction when Child Abduction Convention proceedings commenced in two countries.

Re B [1994] 2 FCR 1142; [1994] 2 FLR 479 CA Improper that Algerian father (abductor) who was not in contempt when attended court be committed to prison until children brought to British Embassy in Algiers.

Re B (H) [1997] 1 FLR 392 HC FamD Return of abducted children to mother in Denmark ordered despite their desire to remain with father in England.

Re B (N) [1993] 1 FCR 271 CA On what constitutes unlawful removal; non-return of child reversed where initial decision based on mistaken finding that return could well expose child to intolerable situation.

Re B-M [1993] 1 FLR 979 HC FamD On when court has jurisdiction under the Hague Child Abduction Convention.

Re C [1989] FCR 197; [1989] 1 FLR 403; (1989) 133 SJ 660 CA Order for return of abducted child where undertakings by father obviated grave risk of harm to child.

Re C (S) (1971) 121 NLJ 569 HC ChD Four day injunction on removal of child (abducted by parent) from jurisdiction so as to allow non-abducting parent to be heard on the matter.

Re D [1988] FCR 585; [1988] 1 FLR 97 HC FamD On power of court to order party to reveal location of abducted child.

Re G [1990] FCR 189; [1989] 2 FLR 475 CA Return of abducted child justified where undertakings by father obviated grave risk of psychological harm to child; nine-year old's desire to remain with mother (abductress) considered but not acted upon.

Re G [1984] FLR 268 CA Child's welfare paramount issue when adjudicating in wardship action springing from parental abduction.

Re G [1990] FCR 973; [1990] 2 FLR 325 HC FamD Registration of Belgian custody order favouring father (mother abductress).

Re G [1995] 2 FCR 22; [1995] 1 FLR 64 HC FamD Non-return of dual-nationality children of two English parents as mother's return would lead to mental deterioration raising adverse risks for children.

Re H [1991] FCR 243; (1990) 140 NLJ 1192; [1990] TLR 644 CA On what constitutes wrongful removal/retention; Child Abduction Convention inapplicable where wrongful removal occurred before its commencement.

Re H [1990] FCR 990; [1990] 2 FLR 439 HC FamD Mother granted interim custody of child in Canada violated own custody rights when brought child to England: return to Canada ordered.

Re J [1989] 3 All ER 590; [1989] Fam 85; [1990] FCR 341; [1990] 1 FLR 276; [1989] 3 WLR HC FamD On ordering that removal of ward from jurisdiction was unlawful (here so ordered).

Re J (1989) 133 SJ 876 HC FamD Declaration that there had been unlawful removal/retention of ward granted at behest of father (who had no custodial rights over ward).

Re J [1991] FCR 129 (also HL) CA Failed appeal by father against decision not to return child rightfully removed from jurisdiction and before father obtained custody order over child.

Re K (1976) 126 NLJ 412t CA Care and control of children to wife-mother who had removed them from Canada to Britain where she intended to marry man with whom presently enjoyed adulterous relationship.

Re K [1995] 2 FLR 550 CA Return of child ordered where grave risk of pyschological harm upon return unproved.

Re K [1996] 1 FCR 24 CA On relevant factors when ordering return of abducted child; absent risk of grave psychological harm order for return of abducted child from place whence abducted left stand.

Re L [1993] 2 FCR 509; [1993] 2 FLR 401 HC FamD Child returned where inter alia father's undertakings meant return did not pose grave risk of physical/psychological harm to child.

Re M [1995] 3 FCR 745; [1995] 1 FLR 1021 CA Return of children a final order (appeal to CA); undertakings are intended to protect children until case finally decided not to be used to impede return of children.

Re M [1995] 2 FCR 265; [1995] 1 FLR 89 CA Return of children justified given father's undertakings which (despite mother's evidence) it was presumed foreign authorities would seek to enforce.

Re M [1995] 3 FCR 99 HC FamD Unsuccessful action pursuant to Child Abduction Convention as father failed to show mother's taking of child was wrongful removal.

Re N [1995] 2 All ER 417; [1995] Fam 96; [1995] 2 FCR 605; [1995] 2 WLR 233 HC FamD Court has duty under Hague Convention on Child Abduction to order child to be held in country even before child arrives.

Re N [1993] 2 FCR 330; [1993] 2 FLR 124 CA On role of court hearing action pursuant to Hague Child Abduction Convention 1980 as implemented.

Re O [1995] 1 FCR 721; [1994] 2 FLR 349 HC FamD On return of children to jurisdiction where enforceability of father's undertakings to English court of considerable dispute (here return of children ordered).

Re O [1997] 2 FCR 465 HC FamD German child of German mother ('abductress') ordered to be returned to Germany at behest of German grandparents who had been caring for child.

Re P [1996] 2 FCR 133; [1995] 1 FLR 831; [1995] TLR 84 CA Court could (and here was right to) issue declaration that removal of child from England was wrongful.

Re P (A and J) (1977) 127 NLJ 1151b CA Return of Italian children (abducted by Italian mother) to Italy ordered where was best for them that their futures be decided in Italian court.

Re R (1981) 2 FLR 416; (1981) 125 SJ 588 CA On appropriate procedure where wardship application made in respect of 'kidnapped' child: child's best interests determinant factor.

Re R [1994] TLR 624 CA Court could order return of child under the Hague Abduction Convention even though child objected to return.

Re R (No 2) [1993] 1 FLR 249 HC FamD Return of child abroad not ordered where father with English care and control order (since 1991) removed child from Canada where mother had been granted custody (in 1992).

Re S [1993] 2 FCR 499; [1994] 1 FLR 297 CA On principles to be applied when dealing with child abduction involving non-Child Abduction Convention country.

Re S [1993] 1 FCR 789 CA On whether or not to order return of abducted children to jurisdiction not party to the Hague Convention.

Re S [1996] 3 FCR 115 HC FamD Illegitimate child in respect of whom father had no custody rights/parental responsibility (though had applied for residence/parental responsibility orders before child removed and later obtained ex parte residence order) held to have been unlawfully removed by mother.

Re S [1996] 1 FLR 660 HC FamD Successful ex parte application for declaration that removal of child from jurisdiction breached Article 12 of the Child Abduction Convention.

Re S [1997] 1 FLR 958 CA Keeping infant child outside UK (place of habitual residence) by maternal relatives of infant child violated the Hague Convention, Article 3 whilst taking the child from the jurisdiction violated the European Convention, Article 12.

Re S [1997] 3 WLR 597 HL Acting in breach of court order and keeping infant child outside UK (place of habitual residence) by maternal relatives of child violated Hague Convention, Article 3; taking the child from the jurisdiction violated the European Convention, Article 12.

Re S [1995] 3 FCR 707; [1995] 1 FLR 858 HC FamD Sequestration of property of friend of mother allowed where friend assisted mother in her non-compliance with order to return children.

Re S [1997] 2 FCR 342; [1997] 1 FLR 486 HC FamD Children allowed have separate representation in Hague Child Abduction Convention hearing.

Re T (1968) 118 NLJ 564t CA Return of abducted children ordered where faced no real risk of harm in consequence.

Re W [1996] 1 FCR 46 HC FamD Return of child ordered where father in affidavit evidence had made out out good defence of consent but failed to do so in his oral testimony.

S v H [1997] 1 FLR 971; (1997) 141 SJ LB 64; [1997] TLR 127 HC FamD Was not breach of custodial rights for mother-custodian to remove from Italy children to whom father only had access rights: summary return not ordered.

S v S [1995] 1 FCR 188; [1994] 2 FLR 681 HC FamD Return of child ordered where taking from non-Convention country had not involved breach of custody rights.

The Ontario Court v M and M [1997] 2 FCR 573; [1997] 1 FLR 475 HC FamD Neither of two children returned to custody of grandmother in Canada (from that of parents in England) as one child faced grave risk of being placed in intolerable situation if returned.

ABDUCTION (habitual residence)

A v A [1993] 1 FCR 829; [1993] 2 FLR 225 HC FamD Children were habitually resident in Australia where had moved there with intention of long-term stay; letters from father showed had acquiesced in mother's taking of children; return of children to place of habitual residence not ordered.

C v S [1990] 2 All ER 449; [1990] 2 FLR 442 (also HL); [1990] TLR 414 CA No wrongful abduction where father has no rights in respect of child when child taken; no wrongful retention where child not habitually resident in jurisdiction from whence taken.

G v G [1991] FCR 12; [1991] 2 FLR 506 CA Court of first hearing overruled and return of children (abducted by mother) to place of habitual residence ordered.

M v M [1997] 2 FLR 263 CA Successful appeal against judge's finding as to habitual residence: on habitual residence.

P v P [1992] 1 FLR 155 HC FamD Children returned to place of habitual residence despite one child objecting/mother's claim that her unhappiness at return would adversely affect children.

Re A (No 2) [1993] 1 FLR 396 CA On proper exercise of discretion not to return child to country of habitual residence.

Re A and others [1996] 1 All ER 24; [1995] 3 FCR 635; [1996] 1 FLR 1; [1996] 1 WLR 25 HC FamD 'Habitual residence' under Hague Convention on Child Abduction intimates voluntary and settled physical presence in signatory country prior to abduction.

Re B [1995] 1 FCR 273; [1994] 2 FLR 915; [1994] TLR 367 HC FamD On determining place of habital residence of child.

Re B (1994) 138 SJ LB 176 HC FamD Removal of child from jurisdiction to place where mother attempted reconciliation did not change child's habitual residence.

Re B [1994] 1 FCR 394 [1993] 1 FLR 993 HC FamD On what constitutes habitual residence/retention/acquiescence for purposes of Hague Child Abduction Convention.

Re E [1989] 1 FLR 135 CA Return of abducted child to country of habitual residence ordered; on allowing child to remain where return ran grave risk of placing child in intolerable situation.

Re F [1992] 1 FLR 548 CA On evidence admissible in child abduction/Hague Convention proceedings; child of persons apparently intending to emigrate to Australia was habitually resident there (after only three months).

Re F [1992] 2 FCR 595 HC FamD On determining place of habitual residence of children.

Re J [1991] FCR 129 (also CA); (1990) 134 SJ 1039; [1990] TLR 566 HL Taking child from foreign jurisdiction not wrongful as mother had sole custody/guardianship of child; habitual residence to be established as of date non-abducting father secured custody order (at which point child habitually already resident elsewhere).

Re J [1990] 2 AC 562 (also HL) CA On where is place of habitual residence for purpose of Child Abduction Convention; unmarried mother's removing child from Western Australia without father's knowledge did not (by virtue of Western Australian Law) come within terms of Child Abduction Convention.

Re M [1996] 1 FLR 887 CA On determining child's place of habitual residence.

Re M [1994] TLR 475 CA Order for return of child to jurisdiction of habitual residence (pursuant to Child Abduction Convention) is final.

Re N [1993] 2 FCR 330; [1993] 2 FLR 124 CA On role of court hearing action pursuant to Hague Child Abduction Convention 1980 as implemented.

Re O [1995] 2 FCR 649; [1993] 2 FLR 594 HC FamD On deciding place of 'habitual residence'.

Re R [1992] 2 FLR 481 CA On determining place of habitual residence of child.

Re S [1991] FCR 656; [1991] 2 FLR 1 CA Habitual residence defined by reference to pre-abduction situation; failed attempt not to have child returned to place from where abducted.

Re S [1997] 1 FCR 588; [1997] TLR 16 CA On habitual residence of/jurisdiction of court in respect of child (Irish citizen habitually resident in England) removed by deceased mother's relations to Ireland from England.

Re S [1997] TLR 426 HL Child was habitually resident in England despite having been removed to Ireland by deceased mother's relatives.

Re S and another [1994] 1 All ER 237; [1994] Fam 70; [1994] 1 FCR 83; [1994] 2 WLR 229 HC FamD Wrongful retention cannot alter habitual residence so that habitual residence becomes place of wrongful retention.

Re V [1996] 3 FCR 173; [1995] 2 FLR 992 HC FamD On determining habitual residence of persons dividing their year between two jurisdictions.

S v S [1993] 1 FCR 13; [1992] 2 FLR 492 CA Reasonable and strongly-held view of child that should not be returned to place of habitual residence justified non-return.

V v B [1991] FCR 451; [1991] 1 FLR 266 HC FamD Order for child whose 'habitual residence' was Australia to be returned to mother there by father (abducter) as no proof of 'grave risk' to child if returned; on awarding costs in abduction action.

W v W [1993] 2 FCR 644; [1993] 2 FLR 211 HC FamD Return of child to country of habitual residence not ordered; ten-month delay in non-abducting parent seeking return of child was acquiescence to wrongful retention.

ABDUCTION (non-Convention country)

Re A [1997] TLR 357 CA Court to be satisfied (as here) that welfare of child would be adequately safeguarded by courts of foreign non-Convention jurisdiction before ordering return of child to that jurisdiction.

Re P [1997] Fam 45; [1996] 3 FCR 233; [1997] 1 FLR 780; (1996) 140 SJ LB 177; [1997] 2 WLR 223 CA Welfare of abducted child the defining criterion when deciding whether to order return of child to place whence came.

ABDUCTION (non-return)

Re F [1996] 1 FCR 379; [1995] 2 FLR 31 CA Mother's removal of child from Colorado wrongful but return not ordered as would present grave risk of psychological harm to child.

Re F [1995] 3 All ER 641 CA Exceptionally Court will exercise discretionary power under Hague Convention on Child Abduction not to summarily return abducted child to country of habitual residence (as required by Convention) where that would entail grave risk to welfare of child.

Re N [1991] FCR 765; [1991] 1 FLR 413 HC FamD On what constitutes grave risk of harm/settling into new surroundings so as to justify non-return of abducted children: order for return of children to place of habitual residence.

Re R [1997] 3 FCR 29 (also CA); [1997] 1 FLR 663 (also CA) HC FamD Non-return of abducted child (who did not wish to return) to Switzerland and non-registration of Swiss care and custody order (which no longer reflected realities of situation).

Re R [1992] 1 FLR 105 HC FamD Could refuse return of abducted child where sufficiently old/mature to truly object to return: here return refused.

S v S [1992] 2 FCR 113; [1992] 2 FLR 31 HC FamD Some but not grave risk of psychological harm did not merit non-return of child; mature child's vehement desire not to be returned a relevant factor: return not ordered.

ABDUCTION (objections of abductee)

Re M [1994] 2 FCR 750; [1994] 1 FLR 390 CA On procedure where children objecting to being returned to country of habitual residence.

Re M [1992] 2 FCR 608 HC FamD Non-return of abducted children in light of their objections to same.

Re M [1994] 2 FLR 126 CA Court did not order return of child abroad where child objected to same.

Re R [1992] 1 FLR 105 HC FamD Could refuse return of abducted child where sufficiently old/mature to truly object to return: here return refused.

ABDUCTION (peremptory return)

Re M [1996] 1 FCR 557; [1996] 1 FLR 478; [1995] TLR 599 CA Peremptory return order made requiring children to be sent back to Dubai.

ABDUCTION (prohibited steps order)

H v H [1994] 1 FLR 530 HC FamD Mother allowed continue with residence/prohibited steps orders applications in respect of children she had abducted and retained.

ABDUCTION (residence order)

H v H [1994] 1 FLR 530 HC FamD Mother allowed continue with residence/prohibited steps orders applications in respect of children she had abducted and retained.

Re M [1994] 2 FCR 1209; [1994] 1 FLR 551 HC FamD Non-recognition of Irish custody order/declaration that removal of children wrongful where English court had already made interim residence orders favouring mother.

ABDUCTION (ward)

Re C [1978] 2 All ER 230; [1978] Fam 105; (1977) 121 SJ 693; [1977] 3 WLR 561 CA Child's welfare of paramount importance where peremptory order sought after kidnapping; child's interests required English court to assume jurisdiction.

Re J [1989] 3 All ER 590; [1989] Fam 85; [1990] FCR 341; [1990] 1 FLR 276; [1989] 3 WLR HC FamD On ordering that removal of ward from jurisdiction was unlawful (here so ordered).

Re L (1983) 4 FLR 368 CA Interim care and control order made in favour of mother who 'kidnapped' own child from United States and had him made ward of court.

Re L [1974] 1 All ER 913; (1973) 123 NLJ 1066t; (1974) 118 SJ 22; [1974] 1 WLR 250 CA Child's welfare in kidnapping case paramount factor (though parent's conduct also factor).

Re T [1968] 3 All ER 411; [1968] Ch 704; (1968) 112 SJ 639; [1968] 3 WLR 430 CA Generally court will not countenance wardship/custody actions on foot of kidnapping by parent.

ABDUCTION (wrongful removal/retention notice)

R v R [1995] 4 All ER 115; [1995] Fam 209; [1996] 1 FCR 480; [1995] 2 FLR 625; [1995] 3 WLR 425 HC FamD 'Wrongful removal/retention' notice under Convention on Child Abduction need not take given form; generally court to ensure parent in state from which child taken knows Convention rights.

ABORTION (general)

Janaway v Salford Health Authority [1988] 3 All ER 1079; [1989] AC 537 (also CA); [1989] 1 FLR 155; (1988) 138 NLJ 348; (1988) 132 SJ 1731; [1988] 3 WLR 1350 HL Conscience provisions of Abortion Act apply only to medical parts of abortion not preliminary arrangements therefor.

Paton v British Pregnancy Advisory Service Trustees and another (1978) 142 JP 497; [1979] QB 276; (1978) 122 SJ 744; [1978] 3 WLR 687 HC QBD Injunction unavailable to husband against wife/abortion charity to prevent same from procuring lawful abortion for wife.

R v Lumley (1911-13) XXII Cox CC 635; (1912) 76 JP 208 CCC Abortionist guilty of murder/manslaughter if did/did not (nor could not reasonably) consider that death or grievous bodily harm would result from actions.

R v Salford Health Authority, ex parte Janaway [1988] 1 FLR 17 HC QBD Conscience provisions of Abortion Act apply only to medical parts of abortion not preliminary arrangements therefor.

R v Salford Health Authority, ex parte Janaway [1989] AC 537 (also HL); [1988] 2 FLR 370; (1988) 132 SJ 265; [1988] 2 WLR 442 CA Conscience provisions of Abortion Act apply not only to medical parts of abortion but preliminary arrangements therefor.

R v Spicer (1955) 39 Cr App R 189 Assizes Could be convicted for procuring miscarriage where sought so to do though means used could not be successful.

ABORTION (ward)

Re B [1991] FCR 889; [1991] 2 FLR 426 HC FamD Abortion on twelve year old ward authorised.

Re G (S) [1991] FCR 753; [1991] 2 FLR 329 HC FamD Unnecessary to obtain declaration that termination lawful before could perform abortion on mental defective.

ABORTION (ward)

Re G-Y [1984] FLR 811 HC FamD Necessary that leave of court be sought before ward allowed to have abortion.

Re P [1986] 1 FLR 272 HC FamD Wardship jurisdiction invoked to order termination of pregnancy of/insertion of contraceptive device into child in care under Children and Young Persons Act 1969.

ACCESS/CONTACT (abduction)

Re T and others [1993] 3 All ER 127; [1993] 2 FLR 617; [1993] 1 WLR 1461 HC FamD Procedure for contact order concerning child abducted by parent from abroad.

ACCESS/CONTACT (adoption)

C v Berkshire County Council [1988] FCR 161; [1987] 2 FLR 210 HC FamD Valid adjournment of juvenile court parental access action until county court decided in pending action whether child to be freed for adoption.

C v H (1979) 123 SJ 537 HC FamD When access/adoption arise to be decided in same action they should both be decided in tandem, not one before the other.

G v G [1993] 2 FLR 306; [1992] TLR 641 HC FamD Where contact and adoption orders being sought by different parties ought to hear cases together.

Hereford and Worcester County Council v D; Hereford and Worcester County Council v H (E) [1991] FCR 56; [1985] FLR 975 HC FamD Controlled access allowed where did not seem access would be problematic/adoption not proved to be best option for child.

Re A (B) [1985] FLR 1008 HC FamD Children's interests required that they remain in foster-care; objectively tested, mother's refusal of consent to adoption not unreasonable; future access by mother a real possibility.

Re B (MF); Re D (1972) 136 JP 259; (1972) 116 SJ 58 CA On contact between adopted child and biological parents.

Re C (1983) 4 FLR 396 HC FamD Order for increased access to child (for whom council had planned adoption) by natural mother who had surmounted drink problem with view to eventually returning child to mother.

Re C [1988] 1 All ER 705; [1989] AC 1; [1988] FCR 484; [1988] 2 FLR 159; (1988) 138 NLJ 64; (1988) 132 SJ 334; [1988] 2 WLR 474 HL Court may provide for future access to natural family in adoption order.

Re C [1993] 3 All ER 259; [1993] Fam 210; [1993] 3 WLR 85 HC FamD Once adoption order made parental contact provisions altered only if fundamental change in circumstances.

Re C [1995] 2 FCR 701 CA Number of times when contact available to natural parents of child placed for adoption reduced at behest of local authority after child freed for adoption.

Re C [1991] FCR 1052; [1991] TLR 404 CA On deciding whether withholding of parental agreement to adoption justified (here was); court to decide parental access issue before deciding whether to free child for adoption.

Re C [1993] 2 FLR 431 HC FamD On procedure as regards natural mother's applying for contact/specific issue order after adoption order made.

Re C [1992] 1 FLR 115 CA On resolving issue of access by parent who has always shown interest in children it is proposed to have adopted; reasonable refusal of consent not made unreasonable through delay for which parent not responsible.

Re C; P and P v C (1969) 113 SJ 721 CA Adoption order approved even though would end access to natural father as order would lead to legitimation of child.

Re D [1973] 3 All ER 1001; [1973] Fam 209; (1974) 138 JP 18; (1973) 123 NLJ 788t; (1973) 117 SJ 696; [1973] 3 WLR 595 HC FamD Persistent failure to discharge parental obligations to be so complete that no benefit in maintaining contact.

Re E [1995] 2 FCR 655; [1995] 1 FLR 57 HC FamD Contact order refused to natural parents of adopted child.

Re F [1990] 3 All ER 580; [1990] Fam 189; [1991] FCR 116; [1990] 2 FLR 478; [1990] 3 WLR 505 HC FamD Court may grant injunction restraining access by natural parents whether as part of adoption order or otherwise.

Re G (1980) 1 FLR 109 HC FamD On approach when adoption sought by natural parent and step-parent; adoption/access hearings (if are both) to be heard together.

Re G [1993] 2 FCR 27; [1992] 1 FLR 642 CA Where parent/prospective adopters seeking access/adoption order applications are to be heard together but that does not apply to connected interim/interlocutory applications.

Re H [1985] FLR 519 CA Adoption applications not to be ued to frustrate local authority actions; access order attached to adoption order only if agreement between parties concerned; father's refusal of consent to adoption unless access condition attached was reasonable.

Re H [1987] 2 FLR 12 HC FamD On ethnic background as factor when dealing with children; long-term fostering with view to adoption (if possible by someone of own ethnic background); access by mother to depend on her co-operation with social worker/what eventual adopters desired.

Re J [1973] 2 All ER 410; [1973] Fam 106; (1973) 137 JP 467; (1973) 117 SJ 372; [1973] 2 WLR 782 HC FamD Exceptionally court may order contact with natural parent after adoption order — court's powers in making such orders are wide; wardship/directions remedies to breach of adoption order terms.

Re M [1986] 1 FLR 51 CA On whether to order post-adoption access between adopted child and natural parents.

Re R [1991] FCR 1006; [1991] 2 FLR 78 CA Adoption ends access rights of natural parents: cannot stay issue of access and even if could should not have made access order six years after adoption.

Re R (G) [1985] FLR 643 CA Valid decision by judge (who hoped contact between child/grandmother would continue) not to add access order to adoption order absent exceptional circumstances.

Re S [1991] FCR 82 (also HC FamD); [1991] 1 FLR 161 CA Juvenile court could be (but here was not) justified in granting natural mother access to child whom local authority seeking to have adopted.

Re S [1975] 1 All ER 109; [1976] Fam 1; (1975) 139 JP 162; (1974) 124 NLJ 1008t; (1975) 119 SJ 11; [1975] 2 WLR 250 CA Adoption order can be qualified by access order.

Re S [1993] 2 FCR 234; [1993] TLR 118 HC FamD On whether/when natural parent to be afforded contact to adopted child.

Re T [1995] TLR 465; [1995] 2 FLR 792 CA On seeking leave to apply for direct/indirect contact with adopted child.

Re W [1979] 3 All ER 154; [1980] Fam 60; (1979) 143 JP 727; (1979) 123 SJ 553; [1979] 3 WLR 252 CA Natural parent cannot challenge merits of local authority decision to make child ward; authority may consider possible future adoption in deciding to disallow parental access to child.

Re W (1987) 131 SJ 915 CA Could (and here did) make access order as part of adoption order.

Re W [1988] FCR 129; [1988] 1 FLR 175 CA On making adoption rather than custodianship order.

ACCESS/CONTACT (alcoholic)

M v J (1977) 127 NLJ 1130t; (1977) 121 SJ 759 HC FamD Successful appeal by alcoholic, unstable father against refusal of application in which sought order for access to own child.

ACCESS/CONTACT (care/custody)

Bates v Morley (1982) 3 FLR 244; (1982) 132 NLJ 65 CA Mother with care and control of ward (father had access) allowed remove child to Canada (wardship ending upon ward quitting country).

Berkshire County Council v B [1997] 1 FLR 171 HC FamD Parental contact could be ordered in care proceedings though local authority care plan envisaged that ultimately there would be no parental contact.

Birmingham City Council v H (No 2) [1993] 1 FLR 883 CA Where mother/son both minors interests of each equally important; here ending of contact between mother/son too Draconian: reasonable supervised access allowed.

Cheshire County Council v B and others [1992] 2 FCR 572 HC FamD Provisions in care and contact orders for six-month review of their implementation was invalid.

Churchard v Churchard [1984] FLR 635 CA No committal of mother/no changes in custody in situation where children (in mother's custody) seeking of own volition to frustrate access attempts by father.

Devon County Council and others v S and others [1993] 2 FCR 36; [1993] 1 FLR 842 HC FamD Caution needed if appointing welfare officer as guardian ad litem; issue for justices in post-rehabiliation contact termination application not whether rehabilitation successful but should care cease.

Devon County Council v C and another [1985] FLR 619 HC FamD Wrong that access of natural parents to child in local authority care continue where child being placed in foster care with possible view to adoption.

Devon County Council v C and another (1985) 129 SJ 483 CA Judge ought to have decided (as court did here) issue of last occasions of maternal access to child in foster-care (not left it to local authority).

F v F [1989] Fam 1; [1989] FCR 232; [1988] 3 WLR 959 HC FamD Non-enforcement of French custody order where was twenty-one month delay before matter came before court and change in attitude of parties over access.

F v Kent County Council and others [1993] 1 FCR 217; [1993] 1 FLR 432; (1992) 136 SJ LB 258; [1992] TLR 394 HC FamD On exercise of discretion to require parties to seek court's leave before making future care/contact application (here wrongly exercised).

G v G and Devon County Council [1989] FCR 454 CA Divorce court could not make second care order where juvenile court had already made valid care order.

Hereford and Worcester Council v Jah [1985] FLR 530 HC FamD Whether parent to be allowed access to child in care depends on whether in child's best interests to allow access.

Kent County Council v C and another [1993] 1 All ER 719; [1993] Fam 57; [1993] 1 FLR 308; [1992] 3 WLR 808 HC FamD Exceptionally no contact between parent and child may be ordered by family proceedings court in care order but cannot make directions regarding care orders.

M v Berkshire County Council [1985] FLR 257 CA On power of juvenile court to order access.

P v Staffordshire County Council [1989] FCR 16 HC FamD Non-invocation of wardship jurisdiction to review exercise of local authority discretion (over access to child in care).

R v Bolton Metropolitan Borough, ex parte B [1985] FLR 343 HC QBD On ending/denying access of parents to child being held in local authority care.

R v Corby Juvenile Court, ex parte M [1987] 1 All ER 992; [1987] 1 FLR 490; (1987) 151 JP 387; (1970) 130 SJ 860; [1987] 1 WLR 55 HC QBD Access provisions of Child Care Act 1980 apply retrospectively to children put in care under earlier enactment.

R v Oxford Justices, ex parte D [1986] 3 All ER 129; [1987] 1 FLR 61; (1986) 150 JP 519; [1987] QB 199; (1970) 130 SJ 525; [1986] 3 WLR 447 HC QBD Putative father may apply for access to illegitimate child in local authority care.

R v West Glamorgan County Council, ex parte T [1990] FCR 142; [1990] 1 FLR 339; (1989) 133 SJ 1545 HC QBD Refusal of judicial review of local authority decision not to serve fresh notice of refusal of access.

Re B [1994] 1 FCR 471 HC FamD Children of mentally unwell mother taken into care (occasional/no access for older/younger child with aim of eventual residence to fathers).

Re B [1993] 1 FCR 363 (also CC) CA On relation between care/contact applications: inappropriate that CC judge halted contact when making care order.

Re B [1993] 1 FCR 363 (also CA) CyCt Contact with natural mother halted when order for care with view to adoption made.

Re B [1993] 1 FLR 421 HC FamD Care order plus interim contact order pending future hearing was permissible.

Re D [1953] 2 All ER 1318; (1954) 118 JP 25 CA Court of summary jurisdiction within which applicant resides may vary access order.

Re D [1988] 2 FLR 106 HC FamD On magistrates' role under the Guardianship of Minors Act 1971 in custody/access applications concerning children in local authority care.

Re F [1994] 2 FCR 1354; [1995] 1 FLR 510 HC FamD Contact order set aside where made in belief that would require parents to allow sibling in care have access to other siblings; on appropriate order to seek in such circumstances.

Re H (K and M) (1972) 116 SJ 664 HC FamD Issue of access (by illegitimate father) to children left to local authority which had passed care resolution in respect of them.

Re L [1985] FLR 95; [1984] TLR 399 CA Access of natural father to child placed in long-term foster care inappropriate: access order quashed.

Re M (1985) 135 NLJ 321c CA Failed application by mother for access to child whom had voluntarily surrendered to care.

Re M and H [1990] 1 AC 686 (also CA); [1989] FCR 65; [1988] 2 FLR 431; (1988) 138 NLJ 226; (1988) 132 SJ 1146; [1988] 3 WLR 45 HL Court could not grant putative father access to children where local authority had taken children into care.

Re M and H [1990] 1 AC 686 (also HL); [1988] FCR 97; [1988] 1 FLR 151; (1987) 131 SJ 1155; [1987] 3 WLR 759 CA Court could not grant putative father access to children where local authority had taken children into care.

Re N [1989] FCR 481; [1989] 2 FLR 106 CA Earlier access order to father did not preclude local authority being given parental rights over child by way of care order.

Re N (C) [1992] 2 FCR 401 HC FamD Court could order that there be no contact between mother and child in care.

Re P [1993] 2 FLR 156 HC FamD On contact/what constitutes reasonable contact.

Re R [1983] 2 All ER 929; (1983) 4 FLR 787; (1984) 134 NLJ 339c; (1983) 127 SJ 509; [1983] 1 WLR 991 CA Court may give any order in child's interest but generally will not amend bona fide local authority decisions.

Re R [1987] FCR 1; (1987) 151 JP 413 HC FamD On ordering adoption application to be dealt with as custodianship application.

Re S [1991] FCR 82 (also HC FamD); [1991] 1 FLR 161 CA Juvenile court could be (but here was not) justified in granting natural mother access to child whom local authority seeking to have adopted.

Re S [1994] 2 FCR 414; [1994] 2 FLR 222 CA Inappropriate for court to grant care order but adjourn contact decision until later date.

Re S; Dyfed County Council v S [1996] 2 FCR 838; (1995) 139 SJ LB 174; [1995] TLR 390 CA No extension of time to mother of child to appeal against phasing out by local authority of her contact with her children (who were in care).

Re T [1997] TLR 2 CA On relevant factors when deciding whether to discharge order for ending of contact between parents and children where latter are in local authority care.

Re W [1988] FCR 129; [1988] 1 FLR 175 CA On making adoption rather than custodianship order.

Re W [1989] FCR 97; [1988] 1 FLR 47; (1988) 132 SJ 1388; [1988] 1 WLR 1157 CA County court order as to care and access improper as justices having made care order only they could discharge same.

Re W (S) [1993] 1 FCR 896 HC FamD Court could upon making care order make another order terminating contact even though parent not given notice latter order would be sought.

Re Y [1988] 1 FLR 299 HC FamD Non-interference by court in local authority decisions regarding children in care of authority.

Re Y [1975] 3 All ER 348; [1976] Fam 125; (1976) 140 JP 19; (1975) 119 SJ 610; [1975] 3 WLR 342 CA Local authority with ward in care subject to control of court.

Salford City Council v C (1982) 3 FLR 153 HC FamD Care and control of child whom disabled parents unable to adequately care for given to local authority but frequent access to parents ordered.

Staffordshire County Council v C and M [1988] FCR 353 HC FamD On rights of putative father as regards seeking access to/custody of illegitimate child.

V-P v V-P (1980) 1 FLR 336 CA Court would reconsider issue of custody if mother (to whom child entrusted) continued to create difficulties over access by father.

W v Ealing London Borough Council [1994] 1 FCR 436; [1993] 2 FLR 788; [1993] TLR 308 CA Appropriate procedure where parental rights/contact orders sought (here unsuccessfully) in respect of ward.

W v Greenwich London Borough Council [1989] FCR 397; [1989] 2 FLR 67; (1989) 133 SJ 388 HC FamD Justices must give reasons for refusing parents access to children in care.

W v Shropshire County Council [1986] 1 FLR 359 (also HC FamD) CA Non-continuation of wardship over child in respect of whom local authoriy sought to bring care proceedings was valid.

ACCESS/CONTACT (child sex abuse)

B v B [1994] 1 FCR 809; [1994] 2 FLR 713 HC FamD On inteviewing childen where sexual abuse suspected.

C v C [1988] FCR 458; [1988] 1 FLR 462 HC FamD Supervised access by father not guilty of sexually abusing daughter but of horseplay with sexual overtones with her.

Cheshire County Council v M [1992] 2 FCR 817; [1993] 1 FLR 463 HC FamD Father who successfully appealed conviction for child sex abuse to which had confessed denied contact order.

H v B [1990] FCR 43 CA Refusal of second period of experimental access pending final decision whether father who had sexually abused child be continuously allowed access.

H v B (No 2) [1990] FCR 366 HC FamD Conditional access to his children allowed of father who had sexually abused those children.

H v H [1989] FCR 257; [1989] 1 FLR 212 CA Defined/supervised access of children allowed (one of whom person granted access had sexually abused).

L v L [1989] FCR 697; [1989] 2 FLR 16 CA Supervised access to father guilty of sex abuse justified as was eventual extended access to grandparents provided they did not raise sex abuse with girl.

Re B [1995] 1 FLR 904; [1994] TLR 671 HC FamD On proving child sex abuse (civil standard) such as to justify ending parental contact/freeing for adoption.

Re B (C) [1995] 1 FLR 622 CA Access order to grandparents (grandfather a convicted child sex abuser) wrong as did not hear oral evidence/court welfare officer on concerns involved (and contained in latter's report).

Re H [1989] 2 FLR 174 CA Continuation of trial access by father to children, one of whom father had sexually abused was justified.

Re L [1996] 2 FCR 352 CA Authorisation to allow finishing of contact ought not to have been made as would not be implemented in near future; on standard of proof in child sex abuse cases; on when interim/final care orders to be deployed.

Re P [1988] FCR 428; [1988] 2 FLR 209 CA Refusal of access to father (suspected of sexually abusing his illegitimate children) set aside; father to seek access as a parent from juvenile court.

Re P [1996] 3 FCR 714; [1996] 2 FLR 333 CA On deciding whether to grant unsupervised contact to children by father not proven on balance of probabilities to have sexually abused one/both of the children.

Re R [1988] FCR 497; [1988] 1 FLR 206 CA Access ought to have been refused to parent discovered to have sexually abused child.

Re W [1994] 2 FCR 759; [1994] 1 FLR 419; [1993] TLR 611 CA Refusal of contact between father and children justified where inter alia rested on possibly mistaken finding in civil action that father had sexually abused his children.

S (KV) v S (GG) [1992] 2 FCR 23; [1992] 2 FLR 361 HC FamD On establishing sexual abuse of child occurred; resumed access to father merited where sexual abuse of child not proved.

S v S [1988] FCR 219; [1988] 1 FLR 213 CA Where father's access to older child (whom had sexually abused) was refused, supervised access to younger children inappropriate.

ACCESS/CONTACT (contempt)

A v N [1997] 2 FCR 475; [1997] 1 FLR 533 CA Committal of mother to prison for persistent non-compliance with contact order was valid — child's welfare not paramount concern in such cases.

C v C [1990] FCR 682; [1990] 1 FLR 462 CA Committal for mother who repeatedly refused to comply with access order made in husband's favour; CC judge rightly dealt with access issue despite commencement of HC wardship proceedings.

D v D [1991] FCR 323; [1991] 2 FLR 34; [1990] TLR 727 CA On committal for non-compliance with access order/arrangement; on inclusion of penal notice in access order.

L v L [1991] FCR 547 CA Improper dispensing with need for service of access order upon alleged contemnor; on proper procedure as regards dealing with contempt in context of access.

P v W [1984] 1 All ER 866; [1984] Fam 32; (1984) 128 SJ 171; [1984] 2 WLR 439 HC FamD Contempt a last stop measure in dealing with access order abuses; summons for such violations to be detailed so defendant aware of abuses charged.

Re P [1991] FCR 283; [1991] 1 FLR 280; [1990] TLR 694 CA Increased access and eventual return of stepfather to family despite earlier sexual abuse of step-child was justified; contempt of local authority solicitor whereby had sought to frustrate access arrangements purged by contemnor.

ACCESS/CONTACT (criminal)

Re Y [1994] 2 FCR 367; [1994] 2 FLR 699 HC FamD Refusal of contact/no future application for contact with children without leave of court where father guilty of manslaughter of mother.

ACCESS/CONTACT (disclosure)

Re W (N) [1994] 1 FCR 121; [1993] 2 FLR 591 HC FamD Father's medical repports disclosed to mother in course of contact application; justices must give reasons for their decisions.

ACCESS/CONTACT (ethnicity)

Re D [1997] 2 FLR 48 CA Valid refusal of contact (for time being) between child of mixed race and his black father (who had been violent towards child's white mother).

Re M [1995] 2 FCR 435; [1995] 1 FLR 546 CA Magistrates Had not considered all relevant facts when allowing discharge of contact order between mixed race child and her black father (mother/new husband white): rehearing ordered.

ACCESS/CONTACT (evidence)

Bolton Metropolitan Borough Council v W [1988] FCR 305 HC FamD Social workers' videos of mother's access visits not privileged (even if were privileged was waived here when put videos in evidence).

R v Franklin [1994] TLR 334 CA Interview evidence ought not to have been admitted given improprieties in procedure regarding access by solicitor to accused (client).

R v Leeds Justices, ex parte Thompson (1983) 4 FLR 773 HC QBD Would be unusual to exclude relevant evidence at any stage before issue finally determined in case involving child's welfare.

Re H; Re K [1989] 2 FLR 313; (1989) 139 NLJ 864 CA Inadmissibility of hearsay evidence of children in matrimonial/guardianship action; historical events proved to be proved on balance of probabilities.

ACCESS/CONTACT (fine)

Thomason v Thomason [1985] FLR 214 HC FamD Fining of mother for breaches of access order inappropriate in the circumstances.

ACCESS/CONTACT (foreign)

Re A [1996] 3 FCR 165; [1996] 1 FLR 561 CA On registrability/enforcement of foreign access order.

Re F [1973] 3 All ER 493; [1973] Fam 198; (1973) 123 NLJ 723t; (1973) 117 SJ 616; [1973] 3 WLR 461 HC FamD Court may provide 'right of access' orders involving/prohibiting foreign travel by child.

ACCESS/CONTACT (foreign decree)

Re G [1993] 3 All ER 657; [1993] Fam 216; [1993] 2 FCR 485; [1993] 1 FLR 669; [1993] TLR 26; [1993] 2 WLR 824 CA Enforcement of foreign access order requires contact order; not available via compliance order against Lord Chancellor's Department.

ACCESS/CONTACT (fostering)

Coventry City Council v T [1986] 2 FLR 301 HC FamD Access by parents to child whom they had repeatedly abused and who was placed with foster parents was inappropriate.

Devon County Council v C and another [1985] FLR 619 HC FamD Wrong that access of natural parents to child in local authority care continue where child being placed in foster care with possible view to adoption.

Devon County Council v C and another (1985) 129 SJ 483 CA Judge ought to have decided (as court did here) issue of last occasions of maternal access to child in foster-care (not left it to local authority).

Re D and H [1997] 1 FLR 841; (1997) 141 SJ LB 44; [1997] TLR 82 CA No termination of contact between natural mother and children being placed in long-term foster-care as was contrary to what local authority proposed.

Re W (M) [1994] 1 FCR 161 CA Fostering of child but with access to father (who had abused/allowed abuse of child though denied it).

ACCESS/CONTACT (general)

Allette v Allette [1986] 2 FLR 427 CA Order for access only by way of mail was a refusal of access appeal against which did not require leave of court.

B (GW) v B (PW) CA (1971) 115 SJ 486 CA Refusal of access to father whose sixteen year old son did not want to see him.

B v B [1988] 1 All ER 652; [1988] 2 FLR 6; (1988) 132 SJ 564; [1988] 1 WLR 526 HC FamD Rights of access violations must take place in contracting state but are not subject to limited operation of Child Abduction Convention as implemented.

B v B [1971] 3 All ER 682; (1971) 121 NLJ 547t; [1971] 1 WLR 1486 CA Welfare of child may demand no access to divorced parent.

B v B (1972) 122 NLJ 1112 CA Interim custody of young girl to father whom wife had deserted but increased access by mother allowed.

B v B and F (B and B intervening) [1968] 3 All ER 232; (1968) 118 NLJ 956; (1968) 112 SJ 481; [1968] 3 WLR 1217 HC PDAD Access only to children of family; 'children of family' only if mutually accepted as such; no resistance to action for access did not mean mutual acceptance.

B v P [1992] 2 FCR 576 HC FamD Contact between father and small child validly refused where inter alia consequent upset to mother would upset child.

B v S (formerly B) (1974) 118 SJ 219 CA Re-hearing of access case necessary on evidence available (all evidence unavailable as judge promised children would not reveal what they said to him in chambers).

C v C [1984] TLR 743 CA Access to each child to be considered individually where parent seeks but is refused access to all children.

C v C [1990] FCR 682; [1990] 1 FLR 462 CA Committal for mother who repeatedly refused to comply with access order made in husband's favour; CC judge rightly dealt with access issue despite commencement of HC wardship proceedings.

Clarke v Clarke and Lindsay (1912-13) 57 SJ 644 CA Divorcée living in adultery not allowed access to her young son who was about to start going to school.

Corkett v Corkett [1985] FLR 708 CA In application for access to several children court to consider access to each child individually.

D v D [1994] 1 FCR 694 HC FamD On when refusal/dismissal of order/application merited in contact case.

E v C [1982] TLR 475 CA Access pre-eminently a matter for trial judge.

Evans v Jackson (1986) 150 JP 593 (also HC FamD) CA Father properly granted access to child though was upsetting for latter as upset occasioned by mother's improper attempts to frustrate access not by access per se.

F v R [1995] 1 FLR 227; [1994] TLR 628 HC FamD Enforcement of contact order validly refused: on task of justices hearing contact order enforcement application.

G v G (1971) 121 NLJ 410t HC PDAD Adulterous husband's extra-marital lover allowed remain in home she shared with adulterer when his children visited (but not allowed stay overnight when children stayed overnight).

Hammond v Hammond (1962) 106 SJ 610 CA Refusal to order access to children by father was merited.

Harris v Pinnington [1995] 3 FCR 35 HC FamD Custodial parent not allowed remove child from jurisdiction as not in child's best interests; staying contact to father ordered.

I v D [1989] FCR 91; [1988] 2 FLR 286 HC FamD Fining of mother for non-compliance with access order quashed as magistrates had not had as first consideration the best interests of child involved.

K v M [1996] 3 FCR 517; [1996] 1 FLR 312 HC FamD Paternity declaration/contact order refused to putative father who had affair with married woman whose marriage nonetheless survived.

L v L (1980) 1 FLR 396 HC FamD Better that reasonable access be initially granted and defined access ordered later if initial arrangements a failure.

Leeds City Council v C [1993] 1 FCR 585; [1993] 1 FLR 269 HC FamD On supervision of contact order.

Lewis v Lewis [1991] 3 All ER 251; [1991] 2 FLR 43 CA Service of access order may only be dispensed with at time order made.

M (P) v M (C) (1971) 115 SJ 444 CA Father refused access to children as was upsetting them/not in their best interests.

M v H and others [1988] 3 All ER 5 HL Courts have jurisdiction to hear custody/access application by parent against third party but statutorily precluded from doing so.

M v M (1980) 1 FLR 77 CA Problems regarding access not good ground on which to remove custody of young child from mother.

Mnguni v Mnguni (1980) 1 FLR 184; (1979) 123 SJ 859 CA Improper that court should decide access application in such a way that resolution of matter essentially left to welfare officer.

Mundul v Mundul (1968) 112 SJ 93 HC PDAD Inappropriate that when access issue pending before HC it should be encumbered with previous decision of divisional court on the matter.

Nottingham County Council v P [1994] Fam 18 (also HC FamD); (1993) 137 SJ LB 147 CA Prohibited steps order cannot be used where contact/residence order appropriate (residence order set aside).

Nottinghamshire County Council v P [1993] 1 FCR 180; [1993] 1 FLR 514; [1992] TLR 519 HC FamD Prohibited steps order not to be used to same end as contact or residence order.

Nottinghamshire County Council v P; Re P [1993] 3 All ER 815; [1994] 1 FCR 624; [1993] 2 FLR 134; [1993] TLR 213; [1993] 3 WLR 637 CA Prohibited steps order not to be used to same end as contact or residence order.

Orford v Orford (1980) 1 FLR 260 CA Court itself to decide access — improper that be left to welfare officer.

Patterson v Walcott [1984] FLR 408; (1984) 148 JP 161 HC FamD On enforcement of child access order made under Guardianship of Minors Act 1971.

Re A [1991] FCR 849; (1991) 141 NLJ 968t; [1991] TLR 329 CA Non-access to natural father justified as was in interests of children.

Re A-K [1997] 2 FCR 563; [1997] TLR 123 CA Valid order for supervised contact with children at Royal Courts of Justice plus requirement that father surrender his passport to his solicitors where was danger father might otherwise abduct children.

Re B [1984] FLR 648 CA On granting of access to parent where other parent vehemently opposed to it (here access refused but possibility of future variation).

Re B [1994] 2 FCR 812; [1994] 2 FLR 1 CA Contact decision not invalid where decided purely on basis of written evidence and submissions of counsel.

Re B [1992] 2 FCR 631 CA Order of custody of gypsy children to itinerant gypsy father with frequent access to mother with settled lifestyle left unchanged.

Re B [1991] FCR 976; [1992] 1 FLR 140; (1991) 141 NLJ 1004t; [1991] TLR 342 CA Non-aggressive/non-violent eccentricity of father did not justify refusal of defined access (so long as did not seek to use access to turn children against mother).

Re B [1997] TLR 367 CA Valid decision to dismiss contact application by father where stepfather threatened to reject mother and child (who could well be damaged thereby) if application allowed continue.

Re C [1985] FLR 804 CA Refusal of access valid as would have deleterious effect on children/ mother and her partner; improper to refuse access until children decide for themselves whether desirable — not a decision for children.

Re C [1996] Fam 79; [1995] 1 FLR 777; [1995] 3 WLR 30 CA County court judge could not amend contact order so as to vary degree of contact.

Re C (1992) 136 SJ LB 252; [1992] TLR 407 HC FamD May be order that there be no contact between child and natural mother; inappropriate to direct guardian ad litem to police rehabilitation programme of child in local authority care.

Re C [1994] 1 FCR 705; [1993] 1 FLR 940 HC FamD On basis for/securing of access to mentally handicapped adult daughter by parent who did not have care of daughter.

Re C [1991] FCR 969; [1992] 1 FLR 309 CA Husband who was not father refused access to child (absence of blood link a factor though not per se a basis for refusing access).

Re C [1991] FCR 518 HC FamD Inappropriate to order liberal access to non-custodial father so that child could get to know him as well as mother (custodian).

Re C (B) [1985] FLR 639 CA Refusal of access to natural father justified as not in child's best interests (father essentially using access to get at mother/mother very anxious about access).

Re D [1993] 1 FCR 964; [1993] 2 FLR 1 CA Contact with father (to which mother vehemently opposed) denied.

Re D [1953] 2 All ER 1318 CCA Court of summary jurisdiction within which applicant resides may vary access order.

Re D (1997) 141 SJ LB 170; [1997] TLR 445 CA Inappropriate for conditions of an injunctive nature to be attached to a contact order.

Re D [1995] 1 FLR 495; [1995] TLR 45 HC FamD Inappropriate that contact order be made absent welfare officer's report/oral evidence where issue of contact in dispute.

Re D [1987] FCR 140; [1987] 2 FLR 365 CA Despite non-observation by local authority of earlier CA decision that child be rehabilitated with mother passage of time since then meant was no longer in child's best interests to have access to mother.

Re Dankbars (1953) 97 SJ 811; [1953] 3 WLR 957 CA Summary court could vary access order in respect of infant at behest of either parent provided either parent living within court's jurisdiction.

Re E [1994] 1 FCR 584; [1994] 1 FLR 146 CA On terminating contact between children and parents (here inappropriately done in context of local authority plans that 'closed' adoption of child take place).

Re E [1987] 1 FLR 368 CA Upset to child caused by difficulties over access created by non-custodial parent could not justify setting aside of order.

Re F [1993] 1 FCR 945; [1993] 2 FLR 677 CA Post-separation contact order refused to transsexual father whose children did not want contact with him.

Re H [1993] TLR 97; [1994] 2 FCR 249 CA On principles as regards deciding contact applications.

Re H [1994] 2 FLR 969 CA On desirability (as here) of mutual contact: contact validly ordered to person who had not sought same.

Re H [1994] 2 FCR 419; [1994] 2 FLR 776 CA Contact order in favour of stepfather.

Re H [1996] 2 FCR 784; [1996] 1 FLR 614 HC FamD Successful appeal against conviction/fining for non-compliance with contact order.

Re H [1992] TLR 433 CA Father refused contact order was nonetheless granted a parental responsibility order.

Re H [1990] FCR 353 CA Care and control to English uncle and aunt/liberal access to foreign mother where child's best interests demanded it.

Re H [1991] FCR 985; [1991] 2 FLR 109 CA Interim care and control of child of dead mother given to maternal grandmother with generous access rights to father.

Re H [1992] 1 FLR 148 CA On deciding whether access should end/be restarted: here visiting access allowed.

Re J [1994] 2 FCR 741 CA Valid refusal to make contact order where judge reasonably decided disadvantages of contact outweighed advantages.

Re J [1994] 1 FLR 729 CA On when leave to appeal required in contact cases; on whether/when to grant contact order.

Re K [1977] 2 All ER 737; (1976) 126 NLJ 1092t; (1976) 120 SJ 752; [1977] 1 WLR 533 HC FamD Financial penalty/prison committal if access order to child in other parent's custody disobeyed.

Re K [1992] 2 FCR 521; [1992] 2 FLR 108 HC FamD Solicitors reported to Law Society where seemed to be encouraging/inciting mother to violate contact order.

Re L [1990] FCR 332; [1989] 2 FLR 359 CA Inappropriate to order that children reside with mother where she had history of frustrating access by father.

Re M [1985] 1 All ER 745; (1985) 149 JP 574; [1985] 2 WLR 811 CA Access order for juvenile court; freeing of child for adoption for magistrates' court.

Re M [1988] FCR 450; [1988] 1 FLR 35 CA Access order properly set aside where parents rarely visited child when had access rights and was in child's best interests to be adopted.

Re M [1994] 2 FCR 968; [1995] 1 FLR 1029 HC FamD Although can dismiss contact application without hearing evidence ought not to have done so here.

Re M [1995] 1 FLR 274 CA On how court to decide whether contact appropriate.

Re M [1995] 1 FCR 753 CA Refusal of contact justified where children did not desire it/was risk that harm it would cause would be greater than the benefits that would accrue.

Re M [1995] 3 FCR 550; [1995] 2 FLR 86 CA On relevant matters for consideration in grandparent's application for leave to seek contact.

Re M (S) [1991] FCR 492; [1991] 2 FLR 333 HC FamD On access by natural father to illegitimate child.

Re N [1991] FCR 1000; [1992] 1 FLR 134; [1991] TLR 357 CA Father denied access where mother refused to comply with access order (so turning child against access) and only other solution was to imprison mother which was not in child's interest.

Re N (1983) 4 FLR 150; (1982) 132 NLJ 273 CA Appropriate that care and control of baby given to local authority until mother's capacities appraised but six month prohibition on access inappropriate: no prohibition ordered.

Re O [1985] FLR 716; (1985) 149 JP 172; [1984] TLR 693 CA Should not have ordered access by putative father to child pending resolution of paternity issue.

Re P [1997] 1 FCR 459; [1996] 2 FLR 314 CA Supervised contact of father to children: risk of ill-health contact posed for mother did not outweigh paramount interests of children in continued contact.

Re P [1994] 1 FCR 285; [1994] 2 FLR 374 HC FamD Contact order justified though mother's psychiatrist recommended no contact and welfare officer recommended direct/indirect contact in report/before court.

Re P (1996) TLR 15/5/96 CA Mother's objection to contact between children and father not per se a valid reason for refusing same where could be in interests off children for contact to be maintained.

Re R [1996] 3 FCR 566 CA On seeking leave to apply for contact.

Re R [1995] 1 FLR 123 CA Consent (contact) order appeal allowed where mother consented after judge intimated there would otherwise be an order in costs against her.

Re R [1993] 1 FCR 954; [1993] 2 FLR 762 CA Eventual contact to be allowed between natural father and child once child made aware of natural father's existence/adjusted to same.

Re R (1996) TLR 19/7/96 CA On relevant factors when deciding whether father to be given leave to apply for contact with his child.

Re R [1993] TLR 183 CA Interests of five year old child (who believed mother's co-habitee to be her father) demanded that child have access to her natural father.

Re R (J) [1995] 3 FCR 289 HC FamD On need for justices to give reasons for their decision in full/interim care order applications: here reasoning defective in place but conclusion (refusal of direct contact) justified.

Re S [1990] FCR 379; [1990] 2 FLR 166 CA On granting access; access ought not to have been refused merely because judge felt would not work.

Re S [1995] 1 FCR 617; [1994] 2 FLR 1057 CA Adjournment of contact action and imposition without notice of requirement to seek court's leave before bringing future action was improper.

Re T [1995] 2 FCR 537; [1995] 2 FLR 251 CA On contact between natural mother and adopted child.

Re W [1993] 2 FCR 731; [1994] 1 FLR 843 HC FamD Decision of justices set aside in contact case where had not conformed to rules regarding giving of reasons for decision made.

Re W [1996] 3 FCR 337 HC FamD Leave of court unnecessary when seeking variation of indirect contact order so that direct contact possible.

Re W [1993] 2 FCR 427 CA On deciding whether to make parental responsibility order; dismissal of father's contact and parental responsibility applications without hearing oral evidence justified and valid.

Re W (a minor) [1989] FCR 41; [1989] 1 FLR 163 HC FamD Non-access to natural father where mother to marry another who was only person child had ever known as father.

Re W (a minor) [1994] 2 FCR 1216; [1994] 2 FLR 441 CA Contact ordered between child and natural father despite mother (who had no right to end contact) stating would not obey order.

Re W and S [1992] 2 FCR 665 HC FamD Non-interference by appellate court in contact decision of inferior court unless obviously mistaken decision.

Rossage v Rossage and others [1960] 1 All ER 600; (1960) 110 LJ 204; (1960) 104 SJ 231 CA Suspending of access not interlocutory hearing so information/belief evidence inadmissible hearsay.

S v E [1993] 1 FCR 729 HC FamD Magistrates could (but here were wrong to) refuse to order access on terms privately arrived at between parties.

S v H [1997] 1 FLR 971; (1997) 141 SJ LB 64; [1997] TLR 127 HC FamD Was not breach of custodial rights for mother-custodian to remove from Italy children to whom father only had access rights: summary return not ordered.

S v M [1997] 1 FLR 980 HL Hearsay evidence of child as to alleged assaults upon him by father validly taken into account when deciding that access to child by father not in child's best interests.

S v Newham London Borough Council and another [1991] FCR 749; [1991] TLR 256 HC FamD Non-physical access could be ordered.

S v P [1997] 2 FCR 185; [1997] 2 FLR 277; [1997] TLR 55 HC FamD Family assistance order that would require local authority to escort children to/from prison where father incarcerated unmerited; indirect contact ordered while father in prison subject to later review upon father's release/re-establishment of life; parental responsibility on behalf of imprisoned father would be too much too soon.

S v S and P [1962] 2 All ER 1; (1962) 112 LJ 272; (1962) 106 SJ 152; [1962] 1 WLR 445 CA Access to person not shown to be unfit to have contact.

Shears v Shears (1973) 117 SJ 33 HC ChD Wife's refusal to allow husband access to child was unreasonable behaviour justifying divorce.

Sheppard v Miller (1982) 3 FLR 124; (1981) 131 NLJ 1236 CA Access to father denied where was upsetting child.

Starling v Starling (1983) 4 FLR 135 CA Was not in child's best interests to resume relationship with father after three and a half year gap (child a baby when last saw father): access order set aside.

T v T [1984] TLR 469 HC FamD On undesirability of fining/imprisoning custodial parent guilty of breach of access order (variation of access order upon investigation into reason for breach was preferable).

T v W [1996] 2 FLR 473 HC FamD Reasons ought to have been given when magistrates refused to give leave to apply for contact order.

Tilmouth v Tilmouth [1985] FLR 239; [1984] TLR 522 HC FamD On form of access orders.

W v B [1991] FCR 499; [1991] TLR 157 HC FamD Court may order contact by way of media that do not involve physical contact.

Williams v Williams (1985) 149 JP 540 CA Proper that father refused access to children indoctrinated against him by mother where psychiatric evidence was that children could be harmed by such access.

Y v B [1995] 3 FCR 49 HC FamD Trial contact unnecessary before magistrates make decision in contact case (can do so on evidence before court).

Y v Kirklees Metropolitan Council [1985] FLR 927 HC FamD On making application for access orders.

ACCESS/CONTACT (grandparent)

Re A [1996] 1 FCR 467; [1995] 2 FLR 153; [1995] TLR 141 CA No presumption that contact between grandparent and grandchild to be granted unless good reason not to.

Re A [1995] 3 FCR 543 HC FamD Failed application by grandmother for contact with grandchild (opposed by parents).

Re B (C) [1995] 1 FLR 622 CA Access order to grandparents (grandfather a convicted child sex abuser) wrong as did not hear oral evidence/court welfare officer on concerns involved (and contained in latter's report).

Re F and R [1995] 1 FLR 524 HC FamD In controverted action where grandparent seeking leave to apply for contact with grandchildren magistrates ought to have heard evidence from each side.

Re H (1977) 121 SJ 253 HC FamD Could order access by person who was neither parent nor guardian so here was open to grandmother to seek access.

Re M [1995] TLR 228 CA Grandmother required leave of court before could seek contact with grandchild in care.

Re S [1996] 3 FCR 30; [1996] 1 FLR 158 CA Contact with paternal grandparents ordered notwithstanding mother's not wanting same.

Re W [1997] 2 FCR 643; [1997] 1 FLR 793 HC FamD On whether (unlike here) to make contact order in favour of grandparent.

ACCESS/CONTACT (guardian)

Devon County Council v Clancy [1985] FLR 1159; (1985) 149 JP 521 CA Magistrates' unjustified deviation from advice of guardian ad litem will generally be overturned upon appeal.

Re C [1995] 2 FCR 451; [1994] 2 FLR 525 HC FamD On availability of guardian ad litem's adoption report in later contact/residence hearings.

ACCESS/CONTACT (indirect)

Re L [1995] 2 FLR 438 HC FamD Indirect contact and parental responsibility orders to transsexual father.

Re M [1990] FCR 785; [1990] TLR 139 CA Indirect contact ordered where direct contact impracticable.

Re O [1996] 1 FCR 317; [1995] 2 FLR 124; [1995] TLR 163 CA On contact/indirect contact.

ACCESS/CONTACT (information)

Re C [1991] FCR 308 CA On private receipt by judge in access proceedings of confidential information pertaining to action.

ACCESS/CONTACT (interim)

Greenwich London Borough Council v H [1997] 1 FCR 527; [1996] 2 FLR 736 HC FamD Interim contact order inappropriate as children probably going to lose contact after full action which would be particularly distressing if had enjoyed interim contact.

H v Stockport Metropolitan Borough Council [1990] FCR 65; (1989) 133 SJ 359 HC FamD Interim access order unavailable pursuant to Child Care Act 1980, Part 1A.

West Glamorgan County Council v P (No 1) [1992] 2 FCR 378; [1992] 2 FLR 369 HC FamD Interim non-access by mother to child pending full hearing was permissible.

ACCESS/CONTACT (legitimacy)

B v A (1982) 3 FLR 27 HC FamD Father properly refused access to his illegitimate children where as was domineering towards mother of whom was step-father which would also create complications.

M v J (1982) 3 FLR 19 HC FamD Father properly refused access to his illegitimate child where access could jeopardise child's welfare.

Re E (P) (1969) 133 JP 137; (1968) 118 NLJ 956t; (1968) 112 SJ 821; [1968] 1 WLR 1913 CA Better that child lose illegitimacy via adoption and so lose contact with putative father than to retain illegitimacy and retain contact.

Re H (C) [1996] 1 FCR 768; [1996] 1 FLR 569 HC FamD Supervised contact order to ex-husband whose wife had child by artificial insemination (using third party's sperm) but of which child ex-husband legally the father.

S v O (1982) 3 FLR 15 HC FamD Father properly awarded access to his illegitimate child.

ACCESS/CONTACT (maintenance)

Bowers v Clarke (1961) 105 SJ 988 CA Was not repudiation of maintenance agreement whereunder maintenance payable and access granted for custodial parent to remove child to Australia.

Foot v Foot [1987] FCR 62 HC FamD Access to children not relevant factor when determining level of maintenance payable in respect of same.

ACCESS/CONTACT (non-custodian)

Re S [1993] 1 FCR 283; [1992] 2 FLR 313 CA On desirability of access between children/non-custodial parent; on religious upbringing of children.

ACCESS/CONTACT (parent)

M v M [1973] 2 All ER 81 HC FamD Child's interests usually demand some access to adoptive/natural parent.

ACCESS/CONTACT (parental responsibility)

Re H [1993] 1 FCR 85; [1993] 1 FLR 484 CA Parental responsibility but not contact order for father (where stepfather strenuously objected to contact order).

Re L [1995] 2 FLR 438 HC FamD Indirect contact and parental responsibility orders to transsexual father.

ACCESS/CONTACT (prisoner)

Re M [1994] 1 FCR 678; [1994] 1 FLR 272; [1993] TLR 557 HC FamD Indirect contact with father in prison approved; requirements that mother read father's letters to child/submit progress reports to father disapproved.

Re N (1975) 119 SJ 423 HC FamD Access to father in prison ordered.

ACCESS/CONTACT (psychiatrist's report)

Re K [1996] 1 FCR 474; [1995] 2 FLR 432; [1995] TLR 199 CA On procedure where judge deems it necessary to obtain psychiatrist's opinion on matters before court in contact action.

ACCESS/CONTACT (religion)

Evans v Jackson (1986) 150 JP 593 (also HC FamD) CA Father properly granted access to child though was upsetting for latter as upset occasioned by mother's improper attempts to frustrate access not by access per se.

Evans v Jackson (1986) 150 JP 593 (also CA) HC FamD Father properly granted access to child though was upsetting for latter as lifestyle of father afforded broader upbringing to child than that of mother and husband who were Jehovah's Witnesses.

Re G (1965) 109 SJ 756 CA Valid decision not to make staying order in respect of Roman Catholic children to whom father living in adultery granted access.

Wright v Wright (1981) 2 FLR 276 CA Refusal of access to father (Jehovah's Witness) merited where mother (Church of England member) very anxious (and anxiety would upset child) that father would seek to indoctrinate child.

ACCESS/CONTACT (sexual deviant)

Dean v Dean (1983) 133 NLJ 421c CA Experimental access between young girl and father imprisoned for sex crimes deemed inappropriate though might later be permissible.

ACCESS/CONTACT (supervised)

H v H [1989] FCR 257; [1989] 1 FLR 212 CA Defined/supervised access of children allowed (one of whom person granted access had sexually abused).

ACCESS/CONTACT (surrogacy)

Re M (a minor) [1997] TLR 301 CA On avaialability of supervised contact available where unsupervised contact not possible.

ACCESS/CONTACT (surrogacy)

A v C [1985] FLR 445 (also CA) HC FamD No access by natural father to child of woman who reneged on commercial surrogacy deal insofar as surrender of child concerned.

ACCESS/CONTACT (transsexual)

L v C [1995] 3 FCR 125 HC FamD Some indirect contact to male-to-female transsexual who had fathered child when a man; general contact application a future possibility.

ACCESS/CONTACT (trial period)

Re B [1994] 1 FCR 905; [1994] 2 FLR 269; [1994] TLR 202 HC FamD Trial period of contact not delay detrimental to child in resolution of case contrary to Children Act 1989, s 1(2).

ACCESS/CONTACT (ward)

M v Berkshire County Council [1985] FLR 257 CA On power of juvenile court to order access.

Re C (1983) 4 FLR 396 HC FamD Order for increased access to child (for whom council had planned adoption) by natural mother who had surmounted drink problem with view to eventually returning child to mother.

Re D (K) [1988] 1 All ER 577; [1988] AC 806; [1988] FCR 657; [1988] 2 FLR 139; (1988) 132 SJ 301; [1988] 2 WLR 398 HL In wardship proceedings child's welfare paramount; parent's right to access is secondary.

Re G [1988] FCR 440; [1988] 1 FLR 305 CA On role of court (regarding evidence and otherwise) in wardship action; father with mental disorder might after treatment be considered for access; wife deserved access but given visiting access because of threat posed by father.

Re H (L) [1986] 2 FLR 306; (1986) 150 JP 417 HC FamD HC could exercise wardship jurisdiction on request of local authority without latter having to show its powers to be insufficient.

Re P (1982) 3 FLR 420; (1982) 132 NLJ 248 CA Court could not order that no application be made in wardship proceedings until full hearing but could require court's leave be given to any steps taken.

Re P [1991] FCR 283; [1991] 1 FLR 280; [1990] TLR 694 CA Increased access and eventual return of stepfather to family despite earlier sexual abuse of step-child was justified; contempt of local authority solicitor whereby had sought to frustrate access arrangements purged by contemnor.

W v Shropshire County Council [1986] 1 FLR 359 (also HC FamD) CA Non-continuation of wardship over child in respect of whom local authority sought to bring care proceedings was valid.

ACCESS/CONTACT (welfare report)

Clode v Clode (1982) 3 FLR 360 CA Confidentiality of welfare report not to be used to bar access of access of party thereto for purpose of bringing appeal.

Re B (C) [1995] 1 FLR 622 CA Access order to grandparents (grandfather a convicted child sex abuser) wrong as did not hear oral evidence/court welfare officer on concerns involved (and contained in latter's report).

Re C [1994] TLR 593 CA On departing from advice given in report of court welfare officer.

Re F [1997] 1 FCR 523 CA Not following court welfare officer's advice perfectly justified.

Re M [1994] TLR 659 CA On when review of magistrates' decision to depart from recommendations of court welfare officer would be merited.

Re S [1993] 2 FCR 325 HC FamD Magistrates to explain why not pusuing course of conduct recommended by court welfare officer.

ADOPTION (access/contact)

C v Berkshire County Council [1988] FCR 161; [1987] 2 FLR 210 HC FamD Valid adjournment of juvenile court parental access action until county court decided in pending action whether child to be freed for adoption.

C v H (1979) 123 SJ 537 HC FamD When access/adoption arise to be decided in same action they should both be decided in tandem, not one before the other.

Hereford and Worcester County Council v H (E) [1985] FLR 975 HC FamD Controlled access allowed where did not seem access would be problematic/adoption not proved to be best option for child.

Re A (B) [1985] FLR 1008 HC FamD Children's interests required that they remain in foster-care; objectively tested, mother's refusal of consent to adoption not unreasonable; future access by mother a real possibility.

Re C (1983) 4 FLR 396 HC FamD Order for increased access to child (for whom council had planned adoption) by natural mother who had surmounted drink problem with view to eventually returning child to mother.

Re C [1988] 1 All ER 705; [1989] AC 1; [1988] FCR 484; [1988] 2 FLR 159; (1988) 138 NLJ 64; (1988) 132 SJ 334; [1988] 2 WLR 474 HL Court may provide for future access to natural family in adoption order.

Re C [1991] FCR 1052; [1991] TLR 404 CA On deciding whether withholding of parental agreement to adoption justified (here was); court to decide parental access issue before deciding whether to free child for adoption.

Re C [1992] 1 FLR 115 CA On resolving issue of access by parent who has always shown interest in children it is proposed to have adopted; reasonable refusal of consent not made unreasonable through delay for which parent not responsible.

Re C; P and P v C (1969) 113 SJ 721 CA Adoption order approved even though would end access to natural father as order would lead to legitimation of child.

Re E [1990] FCR 921; [1990] 2 FLR 397 CA On freeing children for adoption: here order refused though access had been terminated/children formed relationship with prospective adopters.

Re F [1990] 3 All ER 580; [1990] Fam 189; [1991] FCR 116; [1990] 2 FLR 478; [1990] 3 WLR 505 HC FamD Court may grant injunction restraining access by natural parents whether as part of adoption order or otherwise.

Re F [1982] 1 All ER 321; (1982) 3 FLR 101; (1981) 131 NLJ 1053; (1981) 125 SJ 861; [1982] 1 WLR 102 CA Welfare of child paramount in adoption; welfare indicates if consent un/reasonably withheld by parent; adoption order rather than care order where child's welfare demands no access by mother.

Re G (1980) 1 FLR 109 HC FamD On approach when adoption sought by natural parent and step-parent; adoption/access hearings (if are both) to be heard together.

Re G [1993] 2 FCR 27; [1992] 1 FLR 642 CA Where parent/prospective adopters seeking access/adoption order applications are to be heard together but that does not apply to connected interim/interlocutory applications.

Re H [1985] FLR 519 CA Adoption applications not to be ued to frustrate local authority actions; access order attached to adoption order only if agreement between parties concerned; father's refusal of consent to adoption unless access condition attached was reasonable.

Re H [1987] 2 FLR 12 HC FamD On ethnic background as factor when dealing with children; long-term fostering with view to adoption (if possible by someone of own ethnic background); access by mother to depend on her co-operation with social worker/what eventual adopters desired.

Re M [1986] 1 FLR 51 CA On whether to order post-adoption access between adopted child and natural parents.

Re R [1991] FCR 1006; [1991] 2 FLR 78 CA Adoption ends access rights of natural parents: cannot stay issue of access and even if could should not have made access order six years after adoption.

Re S [1991] FCR 82 (also CA) HC FamD Juvenile court not justified in granting natural mother access to child whom local authority seeking to have adopted.

Re S [1975] 1 All ER 109; [1976] Fam 1; (1975) 139 JP 162; (1974) 124 NLJ 1008t; (1975) 119 SJ 11; [1975] 2 WLR 250 CA Adoption order can be qualified by access order.

Re W [1979] 3 All ER 154; [1980] Fam 60; (1979) 143 JP 727; (1979) 123 SJ 553; [1979] 3 WLR 252 CA Natural parent cannot challenge merits of local authority decision to make child ward; authority may consider possible future adoption in deciding to disallow parental access to child.

Re W (1987) 131 SJ 915 CA Could (and here did) make access order as part of adoption order.

Re W [1988] FCR 129; [1988] 1 FLR 175 CA On making adoption rather than custodianship order.

ADOPTION (accommodation adoption)

Re A [1963] 1 All ER 531; (1963) 127 JP 209; (1963) 113 LJ 170; (1963) 107 SJ 114; [1963] 1 WLR 231 HC ChD 'Accommodation' adoptions not allowed (even where in infant's interest).

ADOPTION (agency)

Re S [1985] FLR 579; [1984] TLR 600 CA Breach of prohibition on person other than adoption agency acting as such without permission of HC.

Re W [1995] 4 All ER 282; [1995] Fam 120; [1995] 1 FLR 163; [1995] 2 WLR 458 HC FamD Care order or adoption arranged through adoption agency by third party permissible where parent under disability.

ADOPTION (applicants resident abroad)

R v Adoption Application 121/1984 (1985) 129 SJ 638 HC FamD Could not order adoption of child by couple resident abroad as was no chance for local authority to see them with child in some form of permanent home in England/Wales.

Re M [1965] Ch 203; (1964) 128 JP 522; (1964) 114 LJ 586; (1964) 108 SJ 563; [1964] 3 WLR HC ChD No adoption order where husband frequently abroad on business could not prove had spent three months before adoption hearing living with wife.

Re R (1962) 112 LJ 634; [1962] 1 WLR 1147 CA Adoption order could be made in respect of adopters with British domicile though ordinarily resident abroad.

Re Y [1985] Fam 136; [1986] 1 FLR 152; [1985] 3 WLR 601 HC FamD Absent home in England court could not hear application of couple to adopt wife's children.

ADOPTION (birth certificate)

R v Registrar General, ex parte Smith [1991] 2 All ER 88; [1991] FCR 403; [1991] 1 FLR 255; [1991] 2 QB 393; [1991] 2 WLR 782 CA Absolute statutory duty to provide birth certificate to adopted persons not applicable where it would facilitate crime.

ADOPTION (care/custody)

Bolton Metropolitan Borough Council v B and H [1990] FCR 57; [1989] 2 FLR 349 HC FamD Long-term care pending adoption for children with parents incapable of proper parenting: access to parents until placed with foster-parents; delay in welfare report criticised.

Crossley v Crossley (1953) 117 JP 216; (1953) 97 SJ 249; [1953] 2 WLR 765 HC PDAD Adoption order completely supersedes existing custody order.

H v H [1947] KB 463 HC KBD Justices could dispense with need for consent to adoption of custody having custody of same.

R v Derbyshire County Council, ex parte T [1989] FCR 679; [1990] 1 FLR 237 (also CA); (1989) 133 SJ 1109 HC QBD Notice to former parent needed if child placed with prospective adopters becomes child in care.

R v Derbyshire County Council, ex parte T and another [1990] 1 All ER 792; [1990] Fam 164; [1989] FCR 713; [1990] 1 FLR 237 (also HC QBD); (1989) 133 SJ 1626; [1990] 2 WLR 101 CA Notice to former parent needed if child placed with prospective adopters becomes child in care.

R v Walker and another (1911-12) XXVIII TLR 375 CA Compromise of action in appeal from refusal to order delivery up of illegitimate child to natural parents from those who had adopted child and kept him for ten years.

Re Adoption Application No 41/61 [1962] 3 All ER 553; [1963] Ch 315; (1962) 126 JP 511; (1962) 112 LJ 718; (1962) 106 SJ 571/649; [1962] 3 WLR 997 CA Infant's interests paramount in adoption/custody cases; adjournment of adoption case to hear custody action.

Re Adoption Application No 41/61 (No 2) [1963] 2 All ER 1082; [1964] Ch 48; (1963) 127 JP 440; (1963) 113 LJ 561; (1963) 107 SJ 573; [1963] 3 WLR 357 HC ChD Welfare of infant of paramount consideration in custody/adoption proceedings.

Re Adoption Application No 41/61 (No 2) [1963] 2 All ER 1082; (1962) 112 LJ 505; [1962] 1 WLR 866 HC ChD Welfare of infant of paramount consideration in custody/adoption proceedings.

Re B [1993] 1 FCR 363 (also CA) CyCt Contact with natural mother halted when order for care with view to adoption made.

Re D (1981) 2 FLR 102 CA Adoption order preferable to joint custody order here where natural and step-parent seeking adoption; wishes of children relevant (here wanted adoption): decision contrary to wishes to be explained); child's memories of natural father inadequate reason for refusing adoption.

Re G (1981) 2 FLR 382; (1981) 125 SJ 307 HC FamD Court could order care and control of child (to local authority) with a view to adoption.

Re H [1989] FCR 498 CA On options open to single father of children in care when local authority seeks to have children freed for adoption.

Re H (1985) 129 SJ 84; [1984] TLR 649 CA Instigation of adoption action an abuse of process where used to frustrate local authority in its exercise of its care jurisdiction.

Re L [1990] FCR 471; [1990] 1 FLR 305; (1989) 139 NLJ 1377 CA On determining whether parent's refusal of consent to adoption (as here) unreasonable; on whether custodianship/ adoption order preferable.

Re M [1990] FCR 424; [1990] 1 FLR 291 CA Failed application by teenage father for custody of his child which was being placed for adoption.

Re N [1990] FCR 241; [1990] 1 FLR 58 HC FamD Care and control of black child to white foster-parents, reasonable access to natural father.

Re S [1987] 2 All ER 99; [1987] Fam 98; [1988] FCR 57; [1987] 2 FLR 331; (1987) 151 JP 577; [1987] 2 WLR 977 CA On ordering adoption application to be treated as custodianship application; on ordering disclosure of confidential reports so that parties have time to prepare response at action.

Re S (1987) 131 SJ 133 CA Adoption order made in preference to custodianship order: on relevant factors in arriving at that decision.

Re T [1990] FCR 71 CA Order of care with view to adoption justified where six month' counselling of mother suggested could never properly care for child (even though was some contradictory expert evidence).

Re T (J) [1986] 2 FLR 107 HC FamD Care of child to local authority with view to adoption where older child had died as result of non-accidental injuries while living with mother as member of extended Rastafarian family.

Re W [1988] FCR 129; [1988] 1 FLR 175 CA On making adoption rather than custodianship order.

Re W [1984] FLR 402 CA On relevancy of child's interests in adoption (as opposed to custody) hearing.

ADOPTION (child sex abuse)

Re B [1995] 1 FLR 904; [1994] TLR 671 HC FamD On proving child sex abuse (civil standard) such as to justify ending parental contact/freeing for adoption.

Re P [1987] FCR 123; [1987] 2 FLR 467; (1987) 151 JP 635 CA Local authority granted care order, non-access by parents and right to place child with foster-parents with view to adoption where child born to parents of family with history of sexual abuse of existing children; on role of court.

ADOPTION (consent)

Hampshire County Council v C [1988] FCR 133 CA On determining un/reasonableness of parent's refusal of consent to adoption: here not unreasonably withheld.

Harris v Hawkins [1947] 1 All ER 312; (1947) 111 JP 161 HC KBD Persons whose consent to adoption required.

Hitchcock v WB and others [1952] 2 All ER 119; (1952) 116 JP 401; (1952) 102 LJ 345; [1952] 2 QB 561; (1952) 96 SJ 448; [1952] 1 TLR 1550; (1952) WN (I) 315 HC QBD Test whether consent unreasonably withheld is attitude of person withholding.

L v M (1956) 120 JP 27 HC QBD Natural father's refusal of consent to adoption (where was motivated by spite against natural mother) unreasonable so adoption allowed.

O'Connor and another v A and B [1971] 2 All ER 1230; (1971) 135 JP 492; (1971) 115 SJ 586; [1971] 1 WLR 1227 HL Must balance child's welfare against parent's ability to raise child (and time lapse before appeal) in deciding if consent unreasonably withheld.

Re A (1981) 2 FLR 173 CA Parents' continuous ill-treatment of their child justified dispensing with their consent to adoption.

Re A [1987] 2 All ER 81; [1987] FCR 9; [1987] 2 FLR 184; (1987) 151 JP 458; (1987) 131 SJ 194; [1987] 1 WLR 153 CA Not unreasonable if parents consent to custodianship order not adoption order; consent dispensed with if in child's interests.

Re A (B) [1985] FLR 1008 HC FamD Children's interests required that they remain in foster-care; objectively tested, mother's refusal of consent to adoption not unreasonable; future access by mother a real possibility.

Re Application No 41 of 1974 (1975) 125 NLJ 507t CA Although best future for baby lay with adopters with whom placed mother's withdrawal/refusal of consent to adoption not unreasonable.

Re B [1990] FCR 841; [1990] 2 FLR 383 CA Consent dispensed with where refused on basis that wished to maintain contact with child; grudge against local authority/basis of grudge irrelevant/could be relevant to reasonableness of refusal of consent (here basis of grudge not reasonable).

Re B [1976] 3 All ER 124; [1976] Fam 161; (1976) 126 NLJ 289t; (1976) 120 SJ 199; [1976] 2 WLR 755 HC FamD Welfare of child primary, not paramount consideration in deciding if parental consent to adoption unreasonably withheld.

Re B [1975] 2 All ER 449; [1975] 2 WLR 569 HC FamD Justices may but should not order adoption; invalid adoption where justices fail to consider interests of child/if consent unreasonably withheld and apply wrong test to question of consent.

Re B [1975] Fam 127; (1975) 125 NLJ 14t; (1975) 119 SJ 133 HC FamD Adoption order made in favour of mother/stepfather (and despite father's refusal of consent) revoked where father genuinely wanted to maintain paternal relationship with child.

Re B [1970] 3 All ER 1008; (1971) 135 JP 59; (1970) 120 NLJ 944t; [1971] 1 QB 437; (1970) 114 SJ 786; [1971] 2 WLR 129 CA Test for determining if withholding of consent is unreasonable.

Re B [1967] 3 All ER 629; [1968] Ch 204; (1967) 111 SJ 809; [1967] 3 WLR 1438 HC ChD Absent foreign father consent dispensed with in interests of child.

Re B [1957] 3 All ER 193; (1957) 107 LJ 617; (1957) 101 SJ 679 CA Mother not served notice of application and whose consent dispensed with could appeal to CA.

Re B (G) [1985] FLR 719 CyCt On test as to whether withholding of consent unreasonable (here was); on examination of normal child by psychiatrist.

Re B (MIJ) (1978) 128 NLJ 187b CA Reasonableness of parent's revocation of non-irrevocable consent to be considered in light of changed circumstances since child placed with adopters.

Re C (1982) 3 FLR 95 CA Dispensing with consent to be subject of hearing if controverted; court to decide whether party of whom adverse comments made in report of guardian ad litem to be informed so can prepare rebuttal.

Re C [1964] 3 All ER 483; (1965) 129 JP 62; [1965] 2 QB 449; [1964] 3 WLR 1041 CA In all the circumstances — though primary consideration effect on child — (of whom strong medical evidence to show non-adoption detrimental) consent being unreasonably withheld.

Re C (LP) (1964) 108 SJ 638 CA Mother's refusal of consent to adoption of child by foster parents with whom had lived for two years.

Re D [1977] 1 All ER 145; [1977] AC 602 (also CA); (1977) 127 NLJ 115t; (1977) 121 SJ 35; [1977] 2 WLR 79 HL Unreasonably withholding consent if reasonable parent in same position would not withhold; no appeal on factual issues to Court of Appeal.

Re D [1976] 2 All ER 342; [1977] AC 602 (also HL); (1977) 141 JP 110; (1976) 126 NLJ 265t; [1976] 3 WLR 12 CA Non-consent unreasonable if reasonable person in parent's place would consent.

Re D (1976) 120 SJ 214 CA Gay father's refusal of consent to adoption was not unreasonable as was no immediate danger of son being exposed to gay influences.

Re D [1958] 1 All ER 427; (1958) 122 JP 156; (1958) 108 LJ 168; (1958) 102 SJ 138 CA Child's welfare paramount in deciding if refusal to consent reasonable; putative father does not have rights of lawful father.

Re E [1989] FCR 118; [1989] 1 FLR 126 CA Mother's withholding consent was reasonable where sought to maintain proposed adoptee's relationship with sibling/hoped for eventual rehabilitation with adoptee.

Re El-G (1983) 4 FLR 589 CA Welfare of children demanded that they stay with prospective adopters; on deciding whether parent's refusal of consent unreasonable (here was: dispensed with); on pivotal role of court when it is sought to change arrangements for ward.

Re F [1982] 1 All ER 321; (1982) 3 FLR 101; (1981) 131 NLJ 1053; (1981) 125 SJ 861; [1982] 1 WLR 102 CA Welfare of child paramount in adoption; welfare indicates if consent un/reasonably withheld by parent; adoption order rather than care order where child's welfare demands no access by mother.

Re F [1957] 1 All ER 819; (1957) 121 JP 270; (1957) 107 LJ 282 HC ChD Revocation of consent anytime before order possible and here was reasonable.

Re F [1970] 1 All ER 344; (1969) 119 NLJ 1094t; [1970] 1 WLR 192 CA Father's consent easily dispensed with where in best interests of child and father has seriously misbehaved.

Re F (R), An Infant [1969] 3 All ER 1101; (1969) 133 JP 743; [1970] 1 QB 385; (1969) 113 SJ 835; [1969] 3 WLR 853 CA Leave to appeal out of time against adoption order of which not notified.

Re G [1990] FCR 881; [1990] 2 FLR 429 CA Reconsideration ordered of case where judge refused to dispense with mother's consent as judge failed to carry out proper balancing exercise.

Re H [1985] FLR 519 CA Adoption applications not to be ued to frustrate local authority actions; access order attached to adoption order only if agreement between parties concerned; father's refusal of consent to adoption unless access condition attached was reasonable.

Re H (1982) 3 FLR 386; (1981) 131 NLJ 1264 CA Mother's agreement to adoption properly dispensed with where reasonable mother in same circumstances would have consented.

Re H [1977] 2 All ER 339; (1977) 121 SJ 303; [1977] 1 WLR 471 CA Consent withdrawal possible anytime before order but more difficult/less reasonable as time progresses.

Re H (1974) 124 NLJ 1159t HC FamD Successful appeal by natural father against decision to dispense with his consent to the adoption of his children.

Re H (1989) 133 SJ 569 CA Under parental rights order father of illegitimate children did not enjoy custody rights over same but could oppose their adoption.

Re H and another (No 3) [1991] 2 All ER 185; [1991] Fam 151; [1990] TLR 734; [1991] 2 WLR 763 CA Parental rights order available despite all rights thereunder not capable of being exercised; if neither parent offers suitable home but refuses consent to adoption that is unreasonable and court can dispense with consent.

Re H and Re W (1983) 133 NLJ 1099c; [1983] TLR 1 CA On reasonableness of parent's withholding consent/welfare of child as factor when deciding whether adoption order to be made.

Re H; Re W (1983) 4 FLR 614; (1983) 127 SJ 86 CA On relevancy of child's welfare to decision whether parent's refusal of consent to adoption unreasonable.

Re Hollyman [1945] 1 All ER 290; (1945) 109 JP 95; (1945) 172 LTR 200; (1944-45) LXI TLR 229; (1945) WN (I) 41 CA Consent may be withdrawn up to making of order — conversely must be consent upon making of order.

Re K; Rogers and another v Kuzmicz [1952] 2 All ER 877; (1953) 117 JP 9; (1952) 102 LJ 639; [1953] 1 QB 117; (1952) 96 SJ 764; [1952] 2 TLR 745; (1952) WN (I) 511 CA Generally parent's withholding of consent will be found reasonable.

Re L [1988] FCR 92; [1987] 1 FLR 400 HC FamD Consent being withheld by mentally unwell mother was, using objective test, unreasonably withheld.

Re L [1990] FCR 471; [1990] 1 FLR 305; (1989) 139 NLJ 1377 CA On determining whether parent's refusal of consent to adoption (as here) unreasonable; on whether custodianship/ adoption order preferable.

Re L (1962) 106 SJ 611 CA Consent by mother having difficulty making up her mind regarding adoption of child already placed with proposed adopters was being unreasonably withheld.

Re M (1981) 131 NLJ 241c CA On determining whether parental refusal of consent to adoption reasonably or (as here) unreasonably withheld.

Re M [1985] FLR 921 CA That contact with mother yielding positive results justified finding her non-consent to adoption as reasonable.

Re M [1987] FCR 17 CA Could not order custodianship unless parents agreed/consent dispensed with — here consent dispensed with: on whether adoption/custodianship preferable.

Re M [1955] 2 All ER 911; (1955) 119 JP 535; (1955) 105 LJ 488; [1955] 2 QB 479; (1955) 99 SJ 539; [1955] 3 WLR 320 CA Natural father of illegitimate not 'parent' whose consent to adoption required under Adoption Act 1950, s 2(4)(a).

Re M (1970) 114 SJ 264 CA Father's withholding of consent to adoption of his child by his ex-wife and her new husband was not unreasonable.

Re M (1965) 109 SJ 574 CA Mother's not visiting (four month old) child could be reasonably explained away so her consent to adoption of child could not be dispensed with.

Re O [1965] Ch 23; [1964] 2 WLR 840 CA Putative father though in special position cannot veto adoption of illegitimate child: child's welfare paramount.

Re P [1977] 1 All ER 182; [1977] Fam 25; (1976) 120 SJ 818; [1976] 3 WLR 924 CA Court may dispense with parental agreement to adoption; child's welfare a factor, not paramount.

Re P [1985] FLR 635; [1984] TLR 325 CA Indecisiveness of natural parent may indicate incapacity to act as reasonable parent.

Re P (1963) 107 SJ 55 CA Valid decision that mother's refusal of consent to adoption was unreasonably withheld.

Re P [1962] 3 All ER 789; (1963) 127 JP 18; (1962) 112 LJ 786; (1962) 106 SJ 630; [1962] 1 WLR 1296 HC ChD Obligations of parent to child are moral and financial: consent dispensed with as failure on both grounds.

Re P, An Infant (1954) 118 JP 139 CA Had children's officers statement that intended adopters might claim maintenance from mother for period child stayed with them coerced mother to consent to adoption that consent would have been obviated.

Re R [1987] FCR 104; [1987] 1 FLR 391 CA On deciding whether appropriate to dispense with parental consent to adoption.

Re R [1966] 3 All ER 613; (1967) 131 JP 1; (1965-66) 116 NLJ 1090t; (1966) 110 SJ 652; [1967] 1 WLR 34 HC ChD Consent of parents dispensed with where parents unavailable as abroad and adoption in infant's interests.

Re R (No 2) [1987] FCR 113 HC FamD On whether appropriate to dispense with parental consent to adoption: here was.

Re S (1977) 127 NLJ 16t/739b; (1976) 120 SJ 819 CA Failed appeal by mother against adoption where trial judge found (applying objective test) that she was unreasonably withholding her consent.

Re S [1973] 3 All ER 88 CA Appeal against dispensing with consent to be decided in light of fresh evidence.

Re T [1986] 1 All ER 817; [1986] Fam 160; [1986] 2 FLR 31 (also CC); (1986) 136 NLJ 285; (1986) 130 SJ 88; [1986] 2 WLR 538 CA Notification of parent regulations directory/not mandatory; oral/written consent to adoption precludes natural parent removing child from adopters.

Re T [1986] 2 FLR 31 (also CA) CyCt Written consent of parent to adoption necessary; notification of parent regulations directory/not mandatory; mother's consent being withheld unreasonably.

Re V [1985] FLR 45; (1985) 135 NLJ 708c; (1986) 136 NLJ 516c CA Adoption allowed continue where mother had sought to withdraw consent after initially agreeing.

Re V [1986] 1 All ER 752; [1987] Fam 57; [1987] 2 FLR 89; (1987) 151 JP 145; (1970) 130 SJ 879; [1986] 3 WLR 927 CA Dispensing with reasonably held consent incorrect; no adoption order where access to parent promotes child's welfare.

Re W [1984] FLR 880 CA On deciding if refusal of parental consent to adoption unreasonable: here consent dispensed with to protect welfare of child.

Re W (1982) 3 FLR 75 CA On dispensing with parental agreement as prerequisite to adoption.

Re W (1981) 2 FLR 161 CA Adoption of child by grandparents who had custody for some years (mother consented/consent of father — a criminal — dispensed with).

Re W (1977) 127 NLJ 43; (1976) 120 SJ 857 HC FamD Refusal of adoption of child by mother/her new husband as natural father (who was in prison) refused his consent.

Re W [1971] 2 All ER 49; [1971] AC 682; (1971) 135 JP 259; (1971) 115 SJ 286; [1971] 2 WLR 1011 HL Need not be culpable in withholding consent for it to be unreasonable; welfare of child important factor in deciding if unreasonable.

Re W [1970] 3 All ER 990; (1971) 135 JP 42; (1970) 120 NLJ 480t; [1970] 2 QB 589; (1970) 114 SJ 433; [1970] 3 WLR 175 CA That consent reasonable does not mean non-consent unreasonable; child's welfare relevant only if non-adoption detrimental to same.

Re W [1965] 3 All ER 231; (1965) 129 JP 550; (1965) 115 LJ 677; [1965] 1 WLR 1259 HC ChD Concealment of remarriage from adoption society and concomitant placing of children with adoption society justified dispensing with consent.

Re W (1965) 109 SJ 850 HC ChD On determining whether (as here) withdrawal of consent to adoption was unreasonable.

W and another v D and another (1956) 120 JP 119 HC QBD Mother's consent to adoption dispensed with where objection to adopters unreasonable (mother wanted child placed with parents who did not have child of same sex).

ADOPTION (contact)

G v G [1993] 2 FLR 306; [1992] TLR 641 HC FamD Where contact and adoption orders being sought by different parties ought to hear cases together.

Re B [1993] 1 FCR 363 (also CA) CyCt Contact with natural mother halted when order for care with view to adoption made.

Re B; Re D [1972] 1 All ER 898; (1972) 136 JP 259; (1972) 116 SJ 58; [1972] 1 WLR 102 CA Exceptionally, could be post-adoption contact between adopted child and natural parent/s.

Re C [1987] 2 FLR 383 CA Refusal of consent to adoption unless adoptee maintained contact with sibling not unreasonable; adopters could not be relied upon to ensure same so adoption refused: long-term fostering ordered.

Re C [1993] 3 All ER 259; [1993] Fam 210; [1993] 3 WLR 85 HC FamD Once adoption order made parental contact provisions altered only if fundamental change in circumstances.

Re C [1995] 2 FCR 701 CA Number of times when contact available to natural parents of child placed for adoption reduced at behest of local authority after child freed for adoption.

Re C [1993] 2 FLR 431 HC FamD On procedure as regards natural mother's applying for contact/specific issue order after adoption order made.

Re D [1973] 3 All ER 1001; [1973] Fam 209; (1974) 138 JP 18; (1973) 123 NLJ 788t; (1973) 117 SJ 696; [1973] 3 WLR 595 HC FamD Persistent failure to discharge parental obligations to be so complete that no benefit in maintaining contact.

Re E [1995] 2 FCR 655; [1995] 1 FLR 57 HC FamD Contact order refused to natural parents of adopted child.

Re J [1973] 2 All ER 410; [1973] Fam 106; (1973) 137 JP 467; (1973) 117 SJ 372; [1973] 2 WLR 782 HC FamD Exceptionally court may order contact with natural parent after adoption order — court's powers in making such orders are wide; wardship/directions remedies to breach of adoption order terms.

Re O [1995] 2 FLR 597 HC FamD Adoption order made but contact to natural mother allowed.

Re P [1994] 2 FCR 1306; [1994] 2 FLR 1000; [1994] TLR 426 CA Inappropriate that judge attach contact order to freeing for adoption order.

Re R (G) [1985] FLR 643 CA Valid decision by judge (who hoped contact between child/grandmother would continue) not to add access order to adoption order absent exceptional circumstances.

Re S [1993] 2 FCR 234; [1993] TLR 118 HC FamD On whether/when natural parent to be afforded contact to adopted child.

Re T [1995] 2 FLR 792; [1995] TLR 465 CA On procedure as regards post-adoption seeking of direct/indirect contact with children.

ADOPTION (discharge)

Re B [1995] 1 FLR 1; (1995) 139 SJ LB 176 HC FamD Failed application for setting aside of procedurally regular adoption order thirty-five years after made.

Re B [1995] TLR 181 CA Failed application for setting aside of procedurally regular adoption order thirty-five years after made.

Re K [1994] 2 FLR 557 CA Adoption order (conferring British nationality on foreigner) discharged.

ADOPTION (disclosure)

D v Registrar General [1996] 2 FCR 248; [1996] 1 FLR 707 HC FamD Failed application for order requiring Registrar General to disclose information enabling natural mother to trace adopted child.

D v Registrar General [1997] 2 FCR 240; [1997] 1 FLR 715 CA Failed appeal against refusal of order requiring Registrar General to disclose information enabling natural mother to trace adopted child (such an order would be exceptional).

Lawson and another v Registrar General (1956) 106 LJ ccr204 CyCt Order for discovery of details pertaining to adopted child so that adoptee might be paid legacy left it by godmother.

Re a Subpoena [1996] 3 FCR 190; [1996] 2 FLR 629 HC QBD On disclosure of adoption materials to commissioner for local administration.

Re an Adoption Application [1990] 1 FLR 412; [1990] 1 WLR 520 HC FamD On disclosure of information from adoption proceedings where is in public interest.

Re an ex parte originating summons in an adoption application [1990] 1 All ER 639 HC FamD Procedure for adoption agency when disclosing confidential information relevant to criminal proceedings.

Re D [1995] 1 FLR 631; (1995) 139 SJ LB 13; [1994] TLR 637; [1995] 1 WLR 356 CA Difficult to obtain full disclosure of relevant materials in adoption cases.

Re D and another [1995] 4 All ER 385; [1996] AC 593; [1996] 1 FCR 205; [1995] 2 FLR 687; (1995) 145 NLJ 1612; [1995] TLR 157; [1995] 3 WLR 483 HL Strong presumption exists in favour of full disclosure of relevant materials in adoption cases except where compelling evidence that disclosure would harm child.

Re H [1995] 1 FCR 546; [1995] 1 FLR 236 HC FamD Release of adoption details where applicant seeking to contact adopted half-brother who possibly had genetic disease.

Re H [1995] 2 FCR 711; [1995] 1 FLR 964 HC FamD On disclosure of adoption papers in criminal action.

Re K [1997] 2 FLR 74 HC FamD Order for non-disclosure to natural mother of onetime conviction for serious sexual offence of prospective adopter of child; on test as to deciding whether to order disclosure/non-disclosure.

Re L (1997) 141 SJ LB 21; [1997] TLR 27; [1997] 2 WLR 739 CA Court ought rarely to order disclosure of adoption details to birth family applicant (and here would not so order).

Re S [1987] 2 All ER 99; [1987] Fam 98; [1988] FCR 57; [1987] 2 FLR 331; (1987) 151 JP 577; [1987] 2 WLR 977 CA On ordering adoption application to be treated as custodianship application; on ordering disclosure of confidential reports so that parties have time to prepare response at action.

ADOPTION (ethnicity)

Re H [1987] 2 FLR 12 HC FamD On ethnic background as factor when dealing with children; long-term fostering with view to adoption (if possible by someone of own ethnic background); access by mother to depend on her co-operation with social worker/what eventual adopters desired.

Re J [1987] 1 FLR 455; (1987) 151 JP 243 HC FamD Wardship order continued but adoption/custodianship of child not allowed where natural mother not unreasonably objected to adoption of child by foster parents who were Jehovah's Witnesses/of different race to child.

Re K (J) [1990] FCR 891; [1991] 2 FLR 340 HC FamD Sikh girl left with white foster parents with view to adoption by them as was in girl's best interests.

Re M [1996] 2 FCR 473; [1996] 2 FLR 441 CA Natural parents are the biological parents; return of black boy to black parents in Africa ordered, adoption by white 'second family' not allowed.

Re M [1996] 3 FCR 185 CA Court would not stay order for return of black boy to black parents in Africa until application to European Commisison on Human Rights had been examined (implementation of order already delayed by failed attempt to get leave to appeal from House of Lords).

Re O [1995] 2 FLR 597 HC FamD Adoption order made but contact to natural mother allowed.

Re P [1994] 2 FCR 537 HC FamD Once (white) foster-parents had sought adoption of (black) child issue of care was for court, not local authority (which sought same-race adoption).

ADOPTION (failed placement)

Re P [1996] 3 FCR 657 HC FamD Appropriate arrangements where placement of girl for adoption did not work out but persons with whom placed sought to adopt brother of girl who was also placed with them.

ADOPTION (foreign decree)

Arani (Hineiti Rirerire) v Public Trustee of New Zealand (Lindsay, Matilda and Arani, Whaitiki-tiki, Interveners) [1920] AC 198; [1919] 88 LJPC 160; (1919) 121 LTR 460; (1918-19) XXXV TLR 671 PC Maori adoption of European child approved.

Ayyar (Krishanamurthi) v Ayyar (Krishnamurthi) and another (1926-27) XLIII TLR 363 PC On succession arrangements following adoption according to Hindu practice.

Bhugwandas (Nagindas) v Hurkissondas (Bachoo) (1915-16) XXXII TLR 132 PC On eligibility of adopted son where is partition of family property under Hindu law.

R v Secretary of State for Health, ex parte Luff [1991] FCR 821; [1992] 1 FLR 59 HC QBD Non-quashing of Health Department advice to Home Office that short life expectancy of prospective adopter rendered proposed adoption inappropriate.

Re 'M' (1983) 133 NLJ 556c CA English adoption order made in respect of child already adopted by applicants under South African law.

Re A [1988] 2 FLR 133; [1988] 1 WLR 229 HC FamD On procedure where adopting foreign child who is brought by another from abroad and placed with adoptive parents outside customs zone.

Re an Adoption Application [1992] 1 FLR 341; [1991] TLR 483; [1993] 2 WLR 110 HC FamD Adoption of foreign child allowed despite breaches by adopters of Adoption Act 1976.

Re G [1996] 1 FCR 495; [1995] 2 FLR 534 HC FamD Non-recognition of Paraguayan adoption; foreign mother joined to English adoption proceedings.

Re H [1982] Fam 121; (1983) 4 FLR 85; [1982] 3 WLR 501 HC FamD Court in making adoption order could override immigration decision by Secretary of State where welfare of child sought to be adopted demanded it.

Re H (An Infant) (1973) 123 NLJ 724t CA Adoption of South Vietnamese child ordered despite apparent adoption in Vietnam as procedure in Vietnam not recognised by United Kingdom.

Re K [1997] 2 FCR 389; [1997] 2 FLR 221 CA Adoption order in respect of foreign child set aside in light of flawed adoption process and application for adoption transferred to HC.

Re Marshall; Barclays Bank, Ltd v Marshall and others [1957] 1 All ER 549 HC ChD Succession principles applied to foreign-legitimated children apply to foreign-adopted children.

Re Marshall; Barclays Bank, Ltd v Marshall and others [1957] 3 All ER 172; (1957) 101 SJ 229 CA On status of foreign adopted child under English will.

Re Valentine's Settlement; Valentine and another v Valentine and another (1964) 108 SJ 582; [1964] 3 WLR 768 HC ChD Foreign adoption not recognised in foreign adopter's place of domicile consequently not recognised by English court.

Re Valentine's Settlement; Valentine and others v Valentine and others [1965] 2 All ER 226; (1965) 115 LJ 349; [1965] 2 WLR 1015 CA Foreign adopters to be domiciled in foreign country for foreign adoption to be valid.

Re W [1986] Fam 54; [1986] 1 FLR 179; (1985) 129 SJ 794; [1985] 3 WLR 945 CA On adoption of foreign child by British citizen (here refused).

Re Wilby [1956] 1 All ER 27; (1956) 106 LJ 26; (1956) 100 SJ 75; [1956] 2 WLR 262 HC PDAD Foreign adoption not covered by Adoption Act 1950, s 13; domiciled in England at date of death so deceased's mother could not succeed to estate.

Re Wilson; Grace v Lucas and others [1954] 1 All ER 997; [1954] Ch 733; (1954) 104 LJ 297; (1954) 98 SJ 372; [1954] 2 WLR 1097 HC ChD Succession of adopted child depends on/not on succession/not adoption law.

Suryanarayana (Kannepalli) and others v Venkataramana (Pucha) and another (1905-06) XXII TLR 670 PC Valid adoption where wife authorised by since dead husband to adopt son adopted a second son where first adopted son died.

ADOPTION (fostering)

Devon County Council v C and another (1985) 129 SJ 483 CA Judge ought to have decided (as court did here) issue of last occasions of maternal access to child in foster-care (not left it to local authority).

Devon County Council v C and another [1985] FLR 619 HC FamD Wrong that access of natural parents to child in local authority care continue where child being placed in foster care with possible view to adoption.

Gatehouse v Robinson and Robinson [1986] 1 FLR 504; (1986) 130 SJ 13; [1986] 1 WLR 18 HC QBD Unsuccessful appeal against failed prosecution — for undertaking privately arranged adoption contrary to Adoption Act 1958, s 29, as amended — of foster-parents who had privately arranged fostering relationship.

R v Lancashire County Council, ex parte M [1992] 1 FLR 109 CA Failed application by fosterers for review of local authority decision to take child from fosterers and place with prospective adopters.

Re B (A) [1996] 1 FLR 27; [1995] TLR 472 HC FamD Adoption order favouring foster-father and residence orders favouring him/his cohabitee so both had parental responsibility towards child.

Re B and S [1995] 1 FCR 486 HC FamD Adoption order made to foster-mother after over eleven years fostering despite fosterers' marriage break-down/fosterers keeping husband's adulterous affair secret from local authority.

Re C [1984] FLR 419 (also HC FamD) CA Risk to ward from mother (to whom was close) required care and control of ward be given to local authority which was authorised to place child with foster-parents with view to adoption.

Re C [1984] FLR 419 (also CA) HC FamD Risk to ward from mother (to whom was close) required care and control of ward be given to local authority which was authorised to place child with foster-parents with view to adoption.

Re C [1987] 2 FLR 383 CA Refusal of consent to adoption unless adoptee maintained contact with sibling not unreasonable; adopters could not be relied upon to ensure same so adoption refused: long-term fostering ordered.

Re C [1994] 2 FCR 839; [1994] 2 FLR 513 CA Foster-mother's adoption application to be fully determined before local authority allowed serve notice to remove foster-child from her.

Re H [1987] 2 FLR 12 HC FamD On ethnic background as factor when dealing with children; long-term fostering with view to adoption (if possible by someone of own ethnic background); access by mother to depend on her co-operation with social worker/what eventual adopters desired.

Re H (SM) and H (RA) [1990] FCR 996 CA On preferability of adoption to fostering on long-term basis.

Re P (L) [1990] FCR 147 HC FamD Balancing exercise as to whether children should go to aunt/be adopted by foster mother.

ADOPTION (freeing order)

Devon County Council v B [1997] 1 FLR 591 CA Freeing order invalid as court did not when making order consider basis of parent's refusal to agree to adoption; county court did not have inherent jurisdiction to bolster care order by way of injunctive relief.

In re G (a minor) [1997] 2 All ER 534; [1997] 2 FLR 202; (1997) 147 NLJ 721; (1997) 141 SJ LB 106; [1997] TLR 248; [1997] 2 WLR 747 HL On granting of conditional revocation of freeing order (here granted once care order in respect of child made under the Children Act 1989, s 31).

Re B [1992] 2 FCR 375; [1992] 2 FLR 37 CA Freeing order set aside/new trial ordered where original trial unbalanced/unfair.

Re B (P) [1985] FLR 394 HC FamD On determining whether child ought to be freed for adoption/whether rehabilitation of child in parents' home preferable.

Re C [1994] 2 FCR 485; [1993] 2 FLR 260 CA On deciding whether child should be freed for adoption.

Re C and another [1993] 3 All ER 313; [1994] Fam 1 CA Natural father without parental responsibility not a 'parent' for purpose of residence order; may not apply for residence order as of right after child freed for adoption.

Re E [1990] FCR 921; [1990] 2 FLR 397 CA On freeing children for adoption: here order refused though access had been terminated/children formed relationship with prospective adopters.

Re E [1995] 1 FCR 65; [1995] 1 FLR 382 CA Judge justified in dispensing with consent of mother to adoption of child by single lesbian woman and in not allowing contact.

Re G [1996] 2 FLR 398 CA Care order unavailable where revocation of freeing order sought: could grant/refuse revocation application.

Re G [1997] 2 All ER 534; [1997] 2 Cr App R (S) 721; [1997] 2 FCR 289; [1997] 2 FLR 202; (1997) 147 NLJ 721; (1997) 141 SJ LB 106; [1997] TLR 248; [1997] 2 WLR 747 HL On granting of conditional revocation of freeing order (here granted once care order in respect of child made under the Children Act 1989, s 31).

Re G (M) (a minor) [1996] 2 FCR 761; (1996) 140 SJ LB 147; (1996) TLR 11/6/96 CA Non-revocation of freeing order where proposed adoption did not go through.

Re H [1994] 2 FCR 437; [1993] 2 FLR 325 CA On freeing for adoption/'open' adoption (with parental contact).

Re M [1985] 1 All ER 745; [1985] Fam 60; (1985) 149 JP 574; [1985] 2 WLR 811 CA Access order for juvenile court; freeing of child for adoption for magistrates' court.

Re P [1994] 2 FCR 1306; [1994] 2 FLR 1000; [1994] TLR 426 CA Inappropriate that judge attach contact order to freeing for adoption order.

Re S (minors) [1994] TLR 682 HC FamD In case where interests of siblings conflicted those of child in respect of whom revocation of care was sought allowed take precedence over those of child in respect of whom adoption freeing order sought.

Re U [1993] 2 FCR 64; [1993] 2 FLR 992 CA Valid granting of residence order to grandparents where adoption agency had sought freeing of child for adoption.

ADOPTION (general)

Coventry Corporation v Surrey County Council [1924-35] All ER 689; [1935] AC 199 HL By 'father' the Poor Law Act 1930, s 93(4) included adopted fathers.

H v H [1947] KB 463; [1948] 117 LJR 349; (1947) 176 LTR 281; (1947) LXIII TLR 207; (1947) WN (I) 67 HC KBD Justices could dispense with need for consent to adoption of custody having custody of same.

R v Chelsea Juvenile Court Justices (Re an infant) [1955] 1 All ER 38; [1955] 1 WLR 52 HC QBD Justices have wide power to amend register of births.

R v City of Liverpool Justices, ex parte W [1959] 1 All ER 337; (1959) 123 JP 152; (1959) 109 LJ 105; (1959) 103 SJ 113 HC QBD Certiorari for failure to consider special circumstances prescribed in Marriage Act 1950, s 2(2).

Re A [1994] 1 FCR 104; [1993] 2 FLR 645 CA On rights of natural parent vis-à-vis child freed for adoption.

Re A (R) (1974) 124 NLJ 599t HC FamD Order for adoption by unmarried couple (made without notice of application for same to natural father) set aside.

Re Adoption Application No 41/61 [1962] 3 All ER 553; [1963] Ch 315; (1962) 126 JP 511; (1962) 112 LJ 718; (1962) 106 SJ 571/649; [1962] 3 WLR 997 CA Infant's interests paramount in adoption/custody cases; adjournment of adoption case to hear custody action.

Re Adoption Application No 41/61 [1962] 2 All ER 833; (1962) 126 JP 403 HC ChD Adoption proceedings stayed to allow putative father bring custody action.

Re B [1975] 2 All ER 449; [1975] 2 WLR 569 HC FamD Justices may but should not order adoption; invalid adoption where justices fail to consider interests of child/if consent unreasonably withheld and apply wrong test to question of consent.

Re B [1995] 1 FLR 895 HC FamD On correct approach to deciding adoption cases — child's welfare and other factors relevant: if decide to make residence order (not adoption order) child's welfare paramount concern.

Re B [1995] 3 All ER 333; [1995] Fam 239; [1995] 3 FCR 671; [1995] 2 FLR 1; [1995] 3 WLR 40 CA Adoption order cannot be set aside as based on fundamental mistake in fact unless natural justice denied in adoption process.

Re B (a minor) (1977) 127 NLJ 542t HC FamD Unqualified adoption order made (grandparents of child had sought qualifications but had misbehaved in employing agent to investigate into finances of adopters).

Re B (GA) [1963] 3 All ER 125; [1964] Ch 1; (1963) 127 JP 492; (1963) 113 LJ 562; (1963) 107 SJ 681; [1963] 3 WLR 471 HC ChD Infant spending better part of week with couple while adopter worked was continuously in adopter's care and control.

Re C [1993] 1 FLR 87 HC FamD No adoption order favouring adopters who contravened adoption law.

Re C [1994] 1 WLR 1220 CA Child's welfare paramount when court deciding whether to order child's removal from foster parent.

Re C [1995] TLR 323 CA Unmarried natural father who did not enjoy parental responsibility over his child did not have to be attached to proceedings regarding adoption of same.

Re C [1994] TLR 349 CA Consideration of child's welfare necessary before granting leave to remove proposed adoptee from foster-care.

Re C (CS) [1960] 1 All ER 711; (1960) 124 JP 260; (1960) 110 LJ 316; (1960) 104 SJ 269 HC ChD Child spending three nights with natural mother in three months before adoption action not in continuous care and possession of adopters; as child placed by local authority must be returned to local authority.

Re C and F [1997] 1 FCR 405; [1997] 1 FLR 190; (1996) 140 SJ LB 261; (1996) TLR 28/11/96 CA No stay/injunction on removal of children by adoption agency from prospective adopters whose marriage was disintegrating.

Re C; Re The Adoption of Children Act 1926 [1938] Ch 121 HC ChD Infant in respect of whom neither proposed adopter was older by twenty-one years could be adopted by natural mother alone but not jointly by same and husband (to whom child not related) or alone by latter.

Re D [1990] FCR 615; [1991] 1 FLR 48 CA On deciding application for freeing of child for adoption.

Re D [1991] 3 All ER 461; [1991] Fam 137; [1991] FCR 521 CA Adoption applies to minors but court can consider post-majority benefit; in making adoption order court may not impose conditions on parents which have effect after majority attained.

Re D (a minor) [1991] 2 FLR 66; [1991] TLR 31; [1991] 2 WLR 1215 CA Court could grant adoption where would operate to benefit child after attained majority; court cannot injunct third party communication with adoptee.

Re G (DM) [1962] 2 All ER 546; (1962) 126 JP 363; (1962) 112 LJ 438; (1962) 106 SJ 410 HC ChD Non-severance with natural parents possible; indecent assault conviction did not preclude from adopting; guiding principles in adoption/guardianship case the same.

Re H (1996) TLR 9/5/96 CA On practice as regards deciding of adoption aplications.

Re K [1991] FCR 142; [1991] 1 FLR 57 CA Rehabilitation of child with natural mother ordered after mother had privately arranged 'adoption' of child.

Re L [1991] FCR 297; [1991] 1 FLR 171; [1990] TLR 668 CA Natural father of illegitimate child need not consent to adoption of same/need not be named in adoption application.

Re M [1990] FCR 993; [1991] 1 FLR 458; [1990] TLR 268 CA Adoption agreement set aside where father agreed to mother/stepfather adopting children unaware of mother's terminal illness from which died shortly thereafter.

Re O [1992] 1 FLR 77 CA Father if suitable and willing to be given first chance at bringing up child where mother unable to do so.

Re P [1995] 2 FCR 58; [1994] 1 FLR 771 HC FamD Adoption process allowed continue but had to ascertain views of natural father previously unaware of child's existence.

Re P [1988] FCR 401; [1988] 1 FLR 1 CA Judge had not failed in duty by not interviewing prospective adoptee nor by taking stepfather's drink problem into account.

Re S [1988] 1 FLR 418 CA Adoption by adoptive mother/non-adoptive father merited despite intention by them not to tell child of her origins.

Re S [1988] FCR 343 CA On need to determine wishes of child vis-à-vis adoption; adoptive parents' intention not to tell child of her origins not fatal to adoption application.

Re S [1995] 2 All ER 122; [1994] TLR 220 CA Despite wide powers when making adoption order Court will not impose conditions against express opposition of adopters which would threaten peace and security of child.

Re S (J) [1959] 3 All ER 856; (1960) 124 JP 89; (1960) 110 LJ 57; (1960) 104 SJ 15; [1959] 1 WLR 1218 HC ChD As on appeal no note of evidence before juvenile court re-trial ordered.

Re T [1995] 2 FCR 537; [1995] 2 FLR 251 CA On contact between natural mother and adopted child.

Re T (1982) 3 FLR 183 CA Re-trial of adoption case ordered where judge refused adoption on basis of unrevealed portions of report of guardian ad litem.

Re T [1995] 3 FCR 299 CA Time extension in which to appeal adoption allowed where father seeking to show procedural irregularity in that all reasonable steps not taken to ensure his presence at adoption hearings.

Re W [1962] 2 All ER 875; [1962] Ch 918; (1962) 126 JP 445; (1962) 112 LJ 490; (1962) 106 SJ 720 HC ChD Adoption order where prior care and possession outside jurisdiction if infant still of compulsory school age.

Re W [1995] 1 FCR 714 HC FamD Adoption arranged through Catholic Children's Society (an approved adoption agency) was valid.

Royal Borough of Kensington and Chelsea v Q [1989] 1 FLR 399 HC FamD On using television to advertise for prospective adopters.

ADOPTION (grandchild)

Re A (1987) 151 JP 39 HC FamD Adoption of child by paternal grandmother allowed.

Re A (L) (a minor) (1978) 128 NLJ 564t; (1978) 122 SJ 417 HC FamD Revocation of adoption order where effect on child of breaking tie between him and his paternal grandparents had not been considered.

Re B (A) (An Infant) [1949] 1 All ER 709; [1949] 118 LJR 1032; (1948) LXIV TLR 573 HC ChD Exceptionally adoption of grandchild may be allowed.

Re C (1981) 2 FLR 177 CA Adoption order for persons not related to child in preference to grandparents (granted access) though had latter (as should have) previously been given custody present adoption would never have arisen.

Re M [1985] FLR 664 HC FamD Adoption by rather than custody to grandparents preferable in instant case.

Re O [1985] FLR 546 HC FamD Adoption by grandparents allowed.

Re W (1981) 2 FLR 161 CA Adoption of child by grandparents who had custody for some years (mother consented/consent of father — a criminal — dispensed with).

Re X (D) [1949] Ch 320; (1949) 99 LJ 161; (1949) LXV TLR 210; (1949) WN (I) 140 HC ChD Exceptionally adoption of child by natural grandparents may be allowed.

ADOPTION (great-uncle)

Re C [1989] 1 All ER 395; [1989] FCR 774; [1989] 1 FLR 222; (1989) 133 SJ 20; [1989] 1 WLR 61 CA Great-uncle not 'relative' for purposes of Adoption Act 1976, s 72(1); court ought not to have appointed guardian in respect of wards of court.

ADOPTION (guardian)

R v North Yorkshire County Council, ex parte M (No 2) [1989] FCR 394; [1989] 2 FLR 79 HC QBD On role of guardian ad litem vis-à-vis local authority as regards adoption of child.

Re A (P) [1971] 3 All ER 522; (1972) 136 JP 37; (1971) 121 NLJ 569t; (1971) 115 SJ 586; [1971] 1 WLR 1530 CA Parties in adoption actions have no undeniable right to report of guardian ad litem.

Re B [1983] TLR 619 CA On allowing confidential report of guardian ad litem to affect adoption proceedings.

Re B (A) [1948] 2 All ER 727; [1949] 118 LJR 21 HC ChD Public policy requires that Official Solicitor be guardian ad litem in adoption cases.

Re C [1995] 2 FCR 451; [1994] 2 FLR 525 HC FamD On availability of guardian ad litem's adoption report in later contact/residence hearings.

Re S [1993] 2 FCR 16; [1993] 2 FLR 204 CA Guardian ad litem not allowed reveal details of proposed adoptive father to mother (who was refusing consent to adoption).

Re S [1959] 2 All ER 675; (1959) 109 LJ 509; (1959) 103 SJ 545 HC ChD On status of guardian ad litem appointed by justices.

Re T [1994] 1 FLR 632 (also HC FamD); (1994) 144 NLJ 123 CA Guardian ad litem ought to have been allowed see case record of child whom local authority sought to place with adoptive parents.

Re T [1994] 1 FLR 632 (also CA) HC FamD Guardian ad litem ought to have been allowed see case record of child whom local authority sought to place with adoptive parents.

ADOPTION (homosexual)

Re D (1976) 120 SJ 214 CA Gay father's refusal of consent to adoption was not unreasonable as was no immediate danger of son being exposed to gay influences.

Re W (a minor) [1997] 3 All ER 620; (1997) 141 SJ LB 137; [1997] TLR 282 HC FamD Single woman living in lesbian relationship could apply for adoption of child.

ADOPTION (illegal)

Re G [1995] 3 FCR 26 CA Following on illegal placement of child adoption could only be authorised by HC.

ADOPTION (immigration)

R v Secretary of State for the Home Department, ex parte Brassey and another [1989] FCR 423; [1989] 2 FLR 486; (1989) 133 SJ 388 HC QBD Person born abroad of foreign parents and later adopted abroad by British subject validly denied British passport.

R v Secretary of State for the Home Department, ex parte Khan [1984] FLR 735; (1984) 128 SJ 580; [1984] TLR 228 CA Refusal of entry of child whom sought to adopt quashed as not based on criteria set out in letter from Home Secretary to appellants and complied with by them.

Re A [1996] 3 FCR 1 CA Adoption of non-patrial allowed where was not ploy to circumvent immigration regulations but was bona fide effort to seek ususal benefits of adoption (other than UK citizenship).

Re Adoption Application 58/80 [1982] TLR 139 HC FamD Order for adoption of child in respect of whom immigration authorities had previously refused to extend entry permit.

Re Adoption Application A113/67 [1988] FCR 723 HC FamD Adoption of foreign child allowed despite procedural irregularities.

Re K [1994] 3 All ER 553; [1995] Fam 38; [1994] 2 FCR 617; [1994] TLR 221; [1994] 3 WLR 572 CA Secretary of State has right of appeal against adoption order; adoption proceedings not to substitute immigration proceedings.

Re S (Q) [1997] 1 FCR 9 HC FamD Immigration concerns defeated application for adoption of non-patrial child.

ADOPTION (injunction)

Re Adoption Application No 77/88 [1990] TLR 428 HC FamD Could as part of adoption order injunct natural father from communicating with child/its new parents or from approaching within certain distance of child's new home.

ADOPTION (interim)

Re H (ZH) [1993] 1 FLR 83 HC FamD Interim adoption order favouring adopter who contravened adoption law as child's welfare demanded should remain with her.

Re W (A) [1992] 2 FCR 641; [1993] 1 FLR 62 HC FamD Interim adoption order favouring adopters who flouted adoption law as child's welfare demanded should remain with them.

S and another v Huddersfield Borough Council and another [1974] 3 All ER 296; [1975] Fam 113; (1974) 138 JP 717; (1975) 119 SJ 272; [1975] 2 WLR 697 CA Interim adoption order in father's favour to see if child should be returned to him valid interference with local authority powers/use of probationary period.

ADOPTION (joint custody)

Re S [1977] 3 All ER 671; [1977] Fam 173; (1977) 127 NLJ 368t; (1977) 121 SJ 222; [1977] 2 WLR 919 CA In parent/step-parent adoption case court must consider whether in child's welfare joint custody order preferable.

ADOPTION (legitimacy)

Coventry Corporation v Surrey County Council [1924-35] All ER 689; [1935] AC 199 HL By 'father' the Poor Law Act 1930, s 93(4) included adopted fathers.

Re C---, an Infant [1938] 107 LJCh 65; (1938) 158 LTR 371; (1936-37) LIII TLR 995 HC ChD Under Adoption of Children Act 1926 court could not allow husband and wife to adopt wife's illegitimate child (in respect of whom neither party was twenty-one years older) but could allow wife to adopt child if husband consented.

Re D [1958] 3 All ER 716; (1959) 123 JP 112; (1959) 109 LJ 41; [1959] 1 QB 229; (1959) 103 SJ 33 CA Single mother can adopt own illegitimate child.

Re E (P) (1969) 133 JP 137; (1968) 118 NLJ 956t; (1968) 112 SJ 821; [1968] 1 WLR 1913 CA Better that child lose illegitimacy via adoption and so lose contact with putative father than to retain illegitimacy and retain contact.

Re O (An Infant) [1964] 1 All ER 786; (1964) 114 LJ 252; (1964) 108 SJ 117 CA Natural father did not exercise right of veto over adoption of illegitimate child that would enjoy over legitimate child.

Veasey v Attorney-General (1982) 3 FLR 267 HC FamD Child legitimated upon marriage of parents: post-marital adoption did not affect situation.

ADOPTION (maintenance)

Hackney Union v Tombs; Tombs v Hackney Union (1909) 73 JP 271 Police Ct Valid adoption of child by poor law guardians; adulterous father ordered to pay maintenance.

Re Skinner; Skinner v Carter [1948] 1 All ER 917; [1948] Ch 387; (1948) 112 JP 329; (1948) 98 LJ 273; [1948] 117 LJR 1628; (1948) WN (I) 185 CA Bigamously married adopter could be ordered to pay for child's maintenance.

Re Skinner; Skinner v Carter (1948) 112 JP 116; (1948) 98 LJ 23 HC ChD Bigamously married adopter could not seek maintenance order in respect of child against partner in bigamy (and co-adopter).

ADOPTION (mistake)

Re B [1995] 3 All ER 333; [1995] Fam 239; [1995] 3 FCR 671; [1995] 2 FLR 1; [1995] 3 WLR 40 CA Adoption order cannot be set aside as based on fundamental mistake in fact unless natural justice denied in adoption process.

Re F [1977] 2 All ER 777; [1977] Fam 165; [1977] 2 WLR 488 CA Court need not set aside adoption order made under mistake that adopters were married.

ADOPTION (non-patrial)

Re A [1996] 3 FCR 1 CA Adoption of non-patrial allowed where was not ploy to circumvent immigration regulations but was bona fide effort to seek usual benefits of adoption (other than UK citizenship).

Re Adoption Application [1993] Fam 125; [1993] 1 FLR 947; [1992] 1 WLR 596 HC FamD Adoption of foreign child allowed despite irregularities in procedure as child's interest in remaining with parents greater than that of leaving same.

Re B [1995] 2 FCR 749 HC FamD Refusal to allow adoption of child from The Gambia.

Re H [1996] 2 FCR 597; [1996] 1 FLR 717 HC FamD Adoption order made in respect of non-patrial (despite Home Secretary's objections) as was genuine adoption where welfare of adoptee outweighed public policy considerations.

Re H [1996] 4 All ER 600; [1996] 2 FLR 187; (1996) 140 SJ LB 128; [1997] 1 WLR 791 CA Adoption order in respect of non-patrial despite Home Secretary's objections: test when making adoption more broad-based than that set out by HC FamD.

Re S (Q) [1997] 1 FCR 9 HC FamD Immigration concerns defeeated application for adoption of non-patrial child.

ADOPTION ('parent')

Re C [1996] 2 FCR 129; [1995] 2 FLR 483 CA Parent for purposes of adoption is person with parental responsibility towards child so natural father not parent in instant case.

ADOPTION (parentage)

Re L (No 2) [1991] 1 FLR 29 CrCt On parentage as alternative to adoption.

ADOPTION (progress reports)

Re C [1986] 1 FLR 315 CA Court ought not to have ordered that annual progress reports regarding adopted child be given to natural father.

ADOPTION (prohibited degrees)

Re C, an Infant [1937] 3 All ER 783; (1937) 84 LJ 116 HC ChD Adoption allowed of child within prohibited degrees of consanguinity vis-à-vis female adopter.

ADOPTION (property)

Re Clay's Policy of Assurance; Clay v Earnshaw [1937] 2 All ER 548; (1937) 83 LJ 304 HC ChD Married Women's Property Act 1882 inapplicable to adopted children.

ADOPTION (provisional)

Re R [1962] 3 All ER 238; (1962) 126 JP 498 CA Cannot make full adoption order to person domiciled outside England, only a provisional order.

ADOPTION (publicity)

Re M [1989] 1 FLR 443 HC FamD Wardship not justified just because parents mentally handicapped but was here; no/was restriction on publicity regarding parents (who sought publicity)/fosterers or future adopters; on procedure where party actively seeks publicity in wardship proceedings.

ADOPTION (religion)

Re C (1966) 110 SJ 309 CA Illegitimate child taken from proposed adopters and given into custody of natural father and his wife (although were not of same religion as natural mother).

Re C (MA) [1966] 1 All ER 838 (also HC ChD); (1966) 130 JP 217 (also HC ChD); [1966] 1 WLR 646 CA In adoption-custody cases child's welfare paramount interest; no requirement regarding religious education imposed.

Re C (MA) [1966] 1 All ER 838 (also CA); (1966) 130 JP 217 (also CA) HC ChD In adoption-custody cases child's welfare paramount interest; no requirement regarding religious education imposed.

Re Carroll (1930) 74 SJ 645 HC KBD Child to be adopted by Protestants/brought up as Protestant notwithstanding contrary wishes of Roman Catholic mother.

Re G [1962] 2 All ER 173; (1962) 126 JP 341; (1962) 112 LJ 320; [1962] 2 QB 141; (1962) 106 SJ 282; [1962] 2 WLR 1010 CA Adoption of Protestant child by Jewish parents allowed as in infant's best interests.

Re J [1987] 1 FLR 455; (1987) 151 JP 243 HC FamD Wardship order continued but adoption/custodianship of child not allowed where natural mother not unreasonably objected to adoption of child by foster parents who were Jehovah's Witnesses/of different race to child.

Re S [1995] 2 FCR 177; [1994] 2 FLR 416; (1994) 138 SJ LB 99 CA Non-imposition of blood transfusion condition when ordering adoption of child by couple who were Jehovah's Witnesses.

ADOPTION (residence)

M v C and Calderdale Metropolitan Borough Council [1993] 1 FCR 431; [1993] 1 FLR 505 CA In Children Act 1989 'parent' includes father of illegitimate child but that status lost post-freeing order after which could not seek residence order.

M v C and Calderdale Metropolitan Borough Council [1992] 2 FCR 141 HC FamD Leave of court required before natural father of adopted illegitimate child could seek residence order.

Re Adoption Application No 52/1951 [1951] 2 All ER 931; [1952] Ch 16; (1951) 115 JP 625; (1951) 101 LJ 637; (1951) 95 SJ 711; [1951] 2 TLR 887; (1951) WN (I) 520 HC ChD Residency requires degree of permananecy: three months out of fifteen with intention to retire not residency.

Re C (minors) [1992] TLR 548 CA Natural father seeking residence order not 'parent' under Children Act 1989 of child freed for adoption so required leave of court.

ADOPTION (revocation)

Re A (L) (a minor) (1978) 128 NLJ 564t; (1978) 122 SJ 417 HC FamD Revocation of adoption order where effect on child of breaking tie between him and his paternal grandparents had not been considered.

Re M (R), an infant (1941) WN (I) 244 CA On revocation of adoption order.

ADOPTION (step-parent)

Re B [1975] Fam 127; (1975) 125 NLJ 14t; (1975) 119 SJ 133 HC FamD Adoption order made in favour of mother/stepfather (and despite father's refusal of consent) revoked where father genuinely wanted to maintain paternal relationship with child.

Re G (1980) 1 FLR 109 HC FamD On approach when adoption sought by natural parent and step-parent; adoption/access hearings (if are both) to be heard together.

Re H (1983) 4 FLR 261 HC FamD Initial procedure as regards application for adoption of child by parent/step-parent.

Re S [1977] 3 All ER 671; [1977] Fam 173; (1977) 127 NLJ 368t; (1977) 121 SJ 222; [1977] 2 WLR 919 CA In parent/step-parent adoption case court must consider whether in child's welfare joint custody order preferable.

ADOPTION (succession)

Ayyar (Krishanamurthi) v Ayyar (Krishnamurthi) and another (1926-27) XLIII TLR 363 PC On succession arrangements following adoption according to Hindu practice.

Lali (Musammat) v Dhar (Murli) (1905-06) XXII TLR 460 PC Deceased's gift to adopted son whose adoption was void had no effect.

Re Brinkley's Will Trusts; Westminster Bank v Brinkley and another [1968] 2 WLR 217; [1968] Ch 407 HC ChD Will bequeathing property to grandchildren held not to include adopted grandchildren.

Re Gilpin; Hutchinson v Gilpin (1953) 97 SJ 763 HC ChD Adopted child was intended/allowed to inherit along with testator's other grandchildren.

Re Jebb, decd; Ward-Smith and another v Jebb and others [1966] Ch 666; [1965] 3 WLR 810 CA Will constructed as being intended to benefit adopted grandchild as well as natural grandchildren of testator.

Re Jones's Will Trusts; Jones v Squire (1965) 115 LJ 529 HC ChD Adopted child deemed to have been intended beneficiary under will leaving property to adoptive mother or on death of same to her children.

Re Marshall (deceased); Barclays Bank, Ltd v Marshall and others [1957] 1 All ER 549 HC ChD Succession principles applied to foreign-legitimated children apply to foreign-adopted children.

Re Wilson; Grace v Lucas and others [1954] 1 All ER 997; [1954] Ch 733; (1954) 104 LJ 297; (1954) 98 SJ 372; [1954] 2 WLR 1097 HC ChD Succession of adopted child depends on/not on succession/not adoption law.

ADOPTION (surrogacy)

Adoption Application AA212/86 [1987] 2 FLR 291 HC FamD Adoption order made in respect of surrogate child despite surrogacy arrangement being coloured by transfer of money between parties.

Re an adoption application [1987] 2 All ER 826; [1987] Fam 81; [1987] FCR 161; [1987] 2 FLR 291; (1987) 137 NLJ 267; [1987] 3 WLR 31 HC FamD Surrogacy not contrary to Adoption Act if payments not for profit/reward.

Re W (M) [1996] 3 FCR 128; [1995] 2 FLR 759 HC FamD Adoption order (plus no contact with natural mother) to surrogate parents (husband natural father) of child.

ADOPTION (taking child outside jurisdiction)

Re M [1973] 1 All ER 852; [1973] Fam 66; (1973) 137 JP 339; (1973) 123 NLJ 56t; (1973) 117 SJ 88; [1973] 2 WLR 515 HC FamD Absent provisional adoption order child (even ward) cannot be removed from jurisdiction by applicant adopters.

ADOPTION (ward)

F v S [1973] 1 All ER 722; [1973] Fam 203; (1973) 137 JP 301; (1973) 117 SJ 109; [1973] 2 WLR 178 CA Leave of court needed for adoption of ward; issue for court is will adoption application succeed?

Re C [1985] FLR 1114 CA Failed application by mother for full investigation in wardship of alleged abuse of her son by his adoptive parents.

Re C [1989] FCR 774; [1989] 1 FLR 222; (1989) 133 SJ 20; [1989] 1 WLR 61 CA Great-uncle not 'relative' for purposes of Adoption Act 1976, s 72(1); court ought not to have appointed guardian in respect of wards of court.

Re D (T) [1985] FLR 1150 HC FamD Natural father of illegitimate child in care could not seek invocation by court of its wardship jurisdiction to prevent local authority arranging adoption of child.

Re E [1991] FCR 33 CA Rehabilitation of child discontinued and placement for adoption ordered.

Re K (1981) 2 FLR 381; (1980) 124 SJ 809 HC FamD Local authority not to apply for wardship 'with a view to adoption'.

Re M (D) [1986] 2 FLR 122 (also CA) HC FamD Failed wardship action in which foster-parents sought review of decision of local authority adoption panel.

Re O [1993] 2 FCR 746; [1993] 2 FLR 737 HC FamD Wardship injunction ended upon adoption order being made.

Re P [1990] FCR 260; [1990] 1 FLR 96; (1989) 139 NLJ 1265 CA Mixed race child justifiably removed from home of white foster-mother to that of black foster-parents with view to adoption.

Re P (1982) 3 FLR 420; (1982) 132 NLJ 248 CA Court could not order that no application be made in wardship proceedings until full hearing but could require court's leave be given to any steps taken.

Re R [1991] FCR 805 HC FamD Courts reluctant to (and here did not) interfere with local authority acting in capacity of adoption agency.

Re S (1978) 128 NLJ 1148t; (1978) 122 SJ 759 HC FamD Wardship action in which were seeking decision on issue of care and control of child dismissed as was really an attempt to secure review of adoption order refusal.

Re W [1990] 2 All ER 463; [1990] Fam 156; [1990] FCR 736; [1990] 2 FLR 470; [1990] TLR 161; [1990] 2 WLR 1116 HC FamD Court will not review actions of approved adoption agency via wardship jurisdiction.

Wolverhampton Metropolitan Borough Council v M [1988] FCR 629 HC FamD Child taken from mentally handicapped parents unable to care for him and placed in care with view to adoption (parental access terminated).

ADOPTION (welfare)

Re El-G (1983) 4 FLR 421 HC FamD Welfare of children demanded that they stay with prospective adopters; on deciding whether parent's refusal of consent unreasonable (here was: dispensed with); on pivotal role of court when is sought to change arrangements for ward.

Re F [1982] 1 All ER 321; (1982) 3 FLR 101; (1981) 131 NLJ 1053; (1981) 125 SJ 861; [1982] 1 WLR 102 CA Welfare of child paramount in adoption; welfare indicates if consent un/reasonably withheld by parent; adoption order rather than care order where child's welfare demands no access by mother.

AFFILIATION (corroboration)

R v Newcastle Emlyn Justices and another, ex parte Evans (1963) 107 SJ 416 HC QBD QBD could not decide whether fraud perpetrated on lower court where was conflicting evidence.

S v C (1963) 107 SJ 1022 CA Putative father's admission of two acts of sex with complainant before defendant gave birth to illegitimate child could be corroboration of complainant's evidence in some material particular.

AFFILIATION (general)

Adedigba v Adedigba (1968) 118 NLJ 228t; (1968) 112 SJ 233 CA Court had jusrisdiction in bastardy proceedings regarding child born abroad to mother domiciled abroad.

Batchelor v Smith (1935) 79 SJ 49 HC KBD Revocation of payment ordered pursuant to affiliation order where had come to light since order that mother had committed perjury.

Buckeridge v Hall [1963] 1 All ER 509; (1963) 127 JP 218; (1963) 113 LJ 154; [1963] 1 QB 614; (1963) 107 SJ 96; [1963] 2 WLR 354 HC QBD Affiliation order available for English-born child of woman of foreign domicil normally resident in England.

Clapham v National Assistance Board [1961] 2 All ER 50; (1961) 125 JP 373; (1961) 111 LJ 306; [1961] 2 QB 77; (1961) 105 SJ 234 HC QBD National Assistance Board may seek/obtain affiliation order despite mother's earlier failed attempt.

Corfield v Hodgson [1966] 2 All ER 205; (1966) 130 JP 271; (1965-66) 116 NLJ 810; (1966) 110 SJ 170; [1966] 1 WLR 590 HC QBD Putative father's lies in affiliation case evidence corroborating paternity.

Foy v Brooks [1977] 2 All ER 113; (1977) 141 JP 339; (1976) 120 SJ 768; [1977] 1 WLR 160 HC FamD Purchase of layette incidental to childbirth.

Gaines v W [1968] 1 All ER 189; (1968) 132 JP 146; (1967) 117 NLJ 1190t; [1968] 1 QB 782; (1967) 111 SJ 888; [1968] 2 WLR 139 HC QBD Single woman may seek affiliation order though not single when child born.

Hyde v Hodge [1985] FLR 711 CA Dismissal of affiliation action by HC improper: should have remitted it to justices for dismissal so that applicant would not lose right of appeal to CrCt.

Kane v Littlefair [1985] FLR 859; (1985) 149 JP 312 HC FamD Can make affiliation order against male who was under fourteen years old at time child conceived.

Loxton v Russell (1966) 110 SJ 170 CA On proving in affiliation action that had sex at relevant period.

McGregor v Telford [1914-15] All ER 209; (1915-17) XXV Cox CC 1; (1915) 79 JP 485; [1915] 3 KB 237; [1915] 84 LJKB 1902; (1915-16) 113 LTR 84; (1914-15) XXXI TLR 512; (1915) WN (I) 258 HC KBD Justices can re-hear affiliation order application.

Michael v Gowland [1977] 2 All ER 328; (1976) 120 SJ 857 HC FamD Time limit for stating case is peremptory.

Oldfield v National Assistance Board [1960] 1 All ER 524; (1960) 124 JP 246; (1960) 110 LJ 190; [1960] 1 QB 635; (1960) 104 SJ 169 HC QBD Affiliation order to be such must require payment of money.

Osborn v Sparks (1982) 3 FLR 90 HC FamD On balancing procedure to be exercised when assessing financial provision to be made by father in respect of illegitimate child and its mother.

Payne v Critchley and the National Assistance Board [1962] 1 All ER 619; (1962) 126 JP 162; (1962) 112 LJ 240; [1962] 2 QB 83; (1962) 106 SJ 78 HC QBD Affiliation order providing for payment to National Assistance Board later variable to mother's benefit.

R v Gravesend Justices, ex parte Doodney [1971] 2 All ER 364; (1971) 135 JP 353; (1971) 121 NLJ 152; (1971) 115 SJ 327; [1971] 1 WLR 818 HC QBD That mother resident abroad need not preclude putative father seeking variation in England.

R v Humphreys and others, ex parte Ward [1914-15] All ER 189 (1914-15) XXIV Cox CC 455; (1915) 79 JP 66; [1914] 3 KB 1237; [1915] 84 LJKB 187; (1914-15) 111 LTR 1110; (1913-14) XXX TLR 698 HC KBD Affiliation order can be made in respect of child not born in England or Wales unless child subject to foreign law.

R v Justices of the Peace for Sunderland, ex parte Leslie Hodgkinson [1945] 2 All ER 175; (1945) 109 JP 201; [1945] 114 LJ 359; (1945) 173 LTR 62; (1945) 89 SJ 436; (1944-45) LXI TLR 456; (1945) WN (I) 150 HC KBD Justices can hear second bastardy hearing/admit fresh evidence and make order despite initial refusal.

R v Lancashire Justices, ex parte Tyrer [1924] All ER 304; (1921-25) XXVII Cox CC 711; (1925) 89 JP 17; [1925] 1 KB 200; (1924) 59 LJ 775; [1925] 94 LJCL 331; (1925) 132 LTR 382; (1924-25) 69 SJ 194; (1924-25) XLI TLR 103; (1924) WN (I) 301 HC KBD Need not seek bastardy order in place where customarily/permanently reside.

Robinson v Williams [1964] 3 All ER 12; (1964) 114 LJ 588; [1965] 1 QB 89; (1964) 108 SJ 691; [1964] 3 WLR 563 HC QBD Dismissal of one affiliation application does not preclude later application; new evidence is evidence uncalled (not necessarily discovered since) first trial.

S v E [1967] 1 All ER 593; [1967] 1 QB 367; (1966) 110 SJ 945; [1967] 2 WLR 704 HC QBD Affiliation proceedings are civil proceedings: putative father a compellable witness.

Smith v May (1969) 113 SJ 1000 HC QBD Child found not to be child of marriage on basis of complainant's evidence.

W v K [1988] 1 FLR 86; (1987) 151 JP 589 HC FamD On heavy burden of proof in disproving legitimacy/paternity.

Willett v Wells [1985] 1 All ER 585; [1985] FLR 514; (1985) 149 JP 454; (1985) 129 SJ 17; [1985] 1 WLR 237 HC FamD Money spent by putative father on child is 'money for its maintenance'.

AFFILIATION (legitimacy)

Boyce v Cox [1921] All ER 658; (1921-25) XXVII Cox CC 139; (1921) 85 JP 279; [1922] 1 KB 149; [1922] 91 LJCL 122; (1922) 126 LTR 254; (1921-22) 66 SJ 142; (1921-22) XXXVIII TLR 51; (1921) WN (I) 312 HC KBD Affiliation order available to woman judicially separated from third party against natural father.

AFFILIATION (maintenance)

Boniface v Harris (1983) 147 JP 208 HC FamD Pre-1975 affiliation order could not order payment straight to child.

Dickens v Pattison; R v Camberwell Green Justices, ex parte Pattison and Dickens [1985] FLR 610; (1985) 149 JP 271; (1985) 129 SJ 31 HC FamD Contravention by magistrates of principle that only affiliation payment arrears of less than one year to be enforced.

G (A) v G (T) [1970] 3 All ER 546; (1971) 135 JP 13; [1970] 2 QB 643; [1970] 3 WLR 132 CA Putative father can authorise agent to pay infant's maintenance; proof of agency required before maintenance proceedings can be begun.

G v G (1970) 114 SJ 493 CA On payment by infant of maintenance towards own child (and on proving paid same).

Haroutunian v Jennings (1980) 1 FLR 62; (1977) 121 SJ 663 HC FamD Amount payable under affiliation order (assessed by reference to father's income) may include payment for mother.

Jeffery v Paget (1919) CC Rep VIII 2 CyCt Man married by woman who has entered into maintenance agreement in affiliation action becomes liable for maintenance of said children.

Moore v Ball [1984] 2 All ER 237; [1984] Fam 41; [1984] FLR 555; (1984) 148 JP 425; (1984) 128 SJ 298; [1984] 2 WLR 865 HC FamD Secretary of State can have varied maintenance order payable to Secretary increased by variation.

R v Birkenhead Borough Justices, ex parte Smith [1954] 1 All ER 503; [1954] Crim LR 133t; [1954] Crim LR 297; (1954) 118 JP 203; (1954) 104 LJ 154; (1954) 98 SJ 163 HC QBD US soldier (member of visiting forces) could not be committed to prison for failure to maintain child pursuant to affiliation order.

R v Bow Road Domestic Proceedings Court, ex parte Adedigba [1968] 2 All ER 89; (1968) 118 NLJ 444; [1968] 2 QB 572; (1968) 132 JP 301; [1968] 2 WLR 1143 CA Maintenance order if mother and father resident in England though child born abroad/mother domiciled abroad when child born.

R v Copestake and others, ex parte Wilkinson [1926] All ER 252; (1926) 90 JP 191; [1927] 1 KB 468; [1927] 96 LJCL 65; (1927) 136 LTR 100; (1926) WN (I) 242 CA Under Criminal Justice Administration Act 1914 court could revoke periodic payments ordered in affiliation suit but could not alter paternity decision.

R v Hereford City Justices, ex parte O [1982] 3 All ER 568; (1983) 4 FLR 196; (1982) 126 SJ 496; [1982] TLR 314; [1982] 1 WLR 1252 HC QBD Can appeal to Crown Court on basis of quantum.

Re Harrington; Wilder v Turner [1908-10] All ER 235; [1908] 2 Ch 687; (1907-09) XXI Cox CC 709; (1908) 72 JP 501; [1909] 78 LJCh 27; (1908) 43 LJ 641; (1908-09) XCIX LTR 723; (1907-08) 52 SJ 855; (1908-09) XXV TLR 3; (1908) WN (I) 203 HC ChD Cannot seek arrears of maintenance under affiliation order from estate/representatives of deceased father.

Willett v Wells [1985] 1 All ER 585; [1985] FLR 514; (1985) 149 JP 454; (1985) 129 SJ 17; [1984] TLR 605; [1985] 1 WLR 237 HC FamD Successful appeal against refusal of affiliation order; provision of clothes/food akin to money payment.

APPRENTICE (general)

Gadd v Thompson (1910-11) XXVII TLR 113 HC KBD Reasonable restrictive covenant entered into by infant apprentice could be enforced by injunction.

APPROVED SCHOOL ORDER (general)

Barnsley Corporation v Lancashire County Council [1956] 3 All ER 671; [1957] 1 QB 123; [1956] 3 WLR 820 HC QBD Cannot appeal against approved school order on basis that child's address unknown.

Hamlyn v Pearce [1962] 2 All ER 436; [1962] Crim LR 405t; (1962) 126 JP 350; (1962) 112 LJ 370; [1962] 2 QB 346; (1962) 106 SJ 355; [1962] 3 WLR 136 HC QBD Can only be sent to approved school if under seventeen at time of order.

Isle of Wight County Council v Warwickshire County Council [1953] 1 All ER 525; [1953] 1 QB 553; (1953) 97 SJ 154; [1953] 2 WLR 451 HC QBD Quarter sessions on appeal cannot name local authority within which offence committed by young person of unknown residence.

Mayor, Aldermen and Burgesses of the County Borough of South Shields v Lord Mayor, Aldermen and Citizens of the City of Liverpool [1943] 1 All ER 338; (1943) 107 JP 77; [1943] 112 LJ 318; (1943) 168 LTR 238; (1943) WN (I) 31 HC KBD Time for deciding where reside is time of making the order.

Rugman v Drover [1950] 2 All ER 575; [1951] 1 KB 380; (1950) 94 SJ 595; [1950] 66 (2) TLR 699 HC KBD State of affairs which exists upon appeal is that which existed at time of trial (when were still young person).

BAIL (general)

R v P [1980] Crim LR 796 CrCt Could be bail of child in care (bail denied in circumstances of this case).

BIRTH (concealment)

R v Chick (Florence Irene) (1925-26) 19 Cr App R 57 CCA Three months in second division for infanticide/concealment of birth in light of prisoner's age (twenty) and strong recommendation of mercy by jury.

R v Conroy and Conroy [1954] Crim LR 141 Assizes Jointly tried parents found guilty of murder of newborn child.

R v Rosenberg (1906) 70 JP 264 CCC On elements of offence of concealment of birth.

BIRTH CERTIFICATE (general)

R v Chelsea Juvenile Court Justices (Re an infant) [1955] 1 All ER 38; (1955) 99 SJ 77; [1955] 1 WLR 52 HC QBD Justices have wide power to amend register of births.

R v Registrar General, ex parte Smith [1990] 2 All ER 170; [1990] FCR 561; [1990] 2 FLR 79; [1990] 2 QB 253; [1990] 2 WLR 980 HC QBD Registrar General may refuse to provide information necessary for granting of birth certificate if might be used for future criminal act.

BIRTH CERTIFICATE (transsexual)

Re P and G [1996] 2 FCR 588; [1996] 2 FLR 90 HC QBD Registrar General's refusal to alter birth certificates so as to show male-to-female transsexuals born female was valid.

BLOOD TEST (general)

B (BR) v B (J) [1968] 2 All ER 1023 CA Blood tests ordered if in child's best interests.

M (D) v M (S) and G (M (DA) intervening) [1969] 2 All ER 243; [1969] 1 WLR 843 CA No blood test as not in child's interest/merely to prove wife's adultery.

Re E [1994] 2 FCR 709; [1995] 1 FLR 392 CA Decision to refuse contact unchanged but parental responsibility order made; on directing that blood tests be conducted (only possible where paternity an issue).

S v McC (formerly S) and M (S intervening) [1970] 1 All ER 1162; (1970) 120 NLJ 153t; (1970) 114 SJ 131; [1970] 1 WLR 672 CA Child's best interests relevant in determining if blood test to be required.

W v W [1970] 1 All ER 1157; (1969) 119 NLJ 1044t; (1969) 113 SJ 874; [1970] 1 WLR 682 CA Child's best interests determine if blood test to be required.

BLOOD TEST (guardian)

Re L [1968] 1 All ER 20; (1967) 117 NLJ 1242t; [1967] 3 WLR 1645 CA PDAD judge can order blood test of infant absent guardian ad litem's consent.

BLOOD TEST (legitimacy)

B v B (1968) 118 NLJ 541t CA On jurisdiction as regards ordering blood testing where paternity of child in issue.

B v B and another (1968) 112 SJ 689 CA HC could order administration of blood test in divorce action where paternity was an issue.

B v B and E (B intervening) [1969] 3 All ER 1106; (1969) 119 NLJ 672t; (1969) 113 SJ 625; [1969] 1 WLR 1800 CA Presumption of legitimacy justifies refusing blood test; blood test not ordered where only to support custody claim, only if in child's interests.

Holmes v Holmes (Holmes, by his Guardian, intervening) [1966] 1 WLR 187 HC PDAD Court will not find child accepted into family unless is clearly the case; blood test proved child not child of husband party to action.

L v L (1968) 112 SJ 294 HC PDAD Court could not order blood testing of child in paternity suit between spouses.

M v M (1968) 118 NLJ 1005t CA Blood test only ordered where is in child's interest (not ordered here).

M v M and others (1968) 112 SJ 840 CA Refusal of blood test where ran risk of bastardising child and revealing mother to be liar without actually discovering who the real father was.

McVeigh v Beattie [1988] 2 All ER 500; [1988] Fam 69; [1988] FCR 516; [1988] 2 FLR 67; (1988) 132 SJ 125; [1988] 2 WLR 992 HC FamD Absent reasonable excuse refusal to provide blood sample corroborates claim of parenthood.

O v L [1995] 2 FLR 930 CA On deciding whether to order blood testing (here not ordered).

R v R [1973] 3 All ER 933; (1973) 117 SJ 394; [1973] 1 WLR 1115 HC FamD Referral of blood test applications from registrar to judge.

Re A [1994] 2 FLR 463 CA On inference to be drawn from refusal of blood test in action where paternity at issue.

Re B (C) [1994] 2 FCR 925; [1994] 2 FLR 762 HC FamD Blood testing of child not allowed where mother objected.

Re E [1995] 1 FCR 245; [1994] 2 FLR 548 HC FamD On ordering blood test where paternity in issue.

Re G [1997] 2 FCR 325; [1997] 1 FLR 360 CA Where separated husband refused to have blood test done in respect of child of wife of whom husband claimed he was father, the inference to be drawn was that he was not the father.

Re G (C) [1994] 2 FCR 889 HC FamD On whether/when to order blood testing where paternity in issue (here ordered).

Re H [1996] 4 All ER 28; [1996] 3 FCR 201; [1996] 2 FLR 65; (1996) 146 NLJ 406; [1996] 3 WLR 506 CA On refusing/ordering blood test where paternity in issue.

Re H (1996) TLR 12/3/96 CA Failed appeal against order for blood testing of mother and child where mother did not consent to the testing.

Re L (1967) 111 SJ 908 CA On rebutting presumption of legitimacy; on ordering blood testing where issue of paternity raised.

Re L [1967] 2 All ER 1110; (1967) 111 SJ 717; [1967] 3 WLR 1149 HC PDAD Blood tests ordered of child if in its best interests.

T (H) v T(E) [1971] 1 All ER 590; (1971) 115 SJ 186; [1971] 1 WLR 429 HC PDAD Absent contrary evidence presumption that child of marriage is legitimate; blood test cautiously accepted as proof of paternity.

T v T [1992] TLR 387 CA Child's best interests demanded carrying out of blood test to determine paternity where mother had cast doubts in respect of same.

Turner v Blunden [1986] 2 All ER 75; [1986] Fam 120; [1986] 2 FLR 69; (1986) 150 JP 180; (1986) 130 SJ 184; [1986] 2 WLR 491 HC FamD Blood tests can corroborate allegation of paternity.

BLOOD TEST (parental responsibility order)

Re F [1993] 3 All ER 596; [1993] Fam 314; [1993] 3 WLR 369 CA Court will not order blood tests where parental responsibility application likely to fail; not in child's interests; parent in charge of child opposed.

BLOOD TEST (paternity)

S (an Infant, by her Guardian ad Litem the Official Solicitor to the Supreme Court) v S; W v Official Solicitor (acting as Guardian ad Litem for a male infant named PHW) [1972] AC 24; [1970] 3 WLR 366 HL Blood test desirable in paternity suit.

CARE/CUSTODY (abduction)

Jenkins v Jenkins (1980) 1 FLR 148 CA Return of child to parent granted custody to be ordered where other parent 'snatches' child.

Re B (1983) 4 FLR 472; (1982) 132 NLJ 1172 CA Interim care and control of children to mother pending resolution of wardship/'kidnapping' proceedings appropriate.

Re L (1983) 4 FLR 368 CA Interim care and control order made in favour of mother who 'kidnapped' own child from United States and had him made ward of court.

Re T [1968] 3 All ER 411; [1968] Ch 704; (1968) 112 SJ 639; [1968] 3 WLR 430 CA Generally court will not countenance wardship/custody actions on foot of kidnapping by parent.

CARE/CUSTODY (access/contact)

Bates v Morley (1982) 3 FLR 244; (1982) 132 NLJ 65 CA Mother with care and control of ward (father had access) allowed remove child to Canada (wardship ending upon ward quitting country).

Berkshire County Council v B [1997] 1 FLR 171 HC FamD Parental contact could be ordered in care proceedings though local authority care plan envisaged that ultimately there would be no parental contact.

Birmingham City Council v H (No 2) [1993] 1 FLR 883 CA Where mother/son both minors interests of each equally important; here ending of contact between mother/son too Draconian: reasonable supervised access allowed.

Cheshire County Council v B and others [1992] 2 FCR 572 HC FamD Provisions in care and contact orders for six-month review of their implementation was invalid.

Churchard v Churchard [1984] FLR 635 CA No committal of mother/no changes in custody in situation where children (in mother's custody) seeking of own volition to frustrate access attempts by father.

Devon County Council and others v S and others [1993] 2 FCR 36; [1993] 1 FLR 842 HC FamD Caution needed if appointing welfare officer as guardian ad litem; issue for justices in post-rehabiliation contact termination application not whether rehabilitation successful but should care cease.

Devon County Council v C and another [1985] FLR 619 HC FamD Wrong that access of natural parents to child in local authority care continue where child being placed in foster care with possible view to adoption.

Devon County Council v C and another (1985) 129 SJ 483 CA Judge ought to have decided (as court did here) issue of last occasions of maternal access to child in foster-care (not left it to local authority).

F v F [1989] Fam 1; [1989] FCR 232; [1988] 3 WLR 959 HC FamD Non-enforcement of French custody order where was twenty-one month delay before matter came before court and change in attitude of parties over access.

F v Kent County Council and others [1993] 1 FCR 217; [1993] 1 FLR 432; (1992) 136 SJ LB 258; [1992] TLR 394 HC FamD On exercise of discretion to require parties to seek court's leave before making future care/contact application (here wrongly exercised).

G v G and Devon County Council [1989] FCR 454 CA Divorce court could not make second care order where juvenile court had already made valid care order.

Hereford and Worcester Council v Jah [1985] FLR 530 HC FamD Whether parent to be allowed access to child in care depends on whether in child's best interests to allow access.

Kent County Council v C and another [1993] 1 All ER 719; [1993] Fam 57; [1993] 1 FLR 308; [1992] 3 WLR 808 HC FamD Exceptionally no contact between parent and child may be ordered by family proceedings court in care order but cannot make directions regarding care orders.

M v Berkshire County Council [1985] FLR 257 CA On power of juvenile court to order access.

M v M (1980) 1 FLR 77 CA Problems regarding access not good ground on which to remove custody of young child from mother.

P v Staffordshire County Council [1989] FCR 16 HC FamD Non-invocation of wardship jurisdiction to review exercise of local authority discretion (over access to child in care).

R v Bolton Metropolitan Borough, ex parte B [1985] FLR 343 HC QBD On ending/denying access of parents to child being held in local authority care.

R v Corby Juvenile Court, ex parte M [1987] 1 All ER 992; [1987] 1 FLR 490; (1987) 151 JP 387; (1970) 130 SJ 860; [1987] 1 WLR 55 HC QBD Access provisions of Child Care Act 1980 apply retrospectively to children put in care under earlier enactment.

R v Oxford Justices, ex parte D [1986] 3 All ER 129; [1987] 1 FLR 61; (1986) 150 JP 519; [1987] QB 199; (1970) 130 SJ 525; [1986] 3 WLR 447 HC QBD Putative father may apply for access to illegitimate child in local authority care.

R v West Glamorgan County Council, ex parte T [1990] FCR 142; [1990] 1 FLR 339; (1989) 133 SJ 1545 HC QBD Refusal of judicial review of local authority decision not to serve fresh notice of refusal of access.

Re B [1994] 1 FCR 471 HC FamD Children of mentally unwell mother taken into care (occasional/no access for older/younger child with aim of eventual residence to fathers).

Re B [1993] 1 FCR 363 (also CC) CA On relation between care/contact applications: inappropriate that CC judge halted contact when making care order.

Re B [1993] 1 FLR 421 HC FamD Care order plus interim contact order pending future hearing was permissible.

Re B and another [1993] 3 All ER 524; [1993] Fam 301; [1993] 3 WLR 63 CA Paramount consideration in parental contact case being welfare of children court entitled to consider local authority's plans for children's future.

Re C [1996] 1 FCR 332 HC FamD Care order with provision for declining contact and ultimate adoption properly made (rather than making of no order which would have resulted in child being left with foster-parents).

Re D [1953] 2 All ER 1318; (1954) 118 JP 25 CA Court of summary jurisdiction within which applicant resides may vary access order.

Re D [1988] 2 FLR 106 HC FamD On magistrates' role under the Guardianship of Minors Act 1971 in custody/access applications concerning children in local authority care.

Re F [1994] 2 FCR 1354; [1995] 1 FLR 510 HC FamD Contact order set aside where made in belief that would require parents to allow sibling in care have access to other siblings; on appropriate order to seek in such circumstances.

Re H (K and M) (1972) 116 SJ 664 HC FamD Issue of access (by illegitimate father) to children left to local authority which had passed care resolution in respect of them.

Re K; Re M; Hertfordshire County Council v H [1972] 3 All ER 769; (1972) 136 JP 838 HC FamD Putative father seeking access order after local authority assumes parental rights must be denied.

Re L [1985] FLR 95; [1984] TLR 399 CA Access of natural father to child placed in long-term foster care inappropriate: access order quashed.

Re M (1985) 135 NLJ 321c CA Failed application by mother for access to child whom had voluntarily surrendered to care.

Re M and H [1990] 1 AC 686 (also CA); [1989] FCR 65; [1988] 2 FLR 431; (1988) 138 NLJ 226; (1988) 132 SJ 1146; [1988] 3 WLR 45 HL Court could not grant putative father access to children where local authority had taken children into care.

Re M and H [1990] 1 AC 686 (also HL); [1988] FCR 97; [1988] 1 FLR 151; (1987) 131 SJ 1155; [1987] 3 WLR 759 CA Court could not grant putative father access to children where local authority had taken children into care.

Re N [1989] FCR 481; [1989] 2 FLR 106 CA Earlier access order to father did not preclude local authority being given parental rights over child by way of care order.

Re N (C) [1992] 2 FCR 401 HC FamD Court could order that there be no contact between mother and child in care.

Re P [1993] 2 FLR 156 HC FamD On contact/what constitutes reasonable contact.

Re R [1983] 2 All ER 929; (1983) 4 FLR 787; (1984) 134 NLJ 339c; (1983) 127 SJ 509; [1983] 1 WLR 991 CA Court may give any order in child's interest but generally will not amend bona fide local authority decisions.

Re R [1987] FCR 1; (1987) 151 JP 413 HC FamD On ordering adoption application to be dealt with as custodianship application.

Re S [1991] FCR 82 (also HC FamD); [1991] 1 FLR 161 CA Juvenile court could be (but here was not) justified in granting natural mother access to child whom local authority seeking to have adopted.

Re S [1994] 2 FLR 222 CA Inappropriate for court to grant care order but adjourn contact decision until later date.

Re S [1994] 2 FCR 414 CA Issue of post-care order contact fell completely within parameters of Children At 1989 and was not a matter for court.

Re S; Dyfed County Council v S [1996] 2 FCR 838; (1995) 139 SJ LB 174; [1995] TLR 390 CA No extension of time to mother of child to appeal against phasing out by local authority of her contact with her children (who were in care).

Re T [1997] TLR 2 CA On relevant factors when deciding whether to discharge order for ending of contact between parents and children where latter are in local authority care.

Re T and another [1997] 1 All ER 65; [1997] 1 FLR 517; [1997] 1 WLR 393 CA On when parental contact to child in care may be terminated (here terminated in respect of one of mother's children but not other).

Re W [1988] FCR 129; [1988] 1 FLR 175 CA On making adoption rather than custodianship order.

Re W [1989] FCR 97; [1988] 1 FLR 47; (1988) 132 SJ 1388; [1988] 1 WLR 1157 CA County court order as to care and access improper as justices having made care order only they could discharge same.

Re W (S) [1993] 1 FCR 896 HC FamD Court could upon making care order make another order terminating contact even though parent not given notice latter order would be sought.

Re Y [1988] 1 FLR 299 HC FamD Non-interference by court in local authority decisions regarding children in care of authority.

Re Y [1975] 3 All ER 348; [1976] Fam 125; (1976) 140 JP 19; (1975) 119 SJ 610; [1975] 3 WLR 342 CA Local authority with ward in care subject to control of court.

Salford City Council v C (1982) 3 FLR 153 HC FamD Care and control of child whom disabled parents unable to adequately care for given to local authority but frequent access to parents ordered.

Staffordshire County Council v C and M [1988] FCR 353 HC FamD On rights of putative father as regards seeking access to/custody of illegitimate child.

V-P v V-P (1980) 1 FLR 336 CA Court would reconsider issue of custody if mother (to whom child entrusted) continued to create difficulties over access by father.

W v Ealing London Borough Council [1994] 1 FCR 436; [1993] 2 FLR 788; [1993] TLR 308 CA Appropriate procedure where parental rights/contact orders sought (here unsuccessfully) in respect of ward.

W v Greenwich London Borough Council [1989] FCR 397; [1989] 2 FLR 67; (1989) 133 SJ 388 HC FamD Justices must give reasons for refusing parents access to children in care.

W v Shropshire County Council [1986] 1 FLR 359 (also HC FamD) CA Non-continuation of wardship over child in respect of whom local authoriy sought to bring care proceedings was valid.

CARE/CUSTODY (adoption)

Bolton Metropolitan Borough Council v B and H [1990] FCR 57; [1989] 2 FLR 349 HC FamD Long-term care pending adoption for children with parents incapable of proper parenting: access to parents until placed with foster-parents; delay in welfare report criticised.

Crossley v Crossley (1953) 117 JP 216; (1953) 97 SJ 249; [1953] 2 WLR 765 HC PDAD Adoption order completely supersedes existing custody order.

H v H [1947] KB 463 HC KBD Justices could dispense with need for consent to adoption of custody having custody of same.

R v Derbyshire County Council, ex parte T [1989] FCR 679; [1990] 1 FLR 237 (also CA); (1989) 133 SJ 1109 HC QBD Notice to former parent needed if child placed with prospective adopters becomes child in care.

R v Derbyshire County Council, ex parte T and another [1990] 1 All ER 792; [1990] Fam 164; [1989] FCR 713; [1990] 1 FLR 237 (also HC QBD); (1989) 133 SJ 1626; [1990] 2 WLR 101 CA Notice to former parent needed if child placed with prospective adopters becomes child in care.

R v Walker and another (1911-12) XXVIII TLR 342 HC KBD Refusal to order delivery up of illegitimate child to natural parents from those who had adopted child and kept him for ten years.

Re Adoption Application No 41/61 [1962] 3 All ER 553; [1963] Ch 315; (1962) 126 JP 511; (1962) 112 LJ 718; (1962) 106 SJ 571/649; [1962] 3 WLR 997 CA Infant's interests paramount in adoption/custody cases; adjournment of adoption case to hear custody action.

Re Adoption Application No 41/61 (No 2) [1963] 2 All ER 1082; [1964] Ch 48; (1963) 127 JP 440; (1963) 113 LJ 561; (1963) 107 SJ 573; [1963] 3 WLR 357 HC ChD Welfare of infant of paramount consideration in custody/adoption proceedings.

Re Adoption Application No 41/61 (No 2) [1963] 2 All ER 1082; (1962) 112 LJ 505; [1962] 1 WLR 866 HC ChD Welfare of infant of paramount consideration in custody/adoption proceedings.

Re B [1993] 1 FCR 363 (also CA) CyCt Contact with natural mother halted when order for care with view to adoption made.

Re C [1996] 1 FCR 332 HC FamD Care order with provision for declining contact and ultimate adoption properly made (rather than making of no order which would have resulted in child being left with foster-parents).

Re D (1981) 2 FLR 102 CA Adoption order preferable to joint custody order here where natural and step-parent seeking adoption; wishes of children relevant (here wanted adoption): decision contrary to wishes to be explained); child's memories of natural father inadequate reason for refusing adoption.

Re F [1984] FLR 60; (1984) 134 NLJ 765c; [1983] TLR 535 CA Circumstances merited inluding direction that child being placed in long-term foster care be prepared for adoption.

Re G (1981) 2 FLR 382; (1981) 125 SJ 307 HC FamD Court could order care and control of child (to local authority) with a view to adoption.

Re H [1989] FCR 498 CA On options open to single father of children in care when local authority seeks to have children freed for adoption.

Re H (1985) 129 SJ 84; [1984] TLR 649 CA Instigation of adoption action an abuse of process where used to frustrate local authority in its exercise of its care jurisdiction.

Re L [1990] FCR 471; [1990] 1 FLR 305; (1989) 139 NLJ 1377 CA On determining whether parent's refusal of consent to adoption (as here) unreasonable; on whether custodianship/adoption order preferable.

Re M [1990] FCR 424; [1990] 1 FLR 291 CA Failed application by teenage father for custody of his child which was being placed for adoption.

Re S [1977] 3 All ER 671; [1977] Fam 173; (1977) 127 NLJ 368t; (1977) 121 SJ 222; [1977] 2 WLR 919 CA In parent/step-parent adoption case court must consider whether in child's welfare joint custody order preferable.

Re S [1987] 2 All ER 99; [1987] Fam 98; [1988] FCR 57; [1987] 2 FLR 331; (1987) 151 JP 577; (1987) 131 SJ 133; [1987] 2 WLR 977 CA On ordering adoption application to be treated as custodianship application; on ordering disclosure of confidential reports so that parties have time to prepare response at action.

Re T [1990] FCR 71 CA Order of care with view to adoption justified where six month' counselling of mother suggested could never properly care for child (even though was some contradictory expert evidence).

Re T (J) [1986] 2 FLR 107 HC FamD Care of child to local authority with view to adoption where older child had died as result of non-accidental injuries while living with mother as member of extended Rastafarian family.

Re W [1988] FCR 129; [1988] 1 FLR 175 CA On making adoption rather than custodianship order.

Re W [1984] FLR 402 CA On relevancy of child's interests in adoption (as opposed to custody) hearing.

CARE/CUSTODY (adulterer)

G v G (1962) 106 SJ 858 HC PDAD Child placed with father living in adulterous relationship rather than placed in local authority care.

CARE/CUSTODY (child sex abuse)

B v B (1982) 3 FLR 187 CA Declaration by divorce court that paedophile husband to marriage being terminated was unfit to have custody of child was valid.

Bradford City Metropolitan Council v K [1990] Fam 140; [1990] 2 WLR 532 HC FamD Statements of child to teacher/foster parent regarding sexual abuse by family member not part of res gestae and inadmissible in later care proceedings as was hearsay evidence.

H v Norfolk County Council [1997] 1 FLR 384 CA Local authority not liable for (alleged) abuse suffered by onetime child in its care placed with foster parents.

R v The Inner London Juvenile Court, ex parte G [1988] FCR 316; [1988] 2 FLR 58 HC QBD Non-adjournment of care action until father tried for alleged sexual abuse of subject of care action was valid.

Re B [1996] 1 FCR 229 HC FamD Reliability of child witnesses ultimately a matter for court, not expert witnesses; on prorelevancy of past behaviour to determining whether child likely to suffer significant harm in future.

Re B [1997] 1 FCR 477; [1997] 1 FLR 285; [1997] 3 WLR 1 HC FamD On operation of issue estoppel in care proceedings (here previous finding of child sex abuse at issue).

Re C [1992] 2 FCR 65 HC FamD Expert assessment ordered to see whether parents should keep newborn child where previous five children in care/had been sexually abused (albeit not perhaps by father).

Re G [1996] 2 FCR 505 CA Care orders justified in respect of all children in light of treatment meted out by parents to elder children.

Re G; Re R [1995] 2 FLR 867 CA Could not say that though sexual abuse not proved on the balance of probabilities there was nonetheless a real possibility of future significant harm.

Re H and R [1995] 2 FCR 384 CA On establishing that child abuse has taken place.

Re L [1996] 1 FLR 116; [1995] TLR 379 CA On appropriate standard of proof in child sex abuse case; full care orders (subject to judge's hopes regarding rehabilitation) merited in respect of children whose future was as yet undecided.

Re M [1993] 1 FCR 253; [1993] 1 FLR 822 CA On admissibility and reliability of parental/expert/ evidence in care action arising from ritual child sex abuse claims.

Re M and R [1996] 4 All ER 239; [1996] 2 FCR 617; [1996] 2 FLR 195 CA Balance of probabilities the standard of proof of child abuse in care proceedings; on admissibility of expert evidence on central matters to be resolved in case.

Re P [1987] FCR 123; [1987] 2 FLR 467; (1987) 151 JP 635 CA Local authority granted care order, non-access by parents and right to place child with foster-parents with view to adoption where child born to parents of family with history of sexual abuse of existing children; on role of court.

Re S [1997] 2 FCR 272 CA Limited intervention of husband (alleged sexual abuser) in proceedings where local authority/mother seeking care/residence orders.

Re S, S and A [1995] 2 FLR 244 HC FamD On issue estoppel in child actions: findings at earlier proceedings to which father not party that he had abused children inadmissible in instant action as fact.

CARE/CUSTODY (child-minder)

Sutton London Borough Council v Davis [1995] 1 All ER 53; [1994] Fam 241; [1994] 2 FCR 1129; [1994] 1 FLR 737; (1994) 138 SJ LB 86; [1994] TLR 155; [1994] 2 WLR 721 HC FamD Justices may examine de novo local authority refusal to register child-minder.

CARE/CUSTODY (confidentiality)

Cleveland County Council and another v F [1995] 2 All ER 236; [1995] 3 FCR 174; [1995] 1 FLR 797; [1995] 1 WLR 785 HC FamD Court may direct that putative statements in care proceedings be confidential but existing statute law affords adequate protection.

Oxfordshire County Council and another v P [1995] 2 All ER 225; [1995] Fam 161; [1995] 2 FCR 212; [1995] 1 FLR 552; [1995] TLR 62; [1995] 2 WLR 543 HC FamD Lifting privilege of confidentiality in care proceedings a matter for court not guardian ad litem.

CARE/CUSTODY (consent)

Re A [1987] 2 All ER 81; [1987] FCR 9; [1987] 2 FLR 184; (1987) 151 JP 458; (1987) 131 SJ 194; [1987] 1 WLR 153 CA Not unreasonable if parents consent to custodianship order not adoption order; consent dispensed with if in child's interests.

Re M [1987] 2 All ER 88; [1987] FCR 17; [1987] 1 FLR 465; [1987] 1 WLR 162 CA Custodianship order cannot be made unless parent's agreement got/dispensed with; refusal of consent unreasonable if reasonable parent would not have refused.

CARE/CUSTODY (contempt)

B (B) v B (M) [1969] 1 All ER 891; (1969) 119 NLJ 321 HC PDAD On appropriate way of dealing with father-contemnor who refused to surrender child to custody of mother.

Maynard v Maynard [1984] FLR 85 CA Court could (and here in interim custody application did) hear party in contempt.

Mozley-Stark v Mozley-Stark and Hitchins [1908-10] All ER 643; [1910] 79 LJP 98; (1909-10) 101 LTR 770; (1909-10) XXVI TLR 194 CA Non committal in circumstances for contempt of custody order.

CARE/CUSTODY (contribution)

C v Surrey County Council [1994] 2 FCR 165 HC FamD On making order requiring parent to contribute towards cost of local authority accommodation for child.

R v Essex County Council, ex parte Washington [1987] 1 FLR 148; (1987) 151 JP 258 HC QBD Failed application to have contribution notice rescinded.

CARE/CUSTODY (cruelty)

Re D [1993] 2 FCR 88; [1993] 2 FLR 423 HC FamD Care (not supervision) order appropriate for new child born of man with record of cruelty to own children.

CARE/CUSTODY (discharge)

P v Bradford Metropolitan Borough Council [1996] 2 FCR 227 HC FamD Valid decision by magistrates after heard evidence of mother to stop hearing of application to discharge care orders.

R v Poole Juvenile Court, ex parte P; R v Southwark Juvenile Court, ex parte C [1988] FCR 1; [1988] 1 FLR 8 HC QBD On procedure as regards applications for discharge of care orders.

R v Worcester City Juvenile Court, ex parte F [1989] 1 All ER 500; [1989] FCR 110; [1989] 1 FLR 230; (1988) 132 SJ 1526 HC QBD Upon request juvenile court must disclose reasons for refusing to discharge care order.

Re A [1995] 2 FCR 686; [1995] 1 FLR 599 HC FamD Leave of court not required before child in care could apply for discharge of care order.

Re L (K) [1990] FCR 692 CrCt Care order in respect of child discharged with view to grandparents commencing wardship proceedings.

Re S [1995] 2 FLR 639 CA Courts can (but generally will not) dispute findings of earlier court in application for discharge of care order.

Re S and P [1995] 2 FLR 782 HC FamD Magistrates validly stopped application for discharge of care order after heard mother's evidence.

Re W [1997] 2 FCR 190; [1997] 1 FLR 128 HC FamD Imprisoned father guilty of murder of stepdaughter discharged from care proceedings at mother's request.

CARE/CUSTODY (disclosure)

Nottinghamshire County Council v H [1995] 2 FCR 365; [1995] 1 FLR 115 HC FamD Crown Prosecution Service ordered to disclose documents to local authority alone (local authority in course of care proceedings).

Re A [1996] 1 FCR 533 CA Leave of family court required by (and given to) solicitor who sought to rely on knowledge acquired in onetime care proceedings to aid defence of later unconnected criminal case.

Re C [1997] 2 WLR 322 CA On disclosure to police of material arising in course of care proceedings relevant to later criminal action springing therefrom.

Re C (E) [1996] 3 FCR 521 (also CA); [1996] 2 FLR 123 HC FamD On disclosure to police of evidence in care proceedings.

Re C (E) [1996] 3 FCR 521 (also HC FamD); [1996] 2 FLR 725 CA On ordering disclosure of materials from care proceedings for use in criminal proceedings.

Re G [1996] 3 FCR 77; [1996] 1 FLR 276; (1996) 146 NLJ 85; (1996) 140 SJ LB 10; [1996] 1 WLR 1407 CA No leave necessary before local authority may disclose to police information social worker obtained from parents.

Re L [1996] 1 FCR 419 CA Right that medical report prepared in course of care proceedings be disclosed to police for use in investigating criminal aspects of case.

Re S [1987] 2 All ER 99; [1987] Fam 98; [1988] FCR 57; [1987] 2 FLR 331; (1987) 151 JP 577; [1987] 2 WLR 977 CA On ordering adoption application to be treated as custodianship application; on ordering disclosure of confidential reports so that parties have time to prepare response at action.

Re S and W (1983) 4 FLR 290; (1983) 133 NLJ 512c; [1982] TLR 220 CA Reference in psycharist's report (commissioned by local authority) to case conference reports not a waiver of privilege by authority in respect of said reports.

CARE/CUSTODY (discovery)

R v Greenwich Juvenile Court, ex parte London Borough of Greenwich (1980) 1 FLR 304 HC QBD No machinery for discovery in magistrates' courts; discoverability of documents to be assessed on individual/class (where are classes) basis.

Re C (J) [1996] 1 FCR 434; [1995] 2 FLR 77 HC FamD On discovery in care actions.

CARE/CUSTODY (divorce)

Re Mathieson (1918) 53 LJ 165 CA Non-restoration of custody of child to father (who had voluntarily parted with same) where was not to good of welfare of child.

CARE/CUSTODY (education)

Re S [1977] 3 All ER 582; [1978] QB 120; [1977] 3 WLR 575 CA On meaning of 'care' in Children and Young Persons Act 1969, s 1(2) — here care order made so that boy might enjoy education.

CARE/CUSTODY (emergency protection order)

Re M [1993] 1 FCR 78; [1993] 1 FLR 275 HC FamD Person who had been acting as guardian ad litem could apply for prohibited steps order after emergency protection order lapsed; justices' reasoning/findings in such cases to be recorded.

Re P [1996] 3 FCR 637; [1996] 1 FLR 482 HC FamD On relevant factor when granting emergency protection order: here granted/renewed.

CARE/CUSTODY (estoppel)

Re B [1997] 1 FCR 477; [1997] 1 FLR 285; [1997] 3 WLR 1 HC FamD On operation of issue estoppel in care proceedings (here previous finding of child sex abuse at issue).

Re F [1992] 1 FLR 561 CA Person estopped by custody order to which consented from appealing against same on basis that had not consented thereto.

Re L [1996] 1 FCR 221 HC FamD On limited operation of issue estoppel in child cases; on admissibility of evidence from earlier child sex abuse cases involving cohabitee of woman whose children were subjects of present care proceedings.

Re L (AC) [1971] 3 All ER 743; (1972) 136 JP 19 HC ChD Local authority estopped from objecting to time-barred application by other which it engineered; failure of mother to accept child in care into her supervision not estoppel from later exercising parental rights in action.

Re S, S and A [1995] 2 FLR 244 HC FamD On issue estoppel in child actions: findings at earlier proceedings to which father not party that he had abused children inadmissible in instant action as fact.

CARE/CUSTODY (ethnicity)

Re H [1987] 2 FLR 12 HC FamD On ethnic background as factor when dealing with children; long-term fostering with view to adoption (if possible by someone of own ethnic background); access by mother to depend on her co-operation with social worker/what eventual adopters desired.

Re J [1987] 1 FLR 455; (1987) 151 JP 243 HC FamD Wardship order continued but adoption/custodianship of child not allowed where natural mother not unreasonably objected to adoption of child by foster parents who were Jehovah's Witnesses/of different race to child.

Re P [1994] 2 FCR 537 HC FamD Once (white) foster-parents had sought adoption of (black) child issue of care was for court, not local authority (which sought same-race adoption).

CARE/CUSTODY (evidence)

F v F [1968] 2 All ER 946 CA Evidence of alleged adultery dismissed at divorce trial can be admitted in later custody case.

R v Wood Green Crown Court, ex parte P (1983) 4 FLR 206; [1982] TLR 164 HC QBD On flexible admissibility rules in care actions (here concerning admissibility of medical/welfare reports).

Re G [1995] 2 FCR 120; [1994] 2 FLR 785 CA Rehearing of care application ordered where factual basis of previous decision put in issue by expert evidence.

Re S (1980) 1 FLR 301 HC QBD Evidence of statement by party to action adverse to own/another's interests admissible/inadmissible in evidence.

CARE/CUSTODY (expert evidence)

Re B [1996] 3 FCR 272; [1996] 1 FLR 667 CA Reasoned departure of judge from opinions of expert/guardian ad litem when granting interim care order was valid.

Re G [1994] 2 FCR 106; [1994] 2 FLR 291 HC FamD On disclosure of papers to expert witnesses in care proceedings.

Re M and R [1996] 4 All ER 239; [1996] 2 FCR 617; [1996] 2 FLR 195 CA Balance of probabilities the standard of proof of child abuse in care proceedings; on admissibility of expert evidence on central matters to be resolved in case.

CARE/CUSTODY (foetus)

Re D [1995] 2 FCR 681 HC FamD Court would not expand care proceedings to consider future of unborn child.

CARE/CUSTODY (foreign decree)

McKee v McKee [1951] 1 All ER 942; [1951] AC 352; (1951) 95 SJ 316; [1951] 1 TLR 755; (1951) WN (I) 186 PC Infant's interests paramount in custody case irrespective of foreign court order.

Re F [1989] 1 FLR 335; (1988) 132 SJ 1323 HC FamD Non-enforcement of French custody order but care and control to mother (abductress) with staying access to father.

Re H [1994] 1 All ER 812; [1994] Fam 105; [1994] 2 FCR 351; [1994] 1 FLR 512; [1993] TLR 578; [1994] 2 WLR 269 CA Court not obliged to enforce recognised foreign custody order.

CARE/CUSTODY (fostering)

Re B (A) [1954] 2 All ER 287; (1954) 118 JP 318; [1954] 2 QB 385; (1954) 98 SJ 391; [1954] 3 WLR 1 HC QBD Court cannot review local authority discretionary decision to remove child from foster parents.

Re C (1969) 113 SJ 164 HL Care and control of child to English foster-parents, not natural foreign parents.

Re C [1993] 1 FLR 832 HC FamD Long-term fostering in best interests of child notwithstanding her contrary desires.

Re O (a minor) (1972) 122 NLJ 112t HC FamD Care and control of Ghanian foster-daughter to English fosterers despite desire of natural parents to bring girl back to Ghana.

Re O (a minor) (1973) 123 NLJ 225t CA Care and control of Ghanian foster-daughter to English fosterers despite desire of natural parents to bring girl back to Ghana.

Re Y [1985] FLR 294 HC FamD Mother's wardship application failed where child had been living happily with good foster parents for eight years.

Turney v Turney and Devon County Council (1983) 4 FLR 199; (1981) 131 NLJ 1309 CA Prolonged fostering inappropriate where care order made under Matrimonial Causes Act 1973, s 43, and so constantly reviewable.

CARE/CUSTODY (general)

Adams v Adams [1984] FLR 768; (1984) 134 NLJ 1064 CA Valid to give custody of closely aged children to one of two deserving parents so as to preserve close sibling relationship between children.

Armstrong v Armstrong; Huff v Huff [1986] 1 FLR 95 CA On making custody orders in respect of children resident outside England and Wales.

Ashley v Ashley (1981) 2 FLR 57 CA Procedure to be adopted regarding in-chambers hearings on future of childen to terminated marriage when custody hearing pending.

Attorney General ex rel Tilley v London Borough of Wandsworth [1981] 1 All ER 1162; (1981) 2 FLR 377; [1981] 1 WLR 854 CA Local authority 'assistance' to child includes providing parents accommodation; resolution of authority barring such assistance invalid.

Attorney General ex rel Tilley v London Borough of Wandsworth [1981] 1 All ER 1162 HC ChD Local authority 'assistance' to child includes providing parents accommodation; resolution of authority barring such assistance invalid.

Avon County Council v N [1996] 1 FCR 252 HC FamD Care of children refused to mother even though might have decided otherwise had local authority conducted itself properly thus necessitating instant decision.

B v B [1924] 93, 184; (1924) 130 LTR 754; (1923-24) 68 SJ 457; (1923-24) XL TLR 349; (1924) WN (I) 64 CA On granting access of guilty spouse to children.

B v B (No 2) (1955) 99 SJ 334; [1955] 1 WLR 557 HL HL incompetent to hear infant custody action decided on by CA as did not relate to matrimonial causes/matters.

B v B (1962) 106 SJ 573 HC PDAD Husband could not be expected to live with drug-addicted wife; custody of child taken from drug addicted wife and care and control of child given to paternal grandmother.

B v B and H [1962] 1 All ER 29; (1962) 112 LJ 58; (1961) 105 SJ 969 HC PDAD Custody order in favour of second husband of dead adulteress.

B v B (1969) 133 JP 245 HC PDAD On power of HC as regards hearing appeal from decision of justices to imprison parent for refusing to observe custody order.

B v B (1973) 117 SJ 165 HC FamD Was relevant factor when determining custody action that mother now had relationship/was living with husband's brother.

B v B (1975) 125 NLJ 552t; (1975) 119 SJ 610 CA Custody of children of adulterous mother to their father.

B v B (1976) 120 SJ 97 HC FamD Court to be informed why custody order appeal withdrawn where was prima facie curious custody decision by justices.

B v B (1980) 1 FLR 385 CA Inappropriate that custody conditions include bedtime/babysitting arrangements for children.

B v B (1984) 134 NLJ 863c CA Custody of eleven month old son to father who with his sister and her husband had been looking after son since wife quit matrimonial home.

B v B [1985] FLR 462 CA Failed application by mother for custody of child adequately looked after by father for eleven months — that father made redundant positive in that it freed father to spend more time with child.

B v B [1985] FLR 166; [1984] TLR 509 CA Moral need for father (who could not get job because looking after child) to seek employment not relevant factor in custody hearing.

B v B [1993] 2 All ER 144; [1993] Fam 32; [1993] 1 FLR 238; (1992) 136 SJ LB 156; [1992] 3 WLR 865 CA Child may be returned to foreign jurisdiction despite high degree of intolerability.

B v B [1997] 2 FCR 518; [1997] TLR 295 CA Valid decision to order one child to live with mother and other child with father but order that father not be allowed seek custody of other child without leave of court was improper.

B (M) v B (R) [1968] 3 All ER 170; (1968) 118 NLJ 862; (1968) 112 SJ 504 CA Valid decision to give child into custody of mother where either party could in fairness have been awarded custody.

B v Derbyshire County Council [1992] 2 FCR 14; [1992] 1 FLR 538 HC FamD Res judicata probably inapplicable to local authority's seeking of care orders (and certainly inapplicable here).

B v T [1990] FCR 31 (also CA); [1989] 2 FLR 31 (also CA) HC FamD Custody of baby daughter/young son to mother where justices failed to properly consider relevant issues.

B v T [1990] FCR 31 (also HC FamD); [1989] 2 FLR 31 (also HC FamD) CA Interim care and control of baby girl/young son to mother/father as custody along interim lines apparently not considered by magistrates.

Bagnall v Bagnall and Hobbs (1909-10) 54 SJ 738; (1909-10) XXVI TLR 659 HC PDAD Absent aggravated circumstances court would not deem wife (who had been divorced for her misconduct) unfit to have custody of her children.

Bain v Wood and others (1979) 129 (1) NLJ 365 HL Qualified care and control order in respect of two children committed to local authority care.

Barclays Bank plc v Khaira and another [1993] 1 FLR 343 (also CA); [1992] 1 WLR 623 HC ChD Bank does not normally owe duty of care to person going guarantor on loan to explain entire transaction/ensure have taken impartial advice on what doing.

Barclays Bank plc v Khaira and another [1993] 1 FLR 343 (also HC ChD) CA Non-party to ChD action not allowed appeal decision that bank does not normally owe duty of care to person going guarantor on loan to explain entire transaction/ensure have taken impartial advice on what doing.

Barrett v Young (1981) 131 NLJ 372 CA Custody of children to mother despite father's looking after children for 6 years, for five of which mother had no contact with children.

Bawden v Bawden [1978] 3 All ER 1216; (1979) 143 JP 114; [1979] QB 419; [1978] 3 WLR 798 CA Local authority right to keep child/residual discretion ends once parent requests child's return.

Beaumont v Beaumont [1938] 2 All ER 226; [1938] Ch 551; [1938] 107 LJCh 241; (1938) 158 LTR 494; (1938) 82 SJ 314; (1937-38) LIV TLR 538; (1938) WN (I) 121 HC ChD No statutory entitlement to have custody case heard in HC; HC refusal to exercise inherent jurisdiction while child being kept outside jurisdiction.

Belton v Belton [1987] 2 FLR 343; (1987) 151 JP 679 CA Child's welfare is paramount interest in application to remove from jurisdiction child in respect of whom one divorced parent has custody.

Berkshire County Council v C and others [1993] 1 FCR 608; [1993] Fam 205; [1993] 1 FLR 569 HC FamD Family proceedings court could direct that child be assessed by social worker by certain date.

Berkshire County Council v D-P [1986] 2 FLR 276 (also CA) HC FamD Matters pre-dating birth of child not relevant to care proceedings.

Bilainkin v Bilainkin [1959] 1 All ER 161; (1959) 109 LJ 72; (1959) 103 SJ 90 CA In custody order allowing restricted removal of child from jurisdiction petitioner's promise to return and respondent's permission to leave should be required.

Bird v Bird and others (1984) 148 JP 641 CA Child's welfare (not father's employment prospects) paramount issue in custody action.

Birmingham City Council and others v H [1994] 1 All ER 12; [1994] 2 AC 212; [1994] 1 FCR 896; [1994] 1 FLR 224; (1994) 144 NLJ 17; (1994) 138 SJ LB 13; [1993] TLR 657; [1994] 2 WLR 31 HL In child care case where mother and child are minors interests of mother's child are paramount.

Brixey v Lynas [1997] 1 FCR 220 [1996] 2 FLR 499 HL On whether custody of young child to be given (as here was) to young mother.

Buckley v Buckley [1977] 3 All ER 544 HC FamD Declaration of unfitness for custody to be made before decree absolute.

Buxton v Buxton [1965] 3 All ER 150; (1965) 129 JP 570; (1965) 109 SJ 435; [1965] 3 WLR 1184 HC PDAD Post-separation custody claim could be cruelty.

C v C (1981) 125 SJ 98 CA Private interviews with each parent by judge/subsequent direction by judge to counsel to cross-examine on what had not heard/split custody absent good cause rendered custody order bad.

C v C (No 2) (1981) 125 SJ 844 HC FamD Inappropriate to place child in care when intention of local authority was to allow child to remain with mother.

C v Solihull Metropolitan Borough Council [1993] 1 FLR 290 HC FamD On appropriate order where local authority seeks care of child pending appraisal of parents after child suffered unexplained injury.

Cheshire County Council v P [1993] 2 FCR 397 CA Care order merited where arrangements had been made to move child at risk of significant harm where was to safe environment in Northern Ireland.

Chinchen v Chinchen (1950) 94 SJ 129; (1950) WN (I) 22 CA Custody orders are interlocutory in nature.

Chipperfield v Chipperfield [1952] 1 All ER 1360 HC PDAD Child's welfare paramount in guardianship cases.

Clark v Clark (1970) 114 SJ 318 HC PDAD Court to explain why departing from probation officers' report.

Cleveland County Council v Director of Public Prosecutions and another (1995) 139 SJ LB 13; [1994] TLR 615 HC QBD Court ordering child into local authority care could not specify where child was to be accommodated.

Cliff v Cliff [1948] 2 All ER 760; (1948) LXIV TLR 555 CA On declaration that parent not fit to have custody.

Cooke v Cooke and Sutton London Borough (1982) 3 FLR 396 HC QBD Committing child to local authority care inappropriate where were not circumstances rendering placing of child with parent/another futile/inappropriate.

Croydon London Borough Council v A (No 3) [1992] 2 FLR 350 HC FamD On granting care/supervision order; on appealing against failed application for care order.

Croydon London Borough v N and others [1987] FCR 129; [1987] 2 FLR 61 HC FamD Wrong to treat Children and Young Pesons Act 1969, s 1(2)(bb) as a preliminary matter in care action (and so require preliminary proof that likely that person convicted as criminal would become member of children's household).

D v Berkshire County Council and others [1987] 1 All ER 20 HC FamD In deciding if neglect of child court can look to historical events (even pre-dating birth).

D v Berkshire County Council and others [1987] 1 All ER 20 CA In deciding if neglect of child court can look to historical events (even pre-dating birth).

D v Berkshire County Council and others [1987] 1 All ER 20 HL In deciding if neglect of child court can look to historical events (even pre-dating birth).

D v D (1965) 109 SJ 573 CA Custody of six year old child given to mother upon appeal.

D v D (1981) 2 FLR 74 CA Removal of child against her wishes from father's custody/placing with mother where other child in father's custody a possible bad influence was justifiable; whether to interview child purely a matter for judge.

Devon County Council v S and others [1992] 3 All ER 793; [1992] Fam 176; [1992] 2 FCR 827; [1992] 2 FLR 244; [1992] 3 WLR 273 HC FamD Prolonged care order hearing inappropriate where proposals already favoured by interested parties.

Dicocco v Milne (1983) 4 FLR 247 HC FamD (also CA) On relevant concerns when determining custody action.

Dicocco v Milne (1983) 4 FLR 247 CA (also HC FamD) On relevant concerns when determining custody action.

E v E (1969) 113 SJ 721 CA Apparently final order was in reality interim where question as to whether mother a fit and proper person to have custody of children had not been answered.

E v E and Cheshire County Council (No 2) (1980) 1 FLR 73 CA HC may, but will not lightly (and here did not), vary existing care order in divorce/wardship action.

Ellard v Ellard: Cheshire County Council; Intervener (1979) 143 JP 747 CA On limited interference by HC with decisions of local authority regarding children in local authority care.

Embley v Embley (1965) 109 SJ 131 HC PDAD Refusal of leave to file discretion statement after divorce hearing but pending custody hearing.

Essex County Council v R (TL) and R (KB) (1979) 143 JP 309 HC QBD Failed application for care of children on basis of impeded development of same where was no evidence at close of action that children were actually being impeded in their development.

Ex parte Jarrett (1946) 90 SJ 283; (1945-46) LXII TLR 230; (1946) WN (I) 50 HC KBD Appeal to High Court preferred to mandamus against justices who persistently adjourned mother's application for custody of her children whom she alleged had been wrongfully removed from her custody by her husband.

F v F [1959] 3 All ER 180; (1959) 109 LJ 588; (1959) 103 SJ 659; [1959] 1 WLR 863 HC PDAD On committing of child to local authority care in divorce suit.

F v F (1976) 120 SJ 503 CA On (importance of) jurisdiction of magistrates' courts in context of custody cases.

F v Leeds City Council [1994] 2 FCR 428; [1994] 2 FLR 60; [1994] TLR 138 CA Final care order made in respect of child at risk from child-mother.

F v Suffolk County Council (1981) 2 FLR 208; (1981) 125 SJ 307 HC QBD On applying for care on basis that proper development of child being impaired/neglected (Children and Young Persons Act 1969, s 1(2)).

Flood v Flood [1948] 2 All ER 712; (1948) 112 JP 416; [1948] 117 LJR 1880; (1948) LXIV TLR 474 HC PDAD Children's welfare paramount in custody cases (and maintenance an important element of that).

Floyd v Floyd (1982) 132 NLJ 40 CA Application of principle that custody decisions are to be made in best interests of children.

Galloway v Galloway [1954] 2 All ER 143; (1954) 98 SJ 336; (1954) 98 SJ 336; [1954] 2 WLR 980 CA Custody/maintenance unavailable in respect of child born outside marriage who cannot be legitimated.

Gateshead Metropolitan Borough Council v L and another [1996] 3 All ER 264; [1996] Fam 55; [1996] 3 FCR 582; [1996] 2 FLR 179; [1996] 3 WLR 426 HC FamD On designation of correct local authority in care order.

Goodfellow v Goodfellow (1968) 112 SJ 332 HC PDAD Successful appeal by adulterous wife against vesting of custody in children in father (who because was in army had to entrust their care to his parents): child's welfare paramount concern.

Grainger v Grainger and Clark [1959] 3 All ER 51; (1959) 103 SJ 637 HC PDAD PDAD would not make fresh custody order under Matrimonial Causes Act 1950, s 26(1) as believed could not following re-marriage of spouses to each other gave no opinion on s 26(1) but would not interfere with PDAD's discretion.

Grainger v Grainger and Clark [1959] 3 All ER 51 (also PDAD); (1959) 109 LJ 635; (1959) 103 SJ 855 [1959] 3 WLR 642 CA PDAD would not make fresh custody order under Matrimonial Causes Act 1950, s 26(1) as believed could not following re-marriage of spouses to each other CA gave no opinion on s 26(1) but would not interfere with PDAD's discretion.

H v Cambridgeshire County Council [1997] 1 FCR 569; [1996] 2 FLR 566 HC FamD Mother not given second time leave to show papers to psychiatrist/have psychiatrist observe contact between her/her children.

H v H [1973] 1 All ER 801; [1973] Fam 62; (1973) 137 JP 297; (1972) 122 NLJ 941t; [1973] 2 WLR 525 HC FamD Court could but would not interfere in local authority decisions about child in care.

H v H [1974] 1 All ER 1145; (1974) 124 NLJ 36t; (1974) 118 SJ 219; [1974] 1 WLR 595 CA Private interviews with judge in custody case desirable; guarantee of non-disclosure by judge undesirable.

H v H (1977) 127 NLJ 16t CA On making stayed order in custody proceedings.

H v H (1977) 127 NLJ 840b CA On need to avoid delay in resolution of custody actions.

H v H [1982] TLR 188 CA Custody hearing to be reheard by another judge where first judge had private pre-trial conversation with welfare officer.

Hackney London Borough Council v G [1994] 2 FCR 216 HC FamD On role of court in care proceedings where is agreement as to need for care order but disagreement over facts.

Harben v Harben [1957] 1 All ER 379; (1957) 107 LJ 91; (1957) 101 SJ 150; [1957] 1 WLR 261 HC PDAD Custody order made though children outside jurisdiction.

Havering London Borough Council v S [1986] 1 FLR 489 HC FamD Interim care and control of child subject of wardship action not ordered to mother whose other children already subject of wardship actions as result of apparent abuse by mother's cohabitee.

Hoey v Hoey [1984] 1 All ER 177; [1984] FLR 334; (1984) 128 SJ 132 CA Why reasons needed in child custody cases.

Holtom v Barnet London Borough Council and another [1993] TLR 478 HC QBD Local authority could be sued by person once in its care for negligent discharge of its duties when acting in loco parentis.

Hounslow London Borough Council v A [1993] 1 FLR 702; [1993] 1 WLR 291 HC FamD Interim care order appropriate where father sought residence order and local authority had not yet completed appraisal of father as carer.

Hull v Hull [1960] 1 All ER 378; (1960) 110 LJ 157; (1960) 104 SJ 310 HC PDAD Res judicata stopped husband alleging wife's desertion in post-decree absolute custody case as had decided husband was in desertion but could raise wife's adultery as not raised in divorce suit.

Hunt v Newcombe (1983) 4 FLR 482 CA Change in custody after more than seven years with one custodial parent justified; interviews with children a discretionary matter for judge.

Hurwitt v Hurwitt (1982) 3 FLR 194 CA Letter from director of society for single mothers concerning mother's earning potential could have been admitted (though improbable that would have made difference).

Hutchinson v Hutchinson (1981) 2 FLR 167 HC FamD Valid departure from welfare officer's recommendations where duly considered and reasons given; valid refusal of custody to mother where likely step-father a threat to child.

Jeffrey v Jeffrey (1962) 106 SJ 686 CA Interference with trial judge's exercise of discretion so that custody of child would be given to one of two living parents (and not sibling of father).

Johns v Jones [1978] 3 All ER 1232; [1978] Crim LR 426; (1979) 143 JP 723; (1978) 128 NLJ882t; [1979] QB 411; (1978) 122 SJ 593; [1978] 3 WLR 792 CA Local authority resolution whereby sought to assume parental authority over child (originally voluntarily left with authority) after mother requested return of child was invalid.

Jones (EG) v Jones (EF) [1974] 3 All ER 702; [1974] 1 WLR 1471 CA Not improper that question of custody of children had been decided while divorce suit was pending.

K (formerly D) v D (1974) 118 SJ 50 CA Custody of children to unimpeachable father, not mother who would remove them to Germany to live there with new partner.

L v L (1981) 2 FLR 48 CA Custody of child awarded to emotionally unstable mother in preference to abusive father (who had been looking after child).

L v London Borough of Bexley [1997] 1 FCR 277; [1996] 2 FLR 595 HC FamD On designating appropriate local authority in care order.

Laxton v Laxton and Eaglan [1966] 2 All ER 977 CA Granting custody but delaying care and control order unusual but valid.

Lewisham London Borough Council v Lewisham Juvenile Court Justices (1978) 128 NLJ 1147t CA Child not in care from moment parent who voluntarily placed child in care notifies local authority of withdrawal of consent to same.

London Borough of Brent v McLymont and others (1974) 138 JP 699; (1974) 118 SJ 499 HC QBD Not open to justices making compensation orders in respect of boys who committed offences to determine whether boys ought to have been placed in charge and control of parent by local authority who had boys in its care.

M v Birmingham City Council [1995] 1 FCR 50; [1994] 2 FLR 141 HC FamD Depended on case whether historical/current/future extent of parental control to be used as basis for determining if child beyond such control/care order merited.

M v H and others [1988] 3 All ER 5 HL Courts have jurisdiction to hear custody/access application by parent against third party but statutorily precluded from doing so.

M v M (1905-06) XXII TLR 325 HC PDAD Custody of two children to petitioner (though one born before marriage and petitioner was not father of same).

M v M (1980) 1 FLR 327 CA Care order invalid as local authority/mother not heard on matter.

M v M [1988] FCR 260; [1988] 1 FLR 225 CA Custody decisions to be based on findings of fact (where facts controverted); cannot make ouster order under domestic violence legislation where parties not living together as man and wife.

M v M [1988] FCR 39; [1987] 2 FLR 146; [1987] 1 WLR 404 CA Custody, care and control of twelve year old girl entrusted to father in light inter alia of girl's vehement objections to being returned to mother.

M v M and G (1962) 106 SJ 877 HC PDAD Guilt/innocence of parties as regards marriage break-up here deemed irrelevant to determination of custody issue.

M v Westminster City Council [1985] FLR 325; [1984] TLR 453 HC FamD On making care orders where proper development of child 'is' beng impaired/neglected.

Manchester City Council v B [1996] 1 FLR 324 HC FamD On burden/standard of proof in care action springing from non-accidental injuries to child.

Mathieson v Napier and Wife [1918] 87 LJCh 445; (1918-19) 119 LTR 18 CA Child's best interests superior to father's right to custody.

Millard v Millard and Addis [1945] 2 All ER 525 HC PDAD Parenthood not legitimacy is the prerequisite for custody applications; illegitimate child need not be legitimised before custody order possible.

Milne v D (1983) 133 NLJ 785c CA On appropriate manner in which to resolve custody actions.

Monaco v Monaco (1937) 157 LTR 231 HC ChD Reigning Prince of Monaco granted custody of grandson and injunction restraining former son-in-law from moving same from United Kingdom (where was studying).

Moore v Moore (1982) 132 NLJ 488 CA Custody of children to mother (wife of Army corporal) who would not have to leave camp until suitable council accommodation obtained.

N v C-H [1982] TLR 484 CA On limited role of CA in appeals against custody decisions.

Nash v Nash [1973] 2 All ER 704 CA No restraint on parental custodian pursuing career of her choice.

Newham London Borough Council v AG [1992] 2 FCR 119; [1993] 1 FLR 281 CA On chances of significant harm to child which merit granting of care order.

Northamptonshire County Council v S and others [1993] Fam 136; [1993] 1 FCR 351; [1993] 1 FLR 554; [1992] 3 WLR 1010 HC FamD Construction of Children Act 1989, s 31(2)(a): on making care order on basis that child is presently suffering 'significant harm'.

O'Dare v South Glamorgan County Council (1982) 3 FLR 1 HC FamD On what was meant by 'failed without reasonable cause to discharge the obligations of a parent'.

Oldham Metropolitan Borough Council v E and others [1994] 1 FLR 568; [1994] TLR 150 CA On approach to be adopted where aunt seeking residence order in respect of child whom local authority wish to have adopted (all parties agreeing mother unsuitable carer).

P v H (1976) 120 SJ 199 HC FamD On staying custody orders pending appeal.

P v McK (formerly P) (1973) 123 NLJ 632t CA Generally custody of young children to be given (as here) to mother.

P v P (1969) 119 NLJ 1069t; (1969) 113 SJ 999 CA Appropriate that all parties to custody action be physically seen by judge in action.

P v P (1978) 128 NLJ 86b CA On relevance of preferences of young children to determination of custody cases.

Philips v Philips (1943-44) LX TLR 395; (1944) WN (I) 141 CA Court may order custody of children to successful petitioner for divorce even though children not in jurisdiction at date of order/application for same.

Plant v Plant (1983) 4 FLR 305 CA Care and control to mother whose maternal capacity not questioned (preferable to father having to resign from job and live on social welfare to look after children if given care and control).

Pountney v Morris [1984] FLR 381; (1984) 134 NLJ 863c CA Children's welfare paramount consideration in custody cases.

Pullen v Pullen (1964) 108 SJ 617 CA Failed appeal against magistrates' order for delivery of child on basis that place where was to be delivered was outside jurisdiction of the magistrates.

R v Avon County Court, ex parte K and others [1986] 1 FLR 443 HC QBD On meaning of giving 'first consideration' to child's welfare (Child Care Act 1980, s 18(1)): here local authority failed in duty to give same when decided to close community home.

R v Birmingham Juvenile Court and others , ex parte S and another; R v Birmingham Juvenile Court and others, ex parte P and another [1984] 1 All ER 393; [1984] FLR 343; [1984] 1 WLR 618 HC QBD In renewing care order — unlike bail order — court looks to all the circumstances on each occasion; 28-day care order expires at start of twenty-eighth day.

R v Birmingham Juvenile Court, ex parte S [1984] FamD 93; [1984] 3 WLR 387 HC FamD Two children of same mother/different fathers were both members of same household though one in care and one living with mother and second father.

R v Booth (Lee Timothy) (1989) 11 Cr App R (S) 258; [1989] Crim LR 843 CA Care order must pre-exist any court order restraining local authority in manner of deealing with juvenile in care.

R v Chertsey Justices, ex parte E [1988] FCR 283; [1987] 2 FLR 415 HC QBD On whether/when to discharge care order.

R v Chief Constable of Cheshire, ex parte K [1990] FCR 201; [1990] 1 FLR 70 HC QBD Police not obliged to assist in enforcement of custody order.

R v Croydon Juvenile Court, ex parte M [1988] FCR 11 HC QBD On role of juvenile court when deciding whether care order to be discharged in face of parental opposition.

R v Exeter Juvenile Court, ex parte H and H; R v Waltham Forest Juvenile Court, ex parte B [1988] FCR 474; [1988] 2 FLR 214 HC QBD Was reasonable to hear care action pending criminal proceedings against parent/s.

R v G (Surrey County Council intervening) [1984] Fam 100; [1984] FLR 780; (1984) 128 SJ 662; [1984] 3 WLR 667 CA That children were constantly shuffled between divorced parents meant were 'exceptional circumstances' (Matrimonial Causes Act 1973, s 43(1)) justifying their being placed in care (care authorities could then validly place child with one parent).

R v Gwynedd County Council, ex parte B and another [1992] 3 All ER; [1991] 2 FLR 365; (1991) 141 NLJ 494t; [1991] TLR 181 CA Local authority rights/duties towards child in care end upon child's death.

R v Hertfordshire County Council, ex parte B; R v Bedfordshire County Council, ex parte C [1987] 1 FLR 239; (1987) 151 JP 202 HC QBD On judicial review of care orders (compliance with natural justice, not particular policy, is matter in issue).

R v Lambeth London Borough Council, ex parte Caddell (1997) 141 SJ LB 147; [1997] TLR 348 HC QBD Failed application for after-care assistance from local authority to whose care had been entrusted before turned eighteen, after which moved to another local authority area.

R v Manchester City Magistrates' Court, ex parte Bannister (1983) 4 FLR 717; (1983) 147 JP 516; (1983) 127 SJ 285; [1983] TLR 179 HC QBD Actual place of residence of child is basis on which decide in name of which council care order to be made.

R v Middlesex Justices, ex parte Bond (1931-34) XXIX Cox CC 563; (1932) 96 JP 487; [1933] 1 KB 72; (1933) 102 LJCL 40; (1933) 148 LTR 134; (1932-33) XLIX TLR 18; (1932) WN (I) 212 HC KBD Custody order bad as in matter that was res judicata.

R v New and Wife (1903-04) XX TLR 515 HC KBD Court will pay close consideration to but need not accede to illegitimate child's mother desires as to custody of child.

R v New and Wife (1903-04) XX TLR 583 CA Court will pay close consideration to but need not accede to illegitimate child's mother desires as to custody of child.

R v Newham London Borough Council, ex parte P [1990] 2 All ER 19; [1990] FCR 601; [1990] 1 FLR 404; (1990) 134 SJ 833; [1990] 1 WLR 482 HC QBD Local authority need not make pre-placement inquiries where stay for brief period as does not transfer charge or control.

R v Nottinghamshire County Council [1993] 1 FCR 576 HC FamD Failed appeal against decision of family proceedings court in care action to allow local authority extra time to file evidence.

R v Oxford City Justices, ex parte H [1974] 2 All ER 356; (1974) 138 JP 552; [1975] QB 1; (1974) 118 SJ 442; [1974] 3 WLR 1 HC QBD Putative father can apply for custody where local authority have assumed mother's parental rights.

R v Plymouth Juvenile Court, ex parte F [1987] 1 FLR 169; (1987) 151 JP 355 HC QBD Best interests of child paramount concern when making care order under Children and Young Persons Act 1969, s 32A(1).

R v Solihull Metropolitan Borough Council, ex parte C and others [1984] FLR 363 HC QBD Decision on date on which to close community home quashed where failed to consider future welfare of affected children.

R v Waltham Forest Justices, ex parte B [1989] FCR 341 HC QBD Care orders valid where magistrates disregarded substance of (but not fact that there were) claims by children (relayed to court inter alia by social worker) but still found orders to be merited.

Re A [1994] 2 FCR 125 CA Non-dismissal of local authority from care action where guardian ad litem convinced child would be at risk of significant harm if aunt made carer.

Re A [1955] 2 All ER 202; (1955) 105 LJ 313 CA Child's welfare paramount/natural mother's wishes regarding child's upbringing did not carry special weight.

Re A [1993] 1 FCR 824 HC FamD On extent of risk of significant harm to child necessary before care order will be made.

Re A [1993] 1 FLR 425 HC FamD Aunt did not have to allowed apply for residence order/joined as party in care action.

Re A (An Infant) [1955] 2 All ER 202 CA Child's welfare paramount/natural mother's wishes regarding child's upbringing did not carry special weight.

Re Adoption Application No 41/61 [1962] 3 All ER 553; [1963] Ch 315; (1962) 106 SJ 649 CA Infant's interests paramount in adoption/custody cases; adjournment of adoption case to hear custody action.

Re an Infant (Care and Protection) [1965] Crim LR 486; (1965) 109 SJ 454 HC QBD Parents required to be heard in local authority application for care order.

Re Aster (1955) 99 SJ 276; [1955] 1 WLR 465 CA Welfare of child not wishes of mother of paramount importance in custody cases.

Re B [1993] 1 FLR 543; (1993) 137 SJ LB 13 CA Exceptionally court may review local authority's long-term plans for child in care.

Re B [1974] 3 All ER 915; [1975] Fam 36; (1975) 139 JP 87 HC FamD On exercise of wardship jurisdiction where child in local authority care.

Re B (1989) 133 SJ 1606 CA On need for/what consist of adequate justices' reasons for decision in child custody action.

Re B [1997] 1 FCR 309; [1996] 2 FLR 693 HC FamD On deciding whether care/supervision orders merited.

Re B [1992] 2 FCR 631 CA Order of custody of gypsy children to itinerant gypsy father with frequent access to mother with settled lifestyle left unchanged.

Re B [1962] 1 All ER 872; (1962) 112 LJ 220; (1962) 106 SJ 489 CA Very young child may be given into father's custody.

Re B (1971) 121 NLJ 296 CA On exercise of judicial discretion as to granting of custody.

Re B [1992] TLR 667 CA Court could under the Children Act 1989 consider the long-term plans of a local authority concerning a child entrusted to local authority's care.

Re B [1993] 2 FCR 607 CA Discharge of committal/care/return orders in respect of child whose return to jurisdiction was sought.

Re B (T) [1996] 1 FCR 101; [1995] 2 FLR 801; [1995] TLR 373 CA On whether to adjourn care action where criminal action (in respect of parents) pending: here inappropriately adjourned.

Re C [1983] TLR 711 CA On undesirability of independent welfare reports; on extent of paramountcy of interests of child.

Re C [1997] 1 FLR 544 HC FamD On which local authority is to be designated in local authority care order.

Re C (1987) 151 JP 135 CA Judge did not err in giving care and control of child to drug addict father where mother was schizophrenic and maternal grandparents quite old.

Re C (1997) 141 SJ LB 34; [1997] TLR 41 HC FamD Child in care but living at home was not being 'accommodated' by local authority under Children Act 1989, s 23.

Re C (a minor) (1993) 137 SJ LB 135 HC FamD On assessment of means when determining whether/to what extent parent liable to contribute towards cost of maintaining child in care.

Re C (A) [1966] 1 All ER 560; (1966) 130 JP 146; (1965-66) 116 NLJ 555; (1966) 110 SJ 212; [1966] 1 WLR 415 HC ChD Court will not interfere with valid exercise of local authority discretion regarding child in care.

Re C (B) [1995] 3 FCR 598 HC FamD On determining to which local authority care order ought to be addressed.

Re Collins [1950] 1 All ER 1057; [1950] Ch 498; (1950) 100 LJ 274; (1950) 94 SJ 352; [1950] 66 (1) TLR 1107; (1950) WN (I) 242 CA Child's welfare paramount in guardianship cases: no rule that dead father has right to determine child's religious upbringing.

Re Cullimore (a minor) (1976) 126 NLJ 468t HC FamD Care and control of child to father who had not battered child as was thought (child actually suffering from brittle bone disease).

Re D [1977] 3 All ER 481; [1977] Fam 158; (1977) 141 JP 669; (1977) 127 NLJ 492t; [1977] 2 WLR 1006 HC FamD Child's interest of paramount concern in wardship not care proceedings.

Re D [1987] AC 317 (also HL); (1986) 136 NLJ 513; (1986) 130 SJ 467; [1986] 3 WLR 85 CA Care order in respect of child on foot of maternal damage to child while foetus was justified.

Re D [1987] AC 317 (also CA); [1987] 1 FLR 422; (1987) 151 JP 313; (1986) 136 NLJ 1184; (1970) 130 SJ 984; [1986] 3 WLR 1080 HL Care order in respect of child on foot of maternal damage to child while foetus was justified.

Re D [1953] 2 All ER 1318 CCA Court of summary jurisdiction within which applicant resides may vary access order.

Re E [1994] 1 FCR 584; [1994] 1 FLR 146 CA On terminating contact between children and parents (here inappropriately done in context of local authority plans that 'closed' adoption of child take place).

Re E [1984] 1 All ER 289 (also HC FamD/HL) CA Care of child to local authority; child to be prepared for adoption.

Re E [1991] FCR 1034 CA Judge ought to have ordered residential assessment to aid him in care and control hearings.

Re F [1995] Fam 224; [1995] TLR 79; [1995] 3 WLR 339 CA Improper that mother removed child from US but court would not order return given potentially serious risk to child which that would entail.

Re F [1969] 2 Ch 238; (1969) 113 SJ 486 HC ChD Child's welfare paramount but not sole concern in custody action: care and custody to mother responsible for collapse of marriage.

Re G [1994] 2 FCR 359; [1994] 2 FLR 301 HC FamD Failed application by mother for residence order: local authority allowed place children outside jurisdiction.

Re G [1993] 1 FCR 810 HC FamD Care order made in respect of child despite here strong desire to be allowed remain with father (incapable of properly caring for her).

Re G [1994] 2 FLR 69 HC FamD On role of court where parties agree care order necessary but disagree on facts justifying same; court in care order application free to reconsider issues that arose in related criminal action.

Re G [1995] Fam 16; [1994] 3 WLR 1211 HC FamD On making care order.

Re G (custody) [1992] 2 FCR 279 CA Judge's non-interference with status quo as regards custody of young child justified despite real concerns of father over mother's new cohabitee.

Re H [1990] 1 FLR 51 CA Care and control to maternal aunt/uncle, not mother (though her maternal abilities unquestioned) was justified.

Re H [1991] FCR 616; [1991] 2 FLR 411; [1991] TLR 49 CA Ex parte custody change generally undesirable: pending inter partes hearing child left with parent whom ex parte order favoured.

Re H [1990] FCR 353 CA Care and control to English uncle and aunt/liberal access to foreign mother where child's best interests demanded it.

Re H [1966] 1 All ER 886; (1966) 110 SJ 88; [1966] 1 WLR 381 (also HC ChD) CA Inquiry into state of affairs permissible but not required before returning children to parent in foreign jurisdiction.

Re H [1992] 2 FCR 330; [1993] 1 FLR 440; [1992] TLR 276 HC FamD On taking account of wishes of disturbed but intelligent and capable child in care action.

Re H (S) [1996] 1 FCR 1; [1995] 1 FLR 746 HC FamD Care order appropriate order for local authority to be given over orphan over whom nobody had parental responsibility.

Re H and another; Re S and another [1991] 3 All ER 230; [1991] 2 FLR 262; (1991) 141 NLJ 891; (1991) 135 SJ LB 52; [1991] TLR 298; [1991] 3 WLR 68 HL Removal/retention exclusive events and cannot overlap; removal/retention means removal/retention out of jurisdiction not of custody.

Re J (a minor) [1991] TLR 115 CA On general undesirability/instant desirability of making joint care and control order.

Re Kinseth [1947] 1 All ER 201; [1947] Ch 223; (1947) 111 JP 136; [1947] 116 LJR 642; (1947) 177 LTR 3; (1947) 91 SJ 67; (1947) LXIII TLR 200 HC ChD Wife entitled to benefit under Summary Jurisdiction (Married Women) Act 1895, s 5 and Guardianship of Infants Act 1925, s 3(2).

Re L [1996] 2 FCR 352 CA Authorisation to allow finishing of contact ought not to have been made as would not be implemented in near future; on standard of proof in child sex abuse cases; on when interim/final care orders to be deployed.

Re L [1962] 3 All ER 1; (1962) 112 LJ 536; [1962] 1 WLR 886 CA Child's welfare paramount but parent's conduct material in deciding care/control — here entrusted to innocent party.

Re M [1994] 1 FCR 866 HC FamD On admittance of medical evidence at care hearing; on procedure where guardian ad litem's recommendation contrary to what child desires/where child gives instructions to solicitor contrary to what guardian recommends.

Re M [1997] 1 All ER 263; [1997] Fam 67; [1997] 1 FCR 109 HC FamD Presence of child in England sufficed to give court jurisdiction in care proceedings.

Re M [1996] 2 FLR 84 HC FamD Care order appropriate in respect of abandoned child with special needs in respect of whom nobody had parental responsibility.

Re M (1983) 133 NLJ 513c CA Custody of infant child to good mother (living with man with rape convictions) rather than good father (who had just married twenty-one year old woman).

Re M [1994] 3 All ER 298; [1994] 2 AC 424; [1994] 2 FCR 871; [1994] 2 FLR 577; (1994) 138 SJ LB 168; [1994] TLR 420; [1994] 3 WLR 558 HL That child temporarily in local authority care 'not suffering' does not stop authority seeking care order; relevant time is time when protection procedure initiated.

Re M [1994] 1 All ER 424; [1994] Fam 95; [1994] 1 FCR 849; [1994] 2 WLR 200 CA At time of care order hearing — and not some time previously — child must be suffering.

Re M [1995] 1 FCR 417 CA Residence (not care) order justified where alleged poor treatment unproved by the local authority but judge found other failures on mother's part.

Re M [1994] 1 FLR 73; (1993) 143 NLJ 1567 CA On deciding whether to make care order.

Re M [1961] 1 All ER 201 HC ChD Once child in local authority care under Children Act s 1(1) wardship should cease as court will not interfere with local authority discretion — regardless of Act.

Re M [1961] 1 All ER 788 CA Court retains supervisory jurisdiction but may order that wardship cease upon ward being taken into local authority care.

Re M [1993] TLR 511 CA Cannot make care order on factual basis which had ceased to exist by time of proceedings before court.

Re M (M) [1996] 2 FCR 521 HC FamD Abandonment of child was ill-treatment (hence harm) of same — this plus various health/developmental problems justified care order.

Re M (No 2) [1994] 1 FLR 59 CA On refusal of care order.

Re M and H (No 2) [1988] FCR 107 HC FamD Court could not grant putative father custody of children where local authority had taken children into care.

Re N [1994] 2 FCR 1101; [1994] 2 FLR 992 HC FamD Where experts on both sides recommending care orders/that children not be placed with parents, action in which latter seeking to contest local authority care applications terminated.

Re N (J) and others [1995] 2 FLR 203 HC FamD Refusal of order for preliminary assessment of mother and children for psychotherapy where local authority had frustrated prospects of attendance.

Re O [1971] 2 All ER 744; [1971] Ch 748; (1971) 115 SJ 264; [1971] 2 WLR 784 CA Appellate court to set aside lower court decision if wrong/unfair/contrary to principle.

Re O [1992] 4 All ER 906; [1992] 2 FLR 7; [1992] 1 WLR 912 HC FamD Justices have no inherent order to stay care order; care order may be appropriate remedy for truancy; significant harm from truancy adequate basis for care order.

Re O [1992] 1 FLR 77 CA Father if suitable and willing to be given first chance at bringing up child where mother unable to do so.

Re P [1995] 1 FCR 583 HC FamD On proving danger of significant harm to child such as to justify care order.

Re P [1994] 2 FLR 751 HC FamD Care order refused as local authority failed to prove significant harm to child whose brother died while in parents' care was likely.

Re R [1994] 2 FCR 136 HC FamD On procedure as regards deciding care actions.

Re R [1986] 1 FLR 6 CA On providing court with evidence of criminal/drinking record of parent in custody action.

Re R (1993) 137 SJ LB 180; [1993] TLR 349 CA Order for adoption (contact with natural mother to continue pending same) was valid.

Re R (K) [1963] 3 All ER 337; [1964] Ch 455; (1964) 128 JP 7; (1963) 113 LJ 626; (1963) 107 SJ 1040; [1963] 3 WLR 991 HC ChD Mother reclaiming care of child in authority care ended authority's right to keep child: court free to make interim order placing child in anyone's care.

Re S [1990] FCR 635; [1990] TLR 109 CA Custody of children to be finally determined when mother's post-divorce accommodation/financial situation resolved.

Re S [1997] 1 FCR 490 HC FamD Justices' decision to hold care hearings absent previously ordered psychological appraisal justified by need to avoid undue delay.

Re S [1991] FCR 155; [1991] 2 FLR 388 CA On custody of young children: child's welfare paramount concern.

Re S [1995] 2 FCR 697; [1995] 1 FLR 151 CA Generally where child charged with grave criminal offence is better for trial of that matter to proceed care action.

Re S [1965] 1 All ER 33; (1965) 115 LJ 57; [1965] 1 WLR 94 HC ChD Local authority responsibility to child in care suspended when parents request immediate return; no review of taking of child from foster parents.

Re S [1997] 1 FLR 497 CA In action where father seeking care of and mother seeking residence order in respect of children allegedly sexually abused by father the mother's new husband (in respect of whom past abuse alleged) allowed intervene in action.

Re S [1958] 1 All ER 783; (1958) 122 JP 245; (1958) 102 SJ 250 HC ChD Unless urgent, stay of custody transfer order desirable upon appeal; otherwise postponed transfer to allow for appeal against refusal of stay.

Re S [1959] 1 WLR 921 HC ChD Guardian ad litem in appeal against CyCt adoption order to be guardian ad litem appointed in CyCt.

Re S (J) [1993] 2 FCR 193; [1993] 2 FLR 919 HC FamD On nature, effect, whether and when to grant care/supervision orders: here care order granted.

Re S (minors) [1994] TLR 682 HC FamD In case where interests of siblings conflicted those of child in respect of whom revocation of care was sought allowed take precedence over those of child in respect of whom adoption freeing order sought.

Re S and D [1995] 1 FCR 626; [1995] 2 FLR 456 CA Prohibited steps order invalid as essentially required child to be kept in local authority care: care order substituted.

Re T [1994] 2 FLR 423; [1994] TLR 248 CA Refusal of care order appropriate course if did not approve of local authority care plan; where supervision is conditional the conditions are to be specified in the order.

Re T [1995] 1 FCR 517; [1995] 1 FLR 159 HC QBD Judicial review of decision not to accommodate 'child in need' already taken in by couple.

Re T [1994] 1 FCR 663; [1994] 1 FLR 103 CA Local authority care (not supervision) order merited in respect of child whose daily care was left to parents notwithstanding order.

Re T (1974) 118 SJ 78 HC FamD Failed appeal in custody action on basis that justices had not seen child in their private room.

Re T (KD) [1994] 2 FCR 721 CA Conditional care order not allowed; care order only to be made if court approves of care plan; on role of court vis-à-vis that of local authority in care proceedings; here supervision order preferable to care order.

Re T and T (1956) 120 JP 566 HC ChD Putative father could not make custody application in respect of his illegitimate children under Guardianship of Infants Acts 1886 or 1925.

Re Thain (Margaret Louise), an infant (1924-25) 69 SJ 812 HC QBD Restoration of child to natural father not allowed as possibly not in child's best interests to be moved where only home had known since infancy was that of aunt (child now six).

Re Thain; Re M M Thain; Thain v Taylor [1926] Ch 676 (also CA); (1926) 61 LJ 301; (1926) 95 LJCh 292 (also CA); (1925-26) 70 SJ 504; (1926) WN (I) 91 HC ChD In custody case child's welfare paramount — but not only — consideration.

Re Thain; Thain v Taylor [1926] All ER 384; [1926] Ch 676 (also HC ChD); (1926) 61 LJ 403; (1926) 95 LJCh 292 (also HC ChD); (1926) 135 LTR 99; (1925-26) 70 SJ 634; (1926) WN (I) 150 CA In custody case child's welfare paramount — but not only — consideration.

Re W (1982) 3 FLR 129; (1981) 131 NLJ 1189 CA On relevant factors in application to have parental rights resolution of local authority rescinded.

Re W (1981) 131 NLJ 1288 CA Local authority care resolution deemed not to have lapsed.

Re W (1980) 124 SJ 272 HC FamD Pre-trial hearing between justices, child and social worker who would be giving evidence in pending case concerning child was inappropriate.

Re W [1953] 2 All ER 1337 CA May appeal from summary court to ChD to CA in custody cases under Guardianship of Infants Act 1925, s 31(1)(i).

Re W (a minor) (1982) 126 SJ 725; [1982] TLR 502 CA On duty of welfare officer in child custody case; on whether custody, care and control of mother (as here) to be preferred.

Re W (A) and W (E) (1979) 129 (1) NLJ 420 CA Court would not in instant case exercise its wardship jurisdiction in respect of child in care.

Re W (JC) [1963] 3 All ER 459; [1964] Ch 202; (1963) 127 JP 529; (1963) 107 SJ 617; [1963] 3 WLR 789 CA Magistrates may divide custody/care and control between different parties.

Re W (JC) [1963] 2 All ER 706; [1963] Ch 556; (1963) 113 LJ 656; (1963) 107 SJ 396; [1963] 2 WLR 1471 HC ChD Cannot give custody to one parent and care and control to other.

Re W (SC) (An Infant) (1963) 113 LJ 610 HC ChD On what is meant by the notion of 'custody' in the Guardianship of Infants Act 1965, s 5.

Re X [1996] 3 FCR 91 HC FamD Order that father not be given notice of care proceedings where was in interests of child/family.

Re X's Settlement [1945] 1 All ER 101; [1945] Ch 44; [1945] 114 LJ 305; (1945) 172 LTR 208; (1944-45) LXI TLR 93; (1944) WN (I) 237 HC ChD Scottish and English courts exercise care/custody powers in a complementary way.

Riley v Riley [1986] 2 FLR 429; (1986) 150 JP 439 CA Custody order should not have provided for constant shuffling of child between homes of divorced parents.

Rostron v Rostron (1982) 3 FLR 270; (1981) 131 NLJ 1189 CA Valid decision not to entrust custody of children to mother after they had spent two years with father pursuant to consent order.

S (BD) v S (DJ) [1977] 1 All ER 656; [1977] Fam 109; (1977) 121 SJ 34; [1977] 2 WLR 44 CA Child's interests primary concern in custody cases.

S v Bedfordshire County Council (1977) 127 NLJ 243t HC QBD Valid revocation of care order in respect of normal child from normal home taken into care because not being sent to school by parents who considered all local comprehensive schools unsuitable.

S v Bedfordshire County Council (1977) 127 NLJ 569t CA Care order restored in respect of normal child from normal home originally taken into care because not being sent to school by parents who considered all local comprehensive schools unsuitable.

S v Merton London Borough [1994] 1 FCR 186 HC FamD Improper to make interim care orders absent any evidence in controverted application.

S v S [1949] 1 All ER 285 HC PDAD On declaration of unfitness for guardianship.

S v S (1973) 117 SJ 34 HC FamD Delay to be avoided in custody action; court to see new partners of parents before deciding custody action.

S v S [1986] 1 FLR 492 HC FamD On staying transfer of custody order pending appeal against same.

S v S [1990] 2 FLR 341 CA Inappropriate that care and control of children be awarded absent proposals as to future accommodation of children.

Saward v Wilson (1981) 131 NLJ 69 CA Adverse effect of custody arrangements on welfare of children required reversal of trial judge's giving of custody to father and that it be given instead to mother.

Stephenson v Stephenson [1985] FLR 1140 CA Wrong to take child from caring environment of father and cohabitee and give care and control to previously rather disinterested mother simply because she was natural mother.

Stevenson v Florant [1927] AC 211; (1927) 96 LJPC 1; (1927) 136 LTR 265; (1926-27) XLIII TLR 6 PC In Quebec right of parent to child's custody prevails over that of tuteur.

Surrey County Council v S and others [1973] 3 All ER 1074; (1974) 138 JP 26; [1974] QB 124; (1973) 117 SJ 727; [1973] 3 WLR 579 CA Court may consider evidence of neglect/ill-treatment of child not subject of application and make appropriate order.

T v T (1970) 130 SJ 650 CA Child validly placed with father: recorder correct in looking at contemporaneous, not future best interests of child.

Thompson v Thompson [1987] 1 FLR 374; (1986) 150 JP 625 CA Young child could be placed with father where best interests lay with either parent, even if situation would be different some years later.

Todd (by his next friend Phyllis Thompson) v Davison [1971] 1 All ER 994; [1972] AC 392; (1971) 115 SJ 223; [1971] 2 WLR 898 HL Whether person in custody of parent an issue of fact; if in fact in custody is immaterial if parents cannot exercise proper control.

Townson v Mahon [1984] FLR 690 CA Custody order valid though judge overstressed importance of child being placed in mother's custody.

W v Hertfordshire County Council [1992] 2 FCR 885; [1993] 1 FLR 118; (1992) 136 SJ LB 259; [1992] TLR 431 HC FamD Justices must give reasons when refusing care order.

W v Heywood [1985] FLR 1064 HC QBD On making care order under Children and Young Persons Act 1969, s 7(7) where child is already subject of matrimonial care order.

W v Nottinghamshire County Council (1982) 3 FLR 33 (also CA) HC FamD Mother was not failing to discharge parental obligations; local authority not to rely on same grounds in extending resolution as when first making it.

W v Nottinghamshire County Council [1982] 1 All ER 1; [1982] Fam 53; (1982) 3 FLR 33 (also HC FamD); (1981) 125 SJ 761; [1981] 3 WLR 959 CA No voluntary or involuntary care, merely care; local authority need not rely on same grounds in extending resolution as when first making it.

W v P [1988] FCR 349; [1988] 1 FLR 508 HC FamD On magistrates giving reasons for custody order.

W v Sunderland Borough Council [1980] 2 All ER 514; (1981) 2 FLR 153; (1981) 145 JP 117; [1980] 1 WLR 1101 HC FamD Social worker who is to give evidence in parent's challenge of local authority not to be present if judge sees child privately; parent may 'consistently' fail to act as parent within a short period.

W v W and C [1968] 3 All ER 408; (1968) 118 NLJ 1029; (1968) 112 SJ 639; [1968] 1 WLR 1310 CA Better for 8 year old boy to be with father.

W v W and Hampshire County Council (1981) 2 FLR 68 CA Care order appropriate where neither parent suitable candidates to have custody of child.

Wakeham v Wakeham [1954] 1 All ER 434; (1954) 104 LJ 73; (1954) 98 SJ 127; [1954] 1 WLR 366 CA Custody of child removed from jurisdiction given to father but care and control issue left open.

Webb v Webb [1952] 1 All ER 527; (1952) 116 JP 146; (1952) 96 SJ 135; [1952] 1 TLR 453; (1952) WN (I) 102 HC PDAD To make custody order child must be actual child of parent.

West Glamorgan County Council v P (No 2) [1992] 2 FCR 406; [1993] 1 FLR 407 HC FamD On relevancy of long-term plans of local authority regarding child in care to court making decision regarding parental contact.

Wheatley v London Borough of Waltham Forest [1979] 2 All ER 289; [1980] AC 311; (1979) 143 JP 380; (1979) 123 SJ 270; [1979] 2 WLR 543 HC FamD Decision of local authority to assume parental rights over child within 28 days of parent requesting child is valid.

White v White and Hampshire County Council (1980) 130 NLJ 417c CA Refusal to rescind care order; on practice regarding obtaining views of child/bringing child to psychiatrist in context of care actions.

Williamson v Williamson [1986] 2 FLR 146 CA Irrelevancy to custody action of mother's occupancy of former matrimonial home; custody/care and control to one/other parent disfavoured.

X and others v Bedfordshire County Council; M and another v Newham London Borough Council and others; E v Dorset County Council and other appeals [1995] 3 All ER 353; [1995] 2 AC 633 (also CA); [1995] 3 FCR 337; [1995] 2 FLR 276; [1995] TLR 375; [1995] 3 WLR 152 HL Local authority child care decision cannot be challenged as breach of statutory duty or common law duty of care if in hindsight decision proved mistaken nor is it vicariously liable for actions of social workers and psychiatrists in case.

CARE/CUSTODY (grandparent)

B v B (1962) 106 SJ 573 HC PDAD Husband could not be expected to live with drug-addicted wife; custody of child taken from drug addicted wife and care and control of child given to paternal grandmother.

Pryor v Pryor [1947] 1 All ER 381; [1948] 117 LJR 94; (1947) 177 LTR 329; (1947) LXIII TLR 208; (1947) WN (I) 108 HC PDAD Court could grant custody to grandparents of children who had previously been entrusted to since deceased mother's custody.

Re F (1975) 125 NLJ 1221t CA Custody of child to young father/stepmother with young daughter rather than to elderly grandparents.

Re K [1996] 1 FCR 365; [1995] 1 FLR 675 HC FamD Care (not residence) order appropriate for grandparents looking after grandchildren.

Re M [1985] FLR 664 HC FamD Adoption by rather than custody to grandparents preferable in instant case.

CARE/CUSTODY (guardian)

Oxfordshire County Council and another v P [1995] 2 All ER 225; [1995] Fam 161; [1995] 2 FCR 212; [1995] 1 FLR 552; [1995] TLR 62; [1995] 2 WLR 543 HC FamD Lifting privilege of confidentiality in care proceedings a matter for court not guardian ad litem.

R v Birmingham Juvenile Court, ex parte G and others; R v Birmingham Juvenile Court, ex parte R [1989] 3 All ER 336; [1989] 2 FLR 454; [1990] 2 QB 573; (1989) 133 SJ 1089; [1989] 3 WLR 1024 CA Court must look to welfare of child/hear guardian ad litem before allowing local authority withdraw care order application.

R v Birmingham Juvenile Court, ex parte G and others; R v Birmingham Juvenile Court, ex parte R [1988] 3 All ER 726; [1989] FCR 22; [1988] 2 FLR 423; (1988) 138 NLJ 143; (1988) 132 SJ 1117; [1988] 1 WLR 950 HC QBD As care proceedings not adversarial court may hear guardian ad litem's evidence even if local authority offers no evidence.

R v Epsom Juvenile Court, ex parte G [1988] 1 All ER 329; [1988] FCR 32; [1988] 2 FLR 36; (1988) 132 SJ 54; [1988] 1 WLR 145 HC QBD Usually report of guardian ad litem should be presented as soon as possible before care case begins.

R v Newcastle-upon-Tyne Council, ex parte S and T [1988] FCR 159; [1988] 1 FLR 535 HC QBD On making order that guardians ad litem be appointed to represent children (on basis that conflict between their interests and that of parents).

R v North Yorkshire County Council, ex parte M [1989] 1 All ER 143; [1989] FCR 128; [1989] 1 FLR 203; [1989] QB 411; (1988) 132 SJ 1731; [1988] 3 WLR 1344 HC QBD Local authority must inform guardian ad litem/hear guardian's views about any major changes to circumstances of child in care.

R v Waltham Forest London Borough, ex parte G [1989] 2 FLR 138 HC QBD On juvenile court's role where dispute between local authority/guardian ad litem over psychiatric assessment of children in care seeking discharge of care orders.

R v West Malling Juvenile Court, ex parte K (1986) 150 JP 367; (1970) 130 SJ 650 HC QBD Case ought to hve been adjourned where parent in care action given social worker/guardian ad litem reports containing unexpected material on day of hearing.

Re B [1996] 3 FCR 272; [1996] 1 FLR 667 CA Reasoned departure of judge from opinions of expert/guardian ad litem when granting interim care order was valid.

Re C (1992) 136 SJ LB 252; [1992] TLR 407 HC FamD May be order that there be no contact between child and natural mother; inappropriate to direct guardian ad litem to police rehabilitation programme of child in local authority care.

Re E (C) [1995] 1 FCR 387; [1995] 1 FLR 26 HC FamD Guardian ad litem reappointed to act for child where specified proceedings ceased to be such upon local authority deciding not to seek care/supervision order.

Re F [1995] 3 FCR 601 HC FamD Psychological appraisal of child inappropriate; guardian ad litem ordered to give oral report.

Re H [1959] 3 All ER 746; (1960) 124 JP 74; (1959) 109 LJ 703; (1959) 103 SJ 1003; [1959] 1 WLR 1163 HC ChD Cannot appoint joint guardian just to help in custody application: infant's interests sole determinant.

Re R [1974] 1 All ER 1033; (1974) 124 NLJ 123t; (1974) 118 SJ 78 HC FamD Custody to non-parent/non-guardian.

Re U (T) [1993] 2 FCR 565 HC FamD Magistrates to give reasons for not following guardian ad litem's recommendation; magistrates improperly ordered contact to mother so putting child at risk.

Suwa v Ando (1913) CC Rep II 34 CyCt Articles of Apprenticeship would not be set aside and custody of child given to (foreign) mother where was not in best interests of child/application not brought solely out of interest for child.

CARE/CUSTODY (habitual residence)

Re J [1990] 2 AC 562 (also CA); [1990] 3 WLR 492 HL On where is place of habitual residence for purpose of Child Abduction Convention; unmarried mother's removing child from Western Australia without father's knowledge did not (by virtue of Western Australian Law) come within terms of Child Abduction Convention.

Re M [1997] 1 All ER 263; [1997] Fam 67; [1997] 1 FCR 109; (1996) TLR 10/12/96 HC FamD Presence of child in England sufficed to give court jurisdiction in care proceedings.

Re R [1995] 3 FCR 305; [1995] 1 FLR 711 HC FamD Child either to be habitually resident or present in jurisdiction on relevant day for care order jurisdiction to arise.

CARE/CUSTODY (harbouring)

Krishnan v London Borough of Sutton [1969] 3 All ER 1367; [1970] Ch 181; (1970) 134 JP 75; (1969) 113 SJ 774; [1969] 3 WLR 683 CA Court cannot order local authority to hand child in care to natural parent; harbouring charge unproven.

CARE/CUSTODY (hearsay)

B v X County Council (1991) 141 NLJ 1740t; [1991] TLR 582 HC FamD Hearsay evidence admissible when CrCt hearing appeal against juvenile court care order.

CARE/CUSTODY (HIV-testing)

Re W (a minor) [1995] 2 FCR 184 HC FamD HIV-testing of child at risk ordered as would aid judge in deciding residence application.

CARE/CUSTODY (homosexual)

C v C [1991] FCR 254; [1991] 1 FLR 223 CA On relevancy of mother's lesbian relationship to determination of custody action (plus relevancy of onetime criminal conviction of mother's lesbian partner).

Re P (1983) 4 FLR 401 CA Child whose father could not have custody given into custody of mother in lesbian relationship but arrangement subject to scrutiny of Official Solicitor.

S v S (1980) 1 FLR 143 CA Custody of children properly granted to father where mother's lesbian relationship could cause children acute embarrassment if became known.

CARE/CUSTODY ('household')

N v Birmingham District Council (1984) 148 JP 700; (1984) 128 SJ 447 HC FamD 'Household' determined by reference to circumstances; can be in same 'household' though not in same place.

R v Birmingham Juvenile Court, ex parte N [1984] 2 All ER 688; [1984] FLR 683 HC QBD 'Household' determined by reference to circumstances; can be in same 'household' though not in same place.

CARE/CUSTODY (ill-treatment)

Surrey County Council v S and others [1973] 1 All ER 1027; (1973) 137 JP 395; (1973) 117 SJ 186; [1973] 2 WLR 649 HC QBD Court discovering neglect/ill-treatment of child not subject of action may itself remit case of second child to justices.

CARE/CUSTODY (injunction)

Devon County Council v B [1997] 1 FLR 591 CA Freeing order invalid as court did not when making order consider basis of parent's refusal to agree to adoption; county court did not have inherent jurisdiction to bolster care order by way of injunctive relief.

Re W [1981] 3 All ER 401 CA County court may issue interlocutory injunction in support of custody order when making order.

CARE/CUSTODY (interim)

A v M and Walsall Metropolitan Borough Council [1994] 1 FCR 606; [1993] 2 FLR 244 HC FamD On deciding interim care cases.

B v B (1972) 122 NLJ 1112 CA Interim custody of young girl to father whom wife had deserted but increased access by mother allowed.

Beard v Beard [1981] 1 All ER 783; (1980) 124 SJ 810; [1981] 1 WLR 369 CA Interim care and control order where emergency affecting children may include giving right to enter children's home/excluding another.

Buckinghamshire County Council v M [1994] 1 FCR 859; [1994] 2 FLR 506 CA Interim care order made in respect of child where full care order refused (siblings already subject to interim care orders).

Croydon London Borough Council v A (No 2) [1992] 2 FCR 858; [1992] 2 FLR 348 HC FamD HC cannot/can make care/interim care order pending appeal from failed care application.

D v R [1995] 1 FCR 501 HC FamD On making of interim care order (here unjustified); on need for magistrates to give their reasons for their decision in care action.

E v NSPCC and another [1990] FCR 609; [1990] 2 FLR 379 HC QBD On interim care hearings.

Edwards v Edwards [1986] 1 FLR 205 CA On justifiability of interim custody order.

Edwards v Edwards [1986] 1 FLR 187; (1985) 149 JP 661 HC FamD On relevant factors when making interim custody order.

F v F (1976) 126 NLJ 743t CA Pending divorce action not good reason for adjourning maintenance/custody applications.

G v G (1983) 4 FLR 327; [1982] TLR 321 CA On appealing against interim custody orders.

Gateshead Metropolitan Borough Council v N [1993] 1 FCR 400; [1993] 1 FLR 811 HC FamD On duration of first/successive interim care order/s.

H v N [1990] TLR 36 HC FamD Mother with interim custody order in respect of Canadian child did not have right to remove child from country of residence (Canada).

Hereford and Worcester County Council v R and G [1994] 2 FCR 981 HC FamD Interim care order not supervision order appropriate mechanism whereby to control residence.

Humberside County Council v B [1993] 1 FCR 613; [1993] 1 FLR 257 HC FamD On relevant factors when making interim care order.

Jones v Jones (1974) 124 NLJ 810t; (1974) 118 SJ 598 CA Custody/interim custody orders preferable to postponement of custody action pending divorce action.

Leicestershire County Council v G [1995] 1 FCR 205; [1994] 2 FLR 329 HC FamD Interim care order substituted for interim supervision order where child of family suffered non-accidental injury before care proceedings heard.

Newham London Borough Council v I and Brent London Borough Council [1997] 2 FCR 629 HC FamD On determining designated care authority in care proceedings where children in interim local accommodation care of one authority and mother had since moved to area of another local authority.

Northamptonshire County Council v C [1988] FCR 378 HC QBD No need for child to attend court each time application for extension of interim care order heard.

Northamptonshire County Council v H [1988] 1 All ER 598; [1988] 1 FLR 529; [1988] QB 205; (1988) 132 SJ 263; [1988] 2 WLR 389 HC QBD Additional interim care orders may be made in absence of child over 5 years old if legally represented.

R v Birmingham City Juvenile Court, ex parte Birmingham City Council [1988] 1 All ER 683; [1988] FCR 175 (also HC QBD); [1988] 1 FLR 424; (1987) 131 SJ 1697; [1988] 1 WLR 337 CA Disputed interim care order application to be decided after local authority/parents/guardian heard.

R v Croydon Juvenile Court, ex parte N [1987] 1 FLR 252; (1987) 151 JP 523 HC QBD On procedure (including evidential procedure) where interim care order sought.

Re A [1993] 1 FCR 164 HC FamD Interim care order where appraisal of father as carer for child incomplete; no need here for welfare officer to prepare report in addition to that which guardian ad litem preparing.

Re B (1983) 4 FLR 683 CA Interim custody order varied as in original form would cause disruption in child's life with time divided equally between both parents.

Re B (1983) 4 FLR 472; (1982) 132 NLJ 1172 CA Interim care and control of children to mother pending resolution of wardship/'kidnapping' proceedings appropriate.

Re B [1996] 3 FCR 272; [1996] 1 FLR 667 CA Reasoned departure of judge from opinions of expert/guardian ad litem when granting interim care order was valid.

Re B [1993] 1 FCR 565; [1993] 1 FLR 815 HC FamD Interim care order to local authority (residence order refused to paternal aunt) until alleged sexual abuse by father (mother in psychiatric hospital) investigated.

Re B [1991] FCR 414; [1991] 2 FLR 405 CA Where future of child depended on future of matrimonial home and judge could not make ancillary relief order any custody order made was interim.

Re C [1994] 1 FCR 447 HC FamD Interim supervision order favouring mother of baby pending full care hearing.

Re C [1996] 2 FLR 708; (1996) TLR 3/10/96 CA Residential assessment cannot be ordered when making interim care order.

Re C (a minor) (1996) 140 SJ LB 221 CA Local authority could refuse to make residential assessment of child (in interim care) and its parents.

Re G [1993] 2 FCR 557; [1993] 2 FLR 839; [1993] TLR 441 CA On nature/effect of interim care order and whether/when to grant one.

Re H [1991] FCR 985; [1991] 2 FLR 109 CA Interim care and control of child of dead mother given to maternal grandmother with generous access rights to father.

Re H [1991] FCR 564 CA Interim care order to grandmother merited where was some doubt as to parental abilities of both parents.

Re J [1994] 1 FLR 253 HC FamD On making of (interim) care order where court does not approve of local authority's proposed care plan.

Re Jarvis [1984] FLR 350 HC QBD General non-interference by HC in juvenile court interim care orders.

Re L [1996] 2 FCR 352 CA Authorisation to allow finishing of contact ought not to have been made as would not be implemented in near future; on standard of proof in child sex abuse cases; on when interim/final care orders to be deployed.

Re L [1996] 2 FCR 706; [1996] 2 FLR 742 CA On making interim care order.

Re M [1996] 3 FCR 137; [1996] 2 FLR 464 CA On role of court when/after making interim care order.

Re M [1993] 2 FCR 182; [1993] 2 FLR 406 HC FamD Failed application for leave to appeal against interim care order out of time (generally undesirable).

Re M (No 1) [1994] 1 FLR 54 CA On maintenance of interim care order pending appeal.

Re O [1992] 2 FCR 394; [1993] 1 FLR 860; (1993) 143 NLJ 814 HC FamD Medical examination direction attached to interim care order valid/relevant/mandatory.

Re P [1993] 2 FLR 742 CA On making interim care orders/further interim care orders/final care orders.

Re R (1981) 2 FLR 316 HC FamD Father who refused to part with children (left with him, initially for brief period, sometime after separated from wife) granted interim custody of children pending custody hearing.

Re R (J) [1995] 3 FCR 289 HC FamD On need for justices to give reasons for their decision in full/interim care order applications: here reasoning defective in place but conclusion (refusal of direct contact) justified.

Re S [1993] 2 FCR 475 HC FamD On when interim care orders (as here) justified.

Re W [1990] FCR 540; [1990] 2 FLR 86 CA Inappropriate that interim custody order be made in favour of putative father until question of paternity decided.

Re W [1994] 3 FCR 102; [1994] 2 FLR 892 CA Interim care orders invalid as had been procedural errors when were made.

Re W and L [1987] 2 FLR 67; (1987) 151 JP 222 CA On granting interim care orders.

Re W and W (1983) 4 FLR 686 CA Interim custody order bad for instability caused to children; refusal of exclusion order (that would allow wife/children to return to home from women's refuge).

S v S (1971) 115 SJ 606 CA Interim custody to father where judge based decision in part on suspicions had regarding mother's behaviour was valid.

W v D (1980) 1 FLR 393 CA Child to be returned to care and control of person from whose care and control is snatched unless to do so would endanger child.

X v X (1963) 107 SJ 571 CA Interim custody order uprooting child from foreign country pending divorce action there and placing child with adulterous wife and her lover was improper.

CARE/CUSTODY (interview)

Re M [1995] TLR 395 HC FamD Access to police videos of interviews with child (concerning possible sexual abuse) ordered in civil trial to which video evidence relevant.

CARE/CUSTODY (joint)

Caffell v Caffell [1984] FLR 169 CA On when joint custody appropriate (here was).

Clissold v Clissold (1964) 108 SJ 220 HC PDAD Refusal of joint custody order upon divorce.

Hurst v Hurst [1984] FLR 867 CA Joint custody ordered as in child's best interests.

J v J [1991] FCR 504; [1991] 2 FLR 385 CA Joint care and control exceptional but merited here.

Jussa v Jussa [1972] 2 All ER 600; (1972) 136 JP 499; (1972) 116 SJ 219; [1972] 1 WLR 881 HC FamD Split orders and joint custody order available if in best interests of children.

May v May [1986] 1 FLR 325 CA Joint custody (care and control to father) where both parents equally suitable (notwithstanding mother's adultery).

Re D (1981) 2 FLR 102 CA Adoption order preferable to joint custody order here where natural and step-parent seeking adoption; wishes of children relevant (here wanted adoption): decision contrary to wishes to be explained); child's memories of natural father inadequate reason for refusing adoption.

Re D (1973) 117 SJ 525 HC FamD Joint custody order to husband and wife.

Re J (minors) (1972) 122 NLJ 216t HC FamD Joint custody orders not exceptional.

Re P [1990] FCR 909; [1990] 2 FLR 223; (1990) 134 SJ 661; [1990] 1 WLR 613 CA Joint custody consent order not injunction/injunctive in nature so penal notice order could not be attached thereto.

Re S [1977] 3 All ER 671; [1977] Fam 173; (1977) 127 NLJ 368t; (1977) 121 SJ 222; [1977] 2 WLR 919 CA In parent/step-parent adoption case court must consider whether in child's welfare joint custody order preferable.

CARE/CUSTODY (legitimacy)

Colquitt v Colquitt [1947] 2 All ER 50; (1947) 111 JP 442; (1947) 97 LJ 277; [1948] 117 LJR 897; (1947) 177 LTR 399; (1947) 91 SJ 310; (1947) LXIII TLR 358; (1947) WN (I) 182 HC PDAD Legitimated child is a child of marriage of natural parents; absent decree of legitimacy court can nonetheless make custody order in respect of child legitimated by marriage of natural parents.

G v G (1929) 73 SJ 111; (1928-29) XLV TLR 7 HC PDAD Court could not make custody order in respect of non-legitimated child of parties to divorce action.

Harrison v Harrison [1951] 2 All ER 346; (1951) 115 JP 428; [1951] 2 TLR 242; (1951) WN (I) 387 HC PDAD No custody order possible in respect of illegitimate child (who cannot be legitimised).

Packer v Packer [1953] 2 All ER 127; (1953) 103 LJ 328; (1953) 97 SJ 403; [1953] 3 WLR 33 CA Test whether court may hear custody/maintenance application is parenthood not legitimacy.

Re G (An Infant) [1956] 2 All ER 876; [1956] 1 WLR 911 CA Valid giving of (illegitimate) child into mother's sole care and custody.

Re T (C) (An Infant); Re T (J) (An Infant) [1956] 3 All ER; [1956] 3 WLR 826 HC ChD Cannot hear application by putative father for custody of illegitimate child.

CARE/CUSTODY (maintenance)

Calderdale Borough Council v H and P [1991] 1 FLR 461 HC FamD Statutory care order to local authority, children to reside with grandparents who were to be paid maintenance pending approval as foster-parents when would be paid boarding-out allowance.

Flood v Flood [1948] 2 All ER 712; (1948) 112 JP 416; [1948] 117 LJR 1880; (1948) LXIV TLR 474 HC PDAD Children's welfare paramount in custody cases (and maintenance an important element of that).

Galloway v Galloway [1954] 2 All ER 143; (1954) 104 LJ 328; (1954) 98 SJ 336; [1954] 2 WLR 980 CA Custody/maintenance unavailable in respect of child born outside marriage who cannot be legitimated.

M and another v Wigan Metropolitan Borough Council [1979] 2 All ER 958; [1980] Fam 36; (1980) 1 FLR 45; [1979] 3 WLR 244 HC FamD Parental obligations wider than financial maintenance; consistent failure is not persistent failure; failure tested objectively.

Packer v Packer [1953] 2 All ER 127; (1953) 103 LJ 328; (1953) 97 SJ 403; [1953] 3 WLR 33 CA Test whether court may hear custody/maintenance application is parenthood not legitimacy.

R v Sandbach Justices, ex parte Smith [1950] 2 All ER 781; (1950) 114 JP 514; [1951] 1 KB 62; (1950) 100 LJ 485; (1950) 94 SJ 597; [1950] 66 (2) TLR 291; (1950) WN (I) 397 HC KBD Guadianship proceedings to be brought where respondent lives (unless High Court action); generally no order where child outside jurisdiction.

Re T; Re Guardianship of Infants Acts, 1886-1925 [1953] Ch 787; (1953) 97 SJ 607 HC ChD Appropriate that means of mother (given custody of children) be taken into account when assessing appropriate maintenance for mother.

CARE/CUSTODY (mental health)

R v Kirklees Metropolitan Borough Council, ex parte C [1993] 2 FCR 381; [1993] 2 FLR 187; [1993] TLR 173 CA Local authority could have child in care admitted to mental hospital.

R v Kirklees Metropolitan Borough Council, ex parte C [1992] 2 FCR 321; [1992] 2 FLR 117; [1992] TLR 45 HC QBD Local authority could have child in care admitted to mental hospital.

CARE/CUSTODY (mother)

Bowley v Bowley [1984] FLR 791 CA On desirabilty that young children be in mother's custody (here so ordered).

Re W (1983) 4 FLR 492 (also CA) HC FamD Custody to mother: child's best interests presumed to be with mother unless strong contrary evidence.

Re W (1983) 4 FLR 492 (also HC FamD) CA Custody to mother: attitude of courts to children being in custody of mothers set out.

CARE/CUSTODY (neglect)

Brooks v Blount [1922] All ER 699; (1921-25) XXVII Cox CC 399; (1923) 87 JP 64; [1923] 1 KB 257; [1923] 92 LJCL 302; (1923) 128 LTR 607; (1922-23) 67 SJ 299; (1922-23) XXXIX TLR 168; (1923) WN (I) 14 HC KBD Legal presumption that child in father's custody not displaced by latter entering separation agreement whereby wife paid to take care of child in her custody: father can still be convicted for neglect of child.

Surrey County Council v S and others [1973] 1 All ER 1027; (1973) 137 JP 395; (1973) 117 SJ 186; [1973] 2 WLR 649 HC QBD Court discovering neglect/ill-treatment of child not subject of action may itself remit case of second child to justices.

CARE/CUSTODY (non-parent)

Re R [1974] 1 All ER 1033; (1974) 124 NLJ 123t; (1974) 118 SJ 78 HC FamD Custody to non-parent/non-guardian.

CARE/CUSTODY (Official Solicitor)

P v P (Wiltshire County Council intervening) (1991) 141 NLJ 968t; [1991] TLR 318 CA Official Solicitor to represent child where local authority disputing his future with others.

CARE/CUSTODY (parental responsibility)

Birmingham City Council v D; Birmingham City Council v M [1994] 2 FCR 245; [1994] 2 FLR 502 HC FamD Refusal of care orders in respect of orphans over whom nobody had parental responsibility.

CARE/CUSTODY (place of safety order)

R v A Justice for Lincoln (Kesteven), ex parte M; R v Lincoln (Kesteven) Juvenile Court, ex parte Lincolnshire County Council [1976] 1 All ER 490; (1976) 140 JP 216; (1975) 125 NLJ 1192t; [1976] QB 957; (1976) 120 SJ 8; [1976] 2 WLR 143 HC QBD Local authority place of safety order application following care order to parent not abuse of process.

CARE/CUSTODY (privilege)

Re D [1970] 1 All ER 1088; (1970) 134 JP 387; (1970) 114 SJ 188; [1970] 1 WLR 599 CA Case-records under Boarding-Out of Children Regulations 1955 are generally privileged.

Re L (1996) TLR 22/3/96 HL Expert report prepared for party into child care action was not clothed by professional privilege.

CARE/CUSTODY (provisional)

L v L (1966) 110 SJ 484; [1966] 1 WLR 1079 CA Custody of children given to father subject to review of order (whereby children stayed with mother but had great access to father) three months after was made.

CARE/CUSTODY (publicity)

Essex County Council v Mirror Group Newspapers Ltd [1996] 2 FCR 831; [1996] 1 FLR 585 HC FamD Local authority refused order requiring newspaper to disclose matters pertaining to article on child care case (publication not breaching publicity prohibition).

Re H [1993] TLR 661 CA Interests of children demanded restriction on publicity following their being entrusted to care of transsexual parent.

Re H-S [1994] 3 All ER; [1994] 1 WLR 1141 CA Welfare of children not paramount consideration where their upbringing and press freedom clash.

CARE/CUSTODY (religion)

Allington v Allington [1985] FLR 586 CA On relevant factors when deciding custody application by mother who left child with father (status quo irrelevant here as child apart from mother for only ten weeks).

H v H (1975) 125 NLJ 507t; (1975) 119 SJ 590 CA Successful appeal by English mother against custody of child resident in England being given to Muslim father so that child might be instructed in Islam (mother agnostic).

Jane v Jane (1983) 4 FLR 712 CA Custody to father/care and control to mother justified as latter a Jehovah's Witness opposed to blood transfusions which father could as custodian authorise.

Re B and G [1985] FLR 134 HC FamD Custody of children transferred to mother after over five years as father/stepmother were scientologists.

Re B and G [1985] FLR 493 CA Custody of children properly transferred to mother after over five years where father/stepmother were scientologists.

Re C (MA) [1966] 1 All ER 838 (also HC ChD); (1966) 130 JP 217 (also HC ChD); (1966) 110 SJ 309; [1966] 1 WLR 646 CA In adoption-custody cases child's welfare paramount interest; no requirement regarding religious education imposed.

Re C (MA) [1966] 1 All ER 838 (also CA); (1966) 130 JP 217 (also CA) HC ChD In adoption-custody cases child's welfare paramount interest; no requirement regarding religious education imposed.

Re Cole (1899-1900) XVI TLR 500 HC ChD Custody of children given to (Protestant) uncle where after (Protestant) father's death mother converted to Catholicism.

Re Collins (An Infant) [1950] 1 All ER 1057 CA Child's welfare paramount in guardianship cases: no rule that dead father has right to determine child's religious upbringing.

Re Hopton, an Infant (1901-02) 46 SJ 749 VacCt That petitioner-father under pressure to return abroad did not excuse denying respondent-mother chance to make her case in custody action; child of Protestant father/Catholic mother ordered to be returned to school for next term, not removed during term time and not instructed as Catholic.

Re J [1987] 1 FLR 455; (1987) 151 JP 243 HC FamD Wardship order continued but adoption/custodianship of child not allowed where natural mother not unreasonably objected to adoption of child by foster parents who were Jehovah's Witnesses/of different race to child.

Re T (1981) 2 FLR 239 CA Custody to mother who was Jehovah's Witness subject to various conditions (inter alia that children be allowed blood transfusions if necessary).

Ward v Laverty and another [1924] All ER 319; [1925] AC 101; (1924) 59 LJ 300; [1925] 94 LJPC 17; (1924) 131 LTR 614; (1923-24) 68 SJ 629; (1923-24) XL TLR 600; (1924) WN (I) 177 HL In custody case child's welfare paramount though father's desire as regards religious upbringing a relevant factor.

CARE/CUSTODY (residence)

A v A and Newham London Borough Council [1993] 1 FCR 870 HC FamD Failed appeal by child's paternal aunt against refusal to allow her seek residence order after alleged sexual abuse of child by paternal uncle.

B v B (residence order: restricting applications) [1997] 2 FCR 518 CA Valid decision to order one child to live with mother and other child with father but order that father not be allowed seek custody of other child without leave of court was improper.

G v Kirklees Metropolitan Borough Council [1993] 1 FCR 357; [1993] 1 FLR 805 HC FamD Aunt not joined to care proceedings where could not reasonably hope to secure residence order.

Gateshead Metropolitan Borough Council v B (1996) TLR 19/3/96 HC FamD On deciding where child is resident (in context of application for care order).

Re G and M (contact) [1995] 3 FCR 514 HC FamD Appropriate case in which to substitute conditional residence orders for care orders.

Re H [1994] 3 FCR 183; [1994] 2 FLR 80 HC FamD Grandparents who had enjoyed staying contact granted residence orders: care order to local authority quashed.

CARE/CUSTODY (residential assessment)

Re C [1996] 4 All ER 871; [1997] AC 489; [1997] 1 FCR 149; [1997] 1 FLR 1; (1996) 146 NLJ 1777; [1996] 3 WLR 1098 HL Residential assessment validly ordered in course of care proceedings.

Re C (a minor) (1996) 140 SJ LB 221 CA Local authority could refuse to make residential assessment of child (in interim care) and its parents.

CARE/CUSTODY (secure accommodation)

R v Leicester City Juvenile Justices, ex parte Capenhurst (1985) 149 JP 409; [1984] TLR 764 HC QBD Local authority's report on accommodation available for person of unruly character not binding on court.

Re L [1984] TLR 482 HC FamD Child placed in care under the Family Law Reform Act 1969, s 7(2) could be placed in secure accommodation under the Child Care Act 1980, s 21A without first having to turn to juvenile court.

CARE/CUSTODY (split)

A v A [1984] TLR 286 CA Preferable that children close in age and companionship not be split up in custody cases.

B v B [1991] FCR 1; [1991] 1 FLR 402 HC FamD On whether to place child with mother (in lesbian relationship) or father; on splitting of siblings.

C v C [1988] FCR 411; [1988] 2 FLR 291 CA On desirability of not splitting up siblings in post-divorce custody arrangements.

Jussa v Jussa [1972] 2 All ER 600; (1972) 136 JP 499; (1972) 116 SJ 219; [1972] 1 WLR 881 HC FamD Split orders and joint custody order available if in best interests of children.

P v P [1991] FCR 97 CA Split custody generally undesirable but here deemed appropriate.

Re B (1976) 126 NLJ 1167b CA Custody of one of two children to each parent merited in instant circumstances.

Re P [1991] 1 FLR 337 CA On making split custody order; on significance of report of court welfare officer when determining custody.

Re S [1996] 2 FLR 773 HC FamD On holding of split hearings in care action.

S v S (otherwise D) (1968) 112 SJ 294 CA Split custody orders not to be preferred (and not granted here).

Wild v Wild [1968] 3 All ER 608; (1968) 132 JP 572; (1968) 118 NLJ 1102; (1968) 112 SJ 746; [1968] 3 WLR 1148 HC PDAD Justices cannot under Matrimonial Proceedings (Magistrates' Courts) Act 1960 divide custody and care and control between parents.

CARE/CUSTODY (step-parent)

Re F (1975) 125 NLJ 1221t CA Custody of child to young father/stepmother with young daughter rather than to elderly grandparents.

CARE/CUSTODY (supervision order)

Manchester City Council v R [1996] 3 FCR 118 HC FamD Supervision order in favour of parents who seemed likely to have occasioned subdural haematoma to child on one occasion (probably by shaking/flinging child down) but were otherwise satisfactory parents.

Re A (a minor) [1995] 3 All ER 401; [1995] 2 FCR 114; [1995] 1 FLR 335; (1994) 138 SJ LB 228; [1995] 1 WLR 482 CA Court cannot make care order on application for extension of supervision order; interim care orders are available but only to cover adjournments.

Re B [1997] 1 FCR 309; [1996] 2 FLR 693 HC FamD On deciding whether care/supervision orders merited.

Re C [1992] 2 FCR 341 HC FamD Conditional, experimental, short-term, interim supervision order in favour of parents previously guilty of battering child.

Re O [1997] 2 FCR 17; [1996] 2 FLR 755 HC FamD Improper exercise of discretion where care orders made rather than first trying supervision orders in respect of children supervision of whom was sought by local authority though it did not seek to remove children from their home.

Re R and G [1994] 1 FLR 793 HC FamD Could not give power to take children into care as part of supervision order.

Re S [1996] 2 FCR 719; [1996] 1 FLR 753 CA On when care and when supervision order merited.

Re V [1996] 2 FCR 555; [1996] 1 FLR 776 CA On whether/when care (as here) or supervision order appropriate; supervision order with conditions inappropriate.

CARE/CUSTODY (surname)

R v R [1978] 2 All ER 33; [1977] 1 WLR 1256 CA Custody of child given to mother notwithstanding that this involved surname-change of child to surname of mother's lover.

CARE/CUSTODY (surrogacy)

Re P [1988] FCR 140; [1987] 2 FLR 421 HC FamD On deciding custody where paid surrogate mother refuses to surrender children to natural father and his wife.

CARE/CUSTODY (temporary)

S v S [1991] TLR 281 CA Temporary order concerning children desirable where situation of conflict comes before court — matters can be permanently resolved at later stage when worst of conflict has passed.

CARE/CUSTODY (transsexual)

Re H [1993] TLR 661 CA Interests of children demanded restriction on publicity following their being entrusted to care of transsexual parent.

CARE/CUSTODY (ward)

A v Berkshire County Council [1989] FCR 184; [1989] 1 FLR 273 (also HC FamD) CA Juvenile court-appointed guardian ad litem could not by way of wardship action challenge local authority exercise of care and control powers over child.

A v Berkshire County Council [1989] FCR 180; [1989] 1 FLR 273 (also CA) HC FamD Juvenile court-appointed guardian ad litem could not by way of wardship action challenge local authority exercise of care and control powers over child.

A v Liverpool City Council and another [1981] 2 All ER 385; [1982] AC 363; (1981) 2 FLR 222; (1981) 145 JP 318; (1981) 131 NLJ 576; (1981) 125 SJ 396; [1981] 2 WLR 948 HL Court can review administrative/not substantive validity of local authority exercising discretionary powers.

A-W v E (1974) 124 NLJ 1159t HC FamD On practice as regards bringing normal child who is subject of custody/wardship proceedings to psychiatrist.

B v W (1979) 123 SJ 704 HC FamD Care and control of ward to mother, supervision order to local authority.

Berkshire County Council v D-P [1986] 2 FLR 276 (also HC FamD) CA Care (not wardship) proceedings appropriate where child born drug-dependent as result of mother's drug abuse while pregnant — matters concerning period of pregnancy could be considered.

D v X City Council (No 2) [1985] FLR 279 HC FamD Child in local authority care to be entrusted to care and control of grandmother.

H v H; H v East Sussex County Council (1972) 116 SJ 968 HC FamD Court would not exercise wardship jurisdiction over child in respect of whom local authority care resolution had been made.

I v Barnsley Metropolitan Borough Council [1986] 1 FLR 109 (also HC FamD) CA Wrong to place one of two children in care on basis that one/other was not/was child of mother's cohabitee who had perpetrated serious cruelty on first child.

J and another v C and others [1970] AC 668; [1969] 2 WLR 540 HL Child's welfare paramount in wardship cases: no rule that custody must go to parents who are suitable for same.

J v Devon County Council [1986] 1 FLR 597 HC FamD Non-exercise of wardship jurisdiction in respect of child taken into local authority care pursuant to matrimonial care order.

London Borough of Lewisham v Lewisham Juvenile Court Justices and another [1979] 2 All ER 297; [1980] AC 273; (1979) 143 JP 441; (1979) 129 (1) NLJ 339; (1979) 123 SJ 270; [1979] 2 WLR 513 HL Local authority care not terminated upon request for return by parent but must pass wardship/s 2 resolution.

London Borough of Lewisham v M and others [1981] 3 All ER 307; (1981) 2 FLR 384; (1981) 131 NLJ 878; [1981] 1 WLR 1248 HC FamD Power to commit care of ward to local authority is unfettered.

NSPCC v H and H [1989] FCR 544; [1989] 2 FLR 131 CA On invocation of wardship jurisdiction of HC where is overlapping care action before juvenile court.

R v London Borough of Newham, ex parte McL [1988] 1 FLR 416 HC QBD Wardship proceedings to be recommended by judge giving leave if preferable to judicial review of local authority decision/s regarding child in its care.

Re A (1980) 1 FLR 100; (1979) 123 SJ 553 HC FamD Independent welfare officer to ascertain wishes of child where sought; child's interests (of paramount importance) required that children remain in local authority care.

Re A and E (1980) 1 FLR 312 CA On exercise by court of its wardship jurisdiction where child in local authority care.

Re Andrews [1958] 2 All ER 308; (1958) 108 LJ 425; (1958) 102 SJ 382 HC ChD Wardship concerns a matter for wardship court; PDAD will make care/custody/control decisions on merit regarding ChD ward (and in the course of so doing will remove child from ChD wardship); ChD may hear wardship application despitet PDAD care/custody/control order/s regarding child.

Re B (1981) 2 FLR 412 HC FamD Wardship ought not to have been terminated where parents not afforded opportunity of further meetings with doctor seeking to rehabilitate family.

Re B (1974) 124 NLJ 620t; (1975) 119 SJ 165; [1975] 2 WLR 302 HC FamD Exceptionally court will (and did here) make child in care a ward of court.

Re B (C) [1981] 1 All ER 16; (1981) 145 JP 90; (1981) 125 SJ 219; [1981] 1 WLR 379 CA Court free to decide case in best interests of child where local authority seeks care and control of child in voluntary care.

Re B's Settlement; B v B [1940] Ch 54; [1940] 109 LJCh 20; (1939-40) LVI TLR 30; (1939) WN (I) 347 HC ChD Ward's welfare paramount factor in deciding custody action even if has already been foreign court order regarding custody.

Re C [1984] FLR 419 (also HC FamD) CA Risk to ward from mother (to whom was close) required care and control of ward be given to local authority which was authorised to place child with foster-parents with view to adoption.

Re C [1984] FLR 419 (also CA) HC FamD Risk to ward from mother (to whom was close) required care and control of ward be given to local authority which was authorised to place child with foster-parents with view to adoption.

Re C [1983] 1 All ER 219; (1983) 4 FLR 374; (1983) 133 NLJ 126; (1982) 126 SJ 820; [1982] TLR 394; [1982] 1 WLR 1462 HC FamD Court may invoke wardship powers in respect of child already subject of care order in criminal case.

Re C (1981) 2 FLR 63 CA Welfare of child may merit exercise by HC of its wardship jurisdiction even though juvenile court dismissed local authority care order application.

Re C (1981) 2 FLR 163 CA Care and control of child to father (though had lived with mother with one six-month break since birth); courts loathe to break bond between child and particular parent.

Re C (1979) 129 (2) NLJ 1180c CA On seeking exercise of wardship jurisdiction as way of appealing against decision of lower court not to make care order.

Re D (1978) 128 NLJ 336t; (1978) 122 SJ 193 HC FamD Wardship jurisdiction exercised in respect of child in local authority care.

Re D (1977) 121 SJ 355 HC FamD Wardship jurisdiction assumed after justices had discharged care order in respect of child.

Re E [1991] FCR 33 CA Rehabilitation of child discontinued and placement for adoption ordered.

Re E [1984] 1 All ER 21; (1983) 4 FLR 668; [1983] TLR 47; [1983] 1 WLR 541 CA Court will not use wardship powers to interfere with local authority acts under care order even if care order case pending and no care order as of yet.

Re E [1984] FLR 457 (also CA/HL) HC FamD Care and control off child to father subject to supervision of welfare officer.

Re E (1983) 147 JP 321 CA On exercise by HC of its wardship jurisdiction where children are in care/care action in progress.

Re E (SA) [1984] 1 All ER 289; [1984] FLR 457 (also HC FamD/CA); (1984) 128 SJ 80; [1984] TLR 17; [1984] 1 WLR 156 HL In ward's interests court may follow course of action not argued by parties to case: period of access to ward by father favoured to see if long-term relationship between father/ward possible.

Re G [1963] 3 All ER 370; (1963) 127 JP 549; (1963) 113 LJ 657; (1963) 107 SJ 682; [1963] 1 WLR 1169 HC ChD Courts will exercise wardship powers in line with local authority's proper exercise of discretion over child in care: if care to end court will intervene.

Re H (1977) 121 SJ 645 HC FamD Assumption by HC of wardship jurisdiction even though juvenile court could have done what parents asked (discharged care order).

Re H [1978] 2 All ER 903; [1978] Fam 65; (1978) 142 JP 474; (1978) 122 SJ 230; [1978] 2 WLR 608 CA Wardship order available where seek to supersede care order; Court of Appeal ought not to vary High Court assumption of wardship.

Re J [1984] 1 All ER 29; [1984] FLR 43; (1983) 127 SJ 616; [1983] TLR 488; [1984] 1 WLR 81 CA High Court will use wardship powers to police return of child in care to mother where care order otherwise would not be discharged by juvenile court.

Re K [1977] 1 All ER 647; [1977] Fam 179; (1977) 121 SJ 84; [1977] 2 WLR 33 CA Child's welfare paramount when considering care and control.

Re K [1991] 2 FLR 104 CA Interim care and control order by wardship court precluded need for divorce court to issue same.

Re K (KJS) [1966] 3 All ER 154; (1965-66) 116 NLJ 1173; (1966) 110 SJ 545; [1966] 1 WLR 1241 HC ChD Variation of access order (not wardship order) best course where post-access order access is unsatisfactory.

Re L [1990] FCR 509; [1991] 1 FLR 14; (1990) 134 SJ 545; [1990] TLR 227 CA Improper to exercise wardship jurisdiction in realm reserved by Parliament to discretion of local authority.

Re M [1985] 1 All ER 745; [1985] Fam 60 CA Access order for juvenile court; freeing of child for adoption for magistrates' court.

Re M (1985) 129 SJ 221 CA Failed application to court to exercise its wardship jurisdiction in lieu of local authority exercising its care jurisdiction.

Re M [1961] 1 All ER 201; [1961] Ch 81; (1961) 125 JP 163; (1961) 111 LJ 170 HC ChD Once child in local authority care under Children Act 1948, s 1(1), wardship should cease as court will not interfere with local authority discretion — regardless of Act.

Re M [1961] 1 All ER 788; [1961] Ch 328; (1961) 125 JP 278; (1961) 111 LJ 237 CA Court retains supervisory jurisdiction but may order that wardship cease upon ward being taken into local authority care.

Re M (R) and M (L) [1986] 2 FLR 205 HC FamD Alleged local authority abuse of power to be challenged by way of judicial review.

Re O [1978] 2 All ER 27; [1978] Fam 196 (also HC FamD); (1977) 121 SJ 710; [1977] 3 WLR 725 CA Child's interests paramount consideration in deciding wardship cases.

Re P [1988] FCR 232; [1988] 1 FLR 328 HC FamD Care/control of babies to parents as medical evidence showed injuries suffered by babies easily sufferable absent rough treatment/babies could have copper deficiency syndrome.

Re R [1988] FCR 388; [1987] 2 FLR 401 CA Court could exercise wardship jurisdiction at behest of local authority where juvenile court discharging care order but child still felt to be at risk.

Re S [1987] FCR 85; [1987] 1 FLR 479 CA On making/effect of care order: here wardship should have been discontinued in light of care orders.

Re S [1965] 1 All ER 865; (1965) 129 JP 228; (1965) 115 LJ 265; (1965) 109 SJ 174; [1965] 1 WLR 483 CA Wardship jurisdiction continues over child in local authority care.

Re T [1989] FCR 212 (also HC FamD); [1989] 1 FLR 313 (also CA); (1988) 132 SJ 1117; [1988] 3 WLR 713 HC FamD HC exercised its wardship jurisdiction where was desirable that single court (rather than various juvenile courts) decide on future welfare of all children of family.

Re T [1969] 3 All ER 998; (1969) 113 SJ 774; [1969] 1 WLR 1608 HC ChD Custody of ward sought by person living abroad: interest of ward/comity of nations of increasing/decreasing importance.

Re W (1981) 2 FLR 360; (1981) 131 NLJ 578 HC FamD On when wardship powers will be exercised in respect of child committed to local authority care by juvenile court.

Re W (1985) 129 SJ 269 CA Discharge of wardship order in respect of child in local authority care.

Re W [1979] 3 All ER 154; [1980] Fam 60; (1979) 143 JP 727; (1979) 123 SJ 553; [1979] 3 WLR 252 CA Natural parent cannot challenge merits of local authority decision to make child ward; authority may consider possible future adoption in deciding to disallow parental access to child.

Re W (1985) 129 SJ 523 HC FamD Girl aged just over seventeen who was beyond parental control committed to care of local authority.

Stockport Metropolitan Borough Council v B; Stockport Metropolitan Borough Council v L [1986] 2 FLR 80 HC FamD On need for wardship proceedings for care order to be processed swiftly.

W v Nottinghamshire County Council and another [1986] 1 FLR 565 CA Court will not allow third party to invoke wardship jurisdiction of court where local authority seeking replacement of care orders with supervision orders.

W v Shropshire County Council [1986] 1 FLR 359 (also CA) HC FamD Non-continuation of wardship over child in respect of whom local authoriy sought to bring care proceedings.

CARE/CUSTODY (welfare)

Cadman v Cadman (1982) 3 FLR 275; (1981) 131 NLJ 1310; (1981) 125 SJ 791 CA On role of court welfare officer: appointment of independent social worker to prepare report not in best interests of child so custody order discharged.

Dimino v Dimino [1989] 2 All ER 280 CA Judge's indorsing proposed order on court welfare officer's report before custody hearing a serious but not fatal irregularity.

Elder v Elder [1986] 1 FLR 610 CA On secrecy of judge's private interviews with children; eight month delay in preparation of welfare report deplored; pre-welfare report transfer of custody from mother not generally favoured.

Faulkner v Faulkner (1981) 2 FLR 115; (1979) 123 SJ 751 HC FamD Magistrates could give custody to mother despite welfare officer's contrary recommendation.

Hutchinson v Hutchinson (1981) 2 FLR 167 HC FamD Valid departure from welfare officer's recommendations where duly considered and reasons given; valid refusal of custody to mother where likely step-father a threat to child.

M v M [1990] FCR 80; [1989] 2 FLR 354 CA On when up-to-date welfare officer's report needed by CA; on role of such a report.

R v Birmingham Juvenile Court, ex parte G and others; R v Birmingham Juvenile Court, ex parte R [1989] 3 All ER 336; [1989] 2 FLR 454; [1990] 2 QB 573; (1989) 133 SJ 1089; [1989] 3 WLR 1024 CA Court must look to welfare of child/hear guardian ad litem before allowing local authority withdraw care order application.

R v West Malling Juvenile Court, ex parte K (1986) 150 JP 367; (1970) 130 SJ 650 HC QBD Case ought to hve been adjourned where parent in care action given social worker/guardian ad litem reports containing unexpected material on day of hearing.

Re A [1991] FCR 569; [1991] 2 FLR 394 CA On custody of young children: child's welfare paramount concern.

Re A (1980) 1 FLR 100; (1979) 123 SJ 553 HC FamD Independent welfare officer to ascertain wishes of child where sought; child's interests (of paramount importance) required that children remain in local authority care.

Re A [1993] 1 FCR 164 HC FamD Interim care order where appraisal of father as carer for child incomplete; no need here for welfare officer to prepare report in addition to that which guardian ad litem preparing.

Re C [1983] TLR 711 CA On undesirability of independent welfare reports; on extent of paramountcy of interests of child.

Re S [1992] 2 FCR 554; [1993] 1 FLR 110; (1992) 136 SJ LB 206 CA On roles of guardian ad litem/court welfare officer.

Re T (1980) 1 FLR 59 HC FamD Court when departing from welfare report recommendations must explain why.

S v Oxfordshire County Council [1993] 2 FCR 676; [1993] 1 FLR 452 HC FamD Justices to give reasons in care cases especially if departing from recommendation/report of guardian ad litem/welfare officer.

Scott v Scott [1986] 2 FLR 320; (1986) 150 JP 333 CA On role of court welfare service.

Smith v Smith (1971) 115 SJ 444 HC PDAD Ordering custody away from mother and outside jurisdiction a matter for earnest consideration; welfare officer's report ought to have been available to court deciding custody matters.

Thompson v Thomspon [1986] 1 FLR 212 CA On hearsay in welfare reports.

W v W [1988] FCR 640; [1988] 2 FLR 505 CA Reasons to be given where decide not to adopt course advocated in welfare officers' report.

Webb v Webb [1986] 1 FLR 462 CA On hearsay in welfare report.

CARE/CUSTODY (wishes of child)

Re M [1993] 2 FCR 721; [1994] 1 FLR 749 HC FamD On practice as regards determining what child wants in family law dispute concerning child.

Re P [1992] 2 FCR 681; [1992] TLR 234 CA On significance of what children desire when deciding care and control application.

Re S [1993] 2 All ER 683; [1993] Fam 242; (1992) 142 NLJ 1341; [1992] TLR 390; [1993] 2 WLR 775 CA Exceptionally court may not return child to foreign jurisdiction; question of whether child's wishes to be taken into account one of discretion.

CARE/CUSTODY (withdrawal of application)

London Borough of Southwark v B [1993] 2 FLR 559 CA On deciding whether to allow withdrawal of application for care.

R v Wandsworth West Juvenile Court, ex parte S (1983) 4 FLR 53 HC QBD Child's solicitor could withdraw application to discharge care order though parents had made application; withdrawal did not mean matter res judicata: could be started anew.

R v Wandsworth West Juvenile Court, ex parte S [1984] FLR 713 CA Child's solicitor ought not to have been allowed withdraw application to discharge care order which parents had made.

Re F [1993] 1 FCR 389; [1993] 2 FLR 9 HC FamD On allowing withdrawal of care application.

CARE/CUSTODY (witness)

R v B County Council, ex parte P [1991] 2 All ER 65; [1991] 1 FLR 470; [1991] 1 WLR 221 CA Local authority behaviour open to judicial review if unreasonable or unlawful; though child a compellable witness in care proceedings should not be called if contrary to best interests thereof.

R v Milton Keynes Juvenile Court, ex parte Russell (1979) 143 JP 373; [1979] 1 WLR 1062 HC QBD Parent could be allowed by magistrates to cross-examine witnesses for local authority in care action.

R v Sunderland Juvenile Court, ex parte G [1988] 2 All ER 34; [1988] FCR 193; [1988] 2 FLR 40 (also HC QBD); (1988) 132 SJ 372; [1988] 1 WLR 398 CA Parent may call independent social worker though court may exclude witness.

Re P [1991] FCR 337; (1991) 141 NLJ 163 CA Witness summons could be (but here was not) issued against child subject of care proceedings as was compellable witness; statements by child to police/medics admissible.

CARE/INTERIM (general)

Havering London Borough Council v S [1986] 1 FLR 489 HC FamD Interim care and control of child subject of wardship action not ordered to mother whose other children already subject of wardship actions as result of apparent abuse by mother's cohabitee.

CAUTION (general)

Re A [1989] 3 All ER 610; [1989] Fam 103; [1990] 1 FLR 86; [1989] 3 WLR 900 HC FamD Deciding whether to administer police caution to ward is purely for prosecuting body but court to be party to actual administration.

CHILD (publicity)

Ex parte Crook and another [1995] 1 All ER 537; [1995] 2 Cr App R 212; [1995] Crim LR 509; [1995] 2 FCR 153; (1995) 159 JP 295; (1989) 133 SJ 1577; [1995] 1 WLR 139 CA Judge may receive representations from all legitimate parties before restricting reports of proceedings; interests of children may outweigh freedom of press to publish.

CHILD ABUSE REGISTER (general)

R v East Sussex County Council, ex parte R [1990] FCR 873; [1991] 2 FLR 358 HC QBD Placing (and manner of placing) mother's name on child abuse register not unreasonable.

R v Norfolk County Council, ex parte M [1989] 2 All ER 359; [1989] FCR 667; [1989] QB 619; (1989) 133 SJ 1089 HC QBD Style of child abuse register by local authority and means of registration contrary to natural justice/open to judicial review.

CHILD OF THE FAMILY (foetus)

A v A [1974] 1 All ER 755; [1974] Fam 6; (1974) 118 SJ 77; [1974] 2 WLR 106 HC FamD Cannot treat unborn child as child of family.

CHILD OF THE FAMILY (general)

Bickley v Bickley [1965] 1 WLR 600 CA Deciding whether or not a child is child of family is a jurisdiction to be carefully exercised.

Carron v Carron [1984] FLR 805 CA Children of wife were children of family where lived with wife and her new husband in same household for four years.

D v D (1981) 2 FLR 93 CA Child living with grandparents and visiting mother/stepfather not child of latter family despite inclusion in stepfather's tax returns.

Davis v Davis (1980) 130 NLJ 885c CA Successful appeal against finding that child had been treated as member of the family.

Hodgkins v Hodgkins [1965] 3 All ER 164; (1965) 115 LJ 660; (1965) 109 SJ 899; [1965] 1 WLR 1448 CA Decree nisi stayed pending trial of whether particular child had been accepted as child of family.

M v M (1981) 2 FLR 39 CA Father's occasional behaviour towards child as though were own did not render child 'child of the family'; parties not 'family' after separation.

P (R) v P (P) [1969] 3 All ER 777 Assizes No acceptance of child as family if both parties do not agree (so no liability for maintenance).

R v R [1968] 2 All ER 608; (1968) 118 NLJ 588; (1967) 111 SJ 413; [1968] 2 WLR 1468 HC PDAD Cannot accept child as member of family unless possess all material facts.

Re M (1980) 130 NLJ 1120c CA Standards of ordinary person appropriate basis for deciding whether (unlike here) child was treated as member of the family.

S v S (1969) 119 NLJ 461t; (1969) 113 SJ 426 HC PDAD On what constitutes 'acceptance' of child into family.

Teeling v Teeling [1984] FLR 808 CA Wife's child a child of family as lived with wife/husband for six months; maintenance ordered minimal as responsibility husband assumed for child negligible.

W (RJ) v W (SJ) [1971] 3 All ER 303; [1972] Fam 152; (1972) 116 SJ 58; [1972] 2 WLR 371 Assizes Wife's child treated by husband as child of family is a child of the family.

CHILD SEX ABUSE (adoption)

Re B [1995] 1 FLR 904; [1994] TLR 671 HC FamD On proving child sex abuse (civil standard) such as to justify ending parental contact/freeing for adoption.

CHILD SEX ABUSE (case conference)

R v Harrow Borough Council, ex parte B [1989] FCR 407 HC QBD Not allowing parent to attend case conference (in context of child abuse investigation) not objectionable.

CHILD SEX ABUSE (general)

R v Devon County Council, ex parte L [1991] FCR 599; [1991] 2 FLR 541 HC QBD Failed application for review of local authority 'decision' to caution interested persons of its belief that applicant a child abuser.

R v Lewisham London Borough Council, ex parte P [1991] 3 All ER 529; [1991] FCR 684; [1991] 2 FLR 185; [1991] TLR 93; [1991] 1 WLR 308 HC QBD Parents/custodians may expect fair treatment from local authority/not to be named as alleged child abusers unless child's interests outweigh effects on alleged abuser and their family.

Re B [1995] 1 FLR 904; [1994] TLR 671 HC FamD On proving child sex abuse (civil standard) such as to justify ending parental contact/freeing for adoption.

Re T (No 2) [1997] 2 FCR 55 HC FamD Supervised contact ordered between father (guilty of 'inadvertent touching' of child) and child in case where entire procedure to alleged child sex abuse had been flawed.

R v Chief Constable for the North Wales Police Area Authority and others, ex parte AB and another (1997) 147 NLJ 1061; [1997] TLR 379 HC QBD Valid disclosure by police of information regarding certain paedophiles was lawful as was necessary for protection of public.

CHILD SEX ABUSE (interview)

R v Hove Juvenile Court, ex parte W [1989] FCR 286; [1989] 2 FLR 145 HC QBD On establishing by way of interview evidence that child has been victim of sex abuse.

Re A and B (No 1) (investigation of alleged abuse) [1995] 3 FCR 389 HC FamD On investigation of/child interviews concerning child sex abuse claims.

CHILD SEX ABUSE (register)

R v Devon County Council, ex parte D [1992] 2 FCR 766 HC QBD Local authority's placing child on child protection register and then informing father of what had done at same time telling him of right to appeal decision not unreasonable procedure.

R v Harrow London Borough Council, ex parte D [1990] 3 All ER 12; [1990] Fam 133; [1989] FCR 729; (1989) 133 SJ 1513 CA Placing of person on child abuse register where have made written/not oral representations not contrary to natural justice.

R v Harrow London Borough Council, ex parte D [1989] 2 FLR 51 HC QBD Refusal of judicial review of local authority placing children on 'at risk' register.

R v Norfolk County Council, ex parte X [1989] 2 FLR 120 HC QBD Placing of person on child abuse register was open to judicial review: registering decision quashed.

R v St Alban's Magistrates' Court, ex parte Read [1994] 1 FCR 50 HC QBD Inter partes hearing ordered to enable formerly registered child-minder to challenge her ex parte removal from the register.

CONTEMPT (abduction)

Adami v Adami (1929) 73 SJ 557 HC PDAD Contemnor-husband who had removed child to France released on condition that would not leave country without leave of court, would surrender passport/permit, would not himself, or through another, interfere with child.

Re B [1994] 2 FCR 1142; [1994] 2 FLR 479 CA Improper that Algerian father (abductor) who was not in contempt when attended court be committed to prison until children brought to British Embassy in Algiers.

Re G (1967) 111 SJ 702 HC ChD Contemnor to be released from prison once 'kidnapped' daughter returned to jurisdiction (child to be placed with foster mother pending wardship hearings).

CONTEMPT (access/contact)

C v C [1990] FCR 682; [1990] 1 FLR 462 CA Committal for mother who repeatedly refused to comply with access order made in husband's favour; CC judge rightly dealt with access issue despite commencement of HC wardship proceedings.

D v D [1991] FCR 323; [1991] 2 FLR 34; [1990] TLR 727 CA On committal for non-compliance with access order/arrangement; on inclusion of penal notice in access order.

L v L [1991] FCR 547 CA Improper dispensing with need for service of access order upon alleged contemnor; on proper procedure as regards dealing with contempt in context of access.

P v W [1984] 1 All ER 866; [1984] Fam 32; (1984) 128 SJ 171; [1984] 2 WLR 439 HC FamD Contempt a last stop measure in dealing with access order abuses; summons for such violations to be detailed so defendant aware of abuses charged.

Re P [1991] FCR 283; [1991] 1 FLR 280; [1990] TLR 694 CA Increased access and eventual return of stepfather to family despite earlier sexual abuse of step-child was justified; contempt of local authority solicitor whereby had sought to frustrate access arrangements purged by contemnor.

CONTEMPT (care/custody)

B (B) v B (M) [1969] 1 All ER 891; (1969) 119 NLJ 321 HC PDAD On appropriate way of dealing with father-contemnor who refused to surrender child to custody of mother.

Maynard v Maynard [1984] FLR 85 CA Court could (and here in interim custody application did) hear party in contempt.

Mozley-Stark v Mozley-Stark and Hitchins [1908-10] All ER 643; [1910] 79 LJP 98; (1909-10) 101 LTR 770; (1909-10) XXVI TLR 194 CA Non committal in circumstances for contempt of custody order.

CONTEMPT (contact)

A v N [1997] 2 FCR 475; [1997] 1 FLR 533 CA Committal of mother to prison for persistent non-compliance with contact order was valid — child's welfare not paramount concern in such cases.

CONTEMPT (general)

Hadkinson v Hadkinson [1952] 2 All ER 567 CA Court will not hear contemnor who has disobeyed order regarding child until contempt purged.

Re B [1994] 2 FCR 1142; [1994] 2 FLR 479 CA Improper that Algerian father (abductor) who was not in contempt when attended court be committed to prison until children brought to British Embassy in Algiers.

CONTEMPT (ward)

Re H's Settlement; H v H [1909] 2 Ch 260; [1909] 78 LJCh 745 HC ChD Court can commit ward of court to prison for contempt.

Re W and others [1989] 1 FLR 246 HC FamD Newspapers and their editors found (using criminal standard of proof) not to be guilty of contempt in breaching injunction on publication of articles regarding wardship action.

CORPORAL PUNISHMENT (general)

R v Ferguson (Robert) (1969) 53 Cr App R 637 CA In chastising their children immigrant parents must conform with British standards.

CRIMINAL (abandonment)

Pallin v Buckland (1911-13) XXII Cox CC 545; (1911) 75 JP 362 HC KBD Accused found as matter of fact not to have run away and left children.

R v Boulden [1957] Crim LR 182 Sessions Successful prosecution for abandonment/neglect of children: on what constitutes abandonment/neglect.

R v Boulden (Edward Ernest) (1957) 41 Cr App R 105; [1957] Crim LR 322 CCA On what constitutes 'abandonment' of child under Children and Young Persons Act 1933, s 1(1).

Watson and another v Nikolaisen [1955] 2 All ER 427; (1955) 119 JP 419; (1955) 105 LJ 346; [1955] 2 QB 286; (1955) 99 SJ 370; [1955] 2 WLR 1187 HC QBD Not abandonment of child to give over to people whom trust.

CRIMINAL (abduction)

R v Alexander (1913-14) XXIII Cox CC 138; (1912) 76 JP 215; (1912-13) 107 LTR 240; (1911-12) XXVIII TLR 200 CCA Conviction quashed where trial judge actively encouraged accused to plead guilty to abduction charge.

R v Dootson (Robert) (1995) 16 Cr App R (S) 223; [1994] Crim LR 702 CA Abduction of child not a sex offence under Criminal Justice Act 1991.

R v Jarvis (James) (1901-07) XX Cox CC 249 Assizes Not abduction to passively acquiesce to proposal of under-sixteen year old unmarried girl to join her in her leaving home.

R v Kauffman (1904) 68 JP 189 CCC On elements of offence of abducting under-eighteen year old girl (Criminal Law Amendment Act 1885, s 7).

CRIMINAL (abortion)

R v Lumley (1911-13) XXII Cox CC 635; (1912) 76 JP 208 CCC Abortionist guilty of murder/manslaughter if did/did not (nor could not reasonably) consider that death or grievous bodily harm would result from actions.

R v Spicer (1955) 39 Cr App R 189 Assizes Could be convicted for procuring miscarriage where sought so to do though means used could not be successful.

R v Starkie (1921-22) 16 Cr App R 61; (1922) 86 JP 74; [1922] 2 KB 275; [1922] 91 LJCL 663; (1921-22) 66 SJ 300; (1921-22) XXXVIII TLR 181; (1922) WN (I) 10 CCA Admissibility of evidence pertaining to alternative counts in criminal abortion charge.

CRIMINAL (assault)

Marsh and another v Hodgson [1974] Crim LR 35 CA Parents found jointly liable for unexplained injuries to their infant child.

R v Hilton (John James) [1925] All ER 396; (1925-26) 19 Cr App R 29 CCA Interpretation of Children Act 1908, s 12(1).

R v Smith (David George) [1985] Crim LR 42 CA On relevance of intention to determination whether physical chastisement of child constituted assault occasioning actual bodily harm.

CRIMINAL (child sex abuse)

Bradford City Metropolitan Council v K [1990] Fam 140; [1990] 2 WLR 532 HC FamD Statements of child to teacher/foster parent regarding sexual abuse by family member not part of res gestae and inadmissible in later care proceedings as was hearsay evidence.

Cleveland County Council v A; Cleveland County Council v B [1988] FCR 593 HC FamD On establishing that child has in fact been sexually abused.

Cleveland County Council v D [1988] FCR 615 HC FamD On establishing that child has in fact been sexually abused.

H v H; K v K [1989] 3 All ER 740; [1990] Fam 86; [1989] FCR 356; (1990) 134 SJ 21; [1989] 3 WLR 933 CA Balance of probabilities the standard of proof in child abuse hearings; undue weight given to social worker's interviews with child (but was admissible); unsworn evidence of child inadmissible in matrimonial hearings; hearsay evidence inadmissible in matrimonial action unless parties elect otherwise.

R v Hampshire County Council, ex parte K and another [1990] 2 All ER 129; [1990] FCR 545; [1990] 1 FLR 330; [1990] 2 QB 71; (1989) 133 SJ 1605; [1990] 2 WLR 649 HC QBD Child's interest requires parents be given every opportunity to defend themselves including access to all relevant material.

R v K (DT) [1993] Crim LR 281; [1993] 2 FLR 181; (1992) 136 SJ LB 328; [1992] TLR 591 CA Improper to refuse disclosure of video (interview) evidence without first ascertaining relevance/significance of same.

Re G [1992] 2 FCR 713; [1993] 1 FLR 103 CA Issue estoppel/res judicata inapplicable to Criminal Injuries Compensation Board; compensation could be available to child sex abuse victim whose assailant was not convicted.

Re H [1991] TLR 291 CA On deciding cases concerning child sex abuse allegations.

Re H and R [1996] 1 FCR 509 HL On establishing that child sex abuse has taken place.

CRIMINAL (child-stealing)

R v Austin and others [1981] 1 All ER 374; (1981) 72 Cr App R 104; [1980] Crim LR 716; (1981) 145 JP 145; (1981) 131 NLJ 68 CA Person with right to possession of child exempt from child-stealing but not paid accessories.

R v Burns (James); R v Ralph (Michael Peter); R v Jackson (Stephen Ronald); R v Burns (Sidney) (1984) 79 Cr App R 173 CA Person could be prosecuted for conspiracy to commit offence though immune from prosecution for substantive offence.

R v Jones (James William) [1973] Crim LR 621 CrCt Was not taking child out of possession of parents (contrary to Sexual Offences Act 1956, s 20) to seek to bring girls for walk, aim being to indecently assault them.

R v Jones (William) (1911-13) XXII Cox CC 212; (1911) 75 JP 272 CCC Must prove accused intended to permanently withdraw child from parent to sustain conviction for stealing away child under fourteen.

R v Pryce [1972] Crim LR 307 CA On unlawful detention contrary to the Offences against the Person Act 1861, s 56.

CRIMINAL (concealment of birth)

R v Kersey (Maud) (1907-09) XXI Cox CC 690 Assizes Murder/concealment of birth conviction not possible/possible on evidence though no dead body.

CRIMINAL (conspiracy)

R v Duguid (1907-09) XXI Cox CC 200; (1906) 70 JP 294; (1906) 41 LJ 335; [1906] 75 LJKB 470; (1906) XCIV LTR 887; (1905-06) 50 SJ 465; (1905-06) XXII TLR 506; (1906) WN (I) 100 CCR Was criminal conspiracy on part of person agreeing with mother to remove her child from lawful custody.

CRIMINAL (cruelty)

Butler v Gregory (1901-02) XVIII TLR 370 HC KBD Father of illegitimate child who did not have care/custody of child nor had bastardy proceedings brought against him not father for purposes of Prevention of Cruelty to Children Act 1894, s 23.

Davidson v Davidson [1953] 1 All ER 611; [1953] 1 WLR 387 HC PDAD Abnormal sexual practices to be precisely specified by justices; inadequate consideration of need for corroboration/possibility of acquiescence justified re-trial.

R v Andrews (Paul) (1986) 82 Cr App R 148 CA Wilful neglect of child properly inferred from circumstantial evidence.

R v Bowditch [1991] Crim LR 831 CA On burden of proof as regards proving cruelty to child under Children and Young Persons Act 1933.

R v Byers (Jessie) (1910) 4 Cr App R 5 CCA Manslaughter of child by means of cruel treatment — even though post-cruelty betterment in child's condition.

R v C and another [1990] TLR 344 CA Failed prosecution for cruelty to child where was inadequate evidence of guiltiness.

R v Chalker (Kate) (1910) 4 Cr App R 2 CCA Manslaughter of child by means of consistently cruel treatment.

R v Connor (1907-09) XXI Cox CC 628; (1908) 72 JP 212; [1908] 2 KB 26; (1908) 43 LJ 283; [1908] 77 LJCL 527; (1908) XCVIII LTR 932; (1907-08) 52 SJ 444; (1907-08) XXIV TLR 483 CCR Father in desertion guilty of wilful neglect (failed to provide food/money).

R v Gibbins (David John) [1977] Crim LR 741 CrCt On elements of offence whereby 'expose[d]' child to unnecessary suffering/injury to health contrary to Children and Young Persons Act 1933, s 1(1).

R v Hale (1901-07) XX Cox CC 739; (1905) 69 JP 83; [1905] 1 KB 126; (1904-05) XCI LTR 839; (1904-05) 49 SJ 68; (1904-05) XXI TLR 70; (1904-05) 53 WR 400 CCR Child need not be present at trial concerning cruelty thereto unless evidence of child needed.

R v Hatton (1926-30) XXVIII Cox CC 43; (1925) 89 JP 164; [1925] 2 KB 322; (1925) 60 LJ 705; [1925] 94 LJCL 863; (1925) 133 LTR 735; (1924-25) XLI TLR 637; (1925) WN (I) 199 CCA Interpretation of phrase 'wilfully assaults' in Children Act 1908, s 12(1).

R v Londesborough [1968] Crim LR 171 CA Eighteen months' imprisonment for assault occasioning actual bodily harm to three year old (albeit that offender-mother was poor/of low intelligence/badly brought up).

R v Sheppard (James Martin) (1980) 70 Cr App R 210 CA Must be intentional neglect of child where charged with cruelty to child by reason of wilful neglect.

R v Wills [1990] Crim LR 714 CA On what is meant by treatment of child 'likely' to cause harm in Children and Young Persons Act 1933, s 1.

R v Young (Tara Moira Lisa) (1993) 97 Cr App R 280; (1993) 137 SJ LB 32; [1992] TLR 641 CA Where jury convinced overall that was cruelty (even though disagree on specific incidents) can convict of cruelty to children.

CRIMINAL (encouraging unlawful carnal knowledge of under-sixteen year old)

R v Chainey [1911-13] All ER 701; (1913-14) XXIII Cox CC 620; (1914) 78 JP 127; [1914] 1 KB 137; (1913) 48 LJ 673; [1914] 83 LJKB 306; (1913-14) 109 LTR 752; (1913-14) XXX TLR 51; (1913) WN (I) 318 CCA Criminal neglect of (under sixteen year old) child socialising with immoral persons did not mean guilty of causing/encouraging unlawful carnal knowledge of same.

R v Moon (Frederick); R v Moon (Emily) (1910) 4 Cr App R 171; [1910] 1 KB 818; (1910) 45 LJ 221; (1910) 79 LJKB 505 CCA Not offence under Children Act 1908, s 17 to encourage seduction of girl already seduced.

CRIMINAL (fine)

Leeds City Council v West Yorkshire Metropolitan Police and others [1982] 1 All ER 274; [1983] 1 AC 29; (1982) 74 Cr App R 336; (1982) 146 JP 154; [1982] 2 WLR 186 HL Local authority not liable for fines imposed on child in care nor are parents of that child unless local authority temporarily transfers powers of supervision to them.

CRIMINAL (gross indecency)

R v Francis (Colin Leslie) (1989) 88 Cr App R 127; [1988] Crim LR 528 CA Indecency with or towards children contrary to Indecency with Children Act 1960, s 1(1) requires that act be aimed at children and that accused pleased that children watching.

CRIMINAL (indecent assault on under-sixteen year old)

R v Blackman (John) (1928-29) 21 Cr App R 132 CCA 'Reasonable belief that girl over sixteen' defence open on charge of carnal knowledge did not preclude conviction of under twenty-three year old for indecent assault.

R v Keech (Herbert Joshua) (1928-29) 21 Cr App R 125 CCA Improper that 'reasonable belief that girl over sixteen' defence open on charge of carnal knowledge but not indecent assault (Criminal Law Amendment Act 1922, s 2); no general guidelines on sentencing offenders convicted of underage indecent assault.

R v Maughan (Reginald) (1932-34) 24 Cr App R 130 CCA Not defence to charge of indecent assault on under-sixteen year old that genuinely believed was over sixteen.

CRIMINAL (indecent photographs)

R v Graham-Kerr (John) (1989) 88 Cr App R 302 (1989) 153 JP 171; (1988) 132 SJ 1299; [1988] 1 WLR 1098 CA On elements of crime of taking indecent photographs of child contrary to Protection of Children Act 1978, s 1(1).

R v Owen (Charles William) (1988) 86 Cr App R 291; [1988] Crim LR 120; (1987) 131 SJ 1696; [1988] 1 WLR 134 CA Jury could have regard to age of child in photograph when deciding if photograph obscene: did not have to decide from intrinsic nature of photograph.

CRIMINAL (infanticide)

R v O'Donoghue (1926-30) XXVIII Cox CC 461; (1927) 91 JP 199; (1927) 64 LJ 378; (1928) 97 LJCL 303; (1928) 138 LTR 240; (1927) 71 SJ 897; (1927) WN (I) 289/297 CCA Verdict of infanticide unavailable as child not newborn/over one month old.

R v Smith (KA) [1983] Crim LR 739 CrCt Could be convicted of attempted infanticide under Infanticide Act 1938.

CRIMINAL (kidnap)

R v C [1991] 2 FLR 252; [1990] TLR 714 CA Conviction of father (who took own child outside jurisdiction without consent of mother-joint custodian) for child kidnapping (common law offence)/abduction quashed/upheld.

CRIMINAL (liability for acts of child/young person)

Bowers and another v Smith; Evans and another v Smith; Flack and another v Smith [1953] 1 All ER 320; (1953) 117 JP 106; (1953) 97 SJ 99; [1953] 1 WLR 297 HC QBD Child/young person committing grossly indecent acts without parent's/guardian's knowledge does not justify requiring parent/guardian to enter recognisance to be proper parent, or placing child/young person on probation.

D v Director of Public Prosecutions and other appeals [1995] Crim LR 748; [1995] 3 FCR 725; [1995] 2 FLR 502; (1995) 145 NLJ 560; [1995] TLR 218 HC QBD Compensation orders against local authority quashed as either no finding that local authority had none done all possible to safeguard public/local authority had behaved satisfactorily.

R v Croydon Juvenile Court Justices, ex parte Croydon London Borough Council [1973] 1 All ER 476; [1973] Crim LR 108; (1973) 117 SJ 70; (1973) 137 JP 283; (1972) 122 NLJ 1112t; [1973] QB 426; [1973] 2 WLR 61 HC QBD Ordering local authority to pay fine of child in its care permissible.

CRIMINAL (manslaughter)

R v Byers (Jessie) (1910) 4 Cr App R 5 CCA Manslaughter of child by means of cruel treatment — even though post-cruelty betterment in child's condition.

R v Chalker (Kate) (1910) 4 Cr App R 2 CCA Manslaughter of child by means of consistently cruel treatment.

R v Izod (1901-07) XX Cox CC 690 Assizes Must be criminally negligent to new-born child after born to sustain conviction for manslaughter of same through neglect.

CRIMINAL (murder)

R v Kersey (Maud) (1907-09) XXI Cox CC 690 Assizes Murder/concealment of birth conviction not possible/possible on evidence though no dead body.

R v Walter Gibbins and Edith Rose Proctor (1917-18) 13 Cr App R 134; (1918) 82 JP 287 CCA On neglect of child as basis for conviction of murder of same.

CRIMINAL (neglect)

Brooks v Blount [1922] All ER 699; (1921-25) XXVII Cox CC 399; (1923) 87 JP 64; [1923] 1 KB 257; [1923] 92 LJCL 302; (1923) 128 LTR 607; (1922-23) 67 SJ 299; (1922-23) XXXIX TLR 168; (1923) WN (I) 14 HC KBD Legal presumption that child in father's custody not displaced by latter entering separation agreement whereby wife paid to take care of child in her custody: father can still be convicted for neglect of child.

Liverpool Society for the Prevention of Cruelty to Children v Jones [1914-15] All ER 1073; (1914-15) XXIV Cox CC 434; (1915) 79 JP 20; [1914] 3 KB 813; (1914) 49 LJ 380; [1915] 84 LJKB 222; (1914-15) 111 LTR 806; (1913-14) 58 SJ 723; (1913-14) XXX TLR 584; (1914) WN (I) 270 HC KBD Possible that putative father could be guilty of wilful neglect of child (contrary to Children Act 1908, s 12).

Poole v Stokes [1914-15] All ER 1083; (1914-15) XXIV Cox CC 169; (1914) 78 JP 231; (1914) 49 LJ 159; (1914) 110 LTR 1020; (1913-14) XXX TLR 371; (1914) WN (I) 123 HC KBD Husband could be convicted of wilful neglect where separated wife acting as agent failed to look after children properly.

Price v Price (1926-27) XLIII TLR 609 HC PDAD On timing of bringing of action for wilful neglect to maintain.

R v Boulden [1957] Crim LR 182 Sessions Successful prosecution for abandonment/neglect of children: on what constitutes abandonment/neglect.

R v Connor (1907-09) XXI Cox CC 628; (1908) 72 JP 212; [1908] 2 KB 26; (1908) 43 LJ 283; [1908] 77 LJCL 527; (1908) XCVIII LTR 932; (1907-08) 52 SJ 444; (1907-08) XXIV TLR 483 CCR Father in desertion guilty of wilful neglect (failed to provide food/money).

R v Gibbins (Walter) and Proctor (Edith Rose) (1917-18) 13 Cr App R 134; (1918) 82 JP 287 CCA On neglect of child as basis for conviction of murder of same.

R v Hayles (1969) 53 Cr App R 36; [1969] Crim LR 24; (1968) 118 NLJ 1029t; [1969] 1 QB 364; (1968) 112 SJ 860; [1968] 3 WLR 1106 CA Could be convicted of ill-treatment of child where what had done constituted neglect of same (Children and Young Persons Act 1933, s 1(1)).

R v Perch (Edmund) (1908-09) XXV TLR 401 CCA Finding that were guilty of wilful neglect of children not affected by jury's rider that accused acted through ignorance.

R v Tonks (1915-17) XXV Cox CC 228; (1914-15) 11 Cr App R 284; (1916) 80 JP 165; [1916] 1 KB 443; [1916] 85 LJKB 396; (1915-16) 60 SJ 122; (1915-16) XXXII TLR 137; (1915) WN (I) 387 CCA Not autrefois convict where prosecuted for manslaughter of child (who died from neglect) where had been convicted of wilful neglect of child.

R v Williams (John Owen) (1910) 4 Cr App R 89; (1909-10) XXVI TLR 290 CCA On what constitutes exposure/abandonment of child (Children Act 1908, s 12(1)).

R v Young (Tara Moira Lisa) (1993) 97 Cr App R 280; (1993) 137 SJ LB 32; [1992] TLR 641 CA Where jury convinced overall that was cruelty (even though disagree on specific incidents) can convict of cruelty to children.

CRIMINAL (notice of intended prosecution)

Director of Public Prosecutions v Cottier [1996] 3 All ER 126; [1996] 2 Cr App R 411; [1996] Crim LR 804; [1996] 1 WLR 826 HC QBD Notice to local authority/probation officer of proceedings against children and young persons required once decision to proceed but need not necessarily precede court appearance.

CRIMINAL (probation)

Leicester Corporation v Stoke-on-Trent Corporation (1918-21) XXVI Cox CC 377; (1919) 120 LTR 320 HC KBD On place of residence of young offender in breach of probation order.

CRIMINAL (publicity)

R v Crown Court at Southwark, ex parte Godwin and others [1991] 3 All ER 818; (1992) 94 Cr App R 34; (1992) 156 JP 86; (1991) 141 NLJ 963; [1992] QB 190; (1991) 135 SJ LB 28; [1991] 3 WLR 689 CA Order specifying particular name not to be published so as to protect child an invalid order.

CRIMINAL (reform school order)

Stoke-on-Trent Borough Council v Cheshire County Council [1914-15] All ER 441; (1915-16) 113 LTR 750 HC KBD Person resides where lives (for purpose of Children Act 1908, s 74).

CRIMINAL (residence)

London County Council v Wiltshire County Council (1926-30) XXVIII Cox CC 416; (1927) 137 LTR 526; (1926-27) XLIII TLR 563 HC KBD Young offender held to reside in area where committed offence if no contrary evidence.

CRIMINAL (restriction order)

R v Lee [1993] 2 All ER 170; [1993] Crim LR 65; (1992) 136 SJ LB 222; [1993] 1 WLR 103 CA Court of Appeal may not impose restriction order where CrCt has decided otherwise save in judicial review.

CRIMINAL (sale of cigarettes to under-aged youth)

St Helens MBC v Hill (1992) 156 JP 602; [1992] TLR 150 HC QBD Sale of cigarettes to under-aged youth a strict liability offence: absent owner properly convicted for actions of worker.

CRIMINAL (sexual abuse)

Re P [1989] Crim LR 897 CA Inadmissible evidence does not become admissible just because is put to accused party during cross-examination.

CRIMINAL (street-trading)

Vann v Eatough [1935] All ER 911; (1935) 79 SJ 840 HC KBD Employment of under-age person as street-trader.

CRIMINAL (unlawful carnal knowledge)

R v Banks [1916-17] All ER 356; (1915-17) XXV Cox CC 535; (1916) 80 JP 432; [1916] 2 KB 621; [1916] 85 LJKB 1657; (1916-17) 115 LTR 457; (1916) WN (I) 281 CCA Must show not that could but did believe girl over sixteen to raise defence on that ground.

R v Chapman (1931-34) XXIX Cox CC 407; (1931-32) 23 Cr App R 45; (1931) 95 JP 205; [1931] 2 KB 606; (1931) 100 LJCL 562; (1932) 146 LTR 120; (1931) 75 SJ 660; (1930-31) XLVII TLR 620 CCA Proviso in Criminal Law Amendment Act 1922, s 2 extends reasonable belief that girl over sixteen defence to men who have not reached the age of twenty-four.

R v Chapman [1958] 3 All ER 143; (1958) 42 Cr App R 257; [1958] Crim LR 623; (1958) 122 JP 462; (1958) 108 LJ 586; [1959] 1 QB 100; (1958) 102 SJ 621 CCA 'Unlawful' sex under Sexual Offences Act 1956 s 19(1) means sex outside marriage.

R v Crocker (William) (1922-23) 17 Cr App R 45 CCA Leave to appeal granted in unlawful carnal knowledge case where corroboration point arose.

R v Crocker (William) (1922-23) 17 Cr App R 46 CCA Girl's evidence need not be corroborated in unlawful carnal knowledge case.

R v Dharma (Chandra); R v Slater; R v Hutchinson; R v Court (1905) 69 JP 39; (1905) 40 LJ 238; (1905) XCII LTR 700; (1904-05) 49 SJ 366; (1904-05) XXI TLR 353 CCR Extension by Prevention of Cruelty of Children Act 1904 to limitation on bringing prosecutions under Criminal Law Amendment Act 1885 operated retrospectively as did not create new offence.

R v Fisher (Colin); R v Marshall (Christopher); R v Mitchell (George) (1969) 113 SJ 70; [1969] 2 WLR 452 Assizes Jury cannot convict accused of sex with under-sixteen year old girl where accused being tried for rape.

R v Hewitt (1926-30) XXVIII Cox CC 101; (1925-26) 19 Cr App R 64; (1926) 90 JP 68; (1926) 134 LTR 157; (1925-26) XLII TLR 216; (1925) WN (I) 292 CCA Previous assault on same girl admissible in unlawful carnal knowledge of under sixteen/over fourteen year old girl — time lapse since earlier assault reduces weight of evidence.

R v Marsh (Percy Harold) (1925-26) 19 Cr App R 27 CCA Accused's silence/keeping of letter sent by prosecutrix not corroborative of latter's claim in sexual offence case.

R v Marsh (Ronald William Frank) (1948-49) 33 Cr App R 185 CCA Evidence of previous confession of guilt/sentencing for indecent assault on child admissible in later charge for carnal knowledge of same child.

R v Rider [1954] Crim LR 49; (1954) 118 JP 73 Assizes On what constitutes a charge when deciding whether accused to have benefit of first-time charge proviso in prosecution for having carnal knowledge of under-sixteen year old (Criminal Law Amendment Act 1922, s 2).

R v Sharp (Edward George) (1931-32) 23 Cr App R 7 CCA Six weeks' detention more than appropriate for unlawful carnal knowledge of precocious under-sixteen year old who looked and acted over sixteen.

R v Wakeley [1918-19] All ER 1157; (1918-21) XXVI Cox CC 569; (1920) 84 JP 31; [1920] 1 KB 688; [1920] 89 LJCL 97; (1920) 122 LTR 623 CCA Prosecution began when information laid and information laid within six months of offence so prosecution in time.

CRIMINAL (vaccination)

Over v Harwood (1899-1900) XVI TLR 163; (1899-1900) 48 WR 608 HC QBD On burden of proof where person charged with disobedience of order to have child vaccinated.

Pym v Wilsher (1901) 36 LJ 310; (1900-01) 45 SJ 578; (1900-01) XVII TLR 558; (1901) WN (I) 126; (1900-01) 49 WR 654 HC KBD Prosecution procedures under Vaccination Act 1898 did not apply to failure to vaccinate which occurred during lifetime of Vaccination Act 1867.

CRIMINAL (ward)

Re J [1984] FLR 535; (1984) 128 SJ 280; [1984] TLR 21 HC FamD Pyschiatric test/reports unnecessary/unavailable where sought by mother as evidence on which to challenge prospective testimony of ward in criminal case.

CRIMINAL (wilful neglect)

Oakey v Jackson [1911-13] All ER 681; (1913-14) XXIII Cox CC 734; (1914) 78 JP 87; [1914] 1 KB 216; [1914] 83 LJKB 712; (1914) 110 LTR 41; (1913-14) XXX TLR 92 HC KBD Father preventing surgical operation on child for no good reason could be charged with wilful neglect.

R v Andrews (Paul) (1986) 82 Cr App R 148 CA Wilful neglect of child properly inferred from circumstantial evidence.

R v Sheppard (James Martin) (1980) 70 Cr App R 210 CA Must be intentional neglect of child where charged with cruelty to child by reason of wilful neglect.

R v Sheppard and another [1980] 3 All ER 899; [1981] AC 394; (1981) 72 Cr App R 82; [1981] Crim LR 171; (1981) 145 JP 65; (1980) 130 NLJ 1144; (1980) 124 SJ 864; [1980] 3 WLR 960 HL Wilful neglect not strict liability offence; must be deliberate/reckless failure to provide proper medical care.

R v Watson and Watson (1959) 43 Cr App R 111 Assizes Where husband and wife living together wife can be convicted of manslaughter of child by wilful neglect.

DAMAGES (general)

M v Lester [1966] 1 All ER 207; [1966] 1 WLR 134 HC QBD On damages paid to infants; on Court of Protection.

DIVORCE (child)

Leech v Leech and Dolleman (1972) 116 SJ 274 HC FamD School report desirable (though not given in instant case) when court asked to decide on educational provision for child.

McKernan v McKernan (1970) 114 SJ 284 HC PDAD Must be fairly permanent arrangements in respect of children before court (in divorce action) can declare itself to be satisfied.

DIVORCE (infant)

Stanga v Stanga [1954] 2 All ER 16; (1953) 97 SJ 607; [1953] 3 WLR 609 HC PDAD Non-compliance with serving of notice on infant requirements necessitated re-hearing.

DIVORCE (welfare)

Brown v Matthews [1990] 2 All ER 155; [1990] Ch 662; [1990] 2 WLR 879 CA Court welfare officer's report may be disclosed in later case if necessary for fair trial.

EDUCATION (general)

C v C [1966] 3 All ER 51; (1965-66) 116 NLJ 1204; (1966) 110 SJ 634; [1966] 1 WLR 1418 HC PDAD On obtaining information regarding child's education.

EVIDENCE (corroboration)

R v Crocker (William) (1922-23) 17 Cr App R 46 CCA Girl's evidence need not be corroborated in unlawful carnal knowledge case.

EVIDENCE (general)

B v B [1994] 2 FCR 667; (1994) 138 SJ LB 119; [1994] TLR 271 CA On procedure as regards hearing of children's cases/interviewing of children by judge.

D v D (1981) 2 FLR 74 CA Removal of child against her wishes from father's custody/placing with mother where other child in father's custody a possible bad influence was justifiable; whether to interview child purely a matter for judge.

H v H; K v K [1989] 3 All ER 740; [1990] Fam 86; [1989] FCR 356; (1990) 134 SJ 21; [1989] 3 WLR 933 CA Balance of probabilities the standard of proof in child abuse hearings; undue weight given to social worker's interviews with child (but was admissible); unsworn evidence of child inadmissible in matrimonial hearings; heasay evidence inadmissible in matrimonial action unless parties elect otherwise.

Hunt v Newcombe (1983) 4 FLR 482 CA Interviews with children a discretionary matter for judge; interviews with children a discretionary matter for judge.

R v Dunne (James) (1928-29) 21 Cr App R 176 CCA Conviction quashed where judge conducted unlawful out-of-court examination of child to test whether suitable for her to take oath.

EVIDENCE (hearsay)

Bradford City Metropolitan Council v K [1990] Fam 140; [1990] 2 WLR 532 HC FamD Statements of child to teacher/foster parent regarding sexual abuse by family member not part of res gestae and inadmissible in later care proceedings as was hearsay evidence.

EVIDENCE (interview)

B v B [1994] 1 FCR 809; [1994] 2 FLR 713 HC FamD On interviewing childen where sexual abuse suspected.

Bradford City Metropolitan Council v K [1990] Fam 140; [1990] 2 WLR 532 HC FamD Statements of child to teacher/foster parent regarding sexual abuse by family member not part of res gestae and inadmissible in later care proceedings as was hearsay evidence.

R v Hove Juvenile Court, ex parte W [1989] FCR 286; [1989] 2 FLR 145 HC QBD On establishing by way of interview evidence that child has been victim of sex abuse.

R v K (DT) [1993] Crim LR 281; [1993] 2 FLR 181; (1992) 136 SJ LB 328; [1992] TLR 591 CA Improper to refuse disclosure of video (interview) evidence without first ascertaining relevance/significance of same.

Re B [1990] FCR 469 HC FamD Court's authorisation unnecessary to arrest/detention of over seventeen year old ward.

EVIDENCE (statement)

Bradford City Metropolitan Council v K [1990] Fam 140; [1990] 2 WLR 532 HC FamD Statements of child to teacher/foster parent regarding sexual abuse by family member not part of res gestae and inadmissible in later care proceedings as was hearsay evidence.

EVIDENCE (witness)

R v Hale (1901-07) XX Cox CC 739; (1905) 69 JP 83; (1904-05) XCI LTR 839; (1904-05) 49 SJ 68; (1904-05) 53 WR 400 CCR Child need not be present at trial concerning cruelty thereto unless evidence of child needed.

R v Highbury Corner Magistrates' Court, ex parte Deering [1997] 1 FLR 683; (1997) 161 JP 138 HC QBD Balancing respective interests of accused and child-witness to be done not when making out witness summons but when child to be called.

Re B [1996] 1 FCR 229 HC FamD Reliability of child witnesses ultimately a matter for court, not expert witnesses; on prorelevancy of past behaviour to determining whether child likely to suffer significant harm in future.

Re K and others [1988] 1 All ER; [1988] Fam 1; [1988] 1 FLR 435; (1988) 152 JP 185; (1987) 131 SJ 1697; [1987] 3 WLR 1233 HC FamD Wardship court will not intervene in existing child abuse case; no leave necessary for child to give evidence against parents.

EXCLUSION ORDER (child)

Egan v Egan [1975] 2 All ER 167; [1975] Ch 218; (1975) 119 SJ 220; [1975] 2 WLR 503 HC ChD Injunction available to restrain child entering parent's house.

EXCLUSION ORDER (general)

M v M [1988] FCR 260; [1988] 1 FLR 225 CA Custody decisions to be based on findings of fact (where facts controverted); cannot make ouster order under domestic violence legislation where parties not living together as man and wife.

Re T; T v T [1987] 1 FLR 181 CA HC not in error in considering child's best interests in wardship application and then relying on that as one of four criteria justifying granting of ouster order.

Re W and W (1983) 4 FLR 686 CA Interim custody order bad for instability caused to children; refusal of exclusion order (that would allow wife/children to return to home from women's refuge).

FAMILY ASSISTANCE ORDER (general)

S v P [1997] 2 FCR 185; [1997] 2 FLR 277; [1997] TLR 55 HC FamD Family assistance order that would require local authority to escort children to/from prison where father incarcerated unmerited; indirect contact ordered while father in prison subject to later review upon father's release/re-establishment of life; parental responsibility on behalf of imprisoned father would be too much too soon.

FERTILITY (general)

R v Ethical Committee of St Mary's Hospital (Manchester), ex parte H [1988] 1 FLR 512 HC QBD Failed application for review of decision not to allow party avail of in vitro fertilisation treatment.

FERTILITY (paternity)

Re M [1997] 2 FLR 90 HC FamD Estoppel inapplicable when dealing with question of parentage; non-biological father of child conceived by wife by way of artificial insemination before the Human Fertilisation and Embryology Act 1990 was enacted was not 'parent' of child for purposes of the Child Support Act 1991.

FILTHY CHILD (general)

London County Council v Stansell (1934-39) XXX Cox CC 335 HC KBD Parent liable where child in filthy condition is father if parents living together.

FINANCIAL PROVISION (assessment)

Grantham v Grantham (1948) WN (I) 329 HC KBD On what constituted 'net income' after which level being attained maintenance payable for child under covenant between husband and wife.

FINANCIAL PROVISION (child of the family)

Jobson v Jobson (1964) 108 SJ 56 HC PDAD Inappropriate to look to degree to which father had taken on responsibility for child when deciding whether child accepted as part of family.

FINANCIAL PROVISION (general)

A v A [1995] 1 FCR 309; [1994] 1 FLR 657 HC FamD On financial provision for child; property adjustment order generally inappropriate way of providing for independent child.

FINANCIAL PROVISION (legitimacy)

Galloway v Galloway (Ex parte) [1955] 3 All ER 429; [1956] AC 299; (1955) 105 LJ 728; (1955) 99 SJ 792; [1955] 3 WLR 723 HL 'Children' in Matrimonial Causes Act 1950 includes illegitimate children.

Galloway v Galloway [1954] 2 All ER 143; (1954) 104 LJ 328; (1954) 98 SJ 336; [1954] 2 WLR 980 CA Custody/maintenance action unavailable in respect of child born outside marriage who cannot be legitimated.

FIT PERSON ORDER (general)

R v Darlington Corporation Juvenile Court, ex parte West Hartlepool Corporation [1957] 1 All ER 398; [1957] Crim LR 322; (1957) 101 SJ 172; [1957] 1 WLR 363 HC QBD Fit person order must contain consent of local authority to making thereof.

Re T (AJJ) [1970] 1 All ER 512; [1970] Ch 336; (1970) 134 JP 151; (1970) 120 NLJ 224; (1969) 113 SJ 980; [1970] 2 WLR 433 HC ChD Court will not interfere with local authority discretion as fit person unless acts improperly/contrary to statute.

Re T (AJJ) [1970] 2 All ER 865; [1970] Ch 688; (1970) 134 JP 611; (1970) 114 SJ 550; [1970] 3 WLR 315 CA Only exceptionally will displace local authority discretion as fit person.

FOREIGN ACCESS/CUSTODY ORDER (general)

Re C [1993] 1 FCR 770 HC FamD Enforcement of United States access order.

Re K [1990] FCR 524; [1990] 1 FLR 387 HC FamD Recognition/registration/enforcement of Belgian custody order allowed.

FOSTERING (access/contact)

Coventry City Council v T [1986] 2 FLR 301 HC FamD Access by parents to child whom they had repeatedly abused and who was placed with foster parents was inappropriate.

Devon County Council v C and another [1985] FLR 619 HC FamD Wrong that access of natural parents to child in local authority care continue where child being placed in foster care with possible view to adoption.

Devon County Council v C and another (1985) 129 SJ 483 CA Judge ought to have decided (as court did here) issue of last occasions of maternal access to child in foster-care (not left it to local authority).

Re W (M) [1994] 1 FCR 161 CA Fostering of child but with access to father (who had abused/allowed abuse of child though denied it).

FOSTERING (adoption)

Devon County Council v C and another [1985] FLR 619 HC FamD Wrong that access of natural parents to child in local authority care continue where child being placed in foster care with possible view to adoption.

Devon County Council v C and another (1985) 129 SJ 483 CA Judge ought to have decided (as court did here) issue of last occasions of maternal access to child in foster-care (not left it to local authority).

Gatehouse v Robinson and Robinson [1986] 1 FLR 504; (1986) 130 SJ 13; [1986] 1 WLR 18 HC QBD Unsuccessful appeal against failed prosecution — for undertaking privately arranged adoption contrary to Adoption Act 1958, s 29, as amended — of foster-parents who had privately arranged fostering relationship.

R v Lancashire County Council, ex parte M [1992] 1 FLR 109 CA Failed application by fosterers for review of local authority decision to take child from fosterers and place with prospective adopters.

Re B (A) [1996] 1 FLR 27; [1995] TLR 472 HC FamD Adoption order favouring foster-father and residence orders favouring him/his cohabitee so both had parental responsibility towards child.

Re B and S [1995] 1 FCR 486 HC FamD Adoption order made to foster-mother after over eleven years fostering despite fosterers' marriage break-down/fosterers keeping husband's adulterous affair secret from local authority.

Re C [1984] FLR 419 (also CA) HC FamD Risk to ward from mother (to whom was close) required care and control of ward be given to local authority which was authorised to place child with foster-parents with view to adoption.

Re C [1987] 2 FLR 383 CA Refusal of consent to adoption unless adoptee maintained contact with sibling not unreasonable; adopters could not be relied upon to ensure same so adoption refused: long-term fostering ordered.

Re C [1994] 2 FCR 839; [1994] 2 FLR 513 CA Foster-mother's adoption application to be fully determined before local authority allowed serve notice to remove foster-child from her.

Re C [1984] FLR 419 (also HC FamD) CA Risk to ward from mother (to whom was close) required care and control of ward be given to local authority which was authorised to place child with foster-parents with view to adoption.

Re G [1990] FCR 881; [1990] 2 FLR 429 CA Reconsideration ordered of case where judge refused to dispense with mother's consent as judge failed to carry out proper balancing exercise.

Re H [1987] 2 FLR 12 HC FamD On ethnic background as factor when dealing with children; long-term fostering with view to adoption (if possible by someone of own ethnic background); access by mother to depend on her co-operation with social worker/what eventual adopters desired.

Re H (SM) and H (RA) [1990] FCR 996 CA On preferability of adoption to fostering on long-term basis.

Re K [1988] 2 FLR 205 CA Children of subnormal parents who could not properly care for children ought to have been placed in long-term fostering with view to adoption.

Re P (L) [1990] FCR 147 HC FamD Balancing exercise as to whether children should go to aunt/be adopted by foster mother.

FOSTERING (care/custody)

Re B (A) [1954] 2 All ER 287; (1954) 118 JP 318; [1954] 2 QB 385; (1954) 98 SJ 391; [1954] 3 WLR 1 HC QBD Court cannot review local authority discretionary decision to remove child from foster parents.

Re C (1969) 113 SJ 164 HL Care and control of child to English foster-parents, not natural foreign parents.

Re O (a minor) (1972) 122 NLJ 112t HC FamD Care and control of Ghanian foster-daughter to English fosterers despite desire of natural parents to bring girl back to Ghana.

Re O (a minor) (1973) 123 NLJ 225t CA Care and control of Ghanian foster-daughter to English fosterers despite desire of natural parents to bring girl back to Ghana.

Re Y [1985] FLR 294 HC FamD Mother's wardship application failed where child had been living happily with good foster parents for eight years.

Turney v Turney and Devon County Council (1983) 4 FLR 199; (1981) 131 NLJ 1309 CA Prolonged fostering inappropriate where care order made under Matrimonial Causes Act 1973, s 43, and so constantly reviewable.

FOSTERING (child sex abuse)

H v Norfolk County Council [1997] 1 FLR 384 CA Local authority not liable for (alleged) abuse suffered by onetime child in its care placed with foster parents.

Re P [1987] FCR 123; [1987] 2 FLR 467; (1987) 151 JP 635 CA Local authority granted care order, non-access by parents and right to place child with foster-parents with view to adoption where child born to parents of family with history of sexual abuse of existing children; on role of court.

Re West [1995] 2 FCR 206 HC FamD Prohibition on publication of information regarding actual/possible abuse (physical or sexual) of fostered children of prominent multiple murderers.

FOSTERING (contact)

Re D and H [1997] 1 FLR 841; (1997) 141 SJ LB 44; [1997] TLR 82 CA No termination of contact between natural mother and children being placed in long-term foster-care as was contrary to what local authority proposed.

FOSTERING (ethnicity)

Re H [1987] 2 FLR 12 HC FamD On ethnic background as factor when dealing with children; long-term fostering with view to adoption (if possible by someone of own ethnic background); access by mother to depend on her co-operation with social worker/what eventual adopters desired.

FOSTERING (general)

R v Avon County Council, ex parte Crabtree [1996] 3 FCR 773; [1996] 1 FLR 502 CA Failed appeal against failed application for judicial review of fostering panel decision to deregister applicant as fosterer.

R v Hereford and Worcester County Council, ex parte D [1992] 1 FLR 448 HC QBD Local authority decision to remove child from foster care quashed where did not consult with foster-parent beforehand.

Re A [1987] 2 FLR 429 HC FamD On balance was decided that Nigerian child be left with English foster-parents notwithstanding cultural difficulties.

Re A (B) [1985] FLR 1008 HC FamD Children's interests required that they remain in foster-care; objectively tested, mother's refusal of consent to adoption not unreasonable; future access by mother a real possibility.

Re L [1985] FLR 95; [1984] TLR 399 CA Access of natural father to child placed in long-term foster care inappropriate: access order quashed.

Re P [1994] 2 FCR 1093 HC FamD Discharge of wardship and leave granted for foster parents to seek residence order.

Re R (M) [1966] 3 All ER 58; (1965-66) 116 NLJ 1204; (1966) 110 SJ 670; [1966] 1 WLR 1527 HC ChD Child returned from foster parents to natural mother as in its best interests.

Wallbridge and another v Dorset County Council [1954] 2 All ER 201; [1954] Ch 659; (1954) 118 JP 305; (1954) 104 LJ 345; (1954) 98 SJ 352; [1954] 2 WLR 1068 HC ChD School boarders over whom parents had parental rights/others to whom local authority in loco parentis were not 'foster children' under Public Health Act 1936.

FOSTERING (homosexual)

Re H [1993] 2 FCR 277 HC FamD Local authority ordered to investigate circumstances of child whom lesbian couple seeking to foster.

Re W (1991) 141 NLJ 1263; [1992] 1 WLR 100 CA Publication of fact that ward placed with gay foster parents allowed though restrictions on identifying foster parents/ward.

FOSTERING (maintenance)

Surrey County Council v Battersby [1965] 1 All ER 273; [1965] Crim LR101t; (1965) 129 JP 116; (1965) 115 LJ 125; [1965] 2 QB 194; (1965) 109 SJ 30; [1965] 2 WLR 378 HC QBD Person taking children for more than one month (albeit interrupted by stays with parents) 'proposed' to maintain foster child.

FOSTERING (publicity)

Re C (1969) 119 NLJ 600t HC ChD Failed application by foster parents to restrain broadcasting of television programme concerning ward in their care.

Re M [1989] 1 FLR 443 HC FamD Wardship not justified just because parents mentally handicapped but was here; no/was restriction on publicity regarding parents (who sought publicity)/fosterers or future adopters; on procedure where party actively seeks publicity in wardship proceedings.

Re West [1995] 2 FCR 206 HC FamD Prohibition on publication of information regarding actual/possible abuse (physical or sexual) of fostered children of prominent multiple murderers.

FOSTERING (residence order)

C v Salford City Council and others [1994] 2 FLR 926 HC FamD Fosterers given leave to seek residence order in respect of child whose natural parents objected to adoption by fosterers.

JR v Merton London Borough [1992] 2 FCR 174 (also CA) HC FamD On granting leave to foster parent to seek residence order (here allowed).

Re B (A) [1996] 1 FLR 27; [1995] TLR 472 HC FamD Adoption order favouring foster-father and residence orders favouring him/his cohabitee so both had parental responsibility towards child.

FOSTERING (ward)

Re O (E) (a minor) (1973) 123 NLJ 180t CA Wardship of Nigerian girl to English fosterers.

Re Y [1985] FLR 294 HC FamD Mother's wardship application failed where child had been living happily with good foster parents for eight years.

GENERAL (miscellaneous)

Re H [1991] FCR 896 CA On when (unlike here) is appropriate to order that leave of court be sought before orders in respect of child be sought.

GUARDIAN (access/contact)

Devon County Council v Clancy [1985] FLR 1159; (1985) 149 JP 521 CA Magistrates' unjustified deviation from advice of guardian ad litem will generally be overturned upon appeal.

Re C [1995] 2 FCR 451; [1994] 2 FLR 525 HC FamD On availability of guardian ad litem's adoption report in later contact/residence hearings.

GUARDIAN (adoption)

R v North Yorkshire County Council, ex parte M (No 2) [1989] FCR 394; [1989] 2 FLR 79 HC QBD On role of guardian ad litem vis-à-vis local authority as regards adoption of child.

Re A (P) [1971] 3 All ER 522; (1972) 136 JP 37; (1971) 121 NLJ 569t; (1971) 115 SJ 586; [1971] 1 WLR 1530 CA Parties in adoption actions have no undeniable right to report of guardian ad litem.

Re B [1983] TLR 619 CA On allowing confidential report of guardian ad litem to affect adoption proceedings.

Re B (A) [1948] 2 All ER 727; [1949] 118 LJR 21 HC ChD Public policy requires that Official Solicitor be guardian ad litem in adoption cases.

Re C [1995] 2 FCR 451; [1994] 2 FLR 525 HC FamD On availability of guardian ad litem's adoption report in later contact/residence hearings.

Re T [1994] 1 FLR 632 (also HC FamD); (1994) 144 NLJ 123 CA Guardian ad litem ought to have been allowed see case record of child whom local authority sought to place with adoptive parents.

Re T [1994] 1 FLR 632 (also CA) HC FamD Guardian ad litem ought to have been allowed see case record of child whom local authority sought to place with adoptive parents.

GUARDIAN (alien)

Re D [1943] 2 All ER 411; [1943] Ch 305; [1943] 112 LJ 237; (1944) 94 LJ 61; (1943) 169 LTR 313; (1943) 87 SJ 290; (1942-43) LIX TLR 354; (1943) WN (I) 174 HC ChD Court could appoint guardian of infant alien without property.

GUARDIAN (blood test)

Re L [1968] 1 All ER 20; (1967) 117 NLJ 1242t; [1967] 3 WLR 1645 CA PDAD judge can order blood test of infant absent guardian ad litem's consent.

GUARDIAN (care/custody)

A v Berkshire County Council [1989] FCR 184; [1989] 1 FLR 273 (also HC FamD) CA Juvenile court-appointed guardian ad litem could not by way of wardship action challenge local authority exercise of care and control powers over child.

A v Berkshire County Council [1989] FCR 180; [1989] 1 FLR 273 (also CA) HC FamD Juvenile court-appointed guardian ad litem could not by way of wardship action challenge local authority exercise of care and control powers over child.

Oxfordshire County Council and another v P [1995] 2 All ER 225; [1995] Fam 161; [1995] 2 FCR 212; [1995] 1 FLR 552; [1995] TLR 62; [1995] 2 WLR 543 HC FamD Lifting privilege of confidentiality in care proceedings a matter for court not guardian ad litem.

R v Birmingham Juvenile Court, ex parte G and others; R v Birmingham Juvenile Court, ex parte R [1988] 3 All ER 726; [1989] FCR 22; [1988] 2 FLR 423; (1988) 138 NLJ 143; (1988) 132 SJ 1117; [1988] 1 WLR 950 HC QBD As care proceedings not adversarial court may hear guardian ad litem's evidence even if local authority offers no evidence.

R v Birmingham Juvenile Court, ex parte G and others; R v Birmingham Juvenile Court, ex parte R [1989] 3 All ER 336; [1989] 2 FLR 454; [1990] 2 QB 573; (1989) 133 SJ 1089; [1989] 3 WLR 1024 CA Court must look to welfare of child/hear guardian ad litem before allowing local authority withdraw care order application.

R v Newcastle-upon-Tyne Council, ex parte S and T [1988] FCR 159; [1988] 1 FLR 535 HC QBD On making order that guardians ad litem be appointed to represent children (on basis that conflict between their interests and that of parents).

R v North Yorkshire County Council, ex parte M [1989] 1 All ER 143; [1989] FCR 128; [1989] 1 FLR 203; [1989] QB 411; (1988) 132 SJ 1731; [1988] 3 WLR 1344 HC QBD Local authority must inform guardian ad litem/hear guardian's views about any major changes to circumstances of child in care.

R v Waltham Forest London Borough, ex parte G [1989] 2 FLR 138 HC QBD On juvenile court's role where dispute between local authority/guardian ad litem over psychiatric assessment of children in care seeking discharge of care orders.

R v West Malling Juvenile Court, ex parte K (1986) 150 JP 367; (1970) 130 SJ 650 HC QBD Case ought to hve been adjourned where parent in care action given social worker/guardian ad litem reports containing unexpected material on day of hearing.

Re A [1994] 2 FCR 125 CA Non-dismissal of local authority from care action where guardian ad litem convinced child would be at risk of significant harm if aunt made carer.

Re B [1996] 3 FCR 272; [1996] 1 FLR 667 CA Reasoned departure of judge from opinions of expert/guardian ad litem when granting interim care order was valid.

Re C (1992) 136 SJ LB 252; [1992] TLR 407 HC FamD May be order that there be no contact between child and natural mother; inappropriate to direct guardian ad litem to police rehabilitation programme of child in local authority care.

Re F [1995] 3 FCR 601 HC FamD Psychological appraisal of child inappropriate; guardian ad litem ordered to give oral report.

Re H [1959] 3 All ER 746; (1960) 124 JP 74; (1959) 109 LJ 703; (1959) 103 SJ 1003; [1959] 1 WLR 1163 HC ChD Cannot appoint joint guardian just to help in custody application: infant's interests sole determinant.

Re R [1974] 1 All ER 1033; (1974) 124 NLJ 123t; (1974) 118 SJ 78 HC FamD Custody to non-parent/non-guardian.

Re U (T) [1993] 2 FCR 565 HC FamD Magistrates to give reasons for not following guardian ad litem's recommendation; magistrates improperly ordered contact to mother so putting child at risk.

Suwa v Ando (1913) CC Rep II 34 CyCt Articles of Apprenticeship would not be set aside and custody of child given to (foreign) mother where was not in best interests of child/application not brought solely out of interest for child.

GUARDIAN (costs)

Re C (P) [1961] 2 All ER 308; [1961] Ch 312; (1961) 111 LJ 341 HC ChD Official Solicitor may recover costs from applicants in action where functions as guardian ad litem.

Re G [1982] 2 All ER 32; [1982] TLR 37; [1982] 1 WLR 438 CA Payment of Official Solicitor's costs for acting as guardian ad litem.

GUARDIAN (divorce)

John v John and Goff [1965] 2 All ER 222; (1965) 109 SJ 109; [1965] 2 WLR 714 HC PDAD Non-appointment of guardian ad litem in divorce of infant made decree nisi voidable not void.

GUARDIAN (emergency protection order)

Re M [1993] 1 FCR 78; [1993] 1 FLR 275 HC FamD Person who had been acting as guardian ad litem could apply for prohibited steps order after emergency protection order lapsed; justices' reasoning/findings in such cases to be recorded.

GUARDIAN (legitimacy)

Slingsby (by his Guardian ad litem) v Attorney-General and others (1916-17) XXXIII TLR 120 HL Failed legitimacy action dismissed with costs to be paid by guardian ad litem or next friend.

GUARDIAN (maintenance)

R v Sandbach Justices, ex parte Smith [1950] 2 All ER 781; (1950) 114 JP 514; [1951] 1 KB 62; (1950) 100 LJ 485; (1950) 94 SJ 597; [1950] 66 (2) TLR 291; (1950) WN (I) 397 HC KBD Guardianship proceedings to be brought where respondent lives (unless High Court action); generally no order where child outside jurisdiction.

GUARDIAN (miscellaneous)

Allen v Allen [1948] 2 All ER 413; (1948) 112 JP 355; (1948) LXIV TLR 418 CA Welfare of child paramount in cases under Guardianship of Infants Act 1925.

Chipperfield v Chipperfield [1952] 1 All ER 1360; (1952) 116 JP 337; (1952) 96 SJ 379; [1952] 1 TLR 1519; (1952) WN (I) 272 HC PDAD Child's welfare paramount in guardianship cases.

Devon County Council and others v S and others [1993] 2 FCR 36; [1993] 1 FLR 842 HC FamD Caution needed if appointing welfare officer as guardian ad litem; issue for justices in post-rehabiliation contact termination application not whether rehabilitation successful but should care cease.

Gharib-Ul-Lah v Khalak Singh and others (1902-03) XIX TLR 447 PC Guardian of infants property could not be appointed in respect of infant's interest in property of undivided Mitacshara family.

Kawas (Hanna Eissa) v Kawas (Bishara Elias) and others [1943] 2 All ER 530; [1943] AC 532; (1943) WN (I) 160 PC Consent of infants required to action and as could not consent could be no action.

Khan (Raja Mohammad Muntaz Ali) v Ali Khan (Sakhawat) and Ali Khan (Farhat) (1900-01) XVII TLR 587 PC On powers of guardian as regards giving property rather than maintenance.

M (SE) v M (SV) [1965] 3 All ER 656 HC PDAD If guardian ad litem can be appointed need not be unless in interests of infant.

Massey v Massey (1918) CC Rep VII 90 CyCt Cannot assign guardianship.

R v Barnet Juvenile Court, ex parte Barnet London Borough [1982] TLR 307 HC QBD Local authority not guardian of juvenile entrusted to its care pursuant to the Children and Young Persons Act 1969, ss 7(7) and 20.

R v Cornwall County Council, ex parte Cornwall and Isles of Scilly Guardians ad Litem and Reporting Officers Panel [1992] 2 All ER 471; [1992] 1 FLR 270; (1991) 135 SJ LB 204; [1991] TLR 525; [1992] 1 WLR 427 HC QBD Certiorari available where local authority seeks to circumscribe role of guardian ad litem.

R v Pontlottlyn Juvenile Court, ex parte R [1990] FCR 900; [1991] 2 FLR 86 HC QBD Guardian ad litem appointed after initial refusal as mother misled by court clerk into thinking appointment forthcoming and so had not attended hearing with her solicitor.

Re A, decd; S v A (1941) 164 LTR 230; (1940) 84 SJ 477; (1939-40) LVI TLR 934; (1940) WN (I) 271 HC ChD Mother of illegitimate child could appoint testamentary guardian of same (Guardianship of Infants Act 1925, s 5 and Part 2 of Schedule to Act).

Re B (LH) [1935] All ER 517; [1935] Ch 643 CA Receiver of lunatic's estate authorised to take such steps regarding lunatic's son as lunatic was authorised to do as son's guardian.

Re B (TA) an infant [1970] 3 All ER 705; [1971] Ch 270; (1971) 135 JP 7; (1970) 114 SJ 769; [1970] 3 WLR 835 HC ChD Rôle of appellate court in guardianship cases.

Re Barbour's Settlement; National Westminster Bank Ltd v Barbour and others [1974] 1 All ER 1188 HC ChD Guardian ad litem to decide if corporate trustee fee increase in interests of minor/to be opposed.

Re C (A); C v C [1970] 1 All ER 309; (1970) 120 NLJ 153t; [1970] 1 WLR 288 CA In guardianship cases paramount interest is that of infant.

Re Collins (An Infant) [1950] 1 All ER 1057; [1950] Ch 498; (1950) 100 LJ 274; (1950) 94 SJ 352; [1950] 66 (1) TLR 1107; (1950) WN (I) 242 CA Child's welfare paramount in guardianship cases: no rule that dead father has right to determine child's religious upbringing.

Re D [1973] 2 All ER 993; [1973] Fam 179; [1973] 3 WLR 53 HC FamD Minor's welfare not only relevant factor under Guardianship of Minors Act 1970, ss 1 and 9; only exceptionally may court in wardship case upset existing decision on merits by magistrates.

Re D [1943] 2 All ER 411 HC ChD Need not be property for guardian of infant to be appointed: test is whether infant needs to be safeguarded.

Re F (W) an infant [1969] 3 All ER 595; [1969] 2 Ch 269; (1969) 133 JP 723; [1969] 3 WLR 206 HC ChD No second hearing absent fresh evidence after first dismissed on merits.

Re G [1992] TLR 545 HC FamD On responsibility on guardian ad litem in deciding whether child/ren to be present in court at proceedings concerning them.

Re H [1993] 2 FCR 437; [1993] 2 FLR 552 HC FamD On allowing child to participate in family proceedings without guardian ad litem.

Re H [1959] 3 All ER 746; (1960) 124 JP 74; (1959) 109 LJ 703; (1959) 103 SJ 1003; [1959] 1 WLR 1163 HC ChD Cannot appoint joint guardian just to help in custody application: infant's interests sole determinant.

Re S [1993] 3 All ER 36; [1993] Fam 263; [1993] 2 FCR 1; [1993] 2 FLR 437; (1993) 143 NLJ 435; [1993] TLR 105; [1993] 2 WLR 801 CA Minor may conduct proceedings without guardian ad litem only where understands specific proceedings in issue; parents may be heard by judge on whether minor so understands.

Re S [1992] 2 FCR 554; [1993] 1 FLR 110; (1992) 136 SJ LB 206 CA On roles of guardian ad litem/court welfare officer.

Re S [1959] 2 All ER 675; (1959) 109 LJ 509; (1959) 103 SJ 545 HC ChD On status of guardian ad litem appointed by justices.

Re Whittall; Whittall v Faulkner and another [1973] 3 All ER 35 HC ChD Guardian ad litem to advise on variation of trust affecting infant but court need not follow advice.

S v S [1949] 1 All ER 285 HC PDAD On declaration of unfitness for guardianship.

GUARDIAN (Official Solicitor)

Re C [1984] FLR 419 (also HC FamD) CA On appointing Official Solicitor as guardian ad litem.

Re G [1982] 2 All ER 32; [1982] TLR 37; [1982] 1 WLR 438 CA Payment of Official Solicitor's costs for acting as guardian ad litem.

GUARDIAN (prohibited steps order)

Re M [1993] 1 FCR 78; [1993] 1 FLR 275 HC FamD Person who had been acting as guardian ad litem could apply for prohibited steps order after emergency protection order lapsed; justices' reasoning/findings in such cases to be recorded.

GUARDIAN (report)

R v Epsom Juvenile Court, ex parte G [1988] 1 All ER 329; [1988] FCR 32; [1988] 2 FLR 36; (1988) 132 SJ 54; [1988] 1 WLR 145 HC QBD Usually report of guardian ad litem should be presented as soon as possible before care case begins.

R v Sunderland Juvenile Court, ex parte G [1988] FCR 17; [1988] 2 FLR 41 (also CA); (1987) 131 SJ 1155 HC QBD Guardian ad litem's report may be made available to independent social worker (here was).

Re C (1982) 3 FLR 95 CA Dispensing with consent to be subject of hearing if controverted; court to decide whether party of whom adverse comments made in report of guardian ad litem to be informed so can prepare rebuttal.

Re C [1995] 2 FCR 451; [1994] 2 FLR 525 HC FamD On availability of guardian ad litem's adoption report in later contact/residence hearings.

Re T (1982) 3 FLR 183 CA Re-trial of adoption case ordered where judge refused adoption on basis of unrevealed portions of report of guardian ad litem.

GUARDIAN (unfitness)

S v S [1949] 1 All ER 285; [1949] 118 LJR 1093; (1949) LXV TLR 80; (1949) WN (I) 32 HC PDAD On declaration of unfitness for guardianship.

GUARDIAN (ward)

A v Berkshire County Council [1989] FCR 184; [1989] 1 FLR 273 (also HC FamD) CA Juvenile court-appointed guardian ad litem could not by way of wardship action challenge local authority exercise of care and control powers over child.

A v Berkshire County Council [1989] FCR 180; [1989] 1 FLR 273 (also CA) HC FamD Juvenile court-appointed guardian ad litem could not by way of wardship action challenge local authority exercise of care and control powers over child.

R v North Yorkshire County Council, ex parte M (No 3) [1989] FCR 403; [1989] 2 FLR 82 HC QBD On possibility of post-judicial review invocation of wardship jurisdiction.

Re B [1989] 1 FLR 268 HC FamD On appointment of guardian ad litem in wardship action.

Re H [1994] 4 All ER 762; [1994] Fam 11; [1993] 3 WLR 1109 HC FamD Ward can take part in case minus guardian ad litem.

Re K [1962] 3 All ER 178; (1962) 112 LJ 617; (1962) 106 SJ 721; [1962] 3 WLR 752 HC ChD No entitlement to see reports lodged with guardian ad litem; parties may question maker's of statements in reports.

Re P [1967] 2 All ER 229; (1967) 111 SJ 496; [1967] 1 WLR 818 HC ChD If magistrates make guardianship ruling then should make variations unless not empowered to make order sought; High Court not constrained in wardship case by earlier decision of magistrates.

Re T and others [1989] 1 All ER 297; [1990] Fam 1; [1989] FCR (also HC FamD); [1989] 1 FLR 313 (also HC FamD); (1989) 133 SJ 568; [1989] 2 WLR 954 CA Rôle of guardian ad litem confined to juvenile court proceedings — cannot begin wardship proceedings.

HABEAS CORPUS (general)

Re Carroll (No 2) [1930] All ER 192; (1931) 95 JP 25; [1931] 1 KB 317; (1931) 100 LJCL 113; (1931) 144 LTR 383; (1931) 75 SJ 98; (1930-31) XLVII TLR 125 CA Mother of illegitimate child may require child to be brought up in particular religion; CA considers habeas corpus appeal de novo.

HABITUAL RESIDENCE (general)

Re A [1995] 2 FCR 298; [1995] 1 FLR 767 HC FamD On determining place of habitual residence of child.

Re M [1997] 2 FCR 527 CA On determining habitual residence (as basis for jurisdiction).

INDUSTRIAL SCHOOL (general)

London County Council v Lord Mayor, Etc, of Birmingham [1924] 1 KB 248; [1924] 93 LJCL 65; (1924) 130 LTR 414; (1923-24) XL TLR 76; (1923) WN (I) 302 HC KBD Liability of local authority for maintenance of child in industrial school depended on place of residence of child when committed larceny, not later breach of probation.

Yorkshire West Riding County Council v Colne Corporation (1917-18) 117 LTR 671; (1917-18) 62 SJ 160 HC KBD On residency of child for purposes of determining which authority liable to maintain child at industrial school.

INFANTS (marriage)

Re Queskey; Queskey v Queskey [1946] 1 All ER 717; [1946] Ch 250; (1946) 110 JP 272; (1946) 96 LJ 176; [1947] 116 LJR 182; (1946) 175 LTR 107; (1946) 90 SJ 236; (1945-46) LXII TLR 344; (1946) WN (I) 75 HC ChD No appeal under Guardianship of Infants Act 1925 from justices' refusal of consent to infants marrying.

LEGITIMACY (access/contact)

B v A (1982) 3 FLR 27 HC FamD Father properly refused access to his illegitimate children where as was domineering towards mother of whom was step-father which would also create complications.

M v J (1982) 3 FLR 19 HC FamD Father properly refused access to his illegitimate child where access could jeopardise child's welfare.

Re E (P) (1969) 133 JP 137; (1968) 118 NLJ 956t; (1968) 112 SJ 821; [1968] 1 WLR 1913 CA Better that child lose illegitimacy via adoption and so lose contact with putative father than to retain illegitimacy and retain contact.

Re H (C) [1996] 1 FCR 768; [1996] 1 FLR 569 HC FamD Supervised contact order to ex-husband whose wife had child by artificial insemination (using third party's sperm) but of which child ex-husband legally the father.

S v O (1982) 3 FLR 15 HC FamD Father properly awarded access to his illegitimate child.

LEGITIMACY (adoption)

Coventry Corporation v Surrey County Council [1924-35] All ER 689; [1935] AC 199 HL Adopted child not removeable to place of settlement of natural mother.

Re C, an Infant [1938] 107 LJCh 65; (1938) 158 LTR 371; (1936-37) LIII TLR 995 HC ChD Under Adoption of Children Act 1926 court could not allow husband and wife to adopt wife's illegitimate child (in respect of whom neither party was twenty-one years older) but could allow wife to adopt child if husband consented.

Re D [1958] 3 All ER 716 CA Single mother can adopt own illegitimate child.

Re E (P) (1969) 133 JP 137; (1968) 118 NLJ 956t; (1968) 112 SJ 821; [1968] 1 WLR 1913 CA Better that child lose illegitimacy via adoption and so lose contact with putative father than to retain illegitimacy and retain contact.

Re O (An Infant) [1964] 1 All ER 786; (1964) 114 LJ 252; (1964) 108 SJ 117 CA Natural father did not exercise right of veto over adoption of illegitimate child that would enjoy over legitimate child.

Veasey v Attorney-General (1982) 3 FLR 267 HC FamD Child legitimated upon marriage of parents: post-marital adoption did not affect situation.

LEGITIMACY (affiliation)

Boyce v Cox [1921] All ER 658; (1921-25) XXVII Cox CC 139; (1921) 85 JP 279; [1922] 1 KB 149; [1922] 91 LJCL 122; (1922) 126 LTR 254; (1921-22) 66 SJ 142; (1921-22) XXXVIII TLR 51; (1921) WN (I) 312 HC KBD Affiliation order available to woman judicially separated from third party against natural father.

LEGITIMACY (blood test)

B v B and another (1968) 118 NLJ 541t; (1968) 112 SJ 689 CA HC could order administration of blood test in divorce action where paternity was an issue.

B v B and E (B intervening) [1969] 3 All ER 1106; (1969) 119 NLJ 672t; (1969) 113 SJ 625; [1969] 1 WLR 1800 CA Presumption of legitimacy justifies refusing blood test; blood test not ordered where only to support custody claim, only if in child's interests.

L v L (1968) 112 SJ 294 HC PDAD Court could not order blood testing of child in paternity suit between spouses.

L v L and another (1968) 112 SJ 840 CA Blood test of child could be ordered where issue of paternity arose in divorce proceedings and testing was in child's best interests.

M v M (1968) 118 NLJ 1005t CA Blood test only ordered where is in child's interest (not ordered here).

McVeigh v Beattie [1988] 2 All ER 500; [1988] Fam 69; [1988] FCR 516; [1988] 2 FLR 67; (1988) 132 SJ 125; [1988] 2 WLR 992 HC FamD Absent reasonable excuse refusal to provide blood sample corroborates claim of parenthood.

O v L [1995] 2 FLR 930 CA On deciding whether to order blood testing (here not ordered).

R v R [1973] 3 All ER 933; (1973) 117 SJ 394; [1973] 1 WLR 1115 HC FamD Referral of blood test applications from registrar to judge.

Re A [1994] 2 FLR 463 CA On inference to be drawn from refusal of blood test in action where paternity at issue.

Re B (C) [1994] 2 FCR 925; [1994] 2 FLR 762 HC FamD Blood testing of child not allowed where mother objected.

Re E [1995] 1 FCR 245; [1994] 2 FLR 548 HC FamD On ordering blood test where paternity in issue.

Re G [1997] 2 FCR 325; [1997] 1 FLR 360 CA Where separated father refused to have blood test done in respect of child of wife of whom husband claimed he was father, the inference to be drawn was that he was not the father.

Re G (C) [1994] 2 FCR 889 HC FamD On whether/when to order blood testing where paternity in issue (here ordered).

Re H [1996] 4 All ER 28; [1996] 3 FCR 201; [1996] 2 FLR 65; (1996) 146 NLJ 406; [1996] 3 WLR 506 CA On refusing/ordering blood test where paternity in issue.

Re H (1996) TLR 12/3/96 CA Failed appeal against order for blood testing of mother and child where mother did not consent to the testing.

Re L (1967) 111 SJ 908 CA On rebutting presumption of legitimacy; on ordering blood testing where issue of paternity raised.

Re L [1967] 2 All ER 1110; (1967) 111 SJ 717; [1967] 3 WLR 1149 HC PDAD Blood tests ordered of child if in its best interests.

S (an Infant, by her Guardian ad Litem the Official Solicitor to the Supreme Court) v S; W v Official Solicitor (acting as Guardian ad Litem for a male infant named PHW) [1972] AC 24; [1970] 3 WLR 366 HL Blood test desirable in paternity suit.

T (H) v T (E) [1971] 1 All ER 590; (1971) 115 SJ 186; [1971] 1 WLR 429 HC PDAD Absent contrary evidence presumption that child of marriage is legitimate; blood test cautiously accepted as proof of paternity.

T v T [1992] TLR 387 CA Child's best interests demanded carrying out of blood test to determine paternity where mother had cast doubts in respect of same.

Turner v Blunden [1986] 2 All ER 75; [1986] Fam 120; [1986] 2 FLR 69; (1986) 150 JP 180; (1986) 130 SJ 184; [1986] 2 WLR 491 HC FamD Blood tests can corroborate allegation of paternity.

LEGITIMACY (care/custody)

Colquitt v Colquitt [1947] 2 All ER 50; (1947) 111 JP 442; (1947) 97 LJ 277; [1948] 117 LJR 897; (1947) 177 LTR 399; (1947) 91 SJ 310; (1947) LXIII TLR 358; (1947) WN (I) 182 HC PDAD Legitimated child is a child of marriage of natural parents; absent decree of legitimacy court can nonetheless make custody order in respect of child legitimated by marriage of natural parents.

G v G (1929) 73 SJ 111; (1928-29) XLV TLR 7 HC PDAD Court could not make custody order in respect of non-legitimated child of parties to divorce action.

Harrison v Harrison [1951] 2 All ER 346; (1951) 115 JP 428; [1951] 2 TLR 242; (1951) WN (I) 387 HC PDAD No custody order possible in respect of illegitimate child (who cannot be legitimised).

Re A [1955] 2 All ER 202; (1955) 105 LJ 313 CA Child's welfare paramount/natural mother's wishes regarding child's upbringing did not carry special weight.

Re G (An Infant) [1956] 2 All ER 876; [1956] 1 WLR 911 CA Valid giving of (illegitimate) child into mother's sole care and custody.

Re T (C) (An Infant); Re T (J) (An Infant) [1956] 3 All ER; [1956] 3 WLR 826 HC ChD Cannot hear application by putative father for custody of illegitimate child.

LEGITIMACY (corroboration)

R v Essex Justices, ex parte Da Costa (1939-40) XXXI Cox CC 133 HC KBD Quarter sessions quashing of bastardy order where inadequate corroboration a final decision on the merits.

R v Lincolnshire Justices, ex parte Brett [1926] All ER 275; (1926) 90 JP 149; [1926] 2 KB 192; [1926] 95 LJCL 827; (1926) 135 LTR 141 CA No bastardy order where no corroboration of complainant's evidence.

Reffell v Morton (1906) 70 JP 347; (1905-06) 50 SJ 378 HC KBD On what for purposes of Bastardy Laws Amendment Act 1872, s 4, constitutes corroboration of mother's evidence as to paternity of illegitimate child.

LEGITIMACY (costs)

Cleave v Attorney-General; Headley, Channon and Barclays Bank, Ltd, intervening [1952] 2 All ER 283; (1952) 102 LJ 399; [1952] 2 TLR 174; (1952) WN (I) 346 HC PDAD Costs of failed legitimacy action could be ordered from estate of which interveners trustees.

Re Hartridge [1934] LJNCCR 252 CyCt Legitimacy declaration made but no costs given owing to delay in bringing petitition.

LEGITIMACY (domicile)

Bamgbose (Matthew Olajide) v Daniel (John Bankole) [1955] AC 107; (1954) 98 SJ 732 PC Child legitimate by law of parents' domicile will be deemed legitimate by English courts — even if parents' marriage polygamous.

R v Wilson, Esq (Metropolitan Magistrate) and others, ex parte Pereira [1952] 2 All ER 706; (1952) 116 JP 549; (1952) 102 LJ 595; [1953] 1 QB 59; (1952) 96 SJ 729; [1952] 2 TLR 594; (1952) WN (I) 457 HC QBD Bastardy action cannot be brought where child abroad to mother then domiciled abroad.

Scappaticci v Attorney-General [1955] 1 All ER 193 (1955) 99 SJ 114; [1955] 2 WLR 409 HC PDAD On legitimation by post-birth marriage of parents; on changing domicil.

LEGITIMACY (evidence)

Re Hamer's Estate; Public Trustee v Attorney-General [1937] 1 All ER 130; (1937) 81 SJ 99; (1936-37) LIII TLR 275 HC ChD Statements in will admitted to disprove legitimacy.

LEGITIMACY (general)

Abraham v Attorney-General (1933) 76 LJ 162; (1933) 102 LJP 115; (1933) 149 LTR 539; (1933) 77 SJ 665 HC PDAD Illegitimate child born of British father and Japanese mother in Japan and was later legitimated by their marriage did not automatically acquire British nationality.

Aldrich v Attorney-General (Rogers intervening) [1968] 1 All ER 345; (1967) 117 NLJ 1269t; (1967) 111 SJ 945; [1968] 2 WLR 413 HC PDAD Cannot declare anyone other than petitioner legitimate.

Ampthill Peerage Case [1976] 2 All ER 411; [1977] AC 547; (1976) 120 SJ 367; [1976] 2 WLR 777 HL Cttee for Privileges Absent fraud/collusion legitimacy declaration binds all — even Crown/Lords.

B (otherwise P) v Attorney-General; B (otherwise P) v Attorney-General and others [1965] 3 All ER 253; (1965) 115 LJ 678; (1965) 109 SJ 536; [1966] 2 WLR 58 HC PDAD Cannot order legitimation proceedings be held in camera.

B v Attorney-General (B and others intervening) [1966] 2 All ER 145; (1965) 115 LJ 58; (1966) 110 SJ 309; [1966] 2 WLR 58 HC PDAD On declarations of legitimacy.

B v Attorney-General (B and others intervening) [1965] 2 WLR 871 HC PDAD No power that legitimacy application be heard in camera.

B v Attorney-General (NEB and others intervening) [1965] 1 All ER 62; [1965] 2 WLR 871 HC PDAD Custody order in divorce decree not estoppel to later denial of paternity; wife's/dead man's denial of husband's paternity could be admissible.

Bamgbose (Matthew Olajide) v Daniel (John Bankole) [1955] AC 107; (1954) 98 SJ 732 PC Child legitimate by law of parents' domicile will be deemed legitimate by English courts — even if parents' marriage polygamous.

Barnsley v Marsh (1947) 111 JP 363; (1947) 177 LTR 573; (1947) 91 SJ 561; (1947) LXIII TLR 399; (1947) WN (I) 159 HC KBD On procedure in bastardy proceedings.

Barritt v Attorney-General [1971] 3 All ER 1183; (1971) 115 SJ 889 HC PDAD In camera hearings involve weighing petitioner's and interested third party's rights against public interest in justice being public.

Battle v Attorney-General (Battle GL and Battle AFT intervening) [1949] 118 LJR 1015; (1949) WN (I) 129 HC PDAD Declarations by alleged blood/by legal grandfathers admissible; child legitimated by parents' marriage.

Beresford v Attorney-General (Marquis of Waterford and others cited) (1918) 118 LTR 133; (1917-18) 62 SJ 103 CA Perpetuated testimony allowed in respect of witnesses who were old and unwell.

Blackwell v Attorney-General (1967) 111 SJ 332 HC PDAD Failed legitimacy application.

Burbury v Jackson [1914-17] All ER 531; (1915-17) XXV Cox CC 555; (1916) 80 JP 455; [1917] 1 KB 16; (1916) 51 LJ 517; [1917] 86 LJCL 255; (1916-17) 115 LTR 713; (1916-17) XXXIII TLR 18; (1916) WN (I) 348 HC KBD Evidence of opportunity not per se sufficient to justify bastardy order.

Chowdhury (Habibur Rahman) and another v Chowdhury (Altaf li) and others (1920-21) XXXVII TLR 487 PC On father's acknowledgment/effect of father's acknowledgment of son's legitimacy under Mahomedan law.

Collins v Attorney-General (1931) 145 LTR 551; (1931) 75 SJ 616; (1930-31) XLVII TLR 484 HC PDAD Legitimation of child under German law recognised though father married to third party when illegitimate child born.

Cotton v Cotton and another [1954] 2 All ER 105; (1954) 104 LJ 313; (1954) 98 SJ 320; [1954] 2 WLR 947 CA When challenging legitimacy of child born within marriage must be no reasonable doubt that child not legitimate.

Coventry Corporation v Surrey County Council [1933] 2 KB 384 HC KBD Adopted illegitimate child acquired settlement of place in which adopted father had resided (and from which was irremovable).

Cunliffe v Attorney-General [1934] All ER 186; (1934) 103 LJP 114; (1934) 78 SJ 520 HC PDAD Costs in legitimacy action.

Davy v Attorney-General [1934] All ER 176; (1934) 78 LJ 63; (1934) 103 LJP 115; (1934) 151 LTR 562; (1934) 78 SJ 618; (1933-34) L TLR 588; (1934) WN (I) 164 HC PDAD Declaration of dead father made post litem motam admitted on grounds of natural justice.

Ettenfield v Ettenfield [1939] 2 All ER 743; (1939) 87 LJ 377; (1939) 161 LTR 230; (1939) 83 SJ 459; (1938-39) LV TLR 735; (1939) WN (I) 207 HC PDAD Evidence of non-access admissible whether or not separation agreement under seal.

Ettenfield v Ettenfield [1940] 1 All ER 293; (1940) 89 LJ 68; [1940] 109 LJP 41; (1940) 162 LTR 172; (1940) 84 SJ 59; (1939-40) LVI TLR 315; (1940) WN (I) 43 CA Spouses living together/apart cannot give evidence that would bastardise/legitimise child born inside marriage; post court-ordered/voluntary separation can prove adultery by reference to court order and child's date of birth/can prove by any means other than non-access evidence and child's date of birth (post-order child presumed bastard/post-voluntary separation child presumed legitimate).

Ex parte Adedigba (1967) 117 NLJ 731t HC QBD Maintenance order unavailable where mother domiciled abroad when child born.

Francis v Francis [1959] 3 All ER 206; (1959) 109 LJ 479; (1959) 103 SJ 546; [1959] 3 WLR 447 HC PDAD Custody order to wife as possibility of illegitmacy not enough to counter presumption of legitimacy of child born within marriage.

Galloway (Ex parte) [1955] 3 All ER 429; [1956] AC 299; (1955) 105 LJ 728; (1955) 99 SJ 792; [1955] 3 WLR 723 HL 'Children' in Matrimonial Causes Act 1950 includes illegitimate children.

Galloway v Galloway [1954] 2 All ER 143; (1954) 104 LJ 328; (1954) 98 SJ 336; [1954] 2 WLR 980 CA Custody/maintenance unavailable in respect of child born outside marriage who cannot be legitimated.

Gatty (FA) and Gatty (PV) v Attorney-General (1951) 95 SJ 610; [1951] 2 TLR 599; (1951) WN (I) 433 HC PDAD Failed petition for legitimacy where could not prove validity of father's marriage.

Giltrow v Day [1965] 1 All ER 73; (1965) 129 JP 94; (1965) 115 LJ 58; (1965) 109 SJ 29; [1965] 1 WLR 317 HC QBD Wife living apart from husband in same house was not single woman.

Gordon v Gordon and Bell (1903) LXXXVIII LTR 573 HC PDAD Wife-respondent's filed answer must contain challenge to paternity if is to be allowed raise that issue at custody hearings.

Green v Green (1928) 66 LJ 448; (1929) 98 LJP 58; (1929) 140 LTR 93; (1928) WN (I) 252 HC PDAD Court cannot post-decree nisi make custody order in respect of child born before marriage and never judicially legitimated.

Greenway v Attorney-General (Greenway and others cited) (1927) 71 SJ 882 HC PDAD Failed application to have legitimation petition heard in camera.

Guardians of West Ham Union v Guardians of Holbeach Union [1904] 2 KB 121 CA Under sixteen year old illegitimate child's three year residence in parish meant she was settled there.

Guardians of West Ham Union v Guardians of Holbeach Union [1903] 2 KB 627 HC KBD Under sixteen year old illegitimate child's three year residence in parish meant she was settled there.

Guardians of Woolwich Union v Guardians of Fulham [1906] 2 KB 240 CA On illegitimate child under sixteen acquiring settlement by residence in parish of mother's residence.

Guardians of Woolwich Union v Guardians of Fulham [1905] 2 KB 203 HC KBD Illegitimate child under sixteen cannot acquire independent settlement.

Hadlow v Hadlow (1930) 143 LTR 774; (1930) 74 SJ 582; (1929-30) XLVI TLR 624 HC PDAD Husband's non-access to wife at relevant time proved was not father of child at issue.

Harvey v Anning [1900-03] All ER 1233; (1903) 67 JP 73; (1902-03) LXXXVII LTR 687 HC KBD Being seen walking out together/overheard asking if would acknowledge child as own evidence of paternity.

Hashmi v Hashmi [1971] 3 All ER 1253; [1972] Fam 36; (1971) 115 SJ 928; [1971] 3 WLR 918 Assizes Children of marriage void under English law but recognised in domicile are legitimate.

Hawkins v Attorney-General [1966] 1 All ER 392; (1965-66) 116 NLJ 471; (1966) 110 SJ 445; [1966] 1 WLR 978 HC PDAD Objective test whether parties 'reasonably believed' marriage valid.

Hockaday v Goodenough [1945] 2 All ER 335; (1945) 109 JP 237; (1945) 173 LTR 204; (1945) 89 SJ 392; (1944-45) LXI TLR 510 HC KBD Letter stating would persevere was statement of future intention not condonation of adultery: wife therefore 'single woman'.

Holland v Roberts (1939-40) XXXI Cox CC 38; (1938) 158 LTR 313 CA Evidence showing opportunity inadequate corroboration of allegation of paternity in bastardy action.

Holmes v Holmes (Holmes, by his Guardian, intervening) [1966] 1 WLR 187 HC PDAD Court will not find child accepted into family unless is clearly the case; blood test proved child not child of husband party to action.

In the Matter of a Petition for Declaration of Legitimacy (1927) WN (I) 292 HC PDAD Failed application for legitimacy petition to be heard in camera.

In the Matter of Clayton (Mabel Inez) a proposed Petitioner (1927) 71 SJ 543 HC PDAD Only party seeking to be legitimated can bring legitimation petition; on procedure as regards bringing such a petition.

In the Matter of the Petition of B (A) (1927) 64 LJ 456; (1928) 97 LJP 104; (1927) WN (I) 291 HC PDAD Failed application for legitimacy petition to be heard in camera.

In the Matter of the Petition of D (C) (1928) 138 LTR 208 HC PDAD Application that legitimacy case be heard in camera refused.

Jones v Davies [1900-03] All ER 243; (1900) 35 LJ 601; [1901] 70 LJK/QB 38; (1900-01) LXXXIII LTR 412; [1901] 1 QB 118; (1900-01) 49 WR 136 HC QBD Married woman living with husband cannot be single woman.

Jones v Evans [1945] 1 All ER 19; (1944) 108 JP 170; [1944] KB 582; [1945] 114 LJ 29; (1944) 171 LTR 138; (1943-44) LX TLR 374; (1944) WN (I) 128 HC KBD Loss of consortium/non-condonation meant de facto separation so woman a 'single woman'.

Jones v Thomas [1933] All ER 535; (1934-39) XXX Cox CC 47; (1934) 98 JP 41; [1934] 1 KB 323; (1933) 76 LJ 338; (1934) 103 LJCL 113; (1934) 150 LTR 216 HC KBD That told a lie not conclusive evidence of paternity.

K v K [1992] 2 All ER 727; [1992] 2 FCR 253; [1992] 2 FLR 220; (1992) 136 SJ LB 69; [1992] TLR 73; [1992] 1 WLR 530 CA Judge may confer benefit on person other than child when making order under Guardianship of Minors Act 1971.

K v M [1996] 3 FCR 517; [1996] 1 FLR 312 HC FamD Paternity declaration/contact order refused to putative father who had affair with married woman whose marriage nonetheless survived.

Knowles v Attorney-General [1950] 2 All ER 6; (1950) 100 LJ 288; (1950) 94 SJ 421; [1950] 66 (1) TLR 1188; (1950) WN (I) 288 HC PDAD Cannot obtain legitimation order in respect of one's uncles.

Knowles v Knowles [1962] 1 All ER 659; (1962) 112 LJ 190; (1961) 105 SJ 1011 HC PDAD Post decree nisi (pre decree absolute) conception of child raised presumption of legitimacy.

Kruhlak v Kruhlak [1958] 1 All ER 154; (1958) 122 JP 360; (1958) 108 LJ 122; (1958) 102 SJ 88 HC QBD Judicially separated woman could make application against husband under Bastardy Laws Amendment Act 1872.

L v L [1949] 1 All ER 141 HC PDAD Artficial insemination not approbation; no estoppel where other not misled/does not act to detriment; that nullity decree would bastardise child not ground for refusal.

Leong (Khoo Hooi) v Kwee (Khoo Hean) [1926] AC 529 PC Son not legitimate under special arrangements concerning secondary wives was not legitimate simply because testator treated him as so.

MacDarmaid v Attorney-General [1950] 1 All ER 497; (1950) 100 LJ 118; (1950) 94 SJ 211; [1950] 66 (1) TLR 543; (1950) WN (I) 104 HC PDAD Failed petition for legitimacy declaration where petitioner failed to prove father's first wife died before before petitioner's birth.

Marshall v Malcolm [1916-17] All ER 365; (1918-21) XXVI Cox CC 129; (1918) 82 JP 77; [1918] 87 LJCL 491; (1917-18) 117 LTR 752 HC KBD Woman living apart from husband on active service not single woman.

Maturin (by her Guardian) v Attorney-General (Maturin and Stone by her Guardian cited) [1938] 2 All ER 214; (1938) 82 SJ 275; (1937-38) LIV TLR 627; (1938) WN (I) 135 HC PDAD Petitioning for divorce adequate evidence of non-access.

Mayor, Aldermen and Citizens of Coventry v Surrey County Council [1934] 1 KB 211 CA Adopted illegitimate child did not acquire settlement of place in which adopted father had resided (and from which was irremovable).

Mellery-Pratt v Attorney-General (1969) 113 SJ 656 HC PDAD Rebuttal of presumption of legitimacy must be done beyond reasonable doubt.

Millard v Millard and Addis [1945] 2 All ER 525 HC PDAD Parenthood not legitimacy is the prerequisite for custody applications; illegitimate child need not be legitimised brfore custody order possible.

Mooney v Mooney [1952] 2 All ER 812; (1952) 116 JP 608; (1952) 102 LJ 625; [1953] 1 QB 38; (1952) 96 SJ 730; [1952] 2 TLR 711; (1952) WN (I) 488 HC QBD Wife living separately from husband not a single woman under Bastardy Laws Amendment Act 1872, s 3.

Moore v Hewitt [1947] 2 All ER 270; (1947) 111 JP 483; [1947] KB 831; (1947) 97 LJ 389; [1947] 116 LJR 1276; (1947) 177 LTR 576; (1947) LXIII TLR 476; (1947) WN (I) 224 HC KBD Close relationship of woman with putative father (and no other) corroborative of mother's claim.

Motala and others v Attorney-General and others [1990] 2 FLR 261 HC FamD Legitimacy declaration in respect of persons born of marriage not recognised/recognised where celebrated/ where domiciled.

National Assistance Board v Mitchell [1955] 3 All ER 291; [1955] Crim LR 567; (1955) 119 JP 572; (1955) 105 LJ 697; [1956] 1 QB 53; (1955) 99 SJ 781; [1955] 3 WLR 591 HC QBD National Assistance Board could make bastardy order application inside three years of last pay-out.

National Assistance Board v Tugby [1957] 1 All ER 509; (1957) 121 JP 149; (1957) 107 LJ 171; [1957] 1 QB 506; (1957) 101 SJ 172; [1957] 2 WLR 316 HC QBD National Assistance Board can seek bastardy order without proving mother single woman.

Newbould v Attorney-General [1931] All ER 377; (1931) 71 LJ 205; (1931) 100 LJP 54; (1931) 144 LTR 728; (1931) 75 SJ 174; (1930-31) XLVII TLR 297; (1931) WN (I) 70 HC PDAD Marriage of illegitimate child's parents (following nullification of father's first marriage) legitimated child.

O'Dea v Tetau [1950] 2 All ER 695; (1950) 114 JP 499; [1951] 1 KB 184; (1950) 100 LJ 455; (1950) 94 SJ 505; [1950] 66(2) TLR 339; (1950) WN (I) 447 HC KBD Cannot make affiliation order in respect of child born abroad of mother with foreign domicile.

Packer v Packer [1953] 2 All ER 127; (1953) 103 LJ 328; (1953) 97 SJ 403; [1953] 3 WLR 33 CA Test whether court may hear custody/maintenance application is parenthood not legitimacy.

Prior v Prior (by his guardian) (1970) 114 SJ 72 HC PDAD On when legitimacy hearings may be heard in camera.

R v Howard, ex parte Da Costa [1938] 3 All ER 241; (1938) 102 JP 333; [1938] 2 KB 544; [1938] 107 LJCL 675; (1938) 82 SJ 477; (1937-38) LIV TLR 825; (1938) WN (I) 202 HC KBD Cannot appeal from quarter sessions decision in affiliation action.

R v Justices of the Peace for Sunderland, ex parte Leslie Hodgkinson [1945] 2 All ER 175; (1945) 109 JP 201; [1945] 114 LJ 359; (1945) 173 LTR 62; (1945) 89 SJ 436; (1944-45) LXI TLR 456; (1945) WN (I) 150 HC KBD Justices can hear scond bastardy hearing/admit fresh evidence and make order despite initial refusal.

R v King's Lynn Justices and another, ex parte M [1988] FCR 436; [1988] 2 FLR 79 HC QBD Presumption of husband's paternity rebutted by admission of paternity from wife's lover (even though birth certificate named husband as father).

R v Lancashire Justices, ex parte Tyrer [1924] All ER 304; (1921-25) XXVII Cox CC 711; (1925) 89 JP 17; [1925] 1 KB 200; (1924) 59 LJ 775; [1925] 94 LJCL 331; (1925) 132 LTR 382; (1924-25) 69 SJ 194; (1924-25) XLI TLR 103; (1924) WN (I) 301 HC KBD Need not seek bastardy order in place where customarily/permanently reside.

R v Markham, ex parte Marsh (1923) WN (I) 112 HC KBD Court would not re-hear paternity suit under guise of action for writ of certiorari.

R v Seddon and others (1916) 80 JP 208; (1915-16) XXXII TLR 279; (1916) WN (I) 63 HC KBD Failure (for want of corroboration) of affiliation action does not preclude second such action inside twelve months (Bastardy Laws Amendment Act 1872, s 4).

R v Wilson, Esq (Metropolitan Magistrate) and others, ex parte Pereira [1952] 2 All ER 706; [1953] 1 QB 59 HC QBD Bastardy action cannot be brought where child abroad to mother then domiciled abroad.

Rabot and another v De Silva and others [1909] AC 376; [1909] 78 LJPC 73; (1909) C LTR 242; (1908-09) XXV TLR 332 PC Bequest to wife (former mistress) and children from her original marriage was valid.

Re Adams; Sursham v Farquharson and others [1951] 1 All ER 1037; [1951] 1 TLR 841 HC ChD Ineligibility of legitimated children to proceeds of trust fund.

Re Aldrich (1967) 111 SJ 475 HC PDAD On intervention in legitimacy action (brought by father).

Re Billson's Settlement Trusts [1984] 2 All ER 401; [1984] Ch 409; [1984] 2 WLR 966 CA Legitimated son barred from interest in settlement executed before legitimation.

Re Brodie, decd; Barclays Bank Ltd v Dallas and others [1967] Ch 818; [1967] 2 WLR 1379 HC ChD Properly legitimated child stands in position of child born legitimate as regards inheritance.

Re Bromage; Public v Cuthbert [1935] All ER 80; [1935] Ch 605; (1935) 153 LTR 313; (1935) 79 SJ 418; (1934-35) LI TLR 408 HC ChD Post-separation deed children deemed illegitimate where no evidence of access by husband.

Re C and another [1992] 2 All ER 86 CA Parental rights order available even where few rights under it enforceable; judge may consider prospective enforceability.

Re Green; Green v Meinall (1911) 46 LJ 372; (1911) 80 LJCh 63; (1910-11) 55 SJ 552; (1911) WN (I) 137 HC ChD Children of marriage between man and dead wife's sister were legitimated under Deceased Wife's Sister's Marriage Act 1907 though party to that later marriage died before statute enacted.

Re H [1989] 2 FLR 215 CA On effect of parental rights order obtained by illegitimate's father child pursuant to Family Law Reform Act 1987, s 4.

Re Haynes; Haynes v Carter (1906) XCIV LTR 431 HC ChD Persons reputed to be husband and wife were so but only one of their two children was deemed legitimate.

Re Heath, deceased; Stacey and another v Bird and another [1945] Ch 417; [1946] 115 LJ 120; (1944-45) LXI TLR 554 HC ChD Child born eight month's after mother's first husband died but whose registered father was man with whom mother then cohabiting and later married was legitimated by that later marriage.

Re Hepworth; Rastall v Hepworth [1936] Ch 750; [1936] 105 LJCh 380; (1936) 155 LTR 250; (1936) WN (I) 264 HC ChD Person legitimated after testator dies cannot inherit under testator's will where could not do so absent legitimation.

Re Hoff; Carnley v Hoff [1942] 1 All ER 547; (1943) 93 LJ 20; (1942) 166 LTR 241; (1942) 86 SJ 105; (1941-42) LVIII TLR 247; (1942) WN (I) 90 HC ChD Special power of appointment not a 'disposition' for purposes of Legitimacy Act 1926, s 10(2).

Re Hurll; Angelini v Dick and others [1952] 2 All ER 322; [1952] Ch 722; (1952) 102 LJ 399; (1952) 96 SJ 462; [1952] 2 TLR 85; (1952) WN (I) 354 HC ChD Legitimacy Act 1926, s 8(1) applies to person born when father resides in country where legitimation by later marriage not recognised.

Re Jenion (deceased); Jenion and others v Wynne [1952] 1 All ER 1228; (1952) 102 LJ 273 CA All oral evidence establishing bastardy admissible (here as res gestae not as direct evidence).

Re Leman's Will Trusts; Public Trustee v Leman and another [1946] 115 LJ 89; (1946) 174 LTR 75; (1944-45) LXI TLR 566; (1945) WN (I) 183 HC ChD Son born in March 1886 of mother whose marriage was ended by divorce in October 1885 was legitimate son of that dissolved marriage.

Re Lowe; Stewart v Lowe [1929] 2 Ch 210; (1929) 98 LJCh 440; (1929) 141 LTR 428; (1928-29) XLV TLR 484; (1929) WN (I) 143 HC ChD Issue of dead illegitimate son (whose parents married after his birth) who died before coming into operation of Legitimacy Act 1926 could not take share in grandmother's estate.

Re Luck's Settlement Trusts; Re Luck's Will Trusts; Walker v Luck [1940] Ch 323; [1940] 109 LJP 108; (1940) 162 LTR 192; (1940) WN (I) 56 HC ChD Recognition of foreign decree recognising putative father as father where in place of domicile at child's birth was not so recognised.

Re Luck, Walker v Luck [1940] 3 All ER 307; [1940] Ch 864; [1940] 109 LJP 380; (1941) 164 LTR 172; (1940) WN (I) 257 CA Non-recognition of foreign decree recognising putative father as father where in place of domicile at child's birth was not so recognised.

Re Makein, decd; Makein v Makein and another [1955] 2 WLR 43 HC ChD Illegitimate son not dependant for purposes of Inheritance (Family Provision) Act 1938, s 1(1).

Re Overbury; Sheppard v Matthews and others [1954] 3 All ER 308; [1955] Ch 122; (1954) 104 LJ 728; (1954) 98 SJ 768; [1954] 3 WLR 644 HC ChD Child born after second marriage/within nine months of death of first spouse is presumed to be legitimate child of first spouse.

Re Spence; Spence v Dennis and another [1990] 2 All ER 827; [1990] Ch 652; [1990] FCR 983; [1990] 2 FLR 278; [1990] TLR 288; [1990] 2 WLR 1430 CA Legitimacy not conferred on child of void marriage entered into by parents after child's birth.

Re Spence; Spence v Dennis and another [1989] 2 All ER 679; [1990] Ch 197; [1989] FCR 651; [1990] 1 FLR 286; (1989) 133 SJ 1372/1513; [1989] 3 WLR 834 HC ChD Child born before parents enter void marriage cannot be treated as legitimate.

Re The Legitimacy Act, 1926, and Re Younghusband (1927) 64 LJ ccr54 CyCt Failed application for legitimacy petition to be heard in camera.

Re W [1990] FCR 540; [1990] 2 FLR 86 CA Inappropriate that interim custody order be made in favour of putative father until question of paternity decided.

Re Wicks' Marriage Settlement; Public Trustee v Wicks [1940] Ch 475; [1940] 109 LJCh 163; (1940) 163 LTR 31; (1940) 84 SJ 304; (1940) WN (I) 136 HC ChD Legitimated child was not object of power of appointment applicable to issue of parents' marriage.

Robertson v Robertson and Butt and In the Matter of an Issue: Robertson v Robertson and others (1928) 72 SJ 585 HC PDAD Hearing as to legitimacy of child to be done in open court as public nature of hearing did not mean justice would be unattainable.

Russell v Attorney-General (1949) 99 LJ 259; [1949] 118 LJR 1247; (1949) LXV TLR 369; (1949) WN (I) 226 HC PDAD Validity of marriage presumed absent direct contrary evidence where parties had undergone ceremony of marriage and thereafter corroborated.

S (otherwise U) v Attorney-General (1932) 146 LTR 144; (1931-32) XLVIII TLR 66 HC PDAD Dismissal of legitimacy petition brought on behalf of mentally unsound person.

Sackville-West v Attorney-General (Lord Sackville and others cited) (1909) 44 LJ 695; [1910] 79 LJP 34; (1909-10) XXVI TLR 33; (1909) WN (I) 220 HC KBD Refusal by court to order trial by jury of questions arising under Legitimacy Declaration Act 1858: jury trial provisions of Matrimonial Causes Act 1857, s 28 inapplicable.

Scappaticci v Attorney-General [1955] 1 All ER 193 (1955) 99 SJ 114; [1955] 2 WLR 409 HC PDAD On legitimation by post-birth marriage of parents; on changing domicil.

Scott v The National Society for the Prevention of Cruelty to Children and Parr (1908-09) XXV TLR 789 Assizes Recovery of costs between solicitor and client incurred in slander and bastardy actions.

Sheward v Attorney-General (1964) 114 LJ 374; (1964) 108 SJ 159; [1964] 1 WLR 724 HC PDAD Must comply with Matrimonial Causes Act 1950, s 17(1) and Legitimacy Act 1959, s 2 for legitimacy order under latter to be made in respect of one.

Slingsby (by his Guardian ad litem) v Attorney-General and others (1916-17) XXXIII TLR 120 HL Failed legitimacy action dismissed with costs to be paid by guardian ad litem or next friend.

Stafford v Kidd [1936] 3 All ER 1023; (1934-39) XXX Cox CC 532; (1937) 101 JP 68; [1937] 1 KB 395; (1937) 83 LJ 26; [1937] 106 LJCL 193; (1937) 156 LTR 75; (1937) 81 SJ 16; (1936-37) LIII TLR 169; (1937) WN (I) 17 HC KBD Separation deed raises presumption of non-access: wife had to prove access by husband.

Sydall v Castings, Ltd [1966] 3 All ER 770 CA 'Descendant' generally means legitimate descendants.

T (H) v T(E) [1971] 1 All ER 590; (1971) 115 SJ 186; [1971] 1 WLR 429 HC PDAD Absent contrary evidence presumption that child of marriage is legitimate; blood test cautiously accepted as proof of paternity.

The Guardians of the Poor of Plymouth v Gibbs (1903) 67 JP 61; [1903] 1 KB 177; [1903] 72 LJKB 33; (1902-03) LXXXVII LTR 685; (1902-03) 47 SJ 32; (1902-03) 51 WR 157 HC KBD Union/parish guardians could seek affiliation order against putative father despite mother's re-marriage to man capable of maintaining children.

W v W [1953] 2 All ER 1013 HC PDAD Husband's use of contraceptives does not rebut presumption of legitimacy; legitimacy could be a post-divorce issue when adultery only matter of concern in divorce suit.

Watson v Tuckwell (1947) LXIII TLR 634 HC KBD Wife/mother living completely separately from husband in house and paying keep for self/children was single woman for purposes of Bastardy Laws Amendment Act 1872, s 3.

Webb v Murrel (1904) 68 JP 104 Police Ct Separated married woman can obtain affiliation order against natural father of her illegitimate child as a 'single woman' (Bastardy Laws Amendment Act 1882, s 3).

Whitton v Garner [1965] 1 All ER 70; (1965) 129 JP 92; (1965) 115 LJ 75; (1965) 109 SJ 194; [1965] 1 WLR 313 HC QBD Wife living apart from husband in same house was single woman.

LEGITIMACY (insanity)

S (otherwise U) v Attorney-General (1932) 146 LTR 144; (1931-32) XLVIII TLR 66 HC PDAD Dismissal of legitimacy petition brought on behalf of mentally unsound person.

LEGITIMACY (maintenance)

Bowen v Norman [1938] 2 All ER 776; (1934-39) XXX Cox CC 674; (1938) 102 JP 123; [1938] 1 KB 689; (1938) 85 LJ 396; [1938] 107 LJCL 273; (1938) 158 LTR 257; (1938) 82 SJ 77; (1937-38) LIV TLR 342; (1938) WN (I) 41 HC KBD Maintenance order per se did not establish non-access.

James v Morgan (1909) 73 JP 149; [1909] 1 KB 564; [1909] 78 LJKB 471; (1909) C LTR 238; (1908-09) 53 SJ 245; (1908-09) XXV TLR 267; (1909) WN (I) 31 HC KBD Father's agreement to maintain bastard child ended upon mother's death.

R v Birkenhead Borough Justices, ex parte Smith [1954] 1 All ER 503; [1954] Crim LR 133t; [1954] Crim LR 297; (1954) 118 JP 203; (1954) 104 LJ 154; (1954) 98 SJ 163 HC QBD Cannot commit member of US forces and father of illegitimate child for non-payment of maintenance.

Re Guardianship of Infants Acts 1886 and 1925, and Re B (S), an Infant [1949] Ch 108; (1948) WN (I) 480 HC ChD Maintenance order discharged where was non-access prior to 188 days before child's birth (and child born was mature); maintenance order applied to father as father so where paternity disproved would not issue against him as husband.

Re Wakeman; Wakeman v Wakeman [1947] 2 All ER 74; [1947] Ch 607; (1947) 111 JP 373; (1947) 97 LJ 319; [1947] 116 LJR 1092; (1947) 177 LTR 161; (1947) 91 SJ 339; (1947) LXIII TLR 396; (1947) WN (I) 180 HC ChD On need for fresh evidence when seeking change to maintenance order under Guardianship of Infants Act 1925; here evidence that condoned adultery/allowed illegitimate child to be registered as own admitted.

Taylor v Parry [1951] 1 All ER 355; (1951) 115 JP 119; [1951] 2 KB 442; (1951) 101 LJ 63; (1951) 95 SJ 61; [1951] 1 TLR 509; (1951) WN (I) 94 HC KBD Mother of illegitimate child who marries man other than father of child cannot seek maintenance from that child from husband/ actual father.

Watson v Watson (1953) 97 SJ 746; [1953] 3 WLR 708 HC PDAD Husband's denial of paternity in successful divorce suit did not preclude ex-wife's later seeking maintenance despite her not challenging husband's denial in divorce suit.

LEGITIMACY (nullity)

Dredge v Dredge (otherwise Harrison) [1947] 1 All ER 29 HC PDAD That nullity renders child illegitimate not consideration for court.

LEGITIMACY (ward)

Re S (J) [1980] 1 All ER 1061; [1981] Fam 22; (1981) 2 FLR 146; (1980) 124 SJ 881; [1980] 3 WLR 984 CA Bare declaration of paternity not to be made in wardship case; grounds on which (if possible) to be made.

MAINTENANCE (access/contact)

Bowers v Clarke (1961) 105 SJ 988 CA Was not repudiation of maintenance agreement whereunder maintenance payable and access granted for custodial parent to remove child to Australia.

Foot v Foot [1987] FCR 62 HC FamD Access to children not relevant factor when determining level of maintenance payable in respect of same.

MAINTENANCE (adoption)

Hackney Union v Tombs; Tombs v Hackney Union (1909) 73 JP 271 Police Ct Valid adoption of child by poor law guardians; adulterous father ordered to pay maintenance.

Re Skinner; Skinner v Carter [1948] 1 All ER 917; [1948] Ch 387; (1948) 112 JP 329; (1948) 98 LJ 273; [1948] 117 LJR 1628; (1948) WN (I) 185 CA Bigamously married adopter could be ordered to pay for child's maintenance.

Re Skinner; Skinner v Carter (1948) 112 JP 116; (1948) 98 LJ 23 HC ChD Bigamously married adopter could not seek maintenance order in respect of child against partner in bigamy (and co-adopter).

MAINTENANCE (affiliation)

Dickens v Pattison [1985] FLR 610; (1985) 149 JP 271; (1985) 129 SJ 31 HC FamD Contravention by magistrates of principle that only affiliation payment arrears of less than one year to be enforced.

G (A) v G (T) [1970] 3 All ER 546; (1971) 135 JP 13; [1970] 2 QB 643; [1970] 3 WLR 132 CA Putative father can authorise agent to pay infant's maintenance; proof of agency required before maintenance proceedings can be begun.

G v G (1970) 114 SJ 493 CA On payment by infant of maintenance towards own child (and on proving paid same).

Jeffery v Paget (1919) CC Rep VIII 2 CyCt Man married by woman who has entered into maintenance agreement in affiliation action becomes liable for maintenance of said children.

Moore v Ball [1984] 2 All ER 237; [1984] Fam 41; [1984] FLR 555; (1984) 148 JP 425; (1984) 128 SJ 298; [1984] 2 WLR 865 HC FamD Secretary of State can have varied maintenance order payable to Secretary increased by variation.

R v Birkenhead Borough Justices, ex parte Smith [1954] 1 All ER 503; [1954] Crim LR 297; [1954] Crim L 133t; (1954) 118 JP 203; (1954) 104 LJ 154; (1954) 98 SJ 163 HC QBD US soldier (member of visiting forces) could not be committed to prison for failure to maintain child pursuant to affiliation order.

R v Bow Road Domestic Proceedings Court, ex parte Adedigba [1968] 2 All ER 89; (1968) 118 NLJ 444; [1968] 2 QB 572; (1968) 132 JP 301; [1968] 2 WLR 1143 CA Maintenance order if mother and father resident in England though child born abroad/mother domiciled abroad when child born.

R v Copestake and others, ex parte Wilkinson [1926] All ER 252; (1926) 90 JP 191; [1927] 1 KB 468; [1927] 96 LJCL 65; (1927) 136 LTR 100; (1926) WN (I) 242 CA Under Criminal Justice Administration Act 1914 court could revoke periodic payments ordered in affiliation suit but could not alter paternity decision.

Re Harrington; Wilder v Turner [1908-10] All ER 235; [1908] 2 Ch 687; (1907-09) XXI Cox CC 709; (1908) 72 JP 501; [1909] 78 LJCh 27; (1908) 43 LJ 641; (1908-09) XCIX LTR 723; (1907-08) 52 SJ 855; (1908-09) XXV TLR 3; (1908) WN (I) 203 HC ChD Cannot seek arrears of maintenance under affiliation order from estate/representatives of deceased father.

MAINTENANCE (arrears)

N (S) v T (S) [1994] 3 FCR 229; [1995] 1 FLR 868 HC FamD Rehearing ordered of justices' refusal to remit arrears as approach to deciding case had been defective.

MAINTENANCE (care/custody)

Flood v Flood [1948] 2 All ER 712; (1948) 112 JP 416; [1948] 117 LJR 1880; (1948) LXIV TLR 474 HC PDAD Children's welfare paramount in custody cases (and maintenance an important element of that).

Galloway v Galloway [1954] 2 All ER 143; (1954) 104 LJ 328; (1954) 98 SJ 336; [1954] 2 WLR 980 CA Custody/maintenance unavailable in respect of child born outside marriage who cannot be legitimated.

Re T; Re Guardianship of Infants Acts, 1886-1925 [1953] Ch 787; (1953) 97 SJ 607 HC ChD Appropriate that means of mother (given custody of children) be taken into account when assessing appropriate maintenance for mother.

MAINTENANCE (child of the family)

P (R) v P (P) [1969] 3 All ER 777 Assizes No acceptance of child as family if both parties do not agree (so no liability for maintenance).

MAINTENANCE (child support)

B v M [1994] 1 FCR 769; [1994] 1 FLR 342 CyCt On revocation (during transitional period of Child Support Act 1991) of child maintenance order prior to application to Child Support Agency for child maintenance assessment.

Smith v McInerney [1994] 2 FCR 1086; [1994] 2 FLR 1077 HC FamD Variation of liabilities under separation agreement where husband had been made redundant/was likely to be subject of Child Support Agency assessment.

T v S [1994] 1 FCR 743; [1994] 2 FLR 883 HC FamD Property being held on trust for sale postponed until youngest child ended secondary schoool/turned twenty-one would revert to father at that point.

MAINTENANCE (costs)

Edwards v Edwards [1958] 2 All ER 179; (1958) 108 LJ 315; (1958) 102 SJ 402 HC PDAD Apportioning of costs in light of solicitor's incompetence.

MAINTENANCE (extension)

Norman v Norman [1950] 1 All ER 1082; (1950) 114 JP 299; (1950) 100 LJ 259; (1950) 94 SJ 354; [1950] 66 (1) TLR 1044; (1950) WN (I) 230 HC PDAD Can be extension of expired maintenance order.

MAINTENANCE (fostering)

Surrey County Council v Battersby [1965] 1 All ER 273; [1965] Crim LR101t; (1965) 129 JP 116; (1965) 115 LJ 125; [1965] 2 QB 194; (1965) 109 SJ 30; [1965] 2 WLR 378 HC QBD Person taking children for more than one month (albeit interrupted by stays with parents) 'proposed' to maintain foster child.

MAINTENANCE (general)

Bancroft v Bancroft [1963] 1 All ER 367; (1963) 107 SJ 112; [1963] 2 WLR 309 CA On leave being unnecessary to make maintenance/secured provision application during divorce petition.

Cockburn v Cockburn [1957] 3 All ER 260; (1957) 107 LJ 586; (1957) 101 SJ 798 CA County court judge cannot suspend maintenance order.

Coldingham Parish Council v Smith [1918] 2 KB 90; (1918) WN (I) 112 HC KBD English-domiciled father not responsible for maintenance of pauper lunatic son in Scotland.

Easterbrook v Easterbrook [1957] 2 All ER 117; (1957) 107 LJ 266; (1957) 101 SJ 303; (1943-44) LX TLR 80 HC PDAD On maintenance of children.

Freeman-Thomas v Freeman-Thomas [1963] 1 All ER 17; (1963) 113 LJ 27; (1962) 106 SJ 532; [1963] 2 WLR 107 HC PDAD No retroactive application of maintenance order requiring payment of education costs.

Garner v Garner [1992] 1 FLR 573 CA Variation of periodical payments order justified where child's welfare demands increase in maintenance paid for child.

Hering v Hering and Wilson [1943] 112 LJ 81; (1943) 169 LTR 236; (1942-43) LIX TLR 428; (1943) WN (I) 216 HC PDAD Guilty wife with own estate could be ordered to pay for maintenance of children.

J v J [1993] 1 FCR 471; [1993] 2 FLR 56 HC FamD Ex-cohabitee not 'father' of mother's child so could not be ordered to transfer property to mother for child's benefit.

Jackson v Jackson (1967) 111 SJ 456 HC PDAD Valid finding of wilful neglect to maintain; wife's failure to give notice to putative father of child regarding maintenance action against another precluded making of maintenance order.

K v H [1993] 1 FCR 683; [1993] 2 FLR 61; [1992] TLR 660 HC FamD Court order available to formalise existing well-working private mintenance agreement.

Le Mare v Le Mare [1960] 2 All ER 280; (1960) 110 LJ 399; (1960) 104 SJ 450 HC PDAD Unsecured maintenance available for child over twenty-one.

Meaney v Meaney [1957] 2 All ER 415; (1957) 107 LJ 362; (1957) 101 SJ 482 HC PDAD On jurisdiction of different magistrates' courts to vary/discharge maintenance orders.

Meyer v Meyer [1957] 2 All ER 546; (1957) 121 JP 424; (1957) 107 LJ 442; (1957) 101 SJ 630 HC PDAD Justices can ante-date maintenance order.

Nowell v Nowell [1951] 1 All ER 474; (1951) 115 JP 162; (1951) 101 LJ 119; (1951) 95 SJ 270; [1951] 1 TLR 647; (1951) WN (I) 167 HC PDAD On continuation of maintenance orders: test inerests of child/financial status of parties.

R v High Peak Magistrates' Court, ex parte B [1995] 1 FLR 568 HC FamD On inappropriateness of judicial review of maintenance order as a form of relief when appeal structure exists.

R v R [1988] FCR 307; [1988] 1 FLR 89 CA On assessing appropriate maintenance for children (husband's expenditure on new house was justified here).

R v Rose, ex parte McGibbon (1959) 123 JP 374 HC QBD Jamaican maintenance order could not be rescinded by English court under Maintenance Orders (Facilties for Enforcement) Act 1920.

R v West London Magistrates' Court, ex parte Emmett [1994] 1 FCR 421; [1993] 2 FLR 663 HC FamD On enforceability of registered Irish maintenance order: in-/effective post-/pre-divorce decree absolute.

Re B; B v B [1949] 118 LJR 369; (1949) LXV TLR 142 HC ChD Child who showed no evidence of prematurity despite being born only 188 days after 'father's' return was not child of purported father.

Re Dulles' Settlement Trusts; Dulles v Vidler [1950] 2 All ER 1013; [1951] Ch 265; (1950) 100 LJ 622; (1950) 94 SJ 760; [1950] 66 (2) TLR 1028; (1950) WN (I) 523 CA Party may submit to jurisdiction of courts from abroad; application by infant with mother as best friend treated as mother's application.

Re Dulles' Settlement Trusts; Dulles v Vidler (1951) 101 LJ 302; [1951] 2 TLR 145 CA Foreigner living abroad can submit self to jurisdiction of court in custody proceedings.

Re Guardianship of Infants Acts 1886 and 1925, and Re B (S), an Infant [1949] Ch 108; (1948) WN (I) 480 HC ChD Maintenance order discharged where was non-access prior to 188 days before child's birth (and child born was mature); maintenance order applied to father as father so where paternity disproved would not issue against him as husband.

Re Hambrough's Estate; Hambrough v Hambrough [1909] 2 Ch 620 HC ChD Court cannot order mortgage of interest of infant tenant in tail in remainder so as to secure maintenance for him.

Re McK (1976) 126 NLJ 890t HC FamD Substitution of higher maintenance payments than those required upon variation by Australian court of original maintenance order.

Re Reade-Revell; Crellin v Melling [1929] All ER 506; [1930] 1 Ch 52; (1930) 142 LTR 177 HC ChD No maintenance from trust fund as contingent interest did not carry intermediate income.

Re Scott; Scott v Scott [1902] 1 Ch 918 HC ChD On entitlement of beneficiary children upon attaining age of majority to accumulations of beqeathed property not already paid to them as maintenance.

Re Stern; Stern v Stern [1950] 2 All ER 160; (1950) 114 JP 361; (1950) 94 SJ 420; [1950] 66 (1) TLR 1087 HC ChD No right of appeal against orders by summary court under Children Act 1948, s 53.

Re T [1953] 2 All ER 830; (1953) 117 JP 517; (1953) 103 LJ 604; [1953] 3 WLR 619 HC ChD In deciding infant's maintenance by father, mother's income relevant.

Re W and another [1956] 1 All ER 368; [1956] Ch 384; (1956) 120 JP 210; [1956] 2 WLR 493 CA Mother's income relevant when determining infant's maintenance payable by father.

Riding v Riding [1958] 1 All ER 65; (1958) 108 LJ 56; (1958) 102 SJ 52 CA Committal for non-payment of maintenance is for original amount of order.

S v S [1993] 1 FLR 606 HC FamD On appellate review of child maintenance actions; maintenance order invalid as procedural errors in action.

S v S [1995] 1 FCR 149 HC FamD On need for caution in incurring of costs in financial provision applications: here no capital adjustment between parties who ran up high costs.

Smith v Smith and Brown [1962] 3 All ER 369; (1962) 112 LJ 665; (1962) 106 SJ 610; [1962] 1 WLR 1218 CA No maintenance of child accepted into family justified where marriage short.

Symmons v Symmons [1993] 2 FCR 247; [1993] 1 FLR 317 HC FamD Maintenance undertaking could be (here was) enforceable by way of judgment summons.

Teeling v Teeling [1984] FLR 808 CA Wife's child a child of family as lived with wife/husband for six months; maintenance ordered minimal as responsibility husband assumed for child negligible.

Wheatley v Wheatley [1949] 2 All ER 428; (1949) 113 JP 459; [1950] 1 KB 39; (1949) 99 LJ 414; (1949) LXV TLR 602; (1949) WN (I) 350 HC KBD Maintenance not payable as parties residing under one roof.

Whitcombe v Evans (1932) 74 LJ ccr86 CyCt Agreement by putative father to pay maintenance for child had by married woman was not void for public policy reasons.

MAINTENANCE (legitimacy)

Bowen v Norman [1938] 2 All ER 776; (1934-39) XXX Cox CC 674; (1938) 102 JP 123; [1938] 1 KB 689; (1938) 85 LJ 396; [1938] 107 LJCL 273; (1938) 158 LTR 257; (1938) 82 SJ 77; (1937-38) LIV TLR 342; (1938) WN (I) 41 HC KBD Maintenance order per se did not establish non-access.

James v Morgan (1909) 73 JP 149; [1909] 1 KB 564; [1909] 78 LJKB 471; (1909) C LTR 238; (1908-09) 53 SJ 245; (1908-09) XXV TLR 267; (1909) WN (I) 31 HC KBD Father's agreement to maintain bastard child ended upon mother's death.

Osborn v Sparks (1982) 3 FLR 90 HC FamD On balancing procedure to be exercised when assessing financial provision to be made by father in respect of illegitimate child and its mother.

Packer v Packer [1953] 2 All ER 127; (1953) 103 LJ 328; (1953) 97 SJ 403; [1953] 3 WLR 33 CA Test whether court may hear custody/maintenance application is parenthood not legitimacy.

Re Guardianship of Infants Acts 1886 and 1925, and Re B (S), an Infant [1949] Ch 108; (1948) WN (I) 480 HC ChD Maintenance order discharged where was non-access prior to 188 days before child's birth (and child born was mature); maintenance order applied to father as father so where paternity disproved would not issue against him as husband.

Re Wakeman; Wakeman v Wakeman [1947] 2 All ER 74; [1947] Ch 607; (1947) 111 JP 373; (1947) 97 LJ 319; [1947] 116 LJR 1092; (1947) 177 LTR 161; (1947) 91 SJ 339; (1947) LXIII TLR 396; (1947) WN (I) 180 HC ChD On need for fresh evidence when seeking change to maintenance order under Guardianship of Infants Act 1925; here evidence that condoned adultery/allowed illegitimate child to be registered as own admitted.

Taylor v Parry [1951] 1 All ER 355; (1951) 115 JP 119; [1951] 2 KB 442; (1951) 101 LJ 63; (1951) 95 SJ 61; [1951] 1 TLR 509; (1951) WN (I) 94 HC KBD Mother of illegitimate child who marries man other than father of child cannot seek maintenance from that child from husband/actual father.

Watson v Watson (1953) 97 SJ 746; [1953] 3 WLR 708 HC PDAD Husband's denial of paternity in successful divorce suit did not preclude ex-wife's later seeking maintenance despite her not challenging husband's denial in divorce suit.

MAINTENANCE (separation)

Starkie v Starkie (No 2) [1953] 2 All ER 1519; (1954) 118 JP 59; (1954) 98 SJ 46; [1954] 1 WLR 98 HC PDAD Husband is/is not under duty to maintain child/wife where consensual separation with no maintenance agreement.

MAINTENANCE (social security)

E v C [1996] 1 FCR 612; [1996] 1 FLR 472; [1995] TLR 638 HC FamD Income support/child benefit to be treated as subsistence money — that plus cost of supporting new family justified downward variation of child maintenance order.

Phillips v Peace [1996] 2 FLR 230 HC FamD Lump sum ordered for maintenance of child in circumstances where child support officer (correctly) assessed father's actual income as nil.

MAINTENANCE (tax)

Jefferson v Jefferson [1956] 1 All ER 31; (1956) 106 LJ 8; (1955) 99 SJ 911; [1955] 3 WLR 1001 CA Maintenance 'free of tax' meant that after tax the amount paid should be the amount stated.

Sherdley v Sherdley [1986] 2 All ER 202; [1988] AC 213; [1986] 2 FLR 326; (1986) 150 JP 305; (1986) 136 NLJ 464; (1986) 130 SJ 356; [1986] 1 WLR 732 CA Unless a sham/for avoidance of tax custodial parent can seek periodic payments order against self.

Sherdley v Sherdley [1987] FCR 149; (1987) 151 JP 715; (1987) 131 SJ 504; [1987] 2 WLR 1071 HL Even though was for avoidance of tax custodial parent could seek periodic payments order against self.

MAINTENANCE (ward)

Calderdale Borough Council v H and P [1991] 1 FLR 461 HC FamD Statutory care order to local authority, children to reside with grandparents who were to be paid maintenance pending approval as foster-parents when would be paid boarding-out allowance.

Re K and A [1995] 1 FLR 688 HC FamD No power to order local authority to pay maintenance to grandmother for grandchild in her care/its supervision (and if power existed was inappropriately exercised here).

MARRIAGE (foreign)

Mohamed v Knott [1968] 2 All ER 563; [1968] Crim LR 341t; (1968) 132 JP 349; [1969] 1 QB 1; (1968) 112 SJ 332; [1968] 2 WLR 1446 HC QBD Nigerian Moslem marriage to girl of thirteen valid.

MEDICAL TREATMENT (general)

Gillick v West Norfolk and Wisbech Area Health Authority and another [1984] 1 All ER 365; [1984] FLR 249; (1983) 133 NLJ 888; [1984] QB 681; (1983) 127 SJ 696; [1983] TLR 541 HC QBD Doctor prescribing contraceptives for under-16 year old girl not encouraging unlawful sexual intercourse; contraceptive advice to under-16 year old not interference with parental duties.

Gillick v West Norfolk and Wisbech Area Health Authority and another [1985] 1 All ER 533; [1985] FLR 736; (1985) 135 NLJ 81; (1985) 129 SJ 47; [1984] TLR 744 CA Absent emergency doctor's prescribing contraceptives for under-16 year old girl was interference with parental duties.

Gillick v West Norfolk and Wisbech Area Health Authority and another [1986] Crim LR 113; [1986] 1 FLR 224; (1985) 135 NLJ 1055; (1985) 129 SJ 738 HL Depended on intent of doctor prescribing contraceptives for under-16 year old girl whether was aiding and abetting unlawful sexual intercourse; contraceptive advice to under-16 year old not necessarily interference with parental duties.

R v Cambridge District Health Authority, ex parte B [1995] 2 FCR 485; [1995] 1 FLR 1055 (also HC QBD) CA Health authority's decision not to fund expensive experimental treatment of seriously ill child was reasonable.

Re F (G) [1992] 1 FLR 293 HC FamD On when declaration of legality of hysterectomy on mentally handicapped woman is unnecessary.

Re R (a minor) [1993] 2 FCR 544; [1993] 2 FLR 757 HC FamD Order that in life-threatening situation child of Jehovah's Witnesses could be given blood transfusions.

Re W [1992] 4 All ER 627; [1993] Fam 64; [1992] 2 FCR 785 (also HC FamD); [1993] 1 FLR 1; (1992) 142 NLJ 1124; [1992] 3 WLR 758 CA Court may order medical treatment of minor despite minor's objections.

Re W [1992] 2 FCR 785 (also CA) HC FamD Court may order medical treatment of minor despite minor's objections.

Re W [1993] 2 FCR 187; [1993] 1 FLR 381 HC FamD Proposed sterilisation of applicant's mentally handicapped daughter approved.

South Glamorgan County Council v W and B [1993] 1 FCR 626; [1993] 1 FLR 574 HC FamD Court can order medical care of minor despite minor's (informed) refusal if in minor's best interests.

MEDICAL TREATMENT (religion)

Re S [1993] 1 FLR 376 HC FamD Blood transfusions to child allowed though contrary to principles/wishes of parents (Jehovah's Witnesses).

MEDICAL TREATMENT (sterilisation)

Re G (H) [1993] 1 FCR 553; [1993] 1 FLR 587 HC FamD Child could by father as next friend bring application for authorisation of own sterilisation.

MEDICAL TREATMENT (ward)

Re E [1991] FCR 771; [1991] 2 FLR 585; [1991] TLR 93 HC FamD Leave of court unnecessary for thereapeutic sterilisation of mentally handicapped girl.

MIDWIFE (general)

Davis v Morris (1922-23) XXXIX TLR 454; (1923) WN (I) 139 HC KBD On elements of defence of medical supervision where charged with acting as uncertified midwife (Midwives Act 1902, s 1(2)).

NECESSARIES (general)

Biberfield v Berens [1952] 2 All ER 237; [1952] 2 QB 770; [1952] 2 TLR 39 CA Wife of means deemed not husband's agent of necessity after his actions forced her to leave home.

Hewlings v Graham [1901] 70 LJCh 568; (1901) LXXXIV LTR 497 HC ChD Infant's buying of jewellery (without agreement of guardian) for fiancée whom infant does not later marry is not purchase of necessaries.

JN Nabarro and Sons v Kennedy [1954] 2 All ER 605; [1955] 1 QB 575; (1954) 98 SJ 524 HC QBD Wife can pledge husband's credit for necessaries in respect of costs of action under Married Women's Property Act 1882, s 17.

Nash v Inman [1908] 2 KB 1; [1908] 77 LJCL 626; (1908) XCVIII LTR 658; (1907-08) XXIV TLR 401 CA In suing infant for necessaries must show were apposite to infant's state in life and that infant had inadequate supply of said goods when supplied.

Re Clabon (FW) [1904-07] All ER 1446; (1904-05) XCI LTR 316 HC ChD Poor infant liable like any other to pay for necessaries provided under invalid contract from own property.

Rondeau, Legrand and Co v Marks [1916-17] All ER 664; [1918] 1 KB 75; (1917) 52 LJ 378; [1918] 87 LJCL 215 (also HC KBD); (1917-18) 117 LTR 651; (1917-18) 62 SJ 24; (1917-18) XXXIV TLR 8; (1917) WN (I) 298 CA Husband must provide wife with necessary clothes but need not give them to her.

Rondeau, Legrand and Co v Marks (Louis Marks, Claimant) [1917] 2 KB 636; [1918] 87 LJCL 215 (also CA); (1916-17) 61 SJ 666; (1916-17) XXXIII TLR 529; (1917) WN (I) 268 HC KBD Husband must provide wife with necessary clothes but need not give them to her.

NON-INTERFERENCE WITH CHILD POST-MAJORITY (general)

Re V [1995] 2 FLR 1003 HC FamD Injunction to restrain mother from interfering with child's decision upon attaining majority as to where would live.

PARENTAGE (adoption)

Re L (no 2) [1991] 1 FLR 29 CrCt On parentage as alternative to adoption.

PARENTAGE (general)

Re B [1996] 3 FCR 697; [1996] 2 FLR 15 HC FamD Though no consent to keeping/use of gametes man and woman had jointly undergone fertility treatment so man was parent of children born.

PARENTAL RESPONSIBILITY ORDER (blood tests)

Re F [1993] 3 All ER 596; [1993] Fam 314; [1993] 3 WLR 369 CA Court will not order blood tests where parental responsibility application likely to fail; not in child's interests; parent in charge of child opposed.

PARENTAL RESPONSIBILITY ORDER (contact)

Re H [1993] 1 FCR 85; [1993] 1 FLR 484 CA Parental responsibility but not contact order for father (where stepfather strenuously objected to contact order).

PARENTAL RESPONSIBILITY ORDER (general)

B v B (1980) 1 FLR 87 CA Court must itself decide which school child to attend where divorced parents cannot agree on matter.

B v B [1993] 1 FCR 211; [1992] 2 FLR 327 HC FamD Residence order to grandmother (seeking same with mother's approval) that she might exercise parental responsibility.

Birmingham City Council v H [1993] 1 FCR 247; [1992] 2 FLR 323 HC FamD Residence order carries with it right to exercise parental responsibility.

D v Hereford and Worcester County Council [1991] 2 All ER 177; [1991] Fam 14; [1991] 1 FLR 205; (1990) 134 SJ 1402; [1990] TLR 698; [1991] 2 WLR 753 HC FamD Parental rights order available even if child in care; all relevant facts of concern to court asked to make parental rights order.

D v S [1995] 3 FCR 783 HC FamD On whether/when parental responsibility order appropriate: ill-will between parties not a deciding factor.

R (B) v Ealing London Borough [1985] FLR 999 HC FamD Failed application by mother of children over whom parental rights resolution made to have that resolution determined.

Re A [1996] 1 FCR 562 HC FamD On whether/when (as here) to make parental responsibility order.

Re B [1991] FCR 800 CA Local authority's parental rights in respect of child ended upon child's death.

Re B (C) [1993] 1 FCR 440; [1993] 1 FLR 920 HC FamD On nature/effect of parental reponsibility order: here refusal of order quashed as justices did not fully consider appropriateness of order.

Re C [1991] FCR 856; [1992] 1 FLR 1; (1991) 135 SJ LB 100; [1991] TLR 387 CA On relevant considerations when deciding whether to grant parental rights order: enforceability a relevant, not paramount issue.

Re E [1994] 2 FCR 709; [1995] 1 FLR 392 CA Decision to refuse contact unchanged but parental responsibility order made; on directing that blood tests be conducted (only possible where paternity an issue).

Re G [1995] 2 FCR 53; [1994] 2 FLR 964 CA Failed prohibited steps application by mother to restrain father with custody, care and control of son from sending him to boarding school.

Re G [1994] 2 FCR 1037; [1994] 1 FLR 504 CA On deciding whether to make parental responsibility order.

Re H [1989] 2 FLR 215 CA On effect of parental rights order obtained by illegitimate's father child pursuant to Family Law Reform Act 1987, s 4.

Re H [1992] TLR 433 CA Father refused contact order was nonetheless granted a parental responsibility order.

Re H [1996] 3 FCR 49; [1996] 1 FLR 867 CA Father's non-payment of maintenance did not justify refusal of parental responsibility order.

Re H (1989) 133 SJ 569 CA Under parental rights order father of illegitimate children did not enjoy custody rights over same but could oppose their adoption.

Re H (No 2) [1991] FCR 361 [1991] 1 FLR 214 CA Parental rights order made in respect of father of illegitimate children but his consent to adoption of same dispensed with.

Re H (No 3) [1991] 2 WLR 763 CA Parental rights order made in respect of father of illegitimate children but his consent to adoption of same dispensed with.

Re M [1993] 1 FLR 495; [1992] TLR 518 CA On parental responsibility/habitual residence.

Re O [1997] TLR 334 HC FamD Absent contract/court order could nonetheless acquire joint custody of child (as here) following longtime exercise of parental responsibilities over same.

Re P [1995] 3 FCR 753; [1995] 1 FLR 1048 HC FamD On ending parental responsibility order: father's terminated after non-accidental injuries to child (interests of whom paramount).

Re P [1993] 2 FCR 689; [1994] 1 FLR 578 HC FamD On making parental responsibility order favouring father.

Re S [1995] 3 FCR 225; [1995] 2 FLR 648; [1995] TLR 107 CA On whether/when to grant parental responsibility order to natural father of illegitimate child.

Re S [1995] 3 FCR 564 HC FamD On granting parental responsibility order to unmarried father (here merited).

Re T [1993] 1 FCR 973; [1993] 2 FLR 450 CA Refusal of parental responsibility order and three-year stay on future applications for same merited.

Re W [1993] 2 FCR 427 CA On deciding whether to make parental responsibility order; dismissal of father's contact and parental responsibility applications without hearing oral evidence justified and valid.

S v P [1997] 2 FCR 185; [1997] 2 FLR 277; [1997] TLR 55 HC FamD Family assistance order that would require local authority to escort children to/from prison where father incarcerated unmerited; indirect contact ordered while father in prison subject to later review upon father's release/re-establishment of life; parental responsibility on behalf of imprisoned father would be too much too soon.

S v R [1993] 1 FCR 331 HC FamD On deciding whether to make parental responsibility order.

W v Ealing London Borough Council [1994] 1 FCR 436; [1993] 2 FLR 788; [1993] TLR 308 CA Appropriate procedure where parental rights/contact orders sought (here unsuccessfully) in respect of ward.

PATERNITY (blood test)

Re G (a minor) [1997] 2 FCR 325; [1977] 1 FLR 360 CA Where separated husband refused to have blood test done in respect of child of wife of whom husband claimed he was father, the inference to be drawn was that he was not the father.

PATERNITY (estoppel)

Re M [1997] 2 FLR 90 HC FamD Estoppel inapplicable when dealing with question of parentage; non-biological father of child conceived by wife by way of artificial insemination before the Human Fertilisation and Embryology Act 1990 was enacted was not 'parent' of child for purposes of the Child Support Act 1991.

PLACE OF SAFETY ORDER (care/custody)

R v A Justice for Lincoln (Kesteven), ex parte M; R v Lincoln (Kesteven) Juvenile Court, ex parte Lincolnshire County Council [1976] 1 All ER 490; (1976) 140 JP 216; (1975) 125 NLJ 1192t; [1976] QB 957; (1976) 120 SJ 8; [1976] 2 WLR 143 HC QBD Local authority place of safety order application following care order to parent not abuse of process.

PLACE OF SAFETY ORDER (general)

Nottinghamshire County Council v Q [1982] 2 All ER 641; [1982] Fam 94; (1982) 3 FLR 305; (1982) 126 SJ 309; [1982] 2 WLR 954 HC FamD Appeals against place of safety order under Children and Young Persons Act 1969, s 28, an abuse of process.

Re B (1981) 2 FLR 307; (1980) 124 SJ 81 HC FamD Practice as regards application for place of safety order for ward of court.

PRESUMPTION OF ADVANCEMENT (general)

Shephard v Cartwright (1954) 104 LJ 808; (1954) 98 SJ 868 HL On admissibility in evidence of later acts to rebut the presumption of advancement.

PROHIBITED STEPS ORDER (abduction)

H v H [1994] 1 FLR 530 HC FamD Mother allowed continue with residence/prohibited steps orders applications in respect of children she had abducted and retained.

PROHIBITED STEPS ORDER (general)

Croydon London Borough Council v A and others [1992] 3 All ER 788; [1992] Fam 169; [1992] 2 FCR 481; [1992] 2 FLR 341; (1992) 136 SJ LB 69; [1992] 3 WLR 267 HC FamD Prohibited steps order cannot apply between two adults.

Nottingham County Council v P [1994] Fam 18 (also CA); [1993] 1 FCR 180; [1993] 1 FLR 514; [1992] TLR 519; [1993] 2 WLR 406 HC FamD Prohibited steps order cannot be used where contact/residence order appropriate (residence order made on alternative basis).

Nottinghamshire County Council v P; Re P [1993] 3 All ER 815; [1994] Fam 18 (also HC FamD; [1994] 1 FCR 624; [1993] 2 FLR 134; (1993) 137 SJ LB 147; [1993] TLR 213; [1993] 3 WLR 637 CA Prohibited steps order not to be used to same end as contact or residence order.

Re D [1996] 2 FLR 273 CA Successful appeal against order that husband not stay overnight at matrimonial home after contact to his children.

Re L [1993] 1 FCR 325 HC FamD On determining whether custodial parent to be allowed remove child from jurisdiction.

Re M [1993] 1 FCR 78; [1993] 1 FLR 275 HC FamD Person who had been acting as guardian ad litem could apply for prohibited steps order after emergency protection order lapsed; justices' reasoning/findings in such cases to be recorded.

Re M [1993] 1 FCR 718 CA On determining place of habitual residence (so as to decide whether party could bring residence/prohibited steps actions).

Re S and D [1995] 1 FCR 626; [1995] 2 FLR 456 CA Prohibited steps order invalid as essentially required child to be kept in local authority care: care order substituted.

PUBLICITY (general)

R v Cambridge District Health Authority, ex parte B (No 2) [1996] 1 FLR 375 CA Reporting restrictions lifted so that father might publicise plight of child and so raise money for her treatment.

R v Central Criminal Court, ex parte Godwin and Crook [1995] 1 FLR 132; (1994) 138 SJ LB 199 CA Valid exercise of discretion prohibiting publication of information on trial: prior to making order judge could hear anyone whom considered to have valid interest in matter.

Re B (a minor) [1996] 1 FCR 661 CA Reporting restrictions lifted that father might make money from newspaper publicity and thus ensure could provide continuing medical treatment for child.

RELIGION (access/contact)

Evans v Jackson (1986) 150 JP 593 (also HC FamD) CA Father properly granted access to child though was upsetting for latter as upset occasioned by mother's improper attempts to frustrate access not by access per se.

Evans v Jackson (1986) 150 JP 593 (also CA) HC FamD Father properly granted access to child though was upsetting for latter as lifestyle of father afforded broader upbringing to child than that of mother and husband who were Jehovah's Witnesses.

Re G (1965) 109 SJ 756 CA Valid decision not to make staying order in respect of Roman Catholic children to whom father living in adultery granted access.

Wright v Wright (1981) 2 FLR 276 CA Refusal of access to father (Jehovah's Witness) merited where mother (Church of England member) very anxious (and anxiety would upset child) that father would seek to indoctrinate child.

RELIGION (adoption)

Re C (MA) [1966] 1 All ER 838 (also HC ChD); (1966) 130 JP 217 (also HC ChD); (1966) 110 SJ 309; [1966] 1 WLR 646 CA In adoption-custody cases child's welfare paramount interest; no requirement regarding religious education imposed.

Re C (MA) [1966] 1 All ER 838 (also CA); (1966) 130 JP 217 (also CA) HC ChD In adoption-custody cases child's welfare paramount interest; no requirement regarding religious education imposed.

Re Carroll (1930) 74 SJ 645 HC KBD Child to be adopted by Protestants/brought up as Protestant notwithstanding contrary wishes of Roman Catholic mother.

Re G [1962] 2 All ER 173; (1962) 126 JP 341; (1962) 112 LJ 320; [1962] 2 QB 141; (1962) 106 SJ 282; [1962] 2 WLR 1010 CA Adoption of Protestant child by Jewish parents allowed as in infant's best interests.

Re J [1987] 1 FLR 455; (1987) 151 JP 243 HC FamD Wardship order continued but adoption/custodianship of child not allowed where natural mother not unreasonably objected to adoption of child by foster parents who were Jehovah's Witnesses/of different race to child.

Re S [1995] 2 FCR 177; [1994] 2 FLR 416; (1994) 138 SJ LB 99 CA Non-imposition of blood transfusion condition when ordering adoption of child by couple who were Jehovah's Witnesses.

RELIGION (care/custody)

Allington v Allington [1985] FLR 586 CA On relevant factors when deciding custody application by mother who left child with father (status quo irrelevant here as child apart from mother for only ten weeks).

H v H (1975) 125 NLJ 507t; (1975) 119 SJ 590 CA Successful appeal by English mother against custody of child resident in England being given to Muslim father so that child might be instructed in Islam (mother agnostic).

Jane v Jane (1983) 4 FLR 712 CA Custody to father/care and control to mother justified as latter a Jehovah's Witness opposed to blood transfusions which father could as custodian authorise.

Re B and G [1985] FLR 134 HC FamD Custody of children transferred to mother after over five years as father/stepmother were scientologists.

Re B and G [1985] FLR 493 CA Custody of children properly transferred to mother after over five years where father/stepmother were scientologists.

Re C (MA) [1966] 1 All ER 838 (also HC ChD); (1966) 130 JP 217 (also HC ChD); (1966) 110 SJ 309; [1966] 1 WLR 646 CA In adoption-custody cases child's welfare paramount interest; no requirement regarding religious education imposed.

Re C (MA) [1966] 1 All ER 838 (also CA); (1966) 130 JP 217 (also CA) HC ChD In adoption-custody cases child's welfare paramount interest; no requirement regarding religious education imposed.

Re Cole (1899-1900) XVI TLR 500 HC ChD Custody of children given to (Protestant) uncle where after (Protestant) father's death mother converted to Catholicism.

Re Collins (An Infant) [1950] 1 All ER 1057 CA Child's welfare paramount in guardianship cases: no rule that dead father has right to determine child's religious upbringing.

Re Hopton, an Infant (1901-02) 46 SJ 749 VacCt That petitioner-father under pressure to return abroad did not excuse denying respondent-mother chance to make her case in custody action; child of Protestant father/Catholic mother ordered to be returned to school for next term, not removed during term time and not instructed as Catholic.

Re J [1987] 1 FLR 455; (1987) 151 JP 243 HC FamD Wardship order continued but adoption/custodianship of child not allowed where natural mother not unreasonably objected to adoption of child by foster parents who were Jehovah's Witnesses/of different race to child.

Re T (1981) 2 FLR 239 CA Custody to mother who was Jehovah's Witness subject to various conditions (inter alia that children be allowed blood transfusions if necessary).

Ward v Laverty and another [1924] All ER 319; [1925] AC 101; (1924) 59 LJ 300; [1925] 94 LJPC 17; (1924) 131 LTR 614; (1923-24) 68 SJ 629; (1923-24) XL TLR 600; (1924) WN (I) 177 HL In custody case child's welfare paramount though father's desire as regards religious upbringing a relevant factor.

RELIGION (ethnicity)

Re J [1987] 1 FLR 455; (1987) 151 JP 243 HC FamD Wardship order continued but adoption/custodianship of child not allowed where natural mother not unreasonably objected to adoption of child by foster parents who were Jehovah's Witnesses/of different race to child.

RELIGION (general)

Re Carroll (No 2) [1930] All ER 192; (1931) 95 JP 25; [1931] 1 KB 317; (1931) 100 LJCL 113; (1931) 144 LTR 383; (1931) 75 SJ 98; (1930-31) XLVII TLR 125 CA Mother of illegitimate child may require child to be brought up in particular religion; CA considers habeas corpus appeal de novo.

Re Collins [1950] 1 All ER 1057; [1950] Ch 498; (1950) 100 LJ 274; (1950) 94 SJ 352; [1950] 66 (1) TLR 1107; (1950) WN (I) 242 CA Child's welfare paramount in guardianship cases: no rule that dead father has right to determine child's religious upbringing.

Re R [1993] 2 FCR 525; [1993] 2 FLR 163; [1992] TLR 506 CA Residence order to father rather than religious sect of which father had been/boy was member.

Re S [1993] 1 FCR 283; [1992] 2 FLR 313 CA On desirability of access between children/non-custodial parent; on religious upbringing of children.

RELIGION (medical treatment)

Re S [1993] 1 FLR 376 HC FamD Blood transfusions to child allowed though contrary to principles/wishes of parents (Jehovah's Witnesses).

RELIGION (ward)

F v F [1902] 1 Ch 688 HC ChD Ward removed from guardian's care where guardian changed religion which held at time entrusted with ward.

Re E [1963] 3 All ER 874; (1964) 114 LJ 9; (1964) 108 SJ 75; [1964] 1 WLR 51 HC ChD Mother's desires on religious education important but child's welfare paramount: here two compatible.

Re J [1987] 1 FLR 455; (1987) 151 JP 243 HC FamD Wardship order continued but adoption/custodianship of child not allowed where natural mother not unreasonably objected to adoption of child by foster parents who were Jehovah's Witnesses/of different race to child.

Re W; W v M (1908) 77 LJCh 147 (also CA) HC ChD Variation of wardship order so as to allow two Jewish children to be educated as Christians.

Re W; W v M (1) [1907] 2 Ch 557; (1908) 77 LJCh 147 (also HC ChD); (1907) WN (I) 204 CA Variation of wardship order so as to allow Jewish child (at his behest) to be educated as a Christian but his sister to continue being educated as a Jew.

RESIDENCE ORDER (abduction)

H v H [1994] 1 FLR 530 HC FamD Mother allowed continue with residence/prohibited steps orders applications in respect of children she had abducted and retained.

RESIDENCE ORDER (adoption)

M v C and Calderdale Metropolitan Borough Council [1992] 2 FCR 141 HC FamD Leave of court required before natural father of adopted illegitimate child could seek residence order.

M v C and Calderdale Metropolitan Borough Council [1993] 1 FCR 431; [1993] 1 FLR 505 CA In Children Act 1989 'parent' includes father of illegitimate child but that status lost post-freeing order after which could not seek residence order.

RESIDENCE ORDER (care/custody)

G v Kirklees Metropolitan Borough Council [1993] 1 FCR 357; [1993] 1 FLR 805 HC FamD Aunt not joined to care proceedings where could not reasonably hope to secure residence order.

Gateshead Metropolitan Borough Council v B (1996) TLR 19/3/96 HC FamD On deciding where child is resident (in context of application for care order).

Re G and M (contact) [1995] 3 FCR 514 HC FamD Appropriate case in which to substitute conditional residence orders for care orders.

RESIDENCE ORDER (conditional)

Re G and M (contact) [1995] 3 FCR 514 HC FamD Appropriate case in which to substitute conditional residence orders for care orders.

RESIDENCE ORDER (ex parte)

M v C [1993] 1 FCR 264; [1993] 2 FLR 584 HC FamD On (ex parte) granting of residence orders; on need to give reasons inter alia for not adopting course advocated by court welfare officer.

Re G [1992] 2 FCR 720; [1993] 1 FLR 910; [1992] TLR 468 CA On availability/appropriateness of ex parte interim residence order.

Re P [1993] 2 FCR 417; [1993] 1 FLR 915 CA On availability/appropriateness of ex parte interim residence order.

Re Y [1993] 2 FCR 422 HC FamD Ex parte residence order application merited but three month delay in inter partes hearing unjustified.

RESIDENCE ORDER (fostering)

JR v Merton London Borough [1992] 2 FCR 174 (also HC FamD) CA On granting leave to foster parent to seek residence order (here refused).

Re B (A) [1996] 1 FLR 27; [1995] TLR 472 HC FamD Adoption order favouring foster-father and residence orders favouring him/his cohabitee so both had parental responsibility towards child.

RESIDENCE ORDER (general)

A v A and Newham London Borough Council [1993] 1 FCR 870 HC FamD Failed appeal by child's paternal aunt against refusal to allow her seek residence order after alleged sexual abuse of child by paternal uncle.

B v B [1997] 2 FCR 518; [1997] 1 FLR 139; (1996) TLR 10/10/96; [1997] TLR 295 CA Valid decision to order one child to live with mother and other child with father but order that father not be allowed seek custody of other child without leave of court was improper.

Birmingham City Council v H [1993] 1 FCR 247; [1992] 2 FLR 323 HC FamD Residence order carries with it right to exercise parental responsibility.

C v Salford City Council and others [1994] 2 FLR 926 HC FamD Fosterers given leave to seek residence order in respect of child whose natural parents objected to adoption by fosterers.

Cleveland County Council v Director of Public Prosecutions and another (1995) 139 SJ LB 13; [1994] TLR 615 HC QBD Court ordering child into local authority care could not specify where child was to be accommodated.

H v H (No 2) [1997] 1 FCR 603 HC FamD On determining forum conveniens in shared residence/specific issue application concerning child.

H v H [1995] 2 FCR 469 [1995] 1 FLR 529 CA On deciding whether to grant residence order/leave to remove child from jurisdiction.

M v C [1993] 1 FCR 264; [1993] 2 FLR 584 HC FamD On (ex parte) granting of residence orders; on need to give reasons inter alia for not adopting course advocated by court welfare officer.

N v B [1993] 1 FCR 231 HC FamD Shared residence order (so that could acquire parental responsibility) refused; leave to remove remove children from jurisdiction refused.

North Yorkshire County Council v G [1994] 1 FCR 737; [1993] 2 FLR 732 HC FamD Child's welfare not paramount interest in residence action; brother not allowed become party to action concerning other brother where sought to help mother with little English.

Nottinghamshire County Council v P [1994] Fam 18 (also CA); [1993] 1 FCR 180; [1993] 1 FLR 514; [1992] TLR 519; [1993] 2 WLR 406 HC FamD Prohibited steps order not to be used to same end as contact or residence order.

Nottinghamshire County Council v P; Re P [1993] 3 All ER 815; [1994] Fam 18 (also HC FamD); [1994] 1 FCR 624; [1993] 2 FLR 134; (1993) 137 SJ LB 147; [1993] TLR 213; [1993] 3 WLR 637 CA Prohibited steps order not to be used to same end as contact or residence order.

Oldham Metropolitan Borough Council v E and others [1994] 1 FLR 568; [1994] TLR 150 CA On approach to be adopted where aunt seeking residence order in respect of child whom local authority wish to have adopted (all parties agreeing mother unsuitable carer).

R v Redbridge London Borough Council, ex parte East Sussex County Council [1992] TLR 663 HC QBD Ordinary residence of mentally handicapped twins whose parents had left them in England and returned to Nigeria was deemed not to lie with parents.

Re A [1993] 1 FLR 425 HC FamD Aunt did not have to allowed apply for residence order/joined as party in care action.

Re A and others [1992] 3 All ER 872; [1992] Fam 182; [1992] 2 FLR 154; [1992] TLR 245; [1992] 3 WLR 422 CA Child's welfare not paramount consideration in residence order proceedings.

Re B [1995] 1 FLR 895 HC FamD On correct approach to deciding adoption cases — child's welfare and other factors relevant: if decide to make residence order (not adoption order) child's welfare paramount concern.

Re B (No 1) [1994] 1 FCR 389 HC FamD On relationship between contact/residence orders jurisdiction of court and Child Abduction Convention jurisdiction.

Re B (T) (residence order) [1995] 2 FCR 240 CA Valid decision by judge to retain status quo (three children with father, one with mother) with regular contact by mother to child resident with father.

Re B (W) [1995] 2 FLR 1023 HC FamD Shared residence order refused to non-biological father who had acted as father.

Re B and others [1992] 3 All ER 867; [1992] Fam 162; [1992] 3 WLR 113 CA Court may make residence order to preempt abduction — ex parte if necessary.

Re C [1994] 1 FCR 609 HC FamD Leave to child to seek residence order: on granting leave for same.

Re C [1994] 1 FCR 837; [1994] 1 FLR 26 HC FamD Near-fifteen year old refused residence order facilitating her living separately from parents/refused specific issue order allowing her to go on foreign holiday with friend's family.

Re C [1995] 1 FLR 617 CA Was reasonable to decide residence order application absent welfare officer where report latter provided inconclusive.

Re C [1995] 2 FCR 276 CA On deciding whether or not to adjourn residence application where court welfare officer cannot be present to give oral evidence; on interviewing of child at centre of residence application.

Re C [1996] 1 FCR 461; [1995] 1 FLR 927 HC FamD On judicial approach to application by child to live with separated parent.

Re C (S) [1994] 1 FLR 96 HC FamD Leave given to fourteen year old in local authority care to seek residence order enabling her to live with family of friend.

Re C and another [1993] 3 All ER 313; [1994] Fam 1 CA Natural father without parental responsibility not a 'parent' for purpose of residence order; may not apply for residence order as of right after child freed for adoption.

Re D [1996] 2 FCR 820; [1996] 2 FLR 281 CA Refusal of residence order (effectively an ouster order) set aside as judge had failed to consider contested residence application as such.

Re E [1997] TLR 273 CA Conditional residence order improper.

Re G [1994] 2 FCR 359; [1994] 2 FLR 301 HC FamD Failed application by mother for residence order: local authority allowed place children outside jurisdiction.

Re J [1994] 1 FLR 369 HC FamD On need for magistrate to give reasons in residence case; on magistrates granting stay of residence order pending appeal.

Re J [1997] 1 FCR 325; [1997] 1 FLR 606 HC FamD On making/effecting of ex parte (here residence/recovery) orders.

Re L [1995] 3 FCR 684; [1995] 2 FLR 445 HC FamD On need for magistrates to give reasons for decision in residence order application.

Re M [1995] 1 FCR 417 CA Residence (not care) order justified where alleged poor treatment unproved by the local authority but judge found other failures on mother's part.

Re M [1993] 1 FCR 718 CA On determining place of habitual residence (so as to decide whether party could bring residence/prohibited steps actions).

Re M [1993] 1 FLR 495; [1992] TLR 518 CA On parental responsibility/habitual residence.

Re M [1997] 2 FCR 28 CA Residence order in favour of father (psychiatric patient) but interim residence to mother (pending further order when father well enough to resume caring for children).

Re M [1993] 2 FLR 706 HC FamD Justices did not need to see child properly where was guardian ad litem/had welfare officer's report; reasons to be given where depart from recommendations in welfare officer's report.

Re M (W); B v B [1997] 2 FCR 494; [1997] 1 FLR 132; [1997] 1 FLR 139 CA Separation of siblings justified but order preventing father from making future residence applications was obviated.

Re N [1995] 2 FLR 230 CA On making residence order where not much choice between either of two parents presenting cross-applications.

Re N (minors) [1996] 1 FCR 244 CA Valid decision to allow return of own two children to father against whom step-daughter had made allegations of sexual abuse.

Re O (minors) [1993] 2 FCR 482; [1994] 1 FLR 172 HC FamD Procedural error in ex parte application for leave to seek residence order did not invalidate order made but duration of order (five weeks) too long.

Re P [1994] 2 FCR 1093 HC FamD Discharge of wardship and leave granted for foster parents to seek residence order.

Re R [1993] 2 FCR 525; [1993] 2 FLR 163; [1992] TLR 506 CA Residence order to father rather than religious sect of which father had been/boy was member.

Re R [1995] 3 FCR 334; [1995] 2 FLR 612; [1995] TLR 268 CA Shared residence order approved: judge's consideration of financial implications of making residence order was valid.

Re S [1997] 1 FLR 497 CA In action where father seeking care of and mother seeking residence order in respect of children allegedly sexually abused by father the mother's new husband (in respect of whom past abuse alleged) allowed intervene in action.

Re T [1996] 3 FCR 97; [1996] 2 FLR 352 CA Residence order granted to father in failed application by good mother for leave to remove child abroad set aside.

Re T (C) [1993] 2 FLR 278 CA On allowing child to apply for residence order without next friend: here allowed.

Re T and E [1995] 3 FCR 260; [1995] 1 FLR 581 HC FamD Residence order to father of one of two half-sisters in care as was in her best interest (though joint best interests of the two girls demanded that they be adopted together).

Re W [1993] TLR 225 CA On approach to resolving residence dispute where natural parent and another in dispute over same.

Re W [1992] 2 FCR 603; [1992] 2 FLR 332; [1992] TLR 262 CA Pending residence order hearing four week old baby should have been given to mother even though upset status quo.

Re W [1992] 2 FCR 461 CA On determination of residence order application in light of expressed wishes of children involved.

Re W [1993] 2 FCR 589; [1993] 2 FLR 625 CA Generally preferable that child live with natural parents but not always so.

RESIDENCE ORDER (grandparent)

Re H [1994] 3 FCR 183; [1994] 2 FLR 80 HC FamD Grandparents who had enjoyed staying contact granted residence orders: care order to local authority quashed.

Re K [1996] 1 FCR 365; [1995] 1 FLR 675 HC FamD Care (not residence) order appropriate for grandparents looking after grandchildren.

Re U [1993] 2 FCR 64; [1993] 2 FLR 992 CA Valid granting of residence order to grandparents where adoption agency had sought freeing of child for adoption.

RESIDENCE ORDER (habitual residence)

Re S (1994) 138 SJ LB 221; [1994] TLR 522 HC FamD Court did have jurisdiction to alter continuing order in respect of child now habitually resident abroad.

RESIDENCE ORDER (homosexual)

Re H [1993] 2 FLR 541 HC FamD Application for residence order by lesbian couple, one party to which was mother of baby girl.

RESIDENCE ORDER (immigration)

Re M (a minor) [1995] 2 FCR 793; [1993] 2 FLR 858 HC FamD Immigrant child granted residence order at stepmother's behest.

RESIDENCE ORDER (interim)

Re B [1992] 2 FLR 1 CA Exceptionally can make ex parte interim residence order in respect of abductee and non-abducted children on application by non-abducting parent.

Re G [1992] 2 FCR 720; [1993] 1 FLR 910; [1992] TLR 468 CA On availability/appropriateness of ex parte interim residence order.

Re M [1994] 2 FCR 1209; [1994] 1 FLR 551 HC FamD Non-recognition of Irish custody order/declaration that removal of children wrongful where English court had already made interim residence orders favouring mother.

Re P [1993] 2 FCR 417; [1993] 1 FLR 915 CA On availability/appropriateness of ex parte interim residence order.

RESIDENCE ORDER (shared)

A v A [1995] 1 FCR 91; [1994] 1 FLR 669; [1994] TLR 100 CA On making shared residence order (here merited).

Re H [1996] 3 FCR 321; [1995] 2 FLR 883 CA Shared residence order to stepfather approved.

Re H [1993] 1 FCR 671; [1994] 1 FLR 717 CA On deciding whether/when shared residence order merited (here was not).

RESIDENCE ORDER (welfare report)

M v C [1993] 1 FCR 264; [1993] 2 FLR 584 HC FamD On (ex parte) granting of residence orders; on need to give reasons inter alia for not adopting course advocated by court welfare officer.

Re V [1996] 3 FCR 101; [1995] 2 FLR 1010 CA Valid departure by judge from expert opinion/recommendations of welfare officer.

SAFETY ORDER (general)

R v Bristol Justices, ex parte Broome [1987] 1 All ER 676; [1987] 2 FLR 76; (1987) 151 JP 409; (1987) 131 SJ 102; [1987] 1 WLR 352 HC QBD Police to be heard in application to release child held by constable.

SECURE ACCOMMODATION (general)

E (A) v Staffordshire County Council [1995] 2 FCR 84; (1995) 159 JP 367 HC FamD On relevant factors when determining whether to make secure accommodation order.

Gateshead Metropolitan Borough Council v L and another [1996] 3 All ER 264; [1996] Fam 55; [1996] 3 FCR 582; [1996] 2 FLR 179; [1996] 3 WLR 426 HC FamD On designation of correct local authority in care order.

Hereford and Worcester County Council v S [1993] 1 FCR 653; [1993] 2 FLR 360 HC FamD On availability of secure accommodation order to child subject to mental health order.

R v Slough Juvenile Court, ex parte Royal Berkshire County Council [1984] QB 387; (1983) 127 SJ 841; [1984] 2 WLR 45 HC QBD Secure accommodation order for duration of more than seventy-two hours in respect of child had to be authorised by juvenile court.

Re B [1995] 1 WLR 232 CA On maximum duration (and hence commencement date of particular) secure accommodation order.

Re H [1993] 1 FCR 904 CA On balancing interests of child-mother and her baby in care order application; three-month secure accommodation order in respect of mother merited.

Re W [1995] 2 FCR 708 HC FamD Local authority could make secure accommodation application to family proceedings court in respect of child placed on bail by youth court and entrusted to local authority.

Re W (minor) [1993] TLR 53 HC FamD Secure accommodation order to be for appropriate duration (no more) and reasons must be given for making order.

Re W and D [1995] 3 FCR 806; [1995] 2 FLR 807 HC FamD Secure accommodation order not essential when bail of children facing criminal charges refused: remand to local authority accommodation subject to various conditions appropriate.

SEPARATION (maintenance)

Starkie v Starkie (No 2) [1953] 2 All ER 1519; (1954) 118 JP 59; (1954) 98 SJ 46; [1954] 1 WLR 98 HC PDAD Husband is/is not under duty to maintain child/wife where consensual separation with no maintenance agreement.

SUPERVISION ORDER (care/custody)

Re B [1997] 1 FCR 309; [1996] 2 FLR 693 HC FamD On deciding whether care/supervision orders merited.

SUPERVISION ORDER (general)

Croydon London Borough Council v A (No 3) [1992] 2 FLR 350 HC FamD On granting care/supervision order; on appealing against failed application for care order.

Hereford and Worcester County Council v R and G [1994] 2 FCR 981 HC FamD Interim care order not supervision order appropriate mechanism whereby to control residence.

M v Warwickshire County Council [1994] 2 FCR 121; [1994] 2 FLR 593 HC FamD Six-month supervision order made.

Re B [1996] 3 FCR 446; [1996] 1 FLR 676; [1996] 1 WLR 716 CA Conditional supervision order after mother made certain undertakings improper but amended form of order allowed stand.

Re D [1993] 2 FCR 88; [1993] 2 FLR 423 HC FamD Care (not supervision) order appropriate for new child born of man with record of cruelty to own children.

Re H [1994] 2 FCR 1; [1994] 2 FLR 979 HC FamD Court could not order steps supervisor must take in respect of responsible person subject to supervision order.

Re O [1997] 2 FCR 17; [1996] 2 FLR 755 HC FamD Improper exercise of discretion where care orders made rather than first trying supervision orders in respect of children supervision of whom was sought by local authority though it did not seek to remove children from their home.

Re S [1996] 2 FCR 719; [1996] 1 FLR 753 CA On when care and when supervision order merited.

Re S (J) [1993] 2 FCR 193; [1993] 2 FLR 919 HC FamD On nature, effect, whether and when to grant care/supervision orders: here care order granted.

Re V [1996] 2 FCR 555; [1996] 1 FLR 776 CA On whether/when care (as here) or supervision order appropriate; supervision order with conditions inappropriate.

SUPERVISION ORDER (interim)

Leicestershire County Council v G [1995] 1 FCR 205; [1994] 2 FLR 329 HC FamD Interim care order substituted for interim supervision order where child of family suffered non-accidental injury before care proceedings heard.

SURNAME (care/custody)

R (BM) v R (DN) [1978] 2 All ER 33 CA Change of child's surname permissible where custody given to mother.

R v R [1977] 1 WLR 1256 CA Custody of child given to mother notwithstanding that this involved surname-change of child to surname of mother's lover.

SURNAME (general)

D v B (otherwise D) [1977] 3 All ER 751; [1977] Fam 145; [1977] 2 WLR 1011 HC FamD Other parent's consent required to change of surname of unborn/new-born/unseen/well-known child; child's interests a consideration for court in deciding whether to waive consent.

D v B (otherwise D) (child: surname) [1979] 1 All ER 93; [1979] Fam 38; (1978) 122 SJ 486; [1978] 3 WLR 573 CA Court cannot order mother to execute fresh deed poll.

Dawson v Wearmouth [1997] TLR 468 CA Surname by which child registered of considerable significance when court asked to alter surname of child.

G v A [1995] 2 FCR 223 CyCt Order that children's surname be double-barrelled (natural father's surname plus new surname of re-married mother).

L v F (1978) 128 NLJ 1000t HC FamD Refusal of order allowing children to be styled by name of stepfather, not natural father.

P v N [1997] 2 FCR 65 CyCt Residence order made precluding mother from changing child's surname (that of father) but enabling use of double-barrelled surname (names of father and mother).

R v R (1982) 3 FLR 345 CA Child allowed to use mother's new surname but registered for medical purposes as 'Donna R otherwise T'.

Re B [1996] 1 FLR 791 CA Failed application for children to change surname to that of stepfather (as would have further diminished connection to natural father).

Re D (1978) 128 NLJ 759t CA Child to be known by surname of stepfather and not natural father.

Re D (1977) 127 NLJ 116t; (1977) 121 SJ 35 HC FamD Child to be known by surname of natural father and not stepfather.

Re F [1994] 1 FCR 110; [1993] 2 FLR 837 CA On relevant factors when deciding whether child to be allowed change surname.

Re J [1993] 1 FCR 74; [1993] 1 FLR 699 HC FamD Ex parte surname change application without notice to parents or child (unrepresented by guardian ad litem) allowed.

Re T [1962] 3 All ER 970; (1962) 112 LJ 849; [1962] 3 WLR 1477 HC ChD Right to change infant's surname belongs to natural/legal guardian: unchanged by custody order.

Re T (otherwise H) [1962] 3 All ER 970; [1963] Ch 238; (1962) 106 SJ 1011 HC ChD Right to change infant's surname belongs to natural/legal guardian: unchanged by custody order.

Rice v Rice (1977) 121 SJ 758 CA On irrelevance to determination of custody proceedings of children's using same new surname as that which mother now adopted.

W v A [1981] 1 All ER 100; [1981] Fam 14; (1980) 130 NLJ 1210; (1980) 124 SJ 726; [1981] 2 WLR 124 CA Interests of child paramount in deciding on child's change of name after parents divorce.

Y v Y [1973] 2 All ER 574; [1973] Fam 147; (1973) 117 SJ 506; [1973] 3 WLR 80 HC PDAD Neither parental custodian nor other parent can change child's surname absent agreement/court decision.

SURROGACY (access/contact)

A v C [1985] FLR 445 (also CA) HC FamD No access by natural father to child of woman who reneged on commercial surrogacy deal insofar as surrender of child concerned.

SURROGACY (adoption)

Re an adoption application [1987] 2 All ER 826; [1987] Fam 81; [1987] FCR 161; [1987] 2 FLR 291; (1987) 137 NLJ 267; [1987] 3 WLR 31 HC FamD Surrogacy not contrary to Adoption Act if payments not for profit/reward.

Re W (M) [1996] 3 FCR 128; [1995] 2 FLR 759 HC FamD Adoption order (plus no contact with natural mother) to surrogate parents (husband natural father) of child.

SURROGACY (care/custody)

Re P [1988] FCR 140; [1987] 2 FLR 421 HC FamD On deciding custody where paid surrogate mother refuses to surrender children to natural father and his wife.

SURROGACY (general)

Re Q [1996] 2 FCR 345; [1996] 1 FLR 369 HC FamD Where egg fertilised by anonymous donor's sperm and foetus carried by surrogate mother there was no 'father' whose agreement to parental order being made had to be sought.

SURROGACY (ward)

Re a Baby (1985) 135 NLJ 106 HC FamD Best interests of child still guiding factor in wardship cases involving surrogate children.

Re C [1985] FLR 846 HC FamD Care and control granted husband and wife of surrogate child of which husband natural father.

TAKING CHILD OUTSIDE JURISDICTION (general)

A v A (1980) 1 FLR 380 CA Here was in best interests of child to leave jurisdiction with mother (who had custody) though would probably lose contact with father in consequence.

Andrews v Andrews and Sullivan [1958] 2 All ER 305; (1958) 108 LJ 426; (1958) 102 SJ 384 HC PDAD Only ChD can grant leave for wards of ChD to be taken out of jurisdiction.

Barnes v Tyrrell (1982) 3 FLR 240; (1981) 131 NLJ 1288 CA Mother with custody of children allowed remove them to Australia to where was emigrating.

Belton v Belton [1987] 2 FLR 343; (1987) 151 JP 679 CA Child's welfare is paramount interest in application to remove from jurisdiction child in respect of whom one divorced parent has custody.

Bilainkin v Bilainkin [1959] 1 All ER 161; (1959) 109 LJ 72; (1959) 103 SJ 90 CA In custody order allowing restricted removal of child from jurisdiction petitioner's promise to return and respondent's permission to leave should be required.

Bowers v Clarke (1961) 105 SJ 988 CA Was not repudiation of maintenance agreement whereunder maintenance payable and access granted for custodial parent to remove child to Australia.

Chamberlain v De La Mare (1983) 4 FLR 434 (also CA) HC FamD Mother refused permission to take children from jurisdiction as their best interests demanded they continue contact with father.

H (M) v P (G) [1995] 2 FLR 106 HC FamD On whether to allow removal of child from jurisdiction.

Harris v Pinnington [1995] 3 FCR 35 HC FamD Custodial parent not allowed remove child from jurisdiction as not in child's best interests; staying contact to father ordered.

L v L (1969) 119 NLJ 81t; (1969) 113 SJ 88; [1969] 2 WLR 326 HC PDAD Wife about to seek divorce granted injunction against husband to prevent latter removing couple's children from jurisdiction.

Lonslow v Hennig (formerly Lonslow) [1986] 2 FLR 378 CA Emigrating mother allowed remove children from jurisdiction (though would minimise husband's contact with children) subject to undertaking to return them if so directed.

M v M [1993] 1 FCR 5; [1992] 2 FLR 303; [1992] TLR 398 CA On need to take into account views of children before deciding whether to allow custodial parent remove them from the jurisdiction.

Monaco v Monaco (1937) 157 LTR 231 HC ChD Reigning Prince of Monaco granted custody of grandson and injunction restraining former son-in-law from moving same from United Kingdom (where was studying).

P (LM) (otherwise E) v P (GE) [1970] 3 All ER 659 CA Child's welfare could justify permanently removing from jurisdiction.

Poel v Poel (1970) 114 SJ 720, [1970] 1 WLR 1469 CA Mother with custody of child allowed remove child to New Zealand to where mother emigrating with new husband.

Re B [1994] 2 FCR 309 CA Mother allowed remove children from jurisdiction as would lead to increased likelihood of contact between father/children; otherwise would cause great frustration.

Re Benner (1951) 95 SJ 596; (1951) WN (I) 436 HC ChD American father granted leave to remove wards from UK (where life with mother was uncertain) to US where he and his wife could offer greater certainty.

Re D [1992] 1 All ER 892; [1992] 2 FCR 41; [1992] 1 FLR 637; [1992] 1 WLR 315 CA Court may grant ex parte order for return of child/prohibited steps order forbidding removal of child even if other parent outside jurisdiction/has no assets in jurisdiction.

Re E (An Infant) [1955] 3 All ER 174; [1956] Ch 23; (1955) 105 LJ 601; (1955) 99 SJ 726; [1955] 3 WLR 493 HC ChD Cannot order that child be allowed leave jurisdiction in action under Guardianship of Infants Acts 1886 and 1925; court cannot exercise inherent wardship jurisdiction over non-wards unless made wards under Law Reform (Miscellaneous Provisions) Act 1949.

Re F [1988] 2 FLR 116 CA On deciding whether to allow custodial parent remove child from jurisdiction (here allowed).

Re J [1988] 1 FLR 65 HC FamD Injunction available to prevent mother (of ward) from leaving jurisdiction where appropriate.

Re K [1992] 2 FCR 161; [1992] 2 FLR 98 HC FamD Refusal of unrealistic application by custodial parent to remove child from jurisdiction.

Re L (1968) 118 NLJ 518t CA Wardship over illegitimate child ended so that mother could emigrate to Canada and settle down there to new life — that natural father would lose access to child not ground for continuing wardship.

Re L [1993] 1 FCR 325 HC FamD On determining whether custodial parent to be allowed remove child from jurisdiction.

Re M [1973] 1 All ER 852; [1973] Fam 66; (1973) 137 JP 339; (1973) 123 NLJ 56t; (1973) 117 SJ 88; [1973] 2 WLR 515 HC FamD Absent provisional adoption order child (even ward) cannot be removed from jurisdiction by applicant adopters.

Re O [1962] 2 All ER 10; (1962) 112 LJ 272; (1962) 106 SJ 429; [1962] 1 WLR 724 CA Welfare of children paramount, not only factor: here other factors justified leave to take ward outside jurisdiction.

Re T [1996] 3 FCR 97 CA Residence order granted to father in failed application by good mother for leave to remove child abroad set aside.

Re W [1994] 1 FCR 842 HC FamD That had firm albeit not definitely settled plans as to future adequate basis on which to allow mother take child from jurisdiction.

T v T [1968] 3 All ER 321; (1968) 118 NLJ 1005; (1968) 112 SJ 964; [1968] 1 WLR 1887 HC PDAD Magistrates cannot order/enforce order that children not be removed from jurisdiction.

T v T (1970) 114 SJ 909 CA Father to whom custody of children entrusted allowed emigrate to Australia.

Tyler v Tyler [1990] FCR 22; [1989] 2 FLR 158 CA Refusal to allow mother emigrate with children of whom had joint custody was justified.

WARD (abduction)

Re C [1978] 2 All ER 230; [1978] Fam 105; (1977) 121 SJ 693; [1977] 3 WLR 561 CA Child's welfare of paramount importance where peremptory order sought after kidnapping; child's interests required English court to assume jurisdiction.

Re J [1989] 3 All ER 590; [1989] Fam 85; [1990] FCR 341; [1990] 1 FLR 276; [1989] 3 WLR HC FamD On ordering that removal of ward from jurisdiction was unlawful (here so ordered).

Re L (1983) 4 FLR 368 CA Interim care and control order made in favour of mother who 'kidnapped' own child from United States and had him made ward of court.

Re L [1974] 1 All ER 913; (1973) 123 NLJ 1066t; (1974) 118 SJ 22; [1974] 1 WLR 250 CA Child's welfare in kidnapping case paramount factor (though parent's conduct also factor).

Re R (1981) 2 FLR 416; (1981) 125 SJ 588 CA On appropriate procedure where wardship application made in respect of 'kidnapped' child: child's best interests determinant factor.

Re T [1968] 3 All ER 411; [1968] Ch 704; (1968) 112 SJ 639; [1968] 3 WLR 430 CA Generally court will not countenance wardship/custody actions on foot of kidnapping by parent.

WARD (abortion)

Re B [1991] FCR 889; [1991] 2 FLR 426 HC FamD Abortion on twelve year old ward authorised.

Re G-Y [1984] FLR 811 HC FamD Necessary that leave of court be sought before ward allowed to have abortion.

Re P [1986] 1 FLR 272 HC FamD Wardship jurisdiction invoked to order termination of pregnancy of/insertion of contraceptive device into child in care under Children and Young Persons Act 1969.

WARD (access/contact)

M v Berkshire County Council [1985] FLR 257 CA On power of juvenile court to order access.

Re C (1983) 4 FLR 396 HC FamD Order for increased access to child (for whom council had planned adoption) by natural mother who had surmounted drink problem with view to eventually returning child to mother.

Re D (K) [1988] 1 All ER 577; [1988] AC 806; [1988] FCR 657; [1988] 2 FLR 139; (1988) 132 SJ 301; [1988] 2 WLR 398 HL In wardship proceedings child's welfare paramount; parent's right to access is secondary.

Re G [1988] FCR 440; [1988] 1 FLR 305 CA On role of court (regarding evidence and otherwise) in wardship action; father with mental disorder might after treatment be considered for access; wife deserved access but given visiting access because of threat posed by father.

Re H (L) [1986] 2 FLR 306; (1986) 150 JP 417 HC FamD HC could exercise wardship jurisdiction on request of local authority without latter having to show its powers to be insufficient.

Re P (1982) 3 FLR 420; (1982) 132 NLJ 248 CA Court could not order that no application be made in wardship proceedings until full hearing but could require court's leave be given to any steps taken.

Re P [1991] FCR 283; [1991] 1 FLR 280; [1990] TLR 694 CA Increased access and eventual return of stepfather to family despite earlier sexual abuse of step-child was justified; contempt of local authority solicitor whereby had sought to frustrate access arrangements purged by contemnor.

W v Shropshire County Council [1986] 1 FLR 359 (also HC FamD) CA Non-continuation of wardship over child in respect of whom local authoriy sought to bring care proceedings was valid.

Wolverhampton Metropolitan Borough Council v M [1988] FCR 629 HC FamD Child taken from mentally handicapped parents unable to care for him and placed in care with view to adoption (parental access terminated).

WARD (adoption)

F v S [1973] 1 All ER 722; [1973] Fam 203; (1973) 137 JP 301; (1973) 117 SJ 109; [1973] 2 WLR 178 CA Leave of court needed for adoption of ward; issue for court is will adoption application succeed?

Re C [1985] FLR 1114 CA Failed application by mother for full investigation in wardship of alleged abuse of her son by his adoptive parents.

Re C [1989] FCR 774; [1989] 1 FLR 222; (1989) 133 SJ 20; [1989] 1 WLR 61 CA Great-uncle not 'relative' for purposes of Adoption Act 1976, s 72(1); court ought not to have appointed guardian in respect of wards of court.

Re D (T) [1985] FLR 1150 HC FamD Natural father of illegitimate child in care could not seek invocation by court of its wardship jurisdiction to prevent local authority arranging adoption of child.

Re F [1984] FLR 60; (1984) 134 NLJ 765c; [1983] TLR 535 CA Circumstances merited inluding direction that child being placed in long-term foster care be prepared for adoption.

Re K (1981) 2 FLR 381; (1980) 124 SJ 809 HC FamD Local authority not to apply for wardship 'with a view to adoption'.

Re M (D) [1986] 2 FLR 122 (also HC FamD) CA On judicial review of local authority decision regarding adoption of child in care.

Re O [1978] 1 All ER 145; [1978] Fam 196 (also CA); (1977) 127 NLJ 569t; (1977) 121 SJ 391 HC FamD Exceptional for court to consider wardship application by natural parent in respect of adopted child.

Re O [1993] 2 FCR 746; [1993] 2 FLR 737 HC FamD Wardship injunction ended upon adoption order being made.

Re P [1990] FCR 260; [1990] 1 FLR 96; (1989) 139 NLJ 1265 CA Mixed race child justifiably removed from home of white foster-mother to that of black foster-parents with view to adoption.

Re P (1982) 3 FLR 420; (1982) 132 NLJ 248 CA Court could not order that no application be made in wardship proceedings until full hearing but could require court's leave be given to any steps taken.

Re R [1991] FCR 805 HC FamD Courts reluctant to (and here did not) interfere with local authority acting in capacity of adoption agency.

Re S (1978) 128 NLJ 1148t; (1978) 122 SJ 759 HC FamD Wardship action in which were seeking decision on issue of care and control of child dismissed as was really an attempt to secure review of adoption order refusal.

Re W [1993] 1 FCR 988 HC FamD Adoption order made despite procedural irregularities in manner in which went about adopting foreign child.

Wolverhampton Metropolitan Borough Council v M [1988] FCR 629 HC FamD Child taken from mentally handicapped parents unable to care for him and placed in care with view to adoption (parental access terminated).

WARD (care/custody)

A v Berkshire County Council [1989] FCR 184; [1989] 1 FLR 273 (also HC FamD) CA Juvenile court-appointed guardian ad litem could not by way of wardship action challenge local authority exercise of care and control powers over child.

A v Berkshire County Council [1989] FCR 180; [1989] 1 FLR 273 (also CA) HC FamD Juvenile court-appointed guardian ad litem could not by way of wardship action challenge local authority exercise of care and control powers over child.

A v Liverpool City Council and another [1981] 2 All ER 385; [1982] AC 363; (1981) 2 FLR 222; (1981) 145 JP 318; (1981) 131 NLJ 576; (1981) 125 SJ 396; [1981] 2 WLR 948 HL Court can review administrative/not substantive validity of local authority exercising discretionary powers.

A-W v E (1974) 124 NLJ 1159t HC FamD On practice as regards bringing normal child who is subject of custody/wardship proceedings to psychiatrist.

B v W (1979) 123 SJ 704 HC FamD Care and control of ward to mother, supervision order to local authority.

Berkshire County Council v D-P [1986] 2 FLR 276 (also HC FamD) CA Care (not wardship) proceedings appropriate where child born drug-dependent as result of mother's drug abuse while pregnant — matters concerning period of pregnancy could be considered.

D v X City Council (No 2) [1985] FLR 279 HC FamD Child in local authority care to be entrusted to care and control of grandmother.

E v E and Cheshire County Council (No 2) (1980) 1 FLR 73 CA HC may, but will not lightly (and here did not), vary existing care order in divorce/wardship action.

H v H; H v East Sussex County Council (1972) 116 SJ 968 HC FamD Court would not exercise wardship jurisdiction over child in respect of whom local authority care resolution had been made.

Havering London Borough Council v S [1986] 1 FLR 489 HC FamD Interim care and control of child subject of wardship action not ordered to mother whose other children already subject of wardship actions as result of apparent abuse by mother's cohabitee.

I v Barnsley Metropolitan Borough Council [1986] 1 FLR 109 (also CA) HC FamD One of two children placed in care on basis that one/other was not/was child of mother's cohabitee who had perpetrated serious cruelty on first child.

J and another v C and others [1970] AC 668; [1969] 2 WLR 540 HL Child's welfare paramount in wardship cases: no rule that custody must go to parents who are suitable for same.

J v Devon County Council [1986] 1 FLR 597 HC FamD Non-exercise of wardship jurisdiction in respect of child taken into local authority care pursuant to matrimonial care order.

London Borough of Lewisham v Lewisham Juvenile Court Justices and another [1979] 2 All ER 297; [1980] AC 273; (1979) 143 JP 441; (1979) 129 (1) NLJ 339; (1979) 123 SJ 270; [1979] 2 WLR 513 HL Local authority care not terminated upon request for return by parent but must pass wardship/s 2 resolution.

London Borough of Lewisham v M and others [1981] 3 All ER 307; (1981) 2 FLR 384; (1981) 131 NLJ 878; [1981] 1 WLR 1248 HC FamD Power to commit care of ward to local authority is unfettered.

NSPCC v H and H [1989] FCR 544; [1989] 2 FLR 131 CA On invocation of wardship jurisdiction of HC where is overlapping care action before juvenile court.

R v London Borough of Newham, ex parte McL [1988] FCR 229 HC FamD Wardship proceedings to be recommended by judge giving leave for judicial review of local authority decision regarding child in its care.

Re A (1980) 1 FLR 100; (1979) 123 SJ 553 HC FamD Independent welfare officer to ascertain wishes of child where sought; child's interests (of paramount importance) required that children remain in local authority care.

Re Andrews [1958] 2 All ER 308; [1958] Ch 665; (1958) 108 LJ 425; (1958) 102 SJ 382 HC ChD Wardship concerns a matter for wardship court; PDAD will make care/custody/control decisions on merit regarding ChD ward (and in the course of so doing will remove child from ChD wardship); ChD may hear wardship application despitet PDAD care/custody/control order/s regarding child.

Re B (1981) 2 FLR 412 HC FamD Wardship ought not to have been terminated where parents not afforded opportunity of further meetings with doctor seeking to rehabilitate family.

Re B (1974) 124 NLJ 620t; (1975) 119 SJ 165; [1975] 2 WLR 302 HC FamD Exceptionally court will (and did here) make child in care a ward of court.

Re B (C) [1981] 1 All ER 16; (1981) 145 JP 90; (1981) 125 SJ 219; [1981] 1 WLR 379 CA Court free to decide case in best interests of child where local authority seeks care and control of child in voluntary care.

Re B's Settlement; B v B [1940] Ch 54; [1940] 109 LJCh 20; (1939-40) LVI TLR 30; (1939) WN (I) 347 HC ChD Ward's welfare paramount factor in deciding custody action even if has already been foreign court order regarding custody.

Re C [1984] FLR 419 (also HC FamD) CA Risk to ward from mother (to whom was close) required care and control of ward be given to local authority which was authorised to place child with foster-parents with view to adoption.

Re C [1984] FLR 419 (also CA) HC FamD Risk to ward from mother (to whom was close) required care and control of ward be given to local authority which was authorised to place child with foster-parents with view to adoption.

Re C [1983] 1 All ER 219; (1983) 4 FLR 374; (1983) 133 NLJ 126; (1982) 126 SJ 820; [1982] TLR 394; [1982] 1 WLR 1462 HC FamD Court may invoke wardship powers in respect of child already subject of care order in criminal case.

Re C (1981) 2 FLR 63 CA Welfare of child may merit exercise by HC of its wardship jurisdiction even though juvenile court dismissed local authority care order appliccation.

Re C (1981) 2 FLR 163 CA Care and control of child to father (though had lived with mother with one six-month break since birth); courts loathe to break bond between child and particular parent.

Re C (1979) 129 (2) NLJ 1180c CA On seeking exercise of wardship jurisdiction as way of appealing against decision of lower court not to make care order.

Re D (1978) 128 NLJ 336t; (1978) 122 SJ 193 HC FamD Wardship jurisdiction exercised in respect of child in local authority care.

Re D (1977) 121 SJ 355 HC FamD Wardship jurisdiction assumed after justices had discharged care order in respect of child.

Re E [1991] FCR 33 CA Rehabilitation of child discontinued and placement for adoption ordered.

Re E [1984] 1 All ER 21; (1983) 4 FLR 668; [1983] TLR 47; [1983] 1 WLR 541 CA Court will not use wardship powers to interfere with local authority acts under care order even if care order case pending and no care order as of yet.

Re E [1984] FLR 457 (also CA/HL) HC FamD Care and control off child to father subject to supervision of welfare officer.

Re E [1984] 1 All ER 289 (also HC FamD/HL) CA Care of child to local authority; child to be prepared for adoption.

Re E (1983) 147 JP 321 CA On exercise by HC of its wardship jurisdiction where children are in care/care action in progress.

Re E (D) [1967] Ch 287 HC ChD Court allowed child removed from United States contrary to court order there to remain in care and custody of aunt in England.

Re E (SA) [1984] 1 All ER 289; [1984] FLR 457 (also HC FamD/CA); (1984) 128 SJ 80; [1984] TLR 17; [1984] 1 WLR 156 HL In ward's interests court may follow course of action not argued by parties to case: period of access to ward by father favoured to see if long-term relationship between father/ward possible.

Re G [1963] 3 All ER 370; (1963) 127 JP 549; (1963) 113 LJ 657; (1963) 107 SJ 682; [1963] 1 WLR 1169 HC ChD Courts will exercise wardship powers in line with local authority's proper exercise of discretion over child in care: if care to end court will intervene.

Re H (1977) 121 SJ 645 HC FamD Assumption by HC of wardship jurisdiction even though juvenile court could have done what parents asked (discharged care order).

Re H [1978] 2 All ER 903; [1978] Fam 65; (1978) 142 JP 474; (1978) 122 SJ 230; [1978] 2 WLR 608 CA Wardship order available where seek to supersede care order; Court of Appeal ought not to vary High Court assumption of wardship.

Re J [1984] 1 All ER 29; [1984] FLR 43; (1983) 127 SJ 616; [1983] TLR 488; [1984] 1 WLR 81 CA High Court will use wardship powers to police return of child in care to mother where care order otherwise would not be discharged by juvenile court.

Re K [1977] 1 All ER 647; [1977] Fam 179; (1977) 121 SJ 84; [1977] 2 WLR 33 CA Child's welfare paramount when considering care and control.

Re K [1991] 2 FLR 104 CA Interim care and control order by wardship court precluded need for divorce court to issue same.

Re K (KJS) [1966] 3 All ER 154; (1965-66) 116 NLJ 1173; (1966) 110 SJ 545; [1966] 1 WLR 1241 HC ChD Variation of access order (not wardship order) best course where post-access order access is unsatisfactory.

Re L [1990] FCR 509; [1991] 1 FLR 14; (1990) 134 SJ 545; [1990] TLR 227 CA Improper to exercise wardship jurisdiction in realm reserved by Parliament to discretion of local authority.

Re M [1985] 1 All ER 745; [1985] Fam 60 CA Access order for juvenile court; freeing of child for adoption for magistrates' court.

Re M (1985) 129 SJ 221 CA Failed application to court to exercise its wardship jurisdiction in lieu of local authority exercising its care jurisdiction.

Re M [1961] 1 All ER 201; [1961] Ch 81; (1961) 125 JP 163; (1961) 111 LJ 170 HC ChD Once child in local authority care under Children Act 1948, s 1(1), wardship should cease as court will not interfere with local authority discretion — regardless of Act.

Re M [1961] 1 All ER 788; [1961] Ch 328; (1961) 125 JP 278; (1961) 111 LJ 237 CA Court retains supervisory jurisdiction but may order that wardship cease upon ward being taken into local authority care.

Re M (R) and M (L) [1986] 2 FLR 205 HC FamD Alleged local authority buse of power to be challenged by way of judicial review.

Re O [1978] 2 All ER 27; [1978] Fam 196 (also HC FamD); (1977) 121 SJ 710; [1977] 3 WLR 725 CA Child's interests paramount consideration in deciding wardship cases.

Re P [1988] FCR 232; [1988] 1 FLR 328 HC FamD Care/control of babies to parents as medical evidence showed injuries suffered by babies easily sufferable absent rough treatment/babies could have copper deficiency syndrome.

Re R [1988] FCR 388; [1987] 2 FLR 401 CA Court could exercise wardship jurisdiction at behest of local authority where juvenile court discharging care order but child still felt to be at risk.

Re S [1987] FCR 85; [1987] 1 FLR 479 CA On making/effect of care order: here wardship should have been discontinued in light of care orders.

Re S [1965] 1 All ER 865; (1965) 129 JP 228; (1965) 115 LJ 265; (1965) 109 SJ 174; [1965] 1 WLR 483 CA Wardship jurisdiction continues over child in local authority care.

Re T [1989] FCR 212 (also HC FamD); [1989] 1 FLR 313 (also CA); (1988) 132 SJ 1117; [1988] 3 WLR 713 HC FamD HC exercised its wardship jurisdiction where was desirable that single court (rather than various juvenile courts) decide on future welfare of all children of family.

Re T [1969] 3 All ER 998; (1969) 113 SJ 774; [1969] 1 WLR 1608 HC ChD Custody of ward sought by person living abroad: interest of ward/comity of nations of increasing/decreasing importance.

Re W (1981) 2 FLR 360; (1981) 131 NLJ 578 HC FamD On when wardship powers will be exercised in respect of child committed to local authority care by juvenile court.

Re W (1985) 129 SJ 269 CA Discharge of wardship order in respect of child in local authority care.

Re W [1979] 3 All ER 154; [1980] Fam 60; (1979) 143 JP 727; (1979) 123 SJ 553; [1979] 3 WLR 252 CA Natural parent cannot challenge merits of local authority decision to make child ward; authority may consider possible future adoption in deciding to disallow parental access to child.

Re W (1985) 129 SJ 523 HC FamD Girl aged just over seventeen who was beyond parental control committed to care of local authority.

Re W (A) and W (E) (1979) 129 (1) NLJ 420 CA Court would not in instant case exercise its wardship jurisdiction in respect of child in care.

Stockport Metropolitan Borough Council v B; Stockport Metropolitan Borough Council v L [1986] 2 FLR 80 HC FamD On need for wardship proceedings for care order to be processed swiftly.

W v Nottinghamshire County Council and another [1986] 1 FLR 565 CA Court will not allow third party to invoke wardship jurisdiction of court where local authority seeking replacement of care orders with supervision orders.

W v Shropshire County Council [1986] 1 FLR 359 (also CA) HC FamD Non-continuation of wardship over child in respect of whom local authority sought to bring care proceedings.

WARD (caution)

Re G; Re R [1990] 2 FLR 347 HC FamD Police allowed give formal police caution to wards; on appropriate procedure in such cases.

Re M [1990] FCR 385 HC FamD Social worker required to be present at formal police cautioning of ward (cautioning had to be authorised by court).

WARD (child sex abuse)

Cleveland County Council v E [1988] FCR 625 HC FamD Though local authority had not continued with action court found children not sexually abused and de-warded them.

Re C [1985] FLR 1114 CA Failed application by mother for full investigation in wardship of alleged abuse of her son by his adoptive parents.

Re F [1988] FCR 679; [1988] 2 FLR 123 CA Wardship having harmful effect on children halted where had been no substantial evidence on which to continue it.

Re H [1992] 1 WLR 243 CA Wards (children of two families sharing accommodation) returned to family environment though there was (unsatisfactory) evidence of child abuse against one of them.

Re K and others [1988] 1 All ER; [1988] Fam 1; [1988] 1 FLR 435; (1988) 152 JP 185; (1987) 131 SJ 1697; [1987] 3 WLR 1233 HC FamD Wardship court will not intervene in existing child abuse case; no leave necessary for child to give evidence against parents.

WARD (contempt)

Re H's Settlement; H v H [1909] 2 Ch 260; [1909] 78 LJCh 745 HC ChD Court can commit ward of court to prison for contempt.

Re W and others [1989] 1 FLR 246 HC FamD Newspapers and their editors found (using criminal standard of proof) not to be guilty of contempt in breaching injunction on publication of articles regarding wardship action.

WARD (costs)

Re G [1982] 2 All ER 32; [1982] TLR 37; [1982] 1 WLR 438 CA Payment of Official Solicitor's costs for acting as guardian ad litem.

WARD (disclosure)

Official Solicitor v K and another [1963] 3 All ER 191; (1963) 113 LJ 577; (1963) 107 SJ 616 HL No-one has absolute right to see Official Solicitor's confidential reports but reports only to be so given if in ward's interests.

Re E [1993] 1 FCR 529 CA On disclosure of wardship documents in later wardship action concerning sibling.

Re J [1984] FLR 535; (1984) 128 SJ 280; [1984] TLR 21 HC FamD Pyschiatric test/reports unnecessary/unavailable where sought by mother as evidence on which to challenge prospective testimony of ward in criminal case.

Re M [1993] 1 FCR 476; (1992) 142 NLJ 1233; (1992) 136 SJ LB 253 CA On disclosure of wardship documents for use in later civil action (here against local authority).

Re S and others [1987] 3 All ER 1076; [1987] Fam 199; [1988] 1 FLR 1; [1987] 3 WLR 847 HC FamD Leave of court required for disclosure of records concerning ward even if came into being after wardship made; interest of ward in confidentiality will rarely supersede interest in protecting society from crime; ordinary case records of local authority not subject to disclosure; that privilege not waived because social worker report to court based on records.

WARD (discovery)

Re X and others [1992] Fam 124; [1991] FCR 954; [1992] 1 FLR 84; (1991) 141 NLJ 708; [1991] TLR 146; [1992] 2 WLR 784 HC FamD Definite injury to wardship jurisdiction and lack of real chance of injury to libel action merited refusal of discovery of wardship files for purposes of libel action.

WARD (education)

Re Baker [1961] Ch 303; (1961) 111 LJ 597 HC ChD Non-exercise of court's wardship jurisdiction over infants to enforce school attendance order.

Re D [1987] 3 All ER 717; [1988] 1 FLR 131; (1987) 131 SJ 1485; [1987] 1 WLR 1400 CA Court will not normally intervene in local education authority decision on special education needs of ward save to assist/if invited by authority.

WARD (estoppel)

Re L (AC) [1971] 3 All ER 743; (1972) 136 JP 19 HC ChD Local authority estopped from objecting to time-barred application by other which it engineered; failure of mother to accept child in care into her supervision not estoppel from later exercising parental rights in action.

WARD (ethnicity)

Re J [1987] 1 FLR 455; (1987) 151 JP 243 HC FamD Wardship order continued but adoption/custodianship of child not allowed where natural mother not unreasonably objected to adoption of child by foster parents who were Jehovah's Witnesses/of different race to child.

WARD (ex parte application)

Re H [1986] 1 FLR 132; [1985] 1 WLR 1164 CA On undesirability of ex parte applications in wardship proceedings.

WARD (foetus)

Re F [1988] 2 All ER 193; [1988] Fam 122; [1988] FCR 529; [1988] 2 FLR 307 (also HC FamD); (1988) 138 NLJ 37; (1989) 133 SJ 1088; (1988) 132 SJ 820; [1988] 2 WLR 1288 CA Unborn child cannot be made ward of court.

Re F [1988] 2 FLR 307 (also CA) HC FamD Unborn child cannot be made ward of court.

WARD (foreign decree)

Re E [1967] 2 All ER 881; [1967] 2 WLR 1370 CA Court need not blindly obey foreign court order if not in interests of child.

Re M (B) [1993] 2 FCR 388 HC FamD Foreign child who habitually resided in jurisdiction could be (and here was) made ward of court.

WARD (fostering)

Re O (E) (a minor) (1973) 123 NLJ 180t CA Wardship of Nigerian girl to English fosterers.

Re W (1991) 141 NLJ 1263; [1992] 1 WLR 100 CA Publication of fact that ward placed with gay foster parents allowed though restrictions on identifying foster parents/ward.

Re Y [1985] FLR 294 HC FamD Mother's wardship application failed where child had been living happily with good foster parents for eight years.

WARD (general)

Bates v Morley (1982) 3 FLR 244; (1982) 132 NLJ 65 CA Mother with care and control of ward (father had access) allowed remove child to Canada (wardship ending upon ward quitting country).

Devon County Council v S and another [1995] 1 All ER 243; [1994] Fam 169; [1994] 2 FCR 409; [1994] 1 FLR 355; [1993] TLR 626; [1994] 3 WLR 183 HC FamD Local authority may invite court to exercise wardship powers under inherent jurisdiction.

H v Lambeth London Borough Council [1984] TLR 213 HC FamD On need for leave of court in respect of all significant decisions taken regarding ward.

M v Humberside County Council and another [1979] 2 All ER 744; [1979] Fam 114; (1980) 1 FLR 91; [1979] 3 WLR 234 HC FamD If lower court empowered High Court will only intervene if unusual case; local authority acting outside powers; lower court powers inadequate.

R v North Yorkshire County Council, ex parte M (No 3) [1989] FCR 403; [1989] 2 FLR 82 HC QBD On possibility of post-judicial review invocation of wardship jurisdiction.

Re A [1970] 3 All ER 184; [1970] Ch 665; (1970) 114 SJ 415; [1970] 3 WLR 142 CA Court need not order return if children not in jurisdiction through fraud, they need protection, and other parent can readily come to England.

Re A, an Infant; Allen v Peninsular and Oriental Steamship Co, Ltd, and another (1961) 105 SJ 424 CA Court would not make order to restrain ward on board ship being allowed enter new jurisdiction when ship docked there.

Re A-H [1962] 3 All ER 853; (1962) 112 LJ 816; (1962) 106 SJ 1011; [1962] 3 WLR 1430 HC ChD Non-interference by ChD where orders sought available in existing proceedings before PDAD.

Re Andrews [1958] 2 All ER 308; [1958] Ch 665; (1958) 108 LJ 425; (1958) 102 SJ 382 HC ChD Wardship concerns a matter for wardship court; PDAD will make care/custody/control decisions on merit regarding ChD ward (and in the course of so doing will remove child from ChD wardship); ChD may hear wardship application despitet PDAD care/custody/control order/s regarding child.

Re Arif (Mohamed); Re Singh (Nirbhai) [1968] Ch 643 (also CA) [1968] 2 WLR 1290 (also CA) HC ChD Courts if had wardship jurisdiction over infant refused admission by immigration authorities would not (if those authorities acted properly) exercise its jurisdiction.

Re B [1989] FCR 191; [1988] 1 FLR 484 HC FamD Permissible though inappropriate for court to review local authority decision regarding allocation of staff.

Re B [1962] Ch 201 CA Court would not implore wardship jurisdiction in respect of children over whom statutory body (local education authority) seeking to discharge its duty.

Re C [1984] FLR 419 (also HC FamD) CA Child's interests absolutely paramount in wardship actions.

Re C [1983] TLR 711 CA On undesirability of independent welfare reports; on extent of paramountcy of interests of child.

Re C (no 2) [1990] FCR 220 [1990] 1 FLR 263 CA Judgment in open court (albeit taking steps to protect identity of persons involved in case) required where ordering non-treatment of ward who as result would die.

Re D [1977] 3 All ER 481; [1977] Fam 158; (1977) 141 JP 669; (1977) 127 NLJ 492t; [1977] 2 WLR 1006 HC FamD Child's interest of paramount concern in wardship not care proceedings.

Re D [1973] 2 All ER 993; [1973] Fam 179; [1973] 3 WLR 53 HC FamD Minor's welfare not only relevant factor under Guardianship of Minors Act 1970, ss 1 and 9; only exceptionally may court in wardship case upset existing decision on merits by magistrates.

Re E [1967] 1 All ER 329; (1967) 111 SJ 34; [1967] 2 WLR 445 HC ChD Despite need for comity, child subject to foreign order may if necessary be made ward/put into custody and control here.

Re E (D) [1967] Ch 761; (1967) 111 SJ 352 CA Court allowed child removed from United States contrary to court order there to remain in care and custody of aunt in England.

Re El-G (1983) 4 FLR 421 HC FamD Welfare of children demanded that they stay with prospective adopters; on deciding whether parent's refusal of consent unreasonable (here was: dispensed with); on pivotal role of court when is sought to change arrangements for ward.

Re G [1969] 2 All ER 1135; (1969) 119 NLJ 672; [1969] 1 WLR 1001 HC ChD Forum conveniens for post-divorce wardship case is that where divorce heard.

Re H [1965] 3 All ER 906; [1966] 1 WLR 381 (also CA) HC ChD Children returned to foreign jurisdiction without inquiry into merits of case/foreign court order.

Re H [1966] 1 All ER 886; (1965-66) 116 NLJ 725; [1966] 1 WLR 381 CA Inquiry into state of affairs permissible but not required before returning children to parent in foreign jurisdiction.

Re H (A) [1963] Ch 232 HC ChD On competence/willingness of ChD to make wardship orders in light of connected divorce action in PDAD.

Re H (GJ) [1966] 1 All ER 952; (1965-66) 116 NLJ 697; (1966) 110 SJ 330; [1966] 1 WLR 706 HC ChD Jurisdiction in wardship cases.

Re Kernot [1964] 3 All ER 339; [1965] Ch 217; (1964) 114 LJ 675; (1964) 108 SJ 675; [1964] 3 WLR 1210 HC ChD Factors when deciding forum conveniens.

Re L [1978] 2 All ER 318; (1978) 122 SJ 15; [1978] 1 WLR 181 CA Procedural errors by registrar required re-hearing of wardship case.

Re L [1963] 1 All ER 176; (1963) 107 SJ 35; [1963] 1 WLR 97 HC ChD On proper respondent in wardship cases.

Re L [1962] 3 All ER 1; (1962) 106 SJ 686 CA Child's welfare paramount but parent's conduct material in deciding care/control — here entrusted to innocent party.

Re Liddell's Settlement Trusts; Liddell v Liddell [1936] 1 All ER 239; [1936] Ch 365; (1936) 80 SJ 165; (1935-36) LII TLR 308 CA Sequestration of assets of person domiciled in England/ resident abroad for non-compliance with order to return wards to jurisdiction.

Re M, an infant (1961) 105 SJ 153 CA Prerogative rights of Crown as parens patriae existed notwithstanding enactment of Children Act 1948.

Re N [1967] 1 All ER 161; [1967] Ch 512; (1966) 110 SJ 924; [1967] 2 WLR 691 HC ChD Where urgent can make post-wardship style orders before wardship/issue injunction on Sunday or before writ issued.

Re P (AJ) (1969) 119 NLJ 12; (1968) 112 SJ 861; [1968] 1 WLR 1976 HC ChD HC ChD could in wardship cases make orders contrary to those made by magistrates though was not necessary here.

Re P (GE) [1964] 3 All ER 977; [1965] Ch 568; (1965) 115 LJ 24; (1964) 108 SJ 916; [1965] 2 WLR 1 CA Court has wardship jurisdiction over stateless infant living in England when action begun though later outside jurisdiction.

Re P (GE) [1964] Ch 575; (1964) 114 LJ 474; (1964) 108 SJ 444; [1964] 3 WLR 191 HC ChD Court had no wardship jurisdiction over stateless infant living in England when action begun though later outside jurisdiction.

Re R [1984] TLR 304 CA Court could not re-assess wardship decision in light of ongoing durability of mother's relationship with boyfriend.

Re R (PM) [1968] 1 All ER 691; (1968) 118 NLJ 14t; (1968) 112 SJ 189; [1968] 1 WLR 385 HC ChD On medical examination of ward absent court's consent; on access to wards.

Re S [1983] TLR 550 HC FamD Wardship jurisdiction ought not to be employed on appeal from CyCt.

Re S (M) an infant [1971] 1 All ER 459; [1971] Ch 621; (1970) 120 NLJ 969t; (1971) 115 SJ 93; [1971] 2 WLR 216 HC ChD Scottish court forum conveniens though English proceedings brought first.

Re T; T v T [1987] 1 FLR 181 CA HC not in error in considering child's best interests in wardship application and then relying on that as one of four criteria justifying granting of ouster order.

Re W (1982) 3 FLR 129; (1981) 131 NLJ 1189 CA On relevant factors in application to have parental rights resolution of local authority rescinded.

Re W (1981) 131 NLJ 1288 CA Local authority care resolution deemed not to have lapsed.

WARD (grandparent)

Re L (K) [1990] FCR 692 CrCt Care order in respect of child discharged with view to grandparents commencing wardship proceedings.

WARD (guardian)

R v North Yorkshire County Council, ex parte M (No 3) [1989] FCR 403; [1989] 2 FLR 82 HC QBD On possibility of post-judicial review invocation of wardship jurisdiction.

Re B [1989] 1 FLR 268 HC FamD On appointment of guardian ad litem in wardship action.

Re C [1989] FCR 774; [1989] 1 FLR 222; (1989) 133 SJ 20; [1989] 1 WLR 61 CA Great-uncle not 'relative' for purposes of Adoption Act 1976, s 72(1); court ought not to have appointed guardian in respect of wards of court.

Re C and another [1989] 1 All ER 395 CA Dubious whether court can make guardianship order where existing wardship order.

Re H [1994] 4 All ER 762; [1994] Fam 11; [1993] 3 WLR 1109 HC FamD Ward can take part in case minus guardian ad litem.

Re K [1962] 3 All ER 178; (1962) 112 LJ 617; (1962) 106 SJ 721; [1962] 3 WLR 752 HC ChD No entitlement to see reports lodged with guardian ad litem; parties may question maker's of statements in reports.

Re P [1967] 2 All ER 229; (1967) 111 SJ 496; [1967] 1 WLR 818 HC ChD If magistrates make guardianship ruling then should make variations unless not empowered to make order sought; High Court not constrained in wardship case by earlier decision of magistrates.

Re T [1989] FCR (also HC FamD); [1989] 1 FLR 313 (also HC FamD); (1989) 133 SJ 568 CA Wardship proceedings did not need to be initiated (and ought not to have been initiated by guardian ad litem appointed by juvenile court).

Re T and others [1989] 1 All ER 297; [1990] Fam 1; [1989] 2 WLR 954 CA Rôle of guardian ad litem confined to juvenile court proceedings — cannot begin wardship proceedings.

WARD (habitual residence)

F v S (wardship: jurisdiction) [1993] 2 FLR 686 CA On deciding place of habitual residence of child.

Re W (E) [1992] 2 FCR 441 (also HC FamD) CA On determining place of habitual residence.

Re W (E) [1992] 2 FCR 441 (also CA) HC FamD On determining place of habitual residence.

Re W (E) (No 2) [1993] 1 FCR 710 HC FamD On determining place of habitual residence.

WARD (immigration)

Re A [1991] FCR 1013; [1992] 1 FLR 427 CA Court would not allow wardship action to be used (as here) to frustrate Home Secretary in enforcing immigration law.

Re A (1968) 112 SJ 190 HC ChD Court would not exercise wardship powers in respect of foreign child being dealt with by immigration authorities.

Re A (1968) 112 SJ 295 CA Court would not exercise wardship powers in respect of foreign child being dealt with by immigration authorities.

Re Arif (Mohamed); Re Singh (Nirbhai) [1968] Ch 643 (also HC ChD)[1968] 2 WLR 1290 (also HC ChD) CA Courts if had wardship jurisdiction over infant refused admission by immigration authorities would not (if those authorities acted properly) exercise its jurisdiction.

Re F [1989] 1 All ER 1155; [1990] Fam 125; [1989] FCR 165; [1989] 1 FLR 233 (also HC FamD); (1988) 132 SJ 1269; [1989] 3 WLR 691 CA Use of wardship proceedings to prevent immigration authorities removing child an abuse of process but exceptionally (as here) allowed.

Re F [1989] 1 FLR 233 (also CA); (1989) 133 SJ 1088 HC FamD Use of wardship proceedings to prevent immigration authorities removing child an abuse of process.

Re K and S [1992] 1 FLR 432 HC FamD Court would not allow wardship action to be used (as here) to frustrate Home Secretary in enforcing immigration law.

WARD (injunction)

Re J [1988] 1 FLR 65 HC FamD Injunction available to prevent mother (of ward) from leaving jurisdiction where appropriate.

WARD (interview)

Re B [1990] FCR 469 HC FamD Court's authorisation unnecessary to arrest/detention of over seventeen year old ward.

Re G; Re R [1990] 2 FLR 347 HC FamD Police allowed give formal police caution to wards; on appropriate procedure in such cases.

WARD (legitimacy)

Re S (J) [1980] 1 All ER 1061; [1981] Fam 22; (1981) 2 FLR 146; (1980) 124 SJ 881; [1980] 3 WLR 984 CA Bare declaration of paternity not to be made in wardship case; grounds on which (if possible) to be made.

WARD (maintenance)

Calderdale Borough Council v H and P [1991] 1 FLR 461 HC FamD Statutory care order to local authority, children to reside with grandparents who were to be paid maintenance pending approval as foster-parents when would be paid boarding-out allowance.

Re K and A [1995] 1 FLR 688 HC FamD No power to order local authority to pay maintenance to grandmother for grandchild in her care/its supervision (and if power existed was inappropriately exercised here).

WARD (medical expert)

Re C [1987] 1 FLR 418 HC FamD On role of medical experts/Official Solicitor caring for wards/in wardship proceedings.

WARD (medical treatment)

Re B (1982) 3 FLR 117 (also HC FamD); (1981) 131 NLJ 1112; (1981) 125 SJ 608; [1981] 1 WLR 1421 CA Court ordered operation in respect of new-born Mongol which parents would not authorise: test was best interests of child.

Re B (1982) 3 FLR 117 (also CA) HC QBD Refusal (on basis that not in best interests of child) to order operation on new-born Mongol which parents would not authorise.

Re B [1988] AC 199; [1987] 2 FLR 314 (also HC FamD/CA); (1987) 137 NLJ 432; (1987) 131 SJ 625; [1987] 2 WLR 1213 HL Sterilisation operation of mildly mentally handicapped ward approved as was in best interests of same.

Re C [1989] 2 All ER 782; [1990] Fam 26; [1990] FCR 209; (1989) 139 NLJ 612; (1989) 133 SJ 876; [1989] 3 WLR 240 CA Court may authorise treatment of terminally ill child that eases suffering without prolonging life.

Re E [1991] FCR 771; [1991] 2 FLR 585; [1991] TLR 93 HC FamD Leave of court unnecessary for thereapeutic sterilisation of mentally handicapped girl.

Re M [1988] 2 FLR 497 HC FamD Sterilisation of mentally handicapped ward ordered as was in her best interests never to become pregnant.

Re P [1989] 1 FLR 182 HC FamD Sterilisation of ward ordered where was in her best interests.

WARD (Official Solicitor)

Re C [1987] 1 FLR 418 HC FamD On role of medical experts/Official Solicitor caring for wards/in wardship proceedings.

WARD (place of safety order)

Re B (1981) 2 FLR 307; (1980) 124 SJ 81 HC FamD Practice as regards application for place of safety order for ward of court.

WARD (publicity)

R (Mrs) v Central Independent Television plc [1994] 3 All ER 641; [1994] Fam 192; [1995] 1 FCR 521; [1994] 2 FLR 151; [1994] TLR 92; [1994] 3 WLR 20 CA Parental jurisdiction of court does not extend to injuncting publication touching on child but not addressing care or upbringing.

Re B (A) [1985] FLR 470 HC FamD Exceptionally (as here) court would make universally binding order prohibiting publication of material enabling identification of mother/ward.

Re C (1969) 119 NLJ 600t HC ChD Failed application by foster parents to restrain broadcasting of television programme concerning ward in their care.

Re C (No 1) [1990] 1 FLR 252 CA Blanket ban on publication of any personal information other than that contained in open court judgment given in wardship case of particular public interest.

Re C (No 2) [1989] 2 All ER 791 [1990] Fam 39; (1989) 139 NLJ 613; [1989] 3 WLR 252 CA Injunction prohibiting any publicity about medical treatment to ward justifiable if in interests of ward.

Re Dunhill (1967) 111 SJ 113 HC ChD Wardship summons dismissed where merely issued for publicity purposes.

Re H [1995] 2 FLR 542 HC FamD Permission to report judgment under initials as would compel ward to confront own behaviour/was necessary to safeguard public.

Re L [1988] 1 All ER 418; (1987) 137 NLJ 760; [1988] 1 FLR 255 HC FamD No automatic absolute prohibition of anything about ward.

Re M [1989] 1 FLR 443 HC FamD Wardship not justified just because parents mentally handicapped but was here; no/was restriction on publicity regarding parents (who sought publicity)/fosterers or future adopters; on procedure where party actively seeks publicity in wardship proceedings.

Re M and N [1990] Fam 211; [1990] FCR 395; [1990] 1 FLR 149 (also HC FamD); (1989) 139 NLJ 1154; (1990) 134 SJ 165; [1989] 3 WLR 1136 CA On publication of information (and injunctions available to restrain publication of same) pertaining to wards.

Re M and N [1990] 1 FLR 149 (also CA) HC FamD On publication of information (and injunctions available to restrain publication of same) pertaining to wards.

Re R [1994] 2 FCR 468; [1994] 2 FLR 637 CA On imposition of restraints on reporting of criminal proceedings concerning (abduction of) ward.

Re W [1992] 1 All ER 794; [1992] 1 FLR 99; [1991] TLR 391 CA Publication about ward placement involves balancing press freedom/real public interest and child's interests; sometimes publication may legitimately require disclosure of child's identity.

Re W and others [1989] 1 FLR 246 HC FamD Newspapers and their editors found (using criminal standard of proof) not to be guilty of contempt in breaching injunction on publication of articles regarding wardship action.

Re X (1984) 128 SJ 873; [1984] 1 WLR 1422 HC FamD Court order issued prohibiting revelation of ward's identity or that of parents where was necessary to protect ward.

Re X [1975] 1 All ER; (1974) 124 NLJ 1083t; (1975) 119 SJ 12; [1975] 2 WLR 335 HC FamD Interests of ward not greater than public interest in freedom of publication.

Re Z [1995] 4 All ER 961; [1997] Fam 1 CA Wardship jurisdiction theoretically unlimited but will not be exercised where freedom of publication the dominant interest and child only referred to indirectly.

Re Z [1996] 2 WLR 88 CA Child's welfare took precedence over public interest in freedom to publish: injunction preventing publication of information in relation to child appropriate.

WARD (religion)

F v F [1902] 1 Ch 688 HC ChD Ward removed from guardian's care where guardian changed religion which held at time entrusted with ward.

Re E [1963] 3 All ER 874; (1964) 114 LJ 9; (1964) 108 SJ 75; [1964] 1 WLR 51 HC ChD Mother's desires on religious education important but child's welfare paramount: here two compatible.

Re J [1987] 1 FLR 455; (1987) 151 JP 243 HC FamD Wardship order continued but adoption/custodianship of child not allowed where natural mother not unreasonably objected to adoption of child by foster parents who were Jehovah's Witnesses/of different race to child.

Re W; W v M (1908) 77 LJCh 147 (also CA) HC ChD Variation of wardship order so as to allow two Jewish children to be educated as Christians.

Re W; W v M (1) [1907] 2 Ch 557; (1908) 77 LJCh 147 (also HC ChD); (1907) WN (I) 204 CA Variation of wardship order so as to allow Jewish child (at his behest) to be educated as a Christian but his sister to continue being educated as a Jew.

WARD (secure accommodation)

Re W (S) [1986] 1 FLR 24 HC FamD On ordering that ward over age of seventeen be placed in secure accommodation.

WARD (social worker)

Re C [1985] FLR 56 HC FamD On role of independent social workers.

WARD (soldier)

Re S (J) [1990] 2 All ER 861; [1990] Fam 182; [1990] FCR 961; [1991] 1 FLR 7; [1990] 3 WLR 119 HC FamD Minor subject to military law not suitable candidate for wardship of court.

WARD (sterilisation)

Re B [1987] 2 FLR 314 (also HC FamD/HL); (1987) 137 NLJ 291; (1987) 131 SJ 442 CA Sterilisation operation of mildly mentally handicapped ward approved as was in best interests of same.

Re B [1987] 2 FLR 314 (also CA/HL) HC FamD Sterilisation operation of mildly mentally handicapped ward approved as was in best interests of same.

WARD (supervision)

W v Nottinghamshire County Council and another [1986] 1 FLR 565 CA Court will not allow third party to invoke wardship jurisdiction of court where local authority seeking replacement of care orders with supervision orders.

WARD (surety)

Re H [1991] FCR 45; [1991] 1 FLR 40; [1990] TLR 311 CA On requiring surety for return of abducted children to jurisdiction within certain period.

WARD (surrogacy)

Re a Baby (1985) 135 NLJ 106 HC FamD Best interests of child still guiding factor in wardship cases involving surrogate children.

Re C [1985] FLR 846 HC FamD Care and control granted husband and wife of surrogate child of which husband natural father.

WARD (witness)

Re K and others [1988] 1 All ER; [1988] Fam 1; [1988] 1 FLR 435; (1988) 152 JP 185; (1987) 131 SJ 1697; [1987] 3 WLR 1233 HC FamD Wardship court will not intervene in existing child abuse case; no leave necessary for child to give evidence against parents.

WELFARE REPORT (general)

B v B (1973) 123 NLJ 107t HC FamD On practice as regards requesting reports by welfare officers.

B v M [1990] FCR 581; [1990] 2 FLR 46 CA On disclosure of welfare reports.

Re B (minors) (1977) 127 NLJ 913t HC FamD On desirability of ready availability of welfare officer's reports to parties' lawyers.

Re C [1983] TLR 711 CA On undesirability of independent welfare reports; on extent of paramountcy of interests of child.

Re H (minors) [1990] 2 FLR 172 CA Wardship/property action to be begun in absence of delayed welfare report as was in interests of children involved.

Re P (a minor) [1996] 2 FCR 285 HC FamD Successful appeal against residence/contact orders settled on where made on basis of unsatisfactory court welfare officer's reporrt.

Re S (a minor) [1992] TLR 308 CA Unnecessary to require reports in proceedings from both guardian ad litem and court welfare officer.

Re W (a minor) [1995] TLR 17 CA Appeal against judge's request for welfare report to be prepared ought not to have been brought.

WILFUL NEGLECT (general)

Jackson v Jackson (1967) 111 SJ 456 HC PDAD Valid finding of wilful neglect to maintain; wife's failure to give notice to putative father of child regarding maintenance action against another precluded making of maintenance order.

ALPHABETICAL INDEX

Attorney-General, Russell v (1949) 99 LJ 259; [1949] 118 LJR 1247; (1949) LXV TLR 369; (1949) WN (I) 226 HC PDAD Validity of marriage presumed absent direct contrary evidence where parties had undergone ceremony of marriage and thereafter corroborated.

Attorney-General, S, otherwise U v (1932) 146 LTR 144; (1931-32) XLVIII TLR 66 HC PDAD Petition for declaration of legtimacy dismissed where court not satisfied with evidence regarding parents.

Attorney-General, Sheward v (1964) 114 LJ 374; (1964) 108 SJ 159; [1964] 1 WLR 724 HC PDAD Must comply with Matrimonial Causes Act 1950, s 17(1) and Legitimacy Act 1959, s 2 for legitimacy order under latter to be made in respect of one.

Attorney-General, Veasey v (1982) 3 FLR 267 HC FamD Child legitimated upon marriage of parents: post-marital adoption did not affect situation.

Austin and others, R v [1981] 1 All ER 374; (1981) 72 Cr App R 104; [1980] Crim LR 716; (1981) 145 JP 145; (1981) 131 NLJ 68 CA Person with right to possession of child exempt from child-stealing but not paid accessories.

Avon County Council v N [1996] 1 FCR 252 HC FamD Care of children refused to mother even though might have decided otherwise had local authority conducted itself properly thus necessitating instant decision.

Avon County Council, ex parte Crabtree, R v [1996] 3 FCR 773; [1996] 1 FLR 502 CA Failed appeal against failed application for judicial review of fostering panel decision to deregister applicant as fosterer.

Avon County Court, ex parte K and others, R v [1986] 1 FLR 443 HC QBD On meaning of giving 'first consideration' to child's welfare (Child Care Act 1980, s 18(1)): here local authority failed in duty to give same when decided to close community home.

Ayyar (Krishanamurthi) v Ayyar (Krishnamurthi) and another (1926-27) XLIII TLR 363 PC On succession arrangements following adoption according to Hindu practice.

Ayyar (Krishnamurthi) and another, Ayyar (Krishanamurthi) v (1926-27) XLIII TLR 363 PC On succession arrangements following adoption according to Hindu practice.

B (B) v B (M) [1969] 1 All ER 891; (1969) 119 NLJ 321 HC PDAD On appropriate way of dealing with father-contemnor who refused to surrender child to custody of mother.

B (BR) v B (J) [1968] 2 All ER 1023 CA Blood tests ordered if in child's best interests.

B (GW) v B (PW) CA (1971) 115 SJ 486 CA Refusal of access to father whose sixteen year old son did not want to see him.

B (J), B (BR) v [1968] 2 All ER 1023 CA Blood tests ordered if in child's best interests.

B (M) v B (R) [1968] 3 All ER 170; (1968) 118 NLJ 862; (1968) 112 SJ 504 CA Valid decision to give child into custody of mother where either party could in fairness have been awarded custody.

B (M), B (B) v [1969] 1 All ER 891; (1969) 119 NLJ 321 HC PDAD On appropriate way of dealing with father-contemnor who refused to surrender child to custody of mother.

B (No 2), B v (1955) 99 SJ 334; [1955] 1 WLR 557 HL HL incompetent to hear infant custody action decided on by CA as did not relate to matrimonial causes/matters.

B (No 2), H v [1990] FCR 366 HC FamD Conditional access to his children allowed of father who had sexually abused those children.

B (otherwise D) (child: surname), D v [1979] 1 All ER 93; [1979] Fam 38; (1978) 122 SJ 486; [1978] 3 WLR 573 CA Court cannot order mother to execute fresh deed poll.

B (otherwise D), D v [1977] 3 All ER 751; [1977] Fam 145; [1977] 2 WLR 1011 HC FamD Other parent's consent required to change of surname of unborn/new-born/unseen/well-known child; child's interests a consideration for court in deciding whether to waive consent.

B (otherwise P) v Attorney-General; B (otherwise P) v Attorney-General and others [1965] 3 All ER 253; (1965) 115 LJ 678; (1965) 109 SJ 536; [1966] 2 WLR 58 HC PDAD Cannot order legitimation proceedings be held in camera.

B (PW) CA, B (GW) v (1971) 115 SJ 486 CA Refusal of access to father whose sixteen year old son did not want to see him.

B (R), B (M) v [1968] 3 All ER 170; (1968) 118 NLJ 862; (1968) 112 SJ 504 CA Valid decision to give child into custody of mother where either party could in fairness have been awarded custody.

B (residence order: restricting applications), B v [1997] 2 FCR 518 CA Valid decision to order one child to live with mother and other child with father but order that father not be allowed seek custody of other child without leave of court was improper.

B and another, B v (1968) 112 SJ 689 CA HC could order administration of blood test in divorce action where paternity was an issue.

B and E (B intervening), B v [1969] 3 All ER 1106; (1969) 119 NLJ 672t; (1969) 113 SJ 625; [1969] 1 WLR 1800 CA Presumption of legitimacy justifies refusing blood test; blood test not ordered where only to support custody claim, only if in child's interests.

B and F (B and B intervening), B v [1968] 3 All ER 232; (1968) 118 NLJ 956; (1968) 112 SJ 481; [1968] 3 WLR 1217 HC PDAD Access only to children of family; 'children of family' only if mutually accepted as such; no resistance to action for access did not mean mutual acceptance.

B and H, B v [1962] 1 All ER 29; (1962) 112 LJ 58; (1961) 105 SJ 969 HC PDAD Custody order in favour of second husband of dead adulteress.

B and H, Bolton Metropolitan Borough Council v [1990] FCR 57; [1989] 2 FLR 349 HC FamD Long-term care pending adoption for children with parents incapable of proper parenting: access to parents until placed with foster-parents; delay in welfare report criticised.

B and others, Cheshire County Council v [1992] 2 FCR 572 HC FamD Provisions in care and contact orders for six-month review of their implementation was invalid.

B County Council, ex parte P, R v [1991] 2 All ER 65; [1991] 1 FLR 470; [1991] 1 WLR 221 CA Local authority behaviour open to judicial review if unreasonable or unlawful; though child a compellable witness in care proceedings should not be called if contrary to best interests thereof.

B v A (1982) 3 FLR 27 HC FamD Father properly refused access to his illegitimate children where as was domineering towards mother of whom was step-father which would also create complications.

B v Attorney-General (B and others intervening) [1966] 2 All ER 145; (1965) 115 LJ 58; (1966) 110 SJ 309; [1966] 2 WLR 58 HC PDAD On declarations of legitimacy.

B v Attorney-General (B and others intervening) [1965] 2 WLR 871 HC PDAD No power that legitimacy application be heard in camera.

B v Attorney-General (NEB and others intervening) [1965] 1 All ER 62; [1965] 2 WLR 871 HC PDAD Custody order in divorce decree not estoppel to later denial of paternity; wife's/dead man's denial of husband's paternity could be admissible.

B v B [1924] 93, 184; (1924) 130 LTR 754; (1923-24) 68 SJ 457; (1923-24) XL TLR 349; (1924) WN (I) 64 CA On granting access of guilty spouse to children.

B v B (No 2) (1955) 99 SJ 334; [1955] 1 WLR 557 HL HL incompetent to hear infant custody action decided on by CA as did not relate to matrimonial causes/matters.

B v B (1962) 106 SJ 573 HC PDAD Husband could not be expected to live with drug-addicted wife; custody of child taken from drug addicted wife and care and control of child given to paternal grandmother.

B v B (1969) 133 JP 245 HC PDAD On power of HC as regards hearing appeal from decision of justices to imprison parent for refusing to observe custody order.

B v B [1971] 3 All ER 682; (1971) 121 NLJ 547t; [1971] 1 WLR 1486 CA Welfare of child may demand no access to divorced parent.

B v B (1972) 122 NLJ 1112 CA Interim custody of young girl to father whom wife had deserted but increased access by mother allowed.

B v B (1973) 117 SJ 165 HC FamD Was relevant factor when determining custody action that mother now had relationship/was living with husband's brother.

B v B (1973) 123 NLJ 107t HC FamD On practice as regards requesting reports by welfare officers.

B v B (1975) 125 NLJ 552t; (1975) 119 SJ 610 CA Custody of children of adulterous mother to their father.

B v B (1976) 120 SJ 97 HC FamD Court to be informed why custody order appeal withdrawn where was prima facie curious custody decision by justices.

B v B (1980) 1 FLR 87 CA Court must itself decide which school child to attend where divorced parents cannot agree on matter.

B v B (1980) 1 FLR 385 CA Inappropriate that custody conditions include bedtime/babysitting arrangements for children.

B v B (1982) 3 FLR 187 CA Declaration by divorce court that paedophile husband to marriage being terminated was unfit to have custody of child was valid.

B v B (1984) 134 NLJ 863c CA Custody of eleven month old son to father who with his sister and her husband had been looking after son since wife quit matrimonial home.

B v B [1985] FLR 166; [1984] TLR 509 CA Moral need for father (who could not get job because looking after child) to seek employment not relevant factor in custody hearing.

B v B [1985] FLR 462 CA Failed application by mother for custody of child adequately looked after by father for eleven months — that father made redundant positive in that it freed father to spend more time with child.

B v B [1988] 1 All ER 652; [1988] 2 FLR 6; (1988) 132 SJ 564; [1988] 1 WLR 526 HC FamD Rights of access violations must take place in contracting state but are not subject to limited operation of Child Abduction Convention as implemented.

B v B [1991] FCR 1; [1991] 1 FLR 402 HC FamD On whether to place child with mother (in lesbian relationship) or father; on splitting of siblings.

B v B [1993] 2 All ER 144; [1993] Fam 32; [1993] 1 FLR 238; (1992) 136 SJ LB 156; [1992] 3 WLR 865 CA Child may be returned to foreign jurisdiction despite high degree of intolerability.

B v B [1993] 1 FCR 211; [1992] 2 FLR 327 HC FamD Residence order to grandmother (seeking same with mother's approval) that she might exercise parental responsibility.

B v B [1994] 1 FCR 809; [1994] 2 FLR 713 HC FamD On interviewing childen where sexual abuse suspected.

B v B [1994] 2 FCR 667; (1994) 138 SJ LB 119; [1994] TLR 271 CA On procedure as regards hearing of children's cases/interviewing of children by judge.

B v B [1997] 2 FCR 518; [1997] 1 FLR 139; (1996) TLR 10/10/96; [1997] TLR 295 CA Valid decision to order one child to live with mother and other child with father but order that father not be allowed seek custody of other child without leave of court was improper.

B v B (residence order: restricting applications) [1997] 2 FCR 518 CA Valid decision to order one child to live with mother and other child with father but order that father not be allowed seek custody of other child without leave of court was improper.

B v B and another (1968) 118 NLJ 541t; (1968) 112 SJ 689 CA HC could order administration of blood test in divorce action where paternity was an issue.

B v B and E (B intervening) [1969] 3 All ER 1106; (1969) 119 NLJ 672t; (1969) 113 SJ 625; [1969] 1 WLR 1800 CA Presumption of legitimacy justifies refusing blood test; blood test not ordered where only to support custody claim, only if in child's interests.

B v B and F (B and B intervening) [1968] 3 All ER 232; (1968) 118 NLJ 956; (1968) 112 SJ 481; [1968] 3 WLR 1217 HC PDAD Access only to children of family; 'children of family' only if mutually accepted as such; no resistance to action for access did not mean mutual acceptance.

B v B and H [1962] 1 All ER 29; (1962) 112 LJ 58; (1961) 105 SJ 969 HC PDAD Custody order in favour of second husband of dead adulteress.

B v Derbyshire County Council [1992] 2 FCR 14; [1992] 1 FLR 538 HC FamD Res judicata probably inapplicable to local authority's seeking of care orders (and certainly inapplicable here).

B v K [1993] 1 FCR 382 HC FamD Expressed desire of older children not to return respected by court: return of younger brother consequently not ordered.

B v M [1990] FCR 581; [1990] 2 FLR 46 CA On disclosure of welfare reports.

B v M [1994] 1 FCR 769; [1994] 1 FLR 342 CyCt On revocation (during transitional period of Child Support Act 1991) of child maintenance order prior to application to Child Support Agency for child maintenance assessment.

B v P [1992] 2 FCR 576 HC FamD Contact between father and small child validly refused where inter alia consequent upset to mother would upset child.

B v S (formerly B) (1974) 118 SJ 219 CA Re-hearing of access case necessary on evidence available (all evidence unavailable as judge promised children would not reveal what they said to him in chambers).

B v T [1990] FCR 31 (also HC FamD); [1989] 2 FLR 31 (also HC FamD) CA Interim care and control of baby girl/young son to mother/father as custody along interim lines apparently not considered by magistrates.

B v T [1990] FCR 31 (also CA); [1989] 2 FLR 31 (also CA) HC FamD Custody of baby daughter/young son to mother where justices failed to properly consider relevant issues.

B v W (1979) 123 SJ 704 HC FamD Care and control of ward to mother, supervision order to local authority.

B v X County Council (1991) 141 NLJ 1740t; [1991] TLR 582 HC FamD Hearsay evidence admissible when CrCt hearing appeal against juvenile court care order.

B, Berkshire County Council v [1997] 1 FLR 171 HC FamD Parental contact could be ordered in care proceedings though local authority care plan envisaged that ultimately there would be no parental contact.

B, Devon County Council v [1997] 1 FLR 591 CA Freeing order invalid as court did not when making order consider basis of parent's refusal to agree to adoption; county court did not have inherent jurisdiction to bolster care order by way of injunctive relief.

B, Gateshead Metropolitan Borough Council v (1996) TLR 19/3/96 HC FamD On deciding where child is resident (in context of application for care order).

B, H v [1990] FCR 43 CA Refusal of second period of experimental access pending final decision whether father who had sexually abused child be continuously allowed access.

B, Humberside County Council v [1993] 1 FCR 613; [1993] 1 FLR 257 HC FamD On relevant factors when making interim care order.

B, London Borough of Southwark v [1993] 2 FLR 559 CA On deciding whether to allow withdrawal of application for care.

B, Manchester City Council v [1996] 1 FLR 324 HC FamD On burden/standard of proof in care action springing from non-accidental injuries to child.

B, N v [1993] 1 FCR 231 HC FamD Shared residence order (so that could acquire parental responsibility) refused; leave to remove remove children from jurisdiction refused.

B, Stockport Metropolitan Borough Council v; Stockport Metropolitan Borough Council v L [1986] 2 FLR 80 HC FamD On need for wardship proceedings for care order to be processed swiftly.

B, V v [1991] FCR 451; [1991] 1 FLR 266 HC FamD Order for child whose 'habitual residence' was Australia to be returned to mother there by father (abducter) as no proof of 'grave risk' to child if returned; on awarding costs in abduction action.

B, W v [1991] FCR 499; [1991] TLR 157 HC FamD Court may order contact by way of media that do not involve physical contact.

B, Y v [1995] 3 FCR 49 HC FamD Trial contact unnecessary before magistrates make decision in contact case (can do so on evidence before court).

Bagnall and Hobbs, Bagnall v (1909-10) 54 SJ 738; (1909-10) XXVI TLR 659 HC PDAD Absent aggravated circumstances court would not deem wife (who had been divorced for her misconduct) unfit to have custody of her children.

Bagnall v Bagnall and Hobbs (1909-10) 54 SJ 738; (1909-10) XXVI TLR 659 HC PDAD Absent aggravated circumstances court would not deem wife (who had been divorced for her misconduct) unfit to have custody of her children.

Bain v Wood and others (1979) 129 (1) NLJ 365 HL Qualified care and control order in respect of two children committed to local authority care.

Ball, Moore v [1984] 2 All ER 237; [1984] Fam 41; [1984] FLR 555; (1984) 148 JP 425; (1984) 128 SJ 298; [1984] 2 WLR 865 HC FamD Secretary of State can have varied maintenance order payable to Secretary increased by variation.

Bamgbose (Matthew Olajide) v Daniel (John Bankole) [1955] AC 107; (1954) 98 SJ 732 PC Child legitimate by law of parents' domicile will be deemed legitimate by English courts — even if parents' marriage polygamous.

Bancroft v Bancroft [1963] 1 All ER 367; (1963) 107 SJ 112; [1963] 2 WLR 309 CA On leave being unnecessary to make maintenance/secured provision application during divorce petition.

Banks, R v [1916-17] All ER 356; (1915-17) XXV Cox CC 535; (1916) 80 JP 432; [1916] 2 KB 621; [1916] 85 LJKB 1657; (1916-17) 115 LTR 457; (1916) WN (I) 281 CCA Must show not that could but did believe girl over sixteen to raise defence on that ground.

Barclays Bank plc v Khaira and another [1993] 1 FLR 343 (also CA); [1992] 1 WLR 623 HC ChD Bank does not normally owe duty of care to person going guarantor on loan to explain entire transaction/ensure have taken impartial advice on what doing.

Barclays Bank plc v Khaira and another [1993] 1 FLR 343 (also HC ChD) CA Non-party to ChD action not allowed appeal decision that bank does not normally owe duty of care to person going guarantor on loan to explain entire transaction/ensure have taken impartial advice on what doing.

Barnes v Tyrrell (1982) 3 FLR 240; (1981) 131 NLJ 1288 CA Mother with custody of children allowed remove them to Australia to where was emigrating.

Barnet Juvenile Court, ex parte Barnet London Borough, R v [1982] TLR 307 HC QBD Local authority not guardian of juvenile entrusted to its care pursuant to the Children and Young Persons Act 1969, ss 7(7) and 20.

Barnet London Borough Council and another, Holtom v [1993] TLR 478 HC QBD Local authority could be sued by person once in its care for negligent discharge of its duties when acting in loco parentis.

Barnsley Corporation v Lancashire County Council [1956] 3 All ER 671; [1957] 1 QB 123; [1956] 3 WLR 820 HC QBD Cannot appeal against approved school order on basis that child's address unknown.

Barnsley Metropolitan Borough Council, I v [1986] 1 FLR 109 (also HC FamD) CA Wrong to place one of two children in care on basis that one/other was not/was child of mother's cohabitee who had perpetrated serious cruelty on first child.

Barnsley Metropolitan Borough Council, I v [1986] 1 FLR 109 (also CA) HC FamD One of two children placed in care on basis that one/other was not/was child of mother's cohabitee who had perpetrated serious cruelty on first child.

Barnsley v Marsh (1947) 111 JP 363; (1947) 177 LTR 573; (1947) 91 SJ 561; (1947) LXIII TLR 399; (1947) WN (I) 159 HC KBD On procedure in bastardy proceedings.

Barrett v Young (1981) 131 NLJ 372 CA Custody of children to mother despite father's looking after children for 6 years, for five of which mother had no contact with children.

Barritt v Attorney-General [1971] 3 All ER 1183; (1971) 115 SJ 889 HC PDAD In camera hearings involve weighing petitioner's and interested third party's rights against public interest in justice being public.

Batchelor v Smith (1935) 79 SJ 49 HC KBD Revocation of payment ordered pursuant to affiliation order where had come to light since order that mother had committed perjury.

Bates v Morley (1982) 3 FLR 244; (1982) 132 NLJ 65 CA Mother with care and control of ward (father had access) allowed remove child to Canada (wardship ending upon ward quitting country).

Battersby, Surrey County Council v [1965] 1 All ER 273; [1965] Crim LR101t; (1965) 129 JP 116; (1965) 115 LJ 125; [1965] 2 QB 194; (1965) 109 SJ 30; [1965] 2 WLR 378 HC QBD Person taking children for more than one month (albeit interrupted by stays with parents) 'proposed' to maintain foster child.

Battle v Attorney-General (Battle GL and Battle AFT intervening) [1949] 118 LJR 1015; (1949) WN (I) 129 HC PDAD Declarations by alleged blood/by legal grandfathers admissible; child legitimated by parents' marriage.

Bawden v Bawden [1978] 3 All ER 1216; (1979) 143 JP 114; [1979] QB 419; [1978] 3 WLR 798 CA Local authority right to keep child/residual discretion ends once parent requests child's return.

Beard v Beard [1981] 1 All ER 783; (1980) 124 SJ 810; [1981] 1 WLR 369 CA Interim care and control order where emergency affecting children may include giving right to enter children's home/excluding another.

Beattie, McVeigh v [1988] 2 All ER 500; [1988] Fam 69; [1988] FCR 516; [1988] 2 FLR 67; (1988) 132 SJ 125; [1988] 2 WLR 992 HC FamD Absent reasonable excuse refusal to provide blood sample corroborates claim of parenthood.

Beaumont v Beaumont [1938] 2 All ER 226; [1938] Ch 551; [1938] 107 LJCh 241; (1938) 158 LTR 494; (1938) 82 SJ 314; (1937-38) LIV TLR 538; (1938) WN (I) 121 HC ChD No statutory entitlement to have custody case heard in HC; HC refusal to exercise inherent jurisdiction while child being kept outside jurisdiction.

Bedfordshire County Council, S v (1977) 127 NLJ 243t HC QBD Valid revocation of care order in respect of normal child from normal home taken into care because not being sent to school by parents who considered all local comprehensive schools unsuitable.

Bedfordshire County Council, S v (1977) 127 NLJ 569t CA Care order restored in respect of normal child from normal home originally taken into care because not being sent to school by parents who considered all local comprehensive schools unsuitable.

Bedfordshire County Council, X and others v; M and another v Newham London Borough Council and others; E v Dorset County Council and other appeals [1995] 3 All ER 353; [1995] 2 AC 633 (also CA); [1995] 3 FCR 337; [1995] 2 FLR 276; [1995] TLR 375; [1995] 3 WLR 152 HL Local authority child care decision cannot be challenged as breach of statutory duty or common law duty of care if in hindsight decision proved mistaken nor is it vicariously liable for actions of social workers and psychiatrists in case.

Belton v Belton [1987] 2 FLR 343; (1987) 151 JP 679 CA Child's welfare is paramount interest in application to remove from jurisdiction child in respect of whom one divorced parent has custody.

Berens, Biberfield v [1952] 2 All ER 237; [1952] 2 QB 770; [1952] 2 TLR 39 CA Wife of means deemed not husband's agent of necessity after his actions forced her to leave home.

Beresford v Attorney-General (Marquis of Waterford and others cited) (1918) 118 LTR 133; (1917-18) 62 SJ 103 CA Perpetuated testimony allowed in respect of witnesses who were old and unwell.

Berkshire County Council and others, D v [1987] 1 All ER 20 HL In deciding if neglect of child court can look to historical events (even pre-dating birth).

Berkshire County Council and others, D v [1987] 1 All ER 20 CA In deciding if neglect of child court can look to historical events (even pre-dating birth).

Berkshire County Council and others, D v [1987] 1 All ER 20 HC FamD In deciding if neglect of child court can look to historical events (even pre-dating birth).

Berkshire County Council v B [1997] 1 FLR 171 HC FamD Parental contact could be ordered in care proceedings though local authority care plan envisaged that ultimately there would be no parental contact.

Berkshire County Council v C and others [1993] 1 FCR 608; [1993] Fam 205; [1993] 1 FLR 569 HC FamD Family proceedings court could direct that child be assessed by social worker by certain date.

Berkshire County Council v D-P [1986] 2 FLR 276 (also HC FamD) CA Care (not wardship) proceedings appropriate where child born drug-dependent as result of mother's drug abuse while pregnant — matters concerning period of pregnancy could be considered.

Berkshire County Council v D-P [1986] 2 FLR 276 (also CA) HC FamD Matters pre-dating birth of child not relevant to care proceedings.

Berkshire County Council, A v [1989] FCR 184; [1989] 1 FLR 273 (also HC FamD) CA Juvenile court-appointed guardian ad litem could not by way of wardship action challenge local authority exercise of care and control powers over child.

Berkshire County Council, A v [1989] FCR 180; [1989] 1 FLR 273 (also CA) HC FamD Juvenile court-appointed guardian ad litem could not by way of wardship action challenge local authority exercise of care and control powers over child.

Berkshire County Council, C v [1988] FCR 161; [1987] 2 FLR 210 HC FamD Valid adjournment of juvenile court parental access action until county court decided in pending action whether child to be freed for adoption.

Berkshire County Council, M v [1985] FLR 257 CA On power of juvenile court to order access.

Berry (Thomas Clive), R v [1996] 2 Cr App R 226; [1996] Crim LR 574 CA On application of defence that are child's natural father in context of child abduction case where man was taking child in honest but mistaken belief that was own child.

Bhugwandas (Nagindas) v Hurkissondas (Bachoo) (1915-16) XXXII TLR 132 PC On eligibility of adopted son where is partition of family property under Hindu law.

Biberfield v Berens [1952] 2 All ER 237; [1952] 2 QB 770; [1952] 2 TLR 39 CA Wife of means deemed not husband's agent of necessity after his actions forced her to leave home.

Bickley v Bickley [1965] 1 WLR 600 CA Deciding whether or not a child is child of family is a jurisdiction to be carefully exercised.

Bilainkin v Bilainkin [1959] 1 All ER 161; (1959) 109 LJ 72; (1959) 103 SJ 90 CA In custody order allowing restricted removal of child from jurisdiction petitioner's promise to return and respondent's permission to leave should be required.

Bird and others, Bird v (1984) 148 JP 641 CA Child's welfare (not father's employment prospects) paramount issue in custody action.

Bird v Bird and others (1984) 148 JP 641 CA Child's welfare (not father's employment prospects) paramount issue in custody action.

Birkenhead Borough Justices, ex parte Smith, R v [1954] 1 All ER 503; [1954] Crim LR 133t; [1954] Crim LR 297; (1954) 118 JP 203; (1954) 104 LJ 154; (1954) 98 SJ 163 HC QBD US soldier (member of visiting forces) could not be committed to prison for failure to maintain child pursuant to affiliation order.

Birmingham City Council and others v H [1994] 1 All ER 12; [1994] 2 AC 212; [1994] 1 FCR 896; [1994] 1 FLR 224; (1994) 144 NLJ 17; (1994) 138 SJ LB 13; [1993] TLR 657; [1994] 2 WLR 31 HL In child care case where mother and child are minors interests of mother's child are paramount.

Birmingham City Council v D; Birmingham City Council v M [1994] 2 FCR 245; [1994] 2 FLR 502 HC FamD Refusal of care orders in respect of orphans over whom nobody had parental responsibility.

Birmingham City Council v H [1993] 1 FCR 247; [1992] 2 FLR 323 HC FamD Residence order carries with it right to exercise parental responsibility.

Birmingham City Council v H (No 2) [1993] 1 FLR 883 CA Where mother/son both minors interests of each equally important; here ending of contact between mother/son too Draconian: reasonable supervised access allowed.

Birmingham City Council, M v [1995] 1 FCR 50; [1994] 2 FLR 141 HC FamD Depended on case whether historical/current/future extent of parental control to be used as basis for determining if child beyond such control/care order merited.

Birmingham City Juvenile Court, ex parte Birmingham City Council, R v [1988] 1 All ER 683; [1988] FCR 175 (also HC QBD); [1988] 1 FLR 424; (1987) 131 SJ 1697; [1988] 1 WLR 337 CA Disputed interim care order application to be decided after local authority/parents/guardian heard.

Birmingham District Council, N v (1984) 148 JP 700; (1984) 128 SJ 447 HC FamD 'Household' determined by reference to circumstances; can be in same 'household' though not in same place.

Birmingham Juvenile Court and others , ex parte S and another, R v; R v Birmingham Juvenile Court and others, ex parte P and another [1984] 1 All ER 393; [1984] FLR 343; [1984] 1 WLR 618 HC QBD In renewing care order — unlike bail order — court looks to all the circumstances on each occasion; 28-day care order expires at start of twenty-eighth day.

Birmingham Juvenile Court, ex parte G and others, R v; R v Birmingham Juvenile Court, ex parte R [1989] 3 All ER 336; [1989] 2 FLR 454; [1990] 2 QB 573; (1989) 133 SJ 1089; [1989] 3 WLR 1024 CA Court must look to welfare of child/hear guardian ad litem before allowing local authority withdraw care order application.

Birmingham Juvenile Court, ex parte G and others, R v; R v Birmingham Juvenile Court, ex parte R [1988] 3 All ER 726; [1989] FCR 22; [1988] 2 FLR 423; (1988) 138 NLJ 143; (1988) 132 SJ 1117; [1988] 1 WLR 950 HC QBD As care proceedings not adversarial court may hear guardian ad litem's evidence even if local authority offers no evidence.

Birmingham Juvenile Court, ex parte N, R v [1984] 2 All ER 688; [1984] FLR 683 HC QBD 'Household' determined by reference to circumstances; can be in same 'household' though not in same place.

Birmingham Juvenile Court, ex parte S, R v [1984] FamD 93; [1984] 3 WLR 387 HC FamD Two children of same mother/different fathers were both members of same household though one in care and one living with mother and second father.

Blackman (John), R v (1928-29) 21 Cr App R 132 CCA 'Reasonable belief that girl over sixteen' defence open on charge of carnal knowledge did not preclude conviction of under twenty-three year old for indecent assault.

Blackwell v Attorney-General (1967) 111 SJ 332 HC PDAD Failed legitimacy application.

Blaker, Ashley v (1911-13) XXII Cox CC 208 HC KBD Prosecution to be brought for running away and leaving child within two years of moment of running away.

Blount, Brooks v [1922] All ER 699; (1921-25) XXVII Cox CC 399; (1923) 87 JP 64; [1923] 1 KB 257; [1923] 92 LJCL 302; (1923) 128 LTR 607; (1922-23) 67 SJ 299; (1922-23) XXXIX TLR 168; (1923) WN (I) 14 HC KBD Legal presumption that child in father's custody not displaced by latter entering separation agreement whereby wife paid to take care of child in her custody: father can still be convicted for neglect of child.

Blunden, Turner v [1986] 2 All ER 75; [1986] Fam 120; [1986] 2 FLR 69; (1986) 150 JP 180; (1986) 130 SJ 184; [1986] 2 WLR 491 HC FamD Blood tests can corroborate allegation of paternity.

Bolton Metropolitan Borough Council v B and H [1990] FCR 57; [1989] 2 FLR 349 HC FamD Long-term care pending adoption for children with parents incapable of proper parenting: access to parents until placed with foster-parents; delay in welfare report criticised.

Bolton Metropolitan Borough Council v W [1988] FCR 305 HC FamD Social workers' videos of mother's access visits not privileged (even if were privileged was waived here when put videos in evidence).

Bolton Metropolitan Borough, ex parte B, R v [1985] FLR 343 HC QBD On ending/denying access of parents to child being held in local authority care.

Boniface v Harris (1983) 147 JP 208 HC FamD Pre-1975 affiliation order could not order payment straight to child.

Booth (Lee Timothy), R v (1989) 11 Cr App R (S) 258; [1989] Crim LR 843 CA Care order must pre-exist any court order restraining local authority in manner of deealing with juvenile in care.

Boulden (Edward Ernest), R v (1957) 41 Cr App R 105; [1957] Crim LR 322 CCA On what constitutes 'abandonment' of child under Children and Young Persons Act 1933, s 1(1).

Boulden, R v [1957] Crim LR 182 Sessions Successful prosecution for abandonment/neglect of children: on what constitutes abandonment/neglect.

Bow Road Domestic Proceedings Court, ex parte Adedigba, R v [1968] 2 All ER 89; (1968) 118 NLJ 444; [1968] 2 QB 572; (1968) 132 JP 301; [1968] 2 WLR 1143 CA Maintenance order if mother and father resident in England though child born abroad/mother domiciled abroad when child born.

Bowditch, R v [1991] Crim LR 831 CA On burden of proof as regards proving cruelty to child under Children and Young Persons Act 1933.

Bowen v Norman [1938] 2 All ER 776; (1934-39) XXX Cox CC 674; (1938) 102 JP 123; [1938] 1 KB 689; (1938) 85 LJ 396; [1938] 107 LJCL 273; (1938) 158 LTR 257; (1938) 82 SJ 77; (1937-38) LIV TLR 342; (1938) WN (I) 41 HC KBD Maintenance order per se did not establish non-access.

Bowers and another v Smith; Evans and another v Smith; Flack and another v Smith [1953] 1 All ER 320; (1953) 117 JP 106; (1953) 97 SJ 99; [1953] 1 WLR 297 HC QBD Child/young person committing grossly indecent acts without parent's/guardian's knowledge does not justify requiring parent/guardian to enter recognisance to be proper parent, or placing child/young person on probation.

Bowers v Clarke (1961) 105 SJ 988 CA Was not repudiation of maintenance agreement whereunder maintenance payable and access granted for custodial parent to remove child to Australia.

Bowley v Bowley [1984] FLR 791 CA On desirabilty that young children be in mother's custody (here so ordered).

Boyce v Cox [1921] All ER 658; (1921-25) XXVII Cox CC 139; (1921) 85 JP 279; [1922] 1 KB 149; [1922] 91 LJCL 122; (1922) 126 LTR 254; (1921-22) 66 SJ 142; (1921-22) XXXVIII TLR 51; (1921) WN (I) 312 HC KBD Affiliation order available to woman judicially separated from third party against natural father.

Bradford City Metropolitan Council v K [1990] Fam 140; [1990] 2 WLR 532 HC FamD Statements of child to teacher/foster parent regarding sexual abuse by family member not part of res gestae and inadmissible in later care proceedings as was hearsay evidence.

Bradford City Metropolitan Council v K [1990] Fam 140; [1990] 2 WLR 532 HC FamD Statements of child to teacher/foster parent regarding sexual abuse by family member not part of res gestae and inadmissible in later care proceedings as was hearsay evidence.

Bradford Metropolitan Borough Council, P v [1996] 2 FCR 227 HC FamD Valid decision by magistrates after heard evidence of mother to stop hearing of application to discharge care orders.

Bristol Justices, ex parte Broome, R v [1987] 1 All ER 676; [1987] 2 FLR 76; (1987) 151 JP 409; (1987) 131 SJ 102; [1987] 1 WLR 352 HC QBD Police to be heard in application to release child held by constable.

British Pregnancy Advisory Service Trustees and another, Paton v (1978) 142 JP 497; [1979] QB 276; (1978) 122 SJ 744; [1978] 3 WLR 687 HC QBD Injunction unavailable to husband against wife/abortion charity to prevent same from procuring lawful abortion for wife.

Brixey v Lynas [1997] 1 FCR 220 [1996] 2 FLR 499 HL On whether custody of young child to be given (as here was) to young mother.

Brooks v Blount [1922] All ER 699; (1921-25) XXVII Cox CC 399; (1923) 87 JP 64; [1923] 1 KB 257; [1923] 92 LJCL 302; (1923) 128 LTR 607; (1922-23) 67 SJ 299; (1922-23) XXXIX TLR 168; (1923) WN (I) 14 HC KBD Legal presumption that child in father's custody not displaced by latter entering separation agreement whereby wife paid to take care of child in her custody: father can still be convicted for neglect of child.

Brooks, Foy v [1977] 2 All ER 113; (1977) 141 JP 339; (1976) 120 SJ 768; [1977] 1 WLR 160 HC FamD Purchase of layette incidental to childbirth.

Brown v Matthews [1990] 2 All ER 155; [1990] Ch 662; [1990] 2 WLR 879 CA Court welfare officer's report may be disclosed in later case if necessary for fair trial.

Buckeridge v Hall [1963] 1 All ER 509; (1963) 127 JP 218; (1963) 113 LJ 154; [1963] 1 QB 614; (1963) 107 SJ 96; [1963] 2 WLR 354 HC QBD Affiliation order available for English-born child of woman of foreign domicil normally resident in England.

Buckinghamshire County Council v M [1994] 1 FCR 859; [1994] 2 FLR 506 CA Interim care order made in respect of child where full care order refused (siblings already subject to interim care orders).

Buckland, Pallin v (1911-13) XXII Cox CC 545; (1911) 75 JP 362 HC KBD Accused found as matter of fact not to have run away and left children.

Buckley v Buckley [1977] 3 All ER 544 HC FamD Declaration of unfitness for custody to be made before decree absolute.

Burbury v Jackson [1914-17] All ER 531; (1915-17) XXV Cox CC 555; (1916) 80 JP 455; [1917] 1 KB 16; (1916) 51 LJ 517; [1917] 86 LJCL 255; (1916-17) 115 LTR 713; (1916-17) XXXIII TLR 18; (1916) WN (I) 348 HC KBD Evidence of opportunity not per se sufficient to justify bastardy order.

Burns (James), R v; R v Ralph (Michael Peter); R v Jackson (Stephen Ronald); R v Burns (Sidney) (1984) 79 Cr App R 173 CA Person could be prosecuted for conspiracy to commit offence though immune from prosecution for substantive offence.

Butler v Gregory (1901-02) XVIII TLR 370 HC KBD Father of illegitimate child who did not have care/custody of child nor had bastardy proceedings brought against him not father for purposes of Prevention of Cruelty to Children Act 1894, s 23.

Buxton v Buxton [1965] 3 All ER 150; (1965) 129 JP 570; (1965) 109 SJ 435; [1965] 3 WLR 1184 HC PDAD Post-separation custody claim could be cruelty.

Byers (Jessie), R v (1910) 4 Cr App R 5 CCA Manslaughter of child by means of cruel treatment — even though post-cruelty betterment in child's condition.

C (minors), C v [1992] 1 FLR 163 HC FamD Supervised access by American father of children wrongfully brought to England from New York by mother.

C (No 2), C v (1981) 125 SJ 844 HC FamD Inappropriate to place child in care when intention of local authority was to allow child to remain with mother.

C and another, Devon County Council v [1985] FLR 619 HC FamD Wrong that access of natural parents to child in local authority care continue where child being placed in foster care with possible view to adoption.

C and another, Devon County Council v (1985) 129 SJ 483 CA Judge ought to have decided (as court did here) issue of last occasions of maternal access to child in foster-care (not left it to local authority).

C and another, Kent County Council v [1993] 1 All ER 719; [1993] Fam 57; [1993] 1 FLR 308; [1992] 3 WLR 808 HC FamD Exceptionally no contact between parent and child may be ordered by family proceedings court in care order but cannot make directions regarding care orders.

C and another, R v [1990] TLR 344 CA Failed prosecution for cruelty to child where was inadequate evidence of guiltiness.

C and Calderdale Metropolitan Borough Council, M v [1992] 2 FCR 141 HC FamD Leave of court required before natural father of adopted illegitimate child could seek residence order.

C and Calderdale Metropolitan Borough Council, M v [1993] 1 FCR 431; [1993] 1 FLR 505 CA In Children Act 1989 'parent' includes father of illegitimate child but that status lost post-freeing order after which could not seek residence order.

C and M, Staffordshire County Council v [1988] FCR 353 HC FamD On rights of putative father as regards seeking access to/custody of illegitimate child.

C and others, Berkshire County Council v [1993] 1 FCR 608; [1993] Fam 205; [1993] 1 FLR 569 HC FamD Family proceedings court could direct that child be assessed by social worker by certain date.

C and others, J and another v [1970] AC 668; [1969] 2 WLR 540 HL Child's welfare paramount in wardship cases: no rule that custody must go to parents who are suitable for same.

C v Berkshire County Council [1988] FCR 161; [1987] 2 FLR 210 HC FamD Valid adjournment of juvenile court parental access action until county court decided in pending action whether child to be freed for adoption.

C v C [1966] 3 All ER 51; (1965-66) 116 NLJ 1204; (1966) 110 SJ 634; [1966] 1 WLR 1418 HC PDAD On obtaining information regarding child's education.

C v C (1981) 125 SJ 98 CA Private interviews with each parent by judge/subsequent direction by judge to counsel to cross-examine on what had not heard/split custody absent good cause rendered custody order bad.

C v C [1984] TLR 743 CA Access to each child to be considered individually where parent seeks but is refused access to all children.

C v C [1988] FCR 458; [1988] 1 FLR 462 HC FamD Supervised access by father not guilty of sexually abusing daughter but of horseplay with sexual overtones with her.

C v C [1988] FCR 411; [1988] 2 FLR 291 CA On desirability of not splitting up siblings in post-divorce custody arrangements.

C v C [1989] 2 All ER 465; [1989] 1 WLR 654 CA Parent's right to stop child's removal from Australia a right of custody for purpose of Convention on Child Abduction; Convention does not preclude child's return to country because exposed to grave personal risk where arises from mother's refusal to return.

C v C [1990] FCR 682; [1990] 1 FLR 462 CA Committal for mother who repeatedly refused to comply with access order made in husband's favour; CC judge rightly dealt with access issue despite commencement of HC wardship proceedings.

C v C [1991] FCR 254; [1991] 1 FLR 223 CA On relevancy of mother's lesbian relationship to determination of custody action (plus relevancy of onetime criminal conviction of mother's lesbian partner).

C v C [1994] 1 FCR 6 HC FamD Nine month delay before went to law to seek return of child was acquiescence to retention; delay in custody hearings in Brazil an intolerable situation justifying non-return of child there.

C v C (minors) [1992] 1 FLR 163 HC FamD Supervised access by American father of children wrongfully brought to England from New York by mother.

C v C (No 2) (1981) 125 SJ 844 HC FamD Inappropriate to place child in care when intention of local authority was to allow child to remain with mother.

C v H (1979) 123 SJ 537 HC FamD When access/adoption arise to be decided in same action they should both be decided in tandem, not one before the other.

C v S [1990] 2 All ER 449; [1990] 2 FLR 442 (also HL); [1990] TLR 414 CA No wrongful abduction where father has no rights in respect of child when child taken; no wrongful retention where child not habitually resident in jurisdiction from whence taken.

C v Salford City Council and others [1994] 2 FLR 926 HC FamD Fosterers given leave to seek residence order in respect of child whose natural parents objected to adoption by fosterers.

C v Solihull Metropolitan Borough Council [1993] 1 FLR 290 HC FamD On appropriate order where local authority seeks care of child pending appraisal of parents after child suffered unexplained injury.

C v Surrey County Council [1994] 2 FCR 165 HC FamD On making order requiring parent to contribute towards cost of local authority accommodation for child.

C, A v [1985] FLR 445 (also CA) HC FamD No access by natural father to child of woman who reneged on commercial surrogacy deal insofar as surrender of child concerned.

C, E v [1982] TLR 475 CA Access pre-eminently a matter for trial judge.

C, E v [1996] 1 FCR 612; [1996] 1 FLR 472; [1995] TLR 638 HC FamD Income support/child benefit to be treated as subsistence money — that plus cost of supporting new family justified downward variation of child maintenance order.

C, Hampshire County Council v [1988] FCR 133 CA On determining un/reasonableness of parent's refusal of consent to adoption: here not unreasonably withheld.

C, L v [1995] 3 FCR 125 HC FamD Some indirect contact to male-to-female transsexual who had fathered child when a man; general contact application a future possibility.

C, Leeds City Council v [1993] 1 FCR 585; [1993] 1 FLR 269 HC FamD On supervision of contact order.

C, M v [1993] 1 FCR 264; [1993] 2 FLR 584 HC FamD On (ex parte) granting of residence orders; on need to give reasons inter alia for not adopting course advocated by court welfare officer.

C, Northamptonshire County Council v [1988] FCR 378 HC QBD No need for child to attend court each time application for extension of interim care order heard.

C, R v [1991] 2 FLR 252; [1990] TLR 714 CA Conviction of father (who took own child outside jurisdiction without consent of mother-joint custodian) for child kidnapping (common law offence)/abduction quashed/upheld.

C, S v (1963) 107 SJ 1022 CA Putative father's admission of two acts of sex with complainant before defendant gave birth to illegitimate child could be corroboration of complaiant's evidence in some material particular.

C, Salford City Council v (1982) 3 FLR 153 HC FamD Care and control of child whom disabled parents unable to adequately care for given to local authority but frequent access to parents ordered.

C-H, N v [1982] TLR 484 CA On limited role of CA in appeals against custody decisions.

Cadman v Cadman (1982) 3 FLR 275; (1981) 131 NLJ 1310; (1981) 125 SJ 791 CA On role of court welfare officer: appointment of independent social worker to prepare report not in best interests of child so custody order discharged.

Caffell v Caffell [1984] FLR 169 CA On when joint custody appropriate (here was).

Calderdale Borough Council v H and P [1991] 1 FLR 461 HC FamD Statutory care order to local authority, children to reside with grandparents who were to be paid maintenance pending approval as foster-parents when would be paid boarding-out allowance.

Cambridge District Health Authority, ex parte B (No 2), R v [1996] 1 FLR 375 CA Reporting restrictions lifted so that father might publicise plight of child and so raise money for her treatment.

Cambridge District Health Authority, ex parte B, R v [1995] 2 FCR 485; [1995] 1 FLR 1055 (also HC QBD) CA Health authority's decision not to fund expensive experimental treatment of seriously ill child was reasonable.

Cambridgeshire County Council, H v [1997] 1 FCR 569; [1996] 2 FLR 566 HC FamD Mother not given second time leave to show papers to psychiatrist/have psychiatrist observe contact between her/her children.

Carron v Carron [1984] FLR 805 CA Children of wife were children of family where lived with wife and her new husband in same household for four years.

Cartwright, Shephard v (1954) 104 LJ 808; (1954) 98 SJ 868 HL On admissibility in evidence of later acts to rebut the presumption of advancement.

Castings, Ltd, Sydall v [1966] 3 All ER 770 CA 'Descendant' generally means legitimate descendants.

Central Criminal Court, ex parte Godwin and Crook, R v [1995] 1 FLR 132; (1994) 138 SJ LB 199 CA Valid exercise of discretion prohibiting publication of information on trial: prior to making order judge could hear anyone whom considered to have valid interest in matter.

Central Independent Television plc, R (Mrs) v [1994] 3 All ER 641; [1994] Fam 192; [1995] 1 FCR 521; [1994] 2 FLR 151; [1994] TLR 92; [1994] 3 WLR 20 CA Parental jurisdiction of court does not extend to injuncting publication touching on child but not addressing care or upbringing.

Chainey, R v [1911-13] All ER 701; (1913-14) XXIII Cox CC 620; (1914) 78 JP 127; [1914] 1 KB 137; (1913) 48 LJ 673; [1914] 83 LJKB 306; (1913-14) 109 LTR 752; (1913-14) XXX TLR 51; (1913) WN (I) 318 CCA Criminal neglect of (under sixteen year old) child socialising with immoral persons did not mean guilty of causing/encouraging unlawful carnal knowledge of same.

Chalker (Kate), R v (1910) 4 Cr App R 2 CCA Manslaughter of child by means of consistently cruel treatment.

Chamberlain v De La Mare (1983) 4 FLR 434 (also CA) HC FamD Mother refused permission to take children from jurisdiction as their best interests demanded they continue contact with father.

Chapman, R v (1931-34) XXIX Cox CC 407; (1931-32) 23 Cr App R 45; (1931) 95 JP 205; [1931] 2 KB 606; (1931) 100 LJCL 562; (1932) 146 LTR 120; (1931) 75 SJ 660; (1930-31) XLVII TLR 620 CCA Proviso in Criminal Law Amendment Act 1922, s 2 extends reasonable belief that girl over sixteen defence to men who have not reached the age of twenty-four.

Chapman, R v [1958] 3 All ER 143; (1958) 42 Cr App R 257; [1958] Crim LR 623; (1958) 122 JP 462; (1958) 108 LJ 586; [1959] 1 QB 100; (1958) 102 SJ 621 CCA 'Unlawful' sex under Sexual Offences Act 1956 s 19(1) means sex outside marriage.

Chelsea Juvenile Court Justices (Re an infant), R v [1955] 1 All ER 38; (1955) 99 SJ 77; [1955] 1 WLR 52 HC QBD Justices have wide power to amend register of births.

Chertsey Justices, ex parte E, R v [1988] FCR 283; [1987] 2 FLR 415 HC QBD On whether/when to discharge care order.

Cheshire County Council v B and others [1992] 2 FCR 572 HC FamD Provisions in care and contact orders for six-month review of their implementation was invalid.

Cheshire County Council v M [1992] 2 FCR 817; [1993] 1 FLR 463 HC FamD Father who successfully appealed conviction for child sex abuse to which had confessed denied contact order.

Cheshire County Council v P [1993] 2 FCR 397 CA Care order merited where arrangements had been made to move child at risk of significant harm where was to safe environment in Northern Ireland.

Cheshire County Council, Stoke-on-Trent Borough Council v [1914-15] All ER 441; (1915-16) 113 LTR 750 HC KBD Person resides where lives (for purpose of Children Act 1908, s 74).

Chick (Florence Irene), R v (1925-26) 19 Cr App R 57 CCA Three months in second division for infanticide/concealment of birth in light of prisoner's age (twenty) and strong recommendation of mercy by jury.

Chief Constable of Cheshire, ex parte K, R v [1990] FCR 201; [1990] 1 FLR 70 HC QBD Police not obliged to assist in enforcement of custody order.

Chinchen v Chinchen (1950) 94 SJ 129; (1950) WN (I) 22 CA Custody orders are interlocutory in nature.

Chipperfield v Chipperfield [1952] 1 All ER 1360; (1952) 116 JP 337; (1952) 96 SJ 379; [1952] 1 TLR 1519; (1952) WN (I) 272 HC PDAD Child's welfare paramount in guardianship cases.

Chowdhury (Altaf li) and others, Chowdhury (Habibur Rahman) and another v (1920-21) XXXVII TLR 487 PC On father's acknowledgment/effect of father's acknowledgment of son's legitimacy under Mahomedan law.

Chowdhury (Habibur Rahman) and another v Chowdhury (Altaf li) and others (1920-21) XXXVII TLR 487 PC On father's acknowledgment/effect of father's acknowledgment of son's legitimacy under Mahomedan law.

Churchard v Churchard [1984] FLR 635 CA No committal of mother/no changes in custody in situation where children (in mother's custody) seeking of own volition to frustrate access attempts by father.

City of Liverpool Justices, ex parte W, R v [1959] 1 All ER 337; (1959) 123 JP 152; (1959) 109 LJ 105; (1959) 103 SJ 113 HC QBD Certiorari for failure to consider special circumstances prescribed in Marriage Act 1950, s 2(2).

Clancy, Devon County Council v [1985] FLR 1159; (1985) 149 JP 521 CA Magistrates' unjustified deviation from advice of guardian ad litem will generally be overturned upon appeal.

Clapham v National Assistance Board [1961] 2 All ER 50; (1961) 125 JP 373; (1961) 111 LJ 306; [1961] 2 QB 77; (1961) 105 SJ 234 HC QBD National Assistance Board may seek/obtain affiliation order despite mother's earlier failed attempt.

Clark v Clark (1970) 114 SJ 318 HC PDAD Court to explain why departing from probation officers' report.

Clarke and Lindsay, Clarke v (1912-13) 57 SJ 644 CA Divorcée living in adultery not allowed access to her young son who was about to start going to school.

Clarke v Clarke and Lindsay (1912-13) 57 SJ 644 CA Divorcée living in adultery not allowed access to her young son who was about to start going to school.

Clarke, Bowers v (1961) 105 SJ 988 CA Was not repudiation of maintenance agreement where under maintenance payable and access granted for custodial parent to remove child to Australia.

Cleave v Attorney-General; Headley, Channon and Barclays Bank, Ltd, intervening [1952] 2 All ER 283; (1952) 102 LJ 399; [1952] 2 TLR 174; (1952) WN (I) 346 HC PDAD Costs of failed legitimacy action could be ordered from estate of which interveners trustees.

Cleveland County Council and another v F [1995] 2 All ER 236; [1995] 3 FCR 174; [1995] 1 FLR 797; [1995] 1 WLR 785 HC FamD Court may direct that putative statements in care proceedings be confidential but existing statute law affords adequate protection.

Cleveland County Council v A; Cleveland County Council v B [1988] FCR 593 HC FamD On establishing that child has in fact been sexually abused.

Cleveland County Council v D [1988] FCR 615 HC FamD On establishing that child has in fact been sexually abused.

Cleveland County Council v Director of Public Prosecutions and another (1995) 139 SJ LB 13; [1994] TLR 615 HC QBD Court ordering child into local authority care could not specify where child was to be accommodated.

Cleveland County Council v E [1988] FCR 625 HC FamD Though local authority had not continued with action court found children not sexually abused and de-warded them.

Cliff v Cliff [1948] 2 All ER 760; (1948) LXIV TLR 555 CA On declaration that parent not fit to have custody.

Clissold v Clissold (1964) 108 SJ 220 HC PDAD Refusal of joint custody order upon divorce.

Clode v Clode (1982) 3 FLR 360 CA Confidentiality of welfare report not to be used to bar access of access of party thereto for purpose of bringing appeal.

Cockburn v Cockburn [1957] 3 All ER 260; (1957) 107 LJ 586; (1957) 101 SJ 798 CA County court judge cannot suspend maintenance order.

Coldingham Parish Council v Smith [1918] 2 KB 90; (1918) WN (I) 112 HC KBD English-domiciled father not responsible for maintenance of pauper lunatic son in Scotland.

Collins v Attorney-General (1931) 145 LTR 551; (1931) 75 SJ 616; (1930-31) XLVII TLR 484 HC PDAD Legitimation of child under German law recognised though father married to third party when illegitimate child born.

Colne Corporation, Yorkshire West Riding County Council v (1917-18) 117 LTR 671; (1917-18) 62 SJ 160 HC KBD On residency of child for purposes of determining which authority liable to maintain child at industrial school.

Colquitt v Colquitt [1947] 2 All ER 50; (1947) 111 JP 442; (1947) 97 LJ 277; [1948] 117 LJR 897; (1947) 177 LTR 399; (1947) 91 SJ 310; (1947) LXIII TLR 358; (1947) WN (I) 182 HC PDAD Legitimated child is a child of marriage of natural parents; absent decree of legitimacy court can nonetheless make custody order in respect of child legitimated by marriage of natural parents.

Colville-Hyde, R v [1956] Crim LR 117 Assizes On necessary elements of offence of abduction.

Connor, R v (1907-09) XXI Cox CC 628; (1908) 72 JP 212; [1908] 2 KB 26; (1908) 43 LJ 283; [1908] 77 LJCL 527; (1908) XCVIII LTR 932; (1907-08) 52 SJ 444; (1907-08) XXIV TLR 483 CCR Father in desertion guilty of wilful neglect (failed to provide food/money).

Conroy and Conroy, R v [1954] Crim LR 141 Assizes Jointly tried parents found guilty of murder of newborn child.

Cooke and Sutton London Borough, Cooke v (1982) 3 FLR 396 HC QBD Committing child to local authority care inappropriate where were not circumstances rendering placing of child with parent/another futile/inappropriate.

Cooke v Cooke and Sutton London Borough (1982) 3 FLR 396 HC QBD Committing child to local authority care inappropriate where were not circumstances rendering placing of child with parent/another futile/inappropriate.

Copestake and others, ex parte Wilkinson, R v [1926] All ER 252; (1926) 90 JP 191; [1927] 1 KB 468; [1927] 96 LJCL 65; (1927) 136 LTR 100; (1926) WN (I) 242 CA Under Criminal Justice Administration Act 1914 court could revoke periodic payments ordered in affiliation suit but could not alter paternity decision.

Corby Juvenile Court, ex parte M, R v [1987] 1 All ER 992; [1987] 1 FLR 490; (1987) 151 JP 387; (1970) 130 SJ 860; [1987] 1 WLR 55 HC QBD Access provisions of Child Care Act 1980 apply retrospectively to children put in care under earlier enactment.

Corfield v Hodgson [1966] 2 All ER 205; (1966) 130 JP 271; (1965-66) 116 NLJ 810; (1966) 110 SJ 170; [1966] 1 WLR 590 HC QBD Putative father's lies in affiliation case evidence corroborating paternity.

Corkett v Corkett [1985] FLR 708 CA In application for access to several children court to consider access to ech child individually.

Cornwall County Council, ex parte Cornwall and Isles of Scilly Guardians ad Litem and Reporting Officers Panel, R v [1992] 2 All ER 471; [1992] 1 FLR 270; (1991) 135 SJ LB 204; [1991] TLR 525; [1992] 1 WLR 427 HC QBD Certiorari available where local authority seeks to circumscribe role of guardian ad litem.

Cottier, Director of Public Prosecutions v [1996] 3 All ER 126; [1996] 2 Cr App R 411; [1996] Crim LR 804; [1996] 1 WLR 826 HC QBD Notice to local authority/probation officer of proceedings against children and young persons required once decision to proceed but need not necessarily precede court appearance.

Cotton and another, Cotton v [1954] 2 All ER 105; (1954) 104 LJ 313; (1954) 98 SJ 320; [1954] 2 WLR 947 CA When challenging legitimacy of child born within marriage must be no reasonable doubt that child not legitimate.

Cotton v Cotton and another [1954] 2 All ER 105; (1954) 104 LJ 313; (1954) 98 SJ 320; [1954] 2 WLR 947 CA When challenging legitimacy of child born within marriage must be no reasonable doubt that child not legitimate.

Coventry City Council v T [1986] 2 FLR 301 HC FamD Access by parents to child whom they had repeatedly abused and who was placed with foster parents was inappropriate.

Coventry Corporation v Surrey County Council [1933] 2 KB 384 HC KBD Adopted illegitimate child acquired settlement of place in which adopted father had resided (and from which was irremovable).

Coventry Corporation v Surrey County Council [1924-35] All ER 689 HL By 'father' the Poor Law Act 1930, s 93(4) included adopted fathers.

Cox, Boyce v [1921] All ER 658; (1921-25) XXVII Cox CC 139; (1921) 85 JP 279; [1922] 1 KB 149; [1922] 91 LJCL 122; (1922) 126 LTR 254; (1921-22) 66 SJ 142; (1921-22) XXXVIII TLR 51; (1921) WN (I) 312 HC KBD Affiliation order available to woman judicially separated from third party against natural father.

Critchley and the National Assistance Board, Payne v [1962] 1 All ER 619; (1962) 126 JP 162; (1962) 112 LJ 240; [1962] 2 QB 83; (1962) 106 SJ 78 HC QBD Affiliation order providing for payment to National Assistance Board later variable to mother's benefit.

Crocker (William), R v (1922-23) 17 Cr App R 45 CCA Leave to appeal granted in unlawful carnal knowledge case where corroboration point arose.

Crocker (William), R v (1922-23) 17 Cr App R 46 CCA Girl's evidence need not be corroborated in unlawful carnal knowledge case.

Crossley v Crossley (1953) 117 JP 216; (1953) 97 SJ 249; [1953] 2 WLR 765 HC PDAD Adoption order completely supersedes existing custody order.

Crown Court at Southwark, ex parte Godwin and others, R v [1991] 3 All ER 818; (1992) 94 Cr App R 34; (1992) 156 JP 86; (1991) 141 NLJ 963; [1992] QB 190; (1991) 135 SJ LB 28; [1991] 3 WLR 689 CA Order specifying particular name not to be published so as to protect child an invalid order.

Croydon Juvenile Court Justices, ex parte Croydon London Borough Council, R v [1973] 1 All ER 476; [1973] Crim LR 108; (1973) 117 SJ 70; (1973) 137 JP 283; (1972) 122 NLJ 1112t; [1973] QB 426; [1973] 2 WLR 61 HC QBD Ordering local authority to pay fine of child in its care permissible.

Croydon Juvenile Court, ex parte M, R v [1988] FCR 11 HC QBD On role of juvenile court when deciding whether care order to be discharged in face of parental opposition.

Croydon Juvenile Court, ex parte N, R v [1987] 1 FLR 252; (1987) 151 JP 523 HC QBD On procedure (including evidential procedure) where interim care order sought.

Croydon London Borough Council v A (No 2) [1992] 2 FCR 858; [1992] 2 FLR 348 HC FamD HC cannot/can make care/interim care order pending appeal from failed care application.

Croydon London Borough Council v A (No 3) [1992] 2 FLR 350 HC FamD On granting care/supervision order; on appealing against failed application for care order.

Croydon London Borough Council v A and others [1992] 3 All ER 788; [1992] Fam 169; [1992] 2 FCR 481; [1992] 2 FLR 341; (1992) 136 SJ LB 69; [1992] 3 WLR 267 HC FamD Prohibited steps order cannot apply between two adults.

Croydon London Borough v N and others [1987] FCR 129; [1987] 2 FLR 61 HC FamD Wrong to treat Children and Young Pesons Act 1969, s 1(2)(bb) as a preliminary matter in care action (and so require preliminary proof that likely that person convicted as criminal would become member of children's household).

Cunliffe v Attorney-General [1934] All ER 186; (1934) 103 LJP 114; (1934) 78 SJ 520 HC PDAD Costs in legitimacy action.

D and another, W and another v (1956) 120 JP 119 HC QBD Mother's consent to adoption dispensed with where objection to adopters unreasonable (mother wanted child placed with parents who did not have child of same sex).

D v B (otherwise D) [1977] 3 All ER 751; [1977] Fam 145; [1977] 2 WLR 1011 HC FamD Other parent's consent required to change of surname of unborn/new-born/unseen/well-known child; child's interests a consideration for court in deciding whether to waive consent.

D v B (otherwise D) (child: surname) [1979] 1 All ER 93; [1979] Fam 38; (1978) 122 SJ 486; [1978] 3 WLR 573 CA Court cannot order mother to execute fresh deed poll.

D v Berkshire County Council and others [1987] 1 All ER 20 HL In deciding if neglect of child court can look to historical events (even pre-dating birth).

D v Berkshire County Council and others [1987] 1 All ER 20 CA In deciding if neglect of child court can look to historical events (even pre-dating birth).

D v Berkshire County Council and others [1987] 1 All ER 20 HC FamD In deciding if neglect of child court can look to historical events (even pre-dating birth).

D v D (1965) 109 SJ 573 CA Custody of six year old child given to mother upon appeal.

D v D (1981) 2 FLR 74 CA Removal of child against her wishes from father's custody/placing with mother where other child in father's custody a possible bad influence was justifiable; whether to interview child purely a matter for judge.

D v D (1981) 2 FLR 93 CA Child living with grandparents and visiting mother/stepfather not child of latter family despite inclusion in stepfather's tax returns.

D v D [1991] FCR 323; [1991] 2 FLR 34; [1990] TLR 727 CA On committal for non-compliance with access order/arrangement; on inclusion of penal notice in access order.

D v D [1994] 1 FCR 694 HC FamD On when refusal/dismissal of order/application merited in contact case.

D v D [1994] 1 FCR 654; [1994] 1 FLR 137 CA On applying principles of Child Abduction Convention to case where inapplicable.

D v Director of Public Prosecutions and other appeals [1995] Crim LR 748; [1995] 3 FCR 725; [1995] 2 FLR 502; (1995) 145 NLJ 560; [1995] TLR 218 HC QBD Compensation orders against local authority quashed as either no finding that local authority had none done all possible to safeguard public/local authority had behaved satisfactorily.

D v Hereford and Worcester County Council [1991] 2 All ER 177; [1991] Fam 14; [1991] 1 FLR 205; (1990) 134 SJ 1402; [1990] TLR 698; [1991] 2 WLR 753 HC FamD Parental rights order available even if child in care; all relevant facts of concern to court asked to make parental rights order.

D v R [1995] 1 FCR 501 HC FamD On making of interim care order (here unjustified); on need for magistrates to give their reasons for their decision in care action.

D v Registrar General [1996] 2 FCR 248; [1996] 1 FLR 707 HC FamD Failed application for order requiring Registrar General to disclose information enabling natural mother to trace adopted child.

D v Registrar General [1997] 2 FCR 240; [1997] 1 FLR 715 CA Failed appeal against refusal of order requiring Registrar General to disclose information enabling natural mother to trace adopted child (such an order would be exceptional).

D v S [1995] 3 FCR 783 HC FamD On whether/when parental responsibility order appropriate: ill-will between parties not a deciding factor.

D v X City Council (No 2) [1985] FLR 279 HC FamD Child in local authority care to be entrusted to care and control of grandmother.

D, Birmingham City Council v; Birmingham City Council v M [1994] 2 FCR 245; [1994] 2 FLR 502 HC FamD Refusal of care orders in respect of orphans over whom nobody had parental responsibility.

D, Cleveland County Council v [1988] FCR 615 HC FamD On establishing that child has in fact been sexually abused.

D, Hereford and Worcester County Council v; Hereford and Worcester County Council v H (E) [1991] FCR 56; [1985] FLR 975 HC FamD Controlled access allowed where did not seem access would be problematic/adoption not proved to be best option for child.

D, I v [1989] FCR 91; [1988] 2 FLR 286 HC FamD Fining of mother for non-compliance with access order quashed as magistrates had not had as first consideration the best interests of child involved.

D, K (formerly D) v (1974) 118 SJ 50 CA Custody of children to unimpeachable father, not mother who would remove them to Germany to live there with new partner.

D, Milne v (1983) 133 NLJ 785c CA On appropriate manner in which to resolve custody actions.

D, W v (1980) 1 FLR 393 CA Child to be returned to care and control of person from whose care and control is snatched unless to do so would endanger child.

D-P, Berkshire County Council v [1986] 2 FLR 276 (also HC FamD) CA Care (not wardship) proceedings appropriate where child born drug-dependent as result of mother's drug abuse while pregnant — matters concerning period of pregnancy could be considered.

D-P, Berkshire County Council v [1986] 2 FLR 276 (also CA) HC FamD Matters pre-dating birth of child not relevant to care proceedings.

Daniel (John Bankole), Bamgbose (Matthew Olajide) v [1955] AC 107; (1954) 98 SJ 732 PC Child legitimate by law of parents' domicile will be deemed legitimate by English courts — even if parents' marriage polygamous.

Darlington Corporation Juvenile Court, ex parte West Hartlepool Corporation, R v [1957] 1 All ER 398; [1957] Crim LR 322; (1957) 101 SJ 172; [1957] 1 WLR 363 HC QBD Fit person order must contain consent of local authority to making thereof.

Davidson v Davidson [1953] 1 All ER 611; [1953] 1 WLR 387 HC PDAD Abnormal sexual practices to be precisely specified by justices; inadequate consideration of need for corroboration/possibility of acquiescence justified re-trial.

Davies, Jones v [1900-03] All ER 243; (1900) 35 LJ 601; [1901] 70 LJK/QB 38; (1900-01) LXXXIII LTR 412; [1901] 1 QB 118; (1900-01) 49 WR 136 HC QBD Married woman living with husband cannot be single woman.

Davis v Davis (1980) 130 NLJ 885c CA Successful appeal against finding that child had been treated as member of the family.

Davis v Morris (1922-23) XXXIX TLR 454; (1923) WN (I) 139 HC KBD On elements of defence of medical supervision where charged with acting as uncertified midwife (Midwives Act 1902, s 1(2)).

Davis, Sutton London Borough Council v [1995] 1 All ER 53; [1994] Fam 241; [1994] 2 FCR 1129; [1994] 1 FLR 737; (1994) 138 SJ LB 86; [1994] TLR 155; [1994] 2 WLR 721 HC FamD Justices may examine de novo local authority refusal to register child-minder.

Davison, Todd (by his next friend Phyllis Thompson) v [1971] 1 All ER 994; [1972] AC 392; (1971) 115 SJ 223; [1971] 2 WLR 898 HL Whether person in custody of parent an issue of fact; if in fact in custody is immaterial if parents cannot exercise proper control.

Davy v Attorney-General [1934] All ER 176; (1934) 78 LJ 63; (1934) 103 LJP 115; (1934) 151 LTR 562; (1934) 78 SJ 618; (1933-34) L TLR 588; (1934) WN (I) 164 HC PDAD Declaration of dead father made post litem motam admitted on grounds of natural justice.

Dawson v Wearmouth [1997] TLR 468 CA Surname by which child registered of considerable significance when court asked to alter surname of child.

Day, Giltrow v [1965] 1 All ER 73; (1965) 129 JP 94; (1965) 115 LJ 58; (1965) 109 SJ 29; [1965] 1 WLR 317 HC QBD Wife living apart from husband in same house was not single woman.

De La Mare, Chamberlain v (1983) 4 FLR 434 (also CA) HC FamD Mother refused permission to take children from jurisdiction as their best interests demanded they continue contact with father.

De Silva and others, Rabot and another v [1909] AC 376; [1909] 78 LJPC 73; (1909) C LTR 242; (1908-09) XXV TLR 332 PC Bequest to wife (former mistress) and children from her original marriage was valid.

Dean v Dean (1983) 133 NLJ 421c CA Experimental access between young girl and father imprisoned for sex crimes deemed inappropriate though might later be permissible.

Dennis and another, Re Spence; Spence v [1990] 2 All ER 827; [1990] Ch 652; [1990] FCR 983; [1990] 2 FLR 278; [1990] TLR 288; [1990] 2 WLR 1430 CA Legitimacy not conferred on child of void marriage entered into by parents after child's birth.

Derbyshire County Council, B v [1992] 2 FCR 14; [1992] 1 FLR 538 HC FamD Res judicata probably inapplicable to local authority's seeking of care orders (and certainly inapplicable here).

Derbyshire County Council, ex parte T and another, R v [1990] 1 All ER 792; [1990] Fam 164; [1989] FCR 713; [1990] 1 FLR 237 (also HC QBD); (1989) 133 SJ 1626; [1990] 2 WLR 101 CA Notice to former parent needed if child placed with prospective adopters becomes child in care.

Derbyshire County Council, ex parte T, R v [1989] FCR 679; [1990] 1 FLR 237 (also CA); (1989) 133 SJ 1109 HC QBD Notice to former parent needed if child placed with prospective adopters becomes child in care.

Devon County Council and others v S and others [1993] 2 FCR 36; [1993] 1 FLR 842 HC FamD Caution needed if appointing welfare officer as guardian ad litem; issue for justices in post-rehabiliation contact termination application not whether rehabilitation successful but should care cease.

Devon County Council v B [1997] 1 FLR 591 CA Freeing order invalid as court did not when making order consider basis of parent's refusal to agree to adoption; county court did not have inherent jurisdiction to bolster care order by way of injunctive relief.

Devon County Council v C and another [1985] FLR 619 HC FamD Wrong that access of natural parents to child in local authority care continue where child being placed in foster care with possible view to adoption.

Devon County Council v C and another (1985) 129 SJ 483 CA Judge ought to have decided (as court did here) issue of last occasions of maternal access to child in foster-care (not left it to local authority).

Devon County Council v Clancy [1985] FLR 1159; (1985) 149 JP 521 CA Magistrates' unjustified deviation from advice of guardian ad litem will generally be overturned upon appeal.

Devon County Council v S and another [1995] 1 All ER 243; [1994] Fam 169; [1994] 2 FCR 409; [1994] 1 FLR 355; [1993] TLR 626; [1994] 3 WLR 183 HC FamD Local authority may invite court to exercise wardship powers under inherent jurisdiction.

Devon County Council v S and others [1992] 3 All ER 793; [1992] Fam 176; [1992] 2 FCR 827; [1992] 2 FLR 244; [1992] 3 WLR 273 HC FamD Prolonged care order hearing inappropriate where proposals already favoured by interested parties.

Devon County Council, ex parte D, R v [1992] 2 FCR 766 HC QBD Local authority's placing child on child protection register and then informing father of what had done at same time telling him of right to appeal decision not unreasonable procedure.

Devon County Council, ex parte L, R v [1991] FCR 599; [1991] 2 FLR 541 HC QBD Failed application for review of local authority 'decision' to caution interested persons of its belief that applicant a child abuser.

Devon County Council, J v [1986] 1 FLR 597 HC FamD Non-exercise of wardship jurisdiction in respect of child taken into local authority care pursuant to matrimonial care order.

Dhar (Murli), Lali (Musammat) v (1905-06) XXII TLR 460 PC Deceased's gift to adopted son whose adoption was void had no effect.

Dharma (Chandra), R v; R v Slater; R v Hutchinson; R v Court (1905) 69 JP 39; (1905) 40 LJ 238; (1905) XCII LTR 700; (1904-05) 49 SJ 366; (1904-05) XXI TLR 353 CCR Extension by Prevention of Cruelty of Children Act 1904 to limitation on bringing prosecutions under Criminal Law Amendment Act 1885 operated retrospectively as did not create new offence.

Dickens v Pattison; R v Camberwell Green Justices, ex parte Pattison and Dickens [1985] FLR 610; (1985) 149 JP 271; (1985) 129 SJ 31 HC FamD Contravention by magistrates of principle that only affiliation payment arrears of less than one year to be enforced.

Dicocco v Milne (1983) 4 FLR 247 HC FamD (also CA) On relevant concerns when determining custody action.

Dicocco v Milne (1983) 4 FLR 247 CA (also HC FamD) On relevant concerns when determining custody action.

Dimino v Dimino [1989] 2 All ER 280 CA Judge's indorsing proposed order on court welfare officer's report before custody hearing a serious but not fatal irregularity.

Director of Public Prosecutions and another, Cleveland County Council v (1995) 139 SJ LB 13; [1994] TLR 615 HC QBD Court ordering child into local authority care could not specify where child was to be accommodated.

Director of Public Prosecutions and other appeals, D v [1995] Crim LR 748; [1995] 3 FCR 725; [1995] 2 FLR 502; (1995) 145 NLJ 560; [1995] TLR 218 HC QBD Compensation orders against local authority quashed as either no finding that local authority had none done all possible to safeguard public/local authority had behaved satisfactorily.

Director of Public Prosecutions v Cottier [1996] 3 All ER 126; [1996] 2 Cr App R 411; [1996] Crim LR 804; [1996] 1 WLR 826 HC QBD Notice to local authority/probation officer of proceedings against children and young persons required once decision to proceed but need not necessarily precede court appearance.

Dootson (Robert), R v (1995) 16 Cr App R (S) 223; [1994] Crim LR 702 CA Abduction of child not a sex offence under Criminal Justice Act 1991.

Dorset County Council, Wallbridge and another v [1954] 2 All ER 201; [1954] Ch 659; (1954) 118 JP 305; (1954) 104 LJ 345; (1954) 98 SJ 352; [1954] 2 WLR 1068 HC ChD School boarders over whom parents had parental rights/others to whom local authority in loco parentis were not 'foster children' under Public Health Act 1936.

Dredge (otherwise Harrison), Dredge v [1947] 1 All ER 29 HC PDAD That nullity renders child illegitimate not consideration for court.

Dredge v Dredge (otherwise Harrison) [1947] 1 All ER 29 HC PDAD That nullity renders child illegitimate not consideration for court.

Drover, Rugman v [1950] 2 All ER 575; [1951] 1 KB 380; (1950) 94 SJ 595; [1950] 66 (2) TLR 699 HC KBD State of affairs which exists upon appeal is that which existed at time of trial (when were still young person).

Duguid, R v (1907-09) XXI Cox CC 200; (1906) 70 JP 294; (1906) 41 LJ 335; [1906] 75 LJKB 470; (1906) XCIV LTR 887; (1905-06) 50 SJ 465; (1905-06) XXII TLR 506; (1906) WN (I) 100 CCR Was criminal conspiracy on part of person agreeing with mother to remove her child from lawful custody.

Dunne (James), R v (1928-29) 21 Cr App R 176 CCA Conviction quashed where judge conducted unlawful out-of-court examination of child to test whether suitable for her to take oath.

E (A) v Staffordshire County Council [1995] 2 FCR 84; (1995) 159 JP 367 HC FamD On relevant factors when determining whether to make secure accommodation order.

E and Cheshire County Council (No 2), E v (1980) 1 FLR 73 CA HC may, but will not lightly (and here did not), vary existing care order in divorce/wardship action.

E and others, Oldham Metropolitan Borough Council v [1994] 1 FLR 568; [1994] TLR 150 CA On approach to be adopted where aunt seeking residence order in respect of child whom local authority wish to have adopted (all parties agreeing mother unsuitable carer).

E v C [1982] TLR 475 CA Access pre-eminently a matter for trial judge.

E v C [1996] 1 FCR 612; [1996] 1 FLR 472; [1995] TLR 638 HC FamD Income support/child benefit to be treated as subsistence money — that plus cost of supporting new family justified downward variation of child maintenance order.

E v E (1969) 113 SJ 721 CA Apparently final order was in reality interim where question as to whether mother a fit and proper person to have custody of children had not been answered.

E v E and Cheshire County Council (No 2) (1980) 1 FLR 73 CA HC may, but will not lightly (and here did not), vary existing care order in divorce/wardship action.

E v NSPCC and another [1990] FCR 609; [1990] 2 FLR 379 HC QBD On interim care hearings.

E, A-W v (1974) 124 NLJ 1159t HC FamD On practice as regards bringing normal child who is subject of custody/wardship proceedings to psychiatrist.

E, Cleveland County Council v [1988] FCR 625 HC FamD Though local authority had not continued with action court found children not sexually abused and de-warded them.

E, S v [1967] 1 All ER 593; [1967] 1 QB 367; (1966) 110 SJ 945; [1967] 2 WLR 704 HC QBD Affiliation proceedings are civil proceedings: putative father a compellable witness.

E, S v [1993] 1 FCR 729 HC FamD Magistrates could (but here were wrong to) refuse to order access on terms privately arrived at between parties.

Ealing London Borough Council, W v [1994] 1 FCR 436; [1993] 2 FLR 788; [1993] TLR 308 CA Appropriate procedure where parental rights/contact orders sought (here unsuccessfully) in respect of ward.

Ealing London Borough, R (B) v [1985] FLR 999 HC FamD Failed application by mother of children over whom parental rights resolution made to have that resolution determined.

East Sussex County Council, ex parte R, R v [1990] FCR 873; [1991] 2 FLR 358 HC QBD Placing (and manner of placing) mother's name on child abuse register not unreasonable.

Easterbrook v Easterbrook [1957] 2 All ER 117; (1957) 107 LJ 266; (1957) 101 SJ 303; (1943-44) LX TLR 80 HC PDAD On maintenance of children.

Eatough, Vann v [1935] All ER 911; (1935) 79 SJ 840 HC KBD Employment of under-age person as street-trader.

Edwards v Edwards [1958] 2 All ER 179; (1958) 108 LJ 315; (1958) 102 SJ 402 HC PDAD Apportioning of costs in light of solicitor's incompetence.

Edwards v Edwards [1986] 1 FLR 205 CA On justifiability of interim custody order.

Edwards v Edwards [1986] 1 FLR 187; (1985) 149 JP 661 HC FamD On relevant factors when making interim custody order.

Egan v Egan [1975] 2 All ER 167; [1975] Ch 218; (1975) 119 SJ 220; [1975] 2 WLR 503 HC ChD Injunction available to restrain child entering parent's house.

Elder v Elder [1986] 1 FLR 610 CA On secrecy of judge's private interviews with children; eight month delay in preparation of welfare report deplored; pre-welfare report transfer of custody from mother not generally favoured.

Ellard v Ellard: Cheshire County Council; Intervener (1979) 143 JP 747 CA On limited interference by HC with decisions of local authority regarding children in local authority care.

Ellard: Cheshire County Council; Intervener, Ellard v (1979) 143 JP 747 CA On limited interference by HC with decisions of local authority regarding children in local authority care.

Embley v Embley (1965) 109 SJ 131 HC PDAD Refusal of leave to file discretion statement after divorce hearing but pending custody hearing.

Epsom Juvenile Court, ex parte G, R v [1988] 1 All ER 329; [1988] FCR 32; [1988] 2 FLR 36; (1988) 132 SJ 54; [1988] 1 WLR 145 HC QBD Usually report of guardian ad litem should be presented as soon as possible before care case begins.

Essex County Council v Mirror Group Newspapers Ltd [1996] 2 FCR 831; [1996] 1 FLR 585 HC FamD Local authority refused order requiring newspaper to disclose matters pertaining to article on child care case (publication not breaching publicity prohibition).

Essex County Council v R (TL) and R (KB) (1979) 143 JP 309 HC QBD Failed application for care of children on basis of impeded development of same where was no evidence at close of action that children were actually being impeded in their development.

Essex County Council, ex parte Washington, R v [1987] 1 FLR 148; (1987) 151 JP 258 HC QBD Failed application to have contribution notice rescinded.

Essex Justices, ex parte Da Costa, R v (1939-40) XXXI Cox CC 133 HC KBD Quarter sessions quashing of bastardy order where inadequate corroboration a final decision on the merits.

Ethical Committee of St Mary's Hospital (Manchester), ex parte H, R v [1988] 1 FLR 512 HC QBD Failed application for review of decision not to allow party avail of in vitro fertilisation treatment.

Ettenfield v Ettenfield [1939] 2 All ER 743; (1939) 87 LJ 377; (1939) 161 LTR 230; (1939) 83 SJ 459; (1938-39) LV TLR 735; (1939) WN (I) 207 HC PDAD Evidence of non-access admissible whether or not separation agreement under seal.

Ettenfield v Ettenfield [1940] 1 All ER 293; (1940) 89 LJ 68; [1940] 109 LJP 41; (1940) 162 LTR 172; (1940) 84 SJ 59; (1939-40) LVI TLR 315; (1940) WN (I) 43 CA Spouses living together/apart cannot give evidence that would bastardise/legitimise child born inside marriage; post court-ordered/voluntary separation can prove adultery by reference to court order and child's date of birth/can prove by any means other than non-access evidence and child's date of birth (post-order child presumed bastard/post-voluntary separation child presumed legitimate).

Evans v Evans [1989] FCR 153 CA On bringing applications under Child Abduction Convention: return of child ordered.

Evans v Jackson (1986) 150 JP 593 (also HC FamD) CA Father properly granted access to child though was upsetting for latter as upset occasioned by mother's improper attempts to frustrate access not by access per se.

Evans v Jackson (1986) 150 JP 593 (also CA) HC FamD Father properly granted access to child though was upsetting for latter as lifestyle of father afforded broader upbringing to child than that of mother and husband who were Jehovah's Witnesses.

Evans, Jones v [1945] 1 All ER 19; (1944) 108 JP 170; [1944] KB 582; [1945] 114 LJ 29; (1944) 171 LTR 138; (1943-44) LX TLR 374; (1944) WN (I) 128 HC KBD Loss of consortium/non-condonation meant de facto separation so woman a 'single woman'.

Evans, Whitcombe v (1932) 74 LJ ccr86 CyCt Agreement by putative father to pay maintenance for child had by married woman was not void for public policy reasons.

Ex parte Adedigba (1967) 117 NLJ 731t HC QBD Maintenance order unavailable where mother domiciled abroad when child born.

Ex parte Crook and another [1995] 1 All ER 537; [1995] 2 Cr App R 212; [1995] Crim LR 509; [1995] 2 FCR 153; (1995) 159 JP 295; (1989) 133 SJ 1577; [1995] 1 WLR 139 CA Judge may receive representations from all legitimate parties before restricting reports of proceedings; interests of children may outweigh freedom of press to publish.

Ex parte Jarrett (1946) 90 SJ 283; (1945-46) LXII TLR 230; (1946) WN (I) 50 HC KBD Appeal to High Court preferred to mandamus against justices who persistently adjourned mother's application for custody of her children whom she alleged had been wrongfully removed from her custody by her husband.

Exeter Juvenile Court, ex parte H and H, R v; R v Waltham Forest Juvenile Court, ex parte B [1988] FCR 474; [1988] 2 FLR 214 HC QBD Was reasonable to hear care action pending criminal proceedings against parent/s.

F v F [1902] 1 Ch 688 HC ChD Ward removed from guardian's care where guardian changed religion which held at time entrusted with ward.

F v F [1959] 3 All ER 180; (1959) 109 LJ 588; (1959) 103 SJ 659; [1959] 1 WLR 863 HC PDAD On committing of child to local authority care in divorce suit.

F v F [1968] 2 All ER 946 CA Evidence of alleged adultery dismissed at divorce trial can be admitted in later custody case.

F v F (1976) 120 SJ 503 CA On (importance of) jurisdiction of magistrates' courts in context of custody cases.

F v F (1976) 126 NLJ 743t CA Pending divorce action not good reason for adjourning maintenance/custody applications.

F v F [1989] Fam 1; [1989] FCR 232; [1988] 3 WLR 959 HC FamD Non-enforcement of French custody order where was twenty-one month delay before matter came before court and change in attitude of parties over access.

F v Kent County Council and others [1993] 1 FCR 217; [1993] 1 FLR 432; (1992) 136 SJ LB 258; [1992] TLR 394 HC FamD On exercise of discretion to require parties to seek court's leave before making future care/contact application (here wrongly exercised).

F v Leeds City Council [1994] 2 FCR 428; [1994] 2 FLR 60; [1994] TLR 138 CA Final care order made in respect of child at risk from child-mother.

F v R [1995] 1 FLR 227; [1994] TLR 628 HC FamD Enforcement of contact order validly refused: on task of justices hearing contact order enforcement application.

F v S [1973] 1 All ER 722; [1973] Fam 203; (1973) 137 JP 301; (1973) 117 SJ 109; [1973] 2 WLR 178 CA Leave of court needed for adoption of ward; issue for court is will adoption application succeed?

F v S (wardship: jurisdiction) [1993] 2 FLR 686 CA On deciding place of habitual residence of child.

F v Suffolk County Council (1981) 2 FLR 208; (1981) 125 SJ 307 HC QBD On applying for care on basis that proper development of child being impaired/neglected (Children and Young Persons Act 1969, s 1(2)).

F, Cleveland County Council and another v [1995] 2 All ER 236; [1995] 3 FCR 174; [1995] 1 FLR 797; [1995] 1 WLR 785 HC FamD Court may direct that putative statements in care proceedings be confidential but existing statute law affords adequate protection.

F, L v (1978) 128 NLJ 1000t HC FamD Refusal of order allowing children to be styled by name of stepfather, not natural father.

Faulkner v Faulkner (1981) 2 FLR 115; (1979) 123 SJ 751 HC FamD Magistrates could give custody to mother despite welfare officer's contrary recommendation.

Ferguson (Robert), R v (1969) 53 Cr App R 637 CA In chastising their children immigrant parents must conform with British standards.

Fisher (Colin), R v; R v Marshall (Christopher); R v Mitchell (George) (1969) 113 SJ 70; [1969] 2 WLR 452 Assizes Jury cannot convict accused of sex with under-sixteen year old girl where accused being tried for rape.

Flood v Flood [1948] 2 All ER 712; (1948) 112 JP 416; [1948] 117 LJR 1880; (1948) LXIV TLR 474 HC PDAD Children's welfare paramount in custody cases (and maintenance an important element of that).

Florant, Stevenson v [1927] AC 211; (1927) 96 LJPC 1; (1927) 136 LTR 265; (1926-27) XLIII TLR 6 PC In Quebec right of parent to child's custody prevails over that of tuteur.

Floyd v Floyd (1982) 132 NLJ 40 CA Application of principle that custody decisions are to be made in best interests of children.

Foot v Foot [1987] FCR 62 HC FamD Access to children not relevant factor when determining level of maintenance payable in respect of same.

Foy v Brooks [1977] 2 All ER 113; (1977) 141 JP 339; (1976) 120 SJ 768; [1977] 1 WLR 160 HC FamD Purchase of layette incidental to childbirth.

Francis (Colin Leslie), R v (1989) 88 Cr App R 127; [1988] Crim LR 528 CA Indecency with or towards children contrary to Indecency with Children Act 1960, s 1(1) requires that act be aimed at children and that accused pleased that children watching.

Francis v Francis [1959] 3 All ER 206; (1959) 109 LJ 479; (1959) 103 SJ 546; [1959] 3 WLR 447 HC PDAD Custody order to wife as possibility of illegitmacy not enough to counter presumption of legitimacy of child born within marriage.

Franklin, R v [1994] TLR 334 CA Interview evidence ought not to have been admitted given improprieties in procedure regarding access by solicitor to accused (client).

Freeman-Thomas v Freeman-Thomas [1963] 1 All ER 17; (1963) 113 LJ 27; (1962) 106 SJ 532; [1963] 2 WLR 107 HC PDAD No retroactive application of maintenance order requiring payment of education costs.

G (A) v G (T) [1970] 3 All ER 546; (1971) 135 JP 13; [1970] 2 QB 643; [1970] 3 WLR 132 CA Putative father can authorise agent to pay infant's maintenance; proof of agency required before maintenance proceedings can be begun.

G (Surrey County Council intervening), R v [1984] Fam 100; [1984] FLR 780; (1984) 128 SJ 662; [1984] 3 WLR 667 CA That children were constantly shuffled between divorced parents meant were 'exceptional circumstances' (Matrimonial Causes Act 1973, s 43(1)) justifying their being placed in care (care authorities could then validly place child with one parent).

G (T), G (A) v [1970] 3 All ER 546; (1971) 135 JP 13; [1970] 2 QB 643; [1970] 3 WLR 132 CA Putative father can authorise agent to pay infant's maintenance; proof of agency required before maintenance proceedings can be begun.

G and Devon County Council, G v [1989] FCR 454 CA Divorce court could not make second care order where juvenile court had already made valid care order.

G v A [1995] 2 FCR 223 CyCt Order that children's surname be double-barrelled (natural father's surname plus new surname of re-married mother).

G v G (1929) 73 SJ 111; (1928-29) XLV TLR 7 HC PDAD Court could not make custody order in respect of non-legitimated child of parties to divorce action.

G v G (1962) 106 SJ 858 HC PDAD Child placed with father living in adulterous relationship rather than placed in local authority care.

G v G (1970) 114 SJ 493 CA On payment by infant of maintenance towards own child (and on proving paid same).

G v G (1971) 121 NLJ 410t HC PDAD Adulterous husband's extra-marital lover allowed remain in home she shared with adulterer when his children visited (but not allowed stay overnight when children stayed overnight).

G v G (1983) 4 FLR 327; [1982] TLR 321 CA On appealing against interim custody orders.

G v G [1991] FCR 12; [1991] 2 FLR 506 CA Court of first hearing overruled and return of children (abducted by mother) to place of habitual residence ordered.

G v G [1993] 2 FLR 306; [1992] TLR 641 HC FamD Where contact and adoption orders being sought by different parties ought to hear cases together.

G v G and Devon County Council [1989] FCR 454 CA Divorce court could not make second care order where juvenile court had already made valid care order.

G v Kirklees Metropolitan Borough Council [1993] 1 FCR 357; [1993] 1 FLR 805 HC FamD Aunt not joined to care proceedings where could not reasonably hope to secure residence order.

G, Hackney London Borough Council v [1994] 2 FCR 216 HC FamD On role of court in care proceedings where is agreement as to need for care order but disagreement over facts.

G, Leicestershire County Council v [1995] 1 FCR 205; [1994] 2 FLR 329 HC FamD Interim care order substituted for interim supervision order where child of family suffered non-accidental injury before care proceedings heard.

G, North Yorkshire County Council v [1994] 1 FCR 737; [1993] 2 FLR 732 HC FamD Child's welfare not paramount interest in residence action; brother not allowed become party to action concerning other brother where sought to help mother with little English.

Gadd v Thompson (1910-11) XXVII TLR 113 HC KBD Reasonable restrictive covenant entered into by infant apprentice could be enforced by injunction.

Gaines v W [1968] 1 All ER 189; (1968) 132 JP 146; (1967) 117 NLJ 1190t; [1968] 1 QB 782; (1967) 111 SJ 888; [1968] 2 WLR 139 HC QBD Single woman may seek affiliation order though not single when child born.

Galloway (Ex parte), Galloway v [1955] 3 All ER 429; [1956] AC 299; (1955) 105 LJ 728; (1955) 99 SJ 792; [1955] 3 WLR 723 HL 'Children' in Matrimonial Causes Act 1950 includes illegitimate children.

Galloway v Galloway [1954] 2 All ER 143; (1954) 104 LJ 328; (1954) 98 SJ 336; [1954] 2 WLR 980 CA Custody/maintenance unavailable in respect of child born outside marriage who cannot be legitimated.

Galloway v Galloway (Ex parte) [1955] 3 All ER 429; [1956] AC 299; (1955) 105 LJ 728; (1955) 99 SJ 792; [1955] 3 WLR 723 HL 'Children' in Matrimonial Causes Act 1950 includes illegitimate children.

Garner v Garner [1992] 1 FLR 573 CA Variation of periodical payments order justified where child's welfare demands increase in maintenance paid for child.

Garner, Whitton v [1965] 1 All ER 70; (1965) 129 JP 92; (1965) 115 LJ 75; (1965) 109 SJ 194; [1965] 1 WLR 313 HC QBD Wife living apart from husband in same house was single woman.

Gatehouse v Robinson and Robinson [1986] 1 FLR 504; (1986) 130 SJ 13; [1986] 1 WLR 18 HC QBD Unsuccessful appeal against failed prosecution — for undertaking privately arranged adoption contrary to Adoption Act 1958, s 29, as amended — of foster-parents who had privately arranged fostering relationship.

Gateshead Metropolitan Borough Council v B (1996) TLR 19/3/96 HC FamD On deciding where child is resident (in context of application for care order).

Gateshead Metropolitan Borough Council v L and another [1996] 3 All ER 264; [1996] Fam 55; [1996] 3 FCR 582; [1996] 2 FLR 179; [1996] 3 WLR 426 HC FamD On designation of correct local authority in care order.

Gateshead Metropolitan Borough Council v N [1993] 1 FCR 400; [1993] 1 FLR 811 HC FamD On duration of first/successive interim care order/s.

Gatty (FA) and Gatty (PV) v Attorney-General (1951) 95 SJ 610; [1951] 2 TLR 599; (1951) WN (I) 433 HC PDAD Failed petition for legitimacy where could not prove validity of father's marriage.

Gharib-Ul-Lah v Khalak Singh and others (1902-03) XIX TLR 447 PC Guardian of infants property could not be appointed in respect of infant's interest in property of undivided Mitacshara family.

Gibbins (David John), R v [1977] Crim LR 741 CrCt On elements of offence whereby 'expose[d]' child to unnecessary suffering/injury to health contrary to Children and Young Persons Act 1933, s 1(1).

Gibbins (Walter) and Proctor (Edith Rose), R v (1917-18) 13 Cr App R 134; (1918) 82 JP 287 CCA On neglect of child as basis for conviction of murder of same.

Gibbs, The Guardians of the Poor of Plymouth v (1903) 67 JP 61; [1903] 1 KB 177; [1903] 72 LJKB 33; (1902-03) LXXXVII LTR 685; (1902-03) 47 SJ 32; (1902-03) 51 WR 157 HC KBD Union/parish guardians could seek affiliation order against putative father despite mother's re-marriage to man capable of maintaining children.

Gillick v West Norfolk and Wisbech Area Health Authority and another [1986] Crim LR 113; [1986] 1 FLR 224; (1985) 135 NLJ 1055; (1985) 129 SJ 738 HL Depended on intent of doctor prescribing contraceptives for under-16 year old girl whether was aiding and abetting unlawful sexual intercourse; contraceptive advice to under-16 year old not necessarily interference with parental duties.

Gillick v West Norfolk and Wisbech Area Health Authority and another [1984] 1 All ER 365; [1984] FLR 249; (1983) 133 NLJ 888; [1984] QB 681; (1983) 127 SJ 696; [1983] TLR 541 HC QBD Doctor prescribing contraceptives for under-16 year old girl not encouraging unlawful sexual intercourse; contraceptive advice to under-16 year old not interference with parental duties.

Gillick v West Norfolk and Wisbech Area Health Authority and another [1985] 1 All ER 533; [1985] FLR 736; (1985) 135 NLJ 81; (1985) 129 SJ 47; [1984] TLR 744 CA Absent emergency doctor's prescribing contraceptives for under-16 year old girl was interference with parental duties.

Giltrow v Day [1965] 1 All ER 73; (1965) 129 JP 94; (1965) 115 LJ 58; (1965) 109 SJ 29; [1965] 1 WLR 317 HC QBD Wife living apart from husband in same house was not single woman.

Goodenough, Hockaday v [1945] 2 All ER 335; (1945) 109 JP 237; (1945) 173 LTR 204; (1945) 89 SJ 392; (1944-45) LXI TLR 510 HC KBD Letter stating would persevere was statement of future intention not condonation of adultery: wife therefore 'single woman'.

Goodfellow v Goodfellow (1968) 112 SJ 332 HC PDAD Successful appeal by adulterous wife against vesting of custody in children in father (who because was in army had to entrust their care to his parents): child's welfare paramount concern.

Gordon and Bell, Gordon v (1903) LXXXVIII LTR 573 HC PDAD Wife-respondent's filed answer must contain challenge to paternity if is to be allowed raise that issue at custody hearings.

Gordon v Gordon and Bell (1903) LXXXVIII LTR 573 HC PDAD Wife-respondent's filed answer must contain challenge to paternity if is to be allowed raise that issue at custody hearings.

Gowland, Michael v [1977] 2 All ER 328; (1976) 120 SJ 857 HC FamD Time limit for stating case is peremptory.

Graham, Hewlings v [1901] 70 LJCh 568; (1901) LXXXIV LTR 497 HC ChD Infant's buying of jewellery (without agreement of guardian) for fiancée whom infant does not later marry is not purchase of necessaries.

Graham-Kerr (John), R v (1989) 88 Cr App R 302; (1989) 153 JP 171; (1988) 132 SJ 1299; [1988] 1 WLR 1098 CA On elements of crime of taking indecent photographs of child contrary to Protection of Children Act 1978, s 1(1).

Grainger and Clark, Grainger v [1959] 3 All ER 51; (1959) 103 SJ 637 HC PDAD PDAD would not make fresh custody order under Matrimonial Causes Act 1950, s 26(1) as believed could not following re-marriage of spouses to each other gave no opinion on s 26(1) but would not interfere with PDAD's discretion.

Grainger and Clark, Grainger v [1959] 3 All ER 51 (also PDAD); (1959) 109 LJ 635; (1959) 103 SJ 855 [1959] 3 WLR 642 CA PDAD would not make fresh custody order under Matrimonial Causes Act 1950, s 26(1) as believed could not following re-marriage of spouses to each other CA gave no opinion on s 26(1) but would not interfere with PDAD's discretion.

Grainger v Grainger and Clark [1959] 3 All ER 51; (1959) 103 SJ 637 HC PDAD PDAD would not make fresh custody order under Matrimonial Causes Act 1950, s 26(1) as believed could not following re-marriage of spouses to each other gave no opinion on s 26(1) but would not interfere with PDAD's discretion.

Grainger v Grainger and Clark [1959] 3 All ER 51 (also PDAD); (1959) 109 LJ 635; (1959) 103 SJ 855 [1959] 3 WLR 642 CA PDAD would not make fresh custody order under Matrimonial Causes Act 1950, s 26(1) as believed could not following re-marriage of spouses to each other CA gave no opinion on s 26(1) but would not interfere with PDAD's discretion.

Grantham v Grantham (1948) WN (I) 329 HC KBD On what constituted 'net income' after which level being attained maintenance payable for child under covenant between husband and wife.

Gravesend Justices, ex parte Doodney, R v [1971] 2 All ER 364; (1971) 135 JP 353; (1971) 121 NLJ 152; (1971) 115 SJ 327; [1971] 1 WLR 818 HC QBD That mother resident abroad need not preclude putative father seeking variation in England.

Green v Green (1928) 66 LJ 448; (1929) 98 LJP 58; (1929) 140 LTR 93; (1928) WN (I) 252 HC PDAD Court cannot post-decree nisi make custody order in respect of child born before marriage and never judicially legitimated.

Greenway v Attorney-General (Greenway and others cited) (1927) 71 SJ 882 HC PDAD Failed application to have legitimation petition heard in camera.

Greenwich Juvenile Court, ex parte London Borough of Greenwich, R v (1980) 1 FLR 304 HC QBD No machinery for discovery in magistrates' courts; discoverability of documents to be assessed on individual/class (where are classes) basis.

Greenwich London Borough Council v H [1997] 1 FCR 527; [1996] 2 FLR 736 HC FamD Interim contact order inappropriate as children probably going to lose contact after full action which would be particularly distressing if had enjoyed interim contact.

Greenwich London Borough Council, W v [1989] FCR 397; [1989] 2 FLR 67; (1989) 133 SJ 388 HC FamD Justices must give reasons for refusing parents access to children in care.

Gregory, Butler v (1901-02) XVIII TLR 370 HC KBD Father of illegitimate child who did not have care/custody of child nor had bastardy proceedings brought against him not father for purposes of Prevention of Cruelty to Children Act 1894, s 23.

Griffin, R v [1993] Crim LR 515 CA On respective roles of judge/jury in child abduction case; was possible to find attempted abduction where had arranged boat trip and went to school to request control of children in local authority care.

Guardians of Holbeach Union, Guardians of West Ham Union v [1903] 2 KB 627 HC KBD Under sixteen year old illegitimate child's three year residence in parish meant she was settled there.

Guardians of Holbeach Union, Guardians of West Ham Union v [1904] 2 KB 121 CA Under sixteen year old illegitimate child's three year residence in parish meant she was settled there.

Guardians of Fulham, Guardians of Woolwich Union v [1905] 2 KB 203 HC KBD Illegitimate child under sixteen cannot acquire independent settlement.

Guardians of West Ham Union v Guardians of Holbeach Union [1904] 2 KB 121 CA Under sixteen year old illegitimate child's three year residence in parish meant she was settled there.

Guardians of Fulham, Guardians of Woolwich Union v [1906] 2 KB 240 CA On illegitimate child under sixteen acquiring settlement by residence in parish of mother's residence.

Guardians of Woolwich Union v Guardians of Fulham [1905] 2 KB 203 HC KBD Illegitimate child under sixteen cannot acquire independent settlement.

Guardians of Woolwich Union v Guardians of Fulham [1906] 2 KB 240 CA On illegitimate child under sixteen acquiring settlement by residence in parish of mother's residence.

Gwynedd County Council, ex parte B and another, R v [1992] 3 All ER; [1991] 2 FLR 365; (1991) 141 NLJ 494t; [1991] TLR 181 CA Local authority rights/duties towards child in care end upon child's death.

H (E), Hereford and Worcester County Council v [1985] FLR 975 HC FamD Controlled access allowed where did not seem access would be problematic/adoption not proved to be best option for child.

H (M) v P (G) [1995] 2 FLR 106 HC FamD On whether to allow removal of child from jurisdiction.

H (No 2), Birmingham City Council v [1993] 1 FLR 883 CA Where mother/son both minors interests of each equally important; here ending of contact between mother/son too Draconian: reasonable supervised access allowed.

H (No 2), H v [1997] 1 FCR 603 HC FamD On determining forum conveniens in shared residence/specific issue application concerning child.

H and H, NSPCC v [1989] FCR 544; [1989] 2 FLR 131 CA On invocation of wardship jurisdiction of HC where is overlapping care action before juvenile court.

H and others, M v [1988] 3 All ER 5 HL Courts have jurisdiction to hear custody/access application by parent against third party but statutorily precluded from doing so.

H and P, Calderdale Borough Council v [1991] 1 FLR 461 HC FamD Statutory care order to local authority, children to reside with grandparents who were to be paid maintenance pending approval as foster-parents when would be paid boarding-out allowance.

H v B [1990] FCR 43 CA Refusal of second period of experimental access pending final decision whether father who had sexually abused child be continuously allowed access.

H v B (No 2) [1990] FCR 366 HC FamD Conditional access to his children allowed of father who had sexually abused those children.

H v Cambridgeshire County Council [1997] 1 FCR 569; [1996] 2 FLR 566 HC FamD Mother not given second time leave to show papers to psychiatrist/have psychiatrist observe contact between her/her children.

H v H [1947] KB 463; [1948] 117 LJR 349; (1947) 176 LTR 281; (1947) LXIII TLR 207; (1947) WN (I) 67 HC KBD Justices could dispense with need for consent to adoption of custody having custody of same.

H v H [1973] 1 All ER 801; [1973] Fam 62; (1973) 137 JP 297; (1972) 122 NLJ 941t; [1973] 2 WLR 525 HC FamD Court could but would not interfere in local authority decisions about child in care.

H v H [1974] 1 All ER 1145; (1974) 124 NLJ 36t; (1974) 118 SJ 219; [1974] 1 WLR 595 CA Private interviews with judge in custody case desirable; guarantee of non-disclosure by judge undesirable.

H v H (1975) 125 NLJ 507t; (1975) 119 SJ 590 CA Successful appeal by English mother against custody of child resident in England being given to Muslim father so that child might be instructed in Islam (mother agnostic).

H v H (1977) 127 NLJ 16t CA On making stayed order in custody proceedings.

H v H (1977) 127 NLJ 840b CA On need to avoid delay in resolution of custody actions.

H v H [1982] TLR 188 CA Custody hearing to be reheard by another judge where first judge had private pre-trial conversation with welfare officer.

H v H [1989] FCR 257; [1989] 1 FLR 212 CA Defined/supervised access of children allowed (one of whom person granted access had sexually abused).

H v H [1994] 1 FLR 530 HC FamD Mother allowed continue with residence/prohibited steps orders applications in respect of children she had abducted and retained.

H v H [1996] 2 FLR 570; (1996) 140 SJ LB 207; (1996) TLR 14/8/96 CA On proving acquiescence: here not established.

H v H [1995] 2 FCR 469 [1995] 1 FLR 529 CA On deciding whether to grant residence order/leave to remove child from jurisdiction.

H v H [1997] TLR 196 HL On intention as defining element of acquiescence.

H v H (No 2) [1997] 1 FCR 603 HC FamD On determining forum conveniens in shared residence/specific issue application concerning child.

H v H; H v East Sussex County Council (1972) 116 SJ 968 HC FamD Court would not exercise wardship jurisdiction over child in respect of whom local authority care resolution had been made.

H v H; K v K [1989] 3 All ER 740; [1990] Fam 86; [1989] FCR 356; (1990) 134 SJ 21; [1989] 3 WLR 933 CA Balance of probabilities the standard of proof in child abuse hearings; undue weight given to social worker's interviews with child (but was admissible); unsworn evidence of child inadmissible in matrimonial hearings; hearsay evidence inadmissible in matrimonial action unless parties elect otherwise.

H v Lambeth London Borough Council [1984] TLR 213 HC FamD On need for leave of court in respect of all significant decisions taken regarding ward.

H v N [1990] TLR 36 HC FamD Mother with interim custody order in respect of Canadian child did not have right to remove child from country of residence (Canada).

H v Norfolk County Council [1997] 1 FLR 384 CA Local authority not liable for (alleged) abuse suffered by onetime child in its care placed with foster parents.

H v Stockport Metropolitan Borough Council [1990] FCR 65; (1989) 133 SJ 359 HC FamD Interim access order unavailable pursuant to Child Care Act 1980, Part 1A.

H, Birmingham City Council and others v [1994] 1 All ER 12; [1994] 2 AC 212; [1994] 1 FCR 896; [1994] 1 FLR 224; (1994) 144 NLJ 17; (1994) 138 SJ LB 13; [1993] TLR 657; [1994] 2 WLR 31 HL In child care case where mother and child are minors interests of mother's child are paramount.

H, Birmingham City Council v [1993] 1 FCR 247; [1992] 2 FLR 323 HC FamD Residence order carries with it right to exercise parental responsibility.

H, C v (1979) 123 SJ 537 HC FamD When access/adoption arise to be decided in same action they should both be decided in tandem, not one before the other.

H, Greenwich London Borough Council v [1997] 1 FCR 527; [1996] 2 FLR 736 HC FamD Interim contact order inappropriate as children probably going to lose contact after full action which would be particularly distressing if had enjoyed interim contact.

H, K v [1993] 1 FCR 683; [1993] 2 FLR 61; [1992] TLR 660 HC FamD Court order available to formalise existing well-working private maintenance agreement.

H, Northamptonshire County Council v [1988] 1 All ER 598; [1988] 1 FLR 529; [1988] QB 205; (1988) 132 SJ 263; [1988] 2 WLR 389 HC QBD Additional interim care orders may be made in absence of child over 5 years old if legally represented.

H, Nottinghamshire County Council v [1995] 1 FLR 115; [1995] 2 FCR 365 HC FamD Crown Prosecution Service ordered to disclose documents to local authority alone (local authority in course of care proceedings).

H, P v (1976) 120 SJ 199 HC FamD On staying custody orders pending appeal.

H, S v [1997] 1 FLR 971; (1997) 141 SJ LB 64; [1997] TLR 127 HC FamD Was not breach of custodial rights for mother-custodian to remove from Italy children to whom father only had access rights: summary return not ordered.

Hackney London Borough Council v G [1994] 2 FCR 216 HC FamD On role of court in care proceedings where is agreement as to need for care order but disagreement over facts.

Hackney Union v Tombs; Tombs v Hackney Union (1909) 73 JP 271 Police Ct Valid adoption of child by poor law guardians; adulterous father ordered to pay maintenance.

Hadkinson v Hadkinson [1952] 2 All ER 567 CA Court will not hear contemnor who has disobeyed order regarding child until contempt purged.

Hadlow v Hadlow (1930) 143 LTR 774; (1930) 74 SJ 582; (1929-30) XLVI TLR 624 HC PDAD Husband's non-access to wife at relevant time proved was not father of child at issue.

Hale, R v (1901-07) XX Cox CC 739; (1905) 69 JP 83; [1905] 1 KB 126; (1904-05) XCI LTR 839; (1904-05) 49 SJ 68; (1904-05) XXI TLR 70; (1904-05) 53 WR 400 CCR Child need not be present at trial concerning cruelty thereto unless evidence of child needed.

Hall, Buckeridge v [1963] 1 All ER 509; (1963) 127 JP 218; (1963) 113 LJ 154; [1963] 1 QB 614; (1963) 107 SJ 96; [1963] 2 WLR 354 HC QBD Affiliation order available for English-born child of woman of foreign domicil normally resident in England.

Halton, R v [1925] All ER 396 CCA Words 'wilfully assaults' in Children Act 1908, s 12(1) intended to convey something more than common assault.

Hamlyn v Pearce [1962] 2 All ER 436; [1962] Crim LR 405t; (1962) 126 JP 350; (1962) 112 LJ 370; [1962] 2 QB 346; (1962) 106 SJ 355; [1962] 3 WLR 136 HC QBD Can only be sent to approved school if under seventeen at time of order.

Hammond v Hammond (1962) 106 SJ 610 CA Refusal to order access to children by father was merited.

Hampshire County Council v C [1988] FCR 133 CA On determining un/reasonableness of parent's refusal of consent to adoption: here not unreasonably withheld.

Hampshire County Council, ex parte K and another, R v [1990] 2 All ER 129; [1990] FCR 545; [1990] 1 FLR 330; [1990] 2 QB 71; (1989) 133 SJ 1605; [1990] 2 WLR 649 HC QBD Child's interest requires parents be given every opportunity to defend themselves including access to all relevant material.

Harben v Harben [1957] 1 All ER 379; (1957) 107 LJ 91; (1957) 101 SJ 150; [1957] 1 WLR 261 HC PDAD Custody order made though children ouside jurisdiction.

Haroutunian v Jennings (1980) 1 FLR 62; (1977) 121 SJ 663 HC FamD Amount payable under affiliation order (assessed by reference to father's income) may include payment for mother.

Harris v Hawkins [1947] 1 All ER 312; (1947) 111 JP 161 HC KBD Persons whose consent to adoption required.

Harris v Pinnington [1995] 3 FCR 35 HC FamD Custodial parent not allowed remove child from jurisdiction as not in child's best interests; staying contact to father ordered.

Hereford and Worcester County Council, ex parte D, R v [1992] 1 FLR 448 HC QBD Local authority decision to remove child from foster care quashed where did not consult with foster-parent beforehand.

Hereford City Justices, ex parte O, R v [1982] 3 All ER 568; (1983) 4 FLR 196; (1982) 126 SJ 496; [1982] TLR 314; [1982] 1 WLR 1252 HC QBD Can appeal to Crown Court on basis of quantum.

Hering and Wilson, Hering v [1943] 112 LJ 81; (1943) 169 LTR 236; (1942-43) LIX TLR 428; (1943) WN (I) 216 HC PDAD Guilty wife with own estate could be ordered to pay for maintenance of children.

Hering v Hering and Wilson [1943] 112 LJ 81; (1943) 169 LTR 236; (1942-43) LIX TLR 428; (1943) WN (I) 216 HC PDAD Guilty wife with own estate could be ordered to pay for maintenance of children.

Hertfordshire County Council, ex parte B, R v; R v Bedfordshire County Council, ex parte C [1987] 1 FLR 239; (1987) 151 JP 202 HC QBD On judicial review of care orders (compliance with natural justice, not particular policy, is matter in issue).

Hertfordshire County Council, W v [1992] 2 FCR 885; [1993] 1 FLR 118; (1992) 136 SJ LB 259; [1992] TLR 431 HC FamD Justices must give reasons when refusing care order.

Hewitt, Moore v [1947] 2 All ER 270; (1947) 111 JP 483; [1947] KB 831; (1947) 97 LJ 389; [1947] 116 LJR 1276; (1947) 177 LTR 576; (1947) LXIII TLR 476; (1947) WN (I) 224 HC KBD Close relationship of woman with putative father (and no other) corroborative of mother's claim.

Hewitt, R v (1926-30) XXVIII Cox CC 101; (1925-26) 19 Cr App R 64; (1926) 90 JP 68; (1926) 134 LTR 157; (1925-26) XLII TLR 216; (1925) WN (I) 292 CCA Previous assault on same girl admissible in unlawful carnal knowledge of under sixteen/over fourteen year old girl — time lapse since earlier assault reduces weight of evidence.

Hewlings v Graham [1901] 70 LJCh 568; (1901) LXXXIV LTR 497 HC ChD Infant's buying of jewellery (without agreement of guardian) for fiancée whom infant does not later marry is not purchase of necessaries.

Heywood, W v [1985] FLR 1064 HC QBD On making care order under Children and Young Persons Act 1969, s 7(7) where child is already subject of matrimonial care order.

High Peak Magistrates' Court, ex parte B, R v [1995] 1 FLR 568 HC FamD On inappropriateness of judicial review of maintenance order as a form of relief when appeal structure exists.

Highbury Corner Magistrates' Court, ex parte Deering, R v [1997] 1 FLR 683; (1997) 161 JP 138 HC QBD Balancing respective interests of accused and child-witness to be done not when making out witness summons but when child to be called.

Hill, St Helens MBC v (1992) 156 JP 602; [1992] TLR 150 HC QBD Sale of cigarattes to under-aged youth a strict liability offence: absent owner properly convicted for actions of worker.

Hilton (John James), R v (1925-26) 19 Cr App R 29 CCA Interpretation of Children Act 1908, s 12(1).

Hitchcock v WB and others [1952] 2 All ER 119; (1952) 116 JP 401; (1952) 102 LJ 345; [1952] 2 QB 561; (1952) 96 SJ 448; [1952] 1 TLR 1550; (1952) WN (I) 315 HC QBD Test whether consent unreasonably withheld is attitude of person withholding.

Hockaday v Goodenough [1945] 2 All ER 335; (1945) 109 JP 237; (1945) 173 LTR 204; (1945) 89 SJ 392; (1944-45) LXI TLR 510 HC KBD Letter stating would persevere was statement of future intention not condonation of adultery: wife therefore 'single woman'.

Hodge, Hyde v [1985] FLR 711 CA Dismissal of affiliation action by HC improper: should have remitted it to justices for dismissal so that applicant would not lose right of appeal to CrCt.

Hodgkins v Hodgkins [1965] 3 All ER 164; (1965) 115 LJ 660; (1965) 109 SJ 899; [1965] 1 WLR 1448 CA Decree nisi stayed pending trial of whether particular child had been accepted as child of family.

Hodgson, Corfield v [1966] 2 All ER 205; (1966) 130 JP 271; (1965-66) 116 NLJ 810; (1966) 110 SJ 170; [1966] 1 WLR 590 HC QBD Putative father's lies in affiliation case evidence corroborating paternity.

Hodgson, Marsh and another v [1974] Crim LR 35 CA Parents found jointly liable for unexplained injuries to their infant child.

Hoey v Hoey [1984] 1 All ER 177; [1984] FLR 334; (1984) 128 SJ 132 CA Why reasons needed in child custody cases.

Holland v Roberts (1939-40) XXXI Cox CC 38; (1938) 158 LTR 313 CA Evidence showing opportunity inadequate corroboration of allegation of paternity in bastardy action.

Holmes (Holmes, by his Guardian, intervening), Holmes v [1966] 1 WLR 187 HC PDAD Court will not find child accepted into family unless is clearly the case; blood test proved child not child of husband party to action.

Holmes v Holmes (Holmes, by his Guardian, intervening) [1966] 1 WLR 187 HC PDAD Court will not find child accepted into family unless is clearly the case; blood test proved child not child of husband party to action.

Holtom v Barnet London Borough Council and another [1993] TLR 478 HC QBD Local authority could be sued by person once in its care for negligent discharge of its duties when acting in loco parentis.

Hounslow London Borough Council v A [1993] 1 FLR 702; [1993] 1 WLR 291 HC FamD Interim care order appropriate where father sought residence order and local authority had not yet completed appraisal of father as carer.

Hove Juvenile Court, ex parte W, R v [1989] FCR 286; [1989] 2 FLR 145 HC QBD On establishing by way of interview evidence that child has been victim of sex abuse.

Howard, ex parte Da Costa, R v [1938] 3 All ER 241; (1938) 102 JP 333; [1938] 2 KB 544; [1938] 107 LJCL 675; (1938) 82 SJ 477; (1937-38) LIV TLR 825; (1938) WN (I) 202 HC KBD Cannot appeal from quarter sessions decision in affiliation action.

Huddersfield Borough Council and another, S and another v [1974] 3 All ER 296; [1975] Fam 113; (1974) 138 JP 717; (1975) 119 SJ 272; [1975] 2 WLR 697 CA Interim adoption order in father's favour to see if child should be returned to him valid interference with local authority powers/use of probationary period.

Hull v Hull [1960] 1 All ER 378; (1960) 110 LJ 157; (1960) 104 SJ 310 HC PDAD Res judicata stopped husband alleging wife's desertion in post-decree absolute custody case as had decided husband was in desertion but could raise wife's adultery as not raised in divorce suit.

Humberside County Council and another, M v [1979] 2 All ER 744; [1979] Fam 114; (1980) 1 FLR 91; [1979] 3 WLR 234 HC FamD If lower court empowered High Court will only intervene if unusual case; local authority acting outside powers; lower court powers inadequate.

Humberside County Council v B [1993] 1 FCR 613; [1993] 1 FLR 257 HC FamD On relevant factors when making interim care order.

Humphreys and others, ex parte Ward [1914-15] All ER 189, R v (1914-15) XXIV Cox CC 455; (1915) 79 JP 66; [1914] 3 KB 1237; [1915] 84 LJKB 187; (1914-15) 111 LTR 1110; (1913-14) XXX TLR 698 HC KBD Affiliation order can be made in respect of child not born in England or Wales unless child subject to foreign law.

Hunt v Newcombe (1983) 4 FLR 482 CA Change in custody after more than seven years with one custodial parent justified; interviews with children a discretionary matter for judge.

Hurkissondas (Bachoo), Bhugwandas (Nagindas) v (1915-16) XXXII TLR 132 PC On eligibility of adopted son where is partition of family property under Hindu law.

Hurst v Hurst [1984] FLR 867 CA Joint custody ordered as in child's best interests.

Hurwitt v Hurwitt (1982) 3 FLR 194 CA Letter from director of society for single mothers concerning mother's earning potential could have been admitted (though improbable that would have made difference).

Hutchinson v Hutchinson (1981) 2 FLR 167 HC FamD Valid departure from welfare officer's recommendations where duly considered and reasons given; valid refusal of custody to mother where likely step-father a threat to child.

Hyde v Hodge [1985] FLR 711 CA Dismissal of affiliation action by HC improper: should have remitted it to justices for dismissal so that applicant would not lose right of appeal to CrCt.

I and Brent London Borough Council, Newham London Borough Council v [1997] 2 FCR 629 HC FamD On determining designated care authority in care proceedings where children in interim local accommodation care of one authority and mother had since moved to area of another local authority.

I v Barnsley Metropolitan Borough Council [1986] 1 FLR 109 (also HC FamD) CA Wrong to place one of two children in care on basis that one/other was not/was child of mother's cohabitee who had perpetrated serious cruelty on first child.

I v Barnsley Metropolitan Borough Council [1986] 1 FLR 109 (also CA) HC FamD One of two children placed in care on basis that one/other was not/was child of mother's cohabitee who had perpetrated serious cruelty on first child.

I v D [1989] FCR 91; [1988] 2 FLR 286 HC FamD Fining of mother for non-compliance with access order quashed as magistrates had not had as first consideration the best interests of child involved.

In re G (a minor) [1997] 2 All ER 534; [1997] 2 FLR 202; (1997) 147 NLJ 721; (1997) 141 SJ LB 106; [1997] TLR 248; [1997] 2 WLR 747 HL On granting of conditional revocation of freeing order (here granted once care order in respect of child made under the Children Act 1989, s 31).

In the Matter of a Petition for Declaration of Legitimacy (1927) WN (I) 292 HC PDAD Failed application for legitimacy petition to be heard in camera.

In the Matter of Clayton (Mabel Inez) a proposed Petitioner (1927) 71 SJ 543 HC PDAD Only party seeking to be legitimated can bring legitimation petition; on procedure as regards bringing such a petition.

In the matter of the petition of B (A) (1927) 64 LJ 456; (1928) 97 LJP 104; (1927) WN (I) 291 HC PDAD Failed application for legitimacy petition to be heard in camera.

In the matter of the Petition of D (C) (1928) 138 LTR 208 HC PDAD Application that legitimacy case be heard in camera refused.

Inman, Nash v [1908] 2 KB 1; [1908] 77 LJCL 626; (1908) XCVIII LTR 658; (1907-08) XXIV TLR 401 CA In suing infant for necessaries must show were apposite to infant's state in life and that infant had inadequate supply of said goods when supplied.

Isle of Wight County Council v Warwickshire County Council [1953] 1 All ER 525; [1953] 1 QB 553; (1953) 97 SJ 154; [1953] 2 WLR 451 HC QBD Quarter sessions on appeal cannot name local authority within which offence committed by young person of unknown residence.

Izod, R v (1901-07) XX Cox CC 690 Assizes Must be criminally negligent to new-born child after born to sustain conviction for manslaughter of same through neglect.

J and another v C and others [1970] AC 668; [1969] 2 WLR 540 HL Child's welfare paramount in wardship cases: no rule that custody must go to parents who are suitable for same.

J v Devon County Council [1986] 1 FLR 597 HC FamD Non-exercise of wardship jurisdiction in respect of child taken into local authority care pursuant to matrimonial care order.

J v J [1991] FCR 504; [1991] 2 FLR 385 CA Joint care and control exceptional but merited here.

J v J [1993] 1 FCR 471; [1993] 2 FLR 56 HC FamD Ex-cohabitee not 'father' of mother's child so could not be ordered to transfer property to mother for child's benefit.

J, M v (1982) 3 FLR 19 HC FamD Father properly refused access to his illegitimate child where access could jeopardise child's welfare.

J, M v (1977) 127 NLJ 1130t; (1977) 121 SJ 759 HC FamD Successful appeal by alcoholic, unstable father against refusal of application in which sought order for access to own child.

Jackson v Jackson (1967) 111 SJ 456 HC PDAD Valid finding of wilful neglect to maintain; wife's failure to give notice to putative father of child regarding maintenance action against another precluded making of maintenance order.

Jackson, Burbury v [1914-17] All ER 531; (1915-17) XXV Cox CC 555; (1916) 80 JP 455; [1917] 1 KB 16; (1916) 51 LJ 517; [1917] 86 LJCL 255; (1916-17) 115 LTR 713; (1916-17) XXXIII TLR 18; (1916) WN (I) 348 HC KBD Evidence of opportunity not per se sufficient to justify bastardy order.

Jackson, Evans v (1986) 150 JP 593 (also HC FamD) CA Father properly granted access to child though was upsetting for latter as upset occasioned by mother's improper attempts to frustrate access not by access per se.

Jackson, Evans v (1986) 150 JP 593 (also CA) HC FamD Father properly granted access to child though was upsetting for latter as lifestyle of father afforded broader upbringing to child than that of mother and husband who were Jehovah's Witnesses.

Jackson, Oakey v [1911-13] All ER 681; (1913-14) XXIII Cox CC 734; (1914) 78 JP 87; [1914] 1 KB 216; [1914] 83 LJKB 712; (1914) 110 LTR 41; (1913-14) XXX TLR 92 HC KBD Father preventing surgical operation on child for no good reason could be charged with wilful neglect.

Jah, Hereford and Worcester Council v [1985] FLR 530 HC FamD Whether parent to be allowed access to child in care depends on whether in child's best interests to allow access.

James v Morgan (1909) 73 JP 149; [1909] 1 KB 564; [1909] 78 LJKB 471; (1909) C LTR 238; (1908-09) 53 SJ 245; (1908-09) XXV TLR 267; (1909) WN (I) 31 HC KBD Father's agreement to maintain bastard child ended upon mother's death.

Janaway v Salford Health Authority [1988] 3 All ER 1079; [1989] AC 537 (also CA); [1989] 1 FLR 155; (1988) 138 NLJ 348; (1988) 132 SJ 1731; [1988] 3 WLR 1350 HL Conscience provisions of Abortion Act apply only to medical parts of abortion not preliminary arrangements therefor.

Jane v Jane (1983) 4 FLR 712 CA Custody to father/care and control to mother justified as latter a Jehovah's Witness opposed to blood transfusions which father could as custodian authorise.

Jarvis (James), R v (1901-07) XX Cox CC 249 Assizes Not abduction to passively acquiesce to proposal of under-sixteen year old unmarried girl to join her in her leaving home.

Jefferson v Jefferson [1956] 1 All ER 31; (1956) 106 LJ 8; (1955) 99 SJ 911; [1955] 3 WLR 1001 CA Maintenance 'free of tax' meant that after tax the amount paid should be the amount stated.

Jeffery v Paget (1919) CC Rep VIII 2 CyCt Man married by woman who has entered into maintenance agreement in affiliation action becomes liable for maintenance of said children.

Jeffrey v Jeffrey (1962) 106 SJ 686 CA Interference with trial judge's exercise of discretion so that custody of child would be given to one of two living parents (and not sibling of father).

Jenkins v Jenkins (1980) 1 FLR 148 CA Return of child to parent granted custody to be ordered where other parent 'snatches' child.

Jennings, Haroutunian v (1980) 1 FLR 62; (1977) 121 SJ 663 HC FamD Amount payable under affiliation order (assessed by reference to father's income) may include payment for mother.

Jobson v Jobson (1964) 108 SJ 56 HC PDAD Inappropriate to look to degree to which father had taken on responsibility for child when deciding whether child accepted as part of family.

John and Goff, John v [1965] 2 All ER 222; (1965) 109 SJ 109; [1965] 2 WLR 714 HC PDAD Non-appointment of guardian ad litem in divorce of infant made decree nisi voidable not void.

John v John and Goff [1965] 2 All ER 222; (1965) 109 SJ 109; [1965] 2 WLR 714 HC PDAD Non-appointment of guardian ad litem in divorce of infant made decree nisi voidable not void.

Johns v Jones [1978] 3 All ER 1232; [1978] Crim LR 426; (1979) 143 JP 723; (1978) 128 NLJ882t; [1979] QB 411; (1978) 122 SJ 593; [1978] 3 WLR 792 CA Local authority resolution whereby sought to assume parental authority over child (originally voluntarily left with authority) after mother requested return of child was invalid.

Jones (EF), Jones (EG) v [1974] 3 All ER 702; [1974] 1 WLR 1471 CA Not improper that question of custody of children had been decided while divorce suit was pending.

Jones (EG) v Jones (EF) [1974] 3 All ER 702; [1974] 1 WLR 1471 CA Not improper that question of custody of children had been decided while divorce suit was pending.

Jones (James William), R v [1973] Crim LR 621 CrCt Was not taking child out of possession of parents (contrary to Sexual Offences Act 1956, s 20) to seek to bring girls for walk, aim being to indecently assault them.

Jones (William), R v (1911-13) XXII Cox CC 212; (1911) 75 JP 272 CCC Must prove accused intended to permanently withdraw child from parent to sustain conviction for stealing away child under fourteen.

Jones v Davies [1900-03] All ER 243; (1900) 35 LJ 601; [1901] 70 LJK/QB 38; (1900-01) LXXXIII LTR 412; [1901] 1 QB 118; (1900-01) 49 WR 136 HC QBD Married woman living with husband cannot be single woman.

Jones v Evans [1945] 1 All ER 19; (1944) 108 JP 170; [1944] KB 582; [1945] 114 LJ 29; (1944) 171 LTR 138; (1943-44) LX TLR 374; (1944) WN (I) 128 HC KBD Loss of consortium/non-condonation meant de facto separation so woman a 'single woman'.

Jones v Jones (1974) 124 NLJ 810t; (1974) 118 SJ 598 CA Custody/interim custody orders preferable to postponement of custody action pending divorce action.

Jones v Thomas [1933] All ER 535; (1934-39) XXX Cox CC 47; (1934) 98 JP 41; [1934] 1 KB 323; (1933) 76 LJ 338; (1934) 103 LJCL 113; (1934) 150 LTR 216 HC KBD That told a lie not conclusive evidence of paternity.

Jones, Johns v [1978] 3 All ER 1232; [1978] Crim LR 426; (1979) 143 JP 723; (1978) 128 NLJ882t; [1979] QB 411; (1978) 122 SJ 593; [1978] 3 WLR 792 CA Local authority resolution whereby sought to assume parental authority over child (originally voluntarily left with authority) after mother requested return of child was invalid.

Jones, Liverpool Society for the Prevention of Cruelty to Children v [1914-15] All ER 1073; (1914-15) XXIV Cox CC 434; (1915) 79 JP 20; [1914] 3 KB 813; (1914) 49 LJ 380; [1915] 84 LJKB 222; (1914-15) 111 LTR 806; (1913-14) 58 SJ 723; (1913-14) XXX TLR 584; (1914) WN (I) 270 HC KBD Possible that putative father could be guilty of wilful neglect of child (contrary to Children Act 1908, s 12).

JR v Merton London Borough [1992] 2 FCR 174 (also HC FamD) CA On granting leave to foster parent to seek residence order (here refused).

JR v Merton London Borough [1992] 2 FCR 174 (also CA) HC FamD On granting leave to foster parent to seek residence order (here allowed).

Jussa v Jussa [1972] 2 All ER 600; (1972) 136 JP 499; (1972) 116 SJ 219; [1972] 1 WLR 881 HC FamD Split orders and joint custody order available if in best interests of children.

Justices of the Peace for Sunderland, ex parte Leslie Hodgkinson, R v [1945] 2 All ER 175; (1945) 109 JP 201; [1945] 114 LJ 359; (1945) 173 LTR 62; (1945) 89 SJ 436; (1944-45) LXI TLR 456; (1945) WN (I) 150 HC KBD Justices can hear second bastardy hearing/admit fresh evidence and make order despite initial refusal.

K (DT), R v [1993] Crim LR 281; [1993] 2 FLR 181; (1992) 136 SJ LB 328; [1992] TLR 591 CA Improper to refuse disclosure of video (interview) evidence without first ascertaining relevance/significance of same.

K (formerly D) v D (1974) 118 SJ 50 CA Custody of children to unimpeachable father, not mother who would remove them to Germany to live there with new partner.

K and another, Official Solicitor v [1963] 3 All ER 191; (1963) 113 LJ 577; (1963) 107 SJ 616 HL No-one has absolute right to see Official Solicitor's confidential reports but reports only to be so given if in ward's interests.

K v H [1993] 1 FCR 683; [1993] 2 FLR 61; [1992] TLR 660 HC FamD Court order available to formalise existing well-working private maintenance agreement.

K v K [1992] 2 All ER 727; [1992] 2 FCR 253; [1992] 2 FLR 220; (1992) 136 SJ LB 69; [1992] TLR 73; [1992] 1 WLR 530 CA Judge may confer benefit on person other than child when making order under Guardianship of Minors Act 1971.

K v M [1996] 3 FCR 517; [1996] 1 FLR 312 HC FamD Paternity declaration/contact order refused to putative father who had affair with married woman whose marriage nonetheless survived.

K, B v [1993] 1 FCR 382 HC FamD Expressed desire of older children not to return respected by court: return of younger brother consequently not ordered.

K, Bradford City Metropolitan Council v [1990] Fam 140; [1990] 2 WLR 532 HC FamD Statements of child to teacher/foster parent regarding sexual abuse by family member not part of res gestae and inadmissible in later care proceedings as was hearsay evidence.

K, W v [1988] 1 FLR 86; (1987) 151 JP 589 HC FamD On heavy burden of proof in disproving legitimacy/paternity.

Kane v Littlefair [1985] FLR 859; (1985) 149 JP 312 HC FamD Can make affiliation order against male who was under fourteen years old at time child conceived.

Kauffman, R v (1904) 68 JP 189 CCC On elements of offence of abducting under-eighteen year old girl (Criminal Law Amendment Act 1885, s 7).

Kawas (Bishara Elias) and others, Kawas (Hanna Eissa) v [1943] 2 All ER 530; [1943] AC 532; (1943) WN (I) 160 PC Consent of infants required to action and as could not consent could be no action.

Kawas (Hanna Eissa) v Kawas (Bishara Elias) and others [1943] 2 All ER 530; [1943] AC 532; (1943) WN (I) 160 PC Consent of infants required to action and as could not consent could be no action.

Keech (Herbert Joshua), R v (1928-29) 21 Cr App R 125 CCA Improper that 'reasonable belief that girl over sixteen' defence open on charge of carnal knowledge but not indecent assault (Criminal Law Amendment Act 1922, s 2); no general guidelines on sentencing offenders convicted of underage indecent assault.

Kennedy, JN Nabarro and Sons v [1954] 2 All ER 605; [1955] 1 QB 575; (1954) 98 SJ 524 HC QBD Wife can pledge husband's credit for necessaries in respect of costs of action under Married Women's Property Act 1882, s 17.

Kent County Council and others, F v [1993] 1 FCR 217; [1993] 1 FLR 432; (1992) 136 SJ LB 258; [1992] TLR 394 HC FamD On exercise of discretion to require parties to seek court's leave before making future care/contact application (here wrongly exercised).

Kent County Council v C and another [1993] 1 All ER 719; [1993] Fam 57; [1993] 1 FLR 308; [1992] 3 WLR 808 HC FamD Exceptionally no contact between parent and child may be ordered by family proceedings court in care order but cannot make directions regarding care orders.

Kersey (Maud), R v (1907-09) XXI Cox CC 690 Assizes Murder/concealment of birth conviction not possible/possible on evidence though no dead body.

Khaira and another, Barclays Bank plc v [1993] 1 FLR 343 (also CA); [1992] 1 WLR 623 HC ChD Bank does not normally owe duty of care to person going guarantor on loan to explain entire transaction/ensure have taken impartial advice on what doing.

Khaira and another, Barclays Bank plc v [1993] 1 FLR 343 (also HC ChD) CA Non-party to ChD action not allowed appeal decision that bank does not normally owe duty of care to person going guarantor on loan to explain entire transaction/ensure have taken impartial advice on what doing.

Khalak Singh and others, Gharib-Ul-Lah v (1902-03) XIX TLR 447 PC Guardian of infants property could not be appointed in respect of infant's interest in property of undivided Mitacshara family.

Khan (Raja Mohammad Muntaz Ali) v Ali Khan (Sakhawat) and Ali Khan (Farhat) (1900-01) XVII TLR 587 PC On powers of guardian as regards giving property rather than maintenance.

Kidd, Stafford v [1936] 3 All ER 1023; (1934-39) XXX Cox CC 532; (1937) 101 JP 68; [1937] 1 KB 395; (1937) 83 LJ 26; [1937] 106 LJCL 193; (1937) 156 LTR 75; (1937) 81 SJ 16; (1936-37) LIII TLR 169; (1937) WN (I) 17 HC KBD Separation deed raises presumption of non-access: wife had to prove access by husband.

King's Lynn Justices and another, ex parte M, R v [1988] FCR 436; [1988] 2 FLR 79 HC QBD Presumption of husband's paternity rebutted by admission of paternity from wife's lover (even though birth certificate named husband as father).

Kirklees Metropolitan Borough Council, ex parte C, R v [1992] 2 FCR 321; [1992] 2 FLR 117; [1992] TLR 45 HC QBD Local authority could have child in care admitted to mental hospital.

Kirklees Metropolitan Borough Council, ex parte C, R v [1993] 2 FCR 381; [1993] 2 FLR 187; [1993] TLR 173 CA Local authority could have child in care admitted to mental hospital.

Kirklees Metropolitan Borough Council, G v [1993] 1 FCR 357; [1993] 1 FLR 805 HC FamD Aunt not joined to care proceedings where could not reasonably hope to secure residence order.

Kirklees Metropolitan Council, Y v [1985] FLR 927 HC FamD On making application for access orders.

Knott, Mohamed v [1968] 2 All ER 563; [1968] Crim LR 341t; (1968) 132 JP 349; [1969] 1 QB 1; (1968) 112 SJ 332; [1968] 2 WLR 1446 HC QBD Nigerian Moslem marriage to girl of thirteen valid.

Knowles v Attorney-General [1950] 2 All ER 6; (1950) 100 LJ 288; (1950) 94 SJ 421; [1950] 66 (1) TLR 1188; (1950) WN (I) 288 HC PDAD Cannot obtain legitimation order in respect of one's uncles.

Knowles v Knowles [1962] 1 All ER 659; (1962) 112 LJ 190; (1961) 105 SJ 1011 HC PDAD Post decree nisi (pre decree absolute) conception of child raised presumption of legitimacy.

Krishnan v London Borough of Sutton [1969] 3 All ER 1367; [1970] Ch 181; (1970) 134 JP 75; (1969) 113 SJ 774; [1969] 3 WLR 683 CA Court cannot order local authority to hand child in care to natural parent; harbouring charge unproven.

Kruhlak v Kruhlak [1958] 1 All ER 154; (1958) 122 JP 360; (1958) 108 LJ 122; (1958) 102 SJ 88 HC QBD Judicially separated woman could make application against husband under Bastardy Laws Amendment Act 1872.

Kwee (Khoo Hean), Leong (Khoo Hooi) v [1926] AC 529 PC Son not legitimate under special arrangements concerning secondary wives was not legitimate simply because testator treated him as so.

L and another, Gateshead Metropolitan Borough Council v [1996] 3 All ER 264; [1996] Fam 55; [1996] 3 FCR 582; [1996] 2 FLR 179; [1996] 3 WLR 426 HC FamD On designation of correct local authority in care order.

L and another, L v (1968) 112 SJ 840 CA Blood test of child could be ordered where issue of paternity arose in divorce proceedings and testing was in child's best interests.

L v C [1995] 3 FCR 125 HC FamD Some indirect contact to male-to-female transsexual who had fathered child when a man; general contact application a future possibility.

L v F (1978) 128 NLJ 1000t HC FamD Refusal of order allowing children to be styled by name of stepfather, not natural father.

L v L [1949] 1 All ER 141 HC PDAD Artficial insemination not approbation; no estoppel where other not misled/does not act to detriment; that nullity decree would bastardise child not ground for refusal.

L v L (1966) 110 SJ 484; [1966] 1 WLR 1079 CA Custody of children given to father subject to review of order (whereby children stayed with mother but had great access to father) three months after was made.

L v L (1968) 112 SJ 294 HC PDAD Court could not order blood testing of child in paternity suit between spouses.

L v L (1969) 119 NLJ 81t; (1969) 113 SJ 88; [1969] 2 WLR 326 HC PDAD Wife about to seek divorce granted injunction against husband to prevent latter removing couple's children from jurisdiction.

L v L (1980) 1 FLR 396 HC FamD Better that reasonable access be initially granted and defined access ordered later if initial arrangements a failure.

L v L (1981) 2 FLR 48 CA Custody of child awarded to emotionally unstable mother in preference to abusive father (who had been looking after child).

L v L [1989] FCR 697; [1989] 2 FLR 16 CA Supervised access to father guilty of sex abuse justified as was eventual extended access to grandparents provided they did not raise sex abuse with girl.

L v L [1991] FCR 547 CA Improper dispensing with need for service of access order upon alleged contemnor; on proper procedure as regards dealing with contempt in context of access.

L v L and another (1968) 112 SJ 840 CA Blood test of child could be ordered where issue of paternity arose in divorce proceedings and testing was in child's best interests.

L v London Borough of Bexley [1997] 1 FCR 277; [1996] 2 FLR 595 HC FamD On designating appropriate local authority in care order.

L v M (1956) 120 JP 27 HC QBD Natural father's refusal of consent to adoption (where was motivated by spite against natural mother) unreasonable so adoption allowed.

L, O v [1995] 2 FLR 930 CA On deciding whether to order blood testing (here not ordered).

Lali (Musammat) v Dhar (Murli) (1905-06) XXII TLR 460 PC Deceased's gift to adopted son whose adoption was void had no effect.

Lambeth London Borough Council, ex parte Caddell, R v (1997) 141 SJ LB 147; [1997] TLR 348 HC QBD Failed application for after-care assistance from local authority to whose care had been entrusted before turned eighteen, after which moved to another local authority area.

Lambeth London Borough Council, H v [1984] TLR 213 HC FamD On need for leave of court in respect of all significant decisions taken regarding ward.

Lancashire County Council, Barnsley Corporation v [1956] 3 All ER 671; [1957] 1 QB 123; [1956] 3 WLR 820 HC QBD Cannot appeal against approved school order on basis that child's address unknown.

Lancashire County Council, ex parte M, R v [1992] 1 FLR 109 CA Failed application by fosterers for review of local authority decision to take child from fosterers and place with prospective adopters.

Lancashire Justices, ex parte Tyrer, R v [1924] All ER 304; (1921-25) XXVII Cox CC 711; (1925) 89 JP 17; [1925] 1 KB 200; (1924) 59 LJ 775; [1925] 94 LJCL 331; (1925) 132 LTR 382; (1924-25) 69 SJ 194; (1924-25) XLI TLR 103; (1924) WN (I) 301 HC KBD Need not seek bastardy order in place where customarily/permanently reside.

Laverty and another, Ward v [1924] All ER 319; [1925] AC 101; (1924) 59 LJ 300; [1925] 94 LJPC 17; (1924) 131 LTR 614; (1923-24) 68 SJ 629; (1923-24) XL TLR 600; (1924) WN (I) 177 HL In custody case child's welfare paramount though father's desire as regards religious upbringing a relevant factor.

Lawson and another v Registrar General (1956) 106 LJ ccr204 CyCt Order for discovery of details pertaining to adopted child so that adoptee might be paid legacy left it by godmother.

Laxton and Eaglan, Laxton v [1966] 2 All ER 977 CA Granting custody but delaying care and control order unusual but valid.

Laxton v Laxton and Eaglan [1966] 2 All ER 977 CA Granting custody but delaying care and control order unusual but valid.

Le Mare v Le Mare [1960] 2 All ER 280; (1960) 110 LJ 399; (1960) 104 SJ 450 HC PDAD Unsecured maintenance available for child over twenty-one.

Leather (John Holdsworth), R v (1994) 98 Cr App R 179; [1993] Crim LR 516; [1994] 1 FCR 877; [1993] 2 FLR 770; (1993) 137 SJ LB 54; [1993] TLR 18 CA On what it means to remove child from lawful 'control' (Child Abduction Act 1984, s 2(1))

Lee, R v [1993] 2 All ER 170; [1993] Crim LR 65; (1992) 136 SJ LB 222; [1993] 1 WLR 103 CA Court of Appeal may not impose restriction order where CrCt has decided otherwise save in judicial review.

Leech and Dolleman, Leech v (1972) 116 SJ 274 HC FamD School report desirable (though not given in instant case) when court asked to decide on educational provision for child.

Leech v Leech and Dolleman (1972) 116 SJ 274 HC FamD School report desirable (though not given in instant case) when court asked to decide on educational provision for child.

Leeds City Council v C [1993] 1 FCR 585; [1993] 1 FLR 269 HC FamD On supervision of contact order.

Leeds City Council v West Yorkshire Metropolitan Police and others [1982] 1 All ER 274; [1983] 1 AC 29; (1982) 74 Cr App R 336; (1982) 146 JP 154; [1982] 2 WLR 186 HL Local authority not liable for fines imposed on child in care nor are parents of that child unless local authority temporarily transfers powers of supervision to them.

Leeds City Council, F v [1994] 2 FCR 428; [1994] 2 FLR 60; [1994] TLR 138 CA Final care order made in respect of child at risk from child-mother.

Leeds Justices, ex parte Thompson, R v (1983) 4 FLR 773 HC QBD Would be unusual to exclude relevant evidence at any stage before issue finally determined in case involving child's welfare.

Leicester City Juvenile Justices, ex parte Capenhurst, R v (1985) 149 JP 409; [1984] TLR 764 HC QBD Local authority's report on accommodation available for person of unruly character not binding on court.

Leicester Corporation v Stoke-on-Trent Corporation (1918-21) XXVI Cox CC 377; (1919) 120 LTR 320 HC KBD On place of residence of young offender in breach of probation order.

Leicestershire County Council v G [1995] 1 FCR 205; [1994] 2 FLR 329 HC FamD Interim care order substituted for interim supervision order where child of family suffered non-accidental injury before care proceedings heard.

Leong (Khoo Hooi) v Kwee (Khoo Hean) [1926] AC 529 PC Son not legitimate under special arrangements concerning secondary wives was not legitimate simply because testator treated him as so.

Lester, M v [1966] 1 All ER 207; [1966] 1 WLR 134 HC QBD On damages paid to infants; on Court of Protection.

Lewis v Lewis [1991] 3 All ER 251; [1991] 2 FLR 43 CA Service of access order may only be dispensed with at time order made.

Lewisham Juvenile Court Justices and another, London Borough of Lewisham v [1979] 2 All ER 297; [1980] AC 273; (1979) 143 JP 441; (1979) 129 (1) NLJ 339; (1979) 123 SJ 270; [1979] 2 WLR 513 HL Local authority care not terminated upon request for return by parent but must pass wardship/s 2 resolution.

Lewisham Juvenile Court Justices, Lewisham London Borough Council v (1978) 128 NLJ 1147t CA Child not in care from moment parent who voluntarily placed child in care notifies local authority of withdrawal of consent to same.

Lewisham London Borough Council v Lewisham Juvenile Court Justices (1978) 128 NLJ 1147t CA Child not in care from moment parent who voluntarily placed child in care notifies local authority of withdrawal of consent to same.

Lewisham London Borough Council, ex parte P, R v [1991] 3 All ER 529; [1991] FCR 684; [1991] 2 FLR 185; [1991] TLR 93; [1991] 1 WLR 308 HC QBD Parents/custodians may expect fair treatment from local authority/not to be named as alleged child abusers unless child's interests outweigh effects on alleged abuser and their family.

Lincolnshire Justices, ex parte Brett, R v [1926] All ER 275; (1926) 90 JP 149; [1926] 2 KB 192; [1926] 95 LJCL 827; (1926) 135 LTR 141 CA No bastardy order where no corroboration of complainant's evidence.

Littlefair, Kane v [1985] FLR 859; (1985) 149 JP 312 HC FamD Can make affiliation order against male who was under fourteen years old at time child conceived.

Liverpool City Council and another, A v [1981] 2 All ER 385; [1982] AC 363; (1981) 2 FLR 222; (1981) 145 JP 318; (1981) 131 NLJ 576; (1981) 125 SJ 396; [1981] 2 WLR 948 HL Court can review administrative/not substantive validity of local authority exercising discretionary powers.

Liverpool Society for the Prevention of Cruelty to Children v Jones [1914-15] All ER 1073; (1914-15) XXIV Cox CC 434; (1915) 79 JP 20; [1914] 3 KB 813; (1914) 49 LJ 380; [1915] 84 LJKB 222; (1914-15) 111 LTR 806; (1913-14) 58 SJ 723; (1913-14) XXX TLR 584; (1914) WN (I) 270 HC KBD Possible that putative father could be guilty of wilful neglect of child (contrary to Children Act 1908, s 12).

Londesborough, R v [1968] Crim LR 171 CA Eighteen months' imprisonment for assault occasioning actual bodily harm to three year old (albeit that offender-mother was poor/of low intelligence/badly brought up).

London Borough of Bexley, L v [1997] 1 FCR 277; [1996] 2 FLR 595 HC FamD On designating appropriate local authority in care order.

London Borough of Brent v McLymont and others (1974) 138 JP 699; (1974) 118 SJ 499 HC QBD Not open to justices making compensation orders in respect of boys who committed offences to determine whether boys ought to have been placed in charge and control of parent by local authority who had boys in its care.

London Borough of Lewisham v Lewisham Juvenile Court Justices and another [1979] 2 All ER 297; [1980] AC 273; (1979) 143 JP 441; (1979) 129 (1) NLJ 339; (1979) 123 SJ 270; [1979] 2 WLR 513 HL Local authority care not terminated upon request for return by parent but must pass wardship/s 2 resolution.

London Borough of Lewisham v M and others [1981] 3 All ER 307; (1981) 2 FLR 384; (1981) 131 NLJ 878; [1981] 1 WLR 1248 HC FamD Power to commit care of ward to local authority is unfettered.

London Borough of Newham, ex parte McL, R v [1988] FCR 229 HC FamD Wardship proceedings to be recommended by judge giving leave for judicial review of local authority decision regarding child in its care.

London Borough of Newham,ex parte McL, R v [1988] 1 FLR 416 HC QBD Wardship proceedings to be recommended by judge giving leave if preferable to judicial review of local authority decision/s regarding child in its care.

London Borough of Southwark v B [1993] 2 FLR 559 CA On deciding whether to allow withdrawal of application for care.

London Borough of Sutton, Krishnan v [1969] 3 All ER 1367; [1970] Ch 181; (1970) 134 JP 75; (1969) 113 SJ 774; [1969] 3 WLR 683 CA Court cannot order local authority to hand child in care to natural parent; harbouring charge unproven.

London Borough of Waltham Forest, Wheatley v [1979] 2 All ER 289; [1980] AC 311; (1979) 143 JP 380; (1979) 123 SJ 270; [1979] 2 WLR 543 HC FamD Decision of local authority to assume parental rights over child within 28 days of parent requesting child is valid.

London Borough of Wandsworth, Attorney General ex rel Tilley v [1981] 1 All ER 1162; (1981) 2 FLR 377; [1981] 1 WLR 854 CA Local authority 'assistance' to child includes providing parents accommodation; resolution of authority barring such assistance invalid.

London Borough of Wandsworth, Attorney General ex rel Tilley v [1981] 1 All ER 1162 HC ChD Local authority 'assistance' to child includes providing parents accommodation; resolution of authority barring such assistance invalid.

London County Council v Lord Mayor, Etc, of Birmingham [1924] 1 KB 248; [1924] 93 LJCL 65; (1924) 130 LTR 414; (1923-24) XL TLR 76; (1923) WN (I) 302 HC KBD Liability of local authority for maintenance of child in industrial school depended on place of residence of child when committed larceny, not later breach of probation.

London County Council v Stansell (1934-39) XXX Cox CC 335 HC KBD Parent liable where child in filthy condition is father if parents living together.

London County Council v Wiltshire County Council (1926-30) XXVIII Cox CC 416; (1927) 137 LTR 526; (1926-27) XLIII TLR 563 HC KBD Young offender held to reside in area where committed offence if no contrary evidence.

Lonslow v Hennig (formerly Lonslow) [1986] 2 FLR 378 CA Emigrating mother allowed remove children from jurisdiction (though would minimise husband's contact with children) subject to undertaking to return them if so directed.

Lord Mayor, Aldermen and Citizens of the City of Liverpool, Mayor, Aldermen and Burgesses of the County Borough of South Shields v [1943] 1 All ER 338; (1943) 107 JP 77; [1943] 112 LJ 318; (1943) 168 LTR 238; (1943) WN (I) 31 HC KBD Time for deciding where reside is time of making the order.

Lord Mayor, Etc, of Birmingham, London County Council v [1924] 1 KB 248; [1924] 93 LJCL 65; (1924) 130 LTR 414; (1923-24) XL TLR 76; (1923) WN (I) 302 HC KBD Liability of local authority for maintenance of child in industrial school depended on place of residence of child when committed larceny, not later breach of probation.

Loxton v Russell (1966) 110 SJ 170 CA On proving in affiliation action that had sex at relevant period.

Luck, Re Luck, Walker v [1940] 3 All ER 307; [1940] Ch 864; [1940] 109 LJP 380; (1941) 164 LTR 172; (1940) WN (I) 257 CA Non-recognition of foreign decree recognising putative father as father where in place of domicile at child's birth was not so recognised.

Lumley, R v (1911-13) XXII Cox CC 635; (1912) 76 JP 208 CCC Abortionist guilty of murder/manslaughter if did/did not (nor could not reasonably) consider that death or grievous bodily harm would result from actions.

Lynas [1997] 1 FCR 220, Brixey v [1996] 2 FLR 499 HL On whether custody of young child to be given (as here was) to young mother.

M (C), M (P) v (1971) 115 SJ 444 CA Father refused access to children as was upsetting them/not in their best interests.

M (D) v M (S) and G (M (DA) intervening) [1969] 2 All ER 243; [1969] 1 WLR 843 CA No blood test as not in child's interest/merely to prove wife's adultery.

M (P) v M (C) (1971) 115 SJ 444 CA Father refused access to children as was upsetting them/not in their best interests.

M (S) and G (M (DA) intervening), M (D) v [1969] 2 All ER 243; [1969] 1 WLR 843 CA No blood test as not in child's interest/merely to prove wife's adultery.

M (SE) v M (SV) [1965] 3 All ER 656 HC PDAD If guardian ad litem can be appointed need not be unless in interests of infant.

M (SV), M (SE) v [1965] 3 All ER 656 HC PDAD If guardian ad litem can be appointed need not be unless in interests of infant.

M and another v Wigan Metropolitan Borough Council [1979] 2 All ER 958; [1980] Fam 36; (1980) 1 FLR 45; [1979] 3 WLR 244 HC FamD Parental obligations wider than financial maintenance; consistent failure is not persistent failure; failure tested objectively.

M and G, M v (1962) 106 SJ 877 HC PDAD Guilt/innocence of parties as regards marriage break-up here deemed irrelevant to determination of custody issue.

M and M, The Ontario Court v [1997] 2 FCR 573; [1997] 1 FLR 475 HC FamD Neither of two children returned to custody of grandmother in Canada (from that of parents in England) as one child faced grave risk of being placed in intolerable situation if returned.

M and others, London Borough of Lewisham v [1981] 3 All ER 307; (1981) 2 FLR 384; (1981) 131 NLJ 878; [1981] 1 WLR 1248 HC FamD Power to commit care of ward to local authority is unfettered.

M and others, M v (1968) 112 SJ 840 CA Refusal of blood test where ran risk of bastardising child and revealing mother to be liar without actually discovering who the real father was.

M and Walsall Metropolitan Borough Council, A v [1994] 1 FCR 606; [1993] 2 FLR 244 HC FamD On deciding interim care cases.

M v Berkshire County Council [1985] FLR 257 CA On power of juvenile court to order access.

M v Birmingham City Council [1995] 1 FCR 50; [1994] 2 FLR 141 HC FamD Depended on case whether historical/current/future extent of parental control to be used as basis for determining if child beyond such control/care order merited.

M v C [1993] 1 FCR 264; [1993] 2 FLR 584 HC FamD On (ex parte) granting of residence orders; on need to give reasons inter alia for not adopting course advocated by court welfare officer.

M v C and Calderdale Metropolitan Borough Council [1993] 1 FCR 431; [1993] 1 FLR 505 CA In Children Act 1989 'parent' includes father of illegitimate child but that status lost post-freeing order after which could not seek residence order.

M v C and Calderdale Metropolitan Borough Council [1992] 2 FCR 141 HC FamD Leave of court required before natural father of adopted illegitimate child could seek residence order.

M v H and others [1988] 3 All ER 5 HL Courts have jurisdiction to hear custody/access application by parent against third party but statutorily precluded from doing so.

M v Humberside County Council and another [1979] 2 All ER 744; [1979] Fam 114; (1980) 1 FLR 91; [1979] 3 WLR 234 HC FamD If lower court empowered High Court will only intervene if unusual case; local authority acting outside powers; lower court powers inadequate.

M v J (1977) 127 NLJ 1130t; (1977) 121 SJ 759 HC FamD Successful appeal by alcoholic, unstable father against refusal of application in which sought order for access to own child.

M v J (1982) 3 FLR 19 HC FamD Father properly refused access to his illegitimate child where access could jeopardise child's welfare.

M v Lester [1966] 1 All ER 207; [1966] 1 WLR 134 HC QBD On damages paid to infants; on Court of Protection.

M v M (1905-06) XXII TLR 325 HC PDAD Custody of two children to petitioner (though one born before marriage and petitioner was not father of same).

M v M (1968) 118 NLJ 1005t CA Blood test only ordered where is in child's interest (not ordered here).

M v M [1973] 2 All ER 81 HC FamD Child's interests usually demand some access to adoptive/natural parent.

M v M (1980) 1 FLR 77 CA Problems regarding access not good ground on which to remove custody of young child from mother.

M v M (1980) 1 FLR 327 CA Care order invalid as local authority/mother not heard on matter.

M v M (1981) 2 FLR 39 CA Father's occasional behaviour towards child as though were own did not render child 'child of the family'; parties not 'family' after separation.

M v M (1983) 4 FLR 603 CA Children 'kidnapped' by mother returned to Italian father as their long-term interests demanded it (mother a hard-drinking liar).

M v M [1988] FCR 260; [1988] 1 FLR 225 CA Custody decisions to be based on findings of fact (where facts controverted); cannot make ouster order under domestic violence legislation where parties not living together as man and wife.

M v M [1988] FCR 39; [1987] 2 FLR 146; [1987] 1 WLR 404 CA Custody, care and control of twelve year old girl entrusted to father in light inter alia of girl's vehement objections to being returned to mother.

M v M [1990] FCR 80; [1989] 2 FLR 354 CA On when up-to-date welfare officer's report needed by CA; on role of such a report.

M v M [1993] 1 FCR 5; [1992] 2 FLR 303; [1992] TLR 398 CA On need to take into account views of children before deciding whether to allow custodial parent remove them from the jurisdiction.

M v M [1997] 2 FLR 263 CA Successful appeal against judge's finding as to habitual residence: on habitual residence.

M v M and G (1962) 106 SJ 877 HC PDAD Guilt/innocence of parties as regards marriage break-up here deemed irrelevant to determination of custody issue.

M v M and others (1968) 112 SJ 840 CA Refusal of blood test where ran risk of bastardising child and revealing mother to be liar without actually discovering who the real father was.

M v Warwickshire County Council [1994] 2 FCR 121; [1994] 2 FLR 593 HC FamD Six-month supervision order made.

M v Westminster City Council [1985] FLR 325; [1984] TLR 453 HC FamD On making care orders where proper development of child 'is' beng impaired/neglected.

M, B v [1990] FCR 581; [1990] 2 FLR 46 CA On disclosure of welfare reports.

M, B v [1994] 1 FCR 769; [1994] 1 FLR 342 CyCt On revocation (during transitional period of Child Support Act 1991) of child maintenance order prior to application to Child Support Agency for child maintenance assessment.

M, Buckinghamshire County Council v [1994] 1 FCR 859; [1994] 2 FLR 506 CA Interim care order made in respect of child where full care order refused (siblings already subject to interim care orders).

M, Cheshire County Council v [1992] 2 FCR 817; [1993] 1 FLR 463 HC FamD Father who successfully appealed conviction for child sex abuse to which had confessed denied contact order.

M, K v [1996] 3 FCR 517; [1996] 1 FLR 312 HC FamD Paternity declaration/contact order refused to putative father who had affair with married woman whose marriage nonetheless survived.

M, L v (1956) 120 JP 27 HC QBD Natural father's refusal of consent to adoption (where was motivated by spite against natural mother) unreasonable so adoption allowed.

M, S v [1997] 1 FLR 980 HL Hearsay evidence of child as to alleged assaults upon him by father validly taken into account when deciding that access to child by father not in child's best interests.

M, Wolverhampton Metropolitan Borough Council v [1988] FCR 629 HC FamD Child taken from mentally handicapped parents unable to care for him and placed in care with view to adoption (parental access terminated).

MacDarmaid v Attorney-General [1950] 1 All ER 497; (1950) 100 LJ 118; (1950) 94 SJ 211; [1950] 66 (1) TLR 543; (1950) WN (I) 104 HC PDAD Failed petition for legitimacy declaration where petitioner failed to prove father's first wife died before before petitioner's birth.

Mahon, Townson v [1984] FLR 690 CA Custody order valid though judge overstressed importance of child being placed in mother's custody.

Malcolm, Marshall v [1916-17] All ER 365; (1918-21) XXVI Cox CC 129; (1918) 82 JP 77; [1918] 87 LJCL 491; (1917-18) 117 LTR 752 HC KBD Woman living apart from husband on active service not single woman.

Manchester City Council v B [1996] 1 FLR 324 HC FamD On burden/standard of proof in care action springing from non-accidental injuries to child.

Manchester City Council v R [1996] 3 FCR 118 HC FamD Supervision order in favour of parents who seemed likely to have occasioned subdural haematoma to child on one occasion (probably by shaking/flinging child down) but were otherwise satisfactory parents.

Manchester City Magistrates' Court, ex parte Bannister, R v (1983) 4 FLR 717; (1983) 147 JP 516; (1983) 127 SJ 285; [1983] TLR 179 HC QBD Actual place of residence of child is basis on which decide in name of which council care order to be made.

Markham, ex parte Marsh, R v (1923) WN (I) 112 HC KBD Court would not re-hear paternity suit under guise of action for writ of certiorari.

Marks (Louis Marks, Claimant), Rondeau, Legrand and Co v [1917] 2 KB 636; [1918] 87 LJCL 215 (also CA); (1916-17) 61 SJ 666; (1916-17) XXXIII TLR 529; (1917) WN (I) 268 HC KBD Husband must provide wife with necessary clothes but need not give them to her.

Marks, Rondeau, Legrand and Co v [1916-17] All ER 664; [1918] 1 KB 75; (1917) 52 LJ 378; [1918] 87 LJCL 215 (also HC KBD); (1917-18) 117 LTR 651; (1917-18) 62 SJ 24; (1917-18) XXXIV TLR 8; (1917) WN (I) 298 CA Husband must provide wife with necessary clothes but need not give them to her.

Marsh (Percy Harold), R v (1925-26) 19 Cr App R 27 CCA Accused's silence/keeping of letter sent by prosecutrix not corroborative of latter's claim in sexual offence case.

Marsh (Ronald William Frank), R v (1948-49) 33 Cr App R 185 CCA Evidence of previous confession of guilt/sentencing for indecent assault on child admissible in later charge for carnal knowledge of same child.

Marsh and another v Hodgson [1974] Crim LR 35 CA Parents found jointly liable for unexplained injuries to their infant child.

Marsh, Barnsley v (1947) 111 JP 363; (1947) 177 LTR 573; (1947) 91 SJ 561; (1947) LXIII TLR 399; (1947) WN (I) 159 HC KBD On procedure in bastardy proceedings.

Marshall v Malcolm [1916-17] All ER 365; (1918-21) XXVI Cox CC 129; (1918) 82 JP 77; [1918] 87 LJCL 491; (1917-18) 117 LTR 752 HC KBD Woman living apart from husband on active service not single woman.

Massey v Massey (1918) CC Rep VII 90 CyCt Cannot assign guardianship.

Mathieson v Napier and Wife [1918] 87 LJCh 445; (1918-19) 119 LTR 18 CA Child's best interests superior to father's right to custody.

Matthews, Brown v [1990] 2 All ER 155; [1990] Ch 662; [1990] 2 WLR 879 CA Court welfare officer's report may be disclosed in later case if necessary for fair trial.

Maturin (by her Guardian) v Attorney-General (Maturin and Stone by her Guardian cited) [1938] 2 All ER 214; (1938) 82 SJ 275; (1937-38) LIV TLR 627; (1938) WN (I) 135 HC PDAD Petitioning for divorce adequate evidence of non-access.

Maughan (Reginald), R v (1932-34) 24 Cr App R 130 CCA Not defence to charge of indecent assault on under-sixteen year old that genuinely believed was over sixteen.

May v May [1986] 1 FLR 325 CA Joint custody (care and control to father) where both parents equally suitable (notwithstanding mother's adultery).

May, Smith v (1969) 113 SJ 1000 HC QBD Child found not to be child of marriage on basis of complainant's evidence.

Maynard v Maynard [1984] FLR 85 CA Court could (and here in interim custody application did) hear party in contempt.

Mayor, Aldermen and Burgesses of the County Borough of South Shields v Lord Mayor, Aldermen and Citizens of the City of Liverpool [1943] 1 All ER 338; (1943) 107 JP 77; [1943] 112 LJ 318; (1943) 168 LTR 238; (1943) WN (I) 31 HC KBD Time for deciding where reside is time of making the order.

Mayor, Aldermen and Citizens of Coventry v Surrey County Council [1934] 1 KB 211 CA Adopted illegitimate child did not acquire settlement of place in which adopted father had resided (and from which was irremovable).

Mayor, Aldermen and Citizens of Coventry v Surrey County Council [1935] AC 199 HL Adopted child not removeable to place of settlement of natural mother.

McC (formerly S) and M (S intervening), S v [1970] 1 All ER 1162; (1970) 120 NLJ 153t; (1970) 114 SJ 131; [1970] 1 WLR 672 CA Child's best interests relevant in determining if blood test to be required.

McGregor v Telford [1914-15] All ER 209; (1915-17) XXV Cox CC 1; (1915) 79 JP 485; [1915] 3 KB 237; [1915] 84 LJKB 1902; (1915-16) 113 LTR 84; (1914-15) XXXI TLR 512; (1915) WN (I) 258 HC KBD Justices can re-hear affiliation order application.

McInerney, Smith v [1994] 2 FCR 1086; [1994] 2 FLR 1077 HC FamD Variation of liabilities under separation agreement where husband had been made redundant/was likely to be subject of Child Support Agency assessment.

McK (formerly P), P v (1973) 123 NLJ 632t CA Generally custody of young children to be given (as here) to mother.

McKee v McKee [1951] 1 All ER 942; [1951] AC 352; (1951) 95 SJ 316; [1951] 1 TLR 755; (1951) WN (I) 186 PC Infant's interests paramount in custody case irrespective of foreign court order.

McKernan v McKernan (1970) 114 SJ 284 HC PDAD Must be fairly permanent arrangements in respect of children before court (in divorce action) can declare itself to be satisfied.

McLymont and others, London Borough of Brent v (1974) 138 JP 699; (1974) 118 SJ 499 HC QBD Not open to justices making compensation orders in respect of boys who committed offences to determine whether boys ought to have been placed in charge and control of parent by local authority who had boys in its care

McVeigh v Beattie [1988] 2 All ER 500; [1988] Fam 69; [1988] FCR 516; [1988] 2 FLR 67; (1988) 132 SJ 125; [1988] 2 WLR 992 HC FamD Absent reasonable excuse refusal to provide blood sample corroborates claim of parenthood.

Meaney v Meaney [1957] 2 All ER 415; (1957) 107 LJ 362; (1957) 101 SJ 482 HC PDAD On jurisdiction of different magistrates' courts to vary/discharge maintenance orders.

Mellery-Pratt v Attorney-General (1969) 113 SJ 656 HC PDAD Rebuttal of presumption of legitimacy must be done beyond reasonable doubt.

Merton London Borough, JR v [1992] 2 FCR 174 (also HC FamD) CA On granting leave to foster parent to seek residence order (here refused).

Merton London Borough, JR v [1992] 2 FCR 174 (also CA) HC FamD On granting leave to foster parent to seek residence order (here allowed).

Merton London Borough, S v [1994] 1 FCR 186 HC FamD Improper to make interim care orders absent any evidence in controverted application.

Meyer v Meyer [1957] 2 All ER 546; (1957) 121 JP 424; (1957) 107 LJ 442; (1957) 101 SJ 630 HC PDAD Justices can ante-date maintenance order.

Michael v Gowland [1977] 2 All ER 328; (1976) 120 SJ 857 HC FamD Time limit for stating case is peremptory.

Middlesex Justices, ex parte Bond, R v (1931-34) XXIX Cox CC 563; (1932) 96 JP 487; [1933] 1 KB 72; (1933) 102 LJCL 40; (1933) 148 LTR 134; (1932-33) XLIX TLR 18; (1932) WN (I) 212 HC KBD Custody order bad as in matter that was res judicata.

Millard and Addis, Millard v [1945] 2 All ER 525 HC PDAD Parenthood not legitimacy is the prerequisite for custody applications; illegitimate child need not be legitimised brfore custody order possible.

Millard v Millard and Addis [1945] 2 All ER 525 HC PDAD Parenthood not legitimacy is the prerequisite for custody applications; illegitimate child need not be legitimised brfore custody order possible.

Millard v Millard and Addis [1945] 2 All ER 525 HC PDAD Parenthood not legitimacy is the Miller, Sheppard v (1982) 3 FLR 124; (1981) 131 NLJ 1236 CA Access to father denied where was upsetting child.

Milne v D (1983) 133 NLJ 785c CA On appropriate manner in which to resolve custody actions.

Milne, Dicocco v (1983) 4 FLR 247 HC FamD (also CA) On relevant concerns when determining custody action.

Milne, Dicocco v (1983) 4 FLR 247 CA (also HC FamD) On relevant concerns when determining custody action.

Milton Keynes Juvenile Court, ex parte Russell, R v (1979) 143 JP 373; [1979] 1 WLR 1062 HC QBD Parent could be allowed by magistrates to cross-examine witnesses for local authority in care action.

Mirror Group Newspapers Ltd, Essex County Council v [1996] 2 FCR 831; [1996] 1 FLR 585 HC FamD Local authority refused order requiring newspaper to disclose matters pertaining to article on child care case (publication not breaching publicity prohibition).

Mitchell, National Assistance Board v [1955] 3 All ER 291; [1955] Crim LR 567; (1955) 119 JP 572; (1955) 105 LJ 697; [1956] 1 QB 53; (1955) 99 SJ 781; [1955] 3 WLR 591 HC QBD National Assistance Board could make bastardy order application inside three years of last pay-out.

Mnguni v Mnguni (1980) 1 FLR 184; (1979) 123 SJ 859 CA Improper that court should decide access application in such a way that resolution of matter essentially left to welfare officer.

Mohamed v Knott [1968] 2 All ER 563; [1968] Crim LR 341t; (1968) 132 JP 349; [1969] 1 QB 1; (1968) 112 SJ 332; [1968] 2 WLR 1446 HC QBD Nigerian Moslem marriage to girl of thirteen valid.

Monaco v Monaco (1937) 157 LTR 231 HC ChD Reigning Prince of Monaco granted custody of grandson and injunction restraining former son-in-law from moving same from United Kingdom (where was studying).

Moon (Frederick), R v; R v Moon (Emily) (1910) 4 Cr App R 171; [1910] 1 KB 818; (1910) 45 LJ 221; (1910) 79 LJKB 505 CCA Not offence under Children Act 1908, s 17 to encourage seduction of girl already seduced.

Mooney v Mooney [1952] 2 All ER 812; (1952) 116 JP 608; (1952) 102 LJ 625; [1953] 1 QB 38; (1952) 96 SJ 730; [1952] 2 TLR 711; (1952) WN (I) 488 HC QBD Wife living separately from husband not a single woman under Bastardy Laws Amendment Act 1872, s 3.

Moore v Ball [1984] 2 All ER 237; [1984] Fam 41; [1984] FLR 555; (1984) 148 JP 425; (1984) 128 SJ 298; [1984] 2 WLR 865 HC FamD Secretary of State can have varied maintenance order payable to Secretary increased by variation.

Moore v Hewitt [1947] 2 All ER 270; (1947) 111 JP 483; [1947] KB 831; (1947) 97 LJ 389; [1947] 116 LJR 1276; (1947) 177 LTR 576; (1947) LXIII TLR 476; (1947) WN (I) 224 HC KBD Close relationship of woman with putative father (and no other) corroborative of mother's claim.

Moore v Moore (1982) 132 NLJ 488 CA Custody of children to mother (wife of Army corporal) who would not have to leave camp until suitable council accommodation obtained.

Morgan, James v (1909) 73 JP 149; [1909] 1 KB 564; [1909] 78 LJKB 471; (1909) C LTR 238; (1908-09) 53 SJ 245; (1908-09) XXV TLR 267; (1909) WN (I) 31 HC KBD Father's agreement to maintain bastard child ended upon mother's death.

Morley, Bates v (1982) 3 FLR 244; (1982) 132 NLJ 65 CA Mother with care and control of ward (father had access) allowed remove child to Canada (wardship ending upon ward quitting country).

Morris, Davis v (1922-23) XXXIX TLR 454; (1923) WN (I) 139 HC KBD On elements of defence of medical supervision where charged with acting as uncertified midwife (Midwives Act 1902, s 1(2)).

Morris, Pountney v [1984] FLR 381; (1984) 134 NLJ 863c CA Children's welfare paramount consideration in custody cases.

Morton, Reffell v (1906) 70 JP 347; (1905-06) 50 SJ 378 HC KBD On what for purposes of Bastardy Laws Amendment Act 1872, s 4, constitutes corrobortion of mother's evidence as to paternity of illegitimate child.

Motala and others v Attorney-General and others [1990] 2 FLR 261 HC FamD Legitimacy declaration in respect of persons born of marriage not recognised/recognised where celebrated/ where domiciled.

Mousir, R v [1987] Crim LR 561 CA On what is meant by removing child from 'lawful control' for purposes of Child Abduction Act 1984.

Mozley-Stark and Hitchins, Mozley-Stark v [1908-10] All ER 643; [1910] 79 LJP 98; (1909-10) 101 LTR 770; (1909-10) XXVI TLR 194 CA Non committal in circumstances for contempt of custody order.

Mozley-Stark v Mozley-Stark and Hitchins [1908-10] All ER 643; [1910] 79 LJP 98; (1909-10) 101 LTR 770; (1909-10) XXVI TLR 194 CA Non committal in circumstances for contempt of custody order.

Mundul v Mundul (1968) 112 SJ 93 HC PDAD Inappropriate that when access issue pending before HC it should be encumbered with previous decision of divisional court on the matter.

Murrel, Webb v (1904) 68 JP 104 Police Ct Separated married woman can obtain affiliation order against natural father of her illegitimate child as a 'single woman' (Bastardy Laws Amendment Act 1882, s 3).

N (S) v T (S) [1994] 3 FCR 229; [1995] 1 FLR 868 HC FamD Rehearing ordered of justices' refusal to remit arrears as approach to deciding case had been defective.

N and others, Croydon London Borough v [1987] FCR 129; [1987] 2 FLR 61 HC FamD Wrong to treat Children and Young Pesons Act 1969, s 1(2)(bb) as a preliminary matter in care action (and so require preliminary proof that likely that person convicted as criminal would become member of children's household).

N v B [1993] 1 FCR 231 HC FamD Shared residence order (so that could acquire parental responsibility) refused; leave to remove remove children from jurisdiction refused.

N v Birmingham District Council (1984) 148 JP 700; (1984) 128 SJ 447 HC FamD 'Household' determined by reference to circumstances; can be in same 'household' though not in same place.

N v C-H [1982] TLR 484 CA On limited role of CA in appeals against custody decisions.

N v N [1995] 1 FCR 595; [1995] 1 FLR 107 HC FamD Return ordered in case where psychological risk to children in return/non-return considerable.

N, A v [1997] 2 FCR 475; [1997] 1 FLR 533 CA Committal of mother to prison for persistent non-compliance with contact order was valid — child's welfare not paramount concern in such cases.

N, Avon County Council v [1996] 1 FCR 252 HC FamD Care of children refused to mother even though might have decided otherwise had local authority conducted itself properly thus necessitating instant decision.

N, Gateshead Metropolitan Borough Council v [1993] 1 FCR 400; [1993] 1 FLR 811 HC FamD On duration of first/successive interim care order/s.

N, H v [1990] TLR 36 HC FamD Mother with interim custody order in respect of Canadian child did not have right to remove child from country of residence (Canada).

N, P v [1997] 2 FCR 65 CyCt Residence order made precluding mother from changing child's surname (that of father) but enabling use of double-barrelled surname (names of father and mother).

Nabarro (JN) and Sons v Kennedy [1954] 2 All ER 605; [1955] 1 QB 575; (1954) 98 SJ 524 HC QBD Wife can pledge husband's credit for necessaries in respect of costs of action under Married Women's Property Act 1882, s 17.

Napier and Wife, Mathieson v [1918] 87 LJCh 445; (1918-19) 119 LTR 18 CA Child's best interests superior to father's right to custody.

Nash v Inman [1908] 2 KB 1; [1908] 77 LJCL 626; (1908) XCVIII LTR 658; (1907-08) XXIV TLR 401 CA In suing infant for necessaries must show were apposite to infant's state in life and that infant had inadequate supply of said goods when supplied.

Nash v Nash [1973] 2 All ER 704 CA No restraint on parental custodian pursuing career of her choice.

National Assistance Board v Mitchell [1955] 3 All ER 291; [1955] Crim LR 567; (1955) 119 JP 572; (1955) 105 LJ 697; [1956] 1 QB 53; (1955) 99 SJ 781; [1955] 3 WLR 591 HC QBD National Assistance Board could make bastardy order application inside three years of last pay-out.

National Assistance Board v Tugby [1957] 1 All ER 509; (1957) 121 JP 149; (1957) 107 LJ 171; [1957] 1 QB 506; (1957) 101 SJ 172; [1957] 2 WLR 316 HC QBD National Assistance Board can seek bastardy order without proving mother single woman.

National Assistance Board, Clapham v [1961] 2 All ER 50; (1961) 125 JP 373; (1961) 111 LJ 306; [1961] 2 QB 77; (1961) 105 SJ 234 HC QBD National Assistance Board may seek/obtain affiliation order despite mother's earlier failed attempt.

National Assistance Board, Oldfield v [1960] 1 All ER 524; (1960) 124 JP 246; (1960) 110 LJ 190; [1960] 1 QB 635; (1960) 104 SJ 169 HC QBD Affiliation order to be such must require payment of money.

New and Wife, R v (1903-04) XX TLR 515 HC KBD Court will pay close consideration to but need not accede to illegitimate child's mother desires as to custody of child.

New and Wife, R v (1903-04) XX TLR 583 CA Court will pay close consideration to but need not accede to illegitimate child's mother desires as to custody of child.

Newbould v Attorney-General [1931] All ER 377; (1931) 71 LJ 205; (1931) 100 LJP 54; (1931) 144 LTR 728; (1931) 75 SJ 174; (1930-31) XLVII TLR 297; (1931) WN (I) 70 HC PDAD Marriage of illegitimate child's parents (following nullification of father's first marriage) legitimated child.

Newcastle Emlyn Justices and another, ex parte Evans, R v (1963) 107 SJ 416 HC QBD QBD could not decide whether fraud perpetrated on lower court where was conflicting evidence.

Newcastle-upon-Tyne Council, ex parte S and T, R v [1988] FCR 159; [1988] 1 FLR 535 HC QBD On making order that guardians ad litem be appointed to represent children (on basis that conflict between their interests and that of parents).

Newcombe, Hunt v (1983) 4 FLR 482 CA Change in custody after more than seven years with one custodial parent justified; interviews with children a discretionary matter for judge.

Newham London Borough Council and another, S v [1991] FCR 749; [1991] TLR 256 HC FamD Non-physical access could be ordered.

Newham London Borough Council v AG [1992] 2 FCR 119; [1993] 1 FLR 281 CA On chances of significant harm to child which merit granting of care order.

Newham London Borough Council v I and Brent London Borough Council [1997] 2 FCR 629 HC FamD On determining designated care authority in care proceedings where children in interim local accommodation care of one authority and mother had since moved to area of another local authority.

Newham London Borough Council, ex parte P, R v [1990] 2 All ER 19; [1990] FCR 601; [1990] 1 FLR 404; (1990) 134 SJ 833; [1990] 1 WLR 482 HC QBD Local authority need not make pre-placement inquiries where stay for brief period as does not transfer charge or control.

Nikolaisen, Watson and another v [1955] 2 All ER 427; (1955) 119 JP 419; (1955) 105 LJ 346; [1955] 2 QB 286; (1955) 99 SJ 370; [1955] 2 WLR 1187 HC QBD Not abandonment of child to give over to people whom trust.

Norfolk County Council, ex parte M, R v [1989] 2 All ER 359; [1989] FCR 667; [1989] QB 619; (1989) 133 SJ 1089 HC QBD Style of child abuse register by local authority and means of registration contrary to natural justice/open to judicial review.

Norfolk County Council, ex parte X, R v [1989] 2 FLR 120 HC QBD Placing of person on child abuse register was open to judicial review: registering decision quashed.

Norfolk County Council, H v [1997] 1 FLR 384 CA Local authority not liable for (alleged) abuse suffered by onetime child in its care placed with foster parents.

Norman v Norman [1950] 1 All ER 1082; (1950) 114 JP 299; (1950) 100 LJ 259; (1950) 94 SJ 354; [1950] 66 (1) TLR 1044; (1950) WN (I) 230 HC PDAD Can be extension of expired maintenance order.

Norman, Bowen v [1938] 2 All ER 776; (1934-39) XXX Cox CC 674; (1938) 102 JP 123; [1938] 1 KB 689; (1938) 85 LJ 396; [1938] 107 LJCL 273; (1938) 158 LTR 257; (1938) 82 SJ 77; (1937-38) LIV TLR 342; (1938) WN (I) 41 HC KBD Maintenance order per se did not establish non-access.

North Yorkshire County Council v G [1994] 1 FCR 737; [1993] 2 FLR 732 HC FamD Child's welfare not paramount interest in residence action; brother not allowed become party to action concerning other brother where sought to help mother with little English.

North Yorkshire County Council, ex parte M (No 2), R v [1989] FCR 394; [1989] 2 FLR 79 HC QBD On role of guardian ad litem vis-à-vis local authority as regards adoption of child.

North Yorkshire County Council, ex parte M (No 3), R v [1989] FCR 403; [1989] 2 FLR 82 HC QBD On possibility of post-judicial review invocation of wardship jurisdiction.

North Yorkshire County Council, ex parte M, R v [1989] 1 All ER 143; [1989] FCR 128; [1989] 1 FLR 203; [1989] QB 411; (1988) 132 SJ 1731; [1988] 3 WLR 1344 HC QBD Local authority must inform guardian ad litem/hear guardian's views about any major changes to circumstances of child in care.

Northamptonshire County Council v C [1988] FCR 378 HC QBD No need for child to attend court each time application for extension of interim care order heard.

Northamptonshire County Council v H [1988] 1 All ER 598; [1988] 1 FLR 529; [1988] QB 205; (1988) 132 SJ 263; [1988] 2 WLR 389 HC QBD Additional interim care orders may be made in absence of child over 5 years old if legally represented.

Northamptonshire County Council v S and others [1993] Fam 136; [1993] 1 FCR 351; [1993] 1 FLR 554; [1992] 3 WLR 1010 HC FamD Construction of Children Act 1989, s 31(2) (a): on making care order on basis that child is presently suffering 'significant harm'.

Nottingham County Council v P [1994] Fam 18 (also CA); [1993] 1 FCR 180; [1993] 1 FLR 514; [1992] TLR 519; [1993] 2 WLR 406 HC FamD Prohibited steps order not to be used to same end as contact or residence order.

Nottinghamshire County Council and another, W v [1986] 1 FLR 565 CA Court will not allow third party to invoke wardship jurisdiction of court where local authority seeking replacement of care orders with supervision orders.

Nottinghamshire County Council v H [1995] 1 FLR 115; [1995] 2 FCR 365 HC FamD Crown Prosecution Service ordered to disclose documents to local authority alone (local authority in course of care proceedings).

Nottinghamshire County Council v P; Re P [1993] 3 All ER 815; [1994] Fam 18 (also HC FamD); [1994] 1 FCR 624; [1993] 2 FLR 134; (1993) 137 SJ LB 147; [1993] TLR 213; [1993] 3 WLR 637 CA Prohibited steps order not to be used to same end as contact or residence order.

Nottinghamshire County Council v Q [1982] 2 All ER 641; [1982] Fam 94; (1982) 3 FLR 305; (1982) 126 SJ 309; [1982] 2 WLR 954 HC FamD Appeals against place of safety order under Children and Young Persons Act 1969, s 28, an abuse of process.

Nottinghamshire County Council, R v [1993] 1 FCR 576 HC FamD Failed appeal against decision of family proceedings court in care action to allow local authority extra time to file evidence.

Nottinghamshire County Council, W v [1982] 1 All ER 1; [1982] Fam 53; (1982) 3 FLR 33 (also HC FamD); (1981) 125 SJ 761; [1981] 3 WLR 959 CA No voluntary or involuntary care, merely care; local authority need not rely on same grounds in extending resolution as when first making it.

Nottinghamshire County Council, W v (1982) 3 FLR 33 (also CA) HC FamD Mother was not failing to discharge parental obligations; local authority not to rely on same grounds in extending resolution as when first making it.

Nowell v Nowell [1951] 1 All ER 474; (1951) 115 JP 162; (1951) 101 LJ 119; (1951) 95 SJ 270; [1951] 1 TLR 647; (1951) WN (I) 167 HC PDAD On continuation of maintenance orders: test inerests of child/financial status of parties.

NSPCC and another, E v [1990] FCR 609; [1990] 2 FLR 379 HC QBD On interim care hearings.

NSPCC v H and H [1989] FCR 544; [1989] 2 FLR 131 CA On invocation of wardship jurisdiction of HC where is overlapping care action before juvenile court.

O v L [1995] 2 FLR 930 CA On deciding whether to order blood testing (here not ordered).

O'Connor and another v A and B [1971] 2 All ER 1230; (1971) 135 JP 492; (1971) 115 SJ 586; [1971] 1 WLR 1227 HL Must balance child's welfare against parent's ability to raise child (and time lapse before appeal) in deciding if consent unreasonably withheld.

O'Dare v South Glamorgan County Council (1982) 3 FLR 1 HC FamD On what was meant by 'failed without reasonable cause to discharge the obligations of a parent'.

O'Dea v Tetau [1950] 2 All ER 695; (1950) 114 JP 499; [1951] 1 KB 184; (1950) 100 LJ 455; (1950) 94 SJ 505; [1950] 66(2) TLR 339; (1950) WN (I) 447 HC KBD Cannot make affiliation order in respect of child born abroad of mother with foreign domicile.

O'Donoghue, R v (1926-30) XXVIII Cox CC 461; (1927) 91 JP 199; (1927) 64 LJ 378; (1928) 97 LJCL 303; (1928) 138 LTR 240; (1927) 71 SJ 897; (1927) WN (I) 289/297 CCA Verdict of infanticide unavailable as child not newborn/over one month old.

O, S v (1982) 3 FLR 15 HC FamD Father properly awarded access to his illegitimate child.

Oakey v Jackson [1911-13] All ER 681; (1913-14) XXIII Cox CC 734; (1914) 78 JP 87; [1914] 1 KB 216; [1914] 83 LJKB 712; (1914) 110 LTR 41; (1913-14) XXX TLR 92 HC KBD Father preventing surgical operation on child for no good reason could be charged with wilful neglect.

Official Solicitor v K and another [1963] 3 All ER 191; (1963) 113 LJ 577; (1963) 107 SJ 616 HL No-one has absolute right to see Official Solicitor's confidential reports but reports only to be so given if in ward's interests.

Oldfield v National Assistance Board [1960] 1 All ER 524; (1960) 124 JP 246; (1960) 110 LJ 190; [1960] 1 QB 635; (1960) 104 SJ 169 HC QBD Affiliation order to be such must require payment of money.

Oldham Metropolitan Borough Council v E and others [1994] 1 FLR 568; [1994] TLR 150 CA On approach to be adopted where aunt seeking residence order in respect of child whom local authority wish to have adopted (all parties agreeing mother unsuitable carer).

Orford v Orford (1980) 1 FLR 260 CA Court itself to decide access — improper that be left to welfare officer.

Osborn v Sparks (1982) 3 FLR 90 HC FamD On balancing procedure to be exercised when assessing financial provision to be made by father in respect of illegitimate child and its mother.

Over v Harwood (1899-1900) XVI TLR 163; (1899-1900) 48 WR 608 HC QBD On burden of proof where person charged with disobedience of order to have child vaccinated.

Owen (Charles William), R v (1988) 86 Cr App R 291; [1988] Crim LR 120; (1987) 131 SJ 1696; [1988] 1 WLR 134 CA Jury could have regard to age of child in photograph when deciding if photograph obscene: did not have to decide from intrinsic nature of photograph.

Oxford City Justices, ex parte H, R v [1974] 2 All ER 356; (1974) 138 JP 552; [1975] QB 1; (1974) 118 SJ 442; [1974] 3 WLR 1 HC QBD Putative father can apply for custody where local authority have assumed mother's parental rights.

Oxford Justices, ex parte D, R v [1986] 3 All ER 129; [1987] 1 FLR 61; (1986) 150 JP 519; [1987] QB 199; (1970) 130 SJ 525; [1986] 3 WLR 447 HC QBD Putative father may apply for access to illegitimate child in local authority care.

Oxfordshire County Council and another v P [1995] 2 All ER 225; [1995] Fam 161; [1995] 2 FCR 212; [1995] 1 FLR 552; [1995] TLR 62; [1995] 2 WLR 543 HC FamD Lifting privilege of confidentiality in care proceedings a matter for court not guardian ad litem.

Oxfordshire County Council, S v [1993] 2 FCR 676; [1993] 1 FLR 452 HC FamD Justices to give reasons in care cases especially if departing from recommendation/report of guardian ad litem/welfare officer.

P (G), H (M) v [1995] 2 FLR 106 HC FamD On whether to allow removal of child from jurisdiction.

P (GE), P (LM) (otherwise E) v [1970] 3 All ER 659 CA Child's welfare could justify permanently removing from jurisdiction.

P (LM) (otherwise E) v P (GE) [1970] 3 All ER 659 CA Child's welfare could justify permanently removing from jurisdiction.

P (No 1), West Glamorgan County Council v [1992] 2 FCR 378; [1992] 2 FLR 369 HC FamD Interim non-access by mother to child pending full hearing was permissible.

P (No 2), West Glamorgan County Council v [1992] 2 FCR 406; [1993] 1 FLR 407 HC FamD On relevancy of long-term plans of local authority regarding child in care to court making decision regarding parental contact.

P (P), P (R) v [1969] 3 All ER 777 Assizes No acceptance of child as family if both parties do not agree (so no liability for maintenance).

P (R) v P (P) [1969] 3 All ER 777 Assizes No acceptance of child as family if both parties do not agree (so no liability for maintenance).

P (Wiltshire County Council intervening), P v (1991) 141 NLJ 968t; [1991] TLR 318 CA Official Solicitor to represent child where local authority disputing his future with others.

P v Bradford Metropolitan Borough Council [1996] 2 FCR 227 HC FamD Valid decision by magistrates after heard evidence of mother to stop hearing of application to discharge care orders.

P v H (1976) 120 SJ 199 HC FamD On staying custody orders pending appeal.

P v McK (formerly P) (1973) 123 NLJ 632t CA Generally custody of young children to be given (as here) to mother.

P v N [1997] 2 FCR 65 CyCt Residence order made precluding mother from changing child's surname (that of father) but enabling use of double-barrelled surname (names of father and mother).

P v P (1969) 119 NLJ 1069t; (1969) 113 SJ 999 CA Appropriate that all parties to custody action be physically seen by judge in action.

P v P (1978) 128 NLJ 86b CA On relevance of preferences of young children to determination of custody cases.

P v P [1991] FCR 97 CA Split custody generally undesirable but here deemed appropriate.

P v P [1992] 1 FLR 155 HC FamD Children returned to place of habitual residence despite one child objecting/mother's claim that her unhappiness at return would adversely affect children.

P v P (Wiltshire County Council intervening) (1991) 141 NLJ 968t; [1991] TLR 318 CA Official Solicitor to represent child where local authority disputing his future with others.

P v Staffordshire County Council [1989] FCR 16 HC FamD Non-invocation of wardship jurisdiction to review exercise of local authority discretion (over access to child in care).

P v W [1984] 1 All ER 866; [1984] Fam 32; (1984) 128 SJ 171; [1984] 2 WLR 439 HC FamD Contempt a last stop measure in dealing with access order abuses; summons for such violations to be detailed so defendant aware of abuses charged.

P, B v [1992] 2 FCR 576 HC FamD Contact between father and small child validly refused where inter alia consequent upset to mother would upset child.

P, Cheshire County Council v [1993] 2 FCR 397 CA Care order merited where arrangements had been made to move child at risk of significant harm where was to safe environment in Northern Ireland.

P, Nottingham County Council v [1994] Fam 18 (also CA); [1993] 1 FCR 180; [1993] 1 FLR 514; [1992] TLR 519; [1993] 2 WLR 406 HC FamD Prohibited steps order not to be used to same end as contact or residence order.

P, Nottinghamshire County Council v; Re P [1993] 3 All ER 815; [1994] Fam 18 (also HC FamD); [1994] 1 FCR 624; [1993] 2 FLR 134; (1993) 137 SJ LB 147; [1993] TLR 213; [1993] 3 WLR 637 CA Prohibited steps order not to be used to same end as contact or residence order.

P, Oxfordshire County Council and another v [1995] 2 All ER 225; [1995] Fam 161; [1995] 2 FCR 212; [1995] 1 FLR 552; [1995] TLR 62; [1995] 2 WLR 543 HC FamD Lifting privilege of confidentiality in care proceedings a matter for court not guardian ad litem.

P, R v [1980] Crim LR 796 CrCt Could be bail of child in care (bail denied in circumstances of this case).

P, S v [1997] 2 FCR 185; [1997] 2 FLR 277; [1997] TLR 55 HC FamD Family assistance order that would require local authority to escort children to/from prison where father incarcerated unmerited; indirect contact ordered while father in prison subject to later review upon father's release/re-establishment of life; parental responsibility on behalf of imprisoned father would be too much too soon.

P, W v [1988] FCR 349; [1988] 1 FLR 508 HC FamD On magistrates giving reasons for custody order.

Packer v Packer [1953] 2 All ER 127; (1953) 103 LJ 328; (1953) 97 SJ 403; [1953] 3 WLR 33 CA Test whether court may hear custody/maintenance application is parenthood not legitimacy.

Paget, Jeffery v (1919) CC Rep VIII 2 CyCt Man married by woman who has entered into maintenance agreement in affiliation action becomes liable for maintenance of said children.

Pallin v Buckland (1911-13) XXII Cox CC 545; (1911) 75 JP 362 HC KBD Accused found as matter of fact not to have run away and left children.

Parry, Taylor v [1951] 1 All ER 355; (1951) 115 JP 119; [1951] 2 KB 442; (1951) 101 LJ 63; (1951) 95 SJ 61; [1951] 1 TLR 509; (1951) WN (I) 94 HC KBD Mother of illegitimate child who marries man other than father of child cannot seek maintenance from that child from husband/actual father.

Paton v British Pregnancy Advisory Service Trustees and another (1978) 142 JP 497; [1979] QB 276; (1978) 122 SJ 744; [1978] 3 WLR 687 HC QBD Injunction unavailable to husband against wife/abortion charity to prevent same from procuring lawful abortion for wife.

Patterson v Walcott [1984] FLR 408; (1984) 148 JP 161 HC FamD On enforcement of child access order made under Guardianship of Minors Act 1971.

Pattison, Dickens v; R v Camberwell Green Justices, ex parte Pattison and Dickens [1985] FLR 610; (1985) 149 JP 271; (1985) 129 SJ 31 HC FamD Contravention by magistrates of principle that only affiliation payment arrears of less than one year to be enforced.

Payne v Critchley and the National Assistance Board [1962] 1 All ER 619; (1962) 126 JP 162; (1962) 112 LJ 240; [1962] 2 QB 83; (1962) 106 SJ 78 HC QBD Affiliation order providing for payment to National Assistance Board later variable to mother's benefit.

Peace, Phillips v [1996] 2 FLR 230 HC FamD Lump sum ordered for maintenance of child in circumstances where child support officer (correctly) assessed father's actual income as nil.

Pearce, Hamlyn v [1962] 2 All ER 436; [1962] Crim LR 405t; (1962) 126 JP 350; (1962) 112 LJ 370; [1962] 2 QB 346; (1962) 106 SJ 355; [1962] 3 WLR 136 HC QBD Can only be sent to approved school if under seventeen at time of order.

Perch (Edmund), R v (1908-09) XXV TLR 401 CCA Finding that were guilty of wilful neglect of children not affected by jury's rider that accused acted through ignorance.

Philips v Philips (1943-44) LX TLR 395; (1944) WN (I) 141 CA Court may order custody of children to successfuul petitioner for divorce even though children not in jurisdiction at date of order/application for same.

Phillips v Peace [1996] 2 FLR 230 HC FamD Lump sum ordered for maintenance of child in circumstances where child support officer (correctly) assessed father's actual income as nil.

Pinnington, Harris v [1995] 3 FCR 35 HC FamD Custodial parent not allowed remove child from jurisdiction as not in child's best interests; staying contact to father ordered.

Plant v Plant (1983) 4 FLR 305 CA Care and control to mother whose maternal capacity not questioned (preferable to father having to resign from job and live on social welfare to look after children if given care and control).

Plymouth Juvenile Court, ex parte F, R v [1987] 1 FLR 169; (1987) 151 JP 355 HC QBD Best interests of child paramount concern when making care order under Children and Young Persons Act 1969, s 32A(1).

Poel v Poel (1970) 114 SJ 720; [1970] 1 WLR 1469 CA Mother with custody of child allowed remove child to New Zealand to where mother emigrating with new husband.

Pontlottlyn Juvenile Court, ex parte R, R v [1990] FCR 900; [1991] 2 FLR 86 HC QBD Guardian ad litem appointed after initial refusal as mother misled by court clerk into thinking appointment forthcoming and so had not attended hearing with her solicitor.

Poole Juvenile Court, ex parte P, R v; R v Southwark Juvenile Court, ex parte C [1988] FCR 1; [1988] 1 FLR 8 HC QBD On procedure as regards applications for discharge of care orders.

Poole v Stokes [1914-15] All ER 1083; (1914-15) XXIV Cox CC 169; (1914) 78 JP 231; (1914) 49 LJ 159; (1914) 110 LTR 1020; (1913-14) XXX TLR 371; (1914) WN (I) 123 HC KBD Husband could be convicted of wilful neglect where separated wife acting as agent failed to look after children properly.

Pountney v Morris [1984] FLR 381; (1984) 134 NLJ 863c CA Children's welfare paramount consideration in custody cases.

Powell, R v (1914-15) XXIV Cox CC 229; (1915) 79 JP 272 CCC Need not intend to forever deprive parent of child to be convicted of child abduction.

Price v Price (1926-27) XLIII TLR 609 HC PDAD On timing of bringing of action for wilful neglect to maintain.

Prior (by his guardian), Prior v (1970) 114 SJ 72 HC PDAD On when legitimacy hearings may be heard in camera.

Prior v Prior (by his guardian) (1970) 114 SJ 72 HC PDAD On when legitimacy hearings may be heard in camera.

Pryce, R v [1972] Crim LR 307 CA On unlawful detention contrary to the Offences against the Person Act 1861, s 56.

Pryor v Pryor [1947] 1 All ER 381; [1948] 117 LJR 94; (1947) 177 LTR 329; (1947) LXIII TLR 208; (1947) WN (I) 108 HC PDAD Court could grant custody to grandparents of chidren who had previously been entrusted to since deceased mother's custody.

Public Trustee of New Zealand (Lindsay, Matilda and Arani, Whaitiki-tiki, Interveners), Arani (Hineiti Rirerire) v [1920] AC 198; [1919] 88 LJPC 160; (1919) 121 LTR 460; (1918-19) XXXV TLR 671 PC Maori adoption of European child approved.

Pullen v Pullen (1964) 108 SJ 617 CA Failed appeal against magistrates' order for delivery of child on basis that place where was to be delivered was outside jurisdiction of the magistrates.

Pym v Wilsher (1901) 36 LJ 310; (1900-01) 45 SJ 578; (1900-01) XVII TLR 558; (1901) WN (I) 126; (1900-01) 49 WR 654 HC KBD Prosecution procedures under Vaccination Act 1898 did not apply to failure to vaccinate which occurred during lifetime of Vaccination Act 1867.

Q, Nottinghamshire County Council v [1982] 2 All ER 641; [1982] Fam 94; (1982) 3 FLR 305; (1982) 126 SJ 309; [1982] 2 WLR 954 HC FamD Appeals against place of safety order under Children and Young Persons Act 1969, s 28, an abuse of process.

Q, Royal Borough of Kensington and Chelsea v [1989] 1 FLR 399 HC FamD On using television to advertise for prospective adopters.

R (B) v Ealing London Borough [1985] FLR 999 HC FamD Failed application by mother of children over whom parental rights resolution made to have that resolution determined.

R (Mrs) v Central Independent Television plc [1994] 3 All ER 641; [1994] Fam 192; [1995] 1 FCR 521; [1994] 2 FLR 151; [1994] TLR 92; [1994] 3 WLR 20 CA Parental jurisdiction of court does not extend to injuncting publication touching on child but not addressing care or upbringing.

R (TL) and R (KB), Essex County Council v (1979) 143 JP 309 HC QBD Failed application for care of children on basis of impeded development of same where was no evidence at close of action that children were actually being impeded in their development.

R and G, Hereford and Worcester County Council v [1994] 2 FCR 981 HC FamD Interim care order not supervision order appropriate mechanism whereby to control residence.

R v A Justice for Lincoln (Kesteven), ex parte M; R v Lincoln (Kesteven) Juvenile Court, ex parte Lincolnshire County Council [1976] 1 All ER 490; (1976) 140 JP 216; (1975) 125 NLJ 1192t; [1976] QB 957; (1976) 120 SJ 8; [1976] 2 WLR 143 HC QBD Local authority place of safety order application following care order to parent not abuse of process.

R v Adoption Application 121/1984 (1985) 129 SJ 638 HC FamD Could not order adoption of child by couple resident abroad as was no chance for local authority to see them with child in some form of permanent home in England/Wales.

R v Alexander (1913-14) XXIII Cox CC 138; (1912) 76 JP 215; (1912-13) 107 LTR 240; (1911-12) XXVIII TLR 200 CCA Conviction quashed where trial judge actively encouraged accused to plead guilty to abduction charge.

R v Andrews (Paul) (1986) 82 Cr App R 148 CA Wilful neglect of child properly inferred from circumstantial evidence.

R v Austin and others [1981] 1 All ER 374; (1981) 72 Cr App R 104; [1980] Crim LR 716; (1981) 145 JP 145; (1981) 131 NLJ 68 CA Person with right to possession of child exempt from child-stealing but not paid accessories.

R v Avon County Council, ex parte Crabtree [1996] 3 FCR 773; [1996] 1 FLR 502 CA Failed appeal against failed application for judicial review of fostering panel decision to deregister applicant as fosterer.

R v Avon County Court, ex parte K and others [1986] 1 FLR 443 HC QBD On meaning of giving 'first consideration' to child's welfare (Child Care Act 1980, s 18(1)): here local authority failed in duty to give same when decided to close community home.

R v B County Council, ex parte P [1991] 2 All ER 65; [1991] 1 FLR 470; [1991] 1 WLR 221 CA Local authority behaviour open to judicial review if unreasonable or unlawful; though child a compellable witness in care proceedings should not be called if contrary to best interests thereof.

R v Banks [1916-17] All ER 356; (1915-17) XXV Cox CC 535; (1916) 80 JP 432; [1916] 2 KB 621; [1916] 85 LJKB 1657; (1916-17) 115 LTR 457; (1916) WN (I) 281 CCA Must show not that could but did believe girl over sixteen to raise defence on that ground.

R v Barnet Juvenile Court, ex parte Barnet London Borough [1982] TLR 307 HC QBD Local authority not guardian of juvenile entrusted to its care pursuant to the Children and Young Persons Act 1969, ss 7(7) and 20.

R v Berry (Thomas Clive) [1996] 2 Cr App R 226; [1996] Crim LR 574 CA On application of defence that are child's natural father in context of child abduction case where man was taking child in honest but mistaken belief that was own child.

R v Birkenhead Borough Justices, ex parte Smith [1954] 1 All ER 503; [1954] Crim LR 133t; (1954) 98 SJ 163 HC QBD Cannot commit member of US forces and father of illegitimate child for non-payment of maintenance.

R v Birkenhead Borough Justices, ex parte Smith; R v Birkenhead Justices, ex parte Smith [1954] 1 All ER 503; [1954] Crim LR 133t; [1954] Crim LR 297; (1954) 118 JP 203; (1954) 104 LJ 154; (1954) 98 SJ 163 HC QBD US soldier (member of visiting forces) could not be committed to prison for failure to maintain child pursuant to affiliation order.

R v Birmingham City Juvenile Court, ex parte Birmingham City Council [1988] 1 All ER 683; [1988] FCR 175 (also HC QBD); [1988] 1 FLR 424; (1987) 131 SJ 1697; [1988] 1 WLR 337 CA Disputed interim care order application to be decided after local authority/parents/guardian heard.

R v Birmingham Juvenile Court and others , ex parte S and another; R v Birmingham Juvenile Court and others, ex parte P and another [1984] 1 All ER 393; [1984] FLR 343; [1984] 1 WLR 618 HC QBD In renewing care order — unlike bail order — court looks to all the circumstances on each occasion; 28-day care order expires at start of twenty-eighth day.

R v Birmingham Juvenile Court, ex parte G and others; R v Birmingham Juvenile Court, ex parte R [1989] 3 All ER 336; [1989] 2 FLR 454; [1990] 2 QB 573; (1989) 133 SJ 1089; [1989] 3 WLR 1024 CA Court must look to welfare of child/hear guardian ad litem before allowing local authority withdraw care order application.

R v Birmingham Juvenile Court, ex parte G and others; R v Birmingham Juvenile Court, ex parte R [1988] 3 All ER 726; [1989] FCR 22; [1988] 2 FLR 423; (1988) 138 NLJ 143; (1988) 132 SJ 1117; [1988] 1 WLR 950 HC QBD As care proceedings not adversarial court may hear guardian ad litem's evidence even if local authority offers no evidence.

R v Birmingham Juvenile Court, ex parte N [1984] 2 All ER 688; [1984] FLR 683 HC QBD 'Household' determined by reference to circumstances; can be in same 'household' though not in same place.

R v Birmingham Juvenile Court, ex parte S [1984] FamD 93; [1984] 3 WLR 387 HC FamD Two children of same mother/different fathers were both members of same household though one in care and one living with mother and second father.

R v Blackman (John) (1928-29) 21 Cr App R 132 CCA 'Reasonable belief that girl over sixteen' defence open on charge of carnal knowledge did not preclude conviction of under twenty-three year old for indecent assault.

R v Bolton Metropolitan Borough, ex parte B [1985] FLR 343 HC QBD On ending/denying access of parents to child being held in local authority care.

R v Booth (Lee Timothy) (1989) 11 Cr App R (S) 258; [1989] Crim LR 843 CA Care order must pre-exist any court order restraining local authority in manner of deealing with juvenile in care.

R v Boulden [1957] Crim LR 182 Sessions Successful prosecution for abandonment/neglect of children: on what constitutes abandonment/neglect.

R v Boulden (Edward Ernest) (1957) 41 Cr App R 105; [1957] Crim LR 322 CCA On what constitutes 'abandonment' of child under Children and Young Persons Act 1933, s 1(1).

R v Bow Road Domestic Proceedings Court, ex parte Adedigba [1968] 2 All ER 89; (1968) 118 NLJ 444; [1968] 2 QB 572; (1968) 132 JP 301; [1968] 2 WLR 1143 CA Maintenance order if mother and father resident in England though child born abroad/mother domiciled abroad when child born.

R v Bowditch [1991] Crim LR 831 CA On burden of proof as regards proving cruelty to child under Children and Young Persons Act 1933.

R v Bristol Justices, ex parte Broome [1987] 1 All ER 676; [1987] 2 FLR 76; (1987) 151 JP 409; (1987) 131 SJ 102; [1987] 1 WLR 352 HC QBD Police to be heard in application to release child held by constable.

R v Burns (James); R v Ralph (Michael Peter); R v Jackson (Stephen Ronald); R v Burns (Sidney) (1984) 79 Cr App R 173 CA Person could be prosecuted for conspiracy to commit offence though immune from prosecution for substantive offence.

R v Byers (Jessie) (1910) 4 Cr App R 5 CCA Manslaughter of child by means of cruel treatment — even though post-cruelty betterment in child's condition.

R v C [1991] 2 FLR 252; [1990] TLR 714 CA Conviction of father (who took own child outside jurisdiction without consent of mother-joint custodian) for child kidnapping (common law offence)/abduction quashed/upheld.

R v C and another [1990] TLR 344 CA Failed prosecution for cruelty to child where was inadequate evidence of guiltiness.

R v Cambridge District Health Authority, ex parte B [1995] 2 FCR 485; [1995] 1 FLR 1055 (also HC QBD) CA Health authority's decision not to fund expensive experimental treatment of seriously ill child was reasonable.

R v Cambridge District Health Authority, ex parte B (No 2) [1996] 1 FLR 375 CA Reporting restrictions lifted so that father might publicise plight of child and so raise money for her treatment.

R v Central Criminal Court, ex parte Godwin and Crook [1995] 1 FLR 132; (1994) 138 SJ LB 199 CA Valid exercise of discretion prohibiting publication of information on trial: prior to making order judge could hear anyone whom consisdered to have valid interest in matter.

R v Chainey [1911-13] All ER 701; (1913-14) XXIII Cox CC 620; (1914) 78 JP 127; [1914] 1 KB 137; (1913) 48 LJ 673; [1914] 83 LJKB 306; (1913-14) 109 LTR 752; (1913-14) XXX TLR 51; (1913) WN (I) 318 CCA Criminal neglect of (under sixteen year old) child socialising with immoral persons did not mean guilty of causing/encouraging unlawful carnal knowledge of same.

R v Chalker (Kate) (1910) 4 Cr App R 2 CCA Manslaughter of child by means of consistently cruel treatment.

R v Chapman [1958] 3 All ER 143; (1958) 42 Cr App R 257; [1958] Crim LR 623; (1958) 122 JP 462; (1958) 108 LJ 586; [1959] 1 QB 100; (1958) 102 SJ 621 CCA 'Unlawful' sex under Sexual Offences Act 1956 s 19(1) means sex outside marriage.

R v Chapman (1931-34) XXIX Cox CC 407; (1931-32) 23 Cr App R 45; (1931) 95 JP 205; [1931] 2 KB 606; (1931) 100 LJCL 562; (1932) 146 LTR 120; (1931) 75 SJ 660; (1930-31) XLVII TLR 620 CCA Proviso in Criminal Law Amendment Act 1922, s 2 extends reasonable belief that girl over sixteen defence to men who have not reached the age of twenty-four.

R v Chelsea Juvenile Court Justices (Re an infant) [1955] 1 All ER 38; (1955) 99 SJ 77; [1955] 1 WLR 52 HC QBD Justices have wide power to amend register of births.

R v Chertsey Justices, ex parte E [1988] FCR 283; [1987] 2 FLR 415 HC QBD On whether/when to discharge care order.

R v Chick (Florence Irene) (1925-26) 19 Cr App R 57 CCA Three months in second division for infanticide/concealment of birth in light of prisoner's age (twenty) and strong recommendation of mercy by jury.

R v Chief Constable of Cheshire, ex parte K [1990] FCR 201; [1990] 1 FLR 70 HC QBD Police not obliged to assist in enforcement of custody order.

R v City of Liverpool Justices, ex parte W [1959] 1 All ER 337; (1959) 123 JP 152; (1959) 109 LJ 105; (1959) 103 SJ 113 HC QBD Certiorari for failure to consider special circumstances prescribed in Marriage Act 1950, s 2(2).

R v Colville-Hyde [1956] Crim LR 117 Assizes On necessary elements of offence of abduction.

R v Connor (1907-09) XXI Cox CC 628; (1908) 72 JP 212; [1908] 2 KB 26; (1908) 43 LJ 283; [1908] 77 LJCL 527; (1908) XCVIII LTR 932; (1907-08) 52 SJ 444; (1907-08) XXIV TLR 483 CCR Father in desertion guilty of wilful neglect (failed to provide food/money).

R v Conroy and Conroy [1954] Crim LR 141 Assizes Jointly tried parents found guilty of murder of newborn child.

R v Copestake and others, ex parte Wilkinson [1926] All ER 252; (1926) 90 JP 191; [1927] 1 KB 468; [1927] 96 LJCL 65; (1927) 136 LTR 100; (1926) WN (I) 242 CA Under Criminal Justice Administration Act 1914 court could revoke periodic payments ordered in affiliation suit but could not alter paternity decision.

R v Corby Juvenile Court, ex parte M [1987] 1 All ER 992; [1987] 1 FLR 490; (1987) 151 JP 387; (1970) 130 SJ 860; [1987] 1 WLR 55 HC QBD Access provisions of Child Care Act 1980 apply retrospectively to children put in care under earlier enactment.

R v Cornwall County Council, ex parte Cornwall and Isles of Scilly Guardians ad Litem and Reporting Officers Panel [1992] 2 All ER 471; [1992] 1 FLR 270; (1991) 135 SJ LB 204; [1991] TLR 525; [1992] 1 WLR 427 HC QBD Certiorari available where local authority seeks to circumscribe role of guardian ad litem.

R v Crocker (William) (1922-23) 17 Cr App R 45 CCA Leave to appeal granted in unlawful carnal knowledge case where corroboration point arose.

R v Crocker (William) (1922-23) 17 Cr App R 46 CCA Girl's evidence need not be corroborated in unlawful carnal knowledge case.

R v Crown Court at Southwark, ex parte Godwin and others [1991] 3 All ER 818; (1992) 94 Cr App R 34; (1992) 156 JP 86; (1991) 141 NLJ 963; [1992] QB 190; (1991) 135 SJ LB 28; [1991] 3 WLR 689 CA Order specifying particular name not to be published so as to protect child an invalid order.

R v Croydon Juvenile Court Justices, ex parte Croydon London Borough Council [1973] 1 All ER 476; [1973] Crim LR 108; (1973) 117 SJ 70; (1973) 137 JP 283; (1972) 122 NLJ 1112t; [1973] QB 426; [1973] 2 WLR 61 HC QBD Ordering local authority to pay fine of child in its care permissible.

R v Croydon Juvenile Court, ex parte M [1988] FCR 11 HC QBD On role of juvenile court when deciding whether care order to be discharged in face of parental opposition.

R v Croydon Juvenile Court, ex parte N [1987] 1 FLR 252; (1987) 151 JP 523 HC QBD On procedure (including evidential procedure) where interim care order sought.

R v Darlington Corporation Juvenile Court, ex parte West Hartlepool Corporation [1957] 1 All ER 398; [1957] Crim LR 322; (1957) 101 SJ 172; [1957] 1 WLR 363 HC QBD Fit person order must contain consent of local authority to making thereof.

R v Derbyshire County Council, ex parte T [1989] FCR 679; [1990] 1 FLR 237 (also CA); (1989) 133 SJ 1109 HC QBD Notice to former parent needed if child placed with prospective adopters becomes child in care.

R v Derbyshire County Council, ex parte T and another [1990] 1 All ER 792; [1990] Fam 164; [1989] FCR 713; [1990] 1 FLR 237 (also HC QBD); (1989) 133 SJ 1626; [1990] 2 WLR 101 CA Notice to former parent needed if child placed with prospective adopters becomes child in care.

R v Devon County Council, ex parte D [1992] 2 FCR 766 HC QBD Local authority's placing child on child protection register and then informing father of what had done at same time telling him of right to appeal decision not unreasonable procedure.

R v Devon County Council, ex parte L [1991] FCR 599; [1991] 2 FLR 541 HC QBD Failed application for review of local authority 'decision' to caution interested persons of its belief that applicant a child abuser.

R v Dharma (Chandra); R v Slater; R v Hutchinson; R v Court (1905) 69 JP 39; (1905) 40 LJ 238; (1905) XCII LTR 700; (1904-05) 49 SJ 366; (1904-05) XXI TLR 353 CCR Extension by Prevention of Cruelty of Children Act 1904 to limitation on bringing prosecutions under Criminal Law Amendment Act 1885 operated retrospectively as did not create new offence.

R v Dootson (Robert) (1995) 16 Cr App R (S) 223; [1994] Crim LR 702 CA Abduction of child not a sex offence under Criminal Justice Act 1991.

R v Duguid (1907-09) XXI Cox CC 200; (1906) 70 JP 294; (1906) 41 LJ 335; [1906] 75 LJKB 470; (1906) XCIV LTR 887; (1905-06) 50 SJ 465; (1905-06) XXII TLR 506; (1906) WN (I) 100 CCR Was criminal conspiracy on part of person agreeing with mother to remove her child from lawful custody.

R v Dunne (James) (1928-29) 21 Cr App R 176 CCA Conviction quashed where judge conducted unlawful out-of-court examination of child to test whether suitable for her to take oath.

R v East Sussex County Council, ex parte R [1990] FCR 873; [1991] 2 FLR 358 HC QBD Placing (and manner of placing) mother's name on child abuse register not unreasonable.

R v Epsom Juvenile Court, ex parte G [1988] 1 All ER 329; [1988] FCR 32; [1988] 2 FLR 36; (1988) 132 SJ 54; [1988] 1 WLR 145 HC QBD Usually report of guardian ad litem should be presented as soon as possible before care case begins.

R v Essex County Council, ex parte Washington [1987] 1 FLR 148; (1987) 151 JP 258 HC QBD Failed application to have contribution notice rescinded.

R v Essex Justices, ex parte Da Costa (1939-40) XXXI Cox CC 133 HC KBD Quarter sessions quashing of bastardy order where inadequate corroboration a final decision on the merits.

R v Ethical Committee of St Mary's Hospital (Manchester), ex parte H [1988] 1 FLR 512 HC QBD Failed application for review of decision not to allow party avail of in vitro fertilisation treatment.

R v Exeter Juvenile Court, ex parte H and H; R v Waltham Forest Juvenile Court, ex parte B [1988] FCR 474; [1988] 2 FLR 214 HC QBD Was reasonable to hear care action pending criminal proceedings against parent/s.

R v Ferguson (Robert) (1969) 53 Cr App R 637 CA In chastising their children immigrant parents must conform with British standards.

R v Fisher (Colin); R v Marshall (Christopher); R v Mitchell (George) (1969) 113 SJ 70; [1969] 2 WLR 452 Assizes Jury cannot convict accused of sex with under-sixteen year old girl where accused being tried for rape.

R v Francis (Colin Leslie) (1989) 88 Cr App R 127; [1988] Crim LR 528 CA Indecency with or towards children contrary to Indecency with Children Act 1960, s 1(1) requires that act be aimed at children and that accused pleased that children watching.

R v Franklin [1994] TLR 334 CA Interview evidence ought not to have been admitted given improprieties in procedure regarding access by solicitor to accused (client).

R v G (Surrey County Council intervening) [1984] Fam 100; [1984] FLR 780; (1984) 128 SJ 662; [1984] 3 WLR 667 CA That children were constantly shuffled between divorced parents meant were 'exceptional circumstances' (Matrimonial Causes Act 1973, s 43(1)) justifying their being placed in care (care authorities could then validly place child with one parent).

R v Gibbins (Walter) and Proctor (Edith Rose) (1917-18) 13 Cr App R 134; (1918) 82 JP 287 CCA On neglect of child as basis for conviction of murder of same.

R v Gibbins (David John) [1977] Crim LR 741 CrCt On elements of offence whereby 'expose[d]' child to unnecessary suffering/injury to health contrary to Children and Young Persons Act 1933, s 1(1).

R v Graham-Kerr (John) (1989) 88 Cr App R 302 (1989) 153 JP 171; (1988) 132 SJ 1299; [1988] 1 WLR 1098 CA On elements of crime of taking indecent photographs of child contrary to Protection of Children Act 1978, s 1(1).

R v Gravesend Justices, ex parte Doodney [1971] 2 All ER 364; (1971) 135 JP 353; (1971) 121 NLJ 152; (1971) 115 SJ 327; [1971] 1 WLR 818 HC QBD That mother resident abroad need not preclude putative father seeking variation in England.

R v Greenwich Juvenile Court, ex parte London Borough of Greenwich (1980) 1 FLR 304 HC QBD No machinery for discovery in magistrates' courts; discoverability of documents to be assessed on individual/class (where are classes) basis.

R v Griffin [1993] Crim LR 515 CA On respective roles of judge/jury in child abduction case; was possible to find attempted abduction where had arranged boat trip and went to school to request control of children in local authority care.

R v Gwynedd County Council, ex parte B and another [1992] 3 All ER; [1991] 2 FLR 365; (1991) 141 NLJ 494t; [1991] TLR 181 CA Local authority rights/duties towards child in care end upon child's death.

R v Hale (1901-07) XX Cox CC 739; (1904-05) XXI TLR 70; [1905] 1 KB 126; (1904-05) XCI LTR 839; (1904-05) 49 SJ 68; (1904-05) 53 WR 400; (1905) 69 JP 83 CCR Child need not be present at trial concerning cruelty thereto unless evidence of child needed.

R v Halton [1925] All ER 396 CCA Words 'wilfully assaults' in Children Act 1908, s 12(1) intended to convey something more than common assault.

R v Hampshire County Council, ex parte K and another [1990] 2 All ER 129; [1990] FCR 545; [1990] 1 FLR 330; [1990] 2 QB 71; (1989) 133 SJ 1605; [1990] 2 WLR 649 HC QBD Child's interest requires parents be given every opportunity to defend themselves including access to all relevant material.

R v Harrow Borough Council, ex parte B [1989] FCR 407 HC QBD Not allowing parent to attend case conference (in context of child abuse investigation) not objectionable.

R v Harrow London Borough Council, ex parte D [1990] 3 All ER 12; [1990] Fam 133; [1989] FCR 729; (1989) 133 SJ 1513 CA Placing of person on child abuse register where have made written/not oral representations not contrary to natural justice.

R v Harrow London Borough Council, ex parte D [1989] 2 FLR 51 HC QBD Refusal of judicial review of local authority placing children on 'at risk' register.

R v Hatton (1926-30) XXVIII Cox CC 43; (1925) 89 JP 164; [1925] 2 KB 322; (1925) 60 LJ 705; [1925] 94 LJCL 863; (1925) 133 LTR 735; (1924-25) XLI TLR 637; (1925) WN (I) 199 CCA Interpretation of phrase 'wilfully assaults' in Children Act 1908, s 12(1).

R v Hayles (1969) 53 Cr App R 36; [1969] Crim LR 24; (1968) 118 NLJ 1029t; [1969] 1 QB 364; (1968) 112 SJ 860; [1968] 3 WLR 1106 CA Could be convicted of ill-treatment of child where what had done constituted neglect of same (Children and Young Persons Act 1933, s 1(1)).

R v Hereford and Worcester County Council, ex parte D [1992] 1 FLR 448 HC QBD Local authority decision to remove child from foster care quashed where did not consult with foster-parent beforehand.

R v Hereford City Justices, ex parte O [1982] 3 All ER 568; (1983) 4 FLR 196; (1982) 126 SJ 496; [1982] TLR 314; [1982] 1 WLR 1252 HC QBD Can appeal to Crown Court on basis of quantum.

R v Hertfordshire County Council, ex parte B; R v Bedfordshire County Council, ex parte C [1987] 1 FLR 239; (1987) 151 JP 202 HC QBD On judicial review of care orders (compliance with natural justice, not particular policy, is matter in issue).

R v Hewitt (1926-30) XXVIII Cox CC 101; (1925-26) 19 Cr App R 64; (1926) 90 JP 68; (1926) 134 LTR 157; (1925-26) XLII TLR 216; (1925) WN (I) 292 CCA Previous assault on same girl admissible in unlawful carnal knowledge of under sixteen/over fourteen year old girl — time lapse since earlier assault reduces weight of evidence.

R v High Peak Magistrates' Court, ex parte B [1995] 1 FLR 568 HC FamD On inappropriateness of judicial review of maintenance order as a form of relief when appeal structure exists.

R v Highbury Corner Magistrates' Court, ex parte Deering [1997] 1 FLR 683; (1997) 161 JP 138 HC QBD Balancing respective interests of accused and child-witness to be done not when making out witness summons but when child to be called.

R v Hilton (John James) [1925] All ER 396; (1925-26) 19 Cr App R 29 CCA Interpretation of Children Act 1908, s 12(1).

R v Hove Juvenile Court, ex parte W [1989] FCR 286; [1989] 2 FLR 145 HC QBD On establishing by way of interview evidence that child has been victim of sex abuse.

R v Howard, ex parte Da Costa [1938] 3 All ER 241; (1938) 102 JP 333; [1938] 2 KB 544; [1938] 107 LJCL 675; (1938) 82 SJ 477; (1937-38) LIV TLR 825; (1938) WN (I) 202 HC KBD Cannot appeal from quarter sessions decision in affiliation action.

R v Humphreys and others, ex parte Ward [1914-15] All ER 189 (1914-15) XXIV Cox CC 455; (1915) 79 JP 66; [1914] 3 KB 1237; [1915] 84 LJKB 187; (1914-15) 111 LTR 1110; (1913-14) XXX TLR 698 HC KBD Affiliation order can be made in respect of child not born in England or Wales unless child subject to foreign law.

R v Izod (1901-07) XX Cox CC 690 Assizes Must be criminally negligent to new-born child after born to sustain conviction for manslaughter of same through neglect.

R v Jarvis (James) (1901-07) XX Cox CC 249 Assizes Not abduction to passively acquiesce to proposal of under-sixteen year old unmarried girl to join her in her leaving home.

R v Jones (James William) [1973] Crim LR 621 CrCt Was not taking child out of possession of parents (contrary to Sexual Offences Act 1956, s 20) to seek to bring girls for walk, aim being to indecently assault them.

R v Jones (William) (1911-13) XXII Cox CC 212; (1911) 75 JP 272 CCC Must prove accused intended to permanently withdraw child from parent to sustain conviction for stealing away child under fourteen.

R v Justices of the Peace for Sunderland, ex parte Leslie Hodgkinson [1945] 2 All ER 175; (1945) 109 JP 201; [1945] 114 LJ 359; (1945) 173 LTR 62; (1945) 89 SJ 436; (1944-45) LXI TLR 456; (1945) WN (I) 150 HC KBD Justices can hear scond bastardy hearing/admit fresh evidence and make order despite initial refusal.

R v K (DT) [1993] Crim LR 281; [1993] 2 FLR 181; (1992) 136 SJ LB 328; [1992] TLR 591 CA Improper to refuse disclosure of video (interview) evidence without first ascertaining relevance/ significance of same.

R v Kauffman (1904) 68 JP 189 CCC On elements of offence of abducting under-eighteen year old girl (Criminal Law Amendment Act 1885, s 7).

R v Keech (Herbert Joshua) (1928-29) 21 Cr App R 125 CCA Improper that 'reasonable belief that girl over sixteen' defence open on charge of carnal knowledge but not indecent assault (Criminal Law Amendment Act 1922, s 2); no general guidelines on sentencing offenders convicted of underage indecent assault.

R v Kersey (Maud) (1907-09) XXI Cox CC 690 Assizes Murder/concealment of birth conviction not possible/possible on evidence though no dead body.

R v King's Lynn Justices and another, ex parte M [1988] FCR 436; [1988] 2 FLR 79 HC QBD Presumption of husband's paternity rebutted by admission of paternity from wife's lover (even though birth certificate named husband as father).

R v Kirklees Metropolitan Borough Council, ex parte C [1993] 2 FCR 381; [1993] 2 FLR 187; [1993] TLR 173 CA Local authority could have child in care admitted to mental hospital.

R v Kirklees Metropolitan Borough Council, ex parte C [1992] 2 FCR 321; [1992] 2 FLR 117; [1992] TLR 45 HC QBD Local authority could have child in care admitted to mental hospital.

R v Lambeth London Borough Council, ex parte Caddell (1997) 141 SJ LB 147; [1997] TLR 348 HC QBD Failed application for after-care assistance from local authority to whose care had been entrusted before turned eighteen, after which moved to another local authority area.

R v Lancashire County Council, ex parte M [1992] 1 FLR 109 CA Failed application by fosterers for review of local authority decision to take child from fosterers and place with prospective adopters.

R v Lancashire Justices, ex parte Tyrer [1924] All ER 304; (1921-25) XXVII Cox CC 711; (1925) 89 JP 17; [1925] 1 KB 200; (1924) 59 LJ 775; [1925] 94 LJCL 331; (1925) 132 LTR 382; (1924-25) 69 SJ 194; (1924-25) XLI TLR 103; (1924) WN (I) 301 HC KBD Need not seek bastardy order in place where customarily/permanently reside.

R v Leather (John Holdsworth) (1994) 98 Cr App R 179; [1993] Crim LR 516; [1994] 1 FCR 877; [1993] 2 FLR 770; (1993) 137 SJ LB 54; [1993] TLR 18 CA On what it means to remove child from lawful 'control' (Child Abduction Act 1984, s 2(1)).

R v Lee [1993] 2 All ER 170; [1993] Crim LR 65; (1992) 136 SJ LB 222; [1993] 1 WLR 103 CA Court of Appeal may not impose restriction order where CrCt has decided otherwise save in judicial review.

R v Leeds Justices, ex parte Thompson (1983) 4 FLR 773 HC QBD Would be unusual to exclude relevant evidence at any stage before issue finally determined in case involving child's welfare.

R v Leicester City Juvenile Justices, ex parte Capenhurst (1985) 149 JP 409; [1984] TLR 764 HC QBD Local authority's report on accommodation available for person of unruly character not binding on court.

R v Lewisham London Borough Council, ex parte P [1991] 3 All ER 529; [1991] FCR 684; [1991] 2 FLR 185; [1991] TLR 93; [1991] 1 WLR 308 HC QBD Parents/custodians may expect fair treatment from local authority/not to be named as alleged child abusers unless child's interests outweigh effects on alleged abuser and their family.

R v Lincolnshire Justices, ex parte Brett [1926] All ER 275; (1926) 90 JP 149; [1926] 2 KB 192; [1926] 95 LJCL 827; (1926) 135 LTR 141 CA No bastardy order where no corroboration of complainant's evidence.

R v Londesborough [1968] Crim LR 171 CA Eighteen months' imprisonment for assault occasioning actual bodily harm to three year old (albeit that offender-mother was poor/of low intelligence/badly brought up).

R v London Borough of Newham, ex parte McL [1988] FCR 229 HC FamD Wardship proceedings to be recommended by judge giving leave for judicial review of local authority decision regarding child in its care.

R v London Borough of Newham,ex parte McL [1988] 1 FLR 416 HC QBD Wardship proceedings to be recommended by judge giving leave if preferable to judicial review of local authority decision/s regarding child in its care.

R v Lumley (1911-13) XXII Cox CC 635; (1912) 76 JP 208 CCC Abortionist guilty of murder/manslaughter if did/did not (nor could not reasonably) consider that death or grieveous bodily harm would result from actions.

R v Manchester City Magistrates' Court, ex parte Bannister (1983) 4 FLR 717; (1983) 147 JP 516; (1983) 127 SJ 285; [1983] TLR 179 HC QBD Actual place of residence of child is basis on which decide in name of which council care order to be made.

R v Markham, ex parte Marsh (1923) WN (I) 112 HC KBD Court would not re-hear paternity suit under guise of action for writ of certiorari.

R v Marsh (Percy Harold) (1925-26) 19 Cr App R 27 CCA Accused's silence/keeping of letter sent by prosecutrix not corroborative of latter's claim in sexual offence case.

R v Marsh (Ronald William Frank) (1948-49) 33 Cr App R 185 CCA Evidence of previous confession of guilt/sentencing for indecent assault on child admissible in later charge for carnal knowledge of same child.

R v Maughan (Reginald) (1932-34) 24 Cr App R 130 CCA Not defence to charge of indecent assault on under-sixteen year old that genuinely believed was over sixteen.

R v Middlesex Justices, ex parte Bond (1931-34) XXIX Cox CC 563; (1932) 96 JP 487; [1933] 1 KB 72; (1933) 102 LJCL 40; (1933) 148 LTR 134; (1932-33) XLIX TLR 18; (1932) WN (I) 212 HC KBD Custody order bad as in matter that was res judicata.

R v Milton Keynes Juvenile Court, ex parte Russell (1979) 143 JP 373; [1979] 1 WLR 1062 HC QBD Parent could be allowed by magistrates to cross-examine witnesses for local authority in care action.

R v Moon (Frederick); R v Moon (Emily) (1910) 4 Cr App R 171; [1910] 1 KB 818; (1910) 45 LJ 221; (1910) 79 LJKB 505 CCA Not offence under Children Act 1908, s 17 to encourage seduction of girl already seduced.

R v Mousir [1987] Crim LR 561 CA On what is meant by removing child from 'lawful control' for purposes of Child Abduction Act 1984.

R v New and Wife (1903-04) XX TLR 515 HC KBD Court will pay close consideration to but need not accede to illegitimate child's mother desires as to custody of child.

R v New and Wife (1903-04) XX TLR 583 CA Court will pay close consideration to but need not accede to illegitimate child's mother desires as to custody of child.

R v Newcastle Emlyn Justices and another, ex parte Evans (1963) 107 SJ 416 HC QBD QBD could not decide whether fraud perpetrated on lower court where was conflicting evidence.

R v Newcastle-upon-Tyne Council, ex parte S and T [1988] FCR 159; [1988] 1 FLR 535 HC QBD On making order that guardians ad litem be appointed to represent children (on basis that conflict between their interests and that of parents).

R v Newham London Borough Council, ex parte P [1990] 2 All ER 19; [1990] FCR 601; [1990] 1 FLR 404; (1990) 134 SJ 833; [1990] 1 WLR 482 HC QBD Local authority need not make pre-placement inquiries where stay for brief period as does not transfer charge or control.

R v Norfolk County Council, ex parte M [1989] 2 All ER 359; [1989] FCR 667; [1989] QB 619; (1989) 133 SJ 1089 HC QBD Style of child abuse register by local authority and means of registration contrary to natural justice/open to judicial review.

R v Norfolk County Council, ex parte X [1989] 2 FLR 120 HC QBD Placing of person on child abuse register was open to judicial review: registering decision quashed.

R v North Yorkshire County Council, ex parte M [1989] 1 All ER 143; [1989] FCR 128; [1989] 1 FLR 203; [1989] QB 411; (1988) 132 SJ 1731; [1988] 3 WLR 1344 HC QBD Local authority must inform guardian ad litem/hear guardian's views about any major changes to circumstances of child in care.

R v North Yorkshire County Council, ex parte M (No 2) [1989] FCR 394; [1989] 2 FLR 79 HC QBD On role of guardian ad litem vis-à-vis local authority as regards adoption of child.

R v North Yorkshire County Council, ex parte M (No 3) [1989] FCR 403; [1989] 2 FLR 82 HC QBD On possibility of post-judicial review invocation of wardship jurisdiction.

R v Nottinghamshire County Council [1993] 1 FCR 576 HC FamD Failed appeal against decision of family proceedings court in care action to allow local authority extra time to file evidence.

R v O'Donoghue (1926-30) XXVIII Cox CC 461; (1927) 91 JP 199; (1927) 64 LJ 378; (1928) 97 LJCL 303; (1928) 138 LTR 240; (1927) 71 SJ 897; (1927) WN (I) 289/297 CCA Verdict of infanticide unavailable as child not newborn/over one month old.

R v Owen (Charles William) (1988) 86 Cr App R 291; [1988] Crim LR 120; (1987) 131 SJ 1696; [1988] 1 WLR 134 CA Jury could have regard to age of child in photograph when deciding if photograph obscene: did not have to decide from intrinsic nature of photograph.

R v Oxford City Justices, ex parte H [1974] 2 All ER 356; (1974) 138 JP 552; [1975] QB 1; (1974) 118 SJ 442; [1974] 3 WLR 1 HC QBD Putative father can apply for custody where local authority have assumed mother's parental rights.

R v Oxford Justices, ex parte D [1986] 3 All ER 129; [1987] 1 FLR 61; (1986) 150 JP 519; [1987] QB 199; (1970) 130 SJ 525; [1986] 3 WLR 447 HC QBD Putative father may apply for access to illegitimate child in local authority care.

R v P [1980] Crim LR 796 CrCt Could be bail of child in care (bail denied in circumstances of this case).

R v Perch (Edmund) (1908-09) XXV TLR 401 CCA Finding that were guilty of wilful neglect of children not affected by jury's rider that accused acted through ignorance.

R v Plymouth Juvenile Court, ex parte F [1987] 1 FLR 169; (1987) 151 JP 355 HC QBD Best interests of child paramount concern when making care order under Children and Young Persons Act 1969, s 32A(1).

R v Pontlottlyn Juvenile Court, ex parte R [1990] FCR 900; [1991] 2 FLR 86 HC QBD Guardian ad litem appointed after initial refusal as mother misled by court clerk into thinking appointment forthcoming and so had not attended hearing with her solicitor.

R v Poole Juvenile Court, ex parte P; R v Southwark Juvenile Court, ex parte C [1988] FCR 1; [1988] 1 FLR 8 HC QBD On procedure as regards applications for discharge of care orders.

R v Powell (1914-15) XXIV Cox CC 229; (1915) 79 JP 272 CCC Need not intend to forever deprive parent of child to be convicted of child abduction.

R v Pryce [1972] Crim LR 307 CA On unlawful detention contrary to the Offences against the Person Act 1861, s 56.

R v R (1982) 3 FLR 345 CA Child allowed to use mother's new surname but registered for medical purposes as 'Donna R otherwise T'.

R v R [1978] 2 All ER 33; [1977] 1 WLR 1256 CA Custody of child given to mother notwithstanding that this involved surname-change of child to surname of mother's lover.

R v R [1988] FCR 307; [1988] 1 FLR 89 CA On assessing appropriate maintenance for children (husband's expenditure on new house was justified here).

R v R [1995] 4 ll ER 115; [1995] Fam 209; [1996] 1 FCR 480; [1995] 2 FLR 625; [1995] 3 WLR 425 HC FamD 'Wrongful removal/retention' notice under Convention on Child Abduction need not take given form; generally court to ensure parent in state from which child taken knows Convention rights.

R v R [1973] 3 All ER 933; (1973) 117 SJ 394; [1973] 1 WLR 1115 HC FamD Referral of blood test applications from registrar to judge.

R v R [1968] 2 All ER 608; (1968) 118 NLJ 588; (1967) 111 SJ 413; [1968] 2 WLR 1468 HC PDAD Cannot accept child as member of family unless possess all material facts.

R v Redbridge London Borough Council, ex parte East Sussex County Council [1992] TLR 663 HC QBD Ordinary residence of mentally handicapped twins whose parents had left them in England and returned to Nigeria was deemed not to lie with parents.

R v Registrar General, ex parte Smith [1990] 2 All ER 170; [1990] FCR 561; [1990] 2 FLR 79; [1990] 2 QB 253; [1990] 2 WLR 980 HC QBD Registrar General may refuse to provide information necessary for granting of birth certificate if might be used for future criminal act.

R v Registrar General, ex parte Smith [1991] 2 All ER 88; [1991] FCR 403; [1991] 1 FLR 255; [1991] 2 QB 393; [1991] 2 WLR 782 CA Absolute statutory duty to provide birth certificate to adopted persons not applicable where it would facilitate crime.

R v Rider [1954] Crim LR 49; (1954) 118 JP 73 Assizes On what constitutes a charge when deciding whether accused to have benefit of first-time charge proviso in prosecution for having carnal knowledge of under-sixteen year old (Criminal Law Amendment Act 1922, s 2).

R v Rose, ex parte McGibbon (1959) 123 JP 374 HC QBD Jamaican maintenance order could not be rescinded by English court under Maintenance Orders (Facilties for Enforcement) Act 1920.

R v Rosenberg (1906) 70 JP 264 CCC On elements of offence of concealment of birth.

R v Salford Health Authority, ex parte Janaway [1988] 1 FLR 17 HC QBD Conscience provisions of Abortion Act apply only to medical parts of abortion not preliminary arrangements therefor.

R v Salford Health Authority, ex parte Janaway [1989] AC 537 (also HL); [1988] 2 FLR 370; (1988) 132 SJ 265; [1988] 2 WLR 442 CA Conscience provisions of Abortion Act apply not only to medical parts of abortion but preliminary arrangements therefore.

R v Sandbach Justices, ex parte Smith [1950] 2 All ER 781; (1950) 114 JP 514; [1951] 1 KB 62; (1950) 100 LJ 485; (1950) 94 SJ 597; [1950] 66 (2) TLR 291; (1950) WN (I) 397 HC KBD Guardianship proceedings to be brought where respondent lives (unless High Court action); generally no order where child outside jurisdiction.

R v Secretary of State for Health, ex parte Luff [1991] FCR 821; [1992] 1 FLR 59 HC QBD Non-quashing of Health Department advice to Home Office that short life expectancy of prospective adopter rendered proposed adoption inappropriate.

R v Secretary of State for the Home Department, ex parte Brassey and another [1989] FCR 423; [1989] 2 FLR 486; (1989) 133 SJ 388 HC QBD Person born abroad of foreign parents and later adopted abroad by British subject validly denied British passport.

R v Secretary of State for the Home Department, ex parte Khan [1984] FLR 735; (1984) 128 SJ 580; [1984] TLR 228 CA Refusal of entry of child whom sought to adopt quashed as not based on criteria set out in letter from Home Secretary to appellants and complied with by them.

R v Seddon and others (1916) 80 JP 208; (1915-16) XXXII TLR 279; (1916) WN (I) 63 HC KBD Failure (for want of corroboration) of affiliation action does not preclude second such action inside twelve months (Bastardy Laws Amendment Act 1872, s 4).

R v Sharp (Edward George) (1931-32) 23 Cr App R 7 CCA Six weeks' detention more than appropriate for unlawful carnal knowledge of precocious under-sixteen year old who looked and acted over sixteen.

R v Sheppard (James Martin) (1980) 70 Cr App R 210 CA Must be intentional neglect of child where charged with cruelty to child by reason of wilful neglect.

R v Sheppard and another [1980] 3 All ER 899; [1981] AC 394; (1981) 72 Cr App R 82; [1981] Crim LR 171; (1981) 145 JP 65; (1980) 130 NLJ 1144; (1980) 124 SJ 864; [1980] 3 WLR 960 HL Wilful neglect not strict liability offence; must be deliberate/reckless failure to provide proper medical care.

R v Slough Juvenile Court, ex parte Royal Berkshire County Council [1984] QB 387; (1983) 127 SJ 841; [1984] 2 WLR 45 HC QBD Secure accommodation order for duration of more than seventy-two hours in respect of child had to be authorised by juvenile court.

R v Smith (David George) [1985] Crim LR 42 CA On relevance of intention to detremination whether physical chastisement of child constituted assault occasioing actual bodily harm.

R v Smith (KA) [1983] Crim LR 739 CrCt Could be convicted of attempted infanticide under Infanticide Act 1938.

R v Solihull Metropolitan Borough Council, ex parte C and others [1984] FLR 363 HC QBD Decision on date on which to close community home quashed where failed to consider future welfare of affected children.

R v Spicer (1955) 39 Cr App R 189 Assizes Could be convicted for procuring miscarriage where sought so to do though means used could not be successful.

R v St Alban's Magistrates' Court, ex parte Read [1994] 1 FCR 50 HC QBD Inter partes hearing ordered to enable formerly registered child-minder to challenge her ex parte removal from the register.

R v Starkie (1921-22) 16 Cr App R 61; (1922) 86 JP 74; [1922] 2 KB 275; [1922] 91 LJCL 663; (1921-22) 66 SJ 300; (1921-22) XXXVIII TLR 181; (1922) WN (I) 10 CCA Admissibility of evidence pertaining to alternative counts in criminal abortion charge.

R v Sunderland Juvenile Court, ex parte G [1988] 2 All ER 34; [1988] FCR 193; [1988] 2 FLR 40 (also HC QBD); (1988) 132 SJ 372; [1988] 1 WLR 398 CA Parent may call independent social worker though court may exclude witness.

R v Sunderland Juvenile Court, ex parte G [1988] FCR 17; [1988] 2 FLR 41 (also CA); (1987) 131 SJ 1155 HC QBD Guardian ad litem's report may be made available to independent social worker (here was).

R v Tegerdine [1983] Crim LR 163 CA Putative father was guilty of abduction of child albeit that did so from concern for child.

R v The Inner London Juvenile Court, ex parte G [1988] FCR 316; [1988] 2 FLR 58 HC QBD Non-adjournment of care action until father tried for alleged sexual abuse of subject of care action was valid.

R v Tonks (1915-17) XXV Cox CC 228; (1914-15) 11 Cr App R 284; (1916) 80 JP 165; [1916] 1 KB 443; [1916] 85 LJKB 396; (1915-16) 60 SJ 122; (1915-16) XXXII TLR 137; (1915) WN (I) 387 CCA Not autrefois convict where prosecuted for manslaughter of child (who died from neglect) where had been convicted of wilful neglect of child.

R v Wakeley [1918-19] All ER 1157; (1918-21) XXVI Cox CC 569; (1920) 84 JP 31; [1920] 1 KB 688; [1920] 89 LJCL 97; (1920) 122 LTR 623 CCA Prosecution began when information laid and information laid within six months of offence so prosecution in time.

R v Walker and another (1911-12) XXVIII TLR 342 HC KBD Refusal to order delivery up of illegitimate child to natural parents from those who had adopted child and kept him for ten years.

R v Walker and another (1911-12) XXVIII TLR 375 CA Compromise of action in appeal from refusal to order delivery up of illegitimate child to natural parents from those who had adopted child and kept him for ten years.

R v Waltham Forest Justices, ex parte B [1989] FCR 341 HC QBD Care orders valid where magistrates disregarded substance of (but not fact that there were) claims by children (relayed to court inter alia by social worker) but still found orders to be merited.

R v Waltham Forest London Borough, ex parte G [1989] 2 FLR 138 HC QBD On juvenile court's role where dispute between local authority/guardian ad litem over psychiatric assessment of children in care seeking discharge of care orders.

R v Wandsworth West Juvenile Court, ex parte S (1983) 4 FLR 53 HC QBD Child's solicitor could withdraw application to discharge care order though parents had made application; withdrawal did not mean matter res judicata: could be started anew.

R v Wandsworth West Juvenile Court, ex parte S [1984] FLR 713 CA Child's solicitor ought not to have been allowed withdraw application to discharge care order which parents had made.

R v Watson and Watson (1959) 43 Cr App R 111 Assizes Where husband and wife living together wife can be convicted of manslaughter of child by wilful neglect.

R v West Glamorgan County Council, ex parte T [1990] FCR 142; [1990] 1 FLR 339; (1989) 133 SJ 1545 HC QBD Refusal of judicial review of local authority decision not to serve fresh notice of refusal of access.

R v West London Magistrates' Court, ex parte Emmett [1994] 1 FCR 421; [1993] 2 FLR 663 HC FamD On enforceability of registered Irish maintenance order: in-/effective post-/pre-divorce decree absolute.

R v West Malling Juvenile Court, ex parte K (1986) 150 JP 367; (1970) 130 SJ 650 HC QBD Case ought to hve been adjourned where parent in care action given social worker/guardian ad litem reports containing unexpected material on day of hearing.

R v Williams (John Owen) (1910) 4 Cr App R 89; (1909-10) XXVI TLR 290 CCA On what constitutes exposure/abandonment of child (Children Act 1908, s 12(1)).

R v Wills [1990] Crim LR 714 CA On what is meant by treatment of child 'likely' to cause harm in Children and Young Persons Act 1933, s 1.

R v Wilson, Esq (Metropolitan Magistrate) and others, ex parte Pereira [1952] 2 All ER 706; (1952) 116 JP 549; (1952) 102 LJ 595; [1953] 1 QB 59; (1952) 96 SJ 729; [1952] 2 TLR 594; (1952) WN (I) 457 HC QBD Bastardy action cannot be brought where child abroad to mother then domiciled abroad.

R v Wood Green Crown Court, ex parte P (1983) 4 FLR 206; [1982] TLR 164 HC QBD On flexible admissibility rules in care actions (here concerning admissibility of medical/welfare reports).

R v Worcester City Juvenile Court, ex parte F [1989] 1 All ER 500; [1989] FCR 110; [1989] 1 FLR 230; (1988) 132 SJ 1526 HC QBD Upon request juvenile court must disclose reasons for refusing to discharge care order.

R v Young (Tara Moira Lisa) (1993) 97 Cr App R 280; (1993) 137 SJ LB 32; [1992] TLR 641 CA Where jury convinced overall that was cruelty (even though disagree on specific incidents) can convict of cruelty to children.

R, D v [1995] 1 FCR 501 HC FamD On making of interim care order (here unjustified); on need for magistrates to give their reasons for their decision in care action.

R, F v [1995] 1 FLR 227; [1994] TLR 628 HC FamD Enforcement of contact order validly refused: on task of justices hearing contact order enforcement application.

R, Manchester City Council v [1996] 3 FCR 118 HC FamD Supervision order in favour of parents who seemed likely to have occasioned subdural haematoma to child on one occasion (probably by shaking/flinging child down) but were otherwise satisfactory parents.

R, S v [1993] 1 FCR 331 HC FamD On deciding whether to make parental responsibility order.

Rabot and another v De Silva and others [1909] AC 376; [1909] 78 LJPC 73; (1909) C LTR 242; (1908-09) XXV TLR 332 PC Bequest to wife (former mistress) and children from her original marriage was valid.

Re A [1991] FCR 569; [1991] 2 FLR 394 CA On custody of young children: child's welfare paramount concern.

Re A [1989] 3 All ER 610; [1989] Fam 103; [1990] 1 FLR 86; [1989] 3 WLR 900 HC FamD Deciding whether to administer police caution to ward is purely for prosecuting body but court to be party to actual administration.

Re A [1991] FCR 1013; [1992] 1 FLR 427 CA Court would not allow wardship action to be used (as here) to frustrate Home Secretary in enforcing immigration law.

Re A [1994] 2 FCR 125 CA Non-dismissal of local authority from care action where guardian ad litem convinced child would be at risk of significant harm if aunt made carer.

Re A (1981) 2 FLR 173 CA Parents' continuous ill-treatment of their child justified dispensing with their consent to adoption.

Re A (1980) 1 FLR 100; (1979) 123 SJ 553 HC FamD Independent welfare officer to ascertain wishes of child where sought; child's interests (of paramount importance) required that children remain in local authority care.

Re A (1981) 131 NLJ 1212 CA Return of children to Italian father in Rome ordered of English mother who had taken the children to England.

Re A [1992] TLR 419 CA No order for return of child where had clearly been acquiescence to its removal from Germany.

Re A [1987] 2 FLR 429 HC FamD On balance was decided that Nigerian child be left with English foster-parents notwithstanding cultural difficulties.

Re A [1988] 1 FLR 365 CA Return of child to foreign jurisdiction ordered where was not grave risk that same would expose child to psychological harm.

Re A [1987] 2 All ER 81; [1987] FCR 9; [1987] 2 FLR 184; (1987) 151 JP 458; (1987) 131 SJ 194; [1987] 1 WLR 153 CA Not unreasonable if parents consent to custodianship order not adoption order; consent dispensed with if in child's interests.

Re A (1987) 151 JP 39 HC FamD Adoption of child by paternal grandmother allowed.

Re A [1988] 2 FLR 133; [1988] 1 WLR 229 HC FamD On procedure where adopting foreign child who is brought by another from abroad and placed with adoptive parents outside customs zone.

Re A [1955] 2 All ER 202; (1955) 105 LJ 313 CA Child's welfare paramount/natural mother's wishes regarding child's upbringing did not carry special weight.

Re A [1996] 1 FCR 562 HC FamD On whether/when (as here) to make parental responsibility order.

Re A [1996] 1 FCR 533 CA Leave of family court required by (and given to) solicitor who sought to rely on knowledge acquired in onetime care proceedings to aid defence of later unconnected criminal case.

Re A [1996] 3 FCR 1 CA Adoption of non-patrial allowed where was not ploy to circumvent immigration regulations but was bona fide effort to seek usual benefits of adoption (other than UK citizenship).

Re A [1995] 2 FCR 686; [1995] 1 FLR 599 HC FamD Leave of court not required before child in care could apply for discharge of care order.

Re A [1996] 1 FCR 467; [1995] 2 FLR 153; [1995] TLR 141 CA No presumption that contact between grandparent and grandchild to be granted unless good reason not to.

Re A [1994] 2 FLR 463 CA On inference to be drawn from refusal of blood test in action where paternity at issue.

Re A [1993] 1 FCR 824 HC FamD On extent of risk of significant harm to child necessary before care order will be made.

Re A [1995] 3 FCR 543 HC FamD Failed application by grandmother for contact with grandchild (opposed by parents).

Re A [1996] 3 FCR 165; [1996] 1 FLR 561 CA On registrability/enforcement of foreign access order.

Re A [1970] 3 All ER 184; [1970] Ch 665; (1970) 114 SJ 415; [1970] 3 WLR 142 CA Court need not order return if children not in jurisdiction through fraud, they need protection, and other parent can readily come to England.

Re A (1968) 112 SJ 190 HC ChD Court would not exercise wardship powers in respect of foreign child being dealt with by immigration authorities.

Re A (1968) 112 SJ 295 CA Court would not exercise wardship powers in respect of foreign child being dealt with by immigration authorities.

Re A [1993] 1 FCR 164 HC FamD Interim care order where appraisal of father as carer for child incomplete; no need here for welfare officer to prepare report in addition to that which guardian ad litem preparing.

Re A [1995] 2 FCR 298; [1995] 1 FLR 767 HC FamD On determining place of habitual residence of child.

Re A [1991] FCR 849; (1991) 141 NLJ 968t; [1991] TLR 329 CA Non-access to natural father justified as was in interests of children.

Re A [1994] 1 FCR 104; [1993] 2 FLR 645 CA On rights of natural parent vis-à-vis child freed for adoption.

Re A [1993] 1 FLR 425 HC FamD Aunt did not have to allowed apply for residence order/joined as party in care action.

Re A [1963] 1 All ER 531; (1963) 127 JP 209; (1963) 113 LJ 170; (1963) 107 SJ 114; [1963] 1 WLR 231 HC ChD 'Accommodation' adoptions not allowed (even where in infant's interest).

Re A [1997] TLR 357 CA Court to be satisfied (as here) that welfare of child would be adequately safeguarded by courts of foreign non-Convention jurisdiction before ordering return of child to that jurisdiction.

Re A (a minor) [1995] 3 All ER 401; [1995] 2 FCR 114; [1995] 1 FLR 335; (1994) 138 SJ LB 228; [1995] 1 WLR 482 CA Court cannot make care order on application for extension of supervision order; interim care orders are available but only to cover adjournments.

Re A (An infant) [1955] 2 All ER 202 CA Child's welfare paramount/natural mother's wishes regarding child's upbringing did not carry special weight.

Re A (B) [1985] FLR 1008 HC FamD Children's interests required that they remain in foster-care; objectively tested, mother's refusal of consent to adoption not unreasonable; future access by mother a real possibility.

Re A (L) (a minor) (1978) 128 NLJ 564t; (1978) 122 SJ 417 HC FamD Revocation of adoption order where effect on child of breaking tie between him and his paternal grandparents had not been considered.

Re A (No 2) [1993] 1 FLR 396 CA On proper exercise of discretion not to return child to country of habitual residence.

Re A (P) [1971] 3 All ER 522; (1972) 136 JP 37; (1971) 121 NLJ 569t; (1971) 115 SJ 586; [1971] 1 WLR 1530 CA Parties in adoption actions have no undeniable right to report of guardian ad litem.

Re A (R) (1974) 124 NLJ 599t HC FamD Order for adoption by unmarried couple (made without notice of application for same to natural father) set aside.

Re A (Z) [1993] 1 FCR 733 (also HC FamD) CA On what constitutes acquiescence/wrongful retention.

Re A (Z) [1993] 1 FCR 733 (also CA) HC FamD Mother/aunt had wrongfully retained child when kept child in England/secured ex parte residence and prohibited steps orders: father did not acquiesce to wrongful retention.

Re A and another [1991] FCR 460; [1991] 2 FLR 241; [1991] TLR 19 CA Non-acquiescence by father meant (absent other ground for claim) abducted children had to be returned to jurisdiction from where taken.

Re A and another [1992] 1 All ER 929; [1992] Fam 106; [1992] 2 FCR 97; [1992] 2 FLR 14; [1992] TLR 62; [1992] 2 WLR 536 CA Acquiescence may be active/passive; acquiescence where know other party removing/retaining child, know act is unlawful, know of general rights; acquiescence not a continuing frame of mind so can only be withdrawn immediately after given.

Re A and another (No 2) [1993] 1 All ER 272 [1993] Fam 1; [1993] 1 FCR 293; [1992] 3 WLR 538 CA Acquiescence of father to wrongful removal/retention of children by mother entitles court to consider interests of children in deciding whether or not to order return.

Re A and B (No 1) (investigation of alleged abuse) [1995] 3 FCR 389 HC FamD On investigation of/child interviews concerning child sex abuse claims.

Re A and E (1980) 1 FLR 312 CA On exercise by court of its wardship jurisdiction where child in local authority care.

Re A and others [1992] 3 All ER 872; [1992] Fam 182; [1992] 2 FLR 154; [1992] TLR 245; [1992] 3 WLR 422 CA Child's welfare not paramount consideration in residence order proceedings.

Re A and others [1996] 1 All ER 24; [1995] 3 FCR 635; [1996] 1 FLR 1; [1996] 1 WLR 25 HC FamD 'Habitual residence' under Hague Convention on Child Abduction intimates voluntary and settled physical presence in signatory country prior to abduction.

Re a Baby (1985) 135 NLJ 106 HC FamD Best interests of child still guiding factor in wardship cases involving surrogate children.

Re a Subpoena [1996] 3 FCR 190; [1996] 2 FLR 629 HC QBD On disclosure of adoption materials to commissioner for local administration.

Re A, an Infant; Allen v Peninsular and Oriental Steamship Co, Ltd, and another (1961) 105 SJ 424 CA Court would not make order to restrain ward on board ship being allowed enter new jurisdiction when ship docked there.

Re A, decd; S v A (1941) 164 LTR 230; (1940) 84 SJ 477; (1939-40) LVI TLR 934; (1940) WN (I) 271 HC ChD Mother of illegitimate child could appoint testamentary guardian of same (Guardianship of Infants Act 1925, s 5 and Part 2 of Schedule to Act).

Re A-H [1962] 3 All ER 853; (1962) 112 LJ 816; (1962) 106 SJ 1011; [1962] 3 WLR 1430 HC ChD Non-interference by ChD where orders sought available in existing proceedings before PDAD.

Re A-K [1997] 2 FCR 563; [1997] TLR 123 CA Valid order for supervised contact with children at Royal Courts of Justice plus requirement that father surrender his passport to his solicitors where was danger father might otherwise abduct children.

Re Adams; Sursham v Farquharson and others [1951] 1 All ER 1037; [1951] 1 TLR 841 HC ChD Ineligibility of legitimated children to proceeds of trust fund.

Re Adoption Application [1993] Fam 125; [1993] 1 FLR 947; [1992] 1 WLR 596 HC FamD Adoption of foreign child allowed despite irregularities in procedure as child's interest in remaining with parents greater than that of leaving same.

Re Adoption Application 58/80 [1982] TLR 139 HC FamD Order for adoption of child in respect of whom immigration authorities had previously refused to extend entry permit.

Re Adoption Application A113/67 [1988] FCR 723 HC FamD Adoption of foreign child allowed despite procedural irregularities.

Re Adoption Application No 41/61 [1962] 2 All ER 833; (1962) 126 JP 403 HC ChD Adoption proceedings stayed to allow putative father bring custody action.

Re Adoption Application No 41/61 [1962] 3 All ER 553; [1963] Ch 315; (1962) 126 JP 511; (1962) 112 LJ 718; (1962) 106 SJ 571/649; [1962] 3 WLR 997 CA Infant's interests paramount in adoption/custody cases; adjournment of adoption case to hear custody action.

Re Adoption Application No 41/61 (No 2) [1963] 2 All ER 1082; [1964] Ch 48; (1963) 127 JP 440; (1963) 113 LJ 561; (1963) 107 SJ 573; [1963] 3 WLR 357 HC ChD Welfare of infant of paramount consideration in custody/adoption proceedings.

Re Adoption Application No 41/61 (No 2) [1963] 2 All ER 1082; (1962) 112 LJ 505; [1962] 1 WLR 866 HC ChD Welfare of infant of paramount consideration in custody/adoption proceedings.

Re Adoption Application No 52/1951 [1951] 2 All ER 931; [1952] Ch 16; (1951) 115 JP 625; (1951) 101 LJ 637; (1951) 95 SJ 711; [1951] 2 TLR 887; (1951) WN (I) 520 HC ChD Residency requires degree of permananecy: three months out of fifteen with intention to retire not residency.

Re Adoption Application No 77/88 [1990] TLR 428 HC FamD Could as part of adoption order injunct natural father from communicating with child/its new parents or from approaching within certain distance of child's new home.

Re Aldrich (1967) 111 SJ 475 HC PDAD On intervention in legitimacy action (brought by father).

Re an Adoption Application [1987] 2 All ER 826; [1987] Fam 81; [1987] FCR 161; [1987] 2 FLR 291; (1987) 137 NLJ 267; [1987] 3 WLR 31 HC FamD Surrogacy not contrary to Adoption Act if payments not for profit/reward.

Re an Adoption Application [1990] 1 FLR 412; [1990] 1 WLR 520 HC FamD On disclosure of information from adoption proceedings where is in public interest.

Re an Adoption Application [1992] 1 FLR 341; [1991] TLR 483; [1993] 2 WLR 110 HC FamD Adoption of foreign child allowed despite breaches by adopters of Adoption Act 1976.

Re an ex parte originating summons in an adoption application [1990] 1 All ER 639 HC FamD Procedure for adoption agency when disclosing confidential information relevant to criminal proceedings.

Re an Infant (Care and Protection) [1965] Crim LR 486; (1965) 109 SJ 454 HC QBD Parents required to be heard in local authority application for care order.

Re Andrews [1958] 2 All ER 308; [1958] Ch 665; (1958) 108 LJ 425; (1958) 102 SJ 382 HC ChD Wardship concerns a matter for wardship court; PDAD will make care/custody/control decisions on merit regarding ChD ward (and in the course of so doing will remove child from ChD wardship); ChD may hear wardship application despite PDAD care/custody/control order/s regarding child.

Re Application No 41 of 1974 (1975) 125 NLJ 507t CA Although best future for baby lay with adopters with whom placed mother's withdrawal/refusal of consent to adoption not unreasonable.

Re Arif (Mohamed); Re Singh (Nirbhai) [1968] Ch 643 (also HC ChD) [1968] 2 WLR 1290 (also HC ChD) CA Courts if had wardship jurisdiction over infant refused admission by immigration authorities would not (if those authorities acted properly) exercise its jurisdiction.

Re Arif (Mohamed); Re Singh (Nirbhai) [1968] Ch 643 (also CA) [1968] 2 WLR 1290 (also CA) HC ChD Courts if had wardship jurisdiction over infant refused admission by immigration authorities would not (if those authorities acted properly) exercise its jurisdiction.

Re Aster (1955) 99 SJ 276; [1955] 1 WLR 465 CA Welfare of child not wishes of mother of paramount importance in custody cases.

Re B [1993] 1 FLR 543; (1993) 137 SJ LB 13 CA Exceptionally court may review local authority's long-term plans for child in care.

Re B [1994] 2 FCR 1142; [1994] 2 FLR 479 CA Improper that Algerian father (abductor) who was not in contempt when attended court be committed to prison until children brought to British Embassy in Algiers.

Re B [1993] 2 FCR 607 CA Discharge of committal/care/return orders in respect of child whose return to jurisdiction was sought.

Re B [1995] 3 All ER 333; [1995] Fam 239; [1995] 3 FCR 671; [1995] 2 FLR 1; [1995] 3 WLR 40 CA Adoption order cannot be set aside as based on fundamental mistake in fact unless natural justice denied in adoption process.

Re B [1974] 3 All ER 915; [1975] Fam 36; (1975) 139 JP 87 HC FamD On exercise of wardship jurisdiction where child in local authority care.

Re B (1989) 133 SJ 1606 CA On need for/what consist of adequate justices' reasons for decision in child custody action.

Re B [1990] FCR 469 HC FamD Court's authorisation unnecessary to arrest/detention of over seventeen year old ward.

Re B (1981) 2 FLR 412 HC FamD Wardship ought not to have been terminated where parents not afforded opportunity of further meetings with doctor seeking to rehabilitate family.

Re B (1982) 3 FLR 117 (also HC FamD); (1981) 131 NLJ 1112; (1981) 125 SJ 608; [1981] 1 WLR 1421 CA Court ordered operation in respect of new-born Mongol which parents would not authorise: test was best interests of child.

Re B (1982) 3 FLR 117 (also CA) HC QBD Refusal (on basis that not in best interests of child) to order operation on new-born Mongol which parents would not authorise.

Re B [1983] TLR 619 CA On allowing confidential report of guardian ad litem to affect adoption proceedings.

Re B (1983) 4 FLR 683 CA Interim custody order varied as in original form would cause disruption in child's life with time divided equally between both parents.

Re B [1984] FLR 648 CA On granting of access to parent where other parent vehemently opposed to it (here access refused but possibility of future variation).

Re B (1983) 4 FLR 472; (1982) 132 NLJ 1172 CA Interim care and control of children to mother pending resolution of wardship/'kidnapping' proceedings appropriate.

Re B (1981) 2 FLR 307; (1980) 124 SJ 81 HC FamD Practice as regards application for place of safety order for ward of court.

Re B [1996] 3 FCR 697; [1996] 2 FLR 15 HC FamD Though no consent to keeping/use of gametes man and woman had jointly undergone fertility treatment so man was parent of children born.

Re B [1994] 1 FCR 471 HC FamD Children of mentally unwell mother taken into care (occasional/no access for older/younger child with aim of eventual residence to fathers).

Re B [1990] FCR 841; [1990] 2 FLR 383 CA Consent dispensed with where refused on basis that wished to maintain contact with child; grudge against local authority/basis of grudge irrelevant/ could be relevant to reasonableness of refusal of consent (here basis of grudge not reasonable).

Re B [1976] 3 All ER 124; [1976] Fam 161; (1976) 126 NLJ 289t; (1976) 120 SJ 199; [1976] 2 WLR 755 HC FamD Welfare of child primary, not paramount consideration in deciding if parental consent to adoption unreasonably withheld.

Re B [1988] AC 199; [1987] 2 FLR 314 (also HC FamD/CA); (1987) 137 NLJ 432; (1987) 131 SJ 625; [1987] 2 WLR 1213 HL Sterilisation operation of mildly mentally handicapped ward approved as was in best interests of same.

Re B [1989] FCR 191; [1988] 1 FLR 484 HC FamD Permissible though inappropriate for court to review local authority decision regarding allocation of staff.

Re B [1989] 1 FLR 268 HC FamD On appointment of guardian ad litem in wardship action.

Re B (1976) 126 NLJ 1167b CA Custody of one of two children to each parent merited in instant circumstances.

Re B [1975] 2 All ER 449; [1975] 2 WLR 569 HC FamD Justices may but should not order adoption; invalid adoption where justices fail to consider interests of child/if consent unreasonably withheld and apply wrong test to question of consent.

Re B (1974) 124 NLJ 620t; (1975) 119 SJ 165; [1975] 2 WLR 302 HC FamD Exceptionally court will (and did here) make child in care a ward of court.

Re B [1975] Fam 127; (1975) 125 NLJ 14t; (1975) 119 SJ 133 HC FamD Adoption order made in favour of mother/stepfather (and despite father's refusal of consent) revoked where father genuinely wanted to maintain paternal relationship with child.

Re B [1996] 1 FCR 229 HC FamD Reliability of child witnesses ultimately a matter for court, not expert witnesses; on prorelevancy of past behaviour to determining whether child likely to suffer significant harm in future.

Re B [1995] 1 FCR 273; [1994] 2 FLR 915; [1994] TLR 367 HC FamD On determining place of habital residence of child.

Re B [1995] 2 FCR 749 HC FamD Refusal to allow adoption of child from The Gambia.

Re B [1994] 2 FCR 309 CA Mother allowed remove children from jurisdiction as would lead to increased likelihood of contact between father/children; otherwise would cause great frustration.

Re B [1997] 1 FCR 477; [1997] 1 FLR 285; [1997] 3 WLR 1 HC FamD On operation of issue estoppel in care proceedings (here previous finding of child sex abuse at issue).

Re B (1994) 138 SJ LB 176 HC FamD Removal of child from jurisdiction to place where mother attempted reconciliation did not change child's habitual residence.

Re B [1994] 1 FCR 905; [1994] 2 FLR 269; [1994] TLR 202 HC FamD Trial period of contact not delay detrimental to child in resolution of case contrary to Children Act 1989, s 1(2).

Re B [1995] 2 FCR 505; [1994] 2 FLR 249; (1994) 138 SJ LB 109; [1994] TLR 267 CA Consent to taking of child invalid as obtained by fraud; on meaning of 'rights of custody' in Child Abduction Convention, art 1(b).

Re B [1962] Ch 201 CA Court would not implore wardship jurisdiction in respect of children over whom statutory body (local education authority) seeking to discharge its duty.

Re B [1992] TLR 520 HC FamD Mother could seek return of children to Germany (from whence taken by father) even though took part in post-abduction family law action in England (place to whence children taken).

Re B [1996] 3 FCR 446; [1996] 1 FLR 676; [1996] 1 WLR 716 CA Conditional supervision order after mother made certain undertakings improper but amended form of order allowed stand.

Re B [1996] 3 FCR 272; [1996] 1 FLR 667 CA Reasoned departure of judge from opinions of expert/guardian ad litem when granting interim care order was valid.

Re B [1992] 2 FLR 1 CA Exceptionally can make ex parte interim residence order in respect of abductee and non-abducted children on application by non-abducting parent.

Re B [1970] 3 All ER 1008; (1971) 135 JP 59; (1970) 120 NLJ 944t; [1971] 1 QB 437; (1970) 114 SJ 786; [1971] 2 WLR 129 CA Test for determining if withholding of consent is unreasonable.

Re B [1995] 1 WLR 232 CA On maximum duration (and hence commencement date of particular) secure accommodation order.

Re B [1967] 3 All ER 629; [1968] Ch 204; (1967) 111 SJ 809; [1967] 3 WLR 1438 HC ChD Absent foreign father consent dispensed with in interests of child.

Re B [1991] FCR 800 CA Local authority's parental rights in respect of child ended upon child's death.

Re B [1993] 1 FCR 363 (also CC) CA On relation between care/contact applications: inappropriate that CC judge halted contact when making care order.

Re B [1993] 1 FCR 565; [1993] 1 FLR 815 HC FamD Interim care order to local authority (residence order refused to paternal aunt) until alleged sexual abuse by father (mother in psychiatric hospital) investigated.

Re B [1991] FCR 414; [1991] 2 FLR 405 CA Where future of child depended on future of matrimonial home and judge could not make ancillary relief order any custody order made was interim.

Re B (a minor) [1996] 1 FCR 661 CA Reporting restrictions lifted that father might make money from newspaper publicity and thus ensure could provide continuing medical treatment for child.

Re B (A) [1985] FLR 470 HC FamD Exceptionally (as here) court would make universally binding order prohibiting publication of material enabling identification of mother/ward.

Re B (A) [1948] 2 All ER 727; [1949] 118 LJR 21 HC ChD Public policy requires that Official Solicitor be guardian ad litem in adoption cases.

Re B (A) [1949] 1 All ER 709; [1949] 118 LJR 1032; (1948) LXIV TLR 573 HC ChD Exceptionally adoption of grandchild may be allowed.

Re B (A) [1996] 1 FLR 27; [1995] TLR 472 HC FamD Adoption order favouring foster-father and residence orders favouring him/his cohabitee so both had parental responsibility towards child.

Re B (A) [1954] 2 All ER 287; (1954) 118 JP 318; [1954] 2 QB 385; (1954) 98 SJ 391; [1954] 3 WLR 1 HC QBD Court cannot review local authority discretionary decision to remove child from foster parents.

Re B (C) [1981] 1 All ER 16; (1981) 145 JP 90; (1981) 125 SJ 219; [1981] 1 WLR 379 CA Court free to decide case in best interests of child where local authority seeks care and control of child in voluntary care.

Re B (C) [1994] 2 FCR 925; [1994] 2 FLR 762 HC FamD Blood testing of child not allowed where mother objected.

Re B (C) [1995] 1 FLR 622 CA Access order to grandparents (grandfather a convicted child sex abuser) wrong as did not hear oral evidence/court welfare officer on concerns involved (and contained in latter's report).

Re B (C) [1993] 1 FCR 440; [1993] 1 FLR 920 HC FamD On nature/effect of parental reponsibility order: here refusal of order quashed as justices did not fully consider appropriateness of order.

Re B (G) [1985] FLR 719 CyCt On test as to whether withholding of consent unreasonable (here was); on examination of normal child by psychiatrist.

Re B (GA) [1963] 3 All ER 125; [1964] Ch 1; (1963) 127 JP 492; (1963) 113 LJ 562; (1963) 107 SJ 681; [1963] 3 WLR 471 HC ChD Infant spending better part of week with couple while adopter worked was continuously in adopter's care and control.

Re B (H) [1997] 1 FLR 392 HC FamD Return of abducted children to mother in Denmark ordered despite their desire to remain with father in England.

Re B (LH) [1935] All ER 517; [1935] Ch 643 CA Receiver of lunatic's estate authorised to take such steps regarding lunatic's son as lunatic was authorised to do as son's guardian.

Re B (MIJ) (1978) 128 NLJ 187b CA Reasonableness of parent's revocation of non-irrevocable consent to be considered in light of changed circumstances since child placed with adopters.

Re B (minors) (1977) 127 NLJ 913t HC FamD On desirability of ready availability of welfare officer's reports to parties' lawyers.

Re B (N) [1993] 1 FCR 271 CA On what constitutes unlawful removal; non-return of child reversed where initial decision based on mistaken finding that return could well expose child to intolerable situation.

Re B (No 1) [1994] 1 FCR 389 HC FamD On relationship between contact/residence orders jurisdiction of court and Child Abduction Convention jurisdiction.

Re B (P) [1985] FLR 394 HC FamD On determining whether child ought to be freed for adoption/whether rehabilitation of child in parents' home preferable.

Re B (T) [1996] 1 FCR 101; [1995] 2 FLR 801; [1995] TLR 373 CA On whether to adjourn care action where criminal action (in respect of parents) pending: here inappropriately adjourned.

Re B (T) (residence order) [1995] 2 FCR 240 CA Valid decision by judge to retain status quo (three children with father, one with mother) with regular contact by mother to child resident with father.

Re B (TA) an infant [1970] 3 All ER 705; [1971] Ch 270; (1971) 135 JP 7; (1970) 114 SJ 769; [1970] 3 WLR 835 HC ChD Rôle of appellate court in guardianship cases.

Re B (W) [1995] 2 FLR 1023 HC FamD Shared residence order refused to non-biological father who had acted as father.

Re B [1994] 1 FCR 394 [1993] 1 FLR 993 HC FamD On what constitutes habitual residence/ retention/acquiescence for purposes of Hague Child Abduction Convention.

Re B and another [1993] 3 All ER 524; [1993] Fam 301; [1993] 3 WLR 63 CA Paramount consideration in parental contact case being welfare of children court entitled to consider local authority's plans for children's future.

Re B and G [1985] FLR 134 HC FamD Custody of children transferred to mother after over five years as father/stepmother were scientologists.

Re B and G [1985] FLR 493 CA Custody of children properly transferred to mother after over five years where father/stepmother were scientologists.

Re B and others [1992] 3 All ER 867; [1992] Fam 162; [1992] 3 WLR 113 CA Court may make residence order to preempt abduction — ex parte if necessary.

Re B and S [1995] 1 FCR 486 HC FamD Adoption order made to foster-mother after over eleven years fostering despite fosterers' marriage break-down/fosterers keeping husband's adulterous affair secret from local authority.

Re B's Settlement; B v B [1940] Ch 54; [1940] 109 LJCh 20; (1939-40) LVI TLR 30; (1939) WN (I) 347 HC ChD Ward's welfare paramount factor in deciding custody action even if has already been foreign court order regarding custody.

Re B-M [1993] 1 FLR 979 HC FamD On when court has jurisdiction under the Hague Child Abduction Convention.

Re B; B v B [1949] 118 LJR 369; (1949) LXV TLR 142 HC ChD Child who showed no evidence of prematurity despite being born only 188 days after 'father's' return was not child of purported father.

Re B; Re D [1972] 1 All ER 898; (1972) 136 JP 259; (1972) 116 SJ 58; [1972] 1 WLR 102 CA Exceptionally, could be post-adoption contact between adopted child and natural parent/s.

Re Baker [1961] Ch 303; (1961) 111 LJ 597 HC ChD Non-exercise of court's wardship jurisdiction over infants to enforce school attendance order.

Re Barbour's Settlement; National Westminster Bank Ltd v Barbour and others [1974] 1 All ER 1188 HC ChD Guardian ad litem to decide if corporate trustee fee increase in interests of minor/to be opposed.

Re Benner (1951) 95 SJ 596; (1951) WN (I) 436 HC ChD American father granted leave to remove wards from UK (where life with mother was uncertain) to US where he and his wife could offer greater certainty.

Re Billson's Settlement Trusts [1984] 2 All ER 401; [1984] Ch 409; [1984] 2 WLR 966 CA Legitimated son barred from interest in settlement executed before legitimation.

Re Brinkley's Will Trusts; Westminster Bank v Brinkley and another [1968] 2 WLR 217; [1968] Ch 407 HC ChD Will bequeathing property to grandchildren held not to include adopted grandchildren.

Re Brodie, decd; Barclays Bank Ltd v Dallas and others [1967] Ch 818; [1967] 2 WLR 1379 HC ChD Properly legitimated child stands in position of child born legitimate as regards inheritance.

Re Bromage; Public v Cuthbert [1935] All ER 80; [1935] Ch 605; (1935) 153 LTR 313; (1935) 79 SJ 418; (1934-35) LI TLR 408 HC ChD Post-separation deed children deemed illegitimate where no evidence of access by husband.

Re C [1996] 4 All ER 871; [1997] AC 489; [1997] 1 FCR 149; [1997] 1 FLR 1; (1996) 146 NLJ 1777; [1996] 3 WLR 1098 HL Residential assessment validly ordered in course of care proceedings.

Re C [1994] 1 FCR 609 HC FamD Leave to child to seek residence order: on granting leave for same.

Re C (1982) 3 FLR 95 CA Dispensing with consent to be subject of hearing if controverted; court to decide whether party of whom adverse comments made in report of guardian ad litem to be informed so can prepare rebuttal.

Re C [1984] FLR 419 (also HC FamD) CA Risk to ward from mother (to whom was close) required care and control of ward be given to local authority which was authorised to place child with foster-parents with view to adoption; on appointing Offical Solicitor as guardian ad litem; child's interests absolutely paramount in wardship actions.

Re C [1983] TLR 711 CA On undesirabiliry of independent welfare reports; on extent of paramountcy of interests of child.

Re C [1984] FLR 419 (also CA) HC FamD Risk to ward from mother (to whom was close) required care and control of ward be given to local authority which was authorised to place child with foster-parents with view to adoption.

Re C [1983] 1 All ER 219; (1983) 4 FLR 374; (1983) 133 NLJ 126; (1982) 126 SJ 820; [1982] TLR 394; [1982] 1 WLR 1462 HC FamD Court may invoke wardship powers in respect of child already subject of care order in criminal case.

Re C (1983) 4 FLR 396 HC FamD Order for increased access to child (for whom council had planned adoption) by natural mother who had surmounted drink problem with view to eventually returning child to mother.

Re C (1981) 2 FLR 63 CA Welfare of child may merit exercise by HC of its wardship jurisdiction even though juvenile court dismissed local authority care order application.

Re C (1969) 119 NLJ 600t HC ChD Failed application by foster parents to restrain broadcasting of television programme concerning ward in their care.

Re C (1981) 2 FLR 163 CA Care and control of child to father (though had lived with mother with one six-month break since birth); courts loathe to break bond between child and particular parent.

Re C (1981) 2 FLR 177 CA Adoption order for persons not related to child in preference to grandparents (granted access) though had latter (as should have) previously been given custody present adoption would never have arisen.

Re C [1994] TLR 593 CA On departing from advice given in report of court welfare officer.

Re C (1979) 129 (2) NLJ 1180c CA On seeking exercise of wardship jurisdiction as way of appealing against decision of lower court not to make care order.

Re C [1996] 3 FCR 222 HC FamD Father who stood by during considerable and lengthy preparations made by mother to remove children from US to UK held to have consented to removal.

Re C [1997] 1 FLR 544 HC FamD On which local authority is to be designated in local authority care order.

Re C [1997] 2 WLR 322 CA On disclosure to police of material arising in course of care proceedings relevant to later criminal action springing therefrom.

Re C [1978] 2 All ER 230; [1978] Fam 105; (1977) 121 SJ 693; [1977] 3 WLR 561 CA Child's welfare of paramount importance where peremptory order sought after kidnapping; child's interests required English court to assume jurisdiction.

Re C [1994] 1 FCR 447 HC FamD Interim supervision order favouring mother of baby pending full care hearing.

Re C [1985] FLR 804 CA Refusal of access valid as would have deleterious effect on children/ mother and her partner; improper to refuse access until children decide for themselves whether desirable — not a decision for children.

Re C [1985] FLR 1114 CA Failed application by mother for full investigation in wardship of alleged abuse of her son by his adoptive parents.

Re C [1985] FLR 56 HC FamD On role of independent social workers.

Re C (1987) 151 JP 135 CA Judge did not err in giving care and control of child to drug addict father where mother was schizophrenic and maternal grandparents quite old.

Re C [1987] 1 FLR 418 HC FamD On role of medical experts/Official Solicitor caring for wards/in wardship proceedings.

Re C [1985] FLR 846 HC FamD Care and control granted husband and wife of surrogate child of which husband natural father.

Re C [1988] 1 All ER 705; [1989] AC 1; [1988] FCR 484; [1988] 2 FLR 159; (1988) 138 NLJ 64; (1988) 132 SJ 334; [1988] 2 WLR 474 HL Court may provide for future access to natural family in adoption order.

Re C [1986] 1 FLR 315 CA Court ought not to have ordered that annual progress reports regarding adopted child be given to natural father.

Re C [1987] 2 FLR 383 CA Refusal of consent to adoption unless adoptee maintained contact with sibling not unreasonable; adopters could not be relied upon to ensure same so adoption refused: long-term fostering ordered.

Re C [1989] 2 All ER 782; [1990] Fam 26; [1990] FCR 209; (1989) 139 NLJ 612; (1989) 133 SJ 876; [1989] 3 WLR 240 CA Court may authorise treatment of terminally ill child that eases suffering without prolonging life.

Re C [1989] FCR 774; [1989] FCR 774; [1989] 1 FLR 222; (1989) 133 SJ 20; [1989] 1 WLR 61 CA Great-uncle not 'relative' for purposes of Adoption Act 1976, s 72(1); court ought not to have appointed guardian in respect of wards of court.

Re C [1996] Fam 79; [1995] 1 FLR 777; [1995] 3 WLR 30 CA County court judge could not amend contact order so as to vary degree of contact.

Re C [1996] 2 FCR 129; [1995] 2 FLR 483 CA Parent for purposes of adoption is person with parental responsibility towards child so natural father not parent in instant case.

Re C [1996] 1 FCR 332 HC FamD Care order with provision for declining contact and ultimate adoption properly made (rather than making of no order which would have resulted in child being left with foster-parents).

Re C [1993] 3 All ER 259; [1993] Fam 210; [1993] 3 WLR 85 HC FamD Once adoption order made parental contact provisions altered only if fundamental change in circumstances.

Re C (1992) 136 SJ LB 252; [1992] TLR 407 HC FamD May be order that there be no contact between child and natural mother; inappropriate to direct guardian ad litem to police rehabilitation programme of child in local authority care.

Re C [1994] 2 FCR 485; [1993] 2 FLR 260 CA On deciding whether child should be freed for adoption.

Re C [1996] 1 FLR 414 HC FamD Could not be acquiescence on part of father who had not originally consented to indefinite removal of children.

Re C [1995] 2 FCR 701 CA Number of times when contact available to natural parents of child placed for adoption reduced at behest of local authority after child freed for adoption.

Re C (1969) 113 SJ 164 HL Care and control of child to English foster-parents, not natural foreign parents.

Re C [1991] FCR 856; [1992] 1 FLR 1; (1991) 135 SJ LB 100; [1991] TLR 387 CA On relevant considerations when deciding whether to grant parental rights order: enforceability a relevant, not paramount issue.

Re C [1993] 1 FLR 87 HC FamD No adoption order favouring adopters who contravened adoption law.

Re C [1994] 1 FCR 705; [1993] 1 FLR 940 HC FamD On basis for/securing of access to mentally handicapped adult daughter by parent who did not have care of daughter.

Re C [1991] FCR 1052; [1991] TLR 404 CA On deciding whether withholding of parental agreement to adoption justified (here was); court to decide parental access issue before deciding whether to free child for adoption.

Re C [1995] 2 FCR 451; [1994] 2 FLR 525 HC FamD On availability of guardian ad litem's adoption report in later contact/residence hearings.

Re C [1994] 2 FCR 839; [1994] 2 FLR 513 CA Foster-mother's adoption application to be fully determined before local authority allowed serve notice to remove foster-child from her.

Re C (1997) 141 SJ LB 34; [1997] TLR 41 HC FamD Child in care but living at home was not being 'accommodated' by local authority under Children Act 1989, s 23.

Re C [1993] 1 FLR 832 HC FamD Long-term fostering in best interests of child notwithstanding her contrary desires.

Re C [1992] 2 FCR 65 HC FamD Expert assessment ordered to see whether parents should keep newborn child where previous five children in care/had been sexually abused (albeit not perhaps by father).

Re C [1994] 1 FCR 837; [1994] 1 FLR 26 HC FamD Near-fifteen year old refused residence order facilitating her living separately from parents/refused specific issue order allowing her to go on foreign holiday with friend's family.

Re C [1993] 2 FLR 431 HC FamD On procedure as regards natural mother's applying for contact/specific issue order after adoption order made.

Re C [1994] 1 WLR 1220 CA Child's welfare paramount when court deciding whether to order child's removal from foster parent.

Re C [1995] 1 FLR 617 CA Was reasonable to decide residence order application absent welfare officer where report latter provided inconclusive.

Re C [1993] 1 FCR 770 HC FamD Enforcement of United States access order.

Re C [1992] 1 FLR 115 CA On resolving issue of access by parent who has always shown interest in children it is proposed to have adopted; reasonable refusal of consent not made unreasonable through delay for which parent not responsible.

Re C [1991] FCR 969; [1992] 1 FLR 309 CA Husband who was not father refused access to child (absence of blood link a factor though not per se a basis for refusing access).

Re C [1991] FCR 518 HC FamD Inappropriate to order liberal access to non-custodial father so that child could get to know him as well as mother (custodian).

Re C [1995] 2 FCR 276 CA On deciding whether or not to adjourn residence application where court welfare officer cannot be present to give oral evidence; on interviewing of child at centre of residence application.

Re C [1964] 3 All ER 483; (1965) 129 JP 62; [1965] 2 QB 449; [1964] 3 WLR 1041 CA In all the circumstances — though primary consideration effect on child — (of whom strong medical evidence to show non-adoption detrimental) consent being unreasonably withheld.

Re C [1996] 2 FLR 708; (1996) TLR 3/10/96 CA Residential assessment cannot be ordered when making interim care order.

Re C [1995] TLR 323 CA Unmarried natural father who did not enjoy parental responsibility over his child did not have to be attached to proceedings regarding adoption of same.

Re C [1996] 1 FCR 461; [1995] 1 FLR 927 HC FamD On judicial approach to application by child to live with separated parent.

Re C [1989] FCR 197; [1989] 1 FLR 403; (1989) 133 SJ 660 CA Order for return of abducted child where undertakings by father obviated grave risk of harm to child.

Re C [1994] TLR 349 CA Consideration of child's welfare necessary before granting leave to remove proposed adoptee from foster-care.

Re C [1992] 2 FCR 341 HC FamD Conditional, experimental, short-term, interim supervision order in favour of parents previously guilty of battering child.

Re C [1991] FCR 308 CA On private receipt by judge in access proceedings of confidential information pertaining to action.

Re C (a minor) (1996) 140 SJ LB 221 CA Local authority could refuse to make residential assessment of child (in interim care) and its parents.

Re C (a minor) (1993) 137 SJ LB 135 HC FamD On assessment of means when determining whether/to what extent parent liable to contribute towards cost of maintaining child in care.

Re C (A) [1966] 1 All ER 560; (1966) 130 JP 146; (1965-66) 116 NLJ 555; (1966) 110 SJ 212; [1966] 1 WLR 415 HC ChD Court will not interfere with valid exercise of local authority discretion regarding child in care.

Re C (A); C v C [1970] 1 All ER 309; (1970) 120 NLJ 153t; [1970] 1 WLR 288 CA In guardianship cases paramount interest is that of infant.

Re C (B) [1985] FLR 639 CA Refusal of access to natural father justified as not in child's best interests (father essentially using access to get at mother/mother very anxious about access).

Re C (B) [1995] 3 FCR 598 HC FamD On determining to which local authority care order ought to be addressed.

Re C (CS) [1960] 1 All ER 711; (1960) 124 JP 260; (1960) 110 LJ 316; (1960) 104 SJ 269 HC ChD Child spending three nights with natural mother in three months before adoption action not in continuous care and possession of adopters; as child placed by local authority must be returned to local authority.

Re C (E) [1996] 3 FCR 521 (also CA); [1996] 2 FLR 123 HC FamD On disclosure to police of evidence in care proceedings.

Re C (E) [1996] 3 FCR 521 (also HC FamD); [1996] 2 FLR 725 CA On ordering disclosure of materials from care proceedings for use in criminal proceedings.

Re C (J) [1996] 1 FCR 434; [1995] 2 FLR 77 HC FamD On discovery in care actions.

Re C (LP) (1964) 108 SJ 638 CA Mother's refusal of consent to adoption of child by foster parents with whom had lived for two years.

Re C (MA) [1966] 1 All ER 838 (also HC ChD); (1966) 130 JP 217 (also HC ChD); (1966) 110 SJ 309; [1966] 1 WLR 646 CA In adoption-custody cases child's welfare paramount interest; no requirement regarding religious education imposed.

Re C (MA) [1966] 1 All ER 838 (also CA); (1966) 130 JP 217 (also CA) HC ChD In adoption-custody cases child's welfare paramount interest; no requirement regarding religious education imposed.

Re C (minors) [1992] TLR 548 CA Natural father seeking residence order not 'parent' under Children Act 1989 of child freed for adoption so required leave of court.

Re C (No 1) [1990] 1 FLR 252 CA Blanket ban on publication of any personal information other than that contained in open court judgment given in wardship case of particular public interest.

Re C (No 2) [1989] 2 All ER 791 [1990] Fam 39; (1989) 139 NLJ 613; [1989] 3 WLR 252 CA Injunction prohibiting any publicity about medical treatment to ward justifiable if in interests of ward.

Re C (No 2) [1990] FCR 220 [1990] 1 FLR 263 CA Judgment in open court (albeit taking steps to protect identity of persons involved in case) required where ordering non-treatment of ward who as result would die.

Re C (P) [1961] 2 All ER 308; [1961] Ch 312; (1961) 111 LJ 341 HC ChD Official Solicitor may recover costs from applicants in action where functions as guardian ad litem.

Re C (S) (1971) 121 NLJ 569 HC ChD Four day injunction on removal of child (abducted by parent) from jurisdiction so as to allow non-abducting parent to be heard on the matter.

Re C (S) [1994] 1 FLR 96 HC FamD Leave given to fourteen year old in local authority care to seek residence order enabling her to live with family of friend.

Re C and another [1989] 1 All ER 395 CA Dubious whether court can make guardianship order where existing wardship order.

Re C and another [1993] 3 All ER 313; [1994] Fam 1 CA Natural father without parental responsibility not a 'parent' for purpose of residence order; may not apply for residence order as of right after child freed for adoption.

Re C and another [1992] 2 All ER 86 CA Parental rights order available even where few rights under it enforceable; judge may consider prospective enforceability.

Re C and F [1997] 1 FCR 405; [1997] 1 FLR 190; (1996) 140 SJ LB 261; (1996) TLR 28/11/96 CA No stay/injunction on removal of children by adoption agency from prospective adopters whose marriage was disintegrating.

Re C, An Infant [1938] 107 LJCh 65; (1938) 158 LTR 371; (1936-37) LIII TLR 995 HC ChD Under Adoption of Children Act 1926 court could not allow husband and wife to adopt wife's illegitimate child (in respect of whom neither party was twenty-one years older) but could allow wife to adopt child if husband consented.

Re C, An Infant [1937] 3 All ER 783; (1937) 84 LJ 116 HC ChD Adoption allowed of child within prohibited degrees of consanguinity vis-à-vis female adopter.

Re C; P and P v C (1969) 113 SJ 721 CA Adoption order approved even though would end access to natural father as order would lead to legitimation of child.

Re C; Re The Adoption of Children Act, 1926 [1938] Ch 121 HC ChD Infant in respect of whom neither proposed adopter was older by twenty-one years could be adopted by natural mother alone but not jointly by same and husband (to whom child not related) or alone by latter.

Re Carroll (1930) 74 SJ 645 HC KBD Child to be adopted by Protestants/brought up as Protestant notwithstanding contrary wishes of Roman Catholic mother.

Re Carroll (No 2) [1930] All ER 192; (1931) 95 JP 25; [1931] 1 KB 317; (1931) 100 LJCL 113; (1931) 144 LTR 383; (1931) 75 SJ 98; (1930-31) XLVII TLR 125 CA Mother of illegitimate child may require child to be brought up in particular religion; CA considers habeas corpus appeal de novo.

Re Clabon (FW) [1904-07] All ER 1446; (1904-05) XCI LTR 316 HC ChD Poor infant liable like any other to pay for necessaries provided under invalid contract from own property.

Re Clay's Policy of Assurance; Clay v Earnshaw [1937] 2 All ER 548; (1937) 83 LJ 304 HC ChD Married Women's Property Act 1882 inapplicable to adopted children.

Re Cole (1899-1900) XVI TLR 500 HC ChD Custody of children given to (Protestant) uncle where after (Protestant) father's death mother converted to Catholicism.

Re Collins [1950] 1 All ER 1057; [1950] Ch 498; (1950) 100 LJ 274; (1950) 94 SJ 352; [1950] 66 (1) TLR 1107; (1950) WN (I) 242 CA Child's welfare paramount in guardianship cases: no rule that dead father has right to determine child's religious upbringing.

Re Cullimore (a minor) (1976) 126 NLJ 468t HC FamD Care and control of child to father who had not battered child as was thought (child actually suffering from brittle bone disease).

Re D [1977] 3 All ER 481; [1977] Fam 158; (1977) 141 JP 669; (1977) 127 NLJ 492t; [1977] 2 WLR 1006 HC FamD Child's interest of paramount concern in wardship not care proceedings.

Re D [1990] FCR 615; [1991] 1 FLR 48 CA On deciding application for freeing of child for adoption.

Re D [1953] 2 All ER 1318; (1954) 118 JP 25 CA Court of summary jurisdiction within which applicant resides may vary access order.

Re D (1981) 2 FLR 102 CA Adoption order preferable to joint custody order here where natural and step-parent seeking adoption; wishes of children relevant (here wanted adoption): decision contrary to wishes to be explained); child's memories of natural father inadequate reason for refusing adoption.

Re D (1978) 128 NLJ 336t; (1978) 122 SJ 193 HC FamD Wardship jurisdiction exercised in respect of child in local authority care.

Re D (1978) 128 NLJ 759t CA Child to be known by surname of stepfather and not natural father.

Re D (1977) 127 NLJ 116t; (1977) 121 SJ 35 HC FamD Child to be known by surname of natural father and not stepfather.

Re D [1977] 1 All ER 145; [1977] AC 602 (also CA); (1977) 127 NLJ 115t; (1977) 121 SJ 35; [1977] 2 WLR 79 HL Unreasonably withholding consent if reasonable parent in same position would not withhold; no appeal on factual issues to Court of Appeal.

Re D [1976] 2 All ER 342; [1977] AC 602 (also HL); (1977) 141 JP 110; (1976) 126 NLJ 265t; [1976] 3 WLR 12 CA Non-consent unreasonable if reasonable person in parent's place would consent.

Re D [1987] AC 317 (also HL); (1986) 136 NLJ 513; (1986) 130 SJ 467; [1986] 3 WLR 85 CA Care order in respect of child on foot of maternal damage to child while foetus was justified.

Re D [1987] AC 317 (also CA); [1987] 1 FLR 422; (1987) 151 JP 313; (1986) 136 NLJ 1184; (1970) 130 SJ 984; [1986] 3 WLR 1080 HL Care order in respect of child on foot of maternal damage to child while foetus was justified.

Re D [1987] 3 All ER 717; [1988] 1 FLR 131; (1987) 131 SJ 1485; [1987] 1 WLR 1400 CA Court will not normally intervene in local education authority decision on special education needs of ward save to assist/if invited by authority.

Re D [1988] 2 FLR 106 HC FamD On magistrates' role under the Guardianship of Minors Act 1971 in custody/access applications concerning children in local authority care.

Re D [1988] FCR 585; [1988] 1 FLR 97 HC FamD On power of court to order party to reveal location of abducted child.

Re D [1943] 2 All ER 411; [1943] Ch 305; [1943] 112 LJ 237; (1944) 94 LJ 61; (1943) 169 LTR 313; (1943) 87 SJ 290; (1942-43) LIX TLR 354; (1943) WN (I) 174 HC ChD Court could appoint guardian of infant alien without property.

Re D (1976) 120 SJ 214 CA Gay father's refusal of consent to adoption was not unreasonable as was no immediate danger of son being exposed to gay influences.

Re D [1995] 1 FLR 631; (1995) 139 SJ LB 13; [1994] TLR 637; [1995] 1 WLR 356 CA Difficult to obtain full disclosure of relevant materials in adoption cases.

Re D (1977) 121 SJ 355 HC FamD Wardship jurisdiction assumed after justices had discharged care order in respect of child.

Re D [1996] 2 FLR 273 CA Successful appeal against order that husband not stay overnight at matrimonial home after contact to his children.

Re D [1973] 2 All ER 993; [1973] Fam 179; [1973] 3 WLR 53 HC FamD Minor's welfare not only relevant factor under Guardianship of Minors Act 1970, ss 1 and 9; only exceptionally may court in wardship case upset existing decision on merits by magistrates.

Re D [1970] 1 All ER 1088; (1970) 134 JP 387; (1970) 114 SJ 188; [1970] 1 WLR 599 CA Case-records under Boarding-Out of Children Regulations 1955 are generally privileged.

Re D (1973) 117 SJ 525 HC FamD Joint custody order to husband and wife.

Re D [1993] 2 FCR 88; [1993] 2 FLR 423 HC FamD Care (not supervision) order appropriate for new child born of man with record of cruelty to own children.

Re D [1997] 2 FLR 48 CA Valid refusal of contact (for time being) between child of mixed race and his black father (who had been violent towards child's white mother).

Re D [1992] 1 All ER 892; [1992] 2 FCR 41; [1992] 1 FLR 637; [1992] 1 WLR 315 CA Court may grant ex parte order for return of child/prohibited steps order forbidding removal of child even if other parent outside jurisdiction/has no assets in jurisdiction.

Re D [1991] 3 All ER 461; [1991] Fam 137; [1991] FCR 521 CA Adoption applies to minors but court can consider post-majority benefit; in making adoption order court may not impose conditions on parents which have effect after majority attained.

Re D [1993] 1 FCR 964; [1993] 2 FLR 1 CA Contact with father (to which mother vehemently opposed) denied.

Re D [1958] 3 All ER 716; (1959) 123 JP 112; (1959) 109 LJ 41; [1959] 1 QB 229; (1959) 103 SJ 33 CA Single mother can adopt own illegitimate child.

Re D [1958] 1 All ER 427; (1958) 122 JP 156; (1958) 108 LJ 168; (1958) 102 SJ 138 CA Child's welfare paramount in deciding if refusal to consent reasonable; putative father does not have rights of lawful father.

Re D [1995] 2 FCR 681 HC FamD Court would not expand care proceedings to consider future of unborn child.

Re D [1943] 2 All ER 411 HC ChD Need not be property for guardian of infant to be appointed: test is whether infant needs to be safeguarded.

Re D [1953] 2 All ER 1318 CCA Court of summary jurisdiction within which applicant resides may vary access order.

Re D (1997) 141 SJ LB 170; [1997] TLR 445 CA Inappropriate for conditions of an injunctive nature to be attached to a contact order.

Re D [1996] 2 FCR 820; [1996] 2 FLR 281 CA Refusal of residence order (effectively an ouster order) set aside as judge had failed to consider contested residence application as such.

Re D [1995] 1 FLR 495; [1995] TLR 45 HC FamD Inappropriate that contact order be made absent welfare officer's report/oral evidence where issue of contact in dispute.

Re D [1987] FCR 140; [1987] 2 FLR 365 CA Despite non-observation by local authority of earlier CA decision that child be rehabilitated with mother passage of time since then meant was no longer in child's best interests to have access to mother.

Re D [1973] 3 All ER 1001; [1973] Fam 209; (1974) 138 JP 18; (1973) 123 NLJ 788t; (1973) 117 SJ 696; [1973] 3 WLR 595 HC FamD Persistent failure to discharge parental obligations to be so complete that no benefit in maintaining contact.

Re D (a minor) [1991] 2 FLR 66; [1991] TLR 31; [1991] 2 WLR 1215 CA Court could grant adoption where would operate to benefit child after attained majority; court cannot injunct third party communication with adoptee.

Re D (K) [1988] 1 All ER 577; [1988] AC 806; [1988] FCR 657; [1988] 2 FLR 139; (1988) 132 SJ 301; [1988] 2 WLR 398 HL In wardship proceedings child's welfare paramount; parent's right to access is secondary.

Re D (T) [1985] FLR 1150 HC FamD Natural father of illegitimate child in care could not seek invocation by court of its wardship jurisdiction to prevent local authority arranging adoption of child.

Re D and another [1995] 4 All ER 385; [1996] AC 593; [1996] 1 FCR 205; [1995] 2 FLR 687; (1995) 145 NLJ 1612; [1995] TLR 157; [1995] 3 WLR 483 HL Strong presumption exists in favour of full disclosure of relevant materials in adoption cases except where compelling evidence that disclosure would harm child.

Re D and H [1997] 1 FLR 841; (1997) 141 SJ LB 44; [1997] TLR 82 CA No termination of contact between natural mother and children being placed in long-term foster-care as was contrary to what local authority proposed.

Re Dankbars (1953) 97 SJ 811; [1953] 3 WLR 957 CA Summary court could vary access order in respect of infant at behest of either parent provided either parent living within court's jurisdiction.

Re Dulles' Settlement Trusts; Dulles v Vidler [1950] 2 All ER 1013; [1951] Ch 265; (1950) 100 LJ 622; (1950) 94 SJ 760; [1950] 66 (2) TLR 1028; (1950) WN (I) 523 CA Party may submit to jurisdiction of courts from abroad; application by infant with mother as best friend treated as mother's application.

Re Dulles' Settlement Trusts; Dulles v Vidler (1951) 101 LJ 302; [1951] 2 TLR 145 CA Foreigner living abroad can submit self to jurisdiction of court in custody proceedings.

Re Dunhill (1967) 111 SJ 113 HC ChD Wardship summons dismissed where merely issued for publicity purposes.

Re E [1994] 1 FCR 584; [1994] 1 FLR 146 CA On terminating contact between children and parents (here inappropriately done in context of local authority plans that 'closed' adoption of child take place).

Re E [1991] FCR 33 CA Rehabilitation of child discontinued and placement for adoption ordered.

Re E [1991] FCR 771; [1991] 2 FLR 585; [1991] TLR 93 HC FamD Leave of court unnecessary for thereapeutic sterilisation of mentally handicapped girl.

Re E [1984] 1 All ER 21; (1983) 4 FLR 668; [1983] TLR 47; [1983] 1 WLR 541 CA Court will not use wardship powers to interfere with local authority acts under care order even if care order case pending and no care order as of yet.

Re E [1984] FLR 457 (also CA/HL) HC FamD Care and control off child to father subject to supervision of welfare officer.

Re E [1984] 1 All ER 289 (also HC FamD/HL) CA Care of child to local authority; child to be prepared for adoption.

Re E (1983) 147 JP 321 CA On exercise by HC of its wardship jurisdiction where children are in care/care action in progress.

Re E [1990] FCR 921; [1990] 2 FLR 397 CA On freeing children for adoption: here order refused though access had been terminated/children formed relationship with prospective adopters.

Re E [1987] 1 FLR 368 CA Upset to child caused by difficulties over access created by non-custodial parent could not justify setting aside of order.

Re E [1989] FCR 118; [1989] 1 FLR 126 CA Mother's withholding consent was reasonable where sought to maintain proposed adoptee's relationship with sibling/hoped for eventual rehabilitation with adoptee.

Re E [1989] 1 FLR 135 CA Return of abducted child to country of habitual residence ordered; on allowing child to remain where return ran grave risk of placing child in intolerable situation.

Re E [1955] 3 All ER 174; [1956] Ch 23; (1955) 105 LJ 601; (1955) 99 SJ 726; [1955] 3 WLR 493 HC ChD Cannot order that child be allowed leave jurisdiction in action under Guardianship of Infants Acts 1886 and 1925; court cannot exercise inherent wardship jurisdiction over non-wards unless made wards under Law Reform (Miscellaneous Provisions) Act 1949.

Re E [1991] FCR 1034 CA Judge ought to have ordered residential assessment to aid him in care and control hearings.

Re E [1967] 2 All ER 881; [1967] 2 WLR 1370 CA Court need not blindly obey foreign court order if not in interests of child.

Re E [1967] 1 All ER 329; (1967) 111 SJ 34; [1967] 2 WLR 445 HC ChD Despite need for comity, child subject to foreign order may if necessary be made ward/put into custody and control here.

Re E [1995] 1 FCR 245; [1994] 2 FLR 548 HC FamD On ordering blood test where paternity in issue.

Re E [1963] 3 All ER 874; (1964) 114 LJ 9; (1964) 108 SJ 75; [1964] 1 WLR 51 HC ChD Mother's desires on religious education important but child's welfare paramount: here two compatible.

Re E [1995] 2 FCR 655; [1995] 1 FLR 57 HC FamD Contact order refused to natural parents of adopted child.

Re E [1993] 1 FCR 529 CA On disclosure of wardship documents in later wardship action concerning sibling.

Re E [1995] 1 FCR 65; [1995] 1 FLR 382 CA Judge justified in dispensing with consent of mother to adoption of child by single lesbian woman and in not allowing contact.

Re E [1994] 2 FCR 709; [1995] 1 FLR 392 CA Decision to refuse contact unchanged but parental responsibility order made; on directing that blood tests be conducted (only possible where paternity an issue).

Re E [1997] TLR 273 CA Conditional residence order improper.

Re E (C) [1995] 1 FCR 387; [1995] 1 FLR 26 HC FamD Guardian ad litem reappointed to act for child where specified proceedings ceased to be such upon local authority deciding not to seek care/supervision order.

Re E (D) [1967] Ch 287 HC ChD Court allowed child removed from United States contrary to court order there to remain in care and custody of aunt in England.

Re E (D) [1967] Ch 761; (1967) 111 SJ 352 CA Court allowed child removed from United States contrary to court order there to remain in care and custody of aunt in England.

Re E (P) (1969) 133 JP 137; (1968) 118 NLJ 956t; (1968) 112 SJ 821; [1968] 1 WLR 1913 CA Better that child lose illegitimacy via adoption and so lose contact with putative father than to retain illegitimacy and retain contact.

Re E (SA) [1984] 1 All ER 289; [1984] FLR 457 (also HC FamD/CA); (1984) 128 SJ 80; [1984] TLR 17; [1984] 1 WLR 156 HL In ward's interests court may follow course of action not argued by parties to case: period of access to ward by father favoured to see if long-term relationship between father/ward possible.

Re El-G (1983) 4 FLR 421 HC FamD Welfare of children demanded that they stay with prospective adopters; on deciding whether parent's refusal of consent unreasonable (here was: dispensed with); on pivotal role of court when is sought to change arrangements for ward.

Re El-G (1983) 4 FLR 589 CA Welfare of children demanded that they stay with prospective adopters; on deciding whether parent's refusal of consent unreasonable (here was: dispensed with); on pivotal role of court when is sought to change arrangements for ward.

Re F [1994] 1 FCR 110; [1993] 2 FLR 837 CA On relevant factors when deciding whether child to be allowed change surname.

Re F [1990] 3 All ER 580; [1990] Fam 189; [1991] FCR 116; [1990] 2 FLR 478; [1990] 3 WLR 505 HC FamD Court may grant injunction restraining access by natural parents whether as part of adoption order or otherwise.

Re F [1982] 1 All ER 321; (1982) 3 FLR 101; (1981) 131 NLJ 1053; (1981) 125 SJ 861; [1982] 1 WLR 102 CA Welfare of child paramount in adoption; welfare indicates if consent un/reasonably withheld by parent; adoption order rather than care order where child's welfare demands no access by mother.

Re F [1993] 1 FCR 389; [1993] 2 FLR 9 HC FamD On allowing withdrawal of care application.

Re F [1984] FLR 60; (1984) 134 NLJ 765c; [1983] TLR 535 CA Circumstances merited inluding direction that child being placed in long-term foster care be prepared for adoption.

Re F [1977] 2 All ER 777; [1977] Fam 165; [1977] 2 WLR 488 CA Court need not set aside adoption order made under mistake that adopters were married.

Re F [1988] 2 All ER 193; [1988] Fam 122; [1988] FCR 529; [1988] 2 FLR 307 (also HC FamD); (1988) 138 NLJ 37; (1989) 133 SJ 1088; (1988) 132 SJ 820; [1988] 2 WLR 1288 CA Unborn child cannot be made ward of court.

Re F [1988] 2 FLR 307 (also CA) HC FamD Unborn child cannot be made ward of court.

Re F [1989] 1 FLR 335; (1988) 132 SJ 1323 HC FamD Non-enforcement of French custody order but care and control to mother (abductress) with staying access to father.

Re F [1989] 1 All ER 1155; [1990] Fam 125; [1989] FCR 165; [1989] 1 FLR 233 (also HC FamD); (1988) 132 SJ 1269; [1989] 3 WLR 691 CA Use of wardship proceedings to prevent immigration authorities removing child an abuse of process but exceptionally (as here) allowed.

Re F [1989] 1 FLR 233 (also CA); (1989) 133 SJ 1088 HC FamD Use of wardship proceedings to prevent immigration authorities removing child an abuse of process.

Re F [1988] 2 FLR 116 CA On deciding whether to allow custodial parent remove child from jurisdiction (here allowed).

Re F [1988] FCR 679; [1988] 2 FLR 123 CA Wardship having harmful effect on children halted where had been no substantial evidence on which to continue it.

Re F [1957] 1 All ER 819; (1957) 121 JP 270; (1957) 107 LJ 282 HC ChD Revocation of consent anytime before order possible and here was reasonable.

Re F (1975) 125 NLJ 1221t CA Custody of child to young father/stepmother with young daughter rather than to elderly grandparents.

Re F [1995] Fam 224; [1995] TLR 79; [1995] 3 WLR 339 CA Improper that mother removed child from US but court would not order return given potentially serious risk to child which that would entail.

Re F [1996] 1 FCR 379; [1995] 2 FLR 31 CA Mother's removal of child from Colorado wrongful but return not ordered as would present grave risk of psychological harm to child.

Re F [1973] 3 All ER 493; [1973] Fam 198; (1973) 123 NLJ 723t; (1973) 117 SJ 616; [1973] 3 WLR 461 HC FamD Court may provide 'right of access' orders involving/prohibiting foreign travel by child.

Re F [1992] 1 FLR 548 CA On evidence admissible in child abduction/Hague Convention proceedings; child of persons apparently intending to emigrate to Australia was habitually resident there (after only three months).

Re F [1992] 1 FLR 561 CA Person estopped by custody order to which consented from appealing against same on basis that had not consented thereto.

Re F [1995] 3 All ER 641 CA Exceptionally Court will exercise discretionary power under Hague Convention on Child Abduction not to summarily return abducted child to country of habitual residence (as required by Convention) where that would entail grave risk to welfare of child.

Re F [1993] 3 All ER 596; [1993] Fam 314; [1993] 3 WLR 369 CA Court will not order blood tests where parental responsibility application likely to fail; not in child's interests; parent in charge of child opposed.

Re F [1997] 1 FCR 523 CA Not following court welfare officer's advice perfectly justified.

Re F [1970] 1 All ER 344; (1969) 119 NLJ 1094t; [1970] 1 WLR 192 CA Father's consent easily dispensed with where in best interests of child and father has seriously misbehaved.

Re F [1992] 2 FCR 595 HC FamD On determining place of habitual residence of children.

Re F [1969] 2 Ch 238; (1969) 113 SJ 486 HC ChD Child's welfare paramount but not sole concern in custody action: care and custody to mother responsible for collapse of marriage.

Re F [1994] 2 FCR 1354; [1995] 1 FLR 510 HC FamD Contact order set aside where made in belief that would require parents to allow sibling in care have access to other siblings; on appropriate order to seek in such circumstances.

Re F [1995] 3 FCR 601 HC FamD Psychological appraisal of child inappropriate; guardian ad litem ordered to give oral report.

Re F [1993] 1 FCR 945; [1993] 2 FLR 677 CA Post-separation contact order refused to transsexual father whose children did not want contact with him.

Re F (G) [1992] 1 FLR 293 HC FamD On when declaration of legality of hysterectomy on mentally handicapped woman is unnecessary.

Re F (R) an infant [1969] 3 All ER 1101; (1969) 133 JP 743; [1970] 1 QB 385; (1969) 113 SJ 835; [1969] 3 WLR 853 CA Leave to appeal out of time against adoption order of which not notified.

Re F (W) an infant [1969] 3 All ER 595; [1969] 2 Ch 269; (1969) 133 JP 723; [1969] 3 WLR 206 HC ChD No second hearing absent fresh evidence after first dismissed on merits.

Re F and R [1995] 1 FLR 524 HC FamD In controverted action where grandparent seeking leave to apply for contact with grandchildren magistrates ought to have heard evidence from each side.

Re G [1994] 2 FCR 359; [1994] 2 FLR 301 HC FamD Failed application by mother for residence order: local authority allowed place children outside jurisdiction.

Re G [1993] 1 FCR 810 HC FamD Care order made in respect of child despite here strong desire to be allowed remain with father (incapable of properly caring for her).

Re G [1990] FCR 189; [1989] 2 FLR 475 CA Return of abducted child justified where undertakings by father obviated grave risk of psychological harm to child; nine-year old's desire to remain with mother (abductress) considered but not acted upon.

Re G [1984] FLR 268 CA Child's welfare paramount issue when adjudicating in wardship action springing from parental abduction.

Re G [1996] 3 FCR 77; [1996] 1 FLR 276; (1996) 146 NLJ 85; (1996) 140 SJ LB 10; [1996] 1 WLR 1407 CA No leave necessary before local authority may disclose to police information social worker obtained from parents.

Re G [1982] 2 All ER 32; [1982] TLR 37; [1982] 1 WLR 438 CA Payment of Official Solicitor's costs for acting as guardian ad litem.

Re G (1980) 1 FLR 109 HC FamD On approach when adoption sought by natural parent and step-parent; adoption/access hearings (if are both) to be heard together.

Re G [1990] FCR 973; [1990] 2 FLR 325 HC FamD Registration of Belgian custody order favouring father (mother abductress).

Re G [1988] FCR 440; [1988] 1 FLR 305 CA On role of court (regarding evidence and otherwise) in wardship action; father with mental disorder might after treatment be considered for access; wife deserved access but given visiting access because of threat posed by father.

Re G [1995] 2 FCR 53; [1994] 2 FLR 964 CA Failed prohibited steps application by mother to restrain father with custody, care and control of son from sending him to boarding school.

Re G [1996] 1 FCR 495; [1995] 2 FLR 534 HC FamD Non-recognition of Paraguayan adoption; foreign mother joined to English adoption proceedings.

Re G [1996] 1 FCR 173; [1995] 2 FLR 410 HC FamD Non-return of children where was inordinate delay in seeking return (children two and a half years in jurisdiction).

Re G [1995] 3 FCR 26 CA Following on illegal placement of child adoption could only be authorised by HC.

Re G [1994] 2 FCR 1037; [1994] 1 FLR 504 CA On deciding whether to make parental responsibility order.

Re G [1990] FCR 881; [1990] 2 FLR 429 CA Reconsideration ordered of case where judge refused to dispense with mother's consent as judge failed to carry out proper balancing exercise.

Re G [1994] 2 FLR 69 HC FamD On role of court where parties agree care order necessary but disagree on facts justifying same; court in care order application free to reconsider issues that arose in related criminal action.

Re G (1981) 2 FLR 382; (1981) 125 SJ 307 HC FamD Court could order care and control of child (to local authority) with a view to adoption.

Re G [1995] 2 FCR 120; [1994] 2 FLR 785 CA Rehearing of care application ordered where factual basis of previous decision put in issue by expert evidence.

Re G [1994] 2 FCR 106; [1994] 2 FLR 291 HC FamD On disclosure of papers to expert witnesses in care proceedings.

Re G [1995] Fam 16; [1994] 3 WLR 1211 HC FamD On making care order.

Re G [1993] 3 All ER 657; [1993] Fam 216; [1993] 2 FCR 485; [1993] 1 FLR 669; [1993] TLR 26; [1993] 2 WLR 824 CA Enforcement of foreign access order requires contact order; not available via compliance order against Lord Chancellor's Department.

Re G [1969] 2 All ER 1135; (1969) 119 NLJ 672; [1969] 1 WLR 1001 HC ChD Forum conveniens for post-divorce wardship case is that where divorce heard.

Re G [1992] 2 FCR 713; [1993] 1 FLR 103 CA Issue estoppel/res judicata inapplicable to Criminal Injuries Compensation Board; compensation could be available to child sex abuse victim whose assailant was not convicted.

Re G (1967) 111 SJ 702 HC ChD Contemnor to be released from prison once 'kidnapped' daughter returned to jurisdiction (child to be placed with foster mother pending wardship hearings.

Re G [1992] TLR 545 HC FamD On responsibility on guardian ad litem in deciding whether child/ren to be present in court at proceedings concerning them.

Re G [1993] 2 FCR 27; [1992] 1 FLR 642 CA Where parent/prospective adopters seeking access/adoption order applications are to be heard together but that does not apply to connected interim/interlocutory applications.

Re G (1965) 109 SJ 756 CA Valid decision not to make staying order in respect of Roman Catholic children to whom father living in adultery granted access.

Re G [1963] 3 All ER 370; (1963) 127 JP 549; (1963) 113 LJ 657; (1963) 107 SJ 682; [1963] 1 WLR 1169 HC ChD Courts will exercise wardship powers in line with local authority's proper exercise of discretion over child in care: if care to end court will intervene.

Re G [1995] 2 FCR 22; [1995] 1 FLR 64 HC FamD Non-return of dual-nationality children of two English parents as mother's return would lead to mental deterioration raising adverse risks for children.

Re G [1996] 2 FCR 505 CA Care orders justified in respect of all children in light of treatment meted out by parents to elder children.

Re G [1996] 2 FLR 398 CA Care order unavailable where revocation of freeing order sought: could grant/refuse revocation application.

Re G [1992] 2 FCR 720; [1993] 1 FLR 910; [1992] TLR 468 CA On availability/appropriateness of ex parte interim residence order.

Re G [1962] 2 All ER 173; (1962) 126 JP 341; (1962) 112 LJ 320; [1962] 2 QB 141; (1962) 106 SJ 282; [1962] 2 WLR 1010 CA Adoption of Protestant child by Jewish parents allowed as in infant's best interests.

Re G [1993] 2 FCR 557; [1993] 2 FLR 839; [1993] TLR 441 CA On nature/effect of interim care order and whether/when to grant one.

Re G [1997] 2 All ER 534; [1997] 2 Cr App R (S) 721; [1997] 2 FCR 289; [1997] 2 FLR 202; (1997) 147 NLJ 721; (1997) 141 SJ LB 106; [1997] TLR 248; [1997] 2 WLR 747 HL On granting of conditional revocation of freeing order (here granted once care order in respect of child made under the Children Act 1989, s 31).

Re G (a minor) [1997] 2 FCR 325; [1997] 1 FLR 360 CA Where separated husband refused to have blood test done in respect of child of wife of whom husband claimed he was father, the inference to be drawn was that he was not the father.

Re G (An infant) [1956] 2 All ER 876; [1956] 1 WLR 911 CA Valid giving of (illegitimate) child into mother's sole care and custody.

Re G (C) [1994] 2 FCR 889 HC FamD On whether/when to order blood testing where paternity in issue(here ordered).

Re G (custody) [1992] 2 FCR 279 CA Judge's non-interference with status quo as regards custody of young child justified despite real concerns of father over mother's new cohabitee.

Re G (DM) [1962] 2 All ER 546; (1962) 126 JP 363; (1962) 112 LJ 438; (1962) 106 SJ 410 HC ChD Non-severance with natural parents possible; indecent assault conviction did not preclude from adopting; guiding principles in adoption/guardianship case the same.

Re G (H) [1993] 1 FCR 553; [1993] 1 FLR 587 HC FamD Child could by father as next friend bring application for authorisation of own sterilisation.

Re G (M) (a minor) [1996] 2 FCR 761; (1996) 140 SJ LB 147; (1996) TLR 11/6/96 CA Non-revocation of freeing order where proposed adoption did not go through.

Re G (S) [1991] FCR 753; [1991] 2 FLR 329 HC FamD Unnecessary to obtain declaration that termination lawful before could perform abortion on mental defective.

Re G and M (contact) [1995] 3 FCR 514 HC FamD Appropriate case in which to substitute conditional residence orders for care orders.

Re G-Y [1984] FLR 811 HC FamD Necessary that leave of court be sought before ward allowed to have abortion.

Re G; Re R [1990] 2 FLR 347 HC FamD Police allowed give formal police caution to wards; on appropriate procedure in such cases.

Re G; Re R [1995] 2 FLR 867 CA Could not say that though sexual abuse not proved on the balance of probabilities there was nonetheless a real possibility of future significant harm.

Re Gilpin; Hutchinson v Gilpin (1953) 97 SJ 763 HC ChD Adopted child was intended/allowed to inherit along with testator's other grandchildren.

Re Green; Green v Meinall (1911) 46 LJ 372; (1911) 80 LJCh 63; (1910-11) 55 SJ 552; (1911) WN (I) 137 HC ChD Children of marriage between man and dead wife's sister were legitimated under Deceased Wife's Sister's Marriage Act 1907 though party to that later marriage died before statute enacted.

Re Guardianship of Infants Acts 1886 and 1925, and Re B (S), an Infant [1949] Ch 108; (1948) WN (I) 480 HC ChD Maintenance order discharged where was non-access prior to 188 days before child's birth (and child born was mature); maintenance order applied to father as father so where paternity disproved would not issue against him as husband.

Re H [1993] TLR 97; [1994] 2 FCR 249 CA On principles as regards deciding contact applications.

Re H [1994] 2 FCR 437; [1993] 2 FLR 325 CA On freeing for adoption/'open' adoption (with parental contact).

Re H [1989] FCR 498 CA On options open to single father of children in care when local authority seeks to have children freed for adoption.

Re H [1990] 1 FLR 51 CA Care and control to maternal aunt/uncle, not mother (though her maternal abilities unquestioned) was justified.

Re H [1991] FCR 45; [1991] 1 FLR 40; [1990] TLR 311 CA On requiring surety for return of abducted children to jurisdiction within certain period.

Re H [1985] FLR 519 CA Adoption applications not to be ued to frustrate local authority actions; access order attached to adoption order only if agreement between parties concerned; father's refusal of consent to adoption unless access condition attached was reasonable.

Re H [1989] 2 FLR 174 CA Continuation of trial access by father to children, one of whom father had sexually abused was justified.

Re H [1989] 2 FLR 215 CA On effect of parental rights order obtained by illegitimate's father child pursuant to Family Law Reform Act 1987, s 4.

Re H [1982] Fam 121; (1983) 4 FLR 85; [1982] 3 WLR 501 HC FamD Court in making adoption order could override immigration decision by Secretary of State where welfare of child sought to be adopted demanded it.

Re H (1982) 3 FLR 386; (1981) 131 NLJ 1264 CA Mother's agreement to adoption properly dispensed with where reasonable mother in same circumstances would have consented.

Re H [1996] 4 All ER 28; [1996] 3 FCR 201; [1996] 2 FLR 65; (1996) 146 NLJ 406; [1996] 3 WLR 506 CA On refusing/ordering blood test where paternity in issue.

Re H (1977) 121 SJ 645 HC FamD Assumption by HC of wardship jurisdiction even though juvenile court could have done what parents asked (discharged care order).

Re H [1978] 2 All ER 903; [1978] Fam 65; (1978) 142 JP 474; (1978) 122 SJ 230; [1978] 2 WLR 608 CA Wardship order available where seek to supersede care order; Court of Appeal ought not to vary High Court assumption of wardship.

Re H (1983) 4 FLR 261 HC FamD Initial procedure as regards application for adoption of child by parent/step-parent.

Re H [1977] 2 All ER 339; (1977) 121 SJ 303; [1977] 1 WLR 471 CA Consent withdrawal possible anytime before order but more difficult/less reasonable as time progresses.

Re H (1977) 121 SJ 253 HC FamD Could order access by person who was neither parent nor guardian so here was open to grandmother to seek access.

Re H [1987] 2 FLR 12 HC FamD On ethnic background as factor when dealing with children; long-term fostering with view to adoption (if possible by someone of own ethnic background); access by mother to depend on her co-operation with social worker/what eventual adopters desired.

Re H [1986] 1 FLR 132; [1985] 1 WLR 1164 CA On undesirability of ex parte applications in wardship proceedings.

Re H (1985) 129 SJ 84; [1984] TLR 649 CA Instigation of adoption action an abuse of process where used to frustrate local authority in its exercise of its care jurisdiction.

Re H [1991] TLR 291 CA On deciding cases concerning child sex abuse allegations.

Re H [1994] 2 FCR 1; [1994] 2 FLR 979 HC FamD Court could not order steps supervisor must take in respect of responsible person subject to supervision order.

Re H [1994] 2 FLR 969 CA On desirability (as here) of mutual contact: contact validly ordered to person who had not sought same.

Re H [1995] 1 FCR 546; [1995] 1 FLR 236 HC FamD Release of adoption details where applicant seeking to contact adopted half-brother who possibly had genetic disease.

Re H [1995] 2 FLR 542 HC FamD Permission to report judgment under initials as would compel ward to confront own behaviour/was necessary to safeguard public.

Re H [1993] 2 FCR 437; [1993] 2 FLR 552 HC FamD On allowing child to participate in family proceedings without guardian ad litem.

Re H [1993] 2 FLR 541 HC FamD Application for residence order by lesbian couple, one party to which was mother of baby girl.

Re H [1994] 1 All ER 812; [1994] Fam 105; [1994] 2 FCR 351; [1994] 1 FLR 512; [1993] TLR 578; [1994] 2 WLR 269 CA Court not obliged to enforce recognised foreign custody order.

Re H [1994] 4 All ER 762; [1994] Fam 11; [1993] 3 WLR 1109 HC FamD Ward can take part in case minus guardian ad litem.

Re H (1974) 124 NLJ 1159t HC FamD Successful appeal by natural father against decision to dispense with his consent to the adoption of his children.

Re H [1996] 3 FCR 321; [1995] 2 FLR 883 CA Shared residence order to stepfather approved.

Re H [1994] 3 FCR 183; [1994] 2 FLR 80 HC FamD Grandparents who had enjoyed staying contact granted residence orders: care order to local authority quashed.

Re H [1994] 2 FCR 419; [1994] 2 FLR 776 CA Contact order in favour of stepfather.

Re H [1993] TLR 661 CA Interests of children demanded restriction on publicity following their being entrusted to care of transsexual parent.

Re H [1996] 2 FCR 784; [1996] 1 FLR 614 HC FamD Successful appeal against conviction/fining for non-compliance with contact order.

Re H [1996] 2 FCR 597; [1996] 1 FLR 717 HC FamD Adoption order made in respect of non-patrial (despite Home Secretary's objections) as was genuine adoption where welfare of adoptee outweighed public policy considerations.

Re H [1996] 4 All ER 600; [1996] 2 FLR 187; (1996) 140 SJ LB 128; [1997] 1 WLR 791 CA Adoption order in respect of non-patrial despite Home Secretary's objections: test when making adoption more broad-based than that set out by HC FamD.

Re H [1993] 1 FCR 904 CA On balancing interests of child-mother and her baby in care order application; three-month secure accommodation order in respect of mother merited.

Re H [1992] TLR 433 CA Father refused contact order was nonetheless granted a parental responsibility order.

Re H [1991] FCR 616; [1991] 2 FLR 411; [1991] TLR 49 CA Ex parte custody change generally undesirable: pending inter partes hearing child left with parent whom ex parte order favoured.

Re H [1996] 3 FCR 425 CA On what constitutes acquiescence to abduction (initiating proceedings but not insisting on summary return of children constituted acquiescence).

Re H [1992] 1 WLR 243 CA Wards (children of two families sharing accommodation) returned to family environment though there was (unsatisfactory) evidence of child abuse against one of them.

Re H [1990] FCR 353 CA Care and control to English uncle and aunt/liberal access to foreign mother where child's best interests demanded it.

Re H [1991] FCR 243; (1990) 140 NLJ 1192; [1990] TLR 644 CA On what constitutes wrongful removal/retention; Child Abduction Convention inapplicable where wrongful removal occurred before its commencement.

Re H [1991] FCR 985; [1991] 2 FLR 109 CA Interim care and control of child of dead mother given to maternal grandmother with generous access rights to father.

Re H [1966] 1 All ER 886; (1966) 110 SJ 88; [1966] 1 WLR 381 (also HC ChD) CA Inquiry into state of affairs permissible but not required before returning children to parent in foreign jurisdiction.

Re H [1965] 3 All ER 906; [1966] 1 WLR 381 (also CA) HC ChD Children returned to foreign jurisdiction without inquiry into merits of case/foreign court order.

Re H [1991] FCR 896 CA On when (unlike here) is appropriate to order that leave of court be sought before orders in respect of child be sought.

Re H [1992] 2 FCR 330; [1993] 1 FLR 440; [1992] TLR 276 HC FamD On taking account of wishes of disturbed but intelligent and capable child in care action.

Re H [1993] 1 FCR 85; [1993] 1 FLR 484 CA Parental responsibility but not contact order for father (where stepfather strenuously objected to contact order).

Re H [1992] 1 FLR 148 CA On deciding whether access should end/be restarted: here visiting access allowed.

Re H [1993] 2 FCR 277 HC FamD Local authority ordered to investigate circumstances of child whom lesbian couple seeking to foster.

Re H [1991] FCR 564 CA Interim care order to grandmother merited where was some doubt as to parental abilities of both parents.

Re H [1996] 3 FCR 49; [1996] 1 FLR 867 CA Father's non-payment of maintenance did not justify refusal of parental responsibility order.

Re H [1993] 1 FCR 671; [1994] 1 FLR 717 CA On deciding whether/when shared residence order merited (here was not).

Re H [1966] 1 All ER 886; (1965-66) 116 NLJ 725; [1966] 1 WLR 381 CA Inquiry into state of affairs permissible but not required before returning children to parent in foreign jurisdiction.

Re H [1959] 3 All ER 746; (1960) 124 JP 74; (1959) 109 LJ 703; (1959) 103 SJ 1003; [1959] 1 WLR 1163 HC ChD Cannot appoint joint guardian just to help in custody application: infant's interests sole determinant.

Re H (1996) TLR 9/5/96 CA On practice as regards deciding of adoption applications.

Re H (1996) TLR 12/3/96 CA Failed appeal against order for blood testing of mother and child where mother did not consent to the testing.

Re H [1995] 2 FCR 711; [1995] 1 FLR 964 HC FamD On disclosure of adoption papers in criminal action.

Re H (1989) 133 SJ 569 CA Under parental rights order father of illegitimate children did not enjoy custody rights over same but could oppose their adoption.

Re H [1990] FCR 990; [1990] 2 FLR 439 HC FamD Mother granted interim custody of child in Canada violated own custody rights when brought child to England: return to Canada ordered.

Re H (A) [1963] Ch 232 HC ChD On competence/willingness of ChD to make wardship orders in light of connected divorce action in PDAD.

Re H (An Infant) (1973) 123 NLJ 724t CA Adoption of South Vietnamese child ordered despite apparent adoption in Vietnam as procedure in Vietnam not recognised by United Kingdom.

Re H (C) [1996] 1 FCR 768; [1996] 1 FLR 569 HC FamD Supervised contact order to ex-husband whose wife had child by artificial insemination (using third party's sperm) but of which child ex-husband legally the father.

Re H (GJ) [1966] 1 All ER 952; (1965-66) 116 NLJ 697; (1966) 110 SJ 330; [1966] 1 WLR 706 HC ChD Jurisdiction in wardship cases.

Re H (K and M) (1972) 116 SJ 664 HC FamD Issue of access (by illegitimate father) to children left to local authority which had passed care resolution in respect of them.

Re H (L) [1986] 2 FLR 306; (1986) 150 JP 417 HC FamD HC could exercise wardship jurisdiction on request of local authority without latter having to show its powers to be insufficient.

Re H (minors) [1990] 2 FLR 172 CA Wardship/property action to be begun in absence of delayed welfare report as was in interests of children involved.

Re H (No 2) [1991] FCR 361 [1991] 1 FLR 214 CA Parental rights order made in respect of father of illegitimate children but his consent to adoption of same dispensed with.

Re H (No 3) [1991] 2 WLR 763 CA Parental rights order made in respect of father of illegitimate children but his consent to adoption of same dispensed with.

Re H (S) [1996] 1 FCR 1; [1995] 1 FLR 746 HC FamD Care order appropriate order for local authority to be given over orphan over whom nobody had parental responsibility.

Re H (SM) and H (RA) [1990] FCR 996 CA On preferability of adoption to fostering on long-term basis.

Re H (ZH) [1993] 1 FLR 83 HC FamD Interim adoption order favouring adopter who contravened adoption law as child's welfare demanded should remain with her.

Re H and another (No 3) [1991] 2 All ER 185; [1991] Fam 151; [1990] TLR 734; [1991] 2 WLR 763 CA Parental rights order available despite all rights thereunder not capable of being exercised; if neither parent offers suitable home but refuses consent to adoption that is unreasonable and court can dispense with consent.

Re H and another; Re S and another [1991] 3 All ER 230; [1991] 2 FLR 262; (1991) 141 NLJ 891; (1991) 135 SJ LB 52; [1991] TLR 298; [1991] 3 WLR 68 HL Removal/retention exclusive events and cannot overlap; removal/retention means removal/retention out of jurisdiction not of custody.

Re H and others [1997] 2 All ER 225; [1997] 2 WLR 563; [1997] 2 FCR 257; [1997] 1 FLR 872 HL On what constitutes acquiescence to removal/retention of child for purposes of Child Abduction Convention (as implemented).

Re H and R [1996] 1 FCR 509 HL On establishing that child sex abuse has taken place.

Re H and R [1995] 2 FCR 384 CA On establishing that child abuse has taken place.

Re H and Re W (1983) 133 NLJ 1099c; [1983] TLR 1 CA On reasonableness of parent's withholding consent/welfare of child as factor when deciding whether adoption order to be made.

Re H's Settlement; H v H [1909] 2 Ch 260; [1909] 78 LJCh 745 HC ChD Court can commit ward of court to prison for contempt.

Re H-S [1994] 3 All ER; [1994] 1 WLR 1141 CA Welfare of children not paramount consideration where their upbringing and press freedom clash.

Re H; Re K [1989] 2 FLR 313; (1989) 139 NLJ 864 CA Inadmissibility of hearsay evidence of children in matrimonial/guardianship action; historical events proved to be proved on balance of probabilities.

Re H; Re W (1983) 4 FLR 614; (1983) 127 SJ 86 CA On relevancy of child's welfare to decision whether parent's refusal of consent to adoption unreasonable.

Re Hambrough's Estate; Hambrough v Hambrough [1909] 2 Ch 620 HC ChD Court cannot order mortgage of interest of infant tenant in tail in remainder so as to secure maintenance for him.

Re Hamer's Estate; Public Trustee v Attorney-General [1937] 1 All ER 130; (1937) 81 SJ 99; (1936-37) LIII TLR 275 HC ChD Statements in will admitted to disprove legitimacy.

Re Harrington; Wilder v Turner [1908-10] All ER 235; [1908] 2 Ch 687; (1907-09) XXI Cox CC 709; (1908) 72 JP 501; [1909] 78 LJCh 27; (1908) 43 LJ 641; (1908-09) XCIX LTR 723; (1907-08) 52 SJ 855; (1908-09) XXV TLR 3; (1908) WN (I) 203 HC ChD Cannot seek arrears of maintenance under affiliation order from estate/representatives of deceased father.

Re Hartridge [1934] LJNCCR 252 CyCt Legitimacy declaration made but no costs given owing to delay in bringing petition.

Re Haynes; Haynes v Carter (1906) XCIV LTR 431 HC ChD Persons reputed to be husband and wife were so but only one of their two children was deemed legitimate.

Re Heath, deceased; Stacey and another v Bird and another [1945] Ch 417; [1946] 115 LJ 120; (1944-45) LXI TLR 554 HC ChD Child born eight month's after mother's first husband died but whose registered father was man with whom mother then cohabiting and later married was legitimated by that later marriage.

Re Hepworth; Rastall v Hepworth [1936] Ch 750; [1936] 105 LJCh 380; (1936) 155 LTR 250; (1936) WN (I) 264 HC ChD Person legitimated after testator dies cannot inherit under testator's will where could not do so absent legitimation.

Re Hoff; Carnley v Hoff [1942] 1 All ER 547; (1943) 93 LJ 20; (1942) 166 LTR 241; (1942) 86 SJ 105; (1941-42) LVIII TLR 247, (1942) WN (I) 90 HC ChD Special power of appointment not a 'disposition' for purposes of Legitimacy Act 1926, s 10(2).

Re Hollyman [1945] 1 All ER 290; (1945) 109 JP 95; (1945) 172 LTR 200; (1944-45) LXI TLR 229; (1945) WN (I) 41 CA Consent may be withdrawn up to making of order — conversely must be consent upon making of order.

Re Hopton, an Infant (1901-02) 46 SJ 749 VacCt That petitioner-father under pressure to return abroad did not excuse denying respondent-mother chance to make her case in custody action; child of Protestant father/Catholic mother ordered to be returned to school for next term, not removed during term time and not instructed as Catholic.

Re Hurll; Angelini v Dick and others [1952] 2 All ER 322; [1952] Ch 722; (1952) 102 LJ 399; (1952) 96 SJ 462; [1952] 2 TLR 85; (1952) WN (I) 354 HC ChD Legitimacy Act 1926, s 8(1) applies to person born when father resides in country where legitimation by later marriage not recognised.

Re J [1989] 3 All ER 590; [1989] Fam 85; [1990] FCR 341; [1990] 1 FLR 276; [1989] 3 WLR HC FamD On ordering that removal of ward from jurisdiction was unlawful (here so ordered).

Re J [1994] 2 FCR 741 CA Valid refusal to make contact order where judge reasonably decided disadvantages of contact outweighed advantages.

Re J [1984] FLR 535; (1984) 128 SJ 280; [1984] TLR 21 HC FamD Pyschiatric test/reports unnecessary/unavailable where sought by mother as evidence on which to challenge prospective testimony of ward in criminal case.

Re J [1984] 1 All ER 29; [1984] FLR 43; (1983) 127 SJ 616; [1983] TLR 488; [1984] 1 WLR 81 CA High Court will use wardship powers to police return of child in care to mother where care order otherwise would not be discharged by juvenile court.

Re J [1988] 1 FLR 65 HC FamD Injunction available to prevent mother (of ward) from leaving jurisdiction where appropriate.

Re J (1989) 133 SJ 876 HC FamD Declaration that there had been unlawful removal/retention of ward granted at behest of father (who had no custodial rights over ward).

Re J [1987] 1 FLR 455; (1987) 151 JP 243 HC FamD Wardship order continued but adoption/custodianship of child not allowed where natural mother not unreasonably objected to adoption of child by foster parents who were Jehovah's Witnesses/of different race to child.

Re J [1994] 1 FLR 369 HC FamD On need for magistrate to give reasons in residence case; on magistrates granting stay of residence order pending appeal.

Re J [1973] 2 All ER 410; [1973] Fam 106; (1973) 137 JP 467; (1973) 117 SJ 372; [1973] 2 WLR 782 HC FamD Exceptionally court may order contact with natural parent after adoption order — court's powers in making such orders are wide; wardship/directions remedies to breach of adoption order terms.

Re J [1993] 1 FCR 74; [1993] 1 FLR 699 HC FamD Ex parte surname change application without notice to parents or child (unrepresented by guardian ad litem) allowed.

Re J [1994] 1 FLR 253 HC FamD On making of (interim) care order where court does not approve of local authority's proposed care plan.

Re J [1997] 1 FCR 325; [1997] 1 FLR 606 HC FamD On making/effecting of ex parte (here residence/recovery) orders.

Re J [1991] FCR 129 (also CA); (1990) 134 SJ 1039; [1990] TLR 566 HL Taking child from foreign jurisdiction not wrongful as mother had sole custody/guardianship of child; habitual residence to be established as of date non-abducting father secured custody order (at which point child habitually already resident elsewhere).

Re J [1991] FCR 129 (also HL) CA Failed appeal by father against decision not to return child rightfully removed from jurisdiction and before father obtained custody order over child.

Re J [1990] 2 AC 562 (also CA); [1990] 3 WLR 492 HL On where is place of habitual residence for purpose of Child Abduction Convention; unmarried mother's removing child from Western Australia without father's knowledge did not (by virtue of Western Australian Law) come within terms of Child Abduction Convention.

Re J [1990] 2 AC 562 (also HL) CA On where is place of habitual residence for purpose of Child Abduction Convention; unmarried mother's removing child from Western Australia without father's knowledge did not (by virtue of Western Australian Law) come within terms of Child Abduction Convention.

Re J [1994] 1 FLR 729 CA On when leave to appeal required in contact cases; on whether/when to grant contact order.

Re J (a minor) [1991] TLR 115 CA On general undesirability/instant desirability of making joint care and control order.

Re J (minors) (1972) 122 NLJ 216t HC FamD Joint custody orders not exceptional.

Re Jarvis [1984] FLR 350 HC QBD General non-interference by HC in juvenile court interim care orders.

Re Jebb, decd; Ward-Smith and another v Jebb and others [1966] Ch 666; [1965] 3 WLR 810 CA Will constructed as being intended to benefit adopted grandchild as well as natural grandchildren of testator.

Re Jenion; Jenion and others v Wynne [1952] 1 All ER 1228; (1952) 102 LJ 273 CA All oral evidence establishing bastardy admissible (here as res gestae not as direct evidence).

Re Jones's Will Trusts; Jones v Squire (1965) 115 LJ 529 HC ChD Adopted child deemed to have been intended beneficiary under will leaving property to adoptive mother or on death of same to her children.

Re K [1991] FCR 142; [1991] 1 FLR 57 CA Rehabilitation of child with natural mother ordered after mother had privately arranged 'adoption' of child.

Re K [1990] FCR 524; [1990] 1 FLR 387 HC FamD Recognition/registration/enforcement of Belgian custody order allowed.

Re K [1997] 2 FCR 389; [1997] 2 FLR 221 CA Adoption order in respect of foreign child set aside in light of flawed adoption process and application for adoption transferred to HC.

Re K [1977] 1 All ER 647; [1977] Fam 179; (1977) 121 SJ 84; [1977] 2 WLR 33 CA Child's welfare paramount when considering care and control.

Re K [1977] 2 All ER 737; (1976) 126 NLJ 1092t; (1976) 120 SJ 752; [1977] 1 WLR 533 HC FamD Financial penalty/prison committal if access order to child in other parent's custody disobeyed.

Re K (1976) 126 NLJ 412t CA Care and control of children to wife-mother who had removed them from Canada to Britain where she intended to marry man with whom presently enjoyed adulterous relationship.

Re K [1988] 2 FLR 205 CA Children of subnormal parents who could not properly care for children ought to have been placed in long-term fostering with view to adoption.

Re K [1995] 2 FLR 550 CA Return of child ordered where grave risk of pyschological harm upon return unproved.

Re K [1996] 1 FCR 474; [1995] 2 FLR 432; [1995] TLR 199 CA On procedure where judge deems it necessary to obtain psychiatrist's opinion on matters before court in contact action.

Re K [1996] 1 FCR 24 CA On relevant factors when ordering return of abducted child; absent risk of grave psychological harm order for return of abducted child from place whence abducted left stand.

Re K [1995] 3 FCR 473; [1995] 1 FLR 977 HC FamD Six-month delay in seeking return not acquiescence to taking of child; return ordered despite child's objections; application to hear oral evidence refused.

Re K [1996] 1 FCR 365; [1995] 1 FLR 675 HC FamD Care (not residence) order appropriate for grandparents looking after grandchildren.

Re K [1995] 3 FCR 697; [1995] 2 FLR 211 CA Father's consent to removal meant could not claim wrongful restraint.

Re K [1994] 3 All ER 553; [1995] Fam 38; [1994] 2 FCR 617; [1994] TLR 221; [1994] 3 WLR 572 CA Secretary of State has right of appeal against adoption order; adoption proceedings not to substitute immigration proceedings.

Re K (1981) 2 FLR 381; (1980) 124 SJ 809 HC FamD Local authority not to apply for wardship 'with a view to adoption'.

Re K [1997] 2 FLR 212 HC FamD On proving consent to removal of child (here from US to UK).

Re K [1994] 2 FLR 557 CA Adoption order (conferring British nationality on foreigner) discharged.

Re K [1997] 2 FLR 74 HC FamD Order for non-disclosure to natural mother of onetime conviction for serious sexual offence of prospective adopter of child; on test as to deciding whether to order disclosure/non-disclosure.

Re K [1992] 2 FCR 161; [1992] 2 FLR 98 HC FamD Refusal of unrealistic application by custodial parent to remove child from jurisdiction.

Re K [1992] 2 FCR 521; [1992] 2 FLR 108 HC FamD Solicitors reported to Law Society where seemed to be encouraging/inciting mother to violate contact order.

Re K [1991] 2 FLR 104 CA Interim care and control order by wardship court precluded need for divorce court to issue same.

Re K [1962] 3 All ER 178; (1962) 112 LJ 617; (1962) 106 SJ 721; [1962] 3 WLR 752 HC ChD No entitlement to see reports lodged with guardian ad litem; parties may question maker's of statements in reports.

Re K (J) [1990] FCR 891; [1991] 2 FLR 340 HC FamD Sikh girl left with white foster-parents with view to adoption by them as was in girl's best interests.

Re K (KJS) [1966] 3 All ER 154; (1965-66) 116 NLJ 1173; (1966) 110 SJ 545; [1966] 1 WLR 1241 HC ChD Variation of access order (not wardship order) best course where post-access order access is unsatisfactory.

Re K and A [1995] 1 FLR 688 HC FamD No power to order local authority to pay maintenance to grandmother for grandchild in her care/its supervision (and if power existed was inappropriately exercised here).

Re K and others [1988] 1 All ER; [1988] Fam 1; [1988] 1 FLR 435; (1988) 152 JP 185; (1987) 131 SJ 1697; [1987] 3 WLR 1233 HC FamD Wardship court will not intervene in existing child abuse case; no leave necessary for child to give evidence against parents.

Re K and S [1992] 1 FLR 432 HC FamD Court would not allow wardship action to be used (as here) to frustrate Home Secretary in enforcing immigration law.

Re K; Re M; Hertfordshire County Council v H [1972] 3 All ER 769; (1972) 136 JP 838 HC FamD Putative father seeking access order after local authority assumes parental rights must be denied.

Re K; Rogers and another v Kuzmicz [1952] 2 All ER 877; (1953) 117 JP 9; (1952) 102 LJ 639; [1953] 1 QB 117; (1952) 96 SJ 764; [1952] 2 TLR 745; (1952) WN (I) 511 CA Generally parent's withholding of consent will be found reasonable.

Re Kernot [1964] 3 All ER 339; [1965] Ch 217; (1964) 114 LJ 675; (1964) 108 SJ 675; [1964] 3 WLR 1210 HC ChD Factors when deciding forum conveniens.

Re Kinseth [1947] 1 All ER 201; [1947] Ch 223; (1947) 111 JP 136; [1947] 116 LJR 642; (1947) 177 LTR 3; (1947) 91 SJ 67; (1947) LXIII TLR 200 HC ChD Wife entitled to benefit under Summary Jurisdiction (Married Women) Act 1895, s 5 and Guardianship of Infants Act 1925, s 3(2).

Re L [1991] FCR 297; [1991] 1 FLR 171; [1990] TLR 668 CA Natural father of illegitimate child need not consent to adoption of same/need not be named in adoption application.

Re L [1996] 2 FCR 352 CA Authorisation to allow finishing of contact ought not to have been made as would not be implemented in near future; on standard of proof in child sex abuse cases; on when interim/final care orders to be deployed.

Re L (1983) 4 FLR 368 CA Interim care and control order made in favour of mother who 'kidnapped' own child from United States and had him made ward of court.

Re L [1978] 2 All ER 318; (1978) 122 SJ 15; [1978] 1 WLR 181 CA Procedural errors by registrar required re-hearing of wardship case.

Re L [1985] FLR 95; [1984] TLR 399 CA Access of natural father to child placed in long-term foster care inappropriate: access order quashed.

Re L [1988] FCR 92; [1987] 1 FLR 400 HC FamD Consent being withheld by mentally unwell mother was, using objective test, unreasonably withheld.

Re L [1984] TLR 482 HC FamD Child placed in care under the Family Law Reform Act 1969, s 7(2) could be placed in secure accommodation under the Child Care Act 1980, s 21A without first having to turn to juvenile court.

Re L [1990] FCR 471; [1990] 1 FLR 305; (1989) 139 NLJ 1377 CA On determining whether parent's refusal of consent to adoption (as here) unreasonable; on whether custodianship/adoption order preferable.

Re L [1988] 1 All ER 418; (1987) 137 NLJ 760; [1988] 1 FLR 255 HC FamD No automatic absolute prohibition of anything about ward.

Re L [1996] 1 FLR 116; [1995] TLR 379 CA On appropriate standard of proof in child sex abuse case; full care orders (subject to judge's hopes regarding rehabilitation) merited in respect of children whose future was as yet undecided.

Re L [1996] 1 FCR 221 HC FamD On limited operation of issue estoppel in child cases; on admissibility of evidence from earlier child sex abuse cases involving cohabitee of woman whose children were subjects of present care proceedings.

Re L [1995] 3 FCR 684; [1995] 2 FLR 445 HC FamD On need for magistrates to give reasons for decision in residence order application.

Re L [1996] 1 FCR 419 CA Right that medical report prepared in course of care proceedings be disclosed to police for use in investigating criminal aspects of case.

Re L [1995] 2 FLR 438 HC FamD Indirect contact and parental responsibility orders to transsexual father.

Re L [1974] 1 All ER 913; (1973) 123 NLJ 1066t; (1974) 118 SJ 22; [1974] 1 WLR 250 CA Child's welfare in kidnapping case paramount factor (though parent's conduct also factor).

Re L (1968) 118 NLJ 518t CA Wardship over illegitimate child ended so that mother could emigrate to Canada and settle down there to new life — that natural father would lose access to child not ground for continuing wardship.

Re L [1968] 1 All ER 20; (1967) 117 NLJ 1242t; [1967] 3 WLR 1645 CA PDAD judge can order blood test of infant absent guardian ad litem's consent.

Re L (1967) 111 SJ 908 CA On rebutting presumption of legitimacy; on ordering blood testing where issue of paternity raised.

Re L [1992] 2 FCR 821; [1992] 2 FLR 178 HC FamD Pre-Child Abduction Convention foreign custody order recognised/registered/enforced in England.

Re L [1967] 2 All ER 1110; (1967) 111 SJ 717; [1967] 3 WLR 1149 HC PDAD Blood tests ordered of child if in its best interests.

Re L [1993] 1 FCR 325 HC FamD On determining whether custodial parent to be allowed remove child from jurisdiction.

Re L [1963] 1 All ER 176; (1963) 107 SJ 35; [1963] 1 WLR 97 HC ChD On proper respondent in wardship cases.

Re L [1962] 3 All ER 1; (1962) 106 SJ 686 CA Child's welfare paramount but parent's conduct material in deciding care/control — here entrusted to innocent party.

Re L (1962) 106 SJ 611 CA Consent by mother having difficulty making up her mind regarding adoption of child already placed with proposed adopters was being unreasonably withheld.

Re L [1996] 2 FCR 706; [1996] 2 FLR 742 CA On making interim care order.

Re L [1990] FCR 332; [1989] 2 FLR 359 CA Inappropriate to order that children reside with mother where she had history of frustrating access by father.

Re L [1993] 2 FCR 509; [1993] 2 FLR 401 HC FamD Child returned where inter alia father's undertakings meant return did not pose grave risk of physical/psychological harm to child.

Re L [1962] 3 All ER 1; (1962) 112 LJ 536; [1962] 1 WLR 886 CA Child's welfare paramount but parent's conduct material in deciding care/control — here entrusted to innocent party.

Re L (1996) TLR 22/3/96 HL Expert report prepared for party into child care action was not clothed by professional privilege.

Re L (1997) 141 SJ LB 21; [1997] TLR 27; [1997] 2 WLR 739 CA Court ought rarely to order disclosure of adoption details to birth family applicant (and here would not so order).

Re L [1990] FCR 509; [1991] 1 FLR 14; (1990) 134 SJ 545; [1990] TLR 227 CA Improper to exercise wardship jurisdiction in realm reserved by Parliament to discretion of local authority.

Re L (AC) [1971] 3 All ER 743; (1972) 136 JP 19 HC ChD Local authority estopped from objecting to time-barred application by other which it engineered; failure of mother to accept child in care into her supervision not estoppel from later exercising parental rights in action.

Re L (K) [1990] FCR 692 CrCt Care order in respect of child discharged with view to grandparents commencing wardship proceedings.

Re L (no 2) [1991] 1 FLR 29 CrCt On parentage as alternative to adoption.

Re Leman's Will Trusts; Public Trustee v Leman and another [1946] 115 LJ 89; (1946) 174 LTR 75; (1944-45) LXI TLR 566; (1945) WN (I) 183 HC ChD Son born in March 1886 of mother whose marriage was ended by divorce in October 1885 was legitimate son of that dissolved marriage.

Re Liddell's Settlement Trusts; Liddell v Liddell [1936] 1 All ER 239; [1936] Ch 365; (1936) 80 SJ 165; (1935-36) LII TLR 308 CA Sequestration of assets of person domiciled in England/resident abroad for non-compliance with order to return wards to jurisdiction.

Re Lowe; Stewart v Lowe [1929] 2 Ch 210; (1929) 98 LJCh 440; (1929) 141 LTR 428; (1928-29) XLV TLR 484; (1929) WN (I) 143 HC ChD Issue of dead illegitimate son (whose parents married after his birth) who died before coming into operation of Legitimacy Act 1926 could not take share in grandmother's estate.

Re Luck's Settlement Trusts; Re Luck's Will Trusts; Walker v Luck [1940] Ch 323; [1940] 109 LJP 108; (1940) 162 LTR 192; (1940) WN (I) 56 HC ChD Recognition of foreign decree recognising putative father as father where in place of domicile at child's birth was not so recognised.

Re Luck, Walker v Luck [1940] 3 All ER 307; [1940] Ch 864; [1940] 109 LJP 380; (1941) 164 LTR 172; (1940) WN (I) 257 CA Non-recognition of foreign decree recognising putative father as father where in place of domicile at child's birth was not so recognised.

Re 'M' (1983) 133 NLJ 556c CA English adoption order made in respect of child already adopted by applicants under South African law.

Re M [1994] 1 FCR 866 HC FamD On admittance of medical evidence at care hearing; on procedure where guardian ad litem's recommendation contrary to what child desires/where child gives instructions to solicitor contrary to what guardian recommends.

Re M [1993] 2 FCR 721; [1994] 1 FLR 749 HC FamD On practice as regards determining what child wants in family law dispute concerning child.

Re M [1990] FCR 993; [1991] 1 FLR 458; [1990] TLR 268 CA Adoption agreement set aside where father agreed to mother/stepfather adopting children unaware of mother's terminal illness from which died shortly thereafter.

Re M [1990] FCR 785; [1990] TLR 139 CA Indirect contact ordered where direct contact impracticable.

Re M [1997] 1 All ER 263; [1997] Fam 67; [1997] 1 FCR 109; (1996) TLR 10/12/96 HC FamD Presence of child in England sufficed to give court jurisdiction in care proceedings.

Re M [1990] FCR 385 HC FamD Social worker required to be present at formal police cautioning of ward (cautioning had to be authorised by court).

Re M [1997] 2 FCR 527 CA On determining habitual residence (as basis for jurisdiction).

Re M (1981) 131 NLJ 241c CA On determining whether parental refusal of consent to adoption reasonably or (as here) unreasonably withheld.

Re M (1980) 130 NLJ 1120c CA Standards of ordinary person appropriate basis for deciding whether (unlike here) child was treated as member of the family.

Re M [1996] 2 FLR 84 HC FamD Care order appropriate in respect of abandoned child with special needs in respect of whom nobody had parental responsibility.

Re M [1995] 3 FCR 745; [1995] 1 FLR 1021 CA Return of children a final order (appeal to CA); undertakings are intended to protect children until case finally decided not to be used to impede return of children.

Re M (1983) 133 NLJ 513c CA Custody of infant child to good mother (living with man with rape convictions) rather than good father (who had just married twenty-one year old woman).

Re M [1986] 1 FLR 51 CA On whether to order post-adoption access between adopted child and natural parents.

Re M [1988] 2 FLR 497 HC FamD Sterilisation of mentally handicapped ward ordered as was in her best interests never to become pregnant.

Re M [1990] FCR 424; [1990] 1 FLR 291 CA Failed application by teenage father for custody of his child which was being placed for adoption.

Re M [1985] 1 All ER 745; [1985] Fam 60; (1985) 149 JP 574; [1985] 2 WLR 811 CA Access order for juvenile court; freeing of child for adoption for magistrates' court.

Re M [1985] FLR 921 CA That contact with mother yielding positive results justified finding her non-consent to adoption as reasonable.

Re M (1985) 135 NLJ 321c CA Failed application by mother for access to child whom had voluntarily surrendered to care.

Re M (1985) 129 SJ 221 CA Failed application to court to exercise its wardship jurisdiction in lieu of local authority exercising its care jurisdiction.

Re M [1987] 2 All ER 88; [1987] FCR 17; [1987] 1 FLR 465; [1987] 1 WLR 162 CA Custodianship order cannot be made unless parent's agreement got/dispensed with; refusal of consent unreasonable if reasonable parent would not have refused.

Re M [1989] 1 FLR 443 HC FamD Wardship not justified just because parents mentally handicapped but was here; no/was restriction on publicity regarding parents (who sought publicity)/fosterers or future adopters; on procedure where party actively seeks publicity in wardship proceedings.

Re M [1988] FCR 450; [1988] 1 FLR 35 CA Access order properly set aside where parents rarely visited child when had access rights and was in child's best interests to be adopted.

Re M [1955] 2 All ER 911; (1955) 119 JP 535; (1955) 105 LJ 488; [1955] 2 QB 479; (1955) 99 SJ 539; [1955] 3 WLR 320 CA Natural father of illegitimate not 'parent' whose consent to adoption required under Adoption Act 1950, s 2(4)(a).

Re M [1994] TLR 659 CA On when review of magistrates' decision to depart from recommendations of court welfare officer would be merited.

Re M [1994] 2 FCR 968; [1995] 1 FLR 1029 HC FamD Although can dismiss contact application without hearing evidence ought not to have done so here.

Re M [1995] 1 FLR 274 CA On how court to decide whether contact appropriate.

Re M [1994] 2 FCR 750; [1994] 1 FLR 390 CA On procedure where children objecting to being returned to country of habitual residence.

Re M [1992] 2 FCR 608 HC FamD Non-return of abducted children in light of their objections to same.

Re M [1973] 1 All ER 852; [1973] Fam 66; (1973) 137 JP 339; (1973) 123 NLJ 56t; (1973) 117 SJ 88; [1973] 2 WLR 515 HC FamD Absent provisional adoption order child (even ward) cannot be removed from jurisdiction by applicant adopters.

Re M [1985] FLR 664 HC FamD Adoption by rather than custody to grandparents preferable in instant case.

Re M [1994] 3 All ER 298; [1994] 2 AC 424; [1994] 2 FCR 871; [1994] 2 FLR 577; (1994) 138 SJ LB 168; [1994] TLR 420; [1994] 3 WLR 558 HL That child temporarily in local authority care 'not suffering' does not stop authority seeking care order; relevant time is time when protection procedure initiated.

Re M [1995] 1 FCR 753 CA Refusal of contact justified where children did not desire it/was risk that harm it would cause would be greater than the benefits that would accrue.

Re M [1995] TLR 228 CA Grandmother required leave of court before could seek contact with grandchild in care.

Re M [1994] 2 FLR 126 CA Court did not order return of child abroad where child objected to same.

Re M [1994] 1 All ER 424; [1994] Fam 95; [1994] 1 FCR 849; [1994] 2 WLR 200 CA At time of care order hearing — and not some time previously — child must be suffering.

Re M (1970) 114 SJ 264 CA Father's withholding of consent to adoption of his child by his ex-wife and her new husband was not unreasonable.

Re M [1994] 1 FCR 678; [1994] 1 FLR 272; [1993] TLR 557 HC FamD Indirect contact with father in prison approved; requirements that mother read father's letters to child/submit progress reports to father disapproved.

Re M [1993] 1 FCR 78; [1993] 1 FLR 275 HC FamD Person who had been acting as guardian ad litem could apply for prohibited steps order after emergency protection order lapsed; justices' reasoning/findings in such cases to be recorded.

Re M [1995] 1 FCR 417 CA Residence (not care) order justified where alleged poor treatment unproved by the local authority but judge found other failures on mother's part.

Re M [1997] 2 FLR 90 HC FamD Estoppel inapplicable when dealing with question of parentage; non-biological father of child conceived by wife by way of artificial insemination before the Human Fertilisation and Embryology Act 1990 was enacted was not 'parent' of child for purposes of the Child Support Act 1991.

Re M [1996] 1 FLR 315 HC FamD Non-return of child settled in England whose removal from Greece (to which father acquiesced) not wrongful under Greek law/whose return entailed risk of physical or psychological harm.

Re M [1996] 1 FCR 557; [1996] 1 FLR 478; [1995] TLR 599 CA Peremptory return order made requiring children to be sent back to Dubai.

Re M [1995] 3 FCR 550; [1995] 2 FLR 86 CA On relevant matters for consideration in grandparent's application for leave to seek contact.

Re M [1994] TLR 475 CA Order for return of child to jurisdiction of habitual residence (pursuant to Child Abduction Convention) is final.

Re M [1993] 2 FLR 706 HC FamD Justices did not need to see child properly where was guardian ad litem/had welfare officer's report; reasons to be given where depart from recommendations in welfare officer's report.

Re M (a minor) [1995] 2 FCR 793; [1993] 2 FLR 858 HC FamD Immigrant child granted residence order at stepmother's behest.

Re M (a minor) [1997] TLR 301 CA On avaialability of supervised contact available where unsupervised contact not possible.

Re M (B) [1993] 2 FCR 388 HC FamD Foreign child who habitually resided in jurisdiction could be (and here was) made ward of court.

Re M (D) [1986] 2 FLR 122 (also HC FamD) CA On judicial review of local authority decision regarding adoption of child in care.

Re M (D) [1986] 2 FLR 122 (also CA) HC FamD Failed wardship action in which foster-parents sought review of decision of local authority adoption panel.

Re M (M) [1996] 2 FCR 521 HC FamD Abandonment of child was ill-treatment (hence harm) of same — this plus various health/developmental problems justified care order.

Re M (No 1) [1994] 1 FLR 54 CA On maintenance of interim care order pending appeal.

Re M (No 2) [1994] 1 FLR 59 CA On refusal of care order.

Re M (R) and M (L) [1986] 2 FLR 205 HC FamD Alleged local authority abuse of power to be challenged by way of judicial review.

Re M (R), an infant (1941) WN (I) 244 CA On revocation of adoption order.

Re M (S) [1991] FCR 492; [1991] 2 FLR 333 HC FamD On access by natural father to illegitimate child.

Re M (W); B v B [1997] 2 FCR 494; [1997] 1 FLR 132; [1997] 1 FLR 139 CA Separation of siblings justified but order preventing father from making future residence applications was obviated.

Re M and H [1990] 1 AC 686 (also CA); [1989] FCR 65; [1988] 2 FLR 431; (1988) 138 NLJ 226; (1988) 132 SJ 1146; [1988] 3 WLR 45 HL Court could not grant putative father access to children where local authority had taken children into care.

Re M and H [1990] 1 AC 686 (also HL); [1988] FCR 97; [1988] 1 FLR 151; (1987) 131 SJ 1155; [1987] 3 WLR 759 CA Court could not grant putative father access to children where local authority had taken children into care.

Re M and H (no 2) [1988] FCR 107 HC FamD Court could not grant putative father custody of children where local authority had taken children into care.

Re M and N [1990] Fam 211; [1990] FCR 395; [1990] 1 FLR 149 (also HC FamD); (1989) 139 NLJ 1154; (1990) 134 SJ 165; [1989] 3 WLR 1136 CA On publication of information (and injunctions available to restrain publication of same) pertaining to wards.

Re M and N [1990] 1 FLR 149 (also CA) HC FamD On publication of information (and injunctions available to restrain publication of same) pertaining to wards.

Re M and R [1996] 4 All ER 239; [1996] 2 FCR 617; [1996] 2 FLR 195 CA Balance of probabilities the standard of proof of child abuse in care proceedings; on admissibility of expert evidence on central matters to be resolved in case.

Re M, an infant (1961) 105 SJ 153 CA Prerogative rights of Crown as parens patriae existed notwithstanding enactment of Children Act 1948.

Re Makein, decd; Makein v Makein and another [1955] 2 WLR 43 HC ChD Illegitimate son not dependant for purposes of Inheritance (Family Provision) Act 1938, s 1(1).

Re Marshall; Barclays Bank, Ltd v Marshall and others [1957] 1 All ER 549 HC ChD Succession principles applied to foreign-legitimated children apply to foreign-adopted children.

Re Marshall; Barclays Bank, Ltd v Marshall and others [1957] 3 All ER 172; (1957) 101 SJ 229 CA On status of foreign adopted child under English will.

Re Mathieson (1918) 53 LJ 165 CA Non-restoration of custody of child to father (who had voluntarily parted with same) where was not to good of welfare of child.

Re McK (1976) 126 NLJ 890t HC FamD Substitution of higher maintenance payments than those required upon variation by Australian court of original maintenance order.

Re N [1989] FCR 481; [1989] 2 FLR 106 CA Earlier access order to father did not preclude local authority being given parental rights over child by way of care order.

Re N [1990] FCR 241; [1990] 1 FLR 58 HC FamD Care and control of black child to white foster-parents, reasonable access to natural father.

Re N [1991] FCR 765; [1991] 1 FLR 413 HC FamD On what constitutes grave risk of harm/settling into new surroundings so as to justify non-return of abducted children: order for return of children to place of habitual residence.

Re N (1975) 119 SJ 423 HC FamD Access to father in prison ordered.

Re N [1994] 2 FCR 1101; [1994] 2 FLR 992 HC FamD Where experts on both sides recommending care orders/that children not be placed with parents, action in which latter seeking to contest local authority care applications terminated.

Re N [1995] 2 All ER 417; [1995] Fam 96; [1995] 2 FCR 605; [1995] 2 WLR 233 HC FamD Court has duty under Hague Convention on Child Abduction to order child to be held in country even before child arrives.

Re N [1995] 2 FLR 230 CA On making residence order where not much choice between either of two parents presenting cross-applications.

Re N [1967] 1 All ER 161; [1967] Ch 512; (1966) 110 SJ 924; [1967] 2 WLR 691 HC ChD Where urgent can make post-wardship style orders before wardship/issue injunction on Sunday or before writ issued.

Re N [1991] FCR 1000; [1992] 1 FLR 134; [1991] TLR 357 CA Father denied access where mother refused to comply with access order (so turning child against access) and only other solution was to imprison mother which was not in child's interest.

Re N [1993] 2 FCR 330; [1993] 2 FLR 124 CA On role of court hearing action pursuant to Hague Child Abduction Convention 1980 as implemented.

Re N (1983) 4 FLR 150; (1982) 132 NLJ 273 CA Appropriate that care and control of baby given to local authority until mother's capacities appraised but six month prohibition on access inappropriate: no prohibition ordered.

Re N (C) [1992] 2 FCR 401 HC FamD Court could order that there be no contact between mother and child in care.

Re N (J) and others [1995] 2 FLR 203 HC FamD Refusal of order for preliminary assessment of mother and children for psychotherapy where local authority had frustrated prospects of attendance.

Re N (minors) [1996] 1 FCR 244 CA Valid decision to allow return of own two children to father against whom step-daughter had made allegations of sexual abuse.

Re O [1978] 2 All ER 27; [1978] Fam 196 (also HC FamD); (1977) 121 SJ 710; [1977] 3 WLR 725 CA Child's interests paramount consideration in deciding wardship cases.

Re O [1985] FLR 546 HC FamD Adoption by grandparents allowed.

Re O [1978] 1 All ER 145; [1978] Fam 196 (also CA); (1977) 127 NLJ 569t; (1977) 121 SJ 391 HC FamD Exceptional for court to consider wardship application by natural parent in respect of adopted child.

Re O [1995] 2 FLR 597 HC FamD Adoption order made but contact to natural mother allowed.

Re O [1995] 2 FCR 649; [1993] 2 FLR 594 HC FamD On deciding place of 'habitual residence'.

Re O [1996] 1 FCR 317; [1995] 2 FLR 124; [1995] TLR 163 CA On contact/indirect contact.

Re O [1985] FLR 716; (1985) 149 JP 172; [1984] TLR 693 CA Should not have ordered access by putative father to child pending resolution of paternity issue.

Re O [1995] 1 FCR 721; [1994] 2 FLR 349 HC FamD On return of children to jurisdiction where enforceability of father's undertakings to English court of considerable dispute (here return of children ordered).

Re O [1971] 2 All ER 744; [1971] Ch 748; (1971) 115 SJ 264; [1971] 2 WLR 784 CA Appellate court to set aside lower court decision if wrong/unfair/contrary to principle.

Re O [1992] 4 All ER 906; [1992] 2 FLR 7; [1992] 1 WLR 912 HC FamD Justices have no inherent order to stay care order; care order may be appropriate remedy for truancy; significant harm from truancy adequate basis for care order.

Re O [1992] 1 FLR 77 CA Father if suitable and willing to be given first chance at bringing up child where mother unable to do so.

Re O [1965] Ch 23; [1964] 2 WLR 840 CA Putative father though in special position cannot veto adoption of illegitimate child: child's welfare paramount.

Re O [1997] 2 FCR 17; [1996] 2 FLR 755 HC FamD Improper exercise of discretion where care orders made rather than first trying supervision orders in respect of children supervision of whom was sought by local authority though it did not seek to remove children from their home.

Re O [1997] 1 FLR 924 HC FamD Father found to have consented to/acquiesced in removal of 'abducted' child: no order for return made.

Re O [1962] 2 All ER 10; (1962) 112 LJ 272; (1962) 106 SJ 429; [1962] 1 WLR 724 CA Welfare of children paramount, not only factor: here other factors justified leave to take ward outside jurisdiction.

Re O [1992] 2 FCR 394; [1993] 1 FLR 860; (1993) 143 NLJ 814 HC FamD Medical examination direction attached to interim care order valid/relevant/mandatory.

Re O [1993] 2 FCR 746; [1993] 2 FLR 737 HC FamD Wardship injunction ended upon adoption order being made.

Re O [1997] 2 FCR 465 HC FamD German child of German mother ('abductress') ordered to be returned to Germany at behest of German grandparents who had been caring for child.

Re O [1997] TLR 334 HC FamD Absent contract/court order could nonetheless acquire joint custody of child (as here) following longtime exercise of parental responsibilities over same.

Re O (a minor) (1972) 122 NLJ 112t HC FamD Care and control of Ghanian foster-daughter to English fosterers despite desire of natural parents to bring girl back to Ghana.

Re O (a minor) (1973) 123 NLJ 225t CA Care and control of Ghanian foster-daughter to English fosterers despite desire of natural parents to bring girl back to Ghana.

Re O (An Infant) [1964] 1 All ER 786; (1964) 114 LJ 252; (1964) 108 SJ 117 CA Natural father did not exercise right of veto over adoption of illegitimate child that would enjoy over legitimate child.

Re O (E) (a minor) (1973) 123 NLJ 180t CA Wardship of Nigerian girl to English fosterers.

Re O (minors) [1993] 2 FCR 482; [1994] 1 FLR 172 HC FamD Procedural error in ex parte application for leave to seek residence order did not invalidate order made but duration of order (five weeks) too long.

Re Overbury; Sheppard v Matthews and others [1954] 3 All ER 308; [1955] Ch 122; (1954) 104 LJ 728; (1954) 98 SJ 768; [1954] 3 WLR 644 HC ChD Child born after second marriage/within nine months of death of first spouse is presumed to be legitimate child of first spouse.

Re P [1995] 2 FCR 58; [1994] 1 FLR 771 HC FamD Adoption process allowed continue but had to ascertain views of natural father previously unaware of child's existence.

Re P [1989] Crim LR 897 CA Inadmissible evidence does not become admissible just because is put to accused party during cross-examination.

Re P [1990] FCR 260; [1990] 1 FLR 96; (1989) 139 NLJ 1265 CA Mixed race child justifiably removed from home of white foster-mother to that of black foster-parents with view to adoption.

Re P (1983) 4 FLR 401 CA Child whose father could not have custody given into custody of mother in lesbian relationship but arrangement subject to scrutiny of Official Solicitor.

Re P (1982) 3 FLR 420; (1982) 132 NLJ 248 CA Court could not order that no application be made in wardship proceedings until full hearing but could require court's leave be given to any steps taken.

Re P [1977] 1 All ER 182; [1977] Fam 25; (1976) 120 SJ 818; [1976] 3 WLR 924 CA Court may dispense with parental agreement to adoption; child's welfare a factor, not paramount.

Re P [1990] FCR 909; [1990] 2 FLR 223; (1990) 134 SJ 661; [1990] 1 WLR 613 CA Joint custody consent order not injunction/injunctive in nature so penal notice order could not be attached thereto.

Re P [1985] FLR 635; [1984] TLR 325 CA Indecisiveness of natural parent may indicate incapacity to act as reasonable parent.

Re P [1988] FCR 140; [1987] 2 FLR 421 HC FamD On deciding custody where paid surrogate mother refuses to surrender children to natural father and his wife.

Re P [1988] FCR 401; [1988] 1 FLR 1 CA Judge had not failed in duty by not interviewing prospective adoptee nor by taking stepfather's drink problem into account.

Re P [1988] FCR 428; [1988] 2 FLR 209 CA Refusal of access to father (suspected of sexually abusing his illegitimate children) set aside; father to seek access as a parent from juvenile court.

Re P [1987] FCR 123; [1987] 2 FLR 467; (1987) 151 JP 635 CA Local authority granted care order, non-access by parents and right to place child with foster-parents with view to adoption where child born to parents of family with history of sexual abuse of existing children; on role of court.

Re P [1986] 1 FLR 272 HC FamD Wardship jurisdiction invoked to order termination of pregnancy of/insertion of contraceptive device into child in care under Children and Young Persons Act 1969.

Re P [1988] FCR 232; [1988] 1 FLR 328 HC FamD Care/control of babies to parents as medical evidence showed injuries suffered by babies easily sufferable absent rough treatment/babies could have copper deficiency syndrome.

Re P [1994] 2 FCR 1306; [1994] 2 FLR 1000; [1994] TLR 426 CA Inappropriate that judge attach contact order to freeing for adoption order.

Re P [1994] 2 FCR 537 HC FamD Once (white) foster-parents had sought adoption of (black) child issue of care was for court, not local authority (which sought same-race adoption).

Re P [1995] 1 FCR 583 HC FamD On proving danger of significant harm to child such as to justify care order.

Re P [1996] 3 FCR 637; [1996] 1 FLR 482 HC FamD On relevant factor when granting emergency protection order: here granted/renewed.

Re P [1995] 3 FCR 753; [1995] 1 FLR 1048 HC FamD On ending parental responsibility order: father's terminated after non-accidental injuries to child (interests of whom paramount).

Re P [1996] 3 FCR 714; [1996] 2 FLR 333 CA On deciding whether to grant unsupervised contact to children by father not proven on balance of probabilities to have sexually abused one/both of the children.

Re P [1997] 1 FCR 459; [1996] 2 FLR 314 CA Supervised contact of father to children: risk of ill-health contact posed for mother did not outweigh paramount interests of children in continued contact.

Re P [1994] 1 FCR 285; [1994] 2 FLR 374 HC FamD Contact order justified though mother's psychiatrist recommended no contact and welfare officer recommended direct/indirect contact in report/before court.

Re P [1993] 2 FLR 156 HC FamD On contact/what constitutes reasonable contact.

Re P [1997] Fam 45; [1996] 3 FCR 233; [1997] 1 FLR 780; (1996) 140 SJ LB 177; [1997] 2 WLR 223 CA Welfare of abducted child the defining criterion when deciding whether to order return of child to place whence came.

Re P [1992] 2 FCR 681; [1992] TLR 234 CA On significance of what children desire when deciding care and control application.

Re P [1967] 2 All ER 229; (1967) 111 SJ 496; [1967] 1 WLR 818 HC ChD If magistrates make guardianship ruling then should make variations unless not empowered to make order sought; High Court not constrained in wardship case by earlier decision of magistrates.

Re P [1994] 2 FLR 751 HC FamD Care order refused as local authority failed to prove significant harm to child whose brother died while in parents' care was likely.

Re P [1991] FCR 337; (1991) 141 NLJ 163 CA Witness summons could be (but here was not) issued against child subject of care proceedings as was compellable witness; statements by child to police/medics admissible.

Re P (1963) 107 SJ 55 CA Valid decision that mother's refusal of consent to adoption was unreasonably withheld.

Re P [1994] 2 FCR 1093 HC FamD Discharge of wardship and leave granted for foster parents to seek residence order.

Re P [1991] FCR 283; [1991] 1 FLR 280; [1990] TLR 694 CA Increased access and eventual return of stepfather to family despite earlier sexual abuse of step-child was justified; contempt of local authority solicitor whereby had sought to frustrate access arrangements purged by contemnor.

Re P [1962] 3 All ER 789; (1963) 127 JP 18; (1962) 112 LJ 786; (1962) 106 SJ 630; [1962] 1 WLR 1296 HC ChD Obligations of parent to child are moral and financial: consent dispensed with as failure on both grounds.

Re P [1993] 2 FCR 417; [1993] 1 FLR 915 CA On availability/appropriateness of ex parte interim residence order.

Re P [1993] 2 FLR 742 CA On making interim care orders/further interim care orders/final care orders.

Re P [1993] 2 FCR 689; [1994] 1 FLR 578 HC FamD On making parental responsibility order favouring father.

Re P (1996) TLR 15/5/96 CA Mother's objection to contact between children and father not per se a valid reason for refusing same where could be in interests off children for contact to be maintained.

Re P [1991] 1 FLR 337 CA On making split custody order; on significance of report of court welfare officer when determining custody.

Re P [1996] 2 FCR 133; [1995] 1 FLR 831; [1995] TLR 84 CA Court could (and here was right to) issue declaration that removal of child from England was wrongful.

Re P [1996] 3 FCR 657 HC FamD Appropriate arrangements where placement of girl for adoption did not work out but persons with whom placed sought to adopt brother of girl who was also placed with them.

Re P [1989] 1 FLR 182 HC FamD Sterilisation of ward ordered where was in her best interests.

Re P (A and J) (1977) 127 NLJ 1151b CA Return of Italian children (abducted by Italian mother) to Italy ordered where was best for them that their futures be decided in Italian court.

Re P (a minor) [1996] 2 FCR 285 HC FamD Successful appeal against residence/contact orders settled on where made on basis of unsatisfactory court welfare officer's reporrt.

Re P (AJ) (1969) 119 NLJ 12; (1968) 112 SJ 861; [1968] 1 WLR 1976 HC ChD HC ChD could in wardship cases make orders contrary to those made by magistrates though was not necessary here.

Re P (GE) [1964] 3 All ER 977; [1965] Ch 568; (1965) 115 LJ 24; (1964) 108 SJ 916; [1965] 2 WLR 1 CA Court has wardship jurisdiction over stateless infant living in England when action begun though later outside jurisdiction.

Re P (GE) [1964] Ch 575; (1964) 114 LJ 474; (1964) 108 SJ 444; [1964] 3 WLR 191 HC ChD Court had no wardship jurisdiction over stateless infant living in England when action begun though later outside jurisdiction.

Re P (L) [1990] FCR 147 HC FamD Balancing exercise as to whether children should go to aunt/be adopted by foster mother.

Re P and G [1996] 2 FCR 588; [1996] 2 FLR 90 HC QBD Registrar General's refusal to alter birth certificates so as to show male-to-female transsexuals born female was valid.

Re P, An Infant (1954) 118 JP 139 CA Had children's officers statement that intended adopters might claim maintenance from mother for period child stayed with them coerced mother to consent to adoption that consent would have been obviated.

Re Q [1996] 2 FCR 345; [1996] 1 FLR 369 HC FamD Where egg fertilised by anonymous donor's sperm and foetus carried by surrogate mother there was no 'father' whose agreement to parental order being made had to be sought.

Re Queskey; Queskey v Queskey [1946] 1 All ER 717; [1946] Ch 250; (1946) 110 JP 272; (1946) 96 LJ 176; [1947] 116 LJR 182; (1946) 175 LTR 107; (1946) 90 SJ 236; (1945-46) LXII TLR 344; (1946) WN (I) 75 HC ChD No appeal under Guardianship of Infants Act 1925 from justices' refusal of consent to infants marrying.

Re R [1993] 2 FCR 461; [1994] 1 FLR 190 HC FamD Maintaining contact with children not acquiescence to their retention: return of abducted/wrongfully retained children ordered.

Re R [1994] 2 FCR 136 HC FamD On procedure as regards deciding care actions.

Re R [1993] 2 FCR 525; [1993] 2 FLR 163; [1992] TLR 506 CA Residence order to father rather than religious sect of which father had been/boy was member.

Re R (1981) 2 FLR 416; (1981) 125 SJ 588 CA On appropriate procedure where wardship application made in respect of 'kidnapped' child: child's best interests determinant factor.

Re R [1984] TLR 304 CA Court could not re-assess wardship decision in light of ongoing durability of mother's relationship with boyfriend.

Re R [1983] 2 All ER 929; (1983) 4 FLR 787; (1984) 134 NLJ 339c; (1983) 127 SJ 509; [1983] 1 WLR 991 CA Court may give any order in child's interest but generally will not amend bona fide local authority decisions.

Re R [1997] 3 FCR 29 (also CA); [1997] 1 FLR 663 (also CA) HC FamD Non-return of abducted child (who did not wish to return) to Switzerland and non-registration of Swiss care and custody order (which no longer reflected realities of situation).

Re R [1987] FCR 1; (1987) 151 JP 413 HC FamD On ordering adoption application to be dealt with as custodianship application.

Re R [1987] FCR 104; [1987] 1 FLR 391 CA On deciding whether appropriate to dispense with parental consent to adoption.

Re R [1986] 1 FLR 6 CA On providing court with evidence of criminal/drinking record of parent in custody action.

Re R [1988] FCR 497; [1988] 1 FLR 206 CA Access ought to have been refused to parent discovered to have sexually abused child.

Re R [1988] FCR 388; [1987] 2 FLR 401 CA Court could exercise wardship jurisdiction at behest of local authority where juvenile court discharging care order but child still felt to be at risk.

Re R [1995] 3 FCR 334; [1995] 2 FLR 612; [1995] TLR 268 CA Shared residence order approved: judge's consideration of financial implications of making residence order was valid.

Re R [1996] 3 FCR 566 CA On seeking leave to apply for contact.

Re R [1974] 1 All ER 1033; (1974) 124 NLJ 123t; (1974) 118 SJ 78 HC FamD Custody to non-parent/non-guardian.

Re R [1994] 2 FCR 468; [1994] 2 FLR 637 CA On imposition of restraints on reporting of criminal proceedings concerning (abduction of) ward.

Re R (No 2) [1993] 1 FLR 249 HC FamD Return of child abroad not ordered where father with English care and control order (since 1991) removed child from Canada where mother had been granted custody (in 1992).

Re R (PM) [1968] 1 All ER 691; (1968) 118 NLJ 14t; (1968) 112 SJ 189; [1968] 1 WLR 385 HC ChD On medical examination of ward absent court's consent; on access to wards.

Re R and G [1994] 1 FLR 793 HC FamD Could not give power to take children into care as part of supervision order.

Re Reade-Revell; Crellin v Melling [1929] All ER 506; [1930] 1 Ch 52; (1930) 142 LTR 177 HC ChD No maintenance from trust fund as contingent interest did not carry intermediate income.

Re S [1994] 2 FCR 945; [1994] 1 FLR 819; [1994] TLR 80 CA On determining whether there has been acquiescence.

Re S [1993] 2 FCR 499; [1994] 1 FLR 297 CA On principles to be applied when dealing with child abduction involving non-Child Abduction Convention country.

Re S [1991] FCR 82 (also HC FamD); [1991] 1 FLR 161 CA Juvenile court could be (but here was not) justified in granting natural mother access to child whom local authority seeking to have adopted.

Re S [1991] FCR 82 (also CA) HC FamD Juvenile court not justified in granting natural mother access to child whom local authority seeking to have adopted.

Re S [1990] FCR 379; [1990] 2 FLR 166 CA On granting access; access ought not to have been refused merely because judge felt would not work.

Re S [1990] FCR 635; [1990] TLR 109 CA Custody of children to be finally determined when mother's post-divorce accommodation/financial situation resolved.

Re S [1993] 2 FCR 16; [1993] 2 FLR 204 CA Guardian ad litem not allowed reveal details of proposed adoptive father to mother (who was refusing consent to adoption).

Re S [1983] TLR 550 HC FamD Wardship jurisdiction ougt not to be employed on appeal from CyCt.

Re S (1978) 128 NLJ 1148t; (1978) 122 SJ 759 HC FamD Wardship action in which were seeking decision on issue of care and control of child dismissed as was really an attempt to secure review of adoption order refusal.

Re S [1993] 1 FCR 789 CA On whether or not to order return of abducted children to jurisdiction not party to the Hague Convention.

Re S [1985] FLR 579; [1984] TLR 600 CA Breach of prohibition on person other than adoption agency acting as such without permission of HC.

Re S [1977] 3 All ER 582; [1978] QB 120; [1977] 3 WLR 575 CA On meaning of 'care' in Children and Young Persons Act 1969, s 1(2) — here care order made so that boy might enjoy education.

Re S [1977] 3 All ER 671; [1977] Fam 173; (1977) 127 NLJ 368t; (1977) 121 SJ 222; [1977] 2 WLR 919 CA In parent/step-parent adoption case court must consider whether in child's welfare joint custody order preferable.

Re S (1977) 127 NLJ 16t/739b; (1976) 120 SJ 819 CA Failed appeal by mother against adoption where trial judge found (applying objective test) that she was unreasonably withholding her consent.

Re S [1988] 1 FLR 418 CA Adoption by adoptive mother/non-adoptive father merited despite intention by them not to tell child of her origins.

Re S [1987] 2 All ER 99; [1987] Fam 98; [1988] FCR 57; [1987] 2 FLR 331; (1987) 151 JP 577; (1987) 131 SJ 133; [1987] 2 WLR 977 CA On ordering adoption application to be treated as custodianship application; on ordering disclosure of confidential reports so that parties have time to prepare response at action.

Re S [1987] FCR 85; [1987] 1 FLR 479 CA On making/effect of care order: here wardship should have been discontinued in light of care orders.

Re S [1988] FCR 343 CA On need to determine wishes of child vis-à-vis adoption; adoptive parents' intention not to tell child of her origins not fatal to adoption application.

Re S [1975] 1 All ER 109; [1976] Fam 1; (1975) 139 JP 162; (1974) 124 NLJ 1008t; (1975) 119 SJ 11; [1975] 2 WLR 250 CA Adoption order can be qualified by access order.

Re S [1996] 3 FCR 30; [1996] 1 FLR 158 CA Contact with paternal grandparents ordered notwithstanding mother's not wanting same.

Re S [1995] 3 FCR 225; [1995] 2 FLR 648; [1995] TLR 107 CA On whether/when to grant parental responsibility order to natural father of illegitimate child.

Re S [1995] 2 FLR 639 CA Courts can (but generally will not) dispute findings of earlier court in application for discharge of care order.

Re S [1995] 3 FCR 564 HC FamD On granting parental responsibility order to unmarried father (here merited).

Re S [1995] 2 All ER 122; [1994] TLR 220 CA Despite wide powers when making adoption order Court will not impose conditions against express opposition of adopters which would threaten peace and security of child.

Re S [1996] 3 FCR 115 HC FamD Illegitimate child in respect of whom father had no custody rights/parental responsibility (though had applied for residence/parental responsibility orders before child removed and later obtained ex parte residence order) held to have been unlawfully removed by mother.

Re S [1973] 3 All ER 88 CA Appeal against dispensing with consent to be decided in light of fresh evidence.

Re S (1994) 138 SJ LB 221; [1994] TLR 522 HC FamD Court did have jurisdiction to alter continuing order in respect of child now habitually resident abroad.

Re S [1997] 1 FCR 490 HC FamD Justices' decision to hold care hearings absent previously ordered psychological appraisal justified by need to avoid undue delay.

Re S [1994] 2 FCR 414; [1994] 2 FLR 222 CA Inappropriate for court to grant care order but adjourn contact decision until later date.

Re S [1995] 2 FCR 177; [1994] 2 FLR 416; (1994) 138 SJ LB 99 CA Non-imposition of blood transfusion condition when ordering adoption of child by couple who were Jehovah's Witnesses.

Re S [1994] TLR 80 CA That parent was given defective legal advice is relevant to determination whether there was acquiescence to the alleged abduction.

Re S [1993] 3 All ER 36; [1993] Fam 263; [1993] 2 FCR 1; [1993] 2 FLR 437; (1993) 143 NLJ 435; [1993] TLR 105; [1993] 2 WLR 801 CA Minor may conduct proceedings without guardian ad litem only where understands specific proceedings in issue; parents may be heard by judge on whether minor so understands.

Re S [1993] 2 FCR 475 HC FamD On when interim care orders (as here) justified.

Re S [1996] 1 FLR 660 HC FamD Successful ex parte application for declaration that removal of child from jurisdiction breached Article 12 of the Child Abduction Convention.

Re S [1997] 1 FLR 958 CA Keeping infant child outside UK (place of habitual residence) by maternal relatives of infant child violated the Hague Convention, Article 3 whilst taking the child from the jurisdiction violated the European Convention, Article 12.

Re S [1997] 3 WLR 597 HL Acting in breach of court order and keeping infant child outside UK (place of habitual residence) by maternal relatives of child violated Hague Convention, Article 3; taking the child from the jurisdiction violated the European Convention, Article 12.

Re S [1992] 2 FCR 554; [1993] 1 FLR 110; (1992) 136 SJ LB 206 CA On roles of guardian ad litem/court welfare officer.

Re S [1993] 2 All ER 683; [1993] Fam 242; (1992) 142 NLJ 1341; [1992] TLR 390; [1993] 2 WLR 775 CA Exceptionally court may not return child to foreign jurisdiction; question of whether child's wishes to be taken into account one of discretion.

Re S [1991] FCR 155; [1991] 2 FLR 388 CA On custody of young children: child's welfare paramount concern.

Re S [1993] 1 FLR 376 HC FamD Blood transfusions to child allowed though contrary to principles/wishes of parents (Jehovah's Witnesses).

Re S [1993] 1 FCR 283; [1992] 2 FLR 313 CA On desirability of access between children/non-custodial parent; on religious upbringing of children.

Re S [1994] 1 FLR 82; (1993) 137 SJ LB 188; [1993] TLR 406 HC FamD Where one/other parent agreed to children remaining in jurisdiction for certain time/sought to keep them there for all time there was no acquiescence to their retention even inside period agreed to.

Re S [1991] FCR 656; [1991] 2 FLR 1 CA Habitual residence defined by reference to pre-abduction situation; failed attempt not to have child returned to place from where abducted.

Re S [1995] 2 FCR 697; [1995] 1 FLR 151 CA Generally where child charged with grave criminal offence is better for trial of that matter to proceed care action.

Re S [1965] 1 All ER 33; (1965) 115 LJ 57; [1965] 1 WLR 94 HC ChD Local authority responsibility to child in care suspended when parents request immediate return; no review of taking of child from foster parents.

Re S [1965] 1 All ER 865; (1965) 129 JP 228; (1965) 115 LJ 265; (1965) 109 SJ 174; [1965] 1 WLR 483 CA Wardship jurisdiction continues over child in local authority care.

Re S [1996] 2 FCR 719; [1996] 1 FLR 753 CA On when care and when supervision order merited.

Re S [1995] 3 FCR 707; [1995] 1 FLR 858 HC FamD Sequestration of property of friend of mother allowed where friend assisted mother in her non-compliance with order to return children.

Re S [1997] 2 FCR 342; [1997] 1 FLR 486 HC FamD Children allowed have separate representation in Hague Child Abduction Convention hearing.

Re S [1995] 1 FCR 617; [1994] 2 FLR 1057 CA Adjournment of contact action and imposition without notice of requirement to seek court's leave before bringing future action was improper.

Re S [1996] 2 FLR 773 HC FamD On holding of split hearings in care action.

Re S [1997] 1 FLR 497 CA In action where father seeking care of and mother seeking residence order in respect of children allegedly sexually abused by father the mother's new husband (in respect of whom past abuse alleged) allowed intervene in action.

Re S [1959] 2 All ER 675; (1959) 109 LJ 509; (1959) 103 SJ 545 HC ChD On status of guardian ad litem appointed by justices.

Re S [1958] 1 All ER 783; (1958) 122 JP 245; (1958) 102 SJ 250 HC ChD Unless urgent, stay of custody transfer order desirable upon appeal; otherwise postponed transfer to allow for appeal aginst refusal of stay.

Re S [1993] 2 FCR 234; [1993] TLR 118 HC FamD On whether/when natural parent to be afforded contact to adopted child.

Re S [1997] 1 FCR 588; [1997] TLR 16 CA On habitual residence of/jurisdiction of court in respect of child (Irish citizen habitually resident in England) removed by deceased mother's relations to Ireland from England.

Re S [1959] 1 WLR 921 HC ChD Guardian ad litem in appeal against CyCt adoption order to be guardian ad litem appointed in CyCt.

Re S [1997] TLR 426 HL Child was habitually resident in England despite having been removed to Ireland by deceased mother's relatives.

Re S (1980) 1 FLR 301 HC QBD Evidence of statement by party to action adverse to own/another's interests admissible/inadmissible in evidence.

Re S [1997] 2 FCR 272 CA Limited intervention of husband (alleged sexual abuser) in proceedings where local authority/mother seeking care/residence orders.

Re S [1993] 2 FCR 325 HC FamD Magistrates to explain why not pusuing course of conduct recommended by court welfare officer.

Re S (a minor) [1992] TLR 308 CA Unnecessary to require reports in proceedings from both guardian ad litem and court welfare officer.

Re S (J) [1990] 2 All ER 861; [1990] Fam 182; [1990] FCR 961; [1991] 1 FLR 7; [1990] 3 WLR 119 HC FamD Minor subject to military law not suitable candidate for wardship of court.

Re S (J) [1980] 1 All ER 1061; [1981] Fam 22; (1981) 2 FLR 146; (1980) 124 SJ 881; [1980] 3 WLR 984 CA Bare declaration of paternity not to be made in wardship case; grounds on which (if possible) to be made.

Re S (J) [1993] 2 FCR 193; [1993] 2 FLR 919 HC FamD On nature, effect, whether and when to grant care/supervision orders: here care order granted.

Re S (J) [1959] 3 All ER 856; (1960) 124 JP 89; (1960) 110 LJ 57; (1960) 104 SJ 15; [1959] 1 WLR 1218 HC ChD As on appeal no note of evidence before juvenile court re-trial ordered.

Re S (M) an infant [1971] 1 All ER 459; [1971] Ch 621; (1970) 120 NLJ 969t; (1971) 115 SJ 93; [1971] 2 WLR 216 HC ChD Scottish court forum conveniens though English proceedings brought first.

Re S (minors) [1994] TLR 682 HC FamD In case where interests of siblings conflicted those of child in respect of whom revocation of care was sought allowed take precedence over those of child in respect of whom adoption freeing order sought.

Re S (Q) [1997] 1 FCR 9 HC FamD Immigration concerns defeated application for adoption of non-patrial child.

Re S and another [1994] 1 All ER 237; [1994] Fam 70; [1994] 1 FCR 83; [1994] 2 WLR 229 HC FamD Wrongful retention cannot alter habitual residence so that habitual residence becomes place of wrongful retention.

Re S and D [1995] 1 FCR 626; [1995] 2 FLR 456 CA Prohibited steps order invalid as essentially required child to be kept in local authority care: care order substituted.

Re S and others [1987] 3 All ER 1076; [1987] Fam 199; [1988] 1 FLR 1; [1987] 3 WLR 847 HC FamD Leave of court required for disclosure of records concerning ward even if came into being after wardship made; interest of ward in confidentiality will rarely supersede interest in protecting society from crime; ordinary case records of local authority not subject to disclosure; that privilege not waived because social worker report to court based on records.

Re S and P [1995] 2 FLR 782 HC FamD Magistrates validly stopped application for discharge of care order after heard mother's evidence.

Re S and W (1983) 4 FLR 290; (1983) 133 NLJ 512c; [1982] TLR 220 CA Reference in psycharist's report (commissioned by local authority) to case conference reports not a waiver of privilege by authority in respect of said reports.

Re S, S and A [1995] 2 FLR 244 HC FamD On issue estoppel in child actions: findings at earlier proceedings to which father not party that he had abused children inadmissible in instant action as fact.

Re S; Dyfed County Council v S [1996] 2 FCR 838; (1995) 139 SJ LB 174; [1995] TLR 390 CA No extension of time to mother of child to appeal against phasing out by local authority of her contact with her children (who were in care).

Re Scott; Scott v Scott [1902] 1 Ch 918 HC ChD On entitlement of beneficiary children upon attaining age of majority to accumulations of beqeathed property not already paid to them as maintenance.

Re Skinner; Skinner v Carter [1948] 1 All ER 917; [1948] Ch 387; (1948) 112 JP 329; (1948) 98 LJ 273; [1948] 117 LJR 1628; (1948) WN (I) 185 CA Bigamously married adopter could be ordered to pay for child's maintenance.

Re Skinner; Skinner v Carter (1948) 112 JP 116; (1948) 98 LJ 23 HC ChD Bigamously married adopter could not seek maintenance order in respect of child against partner in bigamy (and co-adopter).

Re Spence; Spence v Dennis and another [1990] 2 All ER 827; [1990] Ch 652; [1990] FCR 983; [1990] 2 FLR 278; [1990] TLR 288; [1990] 2 WLR 1430 CA Legitimacy not conferred on child of void marriage entered into by parents after child's birth.

Re Spence; Spence v Dennis and another [1989] 2 All ER 679; [1990] Ch 197; [1989] FCR 651; [1990] 1 FLR 286; (1989) 133 SJ 1372/1513; [1989] 3 WLR 834 HC ChD Child born before parents enter void marriage cannot be treated as legitimate.

Re Stern; Stern v Stern [1950] 2 All ER 160; (1950) 114 JP 361; (1950) 94 SJ 420; [1950] 66 (1) TLR 1087 HC ChD No right of appeal against orders by summary court under Children Act 1948, s 53.

Re T [1995] 2 FCR 537; [1995] 2 FLR 251 CA On contact between natural mother and adopted child.

Re T [1953] 2 All ER 830; (1953) 117 JP 517; (1953) 103 LJ 604; [1953] 3 WLR 619 HC ChD In deciding infant's maintenance by father, mother's income relevant.

Re T (1982) 3 FLR 183 CA Re-trial of adoption case ordered where judge refused adoption on basis of unrevealed portions of report of guardian ad litem.

Re T (1981) 2 FLR 239 CA Custody to mother who was Jehovah's Witness subject to various conditions (inter alia that children be allowed blood transfusions if necessary).

Re T [1996] 3 FCR 97; [1996] 2 FLR 352 CA Residence order granted to father in failed application by good mother for leave to remove child abroad set aside.

Re T (1980) 1 FLR 59 HC FamD Court when departing from welfare report recommendations must explain why.

Re T [1995] 2 FLR 792; [1995] TLR 465 CA On seeking leave to apply for direct/indirect contact with adopted child.

Re T [1986] 1 All ER 817; [1986] Fam 160; [1986] 2 FLR 31 (also CC); (1986) 136 NLJ 285; (1986) 130 SJ 88; [1986] 2 WLR 538 CA Notification of parent regulations directory/not mandatory; oral/written consent to adoption precludes natural parent removing child from adopters.

Re T [1989] FCR 212 (also HC FamD); [1989] 1 FLR 313 (also CA); (1988) 132 SJ 1117; [1988] 3 WLR 713 HC FamD HC exercised its wardship jurisdiction where was desirable that single court (rather than various juvenile courts) decide on future welfare of all children of family.

Re T [1986] 2 FLR 31 (also CA) CyCt Written consent of parent to adoption necessary; notification of parent regulations directory/not mandatory; mother's consent being withheld unreasonably.

Re T [1995] 3 FCR 299 CA Time extension in which to appeal adoption allowed where father seeking to show procedural irregularity in that all reasonable steps not taken to ensure his presence at adoption hearings.

Re T [1994] 2 FLR 423; [1994] TLR 248 CA Refusal of care order appropriate course if did not approve of local authority care plan; where supervision is conditional the conditions are to be specified in the order.

Re T [1969] 3 All ER 998; (1969) 113 SJ 774; [1969] 1 WLR 1608 HC ChD Custody of ward sought by person living abroad: interest of ward/comity of nations of increasing/decreasing importance.

Re T [1995] 1 FCR 517; [1995] 1 FLR 159 HC QBD Judicial review of decision not to accommodate 'child in need' already taken in by couple.

Re T [1968] 3 All ER 411; [1968] Ch 704; (1968) 112 SJ 639; [1968] 3 WLR 430 CA Generally court will not countenance wardship/custody actions on foot of kidnapping by parent.

Re T (1968) 118 NLJ 564t CA Return of abducted children ordered where faced no real risk of harm in consequence.

Re T [1992] 2 FCR 92 HC FamD Where Child Abduction proceedings started, stopped, re-started/principally used to secure return of mother not child there was acquiescence to non-return of child.

Re T [1994] 1 FCR 663; [1994] 1 FLR 103 CA Local authority care (not supervision) order merited in respect of child whose daily care was left to parents notwithstanding order.

Re T [1993] 1 FCR 973; [1993] 2 FLR 450 CA Refusal of parental responsibility order and three-year stay on future applications for same merited.

Re T [1990] FCR 71 CA Order of care with view to adoption justified where six month' counselling of mother suggested could never properly care for child (even though was some contradictory expert evidence).

Re T (1974) 118 SJ 78 HC FamD Failed appeal in custody action on basis that justices had not seen child in their private room.

Re T [1994] 1 FLR 632 (also HC FamD); (1994) 144 NLJ 123 CA Guardian ad litem ought to have been allowed see case record of child whom local authority sought to place with adoptive parents.

Re T [1994] 1 FLR 632 (also CA) HC FamD Guardian ad litem ought to have been allowed see case record of child whom local authority sought to place with adoptive parents.

Re T [1962] 3 All ER 970; (1962) 112 LJ 849; [1962] 3 WLR 1477 HC ChD Right to change infant's surname belongs to natural/legal guardian: unchanged by custody order.

Re T [1997] TLR 2 CA On relevant factors when deciding whether to discharge order for ending of contact between parents and children where latter are in local authority care.

Re T (AJJ) [1970] 1 All ER 512; [1970] Ch 336; (1970) 134 JP 151; (1970) 120 NLJ 224; (1969) 113 SJ 980; [1970] 2 WLR 433 HC ChD Court will not interfere with local authority discretion as fit person unless acts improperly/contrary to statute.

Re T (AJJ) [1970] 2 All ER 865; [1970] Ch 688; (1970) 134 JP 611; (1970) 114 SJ 550; [1970] 3 WLR 315 CA Only exceptionally will displace local authority discretion as fit person.

Re T (C) [1993] 2 FLR 278 CA On allowing child to apply for residence order without next friend: here allowed.

Re T (C) [1992] 2 FCR 92 HC FamD Where Child Abduction proceedings started, stopped, re-started/principally used to secure return of mother not child there was acquiescence to non-return of child.

Re T (C) (An Infant); Re T (J) (An Infant) [1956] 3 All ER; [1956] 3 WLR 826 HC ChD Cannot hear application by putative father for custody of illegitimate child.

Re T (J) [1986] 2 FLR 107 HC FamD Care of child to local authority with view to adoption where older child had died as result of non-accidental injuries while living with mother as member of extended Rastafarian family.

Re T (KD) [1994] 2 FCR 721 CA Conditional care order not allowed; care order only to be made if court approves of care plan; on role of court vis-à-vis that of local authority in care proceedings; here supervision order preferable to care order.

Re T (No 2) [1997] 2 FCR 55 HC FamD Supervised contact ordered between father (guilty of 'inadvertent touching' of child) and child in case where entire procedure to alleged child sex abuse had been flawed.

Re T (otherwise H) [1962] 3 All ER 970; [1963] Ch 238; (1962) 106 SJ 1011 HC ChD Right to change infant's surname belongs to natural/legal guardian: unchanged by custody order.

Re T and another [1997] 1 All ER 65; [1997] 1 FLR 517; [1997] 1 WLR 393 CA On when parental contact to child in care may be terminated (here terminated in respect of one of mother's children but not other).

Re T and E [1995] 3 FCR 260; [1995] 1 FLR 581 HC FamD Residence order to father of one of two half-sisters in care as was in her best interest (though joint best interests of the two girls demanded that they be adopted together).

Re T and others [1989] 1 All ER 297; [1990] Fam 1; [1989] 1 FLR 313 (also HC FamD); (1989) 133 SJ 568; [1989] 2 WLR 954 CA Rôle of guardian ad litem confined to juvenile court proceedings — cannot begin wardship proceedings.

Re T and others [1993] 3 All ER 127; [1993] 2 FLR 617; [1993] 1 WLR 1461 HC FamD Procedure for contact order concerning child abducted by parent from abroad.

Re T and T (1956) 120 JP 566 HC ChD Putative father could not make custody application in respect of his illegitimate children under Guardianship of Infants Acts 1886 or 1925.

Re T; Re Guardianship of Infants Acts, 1886-1925 [1953] Ch 787; (1953) 97 SJ 607 HC ChD Appropriate that means of mother (given custody of children) be taken into account when assessing appropriate maintenance for mother.

Re T; T v T [1987] 1 FLR 181 CA HC not in error in considering child's best interests in wardship application and then relying on that as one of four criteria justifying granting of ouster order.

Re Thain (Margaret Louise), an infant (1924-25) 69 SJ 812 HC QBD Restoration of child to natural father not allowed as possibly not in child's best interests to be moved where only home had known since infancy was that of aunt (child now six).

Re Thain; Re M M Thain; Thain v Taylor [1926] Ch 676 (also CA); (1926) 61 LJ 301; (1926) 95 LJCh 292 (also CA); (1925-26) 70 SJ 504; (1926) WN (I) 91 HC ChD In custody case child's welfare paramount — but not only — consideration.

Re Thain; Thain v Taylor [1926] All ER 384; [1926] Ch 676 (also HC ChD); (1926) 61 LJ 403; (1926) 95 LJCh 292 (also HC ChD); (1926) 135 LTR 99; (1925-26) 70 SJ 634; (1926) WN (I) 150 CA In custody case child's welfare paramount — but not only — consideration.

Re The Legitimacy Act, 1926, and Re Younghusband (1927) 64 LJ ccr54 CyCt Failed application for legitimacy petition to be heard in camera.

Re U [1993] 2 FCR 64; [1993] 2 FLR 992 CA Valid granting of residence order to grandparents where adoption agency had sought freeing of child for adoption.

Re U (T) [1993] 2 FCR 565 HC FamD Magistrates to give reasons for not following guardian ad litem's recommendation; magistrates improperly ordered contact to mother so putting child at risk.

Re V [1985] FLR 45; (1985) 135 NLJ 708c; (1986) 136 NLJ 516c CA Adoption allowed continue where mother had sought to withdraw consent after initially agreeing.

Re V [1986] 1 All ER 752; [1987] Fam 57; [1987] 2 FLR 89; (1987) 151 JP 145; (1970) 130 SJ 879; [1986] 3 WLR 927 CA Dispensing with reasonably held consent incorrect; no adoption order where access to parent promotes child's welfare.

Re V [1996] 3 FCR 173; [1995] 2 FLR 992 HC FamD On determining habitual residence of persons dividing their year between two jurisdictions.

Re V [1996] 3 FCR 101; [1995] 2 FLR 1010 CA Valid departure by judge from expert opinion/recommendations of welfare officer.

Re V [1995] 2 FLR 1003 HC FamD Injunction to restrain mother from interfering with child's decision upon attaining majority as to where would live.

Re V [1996] 2 FCR 555; [1996] 1 FLR 776 CA On whether/when care (as here) or supervision order appropriate; supervision order with conditions inappropriate.

Re Valentine's Settlement; Valentine and another v Valentine and another (1964) 108 SJ 582; [1964] 3 WLR 768 HC ChD Foreign adoption not recognised in foreign adopter's place of domicile consequently not recognised by English court.

Re Valentine's Settlement; Valentine and others v Valentine and others [1965] 2 All ER 226; (1965) 115 LJ 349; [1965] 2 WLR 1015 CA Foreign adopters to be domiciled in foreign country for foreign adoption to be valid.

Re W (1982) 3 FLR 129; (1981) 131 NLJ 1189 CA On relevant factors in application to have parental rights resolution of local authority rescinded.

Re W (1981) 131 NLJ 1288 CA Local authority care resolution deemed not to have lapsed.

Re W [1990] 2 All ER 463; [1990] Fam 156; [1990] FCR 736; [1990] 2 FLR 470; [1990] TLR 161; [1990] 2 WLR 1116 HC FamD Court will not review actions of approved adoption agency via wardship jurisdiction.

Re W [1993] 1 FCR 988 HC FamD Adoption order made despite procedural irregularities in manner in which went about adopting foreign child.

Re W [1994] 1 FCR 842 HC FamD That had firm albeit not definitely settled plans as to future adequate basis on which to allow mother take child from jurisdiction.

Re W [1990] FCR 540; [1990] 2 FLR 86 CA Inappropriate that interim custody order be made in favour of putative father until question of paternity decided.

Re W [1984] FLR 880 CA On deciding if refusal of parental consent to adoption unreasonable: here consent dispensed with to protect welfare of child.

Re W (1982) 3 FLR 75 CA On dispensing with parental agreement as prerequisite to adoption.

Re W [1981] 3 All ER 401 CA County court may issue interlocutory injunction in support of custody order when making order.

Re W (1981) 2 FLR 360; (1981) 131 NLJ 578 HC FamD On when wardship powers will be exercised in respect of child committed to local authority care by juvenile court.

Re W (1983) 4 FLR 492 (also CA) HC FamD Custody to mother: child's best interests presumed to be with mother unless strong contrary evidence.

Re W (1985) 129 SJ 269 CA Discharge of wardship order in respect of child in local authority care.

Re W (1983) 4 FLR 492 (also HC FamD) CA Custody to mother: attitude of courts to children being in custody of mothers set out.

Re W (1981) 2 FLR 161 CA Adoption of child by grandparents who had custody for some years (mother consented/consent of father — a criminal — dispensed with).

Re W [1979] 3 All ER 154; [1980] Fam 60; (1979) 143 JP 727; (1979) 123 SJ 553; [1979] 3 WLR 252 CA Natural parent cannot challenge merits of local authority decision to make child ward; authority may consider possible future adoption in deciding to disallow parental access to child.

Re W [1997] 2 FCR 643; [1997] 1 FLR 793 HC FamD On whether (unlike here) to make contact order in favour of grandparent.

Re W (1977) 127 NLJ 43; (1976) 120 SJ 857 HC FamD Refusal of adoption of child by mother/her new husband as natural father (who was in prison) refused his consent.

Re W (1987) 131 SJ 915 CA Could (and here did) make access order as part of adoption order.

Re W (1985) 129 SJ 523 HC FamD Girl aged just over seventeen who was beyond parental control committed to care of local authority.

Re W [1988] FCR 129; [1988] 1 FLR 175 CA On making adoption rather than custodianship order.

Re W [1986] Fam 54; [1986] 1 FLR 179; (1985) 129 SJ 794; [1985] 3 WLR 945 CA On adoption of foreign child by British citizen (here refused).

Re W [1989] FCR 97; [1988] 1 FLR 47; (1988) 132 SJ 1388; [1988] 1 WLR 1157 CA County court order as to care and access improper as justices having made care order only they could discharge same.

Re W (1980) 124 SJ 272 HC FamD Pre-trial hearing between justices, child and social worker who would be giving evidence in pending case concerning child was inappropriate.

Re W [1995] 4 All ER 282; [1995] Fam 120; [1995] 1 FLR 163; [1995] 2 WLR 458 HC FamD Care order or adoption arranged through adoption agency by third party permissible where parent under disability.

Re W [1994] 2 FCR 759; [1994] 1 FLR 419; [1993] TLR 611 CA Refusal of contact between father and children justified where inter alia rested on possibly mistaken finding in civil action that father had sexually abused his children.

Re W [1993] 2 FCR 731; [1994] 1 FLR 843 HC FamD Decision of justices set aside in contact case where had not conformed to rules regarding giving of reasons for decision made.

Re W [1996] 3 FCR 337 HC FamD Leave of court unnecessary when seeking variation of indirect contact order so that direct contact possible.

Re W [1993] TLR 225 CA On approach to resolving residence dispute where natural parent and another in dispute over same.

Re W [1971] 2 All ER 49; [1971] AC 682; (1971) 135 JP 259; (1971) 115 SJ 286; [1971] 2 WLR 1011 HL Need not be culpable in withholding consent for it to be unreasonable; welfare of child important factor in deciding if unreasonable.

Re W [1970] 3 All ER 990; (1971) 135 JP 42; (1970) 120 NLJ 480t; [1970] 2 QB 589; (1970) 114 SJ 433; [1970] 3 WLR 175 CA That consent reasonable does not mean non-consent unreasonable; child's welfare relevant only if non-adoption detrimental to same.

Re W [1995] 2 FCR 708 HC FamD Local authority could make secure accommodation application to family proceedings court in respect of child placed on bail by youth court and entrusted to local authority.

Re W [1984] FLR 402 CA On relevancy of child's interests in adoption (as opposed to custody) hearing.

Re W [1992] 4 All ER 627; [1993] Fam 64; [1992] 2 FCR 785 (also HC FamD); [1993] 1 FLR 1; (1992) 142 NLJ 1124; [1992] 3 WLR 758 CA Court may order medical treatment of minor despite minor's objections.

Re W [1992] 2 FCR 785 (also CA) HC FamD Court may order medical treatment of minor despite minor's objections.

Re W [1992] 2 FCR 603; [1992] 2 FLR 332; [1992] TLR 262 CA Pending residence order hearing four week old baby should have been given to mother even though upset status quo.

Re W [1992] 2 FCR 461 CA On determination of residence order application in light of expressed wishes of children involved.

Re W [1992] 1 All ER 794; [1992] 1 FLR 99; [1991] TLR 391 CA Publication about ward placement involves balancing press freedom/real public interest and child's interests; sometimes publication may legitimately require disclosure of child's identity.

Re W [1965] 3 All ER 231; (1965) 129 JP 550; (1965) 115 LJ 677; [1965] 1 WLR 1259 HC ChD Concealment of remarriage from adoption society and concomitant placing of children with adoption society justified dispensing with consent.

Re W [1995] 1 FLR 878 HC FamD On evidential basis required to establish 'consent' defence contained in Hague Child Abduction Convention, art 13(a).

Re W [1993] 2 FCR 187; [1993] 1 FLR 381 HC FamD Proposed sterilisation of applicant's mentally handicapped daughter approved.

Re W [1993] 2 FCR 589; [1993] 2 FLR 625 CA Generally preferable that child live with natural parents but not always so.

Re W [1996] 1 FCR 46 HC FamD Return of child ordered where father in affidavit evidence had made out out good defence of consent but failed to do so in his oral testimony.

Re W (1965) 109 SJ 850 HC ChD On determining whether (as here) withdrawal of consent to adoption was unreasonable.

Re W [1962] 2 All ER 875; [1962] Ch 918; (1962) 126 JP 445; (1962) 112 LJ 490; (1962) 106 SJ 720 HC ChD Adoption order where prior care and possession outside jurisdiction if infant still of compulsory school age.

Re W [1997] 2 FCR 190; [1997] 1 FLR 128 HC FamD Imprisoned father guilty of murder of stepdaughter discharged from care proceedings at mother's request.

Re W [1994] 3 FCR 102; [1994] 2 FLR 892 CA Interim care orders invalid as had been procedural errors when were made.

Re W (1991) 141 NLJ 1263; [1992] 1 WLR 100 CA Publication of fact that ward placed with gay foster parents allowed though restrictions on identifying foster parents/ward.

Re W [1993] 2 FCR 427 CA On deciding whether to make parental responsibility order; dismissal of father's contact and parental responsibility applications without hearing oral evidence justified and valid.

Re W [1995] 1 FCR 714 HC FamD Adoption arranged through Catholic Children's Society (an approved adoption agency) was valid.

Re W [1953] 2 All ER 1337 CA May appeal from summary court to ChD to CA in custody cases under Guardianship of Infants Act 1925, s 31(1)(i).

Re W (a minor) (1982) 126 SJ 725; [1982] TLR 502 CA On duty of welfare officer in child custody case; on whether custody, care and control of mother (as here) to be preferred.

Re W (a minor) [1989] FCR 41; [1989] 1 FLR 163 HC FamD Non-access to natural father where mother to marry another who was only person child had ever known as father.

Re W (a minor) [1997] 3 All ER 620; (1997) 141 SJ LB 137; [1997] TLR 282 HC FamD Single woman living in lesbian relationship could apply for adoption of child.

Re W (a minor) [1995] TLR 17 CA Appeal against judge's request for welfare report to be prepared ought not to have been brought.

Re W (a minor) [1994] 2 FCR 1216; [1994] 2 FLR 441 CA Contact ordered between child and natural father despite mother (who had no right to end contact) stating would not obey order.

Re W (a minor) [1995] 2 FCR 184 HC FamD HIV-testing of child at risk ordered as would aid judge in deciding residence application.

Re W (A) [1992] 2 FCR 641; [1993] 1 FLR 62 HC FamD Interim adoption order favouring adopters who flouted adoption law as child's welfare demanded should remain with them.

Re W (A) and W (E) (1979) 129 (1) NLJ 420 CA Court would not in instant case exercise its wardship jurisdiction in respect of child in care.

Re W (E) [1992] 2 FCR 441 (also HC FamD) CA On determining place of habitual residence.

Re W (E) [1992] 2 FCR 441 (also CA) HC FamD On determining place of habitual residence.

Re W (E) (No 2) [1993] 1 FCR 710 HC FamD On determining place of habitual residence.

Re W (JC) [1963] 3 All ER 459; [1964] Ch 202; (1963) 127 JP 529; (1963) 107 SJ 617; [1963] 3 WLR 789 CA Magistrates may divide custody/care and control between different parties.

Re W (JC) [1963] 2 All ER 706; [1963] Ch 556; (1963) 113 LJ 656; (1963) 107 SJ 396; [1963] 2 WLR 1471 HC ChD Cannot give custody to one parent and care and control to other.

Re W (M) [1996] 3 FCR 128; [1995] 2 FLR 759 HC FamD Adoption order (plus no contact with natural mother) to surrogate parents (husband natural father) of child.

Re W (M) [1994] 1 FCR 161 CA Fostering of child but with access to father (who had abused/allowed abuse of child though denied it).

Re W (minor) [1993] TLR 53 HC FamD Secure accommodation order to be for appropriate duration (no more) and reasons must be given for making order.

Re W (N) [1994] 1 FCR 121; [1993] 2 FLR 591 HC FamD Father's medical reports disclosed to mother in course of contact application; justices must give reasons for their decisions.

Re W (S) [1993] 1 FCR 896 HC FamD Court could upon making care order make another order terminating contact even though parent not given notice latter order would be sought.

Re W (S) [1986] 1 FLR 24 HC FamD On ordering that ward over age of seventeen be placed in secure accommodation.

Re W (SC) (An Infant) (1963) 113 LJ 610 HC ChD On what is meant by the notion of 'custody' in the Guardianship of Infants Act 1965, s 5.

Re W and another [1956] 1 All ER 368; [1956] Ch 384; (1956) 120 JP 210; [1956] 2 WLR 493 CA Mother's income relevant when determining infant's maintenance payable by father.

Re W and D [1995] 3 FCR 806; [1995] 2 FLR 807 HC FamD Secure accommodation order not essential when bail of children facing criminal charges refused: remand to local authority accommodation subject to various conditions appropriate.

Re W and L [1987] 2 FLR 67; (1987) 151 JP 222 CA On granting interim care orders.

Re W and others [1989] 1 FLR 246 HC FamD Newspapers and their editors found (using criminal standard of proof) not to be guilty of contempt in breaching injunction on publication of articles regarding wardship action.

Re W and S [1992] 2 FCR 665 HC FamD Non-interference by appellate court in contact decision of inferior court unless obviously mistaken decision.

Re W and W (1983) 4 FLR 686 CA Interim custody order bad for instability caused to children; refusal of exclusion order (that would allow wife/children to return to home from women's refuge).

Re W; W v M (1908) 77 LJCh 147 (also CA) HC ChD Variation of wardship order so as to allow two Jewish children to be educated as Christians.

Re W; W v M (1) [1907] 2 Ch 557; (1908) 77 LJCh 147 (also HC ChD); (1907) WN (I) 204 CA Variation of wardship order so as to allow Jewish child (at his behest) to be educated as a Christian but his sister to continue being educated as a Jew.

Re Wakeman; Wakeman v Wakeman [1947] 2 All ER 74; [1947] Ch 607; (1947) 111 JP 373; (1947) 97 LJ 319; [1947] 116 LJR 1092; (1947) 177 LTR 161; (1947) 91 SJ 339; (1947) LXIII TLR 396; (1947) WN (I) 180 HC ChD On need for fresh evidence when seeking change to maintenance order under Guardianship of Infants Act 1925; here evidence that condoned adultery/allowed illegitimate child to be registered as own admitted.

Re West [1995] 2 FCR 206 HC FamD Prohibition on publication of information regarding actual/possible abuse (physical or sexual) of fostered children of prominent multiple murderers.

Re Whittall; Whittall v Faulkner and another [1973] 3 All ER 35 HC ChD Guardian ad litem to advise on variation of trust affecting infant but court need not follow advice.

Re Wicks' Marriage Settlement; Public Trustee v Wicks [1940] Ch 475; [1940] 109 LJCh 163; (1940) 163 LTR 31; (1940) 84 SJ 304; (1940) WN (I) 136 HC ChD Legitimated child was not object of power of appointment applicable to issue of parents' marriage.

Re Wilby [1956] 1 All ER 27; (1956) 106 LJ 26; (1956) 100 SJ 75; [1956] 2 WLR 262 HC PDAD Foreign adoption not covered by Adoption Act 1950, s 13; domiciled in England at date of death so deceased's mother could not succeed to estate.

Re Wilson; Grace v Lucas and others [1954] 1 All ER 997; [1954] Ch 733; (1954) 104 LJ 297; (1954) 98 SJ 372; [1954] 2 WLR 1097 HC ChD Succession of adopted child depends on/not on succession/not adoption law.

Re X (1984) 128 SJ 873; [1984] 1 WLR 1422 HC FamD Court order issued prohibiting revelation of ward's identity or that of parents where was necessary to protect ward.

Re X [1996] 3 FCR 91 HC FamD Order that father not be given notice of care proceedings where was in interests of child/family.

Re X [1975] 1 All ER; (1974) 124 NLJ 1083t; (1975) 119 SJ 12; [1975] 2 WLR 335 HC FamD Interests of ward not greater than public interest in freedom of publication.

Re X (D) [1949] Ch 320; (1949) 99 LJ 161; (1949) LXV TLR 210; (1949) WN (I) 140 HC ChD Exceptionally adoption of child by natural grandparents may be allowed.

Re X and others [1992] Fam 124; [1991] FCR 954; [1992] 1 FLR 84; (1991) 141 NLJ 708; [1991] TLR 146; [1992] 2 WLR 784 HC FamD Definite injury to wardship jurisdiction and lack of real chance of injury to libel action merited refusal of discovery of wardship files for purposes of libel action.

Re X's Settlement [1945] 1 All ER 101; [1945] Ch 44; [1945] 114 LJ 305; (1945) 172 LTR 208; (1944-45) LXI TLR 93; (1944) WN (I) 237 HC ChD Scottish and English courts exercise care/custody powers in a complementary way.

Re Y [1985] FLR 294 HC FamD Mother's wardship application failed where child had been living happily with good foster parents for eight years.

Re Y [1985] Fam 136; [1986] 1 FLR 152; [1985] 3 WLR 601 HC FamD Absent home in England court could not hear application of couple to adopt wife's children.

Re Y [1988] 1 FLR 299 HC FamD Non-interference by court in local authority decisions regarding children in care of authority.

Re Y [1975] 3 All ER 348; [1976] Fam 125; (1976) 140 JP 19; (1975) 119 SJ 610; [1975] 3 WLR 342 CA Local authority with ward in care subject to control of court.

Re Y [1994] 2 FCR 367; [1994] 2 FLR 699 HC FamD Refusal of contact/no future application for contact with children without leave of court where father guilty of manslaughter of mother.

Re Y [1993] 2 FCR 422 HC FamD Ex parte residence order application merited but three month delay in inter partes hearing unjustified.

Re Z [1995] 4 All ER 961; [1997] Fam 1 CA Wardship jurisdiction theoretically unlimited but will not be exercised where freedom of publication the dominant interest and child only referred to indirectly.

Re Z [1996] 2 WLR 88 CA Child's welfare took precedence over public interest in freedom to publish: injunction preventing publication of information in relation to child appropriate.

Re Z (A) [1993] 1 FLR 682 CA Acquiescence to 'abduction' established so no order for return.

Redbridge London Borough Council, ex parte East Sussex County Council, R v [1992] TLR 663 HC QBD Ordinary residence of mentally handicapped twins whose parents had left them in England and returned to Nigeria was deemed not to lie with parents.

Reffell v Morton (1906) 70 JP 347; (1905-06) 50 SJ 378 HC KBD On what for purposes of Bastardy Laws Amendment Act 1872, s 4, constitutes corroboration of mother's evidence as to paternity of illegitimate child.

Registrar General, D v [1996] 2 FCR 248; [1996] 1 FLR 707 HC FamD Failed application for order requiring Registrar General to disclose information enabling natural mother to trace adopted child.

Registrar General, D v [1997] 2 FCR 240; [1997] 1 FLR 715 CA Failed appeal against refusal of order requiring Registrar General to disclose information enabling natural mother to trace adopted child (such an order would be exceptional).

Registrar General, ex parte Smith, R v [1990] 2 All ER 170; [1990] FCR 561; [1990] 2 FLR 79; [1990] 2 QB 253; [1990] 2 WLR 980 HC QBD Registrar General may refuse to provide information necessary for granting of birth certificate if might be used for future criminal act.

Registrar General, ex parte Smith, R v [1991] 2 All ER 88; [1991] FCR 403; [1991] 1 FLR 255; [1991] 2 QB 393; [1991] 2 WLR 782 CA Absolute statutory duty to provide birth certificate to adopted persons not applicable where it would facilitate crime.

Registrar General, Lawson and another v (1956) 106 LJ ccr204 CyCt Order for discovery of details pertaining to adopted child so that adoptee might be paid legacy left it by godmother.

Rice v Rice (1977) 121 SJ 758 CA On irrelevance to determination of custody proceedings of children's using same new surname as that which mother now adopted.

Rider, R v [1954] Crim LR 49; (1954) 118 JP 73 Assizes On what constitutes a charge when deciding whether accused to have benefit of first-time charge proviso in prosecution for having carnal knowledge of under-sixteen year old (Criminal Law Amendment Act 1922, s 2).

Riding v Riding [1958] 1 All ER 65; (1958) 108 LJ 56; (1958) 102 SJ 52 CA Committal for non-payment of maintenance is for original amount of order.

Riley v Riley [1986] 2 FLR 429; (1986) 150 JP 439 CA Custody order should not have provided for constant shuffling of child between homes of divorced parents.

Roberts, Holland v (1939-40) XXXI Cox CC 38; (1938) 158 LTR 313 CA Evidence showing opportunity inadequate corroboration of allegation of paternity in bastardy action.

Robertson v Robertson and Butt and In the Matter of an Issue: Robertson v Robertson and others (1928) 72 SJ 585 HC PDAD Hearing as to legitimacy of child to be done in open court as public nature of hearing did not mean justice would be unattainable.

Robinson and Robinson, Gatehouse v [1986] 1 FLR 504; (1986) 130 SJ 13; [1986] 1 WLR 18 HC QBD Unsuccessful appeal against failed prosecution — for undertaking privately arranged adoption contrary to Adoption Act 1958, s 29, as amended — of foster-parents who had privately arranged fostering relationship.

Robinson v Williams [1964] 3 All ER 12; (1964) 114 LJ 588; [1965] 1 QB 89; (1964) 108 SJ 691; [1964] 3 WLR 563 HC QBD Dismissal of one affiliation application does not preclude later application; new evidence is evidence uncalled (not necessarily discovered since) first trial.

Rondeau, Legrand and Co v Marks [1916-17] All ER 664; [1918] 1 KB 75; (1917) 52 LJ 378; [1918] 87 LJCL 215 (also HC KBD); (1917-18) 117 LTR 651; (1917-18) 62 SJ 24; (1917-18) XXXIV TLR 8; (1917) WN (I) 298 CA Husband must provide wife with necessary clothes but need not give them to her.

Rondeau, Legrand and Co v Marks (Louis Marks, Claimant) [1917] 2 KB 636; [1918] 87 LJCL 215 (also CA); (1916-17) 61 SJ 666; (1916-17) XXXIII TLR 529; (1917) WN (I) 268 HC KBD Husband must provide wife with necessary clothes but need not give them to her.

Rose, ex parte McGibbon, R v (1959) 123 JP 374 HC QBD Jamaican maintenance order could not be rescinded by English court under Maintenance Orders (Facilties for Enforcement) Act 1920.

Rosenberg, R v (1906) 70 JP 264 CCC On elements of offence of concealment of birth.

Rossage and others, Rossage v [1960] 1 All ER 600; (1960) 110 LJ 204; (1960) 104 SJ 231 CA Suspending of access not interlocutory hearing so information/belief evidence inadmissible hearsay.

Rossage v Rossage and others [1960] 1 All ER 600; (1960) 110 LJ 204; (1960) 104 SJ 231 CA Suspending of access not interlocutory hearing so information/belief evidence inadmissible hearsay.

Rostron v Rostron (1982) 3 FLR 270; (1981) 131 NLJ 1189 CA Valid decision not to entrust custody of children to mother after they had spent two years with father pursuant to consent order.

Royal Borough of Kensington and Chelsea v Q [1989] 1 FLR 399 HC FamD On using television to advertise for prospective adopters.

Rugman v Drover [1950] 2 All ER 575; [1951] 1 KB 380; (1950) 94 SJ 595; [1950] 66 (2) TLR 699 HC KBD State of affairs which exists upon appeal is that which existed at time of trial (when were still young person).

Russell v Attorney-General (1949) 99 LJ 259; [1949] 118 LJR 1247; (1949) LXV TLR 369; (1949) WN (I) 226 HC PDAD Validity of marriage presumed absent direct contrary evidence where parties had undergone ceremony of marriage and thereafter corroborated.

Russell, Loxton v (1966) 110 SJ 170 CA On proving in affiliation action that had sex at relevant period.

R v Chief Constable for the North Wales Police Area Authority and others, ex parte AB and another (1997) 147 NLJ 1061; [1997] TLR 379 HC QBD Valid disclosure by police of information regarding certain paedophiles was lawful as was necessary for protection of public.

S (an Infant, by her Guardian ad Litem the Official Solicitor to the Supreme Court) v S; W v Official Solicitor (acting as Guardian ad Litem for a male infant named PHW) [1972] AC 24; [1970] 3 WLR 366 HL Blood test desirable in paternity suit.

S (BD) v S (DJ) [1977] 1 All ER 656; [1977] Fam 109; (1977) 121 SJ 34; [1977] 2 WLR 44 CA Child's interests primary concern in custody cases.

S (DJ), S (BD) v [1977] 1 All ER 656; [1977] Fam 109; (1977) 121 SJ 34; [1977] 2 WLR 44 CA Child's interests primary concern in custody cases.

S (formerly B), B v (1974) 118 SJ 219 CA Re-hearing of access case necessary on evidence available (all evidence unavailable as judge promised children would not reveal what they said to him in chambers).

S (GG), S (KV) v [1992] 2 FCR 23; [1992] 2 FLR 361 HC FamD On establishing sexual abuse of child occurred; resumed access to father merited where sexual abuse of child not proved.

S (KV) v S (GG) [1992] 2 FCR 23; [1992] 2 FLR 361 HC FamD On establishing sexual abuse of child occurred; resumed access to father merited where sexual abuse of child not proved.

S (otherwise D), S v (1968) 112 SJ 294 CA Split custody orders not to be preferred (and not granted here).

S (otherwise U) v Attorney-General (1932) 146 LTR 144 HC PDAD Dismissal of legitimacy petition brought on behalf of mentally unsound person.

S (wardship: jurisdiction), F v [1993] 2 FLR 686 CA On deciding place of habitual residence of child.

S and another v Huddersfield Borough Council and another [1974] 3 All ER 296; [1975] Fam 113; (1974) 138 JP 717; (1975) 119 SJ 272; [1975] 2 WLR 697 CA Interim adoption order in father's favour to see if child should be returned to him valid interference with local authority powers/use of probationary period.

S and another, Devon County Council v [1995] 1 All ER 243; [1994] Fam 169; [1994] 2 FCR 409; [1994] 1 FLR 355; [1993] TLR 626; [1994] 3 WLR 183 HC FamD Local authority may invite court to exercise wardship powers under inherent jurisdiction.

S and others, Devon County Council and others v [1993] 2 FCR 36; [1993] 1 FLR 842 HC FamD Caution needed if appointing welfare officer as guardian ad litem; issue for justices in post-rehabiliation contact termination application not whether rehabilitation successful but should care cease.

S and others, Devon County Council v [1992] 3 All ER 793; [1992] Fam 176; [1992] 2 FCR 827; [1992] 2 FLR 244; [1992] 3 WLR 273 HC FamD Prolonged care order hearing inappropriate where proposals already favoured by interested parties.

S and others, Northamptonshire County Council v [1993] Fam 136; [1993] 1 FCR 351; [1993] 1 FLR 554; [1992] 3 WLR 1010 HC FamD Construction of Children Act 1989, s 31(2)(a): on making care order on basis that child is presently suffering 'significant harm'.

S and others, Surrey County Council v [1973] 3 All ER 1074; (1974) 138 JP 26; [1974] QB 124; (1973) 117 SJ 727; [1973] 3 WLR 579 CA Court may consider evidence of neglect/ill-treatment of child not subject of application and make appropriate order.

S and others, Surrey County Council v [1973] 1 All ER 1027; (1973) 137 JP 395; (1973) 117 SJ 186; [1973] 2 WLR 649 HC QBD Court discovering neglect/ill-treatment of child not subject of action may itself remit case of second child to justices.

S and P, S v [1962] 2 All ER 1; (1962) 112 LJ 272; (1962) 106 SJ 152; [1962] 1 WLR 445 CA Access to person not shown to be unfit to have contact.

S v Bedfordshire County Council (1977) 127 NLJ 243t HC QBD Valid revocation of care order in respect of normal child from normal home taken into care because not being sent to school by parents who considered all local comprehensive schools unsuitable.

S v Bedfordshire County Council (1977) 127 NLJ 569t CA Care order restored in respect of normal child from normal home originally taken into care because not being sent to school by parents who considered all local comprehensive schools unsuitable.

S v C (1963) 107 SJ 1022 CA Putative father's admission of two acts of sex with complainant before defendant gave birth to illegitimate child could be corroboration of complaiant's evidence in some material particular.

S v E [1967] 1 All ER 593; [1967] 1 QB 367; (1966) 110 SJ 945; [1967] 2 WLR 704 HC QBD Affiliation proceedings are civil proceedings: putative father a compellable witness.

S v E [1993] 1 FCR 729 HC FamD Magistrates could (but here were wrong to) refuse to order access on terms privately arrived at between parties.

S v H [1997] 1 FLR 971; (1997) 141 SJ LB 64; [1997] TLR 127 HC FamD Was not breach of custodial rights for mother-custodian to remove from Italy children to whom father only had access rights: summary return not ordered.

S v M [1997] 1 FLR 980 HL Hearsay evidence of child as to alleged assaults upon him by father validly taken into account when deciding that access to child by father not in child's best interests.

S v McC (formerly S) and M (S intervening) [1970] 1 All ER 1162; (1970) 120 NLJ 153t; (1970) 114 SJ 131; [1970] 1 WLR 672 CA Child's best interests relevant in determining if blood test to be required.

S v Merton London Borough [1994] 1 FCR 186 HC FamD Improper to make interim care orders absent any evidence in controverted application.

S v Newham London Borough Council and another [1991] FCR 749; [1991] TLR 256 HC FamD Non-physical access could be ordered.

S v O (1982) 3 FLR 15 HC FamD Father properly awarded access to his illegitimate child.

S v Oxfordshire County Council [1993] 2 FCR 676; [1993] 1 FLR 452 HC FamD Justices to give reasons in care cases especially if departing from recommendation/report of guardian ad litem/welfare officer.

S v P [1997] 2 FCR 185; [1997] 2 FLR 277; [1997] TLR 55 HC FamD Family assistance order that would require local authority to escort children to/from prison where father incarcerated unmerited; indirect contact ordered while father in prison subject to later review upon father's release/re-establishment of life; parental responsibility on behalf of imprisoned father would be too much too soon.

S v R [1993] 1 FCR 331 HC FamD On deciding whether to make parental responsibility order.

S v S [1990] 2 FLR 341 CA Inappropriate that care and control of children be awarded absent proposals as to future accommodation of children.

S v S [1986] 1 FLR 492 HC FamD On staying transfer of custody order pending appeal against same.

S v S [1988] FCR 219; [1988] 1 FLR 213 CA Where father's access to older child (whom had sexually abused) was refused, supervised access to younger children inappropriate.

S v S (1973) 117 SJ 34 HC FamD Delay to be avoided in custody action; court to see new partners of parents before deciding custody action.

S v S [1995] 1 FCR 188; [1994] 2 FLR 681 HC FamD Return of child ordered where taking from non-Convention country had not involved breach of custody rights.

S v S [1995] 1 FCR 149 HC FamD On need for caution in incurring of costs in financial provision applications: here no capital adjustment between parties who ran up high costs.

S v S (1971) 115 SJ 606 CA Interim custody to father where judge based decision in part on suspicions had regarding mother's behaviour was valid.

S v S (1969) 119 NLJ 461t; (1969) 113 SJ 426 HC PDAD On what constitutes 'acceptance' of child into family.

S v S [1992] 2 FCR 113; [1992] 2 FLR 31 HC FamD Some but not grave risk of psychological harm did not merit non-return of child; mature child's vehement desire not to be returned a relevant factor: return not ordered.

S v S [1991] TLR 281 CA Temporary order concerning children desirable where situation of conflict comes before court — matters can be permanently resolved at later stage when worst of conflict has passed.

S v S [1993] 1 FLR 606 HC FamD On appellate review of child maintenance actions; maintenance order invalid as procedural errors in action.

S v S [1993] 1 FCR 13; [1992] 2 FLR 492 CA Reasonable and strongly-held view of child that should not be returned to place of habitual residence justified non-return.

S v S [1949] 1 All ER 285; [1949] 118 LJR 1093; (1949) LXV TLR 80; (1949) WN (I) 32 HC PDAD On declaration of unfitness for guardianship.

S v S (1980) 1 FLR 143 CA Custody of children properly granted to father where mother's lesbian relationship could cause children acute embarrassment if became known.

S v S (otherwise D) (1968) 112 SJ 294 CA Split custody orders not to be preferred (and not granted here).

S v S and P [1962] 2 All ER 1; (1962) 112 LJ 272; (1962) 106 SJ 152; [1962] 1 WLR 445 CA Access to person not shown to be unfit to have contact.

S, C v [1990] 2 All ER 449; [1990] 2 FLR 442 (also HL); [1990] TLR 414 CA No wrongful abduction where father has no rights in respect of child when child taken; no wrongful retention where child not habitually resident in jurisdiction from whence taken.

S, D v [1995] 3 FCR 783 HC FamD On whether/when parental responsibility order appropriate: ill-will between parties not a deciding factor.

S, F v [1973] 1 All ER 722; [1973] Fam 203; (1973) 137 JP 301; (1973) 117 SJ 109; [1973] 2 WLR 178 CA Leave of court needed for adoption of ward; issue for court is will adoption application succeed?

S, Havering London Borough Council v [1986] 1 FLR 489 HC FamD Interim care and control of child subject of wardship action not ordered to mother whose other children already subject of wardship actions as result of apparent abuse by mother's cohabitee.

S, Hereford and Worcester County Council v [1993] 1 FCR 653; [1993] 2 FLR 360 HC FamD On availability of secure accommodation order to child subject to mental health order.

S, otherwise U v Attorney-General (1931-32) XLVIII TLR 66 HC PDAD Petition for declaration of legtimacy dismissed where court not satisfied with evidence regarding parents.

S, S (an Infant, by her Guardian ad Litem the Official Solicitor to the Supreme Court) v; W v Official Solicitor (acting as Guardian ad Litem for a male infant named PHW) [1972] AC 24; [1970] 3 WLR 366 HL Blood test desirable in paternity suit.

S, T v [1994] 1 FCR 743; [1994] 2 FLR 883 HC FamD Property being held on trust for sale postponed until youngest child ended secondary school/turned twenty-one would revert to father at that point.

Sackville-West v Attorney-General (Lord Sackville and others cited) (1909) 44 LJ 695; [1910] 79 LJP 34; (1909-10) XXVI TLR 33; (1909) WN (I) 220 HC KBD Refusal by court to order trial by jury of questions arising under Legitimacy Declaration Act 1858: jury trial provisions of Matrimonial Causes Act 1857, s 28 inapplicable.

Salford City Council and others, C v [1994] 2 FLR 926 HC FamD Fosterers given leave to seek residence order in respect of child whose natural parents objected to adoption by fosterers.

Salford City Council v C (1982) 3 FLR 153 HC FamD Care and control of child whom disabled parents unable to adequately care for given to local authority but frequent access to parents ordered.

Salford Health Authority, ex parte Janaway, R v [1988] 1 FLR 17 HC QBD Conscience provisions of Abortion Act apply only to medical parts of abortion not preliminary arrangements therefor.

Salford Health Authority, ex parte Janaway, R v [1989] AC 537 (also HL); [1988] 2 FLR 370; (1988) 132 SJ 265; [1988] 2 WLR 442 CA Conscience provisions of Abortion Act apply not only to medical parts of abortion but preliminary arrangements therefor.

Salford Health Authority, Janaway v [1988] 3 All ER 1079; [1989] AC 537 (also CA); [1989] 1 FLR 155; (1988) 138 NLJ 348; (1988) 132 SJ 1731; [1988] 3 WLR 1350 HL Conscience provisions of Abortion Act apply only to medical parts of abortion not preliminary arrangements therefor.

Sandbach Justices, ex parte Smith, R v [1950] 2 All ER 781; (1950) 114 JP 514; [1951] 1 KB 62; (1950) 100 LJ 485; (1950) 94 SJ 597; [1950] 66 (2) TLR 291; (1950) WN (I) 397 HC KBD Guardianship proceedings to be brought where respondent lives (unless High Court action); generally no order where child outside jurisdiction.

Saward v Wilson (1981) 131 NLJ 69 CA Adverse effect of custody arrangements on welfare of children required reversal of trial judge's giving of custody to father and that it be given instead to mother.

Scappaticci v Attorney-General [1955] 1 All ER 193 (1955) 99 SJ 114; [1955] 2 WLR 409 HC PDAD On legitimation by post-birth marriage of parents; on changing domicil.

Scott v Scott [1986] 2 FLR 320; (1986) 150 JP 333 CA On role of court welfare service.

Scott v The National Society for the Prevention of Cruelty to Children and Parr (1908-09) XXV TLR 789 Assizes Recovery of costs between solicitor and client incurred in slander and bastardy actions.

Secretary of State for Health, ex parte Luff, R v [1991] FCR 821; [1992] 1 FLR 59 HC QBD Non-quashing of Health Department advice to Home Office that short life expectancy of prospective adopter rendered proposed adoption inappropriate.

Secretary of State for the Home Department, ex parte Brassey and another, R v [1989] FCR 423; [1989] 2 FLR 486; (1989) 133 SJ 388 HC QBD Person born abroad of foreign parents and later adopted abroad by British subject validly denied British passport.

Secretary of State for the Home Department, ex parte Khan, R v [1984] FLR 735; (1984) 128 SJ 580; [1984] TLR 228 CA Refusal of entry of child whom sought to adopt quashed as not based on criteria set out in letter from Home Secretary to appellants and complied with by them.

Seddon and others, R v (1916) 80 JP 208; (1915-16) XXXII TLR 279; (1916) WN (I) 63 HC KBD Failure (for want of corroboration) of affiliation action does not preclude second such action inside twelve months (Bastardy Laws Amendment Act 1872, s 4).

Sharp (Edward George), R v (1931-32) 23 Cr App R 7 CCA Six weeks' detention more than appropriate for unlawful carnal knowledge of precocious under-sixteen year old who looked and acted over sixteen.

Shears v Shears (1973) 117 SJ 33 HC ChD Wife's refusal to allow husband access to child was unreasonable behaviour justifying divorce.

Shephard v Cartwright (1954) 104 LJ 808; (1954) 98 SJ 868 HL On admissibility in evidence of later acts to rebut the presumption of advancement.

Sheppard (James Martin), R v (1980) 70 Cr App R 210 CA Must be intentional neglect of child where charged with cruelty to child by reason of wilful neglect.

Sheppard and another, R v [1980] 3 All ER 899; [1981] AC 394; (1981) 72 Cr App R 82; [1981] Crim LR 171; (1981) 145 JP 65; (1980) 130 NLJ 1144; (1980) 124 SJ 864; [1980] 3 WLR 960 HL Wilful neglect not strict liability offence; must be deliberate/reckless failure to provide proper medical care.

Sheppard v Miller (1982) 3 FLR 124; (1981) 131 NLJ 1236 CA Access to father denied where was upsetting child.

Sherdley v Sherdley [1986] 2 All ER 202; [1988] AC 213; [1986] 2 FLR 326; (1986) 150 JP 305; (1986) 136 NLJ 464; (1986) 130 SJ 356; [1986] 1 WLR 732 CA Unless a sham/for avoidance of tax custodial parent can seek periodic payments order against self.

Sherdley v Sherdley [1987] FCR 149; (1987) 151 JP 715; (1987) 131 SJ 504; [1987] 2 WLR 1071 HL Even though was for avoidance of tax custodial parent could seek periodic payments order against self.

Sheward v Attorney-General (1964) 114 LJ 374; (1964) 108 SJ 159; [1964] 1 WLR 724 HC PDAD Must comply with Matrimonial Causes Act 1950, s 17(1) and Legitimacy Act 1959, s 2 for legitimacy order under latter to be made in respect of one.

Shropshire County Council, W v [1986] 1 FLR 359 (also HC FamD) CA Non-continuation of wardship over child in respect of whom local authority sought to bring care proceedings was valid.

Shropshire County Council, W v [1986] 1 FLR 359 (also CA) HC FamD Non-continuation of wardship over child in respect of whom local authority sought to bring care proceedings.

Slingsby (by his Guardian ad litem) v Attorney-General and others (1916-17) XXXIII TLR 120 HL Failed legitimacy action dismissed with costs to be paid by guardian ad litem or next friend.

Slough Juvenile Court, ex parte Royal Berkshire County Council, R v [1984] QB 387; (1983) 127 SJ 841; [1984] 2 WLR 45 HC QBD Secure accommodation order for duration of more than seventy-two hours in respect of child had to be authorised by juvenile court.

Smith (David George), R v [1985] Crim LR 42 CA On relevance of intention to determination whether physical chastisement of child constituted assault occasioning actual bodily harm.

Smith (KA), R v [1983] Crim LR 739 CrCt Could be convicted of attempted infanticide under Infanticide Act 1938.

Smith and Brown, Smith v [1962] 3 All ER 369; (1962) 112 LJ 665; (1962) 106 SJ 610; [1962] 1 WLR 1218 CA No maintenance of child accepted into family justified where marriage short.

Smith v May (1969) 113 SJ 1000 HC QBD Child found not to be child of marriage on basis of complainant's evidence.

Smith v McInerney [1994] 2 FCR 1086; [1994] 2 FLR 1077 HC FamD Variation of liabilities under separation agreement where husband had been made redundant/was likely to be subject of Child Support Agency assessment.

Smith v Smith (1971) 115 SJ 444 HC PDAD Ordering custody away from mother and outside jurisdiction a matter for earnest consideration; welfare officer's report ought to have been available to court deciding custody matters.

Smith v Smith and Brown [1962] 3 All ER 369; (1962) 112 LJ 665; (1962) 106 SJ 610; [1962] 1 WLR 1218 CA No maintenance of child accepted into family justified where marriage short.

Smith, Batchelor v (1935) 79 SJ 49 HC KBD Revocation of payment ordered pursuant to affiliation order where had come to light since order that mother had committed perjury.

Smith, Bowers and another v; Evans and another v Smith; Flack and another v Smith [1953] 1 All ER 320; (1953) 117 JP 106; (1953) 97 SJ 99; [1953] 1 WLR 297 HC QBD Child/young person committing grossly indecent acts without parent's/guardian's knowledge does not justify requiring parent/guardian to enter recognisance to be proper parent, or placing child/young person on probation.

Smith, Coldingham Parish Council v [1918] 2 KB 90; (1918) WN (I) 112 HC KBD English-domiciled father not responsible for maintenance of pauper lunatic son in Scotland.

Solihull Metropolitan Borough Council, C v [1993] 1 FLR 290 HC FamD On appropriate order where local authority seeks care of child pending appraisal of parents after child suffered unexplained injury.

Solihull Metropolitan Borough Council, ex parte C and others, R v [1984] FLR 363 HC QBD Decision on date on which to close community home quashed where failed to consider future welfare of affected children.

South Glamorgan County Council v W and B [1993] 1 FCR 626; [1993] 1 FLR 574 HC FamD Court can order medical care of minor despite minor's (informed) refusal if in minor's best interests.

South Glamorgan County Council, O'Dare v (1982) 3 FLR 1 HC FamD On what was meant by 'failed without reasonable cause to discharge the obligations of a parent'.

Sparks, Osborn v (1982) 3 FLR 90 HC FamD On balancing procedure to be exercised when assessing financial provision to be made by father in respect of illegitimate child and its mother.

Spicer, R v (1955) 39 Cr App R 189 Assizes Could be convicted for procuring miscarriage where sought so to do though means used could not be successful.

St Alban's Magistrates' Court, ex parte Read, R v [1994] 1 FCR 50 HC QBD Inter partes hearing ordered to enable formerly registered child-minder to challenge her ex parte removal from the register.

St Helens MBC v Hill (1992) 156 JP 602; [1992] TLR 150 HC QBD Sale of cigarattes to under-aged youth a strict liability offence: absent owner properly convicted for actions of worker.

Stafford v Kidd [1936] 3 All ER 1023; (1934-39) XXX Cox CC 532; (1937) 101 JP 68; [1937] 1 KB 395; (1937) 83 LJ 26; [1937] 106 LJCL 193; (1937) 156 LTR 75; (1937) 81 SJ 16; (1936-37) LIII TLR 169; (1937) WN (I) 17 HC KBD Separation deed raises presumption of non-access: wife had to prove access by husband.

Staffordshire County Council v C and M [1988] FCR 353 HC FamD On rights of putative father as regards seeking access to/custody of illegitimate child.

Staffordshire County Council, E (A) v [1995] 2 FCR 84; (1995) 159 JP 367 HC FamD On relevant factors when determining whether to make secure accommodation order.

Staffordshire County Council, P v [1989] FCR 16 HC FamD Non-invocation of wardship jurisdiction to review exercise of local authority discretion (over access to child in care).

Stanga v Stanga [1954] 2 All ER 16; (1953) 97 SJ 607; [1953] 3 WLR 609 HC PDAD Non-compliance with serving of notice on infant requirements necessitated re-hearing.

Stansell, London County Council v (1934-39) XXX Cox CC 335 HC KBD Parent liable where child in filthy condition is father if parents living together.

Starkie (No 2), Starkie v [1953] 2 All ER 1519; (1954) 118 JP 59; (1954) 98 SJ 46; [1954] 1 WLR 98 HC PDAD Husband is/is not under duty to maintain child/wife where consensual separation with no maintenance agreement.

Starkie v Starkie (No 2) [1953] 2 All ER 1519; (1954) 118 JP 59; (1954) 98 SJ 46; [1954] 1 WLR 98 HC PDAD Husband is/is not under duty to maintain child/wife where consensual separation with no maintenance agreement.

Starkie, R v (1921-22) 16 Cr App R 61; (1922) 86 JP 74; [1922] 2 KB 275; [1922] 91 LJCL 663; (1921-22) 66 SJ 300; (1921-22) XXXVIII TLR 181; (1922) WN (I) 10 CCA Admissibility of evidence pertaining to alternative counts in criminal abortion charge.

Starling v Starling (1983) 4 FLR 135 CA Was not in child's best interests to resume relationship with father after three and a half year gap (child a baby when last saw father): access order set aside.

Stephenson v Stephenson [1985] FLR 1140 CA Wrong to take child from caring environment of father and cohabitee and give care and control to previously rather disinterested mother simply because she was natural mother.

Stevenson v Florant [1927] AC 211; (1927) 96 LJPC 1; (1927) 136 LTR 265; (1926-27) XLIII TLR 6 PC In Quebec right of parent to child's custody prevails over that of tuteur.

Stockport Metropolitan Borough Council v B; Stockport Metropolitan Borough Council v L [1986] 2 FLR 80 HC FamD On need for wardship proceedings for care order to be processed swiftly.

Stockport Metropolitan Borough Council, H v [1990] FCR 65; (1989) 133 SJ 359 HC FamD Interim access order unavailable pursuant to Child Care Act 1980, Part 1A.

Stoke-on-Trent Borough Council v Cheshire County Council [1914-15] All ER 441; (1915-16) 113 LTR 750 HC KBD Person resides where lives (for purpose of Children Act 1908, s 74).

W v P [1988] FCR 349; [1988] 1 FLR 508 HC FamD On magistrates giving reasons for custody order.

W v Shropshire County Council [1986] 1 FLR 359 (also HC FamD) CA Non-continuation of wardship over child in respect of whom local authority sought to bring care proceedings was valid.

W v Shropshire County Council [1986] 1 FLR 359 (also CA) HC FamD Non-continuation of wardship over child in respect of whom local authority sought to bring care proceedings.

W v Sunderland Borough Council [1980] 2 All ER 514; (1981) 2 FLR 153; (1981) 145 JP 117; [1980] 1 WLR 1101 HC FamD Social worker who is to give evidence in parent's challenge of local authority not to be present if judge sees child privately; parent may 'consistently' fail to act as parent within a short period.

W v W [1953] 2 All ER 1013 HC PDAD Husband's use of contraceptives does not rebut presumption of legitimacy; legitimacy could be a post-divorce issue when adultery only matter of concern in divorce suit.

W v W [1993] 2 FCR 644; [1993] 2 FLR 211 HC FamD Return of child to country of habitual residence not ordered; ten-month delay in non-abducting parent seeking return of child was acquiescence to wrongful retention.

W v W [1988] FCR 640; [1988] 2 FLR 505 CA Reasons to be given where decide not to adopt course advocated in welfare officers' report.

W v W [1970] 1 All ER 1157; (1969) 119 NLJ 1044t; (1969) 113 SJ 874; [1970] 1 WLR 682 CA Child's best interests determine if blood test to be required.

W v W [1992] 2 FCR 502 HC FamD Was acquiescence to non-return of children where father (unaware of Child Abduction Convention) agreed to mother keeping children.

W v W and C [1968] 3 All ER 408; (1968) 118 NLJ 1029; (1968) 112 SJ 639; [1968] 1 WLR 1310 CA Better for 8 year old boy to be with father.

W v W and Hampshire County Council (1981) 2 FLR 68 CA Care order appropriate where neither parent suitable candidates to have custody of child.

W, B v (1979) 123 SJ 704 HC FamD Care and control of ward to mother, supervision order to local authority.

W, Bolton Metropolitan Borough Council v [1988] FCR 305 HC FamD Social workers' videos of mother's access visits not privileged (even if were privileged was waived here when put videos in evidence).

W, Gaines v [1968] 1 All ER 189; (1968) 132 JP 146; (1967) 117 NLJ 1190t; [1968] 1 QB 782; (1967) 111 SJ 888; [1968] 2 WLR 139 HC QBD Single woman may seek affiliation order though not single when child born.

W, P v [1984] 1 All ER 866; [1984] Fam 32; (1984) 128 SJ 171; [1984] 2 WLR 439 HC FamD Contempt a last stop measure in dealing with access order abuses; summons for such violations to be detailed so defendant aware of abuses charged.

W, T v [1996] 2 FLR 473 HC FamD Reasons ought to have been given when magistrates refused to give leave to apply for contact order.

Wakeham v Wakeham [1954] 1 All ER 434; (1954) 104 LJ 73; (1954) 98 SJ 127; [1954] 1 WLR 366 CA Custody of child removed from jurisdiction given to father but care and control issue left open.

Wakeley, R v [1918-19] All ER 1157; (1918-21) XXVI Cox CC 569; (1920) 84 JP 31; [1920] 1 KB 688; [1920] 89 LJCL 97; (1920) 122 LTR 623 CCA Prosecution began when information laid and information laid within six months of offence so prosecution in time.

Walcott, Patterson v [1984] FLR 408; (1984) 148 JP 161 HC FamD On enforcement of child access order made under Guardianship of Minors Act 1971.

Walker and another, R v (1911-12) XXVIII TLR 342 HC KBD Refusal to order delivery up of illegitimate child to natural parents from those who had adopted child and kept him for ten years.

Walker and another, R v (1911-12) XXVIII TLR 375 CA Compromise of action in appeal from refusal to order delivery up of illegitimate child to natural parents from those who had adopted child and kept him for ten years.

Wallbridge and another v Dorset County Council [1954] 2 All ER 201; [1954] Ch 659; (1954) 118 JP 305; (1954) 104 LJ 345; (1954) 98 SJ 352; [1954] 2 WLR 1068 HC ChD School boarders over whom parents had parental rights/others to whom local authority in loco parentis were not 'foster children' under Public Health Act 1936.

Waltham Forest Justices, ex parte B, R v [1989] FCR 341 HC QBD Care orders valid where magistrates disregarded substance of (but not fact that there were) claims by children (relayed to court inter alia by social worker) but still found orders to be merited.

Waltham Forest London Borough, ex parte G, R v [1989] 2 FLR 138 HC QBD On juvenile court's role where dispute between local authority/guardian ad litem over psychiatric assessment of children in care seeking discharge of care orders.

Wandsworth West Juvenile Court, ex parte S, R v (1983) 4 FLR 53 HC QBD Child's solicitor could withdraw application to discharge care order though parents had made application; withdrawal did not mean matter res judicata: could be started anew.

Wandsworth West Juvenile Court, ex parte S, R v [1984] FLR 713 CA Child's solicitor ought not to have been allowed withdraw application to discharge care order which parents had made.

Ward v Laverty and another [1924] All ER 319; [1925] AC 101; (1924) 59 LJ 300; [1925] 94 LJPC 17; (1924) 131 LTR 614; (1923-24) 68 SJ 629; (1923-24) XL TLR 600; (1924) WN (I) 177 HL In custody case child's welfare paramount though father's desire as regards religious upbringing a relevant factor.

Warwickshire County Council, Isle of Wight County Council v [1953] 1 All ER 525; [1953] 1 QB 553; (1953) 97 SJ 154; [1953] 2 WLR 451 HC QBD Quarter sessions on appeal cannot name local authority within which offence committed by young person of unknown residence.

Warwickshire County Council, M v [1994] 2 FCR 121; [1994] 2 FLR 593 HC FamD Six-month supervision order made.

Watson and another v Nikolaisen [1955] 2 All ER 427; (1955) 119 JP 419; (1955) 105 LJ 346; [1955] 2 QB 286; (1955) 99 SJ 370; [1955] 2 WLR 1187 HC QBD Not abandonment of child to give over to people whom trust.

Watson and Watson, R v (1959) 43 Cr App R 111 Assizes Where husband and wife living together wife can be convicted of manslaughter of child by wilful neglect.

Watson v Tuckwell (1947) LXIII TLR 634 HC KBD Wife/mother living completely separately from husband in house and paying keep for self/children was single woman for purposes of Bastardy Laws Amendment Act 1872, s 3.

Watson v Watson (1953) 97 SJ 746; [1953] 3 WLR 708 HC PDAD Husband's denial of paternity in successful divorce suit did not preclude ex-wife's later seeking maintenance despite her not challenging husband's denial in divorce suit.

WB and others, Hitchcock v [1952] 2 All ER 119; (1952) 116 JP 401; (1952) 102 LJ 345; [1952] 2 QB 561; (1952) 96 SJ 448; [1952] 1 TLR 1550; (1952) WN (I) 315 HC QBD Test whether consent unreasonably withheld is attitude of person withholding.

Wearmouth, Dawson v [1997] TLR 468 CA Surname by which child registered of considerable significance when court asked to alter surname of child.

Webb v Murrel (1904) 68 JP 104 Police Ct Separated married woman can obtain affiliation order against natural father of her illegitimate child as a 'single woman' (Bastardy Laws Amendment Act 1882, s 3).

Webb v Webb [1986] 1 FLR 462 CA On hearsay in welfare report.

Webb v Webb [1952] 1 All ER 527; (1952) 116 JP 146; (1952) 96 SJ 135; [1952] 1 TLR 453; (1952) WN (I) 102 HC PDAD To make custody order child must be actual child of parent.

Wells, Willett v [1985] 1 All ER 585; [1985] FLR 514; (1985) 149 JP 454; (1985) 129 SJ 17; [1985] 1 WLR 237 HC FamD Money spent by putative father on child is 'money for its maintenance'.

West Glamorgan County Council v P (No 1) [1992] 2 FCR 378; [1992] 2 FLR 369 HC FamD Interim non-access by mother to child pending full hearing was permissible.

West Glamorgan County Council v P (No 2) [1992] 2 FCR 406; [1993] 1 FLR 407 HC FamD On relevancy of long-term plans of local authority regarding child in care to court making decision regarding parental contact.

West Glamorgan County Council, ex parte T, R v [1990] FCR 142; [1990] 1 FLR 339; (1989) 133 SJ 1545 HC QBD Refusal of judicial review of local authority decision not to serve fresh notice of refusal of access.

West London Magistrates' Court, ex parte Emmett, R v [1994] 1 FCR 421; [1993] 2 FLR 663 HC FamD On enforceability of registered Irish maintenance order: in-/effective post-/pre-divorce decree absolute.

West Malling Juvenile Court, ex parte K, R v (1986) 150 JP 367; (1970) 130 SJ 650 HC QBD Case ought to have been adjourned where parent in care action given social worker/guardian ad litem reports containing unexpected material on day of hearing.

West Norfolk and Wisbech Area Health Authority and another, Gillick v [1984] 1 All ER 365; [1984] FLR 249; (1983) 133 NLJ 888; [1984] QB 681; (1983) 127 SJ 696; [1983] TLR 541 HC QBD Doctor prescribing contraceptives for under-16 year old girl not encouraging unlawful sexual intercourse; contraceptive advice to under-16 year old not interference with parental duties.

West Norfolk and Wisbech Area Health Authority and another, Gillick v [1985] 1 All ER 533; [1985] FLR 736; (1985) 135 NLJ 81; (1985) 129 SJ 47; [1984] TLR 744 CA Absent emergency doctor's prescribing contraceptives for under-16 year old girl was interference with parental duties.

West Norfolk and Wisbech Area Health Authority and another, Gillick v [1986] Crim LR 113; [1986] 1 FLR 224; (1985) 135 NLJ 1055; (1985) 129 SJ 738 HL Depended on intent of doctor prescribing contraceptives for under-16 year old girl whether was aiding and abetting unlawful sexual intercourse; contraceptive advice to under-16 year old not necessarily interference with parental duties.

West Yorkshire Metropolitan Police and others, Leeds City Council v [1982] 1 All ER 274; [1983] 1 AC 29; (1982) 74 Cr App R 336; (1982) 146 JP 154; [1982] 2 WLR 186 HL Local authority not liable for fines imposed on child in care nor are parents of that child unless local authority temporarily transfers powers of supervision to them.

Westminster City Council, M v [1985] FLR 325; [1984] TLR 453 HC FamD On making care orders where proper development of child 'is' beng impaired/neglected.

Wheatley v London Borough of Waltham Forest [1979] 2 All ER 289; [1980] AC 311; (1979) 143 JP 380; (1979) 123 SJ 270; [1979] 2 WLR 543 HC FamD Decision of local authority to assume parental rights over child within 28 days of parent requesting child is valid.

Wheatley v Wheatley [1949] 2 All ER 428; (1949) 113 JP 459; [1950] 1 KB 39; (1949) 99 LJ 414; (1949) LXV TLR 602; (1949) WN (I) 350 HC KBD Maintenance not payable as parties residing under one roof.

Whitcombe v Evans (1932) 74 LJ ccr86 CyCt Agreement by putative father to pay maintenance for child had by married woman was not void for public policy reasons.

White and Hampshire County Council, White v (1980) 130 NLJ 417c CA Refusal to rescind care order; on practice regarding obtaining views of child/bringing child to psychiatrist in context of care actions.

White v White and Hampshire County Council (1980) 130 NLJ 417c CA Refusal to rescind care order; on practice regarding obtaining views of child/bringing child to psychiatrist in context of care actions.

Whitton v Garner [1965] 1 All ER 70; (1965) 129 JP 92; (1965) 115 LJ 75; (1965) 109 SJ 194; [1965] 1 WLR 313 HC QBD Wife living apart from husband in same house was single woman.

Wigan Metropolitan Borough Council, M and another v [1979] 2 All ER 958; [1980] Fam 36; (1980) 1 FLR 45; [1979] 3 WLR 244 HC FamD Parental obligations wider than financial maintenance; consistent failure is not persistent failure; failure tested objectively.

Wild v Wild [1968] 3 All ER 608; (1968) 132 JP 572; (1968) 118 NLJ 1102; (1968) 112 SJ 746; [1968] 3 WLR 1148 HC PDAD Justices cannot under Matrimonial Proceedings (Magistrates' Courts) Act 1960 divide custody and care and control between parents.

Willett v Wells [1985] 1 All ER 585; [1985] FLR 514; (1985) 149 JP 454; (1985) 129 SJ 17; [1984] TLR 605; [1985] 1 WLR 237 HC FamD Successful appeal against refusal of affiliation order; provision of clothes/food akin to money payment.

Williams (John Owen), R v (1910) 4 Cr App R 89; (1909-10) XXVI TLR 290 CCA On what constitutes exposure/abandonment of child (Children Act 1908, s 12(1)).

Williams v Williams (1985) 149 JP 540 CA Proper that father refused access to children indoctrinated against him by mother where psychiatric evidence was that children could be harmed by such access.

Williams, Robinson v [1964] 3 All ER 12; (1964) 114 LJ 588; [1965] 1 QB 89; (1964) 108 SJ 691; [1964] 3 WLR 563 HC QBD Dismissal of one affiliation application does not preclude later application; new evidence is evidence uncalled (not necessarily discovered since) first trial.

Williamson v Williamson [1986] 2 FLR 146 CA Irrelevancy to custody action of mother's occupancy of former matrimonial home; custody/care and control to one/other parent disfavoured.

Wills, R v [1990] Crim LR 714 CA On what is meant by treatment of child 'likely' to cause harm in Children and Young Persons Act 1933, s 1.

Wilsher, Pym v (1901) 36 LJ 310; (1900-01) 45 SJ 578; (1900-01) XVII TLR 558; (1901) WN (I) 126; (1900-01) 49 WR 654 HC KBD Prosecution procedures under Vaccination Act 1898 did not apply to failure to vaccinate which occurred during lifetime of Vaccination Act 1867.

Wilson, Esq (Metropolitan Magistrate) and others, ex parte Pereira, R v [1952] 2 All ER 706; (1952) 116 JP 549; (1952) 102 LJ 595; [1953] 1 QB 59; (1952) 96 SJ 729; [1952] 2 TLR 594; (1952) WN (I) 457 HC QBD Bastardy action cannot be brought where child abroad to mother then domiciled abroad.

Wilson, Saward v (1981) 131 NLJ 69 CA Adverse effect of custody arrangements on welfare of children required reversal of trial judge's giving of custody to father and that it be given instead to mother.

Wiltshire County Council, London County Council v (1926-30) XXVIII Cox CC 416; (1927) 137 LTR 526; (1926-27) XLIII TLR 563 HC KBD Young offender held to reside in area where committed offence if no contrary evidence.

Wolverhampton Metropolitan Borough Council v M [1988] FCR 629 HC FamD Child taken from mentally handicapped parents unable to care for him and placed in care with view to adoption (parental access terminated).

Wood and others, Bain v (1979) 129 (1) NLJ 365 HL Qualified care and control order in respect of two children committed to local authority care.

Wood Green Crown Court, ex parte P, R v (1983) 4 FLR 206; [1982] TLR 164 HC QBD On flexible admissibility rules in care actions (here concerning admissibility of medical/welfare reports).

Worcester City Juvenile Court, ex parte F, R v [1989] 1 All ER 500; [1989] FCR 110; [1989] 1 FLR 230; (1988) 132 SJ 1526 HC QBD Upon request juvenile court must disclose reasons for refusing to discharge care order.

Wright v Wright (1981) 2 FLR 276 CA Refusal of access to father (Jehovah's Witness) merited where mother (Church of England member) very anxious (and anxiety would upset child) that father would seek to indoctrinate child.

X and others v Bedfordshire County Council; M and another v Newham London Borough Council and others; E v Dorset County Council and other appeals [1995] 3 All ER 353; [1995] 2 AC 633 (also CA); [1995] 3 FCR 337; [1995] 2 FLR 276; [1995] TLR 375; [1995] 3 WLR 152 HL Local authority child care decision cannot be challenged as breach of statutory duty or common law duty of care if in hindsight decision proved mistaken nor is it vicariously liable for actions of social workers and psychiatrists in case.

X City Council (No 2), D v [1985] FLR 279 HC FamD Child in local authority care to be entrusted to care and control of grandmother.

X County Council, B v (1991) 141 NLJ 1740t; [1991] TLR 582 HC FamD Hearsay evidence admissible when CrCt hearing appeal against juvenile court care order.

X v X (1963) 107 SJ 571 CA Interim custody order uprooting child from foreign country pending divorce action there and placing child with adulterous wife and her lover was improper.

Y v B [1995] 3 FCR 49 HC FamD Trial contact unnecessary before magistrates make decision in contact case (can do so on evidence before court).

Y v Kirklees Metropolitan Council [1985] FLR 927 HC FamD On making application for access orders.

Y v Y [1973] 2 All ER 574; [1973] Fam 147; (1973) 117 SJ 506; [1973] 3 WLR 80 HC PDAD Neither parental custodian nor other parent can change child's surname absent agreement/court decision.

Yorkshire West Riding County Council v Colne Corporation (1917-18) 117 LTR 671; (1917-18) 62 SJ 160 HC KBD On residency of child for purposes of determining which authority liable to maintain child at industrial school.

Young (Tara Moira Lisa), R v (1993) 97 Cr App R 280; (1993) 137 SJ LB 32; [1992] TLR 641 CA Where jury convinced overall that was cruelty (even though disagree on specific incidents) can convict of cruelty to children.

Young, Barrett v (1981) 131 NLJ 372 CA Custody of children to mother despite father's looking after children for 6 years, for five of which mother had no contact with children.